IRISH HOTELS FEDERATION

IRISH HOTELS FEDERATION

13 Northbrook Road, Dublin 6, Ireland
Telephone +353 1 497 6459   Fax: +353 1 497 4613

Be Our Guest

2002

Featuring over 1,000 Hotels & Guesthouses

as well as details on Golfing, Angling, Conference Facilities and Touring Maps

irelandhotels.com
log on and book in

The Irish Hotels Federation does not accept any responsibility for errors, omissions or any information whatsoever in the Guide and members and users of the Guide are requested to consult page 20 hereof for further information.

When dialing Ireland from abroad, please use the following codes:
Republic of Ireland: 00 353 + local code (drop the 0)
Northern Ireland: 00 44 + local code (drop the 0)
If dialling Northern Ireland directly from the Republic of Ireland
replace the prefix code 028 with the code 048.

Printed & Published by The Wood Printcraft Group, Greencastle Parade, Clonshaugh, Dublin 17.
Tel: +353 1 847 0011. Fax: +353 1 847 5570.
Design & Origination by Printcraft Imaging, Unit 95 Malahide Road Industrial Park, Malahide Road, Dublin 17.

BE OUR GUEST

GUINNESS.

FACILITIES

🛏	Total number of rooms
♦	Number of rooms with bath/shower and toilet
☎	Direct dial facilities
⬜	TV in all bedrooms
⬍	Elevator/Lift
T	Can be booked through travel agent / tourist office and commission paid
🛝	Childrens playground
🐎	Childrens playroom
C	Price reduction for children
🛁	Babysitter service
CM	Childrens meals
CS	Creche
✳	Garden for visitors use
🏊	Indoor swimming pool
🏊	Outdoor swimming pool
🧖	Sauna
🏋	Gym
🏠	Leisure Complex (including sauna / swimming pool / gym)
🎾	Tennis court - hard / grass

🎱	Games room
禾	Squash court
↻	Horse riding/pony trekking on site or nearby
⛳9	9-hole golf course on site
⛳18	18-hole golf course on site
🎣	Angling on site or nearby
🎵	Evening Entertainment
P	Car parking
🐾	Facilities for pets
S	Price reduction for senior citizens excl. July/August and subject to availability
♇	Wine Licence only
🍾	Dispense Bar Service only
🍺	Licensed to sell all alcoholic drink
alc	À la carte meals provided
☕	Tea/coffee making facilities in bedroom
♿	Facilities and services are accessible to disabled persons
🦽	Suitable for disabled persons, with the assistance of one helper
Inet	Modem access in room
FAX	Fax machine in room
☺	Special Offer

 Denotes that premises are members of the Irish Hotels Federation as at 18 September 2001.

 Denotes that premises are members of the Northern Ireland Hotels Federation as at 18 September 2001.

ACTIVITY SECTIONS

Green symbols Illustrated below denote that the hotel or guesthouse is included in a particular activity section. Further details of the facilities available and the arrangements made on behalf of guests for participation in these activities are shown on pages 409 to 461.

 ✓ Golf   🎣 Angling   🏆 Conference

MARKETING GROUPS

Many of the hotels and guesthouses in the guide are members of Marketing Groups. Those properties which are members of the Marketing Groups will have the name of the group displayed within their entry. Some of these groups operate a central reservation system and can make reservations for you.

SELECTING YOUR HOTEL AND GUESTHOUSE

REGIONS

Begin by selecting the region(s) you wish to visit. This guide divides into eight separate Regions – North, East Coast, Midlands & Lakelands, South East, South West, Shannon, West and North West – and they are represented in that order.

COUNTIES

Within each region, counties are presented alphabetically.

LOCATIONS – CITIES, TOWNS, VILLAGES

Within counties, locations are also presented alphabetically, see Index Pages 4 & 6.

PREMISES

Hotels and guesthouses are also presented in alphabetical order, see Index Pages 484 to 496.

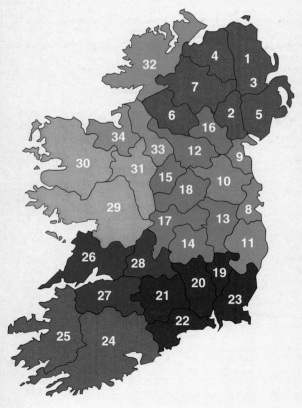

	COUNTIES	REGION	PAGES
1	ANTRIM	North	Page 30 to 37
2	ARMAGH	North	Page 37 to 37
3	BELFAST CITY	North	Page 38 to 42
4	DERRY	North	Page 42 to 45
5	DOWN	North	Page 46 to 50
6	FERMANAGH	North	Page 50 to 51
7	TYRONE	North	Page 52 to 52
8	DUBLIN	East Coast	Page 56 to 117
9	LOUTH	East Coast	Page 117 to 121
10	MEATH	East Coast	Page 121 to 126
11	WICKLOW	East Coast	Page 126 to 138
12	CAVAN	Midlands & Lakelands	Page 140 to 142
13	KILDARE	Midlands & Lakelands	Page 143 to 148
14	LAOIS	Midlands & Lakelands	Page 148 to 150
15	LONGFORD	Midlands & Lakelands	Page 150 to 150
16	MONAGHAN	Midlands & Lakelands	Page 151 to 152
17	OFFALY	Midlands & Lakelands	Page 152 to 156
18	WESTMEATH	Midlands & Lakelands	Page 156 to 159
19	CARLOW	South East	Page 161 to 168
20	KILKENNY	South East	Page 168 to 171
21	TIPPERARY SOUTH	South East	Page 172 to 179
22	WATERFORD	South East	Page 179 to 192
23	WEXFORD	South East	Page 192 to 204
24	CORK	South West	Page 206 to 249
25	KERRY	South West	Page 249 to 296
26	CLARE	Shannon	Page 298 to 320
27	LIMERICK	Shannon	Page 321 to 329
28	TIPPERARY NORTH	Shannon	Page 329 to 332
29	GALWAY	West	Page 334 to 371
30	MAYO	West	Page 372 to 383
31	ROSCOMMON	West	Page 384 to 386
32	DONEGAL	North West	Page 388 to 399
33	LEITRIM	North West	Page 400 to 402
34	SLIGO	North West	Page 402 to 407

AVOCA
HANDWEAVERS

Welcome to the colourful world of Avoca, where our seven magical shops are crammed with beautiful things, most of which are made exclusively by Avoca. Savour our restaurants where our delicious lunches are legendary. Visit any one of our shops and be sure of a warm welcome and an experience with a difference.

Tel: 01 286 7466
Fax: 01 286 2367
Open 7 Days

Kilmacanogue	**Avoca Village**	**Powerscourt House Shop**	**Molls Gap**	**Bunratty**	**Letterfrack**	**Suffolk St.**
Bray, Co. Wicklow	Avoca Co. Wicklow	Enniskerry Co. Wicklow	Killarney, Co. Kerry	Co. Clare	Co. Galway	Dublin 2.

irelandhotels.com
log on and book in

To view any of the hotels and guesthouses featured in this guide, just log on at

www.irelandhotels.com

And, did you know that you can book many of these hotels and guesthouses online?

Just log on and book in

And while you're there, don't forget to check out our Special Offers section.

IRISH
HOTELS
FEDERATION

Be Our Guest

log on and book in

GUINNESS.
SUPPORTING IRISH TOURISM

NIHF

Bord Fáilte
Irish Tourist Board

Northern Ireland
Tourist Board

Mary Fitzgerald
President, Irish Hotels Federation

Hotels and Guesthouses in Ireland are very special. The majority are family owned with the proprietor and members of the family there to welcome guests and to extend to them renowned Irish hospitality. Even when they are owned by a company, or are part of a group, they still retain the character and ambience of a family premises - a place where you will be truly welcome.

The Irish hotel is unique, in that more often than not, it acts as a social centre for the community. Hotels offer a lot more than just a bed and a meal - they are fully fledged social, leisure, business and community centres with every imaginable facility and amenity, providing food, accommodation, sports, leisure facilities, entertainment and other attractions.

If you are moving around the country, you'll find that "Be Our Guest" is an invaluable help in choosing your next location.

Ireland's hoteliers and guesthouse owners want to welcome you and want

to play their part in ensuring that your stay in Ireland is a happy one. We hope that you will stay with us and that you will use this guide to select the hotel or guesthouse of your choice, so that we can personally invite you to -

Be Our Guest

Ní haon ní coitianta é an Óstlann nó an Teach Lóistín in Éirinn. Is i seilbh teaghlaigh iad a bhformhór acu agus bíonn an t-úinéir agus baill den teaghlach romhat chun fáilte Uí Cheallaigh a chur romhat. Fiú nuair is le comhlacht iad, nó is cuid de ghrúpa iad, baineann meon agus atmaisféar áitreabh teaghlaigh leo – áiteanna ina gcuirfí fíorchaoin fáilte romhat.

Rud ar leith is ea an óstlann in Éirinn agus is dócha ná a mhalairt go bhfeidhmíonn sí mar lárionad sóisialta don phobal. Cuireann an óstlann i bhfad níos mó ná leaba agus béile ar fáil - is lárionad sóisialta,a siamsaíochta, gnó agus pobail ar fheabhas í chomh maith agus gach aon áis faoin spéir aici, a chuireann bia, lóistín, imeachtaí spóirt, áiseanna siamsíochta agus só agus tarraingtí nach iad ar fáil.

Agus tú ag taisteal timpeall na tíre gheobhaidh tú amach go mbeidh "Bí i d'Aoi Againn" an-áisiúil agus an chéad suíomh eile á roghnú agat.

Is mian le hóstlannaithe agus le lucht tithe lóistín na hÉireann fáilte a chur romhat agus a bheith in ann a dheimhniú go mbainfidh tú sult as do sheal in Éirinn. Tá súil againn go bhfanfaidh tú linn agus go mbainfidh tú leas as an treoir seo chun do rogha óstlann nó teach lóistin a aimsiú, i dtreo is go mbeimid in ann a rá leat go pearsanta -

Be Our Guest

Les hôtels et les pensions en Irlande sont d'un caractère particulier.

Ils sont très souvent gérés par le propriétaire et des membres de sa famille, présents pour accueillir les visiteurs et leur faire découvrir la célèbre hospitalité irlandaise. Même s'ils appartiennent à une entreprise ou font partie d'un groupe de sociétés, ils possèdent toujours ce caractère et cette ambiance des lieux familiaux - un endroit où vous serez sincèrement bien accueillis.

L'hôtel irlandais est unique en ce qu'il joue très souvent le rôle de centre social pour la communauté. Les hôtels offrent beaucoup plus qu'un lit et un repas - ce sont, pour la communauté, de véritables centres sociaux, de loisirs et d'affaires, équipés de toutes les infrastructures et installations imaginables. Ils vous proposent le gîte et le couvert, mais aussi activités sportives et de loisir, divertissements et autres attractions.

Si vous voyagez dans le pays, vous trouverez que le guide "Be Our Guest" est d'une aide précieuse pour vous aider à choisir votre prochaine destination.

Les hôteliers et les propriétaires de pensions irlandais veulent vous accueillir et être là pour vous assurer un séjour agréable en Irlande. Nous espérons que vous resterez avec nous et que vous utiliserez ce guide pour sélectionner l'hôtel ou la pension de votre choix, afin que nous ayons le plaisir de vous compter parmi nos visiteurs.

Be Our Guest

Die Hotels und Pensionen in Irland sind von ganz besonderer Art.

Zum größten Teil handelt es sich dabei um private Familienbetriebe, in denen der Besitzer und die Familienmitglieder ihre Gäste mit der vielgerühmten irischen Gastfreundschaft willkommen heißen. Aber auch wenn sich diese Häuser in Unternehmensbesitz befinden oder einer Kette angehören, strahlen sie dennoch den Charakter und die Atmosphäre von Familienbetrieben aus - ein Ort, an dem Sie immer herzlich willkommen sind.

Hotels in Irland sind einzig in ihrer Art und dienen oftmals als Mittelpunkt geselliger Treffen. Hotels haben viel mehr zu bieten als nur ein Bett und eine Mahlzeit - sie sind Gesellschafts-, Freizeit-, Geschäfts- und öffentlicher Treffpunkt mit allen nur erdenklichen Einrichtungen und Annehmlichkeiten, angefangen bei Essen, Unterkunft, Sport und Freizeitmöglichkeiten bis zur Unterhaltung und anderen Anziehungspunkten.

Auf Ihren Reisen im Land werden Sie feststellen, daß Ihnen der "Be Our Guest"-Führer eine wertvolle Hilfe bei der Suche nach der nächstgelegenen Unterkunft leistet.

Irlands Hotel- und Pensionsbesitzer heißen Sie gerne willkommen und möchten ihren Anteil dazu beitragen, daß Ihnen Ihr Aufenthalt in Irland in angenehmer Erinnerung bleibt. Wir hoffen, daß Sie uns besuchen werden und diesen Führer bei der Auswahl Ihres Hotels oder Ihrer Pension zu Rate ziehen, so daß wir Sie persönlich willkommen heißen können.

Be Our Guest

irelandhotels.com
log on and book in

IRISH
HOTELS
FEDERATION

live
life
to
the
power
of

Ireland's Tourist Information Network

WELCOME

to the Holiday Regions of Ireland.

You are invited to avail of the services provided by our Tourist Information Network. In addition to the detailed information on what to see and do in the area, helpful diary of events and the convenient room reservation service, they also provide a wide range of other services. All are designed to aid you, both in your holiday planning and in helping you to enjoy to the full, all that Ireland's holiday regions have to offer.

Our services at a glance.

- Accommodation Booking Service
- Guide Books for sale
- Local and National information
- Map sales
- Stamps, postcards and phone-cards

- Bureau de change Facilities
- Itinerary and route planning
- Local Craft
- Souvenirs and gifts
- What's on in the area and nationally

Multi lingual facilities are available in many offices while some tourist offices may not provide all of the service or facilities listed here.

Follow the Shamrock

Check for the Shamrock Sign on all accommodation. It is your guarantee that premises on which it is displayed provide accommodation which is inspected and whose standards are fully approved and regulated by agencies supervised by Bord Failte - the Irish Tourist Board. Of course all accommodation booked on your behalf through Tourist Information Offices is fully approved and regulated in this manner.

Ask for our free guide to the locations and phone numbers of all 122 Tourist Information Offices throughout the Island of Ireland - your best call to access better service leading to a happier holiday.

BORD FÁILTE – IRISH TOURIST BOARD

www.ireland.travel.ie

IRELAND

Dublin
Bord Fáilte - Irish Tourist Board,
Baggot Street Bridge, Dublin 2
Tel: 1850 23 03 30
Fax: 01 - 602 4100

NORTHERN IRELAND

Belfast
Bord Fáilte - Irish Tourist Board,
53 Castle Street, Belfast BT1 1GH
Tel: 028 - 9032 7888
Fax: 028 - 9024 0201

Derry
Bord Fáilte - Irish Tourist Board,
44 Foyle Street, Derry BT48 6AT
Tel: 028 - 7136 9501
Fax: 028 - 7136 9501

If dialling Northern Ireland directly from the Republic of Ireland the code 048 followed by the telephone number is sufficient.

NORTHERN IRELAND TOURIST BOARD

www.discovernorthernireland.ie

Belfast
Northern Ireland Tourist Board,
59 North Street, Belfast BT1 1NB
Tel: 028 - 9023 1221
Fax: 028 - 9024 0960

Dublin
Northern Ireland Tourist Board,
16 Nassau Street, Dublin 2
Tel: 01 - 679 1977
Fax: 01 - 679 1863

TOURISM IRELAND –
EUROPE

Austria
Tourism Ireland
Libellenweg 1, A-1140 Vienna
Tel: 01 - 501596000
Fax: 01 - 911 37 65

Belgium
Tourism Ireland,
Avenue Louise 327 Louizalaan
1050 Brussels
Tel: 02 - 275 01 71
Fax: 02 - 642 98 51

Britain
Britain Visitor Centre,
1 Regent Street, London SW1Y 4XT
Tel: 0800 039 7000
Fax: 0207 493 9065

Tourism Ireland
James Millar House
98 West George Street 7th Floor
Glasgow G2 1PJ
Tel: 0141 - 572 4030
Fax: 0141 - 572 4033

Denmark
Tourism Ireland
'Klostergaarden', Amagertorv 29B, 3,
DK 1160 Copenhagen K
Tel: 033 15 80 45
Fax: 033 32 44 01

Finland
Tourism Ireland,
Erottajankatu 7A, PL33, 00130 Helsinki
Tel: 09 - 608 966
Fax: 09 - 646 022

France
Tourism Ireland,
33 rue de Miromesnil, 75008 Paris
Tel: 01 - 70 20 00 20
Fax: 01 - 47 42 01 64

Germany
Tourism Ireland,
Untermainanlage 7,
D-60329 Frankfurt am Main
Tel: 069 - 66 80 09 50
Fax: 069 - 92 31 85 88

Italy
Tourism Ireland,
Via S. Maria Segreta 6, 20123 Milano
Tel: 02 - 482 96 060
Fax: 02 - 869 03 96

The Netherlands
Tourism Ireland,
Spuistraat 104, 1012VA Amsterdam
Tel: 020 - 504 06 89
Fax: 020 - 620 80 89

Norway
Tourism Ireland,
Postboks 6691, St. Olavs Plass
N-0129 Oslo
Tel: 022 - 20 26 40
Fax: 022 - 20 26 41

Portugal
Tourism Ireland,
Rua da Imprensa a Estrela 1-4°
1200 Lisboa
Tel: 021 - 392 94 40
Fax: 021 - 397 73 63

Spain
Tourism Ireland,
Paseo de la Castellana 46,
3™ Planta, 28046 Madrid
Tel: 091 - 745 64 20
Fax: 091 - 577 69 34

Sweden
Tourism Ireland,
Stora Nygatan 40,
SE 111 27 Stockholm
Tel: 08 662 8510
Fax: 08 233 727

Switzerland
Ireland Mailshop,
Markus Fluehmann AG
Industrie Nord 9
CH-5634 Merenschwand
Tel: 011 21 04 153
Fax: 056 675 75 80 - IRLAND

TOURISM IRELAND –
REST OF THE WORLD

USA
Tourism Ireland
345 Park Avenue,
New York NY 10154
Tel: 1800 22 36 470
Fax: 212 - 371 9052

Canada
Tourism Ireland
2 Bloor St. West
Suite 1501
Toronto, ON M4W 3E2
Tel: 416 - 925 6368
Fax: 416 - 925 6033

South Africa
Tourism Ireland,
c/o Development Promotions
Everite House, 7th Floor,
20, De Korte Street,
Braamfontein 2001
Johannesburg
Tel: 011 - 339 4865
Fax: 011 - 339 2474

New Zealand
Tourism Ireland,
6th Floor, 18 Shortland Street,
Private Bag 92136,
Auckland 1
Tel: 09 - 379 8720
Fax: 09 - 302 2420

Australia
Tourism Ireland,
5th Level, 36 Carrington Street,
Sydney, NSW 2000
Tel: 02 - 9299 6177
Fax: 02 - 9299 6323

Japan
Tourism Ireland,
2-10-7 Kojimachi,
Chiyoda-ku, Tokyo 102 - 0083
Tel: 03 - 5275 1611
Fax: 03 - 5275 1623

irelandhotels.com
log on and book in

To view any of the hotels and guesthouses featured in this guide, just log on at
www.irelandhotels.com

And, did you know that you can book many of these hotels and guesthouses online?

Just log on and book in

And while you're there, don't forget to check out our Special Offers section.

IRISH
HOTELS
FEDERATION

Be Our Guest

LOCAL TOURIST INFORMATION OFFICES

The offices below operate throughout the year; approximately one hundred others are open during the summer months.

Aran Islands
Kilronan
Tel: 099 - 61263
Armagh
40 English Street
Tel: 028 - 3752 1800
Fax: 028 - 3752 8329
Athlone
Tel: 0902 - 94630
Belfast
47 Donegall Place
Tel: 028 - 9024 6609
Fax: 028 - 9031 2424
www.gotobelfast.com
Blarney
Tel: 021 - 438 1624
Newgrange
Bru na Boinne Visitor Centre
Donore, Co. Meath
Tel: 041 - 988 0305
Carlow
College Street
Tel: 0503 - 31554
Clonmel
Town Centre
Tel: 052 - 22960
Cork City
Aras Fáilte,
Grand Parade
Tel: 021 - 425 5100
Fax: 021 - 425 5199
Derry
44 Foyle Street
Tel: 028 - 7126 7284
Fax: 028 - 7137 7992
Dublin
Dublin Tourism Centre,
Suffolk Street, Dublin 2
Ferry Terminal,
Dun Laoghaire Harbour
Arrivals Hall, Dublin Airport
Baggot St. Bridge, Dublin 2
The Square Shopping Centre,
Tallaght
O'Connell Street, Dublin 1
E-mail:
information@dublintourism.ie
Internet: www.visitdublin.com

For reservations in Dublin
contact Ireland Reservations
Freephone
Tel: 1800 668 668 66
Dundalk
Jocelyn Street
Tel: 042 - 933 5484
Fax: 042 - 933 8070
Dungarvan
Town Centre
Tel: 058 - 41741
Ennis
Arthur's Row
Tel: 065 - 682 8366
Enniskillen
Wellington Road
Tel: 028 - 6632 3110
Fax: 028 - 6632 5511
Galway
Forster Street
Tel: 091 - 537700
Fax: 091 - 537733
Giant's Causeway
Bushmills
Tel: 028 - 2073 1855
Fax: 028 - 2073 2537
Gorey
Town Centre
Tel: 055 - 21248
Kilkenny
Rose Inn Street
Tel: 056 - 51500
Fax: 056 - 63955
Killarney
Beech Road
Tel: 064 - 31633
Fax: 064 - 34506
Killymaddy
Dungannon (off A4)
Tel: 028 - 8776 7259
Letterkenny
Derry Road
Tel: 074 - 21160
Fax: 074 - 25180
Limerick City
Arthur's Quay
Tel: 061 - 317522
Fax: 061 - 317939

Mullingar
Market House
Tel: 044 - 48650
Fax: 044 - 40413
Newcastle (Co. Down)
10-14 Central Promenade
Tel: 028 - 4372 2222
Fax: 028 - 4372 2400
Omagh
1 Market Street
Tel: 028 - 8224 7831
Fax: 028 - 8224 0774
Rosslare, Kilrane
Tel: 053 - 33622 /33232
Fax: 053 - 33421
Shannon Airport
Tel: 061 - 471664
Skibbereen
North Street
Tel: 028 - 21766
Fax: 028 - 21353
Sligo
Temple Street
Tel: 071 - 61201
Fax: 071 - 60360
Tralee
Ashe Hall
Tel: 066 - 7121288
Tullamore
Tullamore Dew
Heritage Centre
Bury Quay
Tel: 0506 - 52617
Waterford
The Granary
Tel: 051 - 875823
Fax: 051 - 876720
Waterford Crystal
Tel: 051 - 358397
Westport
James Street
Tel: 098 - 25711
Fax: 098 - 26709
Wexford
Crescent Quay
Tel: 053 - 23111
Fax: 053 - 41743
Wicklow
Fitzwilliam Square
Tel: 0404 - 69117
Fax: 0404 - 69118

How quickly they grow when you're not around to watch them. (Now imagine that's your savings rather than your third cousin.) At Bank of Ireland, we know a thing or two about growth over time. When we first opened our doors in 1783 the United States was six years short of inaugurating its first president, the word Australia had never been uttered, and the Irish 'diaspora' had yet to disperse. The world has grown up since then; we've changed to reflect it. Which is where our menu of currency savings accounts comes in - allowing non-residents to enjoy the many benefits of a savings account with Ireland's longest-standing bank. Benefits like high yield, secure returns, first and foremost; also genuinely professional customer service and the freedom to operate your chosen account in the currency that suits you best (thereby steering clear of exchange rate complications). Last but not least, you'll have the satisfaction of knowing you hold your own full-service bank account back in Ireland. Guaranteeing you many, many happy returns. To find out more, call us on +353 1 829 0122 or email us at fdd@boitib.com

Bank of Ireland Treasury & International Banking – IACT Financial Institution of the Year **2000**

Bank of Ireland
Treasury & International Banking

INTRODUCTION

> It is essential that when booking your accommodation you request the "Be Our Guest 2002" Rate

Our Guide features a broad selection of Irish Hotels, including stately Country Houses, luxurious Castles, old-world Inns and homely Guesthouses. The majority of these hotels and guesthouses are members of the Irish Hotels Federation or the Northern Ireland Hotels Federation and we hope that the illustrations and descriptions of these premises and the amenities they offer will help you to choose the most suitable premises for your holiday.

All of the hotels and guesthouses featured in the Guide at the time of going to print (10th Oct 2001) have been registered or are awaiting registration by Bord Failte / Irish Tourist Board or by the Northern Ireland Tourist Board, in accordance with the Statutory Registration Regulations which they administer. *(See also Activity Sections pages 409-461)*

RATES

The only rates featured in this publication relate to Per Person Sharing or a Room Rate.

<u>Per Person Sharing:</u> relates to the cost of Bed & Full Breakfast per person per night, on the basis of two persons occupying a double/twin bedded room, most having private bath/shower.

<u>Room Rate:</u> relates to the cost of a room per night. There may be a restriction on the number of persons allowed to share the room. It is advisable to check this when making your reservation.

The rates range from minimum to maximum and are those generally in operation throughout the year, but may not apply during special occasions such as Public Holiday Weekends, Christmas and New Year, International Events, Major Festivals and Sporting Fixtures, or on such other occasions as individual premises may decide.

These are guideline rates, please ensure that you contact the premises to vertify the rates applicable to your reservation.

Rates are inclusive of Value Added Taxes at current (2001) rates and Services Charges (if any).

Supplements may be payable for suites or superior / de luxe rooms. Also, where single or double / twin bedded rooms are occupied by one person, a supplement may be payable. Correspondingly, if more than two persons share a family room, special reduced rates may be arranged.

In the case of hotels and guesthouses in the Republic of Ireland, rates are quoted in € (Euro). (For your information, equivalent rates are also shown in the former currency of IR£). Whereas in Northern Ireland rates are quoted in STG£.

STANDARD SPECIAL OFFERS (Per Person Sharing)

Many of the hotels / guesthouses in the Guide feature special offers :

- **Weekend Specials** include 2 nights' accommodation, 2 Breakfasts and 1 Dinner.
- **Midweek Specials** include 3 nights' accommodation and 3 breakfasts.
- **Weekly Partial Board** includes 7 nights' accommodation, 7 breakfasts and 7 dinners.

Alternative Special Offers may be featured

HOTEL CLASSIFICATION

ONE STAR ★

Here you can enjoy the comforts of a pleasantly simple hotel where a warm welcome prevails. These premises offer all the mandatory services and facilities to a satisfactory standard, necessary for a most enjoyable and relaxed visit. Some guest rooms have a private bathroom with a bath or a shower.

TWO STAR ★★

These are more likely to be family operated premises, selected for their charm and their comfortable facilities.

All guest rooms have a telephone and most have a private bathroom with a bath and / or shower. Full dining facilities are available, representing excellent value and good wholesome food.

Dúchas Heritage Card

...the way to explore Ireland's heritage

Adult	IR£15	€19.04
Senior Citizen	IR£10	€12.69
Child/Student	IR£6	€7.60
Family	IR£36	€45.71

Unlimited admission for one year
to over 70 heritage sites

For more information...

email: heritagecard@ealga.ie
web: www.heritageireland.ie
Tel: +353 1 647 2461
Fax: +353 1 661 6764

**An Roinn Ealaíon, Oidhreachta,
Gaeltachta agus Oileán**
Department of Arts, Heritage,
Gaeltacht and the Islands

Dúchas
The Heritage Service

National Heritage Week 1-8 September, 2002

THREE STAR ★★★

These range from small, family operated premises to larger, modern hotels. Guest rooms are well decorated with the emphasis on comfort and all have a private bathroom with a bath and/or shower. Some hotels may also have colour TV, direct dial phones, hairdryers, tea/coffee facilities and room service. Many hotels also have leisure facilities, car parking, safety deposit boxes.

Restaurants offer high standards of cuisine in relaxed and hospitable surroundings. Table d'hôte and / or à la carte dinner menus are available.

FOUR STAR ★★★★

These include contemporary hotels of excellent quality and charming period houses renovated to very high standards complete with all modern comforts. All guest

GUESTHOUSE CLASSIFICATION

ONE STAR ★

These premises meet all the mandatory requirements for guesthouses and offer simple accommodation, facilities and services to a satisfactory standard. Restaurant facilities are available in some guesthouses.

TWO STAR ★★

Half or more of the guest rooms have private bathroom with bath and / or shower. Guesthouse facilities include a reading / writing room or lounge area for residents' use. Restaurant facilities are available in some guesthouses.

THREE STAR ★★★

All guest rooms have private bathroom with bath and / or shower and direct dial telephone. Guesthouse facilities include a TV lounge, travellers cheques are exchanged and major credit cards are accepted. Restaurant facilities are available in some guesthouses.

FOUR STAR ★★★★

This is the top classification for guesthouses in Ireland. Guest accommodation includes half suites and all guest rooms have private bathroom with bath and / or shower, direct dial telephone, colour TV and radio. Room service offers full breakfast. Many premises provide dinner, with table d'hôte and / or à la carte menus. Guesthouse facilities include car parking, safety deposit boxes, fax.

accommodation is luxurious with suites and half suites available in most cases. Restaurant facilities provide excellent cuisine and service for the discerning diner. Table d'hôte and / or à la carte lunch and dinner menus are available.

FIVE STAR ★★★★★

These include Ireland's most luxurious hotels, all of which are of high international standard. They range from elegant, stately castles to prestigious country clubs and top class city hotels catering for both the business and tourist visitor. All guest accommodation is luxurious and spacious suites are also available.

These fine hotels boast of some of the country's best restaurants and offer table d'hôte and / or à la carte lunch and dinner menus. Exceptional service and a personalised welcome are the norm in these hotels.

OPENING DATES

Some of the premises featured in the guide were not open at the guide print date (10 October 2001). The planned date of opening as supplied by these premises is displayed.

Hotels and Guesthouses may have the symbols, U, N, R, P, CR for the following reasons:

U Under the terms of the classification scheme a premises may opt to remain unclassified and will be shown U in this guide. Of course these premises meet all the mandatory requirements for hotel/guesthouse registration.

N These are premises that have recently registered with Bord Fáilte / Northern Irish Tourist Board but, at the time of going to print, have not been long enough in operation for their standards to be fully assessed.

R These premises were undergoing major refurbishment at the time of printing this guide. Their classification will be assessed when the work is completed.

P Applied to Bord Fáilte/Northern Ireland Tourist Board for registration at time of going to print.

CR Classification Rescinded - At the time of going to print (10 October 2001) the classification of these properties had been rescinded and the registration was under review by Bord Fáilte.

RESERVATIONS

Courtesy Onward Reservations

If you are moving around the country, the premises in which you are staying will be delighted to help you select and make your next accommodation reservation from the Be Our Guest Guide.

The following are other ways in which a booking can be made :

1. Advance enquiries and reservations may be made directly to the premises by phone, fax, e-mail or letter and details of the reservation should be confirmed by both parties. A deposit should be forwarded if requested.

2. Book your accommodation **online** at:

**which features all premises
listed in the Be Our Guest guide.**

www.irelandhotels.com

3. Some of the hotels and guesthouses in the Guide participate in a Central Reservations system which may be indicated in their entry.

4. Travel Agent - your travel agent will normally make a booking on your behalf without extra charge where the premises pays travel agents' commission (this is indicated by the symbol ⊤ in the Guide). In other cases, agents will usually charge a small fee to cover the cost of telephone calls and administration.

5. Some Irish Tourist Board offices listed in this guide (see pages 12 & 13) operate an enquiry and booking service and will make an accommodation reservation on your behalf.

COMPLAINTS

Should there be cause for complaint, the matter should be brought to the notice of the Management of the premises in the first instance. **Failing satisfaction, the matter should be referred to the Tourist Information Office concerned (see list on pages 12 & 13) or The Irish Tourist Board, Baggot Street Bridge, Dublin 2.** In the case of Northern Ireland premises, complaints should be addressed to the Customer Relations Section, **Northern Ireland Tourist Board, 59 North Street, Belfast BT1 1NB.**

ERRORS AND OMISSIONS

The information contained in the accommodation section has been supplied by individual premises. While reasonable care has been taken in compiling the information supplied and ensuring its accuracy and compliance with consumer protection laws, the Irish Hotels Federation cannot accept any responsibility for any errors, omissions or misinformation regarding accommodation, facilities, prices, services, classification or any other information whatsover in the Guide and shall have no liability whatsoever and howsoever arising to any person for any loss, whether direct, indirect, economic or consequential, or damages, actions, proceedings, costs, claims, expenses or demands arising therefrom.

The listing of any premises in this guide is not and should not be taken as a recommendation from the IHF or a representation that the premises will be suitable for your purposes.

THINK ABOUT INSURANCE

We strongly advise you to take out an insurance policy against accidents, cancellations, delays, loss of property and medical expenses. Such travel and holiday insurance policies are available quite cheaply and are worth every penny for peace of mind alone.

CANCELLATIONS

Should it be necessary to amend or cancel your reservation, please advise the premises immediately, as there may be a cancellation penalty. Please establish, when making a reservation, what cancellation policy applies.

Blarney Woollen Mills
The Great Irish Shopping Experience

Ireland has a thousand places you'll want to visit, but only one magical shopping experience which you simply cannot miss. When you visit any Blarney Woollen Mills store you will find a traditional store full of classic clothing and gifts. Great names like Waterford Crystal, Belleek, Royal Tara, Irish Dresden and many more fill the giftware shelves, alongside an amazing collection of sweaters and accessories, woollen rugs and throws, Irish tweeds and linen and and and.....

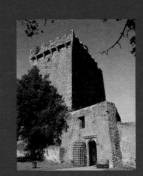

Blarney, Co. Cork • Bunratty, Co. Clare • 21/22 Nassau St., Dublin 2
el: 021 4385280 • www.blarneywoollenmills.ie • Email: blarney@blarney.ie

SAMPLE ENTRY

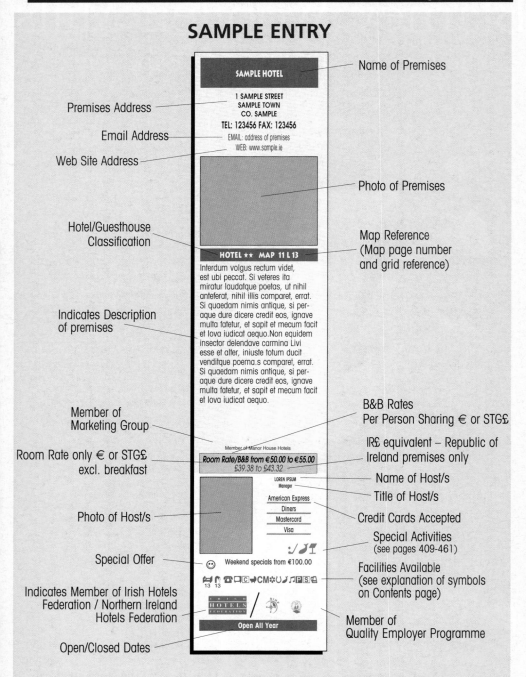

Name of Premises

Premises Address

Email Address

Web Site Address

Photo of Premises

Hotel/Guesthouse Classification

Map Reference (Map page number and grid reference)

Indicates Description of premises

Member of Marketing Group

B&B Rates Per Person Sharing € or STG£

Room Rate only € or STG£ excl. breakfast

IR£ equivalent – Republic of Ireland premises only

Name of Host/s

Title of Host/s

Photo of Host/s

Credit Cards Accepted

Special Activities (see pages 409-461)

Special Offer

Facilities Available (see explanation of symbols on Contents page)

Indicates Member of Irish Hotels Federation / Northern Ireland Hotels Federation

Member of Quality Employer Programme

Open/Closed Dates

Content inside the sample entry:

SAMPLE HOTEL

1 SAMPLE STREET
SAMPLE TOWN
CO. SAMPLE
TEL: 123456 FAX: 123456
EMAIL: address of premises
WEB: www.sample.ie

HOTEL ★★ MAP 11 L 13

Interdum volgus rectum videt, est ubi peccat. Si veteres ita miratur laudatque poetas, ut nihil anteferat, nihil illis comparet, errat. Si quaedam nimis antique, si per-aque dure dicere credit eos, ignave multa fatetur, et sapit et mecum facit et lova iudicat aequo.Non equidem insector delendave carmina Livi esse et alter, iniuste totum ducit venditque poema.s comparet, errat. Si quaedam nimis antique, si per-aque dure dicere credit eos, ignave multa fatetur, et sapit et mecum facit et lova iudicat aequo.

Member of Manor House Hotels

Room Rate/B&B from €50.00 to €55.00
£39.38 to £43.32

LOREN IPSUM
Manager

American Express
Diners
Mastercard
Visa

Weekend specials from €100.00

13 13

IRISH HOTELS FEDERATION

Open All Year

follow in a giant's footsteps.
start with his breakfast.

Next time you fancy a holiday break, try Northern Ireland for size. The massive, mysterious Giant's Causeway (built by giant Finn MacCool, some say, to reach his lady love in Scotland) will take your breath away. And just wait till you see the size of the breakfasts we serve here. One on its own is enough to keep you going for a whole holiday!

We're big on welcomes, too. Nobody's a stranger for long in Northern Ireland - because making new friends is one of our favourite hobbies. Just you try *not* joining in with the music, the singing and the chat when you spend an evening in one of our pubs!

It's ever so easy to get here - and there's so much to see and do you'll never, ever find yourself at a loose end.

Enjoy a wander along one of our beautiful, uncrowded beaches. Take a picnic to your very own secret, hideaway glen (there are nine in County Antrim alone!) or head for our magnificent rolling hills and blow a few cobwebs away.

Come and live it up in our superb restaurants, famous theatres and night clubs. Stroll our first class shopping avenues. Feed your mind in our heritage parks, galleries and museums. Come pony trekking, mountain biking or hang gliding. Or relax on a boating holiday, an angling break or a golfing package.

If you want much, much more from your next holiday or short break ring the CallSave number below.

It's easy to find out more. **CallSave**

1850 230 230

(Mon - Fri, 9.15am - 5.30pm. Sat, 10am - 5pm.)

Ireland

Northern Ireland Tourist Board

16 Nassau Street, Dublin 2.

www.discovernorthernireland.com

QUALITY EMPLOYER PROGRAMME SYMBOL
AN ASSURANCE TO GUESTS OF THE HIGHEST
STANDARDS OF EMPLOYMENT

Readers will notice our Quality Employer Programme (QEP) logo in the right hand corner of a large number of hotel and guesthouse entries throughout this guide. It is an assurance to you, as a guest, that the property you choose offers excellence in all standards of employment and treatment of staff. This ultimately benefits all guests, as the staff in these premises enjoy high job satisfaction, which in turn leads to an enhanced quality of service for you to experience.

The QEP is a defined code of practice with standards set in all areas of employment including; training, personnel relations, rostering and the arrangement of work hours. It also makes recommendations on meals, uniforms and pensions. Once a property has fulfilled all elements of the programme, it faces an annual review to ensure that standards are achieved and maintained. The QEP development by the Irish Hotels Federation is, in effect, a guarantee to you that the accredited properties have reached an important standard in relation to all their employment practices in these areas. It also means that staff are trained to carry out their job to set criteria and receive ongoing training to update their skills. All in all, this means a better service for guests.

The QEP status enjoyed by the properties in this guide also means that they attract the highest calibre of staff. Highly skilled staff in the hospitality sector want to work in the best of hotels and guesthouses, so that they can experience the best conditions of employment and career progression.

So you when you choose a QEP hotel or guesthouse, you can be assured you will experience Irish hospitality and friendliness at its best.

SWING

- Ireland's most renowned golf company. We service a number of major tour operators and corporations from around the World and have many satisfied repeat individual customers. Our record speaks for itself.

- Contact us to arrange your tee times in any part of Ireland. Our professional staff are on hand to give you a quality service. All size groups are catered for.

- Consultancy and Event Management is available to organisations and tour operators and help is provided with familiarsation trips.

- Transparencies and brochures are provided.

Phone: +353 (0)66 7125733
Fax: +353 (0)66 7123651
Email: swing@iol.ie
Web: www.swinggolfireland.com
Address: South West Ireland Golf Ltd, 24 Denny Street, Tralee, Co. Kerry, Ireland.

Donegal

Take a horse for a gallop down a beach in Donegal , and you'll run out of horse long before you run out of beach.

Take a seat around the bar in any of hundreds of village bars, and don't be surprised if the evening stretches long into the night.

Take a walk, in any direction, and expect to want to just keep on going.

Take a look over a harbour wall, and watch fish being landed fresh from the ocean. Then find a little restaurant, and savour it.

Take a bag of golf clubs, and measure yourself against some of the world's finest links courses, if you can keep your eye off the view.

Take the plunge and prepare all your senses for a workout. Visit Donegal!

FREE Brochure with Fantastic Special Holiday Offers Now Available

www.Donegal.direct.ie

☏ 074 21160

follow in a giant's footsteps.
start with his breakfast.

Next time you fancy a holiday break, try Northern Ireland for size. The massive, mysterious Giant's Causeway (built by giant Finn MacCool, some say, to reach his lady love in Scotland) will take your breath away. And just wait till you see the size of the breakfasts we serve here. One on its own is enough to keep you going for a whole holiday!

We're big on welcomes, too. Nobody's a stranger for long in Northern Ireland - because making new friends is one of our favourite hobbies. Just you try *not* joining in with the music, the singing and the chat when you spend an evening in one of our pubs!

It's ever so easy to get here - and there's so much to see and do you'll never, ever find yourself at a loose end.

Enjoy a wander along one of our beautiful, uncrowded beaches. Take a picnic to your very own secret, hideaway glen (there are nine in County Antrim alone!) or head for our magnificent rolling hills and blow a few cobwebs away.

Come and live it up in our superb restaurants, famous theatres and night clubs. Stroll our first class shopping avenues. Feed your mind in our heritage parks, galleries and museums. Come pony trekking, mountain biking or hang gliding. Or relax on a boating holiday, an angling break or a golfing package.

If you want much, much more from your next holiday or short break ring the CallSave number below.

It's easy to find out more. **CallSave**
1850 230 230
(Mon - Fri, 9.15am - 5.30pm. Sat, 10am - 5pm.)

Ireland

Northern Ireland
Tourist Board

16 Nassau Street, Dublin 2.

CROCKATINNEY GUEST HOUSE

80 WHITEPARK ROAD,
BALLYCASTLE,
CO. ANTRIM BT54 6LP
TEL: 028-2076 8801 FAX: 028-2076 9523
EMAIL: crockatinneyguesthouse@hotmail.com
WEB: www.crockatinneyguesthouse.co.uk

GUESTHOUSE ★★★ MAP 15 O 21

Crockatinney is a secluded, luxury guesthouse with panoramic views to Rathlin Island, Scotland, Fairhead and Knocklayde Mountain. It stands on 57 acres of wild countryside, with its own fishing lake and famine graveyard dating back to the 1800s. It is located on B15, en route to Carrick-A-Rede rope bridge and Giants Causeway and is a perfect base for visiting the Glens. Each room has its own balcony, TV and is en suite.

B&B from £25.00 to £30.00

ROISIN MCGINN
MANAGERESS

Mastercard
Visa

✓

🏠👥📺T C CM❄♨🅿🅰️♿
6   6

NIHF

Closed 30 September - 31 March

ADAIR ARMS HOTEL

BALLYMONEY ROAD,
BALLYMENA,
CO. ANTRIM BT43 5BS
TEL: 028-2565 3674 FAX: 028-2564 0436
EMAIL: reservations@adairarms.com
WEB: www.adairarms.com

HOTEL ★★★ MAP 15 O 19

A warm welcome awaits you at the Adair Arms Hotel, which is owned and run by the McLarnon Family. The hotel was built in 1846 by Sir Robert Adair, and designed by the famous architect Charles Lanyon. Situated in the heart of Ballymena, ideally located for touring the romantic Glens of Antrim, Slemish Mountain and North Antrim Coast. The hotel has recently been refurbished and has the added attraction of a new 18 hole golf course within one mile - courtesy transport provided for guests.

B&B from £35.00 to £42.50

G MCLARNON
MANAGER/PROPRIETOR

American Express
Diners
Mastercard
Visa

✓

 Weekend specials from £75.00

🏠👥☎📺T C ➡CMU♨🎵🅿🅰️
44   44

NIHF

Closed 25 - 26 December

BAYVIEW HOTEL

2 BAYHEAD ROAD,
PORTBALLINTRAE,
BUSHMILLS, BT57 8RZ
TEL: 028-2073 4100 FAX: 028-2073 4330
EMAIL: info@bayviewhotelni.com
WEB: www.bayviewhotelni.com

HOTEL N MAP 14 N 21

Opening December 2001, the Bayview Hotel is situated in the heart of the picturesque village of Portballintrae, one mile from Bushmills. Overlooking the Atlantic Ocean and close to the Giants Causeway and Old Bushmills Distillery, with 25 luxurious bedrooms, Conference Facilities, Restaurant and Bar. This small luxury hotel will be the ideal destination for conferencing, golfing, business, incentive travel and leisure.

Member of North Coast Hotels Ltd.

B&B from £37.50 to £55.00

MARY O'NEILL
GROUP MARKETING MANAGER

American Express
Diners
Mastercard
Visa

✓🍴

 Weekend specials from £95.00

🏠👥☎📺T C CMP🅰️🍴 inet
25   25

NIHF

Open All Year

B&B rates are Stg£ per person sharing per night incl. Breakfast

BUSHMILLS INN

9 DUNLUCE ROAD,
BUSHMILLS,
CO. ANTRIM BT57 8QG
TEL: 028-2073 2339 FAX: 028-2073 2048
EMAIL: mail@bushmillsinn.com
WEB: www.bushmillsinn.com

HOTEL ★★★ MAP 14 N 21

"It's one of those places where you hope it rains all day so you have an excuse to snuggle indoors." At the home of the world's oldest distillery between the Giant's Causeway and Royal Portrush Golf Club this award winning hotel and restaurant, with its open peat fires, pitched pine and gas lights, has been outstandingly successful in re-creating its origins as an old coaching inn and mill house.

Member of Ireland's Blue Book

B&B from £44.00 to £64.00

ALAN DUNLOP & STELLA MINOGUE
MANAGERS

American Express
Mastercard
Visa

32 32

  Inet
NIHF

Open All Year

CAUSEWAY HOTEL

40 CAUSEWAY ROAD,
BUSHMILLS,
CO. ANTRIM BT57 8SU
TEL: 028-2073 1226 FAX: 028-2073 2552
EMAIL: reception@giants-causeway-hotel.com
WEB: www.giants-causeway-hotel.com

HOTEL ★★ MAP 14 N 21

Situated on the North Antrim Coast at the entrance to the world famous Giant's Causeway and the new visitors' centre, this old family hotel established in 1836 has been tastefully renovated and restored to provide modern facilities while retaining its old grandeur and charm. The 28 centrally heated bedrooms have TV, telephone, tea/coffee making facilities and bathrooms en suite.

B&B from £32.50 to £35.00

STANLEY ARMSTRONG
PROPRIETOR

Mastercard
Visa

Weekend Specials from £85.00pp

28 28

NIHF

Open All Year

Room rates are Stg£ per room per night

LONDONDERRY ARMS HOTEL

20 HARBOUR ROAD,
CARNLOUGH,
CO. ANTRIM BT44 0EU
TEL: 028-2888 5255 FAX: 028-2888 5263
EMAIL: lda@glensofantrim.com
WEB: www.glensofantrim.com

HOTEL ★★★ MAP 15 P 20

This beautiful Georgian hotel was built in 1847. Once owned by Sir Winston Churchill, it is now owned and managed by Mr Frank O'Neill. With its open log fires, private lounges and award-winning restaurant this premier hotel in the Glens of Antrim is the perfect place to stay and discover the north eastern part of Ireland. Member of Irish Country Hotels.

Member of Northern Ireland's Best Kept Secrets

B&B from £42.50 to £50.00

FRANK O'NEILL
PROPRIETOR

American Express
Diners
Mastercard
Visa

☺ Weekend specials from £75.00

35 35

Open All Year

DOBBINS INN HOTEL

6/8 HIGH STREET,
CARRICKFERGUS,
CO. ANTRIM BT38 7AF
TEL: 028-9335 1905 FAX: 028-9335 1905
EMAIL: info@dobbinsinnhotel.co.uk
WEB: www.dobbinsinnhotel.co.uk

HOTEL ★★ MAP 15 P 18

A family run hotel, built in the 15th century and with its own ghost 'Maud', the hotel has 15 en suite rooms with tea/coffee facilities, colour TV and trouser press. Meals are served all day in the Paul Jones Lounge or the de Courcy Restaurant. Recently refurbished, the hotel has regular evening entertainment. Well located for a pleasant drive to the Giants Causeway or for a day's shopping in Belfast.

B&B from £34.00 to £44.00

MR & MRS FALLIS

American Express
Mastercard
Visa

15 15

Closed 25 - 27 December

KEEF HALLA COUNTRY HOUSE

20 TULLY ROAD,
NUTTS CORNER, CRUMLIN,
CO. ANTRIM BT29 4SW
TEL: 028-9082 5491 FAX: 028-9082 5940
EMAIL: info@keefhalla.com
WEB: www.keefhalla.com

GUESTHOUSE ★★★★ MAP 15 P 18

Keef Halla Country House is the nearest 4**** guesthouse to Belfast International Airport. All 7 bedrooms are elegantly decorated and include satellite TV, direct dial phone, trouser press, tea/coffee and refreshments. It is ideal for business people and holiday travellers requiring a central base for visiting Northern Ireland. We are conviently located to Antrim, Belfast, Crumlin, Dunadry, Lisburn and Templepatrick. Excellent value for money. Located on A26.

B&B from £22.50 to £25.00

CHARLES & SIOBHAN KELLY
OWNERS

American Express
Mastercard
Visa

7 7

Open All Year

B&B rates are Stg£ per person sharing per night incl. Breakfast

CAUSEWAY COAST HOTEL & CONFERENCE CENTRE

36 BALLYREAGH ROAD,
PORTRUSH,
CO. ANTRIM BT56 8LR
TEL: 028-7082 2435 FAX: 028-7082 4495
EMAIL: info@causewaycoast.com
WEB: www.causewaycoast.com

HOTEL ★★★ MAP 14 N 21

Located one mile from Royal Portrush Golf Course on the coast road between Portrush and Portstewart, overlooking the Atlantic Ocean and within easy reach of the Giant's Causeway, Carrick-a-Rede Rope Bridge and Dunluce Castle. Ideal base to relax and play golf at Royal Portrush, Portstewart, Castlerock, Ballycastle, Bushfoot, Gracehill and Galgorm Castle Golf Courses. Private car park. Sister hotel "Bayview Hotel Portballintrae, Bushmills" opening December 2001.

Member of North Coast Hotels Ltd.

B&B from £37.50 to £45.00

MARY O'NEILL
GROUP MARKETING MANAGER

American Express
Mastercard
Visa

Weekend specials from £95.00

🛏️ 📞 ⊓ T C CM❄ ∪ 🅿️ 📧 abc ♿
21 21

Open All Year

CLARMONT

10 LANSDOWNE CRESCENT,
PORTRUSH,
CO. ANTRIM BT56 8AY
TEL: 028-7082 2397 FAX: 028-7082 2397
EMAIL: clarmont10@hotmail.com
WEB: www.clarmont.com

GUESTHOUSE ★★ MAP 14 N 21

Clarmont, a spacious period townhouse, situated on Lansdowne Crescent, an award winning Victorian stucco-style resort terrace, designed to take maximum advantage of its seafront position on the famous Causeway Coast. With the renowned Royal Portrush Golf Club on its doorstep, the Clarmont enjoys an international golfing clientele. Also an ideal base for enjoying the many splendours & attractions of Ireland's North Coast. Convenient to pubs & restaurants. Ample parking.

B&B from £20.00 to £30.00

DECLAN PAUL CORMACK
OWNER

Mastercard
Visa

🛏️ 📞 ⊓ T C CM ∪ 🍴 S ♿
10 10

Open All Year

Room rates are Stg£ per room per night

COMFORT HOTEL PORTRUSH

73 MAIN STREET,
PORTRUSH,
CO. ANTRIM BT56 8BN
TEL: 028-7082 6100 FAX: 028-7082 6160
EMAIL: info@comforthotelportrush.com
WEB: www.comforthotelportrush.com

HOTEL ★★★ MAP 14 N 21

The 3*** Comfort Hotel Portrush opened February 2001, situated overlooking the Atlantic Ocean in the centre of Portrush. 50 en suite bedrooms with interlinking and ambulant disabled rooms, lift and private car park. Ideal base for golfing, walking, cycling, angling, sightseeing, families, tour parties and conferences. Golf at Royal Portrush, Portstewart, Castlerock, Ballycastle and Galgorm Golf Courses. Sister hotel "Bayview Hotel Portballintrae, Bushmills" opening December 2001.

Member of Choice Hotels Europe

B&B from £37.50 to £37.50

MARY O'NEILL
GROUP MARKETING MANAGER

American Express
Diners
Mastercard
Visa

50 50   Inet

Open All Year

EGLINTON HOTEL

49 EGLINTON STREET,
PORTRUSH,
CO. ANTRIM BT56 8DZ
TEL: 028-7082 2371 FAX: 028-7082 3155
EMAIL: reservations@eglintonhotel.com
WEB: www.eglintonhotel.com

HOTEL ★★ MAP 14 N 21

The Eglinton Hotel, situated in the centre of Portrush, is ideally situated to allow you to enjoy famous landmarks, beaches, golf courses, watersports, or indeed any adventurous sports. The hotel has lounges and a grill room. All rooms are en suite with colour TV, tea/coffee facility, DD phone and also a number of large family rooms are available.

B&B from £30.00 to £35.00

RAYMOND GRAY
PROPRIETOR

American Express
Mastercard
Visa

29 29

Open All Year

MAGHERABUOY HOUSE HOTEL

41 MAGHERABOY ROAD,
PORTRUSH,
CO. ANTRIM BT56 8NX
TEL: 028-7082 3507 FAX: 028-7082 4687
EMAIL: admin@magherabuoy.co.uk
WEB: www.magherabuoy.co.uk

HOTEL ★★★ MAP 14 N 21

Overnight in the centre of the Causeway Coast's golfers dream. The Magherabuoy is only a short driving time to Royal Portrush, Portstewart and Castlerock Golf Clubs. Quality location with views over Portrush Town. Members of A Taste of Ulster boasting best of Ulster produce. Unique to the Magherabuoy is on-site aromatheraphy/reflexology and our own specialist cook shop. NITB Welcome Host Gold Award winners 1999, 2000 & 2001.

B&B from £30.00 to £50.00

T. CLARKE
GENERAL MANAGER

American Express
Diners
Mastercard
Visa

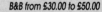

 Weekend specials from £100.00

38 38

Closed 24 - 26 December

B&B rates are Stg£ per person sharing per night incl. Breakfast

PENINSULA HOTEL

15 EGLINTON STREET,
PORTRUSH,
CO. ANTRIM BT56 8DX
TEL: 028-7082 2293 FAX: 028-7082 4315
EMAIL: reservations@peninsulahotel.co.uk
WEB: www.peninsulahotel.co.uk

HOTEL ★★ MAP 14 N 21

The Peninsula Hotel, situated in the centre of Portrush is ideally located to allow you to enjoy the delights of the Causeway Coast including the world famous Giants Causeway. Our bedrooms are warmly decorated with the finest of fittings to ensure comfort for all our guests. The hotel is wheelchair friendly throughout with a passenger lift to all floors. Excellent food served in our Galley Bistro. Less than 10 min walk to Royal Portrush Golf Club.

B&B from £35.00 to £50.00

GERALDINE DOHERTY
GENERAL MANAGER

American Express
Mastercard
Visa

 Weekend specials from £75.00

25 25

Open All Year

WINDSOR HOUSE

67-71 MAIN STREET,
PORTRUSH,
CO. ANTRIM BT56 8BN
TEL: 028-7082 3793 FAX: 028-7082 4625
EMAIL: stay@windsorguesthouse.com
WEB: www.windsorguesthouse.com

GUESTHOUSE ★★ MAP 14 N 21

Windsor House, a grand period townhouse located in the heart of Portrush retains superb sea views and offers the discerning visitor an ideal base from which to explore the world famous Causeway Coast. Large rooms with ornate high ceilings and spacious lounges and dining areas are all welcome features. With renowned home cooking, and being family run, the Windsor offers that little bit extra to ensure your stay will be very memorable.

Member of Causeway Coast & Glens

B&B from £22.00 to £25.00

MARK & AMANDA HOLMES

Mastercard
Visa

 Week partial board from £199.00

27 7

Open All Year

THE CAUSEWAY COAST & GLENS

"Relaxation and stimulation, an area with a unique fusion of unsurpassed beauty, tangible heritage, the great outdoors, craic and family fun. Come on, discover the magic for yourself!"

www.causewaycoastandglens.com

Causeway Coast and Antrim Glens Ltd.
11 Lodge Road, Coleraine,
Co. Londonderry, BT52 1LU
Northern Ireland
Email: mail@causewaycoastandglens.com
Tel: (028) 7032 7720

BALLYMAC

7A ROCK ROAD,
STONEYFORD,
CO. ANTRIM BT28 3SU
TEL: 028-9264 8313 FAX: 028-9264 8312
EMAIL: info@ballymachotel.co.uk
WEB: www.ballymachotel.co.uk

HOTEL ★★ MAP 15 O 18

The Ballymac Hotel set amid tranquil surroundings. Spectacularly reincarnated, the contemporary designed 15 en suite bedrooms with excellent facilities including DD phones, modem facilities, hairdryers, TVs and hospitality trays. Our Grill Bar/Lounge à la carte restaurant feature outstanding cuisine along with an extensive wine list. The Ballymac also boasts well-equipped function suites suitable for weddings, parties, trade shows and conferences. Extensive private parking is available in our grounds.

B&B from £30.00 to £42.50

CATHY MULDOON
GENERAL MANAGER

American Express
Mastercard
Visa

15 15

Closed 25 December

HILTON TEMPLEPATRICK

CASTLE UPTON ESTATE,
TEMPLEPATRICK,
CO. ANTRIM BT39 0DD
TEL: 028-9443 5500 FAX: 028-9443 5511
EMAIL: hilton_templepatrick@hilton.com
WEB: www.hilton.com

HOTEL ★★★★ MAP 15 O 18

Hilton Templepatrick, set in 220 acres of parkland, just 10 mins from Belfast International Airport is the perfect retreat for a short break. 130 en suite rooms offering views of the surrounding countryside. All rooms are equipped with satellite TV, phone, trouser press, hairdryer and hospitality tray. Dine in style in one of the hotel's restaurants or bars. Play a round of golf on the hotel's own 18 hole championship course or relax in the LivingWell Health Club.

Room Rate from £70.00 to £185.00

MATTHEW MULLAN
GENERAL MANAGER

American Express
Diners
Mastercard
Visa

130 130

Open All Year

TEMPLETON HOTEL

882 ANTRIM RD, TEMPLEPATRICK,
BALLYCLARE,
CO. ANTRIM BT39 0AH
TEL: 028-9443 2984 FAX: 028-9443 3406

HOTEL ★★★ MAP 15 O 18

This luxury hotel is in a prime location close to Belfast International Airport, Belfast City Centre and Larne Harbour. Mixing the best of modern facilities with the appeal of yesterday, the hotel offers total quality for all tastes and needs. Upton Grill Room serving lunch and dinner daily, Templeton à la carte restaurant, spacious lounge, 24 bedrooms including executive suites and family rooms, Sam's Bar with pub grub. Late bar on Friday and Saturday evenings.

B&B from £40.00 to £65.00

ALISON MCCOURT/CLAIRE KERR
GEN MANAGER/MRKTG MANAGER

American Express
Diners
Mastercard
Visa

24 24

Closed 25 - 26 December

B&B rates are Stg£ per person sharing per night incl. Breakfast

O'NEILL ARMS HOTEL

**20-22 MAIN STREET,
TOOMEBRIDGE,
CO. ANTRIM. BT41 3TQ**
TEL: 028-7965 0202 FAX: 028-7965 0970

HOTEL ★ MAP 14 N 18

Situated on the main road from Belfast (28 miles) to Derry (43 miles) via the International Airport (15 miles) and less than 40 mins from the North Coast. The O'Neill Arms is ideally located for the exploration of Northern Ireland. Nearby there is a championship golf course, forest walks and excellent coarse fishing. The hotel itself provides extensive carparking and beautiful gardens; and good food is served daily in our restaurant. The O'Neill Arms Hotel awaits you with a warm welcome all year round.

B&B from £30.00 to £35.00

DERMOT MCLARNON
PROPRIETOR

American Express
Diners
Mastercard
Visa

11   11

Closed 25 December

CHARLEMONT ARMS HOTEL

**57-65 ENGLISH STREET,
ARMAGH,
CO. ARMAGH BT 61 7LB**
TEL: 028-3752 2028 FAX: 028-3752 6979
EMAIL: info@charlemontarmshotel.com
WEB: www.charlemontarmshotel.com

HOTEL ★ MAP 14 N 16

A family run hotel set in the city centre which has completed major refurbishment. Convenient to shops, 18-hole golf course, leisure centre and all major tourist attractions including the 2 Cathedrals and other places of historic interest. 30 en suite bedrooms including one for the disabled, a 60 seat restaurant, 80 seat lounge bar, Turner's theme bar and Basement Café / Winebar that offers a unique dining experience for Armagh.

B&B from £50.00 to £70.00

THE FORSTER FAMILY

Mastercard
Visa

30   30

Closed 25 - 26 December

ASHBURN HOTEL

**81 WILLIAM STREET,
LURGAN,
CO. ARMAGH BT66 6JB**
TEL: 028-3832 5711 FAX: 028-3834 7194
EMAIL: info@theashburnhotel.com
WEB: www.theashburnhotel.com

HOTEL ★ MAP 15 O 17

Owned and managed by the McConaghy Family, the Ashburn Hotel is friendly and efficient. Conveniently situated with easy access to the motorway (M1), rail network and town centre. An ideal base for angling or golfing trips - 5 miles from the River Bann and 1 mile from local golf course. All bedrooms are en suite with colour TV, direct dial telephone and hospitality tray. Entertainment each weekend in our popular nightclub.

B&B from £29.50 to £29.50

JOHN F. MCCONAGHY

Mastercard
Visa

12   12

Closed 24 - 26 December

BALMORAL HOTEL

BLACKS ROAD,
DUNMURRY,
BELFAST BT10 0NF

TEL: 028-9030 1234 FAX: 028-9060 1455
EMAIL: info@balmoralhotelbelfast.co.uk

HOTEL ★★ MAP 15 P 18

Situated 4 miles via motorway from Belfast City Centre the Balmoral Hotel offers 44 en suite rooms, 8 of which are equipped with disabled facilities. All rooms have been designed with the guest in mind, each featuring remote control TV, radio, DD phone and hospitality tray. From the moment you arrive at the Balmoral Hotel you can expect the warmest of welcomes. The hotel offers spacious lounges inviting you to sit and relax. Food served all day in the Lady Anne, to fine dining in the hotel restaurant.

B&B from £25.00 to £37.50

CATHERINE & EUGENE MCKEEVER

American Express
Diners
Mastercard
Visa

🛏️ 44 44

Open All Year

CORR'S CORNER HOTEL

315 BALLYCLARE ROAD,
NEWTOWNABBEY,
CO. ANTRIM BT36 4TQ

TEL: 028-9084 9221 FAX: 028-9083 2118
EMAIL: info@corrscorner.com
WEB: www.corrscorner.com

HOTEL ★★ MAP 15 P 18

Corr's Corner is a family-run business located 7 miles north of Belfast at the M2 and A8 junction, 14 miles from Larne Harbour and Belfast International Airport. The hotel has 30 en suite rooms with 2 rooms specifically designed for guests with disabilities. Meals are served all day in the Lady R Bar and the Corriander Room Restaurant. The Ballyhenry Lounge is open every evening and the Cedar Room caters for meetings and private parties up to 60 persons.

Room Rate from £45.00 to £55.00

CATHERINE & EUGENE MCKEEVER

American Express
Diners
Mastercard
Visa

🛏️ 30 30

Closed 25 - 27 December

DUKES HOTEL

65/67 UNIVERSITY STREET,
BELFAST BT7 1HL

TEL: 028-9023 6666 FAX: 028-9023 7177
EMAIL: info@dukes-hotel-belfast.co.uk
WEB: www.dukeshotelbelfast.com

HOTEL ★★★ MAP 15 P 18

A bright new modern hotel constructed within one of Belfast's more distinguished Victorian buildings. Beside Queen's University, Ulster Museum, Botanic Gardens and less than 1 mile from the city centre. Golf courses only minutes away. 20 luxury en suite bedrooms, all with satellite TV, hairdryers and direct dial telephones. Gymnasium and saunas also available. Elegant restaurant serving local cuisine. Popular bar for the smart set. A friendly welcome and service is guaranteed.

B&B from £35.00 to £55.00

MICHAEL CAFOLLA
GENERAL MANAGER

American Express
Diners
Mastercard
Visa

🛏️ 20 20

Open All Year

B&B rates are Stg£ per person sharing per night incl. Breakfast

DUNADRY HOTEL AND COUNTRY CLUB

2 ISLANDREAGH DRIVE,
DUNADRY,
CO. ANTRIM BT41 2HA

TEL: 028-9443 4343 FAX: 028-9443 3389
EMAIL: mooneyhotelgroup@talk21.com
WEB: www.mooneyhotelgroup.com

HOTEL ★★★★ MAP 15 O 18

Truly the place to stay if you're looking for warm hospitality, comfort, charm, relaxation, imaginative gourmet cuisine. Millions of activities to choose from. Awarded Les Routiers Hotel of the year 1999. Luxurious bedrooms, beautiful food in Mill Race Bistro and fine dining restaurant, superb country club and swimming pool. Cycling, fishing, country walking, horse riding and golf available on site or on request. 5 minutes from Belfast Intl Airport. Central reservations @ 02890 385050.

B&B from £40.00 to £75.00

ROBERT MOONEY
GENERAL MANAGER

American Express
Diners
Mastercard
Visa

Weekend specials from £105.00

83 83

Closed 24 - 26 December

FITZWILLIAM INTERNATIONAL HOTEL

BELFAST INTERNATIONAL AIRPORT,
BELFAST BT29 4ZY

TEL: 028-9445 7000 FAX: 028-9442 3500
EMAIL: reception@fitzwilliaminternational.com
WEB: www.fitzwilliaminternational.com

HOTEL ★★★★ MAP 15 P 18

By Belfast International Airport and 50m from anywhere in the world, the Fitzwilliam International offers unsurpassed quality, careful attention to detail and cutting edge service. Belfast's only airport hotel, provides a unique dining experience in Circles Restaurant, headed by the huge talent of head chef, Nigel Broom. Luxurious, contemporary and stylish, describes perfectly the Fitzwilliam International experience. Cycling, golf (courtesy transport provided), fishing and watersports available on site or by request.

Member of UTELL

B&B from £40.00 to £85.00

CALUM MACLACHLAN
GENERAL MANAGER

American Express
Diners
Mastercard
Visa

Free room upgrade, 3 nights, Fri-Sun, for the price of 2.

106 106

Open All Year

HASTINGS EUROPA HOTEL

GREAT VICTORIA STREET,
BELFAST BT2 7AP

TEL: 028-9032 7000 FAX: 028-9032 7800
EMAIL: res@eur.hastingshotels.com
WEB: www.hastingshotels.com

HOTEL ★★★★ MAP 15 P 18

This international 4**** hotel is located in the heart of Belfast within walking distance of the shopping, entertainment and theatre districts. Having completed a £6m extension programme the hotel offers executive accommodation in addition to 2 restaurants, 2 bars, a nightclub and beauty salon. The Brasserie Restaurant offers an extensive bistro menu and is open from 6am - midnight, whilst the Gallery Restaurant offers fine dining and à la carte menu alternatives. This world famous hotel provides spacious elegance, luxury and style.

Member of UTELL International

B&B from £50.00 to £87.00

JOHN D TONER
DIRECTOR & GENERAL MANAGER

American Express
Diners
Mastercard
Visa

Weekend specials from £99.00
(2nts B&B + 1Dinner)

240 240

Closed 24 - 26 December

Room rates are Stg£ per room per night

HILTON BELFAST

4 LANYON PLACE,
BELFAST BT1 3LP

TEL: 028-9027 7000 FAX: 028-9027 7277
EMAIL: hilton_belfast@hilton.com
WEB: www.hilton.com

HOTEL ★★★★★ MAP 15 P 18

Along with the magnificent Waterfront Hall, you will find Hilton Belfast, a contemporary 5***** hotel in an enviable location. The hotel has been designed to offer the discerning guest every level of comfort and convenience and is within easy reach of many of Belfast's most famous attractions, including the Odyssey, an exciting new entertainment complex, just 5 minutes walk from the hotel.

Room Rate from £165.00 to £500.00

MATTHEW MULLAN
GENERAL MANAGER

American Express
Diners
Mastercard
Visa

195 195

Inet FAX

Open All Year

HOLIDAY INN BELFAST

22 ORMEAU AVENUE,
BELFAST BT2 8HS

TEL: 028-9027 1706 FAX: 028-9062 6546

WEB: www.holidayinn.com

HOTEL ★★★★ MAP 15 P 18

A modern hotel situated in the heart of Belfast's City centre, and ideally located for city centre shops, restaurants, Odyssey Centre, Opera House, Belfast Zoo, Botanic Gardens/Ulster Museum, City Hall & the Waterfront Hall. This newly built hotel offers residents superior air-conditioned bedrooms, the contemporary Junction Restaurant and Bar, a superb Health and Leisure Centre. There is also a Pay Car Park on site & an NCP car park behind the hotel.

Member of Bass Hotels & Resorts

B&B from £43.00 to £77.45

ADRIAN MCLAUGHLIN
GENERAL MANAGER

American Express
Diners
Mastercard
Visa

Weekend specials from £99.00

170 170

ald Inet

Open All Year

JURYS INN BELFAST

FISHERWICK PLACE,
GREAT VICTORIA ST,
BELFAST BT2 7AP

TEL: 028-9053 3500 FAX: 028-9053 3511
EMAIL: jurysinnbelfast@jurysdoyle.com
WEB: www.jurysdoyle.com

HOTEL ★★★ MAP 15 P 18

Located in the centre of Belfast, adjacent to the Opera House, the City Hall and the city's main commercial district. Just two minute's walk away are the prime shopping areas of Donegall Place and the Castlecourt Centre, while the city's golden mile, with its myriad lively bars and restaurants, is also within walking distance.

Room Rate from £71.00 to £71.00

MARGARET NAGLE
GENERAL MANAGER

American Express
Diners
Mastercard
Visa

190 190

Closed 24 - 26 December

B&B rates are Stg£ per person sharing per night incl. Breakfast

LA MON HOTEL & COUNTRY CLUB

41 GRANSHA ROAD,
CASTLEREAGH,
BELFAST BT23 5RF

TEL: 028-9044 8631 FAX: 028-9044 8026
EMAIL: info@lamon.co.uk
WEB: www.lamon.co.uk

HOTEL ★★★ MAP 15 P 18

This charming family-run hotel offers 71 contemporary en suite bedrooms, excellent banqueting and conference facilities in a rural setting just 5 miles from Belfast City centre. Guests may relax and unwind using luxurious leisure facilities including gymnasium, swimming pool, jacuzzi and sauna. A range of dining options is available with table d'hôte and à la carte menus. Casual dining with a cosmopolitan flavour is also available in our lively bistro. An ideal venue for business or leisure.

Room Rate from £80.00 to £125.00

FRANCIS BRADY
MANAGING DIRECTOR

American Express
Mastercard
Visa

☺ Weekend specials from £99.00

71 71 🛏️🛎️📞☎️📠🅣🅐🛁🅒●CMCS❖
🔊�📺🔌🚭⛽🅟🖲️ ⌚ inet
NIHE

Open All Year

LANSDOWNE HOTEL

657-659 ANTRIM ROAD,
BELFAST BT15 4EF

TEL: 028-9077 3317 FAX: 028-9078 1588
EMAIL: info@the-lansdowne.co.uk
WEB: www.the-lansdowne.co.uk

HOTEL ★★★ MAP 15 P 18

The new Lansdowne Hotel, refurbished in December 2001, located 2.5 miles north of the city centre. Belfast Castle, Fortwilliam Golf Course, Cave Hill Country Park and Belfast Zoo are but a stone's throw away. The bar and restaurant co-exist in a fusion of modern and contemporary design. With wonderfully landscaped gardens and children's play area, our conservatory restaurant is not to be missed, or relax and have a drink in our lounge bar.

B&B from £30.00 to £37.50

MICHAEL CAFOLLA
GENERAL MANAGER

American Express
Diners
Mastercard
Visa

25 25 🛏️🛎️📞☎️🔌🅣CMP🅢🛁▪️

Open All Year

MCCAUSLAND HOTEL

34-38 VICTORIA STREET,
BELFAST BT1 3GH

TEL: 028-9022 0200 FAX: 028-9022 0220
EMAIL: info@mccauslandhotel.com
WEB: www.mccauslandhotel.com

HOTEL ★★★★ MAP 15 P 18

The McCausland Hotel, a magnificent classical Italianate building which exudes a style that follows through to a beautiful contemporary interior. Bedrooms offer luxury & comfort complete with Neutrogena® toiletries. Modern Irish dishes can be enjoyed in the hotels brasserie & drinks in the café bar. Close to museums, theatres, shopping, Odyssey Arena & Waterfront Hall. Sister properties Hibernian, Dublin & Woodstock, Ennis (near Shannon) Co. Clare. GDS Acc code:LX. UK Toll free Access 00 800 525 48000.

Member of Small Luxury Hotels of the World

Room Rate from £110.00 to £190.00

NIALL COFFEY
GENERAL MANAGER

American Express
Diners
Mastercard
Visa

☺ Weekend specials from £99.00

61 61 🛏️🛎️📞☎️🔌🅣🅒●CMU♪🎵🅟🅢
🅐🄰🄲▪️🅢 inet
NIHE

Closed 24 - 26 December

Room rates are Stg£ per room per night

PARK AVENUE HOTEL

158 HOLYWOOD ROAD,
BELFAST BT4 1PB

TEL: 028-9065 6520 FAX: 028-9047 1417
EMAIL: frontdesk@parkavenuehotel.co.uk
WEB: www.parkavenuehotel.co.uk

HOTEL ★★★ MAP 15 P 18

The Park Avenue Hotel has recently been refurbished. 56 rooms with en suite facilities, including TV with satellite channels. Disabled facilities. Free parking. The Griffin Restaurant offers an extensive menu to suit all tastebuds. Alternatively our bistro menu is served daily in Gelston's Corner Bar. 5 minutes from Belfast City Airport. 10 minutes from city centre. Also in close proximity to the Odyssey Arena and Waterfront Hall. Excellent links to outer ring roads and all transport stations and ferry terminals.

B&B from £30.00 to £39.50

ANGELA REID
FRONT OFFICE/CONFERENCE MANAGER

American Express
Mastercard
Visa

56 56

Inet
NIHF

Closed 25 December

WELLINGTON PARK HOTEL

21 MALONE ROAD,
BELFAST BT9 6RU

TEL: 028-9038 1111 FAX: 028-9066 5410
EMAIL: mooneyhotelgroup@talk21.com
WEB: www.mooneyhotelgroup.com

HOTEL ★★★★ MAP 15 P 18

The ideal place to stay when you come to Belfast. Located 5 minutes from the city centre, in the fashionable area of South Belfast, the city's most popular venues are at our doorstep: King's Hall, Waterfront Hall, Odyssey complex, museums, theatres... Designed to international standards, the hotel is renowned for its elegant and relaxed atmosphere and its luxurious suites. You can also enjoy fine cuisine in the Piper's Bistro. Central Reservations 028-9038 5050.

Member of Best Western Hotels

B&B from £40.00 to £75.00

ARTHUR MOONEY
GENERAL MANAGER

American Express
Diners
Mastercard
Visa

☺ Weekend specials from £95.00

75 75

Inet FAX
NIHF

Closed 24 - 26 December

BROWN TROUT GOLF & COUNTRY INN

209 AGIVEY ROAD,
AGHADOWEY, COLERAINE,
CO. DERRY BT51 4AD

TEL: 028-7086 8209 FAX: 028-7086 8878
EMAIL: bill@browntroutinn.com
WEB: www.browntroutinn.com

HOTEL ★★★ MAP 14 N 20

The Brown Trout Golf and Country Inn nestles near the River Bann only 12.8km from the picturesque Causeway Coast. This old inn with 15 rooms, and four 5 star cottages, is Northern Ireland's first golf hotel. Bill, Gerry, Jane or Joanna will happily organise golf, horseriding and fishing packages with professional tuition if required or you can just enjoy a relaxing break and the craic with the locals. The warm hospitality and 'Taste of Ulster' restaurant will make your stay enjoyable.

Member of Irish Country Hotels

B&B from £30.00 to £42.50

BILL O'HARA
OWNER

American Express
Diners
Mastercard
Visa

15 15

NIHF

Open All Year

B&B rates are Stg£ per person sharing per night incl. Breakfast

BOHILL HOTEL & COUNTRY CLUB

69 CLOYFIN ROAD,
COLERAINE,
CO. LONDONDERRY BT52 2NY
TEL: 028-7034 4406 FAX: 028-7035 2424
EMAIL: bohill@nildram.co.uk

HOTEL ★★★ MAP 14 N 21

At the gateway to the Causeway Coast stands the Bohill Hotel bringing together the elegance of a Country House Hotel with the best of today's modern facilities. The hotel's restaurant holds the "Taste of Ulster" award. Guests enjoy modern bedrooms as one would expect in a luxurious hotel. To compliment, the hotel boasts the largest private hotel pool and leisure facilities in the area. Private gardens surround the hotel.

B&B from £35.00 to £55.00

DONAL MACAULEY
MANAGING DIRECTOR

Diners
Mastercard
Visa

☺ Weekend specials from £90.00

36 36

Open All Year

BEECH HILL COUNTRY HOUSE HOTEL

32 ARDMORE ROAD,
DERRY BT47 3QP

TEL: 028-7134 9279 FAX: 028-7134 5366
EMAIL: info@beech-hill.com
WEB: www.beech-hill.com

HOTEL ★★★★ MAP 14 L 20

Beech Hill is a privately owned country house hotel, 2mls from Londonderry. It retains the elegance of country living, restored to create a hotel of charm, character and style. Its ambience is complemented by the surrounding grounds, planted with a myriad trees, including beech - after which the hotel is named. Winners of British Airways Best Catering - 1994. CMV & Associates 00353 1 295 8900. Best Kept Secrets of Northern Ireland. Sauna, Steamroom, jacuzzi & fitness suites.

Member of Manor House Hotels

B&B from £50.00 to £70.00

SEAMUS DONNELLY
PROPRIETOR

American Express
Mastercard
Visa

27 27

Closed 24 - 26 December

Room rates are Stg£ per room per night

BEST WESTERN WHITE HORSE HOTEL

68 CLOONEY ROAD,
DERRY BT47 3PA

TEL: 028-7186 0606 FAX: 028-7186 0371
EMAIL: info@white-horse.demon.co.uk
WEB: www.whitehorse-hotel.com

HOTEL ★★ MAP 14 L 20

A luxury family-run hotel with 57 bedrooms including 3 executive suites and new (2001) leisure centre. The hotel is ideal for pleasure and business with 4 conference centres, 22m pool with children's section, gymnasium, aerobics studio, sauna and steam rooms, spa, jacuzzi and beauty. Only 10 minutes from the airport and city centre and on the main route to the Giants Causeway. Award winning restaurant and bar and keen room rates. AA Selected ♦♦♦.

Member of Best Western Hotels

B&B from £30.00 to £90.00

SHEILA HUNTER
GENERAL MANAGER

American Express
Diners
Mastercard
Visa

57 57

Open All Year

CITY HOTEL

QUEENS QUAY,
DERRY,
CO. DERRY

TEL: 01-214 4800 FAX: 01-214 4805
EMAIL: res@ho-gsh.com
WEB: www.greatsouthernhotels.com

UNDER CONSTRUCTION - OPENING MAY 2002

HOTEL P MAP 14 L 20

The new City Hotel, Derry offers an ideal location for touring the north west. The 145 bedroomed hotel overlooks the River Foyle on Queens Quay. It is close to the famous city walls. It has extensive conference and leisure facilities.

Member of Great Southern Hotels

Room Rate from £50.00 to £120.00

CATHERINE CRONIN
SALES MANAGER

American Express
Diners
Mastercard
Visa

☺ Weekend specials from £75.00

145 145

Closed 01 January - 30 June

QUALITY HOTEL DA VINCIS

15 CULMORE ROAD,
DERRY BT48 8JB

TEL: 028-7127 9111 FAX: 028-7127 9222
EMAIL: info@davincishotel.com
WEB: www.davincishotel.com

HOTEL ★★★ MAP 14 L 20

Conveniently situated only five minutes from the city centre, Quality Hotel Da Vinci's provides the ultimate in luxury and service. The hotel features 70 well appointed modern rooms, an award winning bar and restaurant à la carte and is home to Derry's premier nightspot, The Spirit Bar. Rooms are spacious and can accommodate up to four adults making it a perfect choice for families or groups. On-site secure parking available.

Member of Choice Hotels Ireland

Room Rate from £59.00 to £80.00

CIARAN O'NEILL
GENERAL MANAGER

American Express
Diners
Mastercard
Visa

☺ Weekend specials from £69.00 p.p.s

70 70

Closed 24 - 26 December

B&B rates are Stg£ per person sharing per night incl. Breakfast

TOWER HOTEL DERRY

THE DIAMOND,
DERRY CITY

TEL: 028-7137 1000 FAX: 028-7137 1234

WEB: www.towerhotelgroup.ie

UNDER CONSTRUCTION - OPENING FEBRUARY 2002

HOTEL P   MAP 14 L 20

A Tower Group Hotel - Tower Hotel Derry, located just off the Diamond in the heart of the city, will open in February 2002. The hotel is excellently situated for visiting the many tourist attractions, which include St. Columb's Cathedral as well as being an ideal base to tour the rest of County Derry. Facilities will include 94 bedrooms with state of the art amenities, Mediterranean style bistro, café bar, conference and business centre and an in-house fitness facility.

Member of Tower Hotel Group

B&B from £40.00 to £50.00

IAN HYLAND

American Express
Diners
Mastercard
Visa

☺ Weekend specials from £79.00

94   94

Closed 24 - 27 December

WALSH'S HOTEL

MAIN STREET,
MAGHERA,
DERRY BT46 5BN

TEL: 028-7954 9100 FAX: 028-7964 4222
EMAIL: info@walshshotel.com
WEB: www.walshshotel.com

HOTEL P   MAP 14 N 19

Walsh's Hotel has been totally refurbished to the status of a three star traditional style hotel. All 15 bedrooms have their own unique character. Each is en suite and is equipped with Telephone, TV, Iron/Trouser Press, Hairdryer, Hospitality tray and internet access. Jacks Bar serves food all day or you can dine in the Silver Hill Restaurant offering excellent cuisine. Located at the foot of the Sperrin Mountains, Walsh's Hotel is ideal for fishing, golfing or simply touring.

B&B from £35.00 to £45.00

KIERAN/ADRIAN BRADLEY & MICHAEL
MCLOUGHLIN DIRECTORS

Mastercard
Visa

☺ Special offers see web site

15   15

Open All Year

EDGEWATER HOTEL

88 STRAND ROAD,
PORTSTEWART,
CO. DERRY BT55 7LZ

TEL: 028-7083 3314 FAX: 028-7083 2224
EMAIL: edgewater.hotel@virgin.net
WEB: www.edgehotel.com

HOTEL ★★   MAP 14 M 21

Adjacent to Portstewart Golf Club, the hotel is magnificently situated overlooking spectacular views of Portstewart Strand, Hills of Donegal and Atlantic Ocean. All 28 en suite rooms (incl 6 suites with sea views) contain colour TV, radio, direct dial phone and tea/coffee facilities. Indulge in dinner in O'Malleys split level restaurant or relax and enjoy a bar snack in the Inishtrahull Lounge, both with picture windows capturing breathtaking views.

B&B from £30.00 to £45.00

KEVIN O'MALLEY
PROPRIETOR

American Express
Diners
Mastercard
Visa

☺ Weekend specials from £75.00

28   28

Open All Year

Room rates are Stg£ per room per night

CAIRN BAY LODGE

THE CAIRN, 278 SEACLIFF ROAD,
BANGOR,
CO. DOWN BT20 5HS
TEL: 028-9146 7636 FAX: 028-9145 7728
EMAIL: info@cairnbaylodge.com
WEB: www.cairnbaylodge.com

GUESTHOUSE ★★★ MAP 15 Q 18

Award winning guesthouse set in extensive gardens directly overlooking Ballyholme Bay and National Trust property Ballymacormick Point. The Lodge is family run, offering the highest standards of food, accommodation and service in luxurious surroundings. An oasis of calm yet only 10 minutes walk from Bangor Town Centre and Marina. 50m from Ballyholme Yacht Club, 5 golf courses within 5 miles and resident beauty therapist. Perfect for business or pleasure.

B&B from £25.00 to £30.00

CHRIS & JENNY MULLEN
PROPRIETOR

Mastercard
Visa

3   3

Open All Year

ROYAL HOTEL

26/28 QUAY STREET,
BANGOR,
CO. DOWN BT20 5ED
TEL: 028-9127 1866 FAX: 028-9146 7810
EMAIL: royalhotelbangor@cs.com
WEB: www.the-royal-hotel.com

HOTEL ★★ MAP 15 Q 18

Overlooking Bangor Marina this family run hotel is probably the best known landmark on Bangor's seafront. All 50 rooms are en suite and include 7 executive suites. Satellite TV, direct dial phone, courtesy tray and hairdryer are all standard throughout. Renowned for superb food served in a variety of atmospheric restaurants and bars. Nightclub, conference and banqueting facilities. 15 minutes from Belfast City Airport. Direct rail link from Dublin and Derry.

B&B from £40.00 to £45.00

PAUL DONEGAN
PROPRIETOR

American Express
Diners
Mastercard
Visa

☺ Weekend specials from £59.00

50   50

Closed 25 - 26 December

SHELLEVEN HOUSE

61 PRINCETOWN ROAD,
BANGOR BT20 3TA,
CO. DOWN
TEL: 028-9127 1777 FAX: 028-9127 1777
EMAIL: shellevenhouse@aol.com
WEB: www.shelleven.com

GUESTHOUSE ★★★ MAP 15 Q 18

An end of terrace Victorian house set back from Princetown Road, with garden and private parking, convenient to the marina, seafront and shops. We have 11 rooms, all en suite. The front rooms have a view of Bangor Bay and the Irish Sea beyond. Train and bus station is 5 minutes away, with direct link to the Dublin train service, and the city airport. Tee off times can be arranged at several local golf courses.

B&B from £23.00 to £27.50

MARY WESTON

Mastercard
Visa

☺ Weekend specials from £60.00

11   11

Open All Year

B&B rates are Stg£ per person sharing per night incl. Breakfast

TARA GUEST HOUSE

51 PRINCETOWN ROAD,
BANGOR,
CO. DOWN BT20 3TA
TEL: 028-9146 8924 FAX: 028-9146 9870
EMAIL: taraguesthouse@lineone.net
WEB: www.taraguesthouse.co.uk

GUESTHOUSE ★★ MAP 15 Q 18

10 en suite rooms in a quiet area close to all amenities. All rooms are en suite and comfortably furnished with telephone, TV, radio and tea/coffee making facilities. A friendly atmosphere and warm welcome assured.

B&B from £22.50 to £22.50

WILLIAM SPENCE

American Express
Mastercard
Visa

10 10

Closed 24 - 28 December

KILMOREY ARMS HOTEL

41-43 GREENCASTLE STREET,
KILKEEL,
CO. DOWN BT34 4BH
TEL: 028-4176 2220 FAX: 028-4176 5399
EMAIL: info@kilmoreyarmshotel.co.uk
WEB: www.kilmoreyarmshotel.co.uk

HOTEL ★★ MAP 12 P 15

Set in the middle of Kilkeel, home to Northern Irelands largest fishing fleet. We are perfectly placed to allow you to explore the beautiful mountains of Mourne. If golf is your passion, championship courses are within easy reach including Royal County Down. Only 30 minutes from Newry and 1 hour from Belfast by car. We can also be reached by regular bus service.

Member of Mourne Activity Breaks

B&B from £20.00 to £23.75

PETER HOUSTON

American Express
Mastercard
Visa

26 26

Open All Year

BURRENDALE HOTEL AND COUNTRY CLUB

51 CASTLEWELLAN ROAD,
NEWCASTLE,
CO. DOWN BT33 0JY
TEL: 028-4372 2599 FAX: 028-4372 2328
EMAIL: reservations@burrendale.com
WEB: www.burrendale.com

HOTEL ★★★ MAP 12 P 16

At the foot of the Mournes, the Burrendale is the ideal location for your family, golfing holiday or short break. The hotel comprises of a Country Club, Beauty Salon, à la carte Vine Restaurant, bistro style Cottage Kitchen Restaurant, Cottage Bar and excellent banqueting / conference facilities. In close proximity are 15 golf courses including Royal County Down, golden beaches, nature walks, forest parks and pony trekking. Superb hospitality awaits you.

B&B from £50.00 to £65.00

KEM AKKARI / SEAN SMALL
GENERAL MANAGER/OWNER

American Express
Diners
Mastercard
Visa

Weekend specials from £97.00

69 69

Open All Year

B&B rates are Stg£ per person sharing per night incl. Breakfast

CANAL COURT HOTEL

MERCHANTS QUAY,
NEWRY,
CO. DOWN BT35 8HF
TEL: 028-3025 1234 FAX: 028-3025 1177
EMAIL: manager@canalcourthotel.com
WEB: www.canalcourthotel.com

HOTEL ★★★★   MAP 12 O 15

British Airways award winning Canal Court Hotel. 51 en suite rooms with satellite TV, hospitality trays, hairdryer, direct dial phone and ironing facilities. The Old Mill Restaurant is one of the finest in the area, the Granary Bar has carvery and bar snacks served daily. Conference facilities for up to 300 people with superb suites for wedding receptions and private functions. Health and leisure complex incorporating gym, swimming pools, jacuzzi, sauna and steam room.

B&B from £55.00 to £65.00

MICHELLE BARRETT
GENERAL MANAGER

American Express
Diners
Mastercard
Visa

🛏️🍴📞🖥️🅿️T🅒CM🔥🖥️🎣♫
51 51
🅿️🅐a/c♿

NIHE

Closed 25 December

NARROWS

8 SHORE ROAD,
PORTAFERRY,
CO. DOWN BT22 1JY
TEL: 028-4272 8148 FAX: 028-4272 8105
EMAIL: reservations@narrows.co.uk
WEB: www.narrows.co.uk

GUESTHOUSE ★★★   MAP 15 Q 17

In the five years since it opened, The Narrows has taken the Northern Ireland hospitality industry by storm. With numerous awards and reviews for its architecture, cuisine, accommodation, accessibility and conference facilities, you will see why our guests keep coming back. Our 13 en suite rooms, restaurant and conference room all have stunning views of Strangford Lough. British Airways Tourism Award for Best Catering in Northern Ireland. AA 2 Rosettes. Sauna and walled garden for your relaxation.

Member of Kingdoms of Down

B&B from £42.50 to £45.00

WILL BROWN

American Express
Mastercard
Visa

☺ Weekend specials from £89.00

🛏️🍴📞🖥️🅿️T🅒CM✻🖥️🅿️
13 13
a/d♿ Inet FAX

NIHE

Open All Year

Room rates are Stg£ per room per night

COs. DOWN - FERMANAGH
PORTAFERRY - BELLEEK / ENNISKILLEN

PORTAFERRY HOTEL

10 THE STRAND,
PORTAFERRY,
CO.DOWN BT22 1PE
TEL: 028-4272 8231 FAX: 028-4272 8999
EMAIL: info@portaferryhotel.com
WEB: www.portaferryhotel.com

HOTEL ★★★ MAP 15 Q 17

Loughside hotel in spectacular setting. Award winning cuisine and fine wines. Explore or simply relax and do nothing; just peace and tranquillity. BA Toursim Endeavour Award, RAC Restaurant of the Year Award, AA rosette, Taste of Ulster, Good Hotel Guide. 29 mile from Belfast

B&B from £45.00 to £50.00

JOHN & MARY HERLIHY
PROPRIETORS

American Express
Diners
Mastercard
Visa

14 14

Open All Year

HOTEL CARLTON

2 MAIN STREET,
BELLEEK,
CO. FERMANAGH BT93 3FX
TEL: 028-6865 8282 FAX: 028-6865 9005
EMAIL: reception@hotelcarlton.co.uk
WEB: www.hotelcarlton.co.uk

HOTEL ★★ MAP 13 I 17

The Hotel Carlton's setting on the banks of the River Erne in the heart of the Irish lake district is quite simply breathtaking. Also on the steps of one of Ireland's most famous landmarks, Belleek Pottery, Ireland's oldest pottery. Ideally situated for visitors who wish to tour the nearby counties of Donegal, Sligo, Tyrone and Leitrim. The Hotel Carlton has recently been completely rebuilt in a traditional style and boasts 19 luxurious well appointed en suite rooms.

Member of MinOtel Ireland Hotel Group

B&B from £30.00 to £37.50

THE GALLAGHER & ROONEY FAMILY

American Express
Mastercard
Visa

19 19

Closed 24 - 25 December

KILLYHEVLIN HOTEL

DUBLIN ROAD,
ENNISKILLEN,
CO. FERMANAGH BT74 6RW
TEL: 028-6632 3481 FAX: 028-6632 4726
EMAIL: info@killyhevlin.com
WEB: www.killyhevlin.com

HOTEL ★★★★ MAP 11 K 16

Killyhevlin Hotel and chalets are situated on the shores of beautiful Lough Erne, making it a terrific location at the gateway to the West and an ideal base for exploring the many sights of Fermanagh. All 43 bedrooms plus the Belmore Suite are fitted to a high standard, all en suite, with satellite TV, direct dial phone, radio and tea facilities. Our scenic lounge and restaurant offer a wide variety of menus. Lunchtime buffet, bar snacks all day. Evenings, table d'hôte or à la carte.

B&B from £42.50 to £55.00

RODNEY J. WATSON
MANAGING DIRECTOR

American Express
Diners
Mastercard
Visa

☺ Weekend specials from £89.50

43 43

Closed 24 - 26 December

B&B rates are Stg£ per person sharing per night incl. Breakfast

MANOR HOUSE COUNTRY HOTEL

KILLADEAS,
ENNISKILLEN,
CO. FERMANAGH BT94 1NY
TEL: 028-6862 2211 FAX: 028-6862 1545
EMAIL: info@manor-house-hotel.com
WEB: www.manor-house-hotel.com

HOTEL ★★★★ MAP 14 K 16

This fine Victorian country mansion is beautifully situated in the Fermanagh countryside on the shores of lower Lough Erne. The hotel has been extensively refurbished to provide extreme comfort in splendid stately surroundings. All rooms are en suite with satellite TV, direct dial phone and tea making facilities. This is the ideal location for a break away where you can enjoy a range of activities in our ultra modern leisure complex including swimming pool.

B&B from £55.00 to £61.00

DAVID BEGLEY
GENERAL MANAGER

American Express
Mastercard
Visa

☺ Weekend specials from £95.00

46   46

Open All Year

RAILWAY HOTEL

34 FORTHILL STREET,
ENNISKILLEN,
CO. FERMANAGH BT74 6AJ
TEL: 028-6632 2084 FAX: 028-6632 7480
EMAIL: enquiries@railwayhotelenniskillen.com
WEB: www.railwayhotelenniskillen.com

HOTEL ★ MAP 11 K 16

James Crozier and Owen McKenna new owners of the Railway Hotel, are clearly succeeding in continuing the tradition of hospitality established through 150 years of family ownership. Guests have the choice of 19 well appointed bedrooms, all en suite, with Sky TV and telephone. A full range of meals is available, in style in the Dining Car Restaurant, which has an excellent reputation for food. Friendly staff and cosy atmosphere ensures a memorable breakaway for everyone.

B&B from £25.00 to £32.50

JAMES CROZIER/OWEN McKENNA
OWNERS

Mastercard
Visa

19   19

Closed 25 - 26 December

MAHONS HOTEL

ENNISKILLEN ROAD,
IRVINESTOWN,
CO. FERMANAGH
TEL: 028-6862 1656 FAX: 028-6862 8344
EMAIL: info@mahonshotel.co.uk
WEB: www.mahonshotel.co.uk

HOTEL ★★ MAP 13 K 17

Situated in the heart of the Fermanagh Lakeland. Ideal base for visiting all major tourist attractions - Belleek Pottery 20 minutes, Marble Arch Caves 30 minutes, Necarne Equestrian Centre 5 minutes, Lough Erne 5 minutes, Donegal 20 minutes. All rooms en suite, TV, tea making facilities. Bushmills Bar of the Year winner, entertainment at weekends, private car park. Family run from 1883. Visit us in our second century. Cycling, horseriding, tennis and golf all available.

Member of Fermanagh Lakeland Hotels

B&B from £34.00 to £37.00

JOE MAHON
MANAGER

American Express
Mastercard
Visa

☺ Weekend specials from £69.50

18   18

Open All Year

SILVERBIRCH HOTEL

5 GORTIN ROAD,
OMAGH,
CO. TYRONE BT79 7DH
TEL: 028-8224 2520 FAX: 028-8224 9061
EMAIL: info@silverbirchhotel.com
WEB: www.silverbirchhotel.com

HOTEL ★★★ MAP 14 L 18

The hotel is situated on the outskirts of Omagh on the B48 leading to the Gortin Glens, Ulster History Park, Sperrins and the Ulster American Folk Park. Set in its own spacious and mature grounds, the hotel now has 40 new en suite bedrooms to 3*** standard. Other facilities include Buttery Grill all day, newly refurbished dining room, function suite for 250 guests for weddings, dinners or conferences. Award winning leisure centre 300 metres away.

B&B from £38.00 to £48.00

ALLAN DUNCAN
MANAGER

American Express
Diners
Mastercard
Visa

 Weekend specials from £79.00

46 46

NIHF

Closed 25 December

VISITORS TO IRELAND

Ireland is a beautiful country. It is known as the 'Emerald Isle' because of its lush green fields and breath-taking scenery.

Every year people from all over the world come to Ireland to meet the friendly local people and enjoy our unspoiled natural landscape.

We love to share the beauty of our island with as many people as we can and we try to keep our country clean and 'green', both for ourselves, who live here, and for you, our guests.

Please help us to protect the natural beauty of our land, by respecting the environment, and doing as much as possible to keep it clean and unspoiled.

B&B rates are Stg£ per person sharing per night incl. Breakfast

As one of the oldest cities in Europe, Dublin provides the visitor with a multitude of cultural riches, from the ancient to the avant-garde: from history, architecture, literature, art and archaeology to the performing arts. Monuments in literature and in stone mark the history, writers, poets and people of Dublin. Medieval, Georgian and modern architecture provide a backdrop to a friendly, bustling port which can boast literary giants such as Wilde, Shaw, Joyce, Yeats, Beckett and O'Casey as native sons. Spawned by the need to ford the river Liffey, fortified by the Danes, developed by the Normans, adorned with fine buildings by the Anglo-Irish, the city has grown in stature and elegance over the century.

When it comes to entertainment, Dubliners with their natural friendly and fun-craving attitude, certainly know how to entertain. The quintessential 'Dublin Pub' provides the focal point of Dublin social life, illuminating the vibrant hues of Dubliners and their culture. It is a place where conversations and "craic" flow freely, unleashing the unique atmosphere that is at the heart of Dublin and its friendly people. Just a twenty-minute journey will bring the visitor from the bustling city centre to the charming coastal towns and villages of the county. These towns and villages provide boundless opportunities for craft-shopping, water-sports, seafood dining and picturesque walks against the spectacular background of Dublin Bay.

Whatever your heart desires, Dublin provides a superb location for all the above activities and many more besides.

Website: http://www.visitdublin.com

Reservations and Information may be obtained by visiting one of our Information Centres:

- Dublin Tourism Centre, Suffolk St.,
- Arrivals Hall, Dublin Airport,
- Ferry Terminal,
  Dun Laoghaire Harbour,
- Baggot St Bridge.
- O'Connell Street.

GUINNESS.

St. Patrick's Day Festival, Dublin.
March

Guinness Blues Festival, Dublin.
July

Kerrygold Horseshow, R.D.S. Dublin.
August

Guinness All-Ireland Hurling Championship Final, Croke Park, Dublin.
September

All-Ireland Football Championship Final, Croke Park, Dublin.
September

Dublin Theatre Festival, Dublin.
October

Event details correct at time of going to press

The 'wee county' as Louth is affectionately known, boasts a wide variety of activities and attractions in an area of natural scenic beauty and offers a truly unique, memorable holiday experience.

Adventure & Activity

Louth is a haven for adventure and water sports enthusiasts. The county boasts four top class adventure centres offering a diverse range of activities including sailing, canoeing, archery, banana skiing, windsurfing, kayaking, orienteering, abseiling, pier jumping, climbing and gorge & hill walking, to name but a few. The historic Cooley Peninsula is a natural paradise for adventure seekers. The legendary Cooley's provide the scenic backdrop as well as the perfect terrain for an action packed adventure breakaway.

Further down the coast at Clogherhead the soft sandy beaches and rugged coastline allow the visitor to enjoy canoeing and surfing at sea and hiking and orienteering on land.

Just one hour from both Dublin and Belfast; Louth with its vast range of accommodation, services and attractions makes it the ideal venue for corporate team building courses. Each adventure centre also caters for corporate groups offering team building courses and outdoor management development and training services.

Sailing is yet another activity to be indulged in. The excellent mooring facilities at Carlingford Marina ensure that visiting sailors to the area are well catered for while Carlingford Yacht charter and sea School operates two ocean going cruisers for yacht chartering and sail training.

Walking

The principle long distance walking route is the 'Tain Way'. This 40km route encircles the Cooley Peninsula and is named after the legendary event, the Tain Bo Cuailgne or the Cattle raid of Cooley. Shorter rural walks can also be enjoyed at Ravensdale, Townley Hall and Slieve Foye Forest Parks, the Boyne walk and Rathesker lakeside walk.

Cycling

Louth is ideal for the cycling tourist with many flat roads and varied and attractive cycling routes. The Tain Trail, Irelandis longest and most historic cycling route stretches from Rathcroghan in Roscommon to the Cooley Peninsula and runs through much of the county. Other routes include the Oriel trail, the Cooley cycle and the Louth coastal cycle.

Equestrian

If you are a casual rider, a horse handling expert of just enjoy the invigorating outdoor lifestyle you will be well catered for at Louth's two excellent A.I. R. E approved equestrian centres.

Golf

In County Louth, golf is part of the way of life. Louth has nine golf courses all of different variety from the idyllic parkland settings to the world famous links at Baltray. Although some of these courses are as testing as any in Ireland the main challenge is simply to keep your eye on the ball amid such splendid surroundings.

Angling

There are a number of well-established angling centres in Louth and a host of excellent fishing venues that will cater for the needs of all anglers. The main angling centres include Castlebellingham and Dundalk. There are also a number of smaller towns and villages in Louth, which would act as suitable bases for your angling trip. Game, sea and coarse angling can all be enjoyed in the wee county.

Gardens

Whether you are starting out or a seasoned gardening enthusiast there is no better way to gain more knowledge and get inspiration than to visit some of the many gardens that Ireland has become famous for. Whatever the season each garden has something to offer. County Louth is no exception to this and boasts four interesting gardens open to visitors as well as its very own gardening school.

Gourmet Cookery

Louth is home to two prestigious cookery schools, Ghan House and An Grianan. Both schools offer a range of interesting courses and provide first class accommodation on site.

Fine Dining & Entertainment

With a great selection of restaurants, entertainment venues and hostelries to suit all tastes Louth makes the perfect short breaks destination.

or log on to www.louthholidays.com

EAST COAST & MIDLANDS TOURISM

Ireland

LOUTH
Bet you didn't know...

Louth – Just one hour from Dublin.

Dublin

GOLFING

COOKERY

SAILING

WALKING

CYCLING

ADVENTURE

ANGLING

EQUESTRIAN

For a free brochure featuring:

LOUTH BREAKAWAYS
FEATURES OVER 40 QUALITY SHORT BREAKS IN LOUTH

- **Great value short breaks**
- **Family breaks**
- **Activity/Adventure breaks**
- **Cookery breaks**
- **Cycling holidays**
- **Equestrian breaks**
- **Gardening holidays**
- **Golfing breaks**
- **Sailing holidays**

Call: +353 42 933 5484.
+353 41 983 7070
+353 42 937 3033
Email: dundalktouristoffice@eircom.net

www.louthholidays.com

BRACKEN COURT HOTEL

BRIDGE STREET,
BALBRIGGAN,
CO. DUBLIN

TEL: 01-841 3333 FAX: 01-841 5118
EMAIL: info@brackencourt.ie
WEB: www.brackencourt.ie

HOTEL N MAP 12 O 12

The newly built Bracken Court Hotel is conveniently located in the seaside town of Balbriggan, 35 minutes north of Dublin City and 15 minutes from Dublin Airport making it an ideal location for access to the city, airport and as a gateway to the north. The 40 bedroom hotel provides luxurious surroundings where comfort and a wide range of facilities combine to satisfy the needs of both business and leisure guest.

B&B from €69.00 to €99.00
£54.34 to £77.96

LUKE MORIARTY
OWNER

American Express
Diners
Mastercard
Visa

Weekend specials from €146.00

40 40

a/c inet

Open All Year

RADISSON SAS ST HELEN'S HOTEL

STILLORGAN ROAD,
CO. DUBLIN

TEL: 01-218 6000 FAX: 01-218 6010
EMAIL: info.dublin@radissonsas.com
WEB: www.radissonsas.com

HOTEL ★★★★★ MAP 8 O 11

Situated on four acres of parkland with formal gardens to the front and rear. The hotel consists of a historic listed house, blended with a new bedroom wing of 151 bedrooms. The hotel has 2 restaurants, 2 bars and a fitness room, snooker room, health and beauty clinic, extensive meeting rooms and free car parking.

Member of Radisson SAS Hotels and Resorts
B&B from €185.00 to €255.00
£145.67 to £200.79

SUSANNE HAZENBERG
GENERAL MANAGER

American Express
Diners
Mastercard
Visa

151 151

inet

Open All Year

STILLORGAN PARK HOTEL

STILLORGAN ROAD,
BLACKROCK,
CO. DUBLIN

TEL: 01-288 1621 FAX: 01-283 1610
EMAIL: sales@stillorganpark.com
WEB: www.stillorganpark.com

HOTEL ★★★ MAP 8 O 11

Dublin's premier hotel for the southside. After an investment of £12 million, this contemporary property now boasts 125 en suite fully air-conditioned bedrooms, a new fully equipped conference and banqueting centre catering for up to 500 delegates, a superb Mediterranean style restaurant and a comfortable bar. Located just a few minutes from Dublin's city centre on main N11, parking for 350 cars. 20 minutes from Druids Glen Golf Course. AA 4****. Awarded the hygiene mark.

B&B from €97.50 to €110.00
£76.79 to £86.63

RONAN DORAN
MANAGING DIRECTOR

American Express
Diners
Mastercard
Visa

Weekend specials from €171.41

125 125

a/c inet

Open All Year

B&B rates are per person sharing per night incl. Breakfast

AIRPORT VIEW

COLD WINTERS,
BLAKES CROSS,
CO. DUBLIN

TEL: 01-843 8756 FAX: 01-807 1949
EMAIL: gerrybutterly@hotmail.com
WEB: www.airportviewguesthouse.com

GUESTHOUSE ★★★ MAP 8 O 11

Airport View newly built luxurious guesthouse situated 4.5 miles from Dublin Airport, on a 7 acre site. Incorporates 4 poster bedroom with jacuzzi, TV lounge, conference room, snooker room, restaurant. All rooms en suite, TV, tea/coffee, fax and computer outlet facilities. Private car park, golf packages available. Airport View is conveniently located 50 yds off the main Dublin-Belfast road. It has all the features of a luxury hotel.

B&B from € 40.00 to € 47.50
£31.50 to £37.40

GERARD BUTTERLY/ ANNEMARIE BEGGS
PROPRIETOR

| Mastercard |
| Visa |

🛏🅵☎🖥🆃🅰🅲🍴CM❄🔍☂🅹🅿
10 10
Ⓢ🆈ald 🖥 Inet FAX

Closed 24 - 25 December

TUDOR HOUSE

DALKEY,
CO. DUBLIN

TEL: 01-285 1528 FAX: 01-284 8133
EMAIL: tudorhousedalkey@hotmail.com

GUESTHOUSE ★★★★ MAP 8 P 11

An elegant listed manor house with secluded grounds in the heart of Dalkey. Period ambience and personal friendly service are the hallmarks of Tudor House. Bedrooms are individually decorated and enjoy views of Dublin Bay. Dalkey is a charming heritage town with Norman castles and quaint harbours. It has many excellent restaurants and pubs. It is 3km from Dun Laoghaire Ferry Port and offers rapid access to Dublin City.

B&B from € 49.00 to € 58.00
£38.59 to £45.68

KATIE HAYDON
OWNER

| Mastercard |
| Visa |

🛏🅵☎🖥🆃❄🅹🅿
6   6

IRISH HOTELS FEDERATION

Open All Year

Room rates are per room per night

WATERSIDE HOTEL

DONABATE,
CO. DUBLIN

TEL: 01-843 6153 FAX: 01-843 6111
EMAIL: info@thewatersidehotel.com
WEB: www.thewatersidehotel.com

HOTEL U MAP 12 O 12

Situated only 10 minutes from Dublin Airport and 11 miles from the city centre on the beach. You'll find The Waterside Hotel adorned by 6 beautiful golf courses. Our club house bar offers ambience, comfort and quality service and the new Links Restaurant offers the best of international cuisine from our extensive à la carte menu. Our newly refurbished en suite bedrooms boast spectacular views of Lambay Island, Howth Head and the lush fairways of the adjoining links golf course. Breakfast served till noon. Live music at weekends.

B&B from €40.00 to €75.00
£31.50 to £59.07

PAULA BALDWIN
PROPRIETOR

Mastercard
Visa

18 18

HOTELS
FEDERATION

Closed 24 - 26 December

GREAT SOUTHERN HOTEL DUBLIN AIRPORT

DUBLIN AIRPORT,
CO. DUBLIN

TEL: 01-844 6000 FAX: 01-844 6001
EMAIL: res@dubairport-gsh.com
WEB: www.greatsouthernhotels.com

HOTEL U MAP 12 O 11

Situated within the airport complex, just two minutes from the main terminal, the Great Southern Hotel provides a tranquil haven for the busy traveller. The guestrooms have every convenience and Potters Restaurant and Clancy's Bar allow guests unwind in stylish surroundings. The hotel has a wide range of conference rooms. Bookable worldwide through UTELL International or Central Reservations on 01-214 4800.

Room Rate from €190.00 to €190.00
£149.61 to £149.61

EAMON DALY
GENERAL MANAGER

American Express
Diners
Mastercard
Visa

147 147

HOTELS
FEDERATION

Closed 24 - 26 December

HOLIDAY INN DUBLIN AIRPORT

DUBLIN AIRPORT,
CO. DUBLIN

TEL: 01-808 0500 FAX: 01-844 6002
EMAIL: gm1767@forte-hotels.com
WEB: www.holiday-inn.co.uk

HOTEL ★★★★ MAP 12 O 11

A modern hotel located on the airport complex, offering a choice of standard and superior accommodation, 11.27km from the city centre. All rooms offer tea/coffee making facilites, mini-bar, trouser press, hairdryer, TV and pay movies. 24hr courtesy coach to and from the airport. Superb choice of dining options including the Bistro Restaurant, Sampans Oriental Restaurant, Café Express Lounge and 24hr room service. The Bodhran Bar (traditional Irish Pub) has live music at weekends. Residents may use the ALSAA Leisure Centre swimming pool.

Member of Six Continents Hotels
B&B from €85.00 to €124.50
£66.94 to £98.05

BRIAN THORNTON
GENERAL MANAGER

American Express
Diners
Mastercard
Visa

☺ Weekend specials from €169.00

249 249

HOTELS
FEDERATION

Closed 24 - 25 December

B&B rates are per person sharing per night incl. Breakfast

AARONMOR GUESTHOUSE

1B/1C SANDYMOUNT AVENUE,
BALLSBRIDGE,
DUBLIN 4
TEL: 01-668 7972 FAX: 01-668 2377
EMAIL: aaronmor@indigo.ie

GUESTHOUSE ★★★ MAP 8 O 11

Welcome to Aaronmor, we trust your stay will have pleasant memories. Turn of century home in fashionable Ballsbridge. All rooms en suite, centrally heated, direct dial phones, fax, tea/coffee facilities. Private car park. Convenient R.D.S. showgrounds, Lansdowne Rugby Club, Point Depot, embassies, museums, car ferries, airport, bus/train service. 10 mins city centre. Enjoy our relaxed atmosphere. Traditional Irish breakfast. Lift to all floors. AA ♦♦♦♦

B&B from €35.00 to €60.00
£27.56 to £47.25

BETTY & MICHAEL DUNNE

American Express
Mastercard
Visa

17 17

Closed 24 - 26 December

ABBERLEY COURT HOTEL

BELGARD ROAD,
TALLAGHT,
DUBLIN 24
TEL: 01-459 6000 FAX: 01-462 1000
EMAIL: abberley@iol.ie
WEB: www.abberley.ie

HOTEL ★★★ MAP 8 O 11

The Abberley Court Hotel is a recently built hotel situated at the foothills of the Dublin Mountains, beside The Square towncentre in Tallaght. The facilities include 40 en suite bedrooms, Kilcawleys Traditional Irish pub, The Leaf Chinese Restaurant. Conference/meeting/training facilities with private car parking. Activities in the locality include golf, pitch & putt, ten pin bowling, horse riding, pony trekking, fishing, watersports.

B&B from €38.09 to €62.21
£30.00 to £49.00

KAREN GARRY & MAIREAD SLYE

American Express
Diners
Mastercard
Visa

40 40

Closed 25 - 30 December

FINGAL

Dublin • Ireland
Rural Charm at the Gates of Dublin

www.fingal-dublin.com
For further information contact:

FINGAL TOURISM
Mainscourt
Main Street
Swords
Fingal
Co. Dublin

Tel: +353 1 8400077
Email: info@fingaltourism.ie
Web: www.fingal-dublin.com

Room rates are per room per night

ABBEY HOTEL

52 MIDDLE ABBEY STREET,
DUBLIN 1

TEL: 01-872 8188 FAX: 01-872 8585
EMAIL: reservations@abbeyhotel.com
WEB: www.abbey-hotel.com

HOTEL ★★ MAP 8 O 11

Small, intimate hotel in the heart of Dublin city centre. It is close to all main shopping areas and night life. The stylish rooms are decorated to high standard. The hotel offers a full à la carte menu daily to 9pm. Only minutes walk from O'Connell Street and Temple Bar. Facilities include TV, telephone, car park, bar, restaurant, entertainment and lift. 21 rooms all en suite.

B&B from €58.00 to €115.00
£45.68 to £90.57

SHEILA O'RIORDAN
GENERAL MANAGER

American Express
Mastercard
Visa

21 21

Closed 24 - 27 December

ABERDEEN LODGE

53 PARK AVENUE, OFF AILESBURY ROAD,
BALLSBRIDGE,
DUBLIN 4

TEL: 01-283 8155 FAX: 01-283 7877
EMAIL: aberdeen@iol.ie
WEB: www.halpinsprivatehotels.com

GUESTHOUSE ★★★★ MAP 8 O 11

Award-winning, 4★★★★, a luxurious combination of Edwardian grace, fine food, modern comforts, all that one expects of a private hotel, aircon suites with jacuzzi, executive facilities, landscaped gardens and guest carpark. Close to city centre, airport and car ferry terminals by DART or bus. Accolades - RAC AAA, Best Loved Hotels, Green Book, Johansens. Sister property of Merrion Hall, Blakes and Halpins Hotel. USA toll free 1800 617 3178. UK free phone 0800 096 4748.

Member of Relais du Silence
B&B from €45.00 to €90.00
£35.44 to £70.88

PAT HALPIN
PROPRIETOR

American Express
Diners
Mastercard
Visa

20 20

Inet FAX

HOTELS
FEDERATION

Open All Year

ABRAE COURT

9 ZION ROAD,
RATHGAR,
DUBLIN 6

TEL: 01-492 2242 FAX: 01-492 3944
EMAIL: abrae@eircom.net
WEB: www.abraecourt.com

GUESTHOUSE ★★★ MAP 8 O 11

Built in 1864, family run, 3★★★ Victorian guesthouse is located in the prestigious residential area of Rathgar, just ten minutes from the heart of Dublin City. Guestrooms are furnished with en suite bathroom, colour TV, direct dial phone and coffee/tea making facilities. Laundry service and a lock up car park are available. Bus routes, a good selection of restaurants, pubs, tourist attractions and various sports.

B&B from €34.50 to €49.50
£27.17 to £38.98

NEVILLE KEEGAN
OWNER

Mastercard
Visa

14 14

HOTELS
FEDERATION

Closed 22 - 28 December

B&B rates are per person sharing per night incl. Breakfast

ACADEMY HOTEL

FINDLATER PLACE,
OFF O'CONNELL STREET,
DUBLIN 1

TEL: 01-878 0666 FAX: 01-878 0600

EMAIL: stay@academy-hotel.ie
WEB: www.academy-hotel.ie

HOTEL U   MAP 8 O 11

The natural choice for the discerning visitor to Dublin, we offer the ultimate in comfort & convenience. Located off the city's main thoroughfare, O'Connell Street, only a short stroll from the very best of international shopping, galleries, theatres and the cosmopolitan area of Temple Bar. Our beautifully appointed en suite, air conditioned rooms represent the perfect retreat after a demanding meeting or a hectic day of shopping or sightseeing. Free parking, bar, restaurant & Conference facilities. GDS Access Code: HK

B&B from €49.00 to €99.00
£38.59 to £77.97

JOSEPH COMERFORD
PROPRIETOR

American Express
Diners
Mastercard
Visa

Midweek specials from €129.00

98 98

Inet FAX

IRISH HOTELS FEDERATION

Open All Year

ADAMS TRINITY HOTEL

28 DAME STREET,
DUBLIN 2

TEL: 01-670 7100 FAX: 01-670 7101

EMAIL: reservations.adamstrinity@indigo.ie
WEB: www.adamstrinity.com

HOTEL ★★★   MAP 8 O 11

What better location in Dublin than the Adams Trinity Hotel? Located midway between Dublin Castle, Grafton Street and Trinity College; it faces the vibrant Temple Bar area. Traditional style bedrooms are finished to an exceptionally luxurious standard. The hotel features the Mercantile Bar and Restaurant, O'Brien's Traditional Bar and café style Brokers Bar. The Adams Trinity Hotel offers all guests that same personal attention and warmth, it has that little something special.

B&B from €62.85 to €95.23
£49.50 to £75.00

FRAN RYDER/PETER HANAHOE
PROPRIETORS

American Express
Diners
Mastercard
Visa

28 28

IRISH HOTELS FEDERATION

Closed 24 - 27 December

AISHLING HOUSE

19/20 ST. LAWRENCE ROAD,
CLONTARF,
DUBLIN 3

TEL: 01-833 9097 FAX: 01-833 8400

EMAIL: info@aishlinghouse.com
WEB: www.aishlinghouse.com

GUESTHOUSE ★★★   MAP 8 O 11

Elegant listed family-run Victorian residence, situated in Clontarf, north Dublin's most exclusive suburb. Ideally located only minutes drive from Point Theatre, City centre and Dublin Port, yet only 15 mins from airport. Numerous golf courses nearby and short walk to Leisure complex. Tranquil elegant lounge, half acre grounds, child's play area, car park, fax facilities. We offer superb luxury accommodation at affordable prices. A treasure of outstanding quality.

B&B from €35.00 to €45.00
£27.56 to £35.44

ROBERT & FRANCES ENGLISH
OWNERS

Mastercard
Visa

Midweek specials from €100.00

9 9

IRISH HOTELS FEDERATION

Open All Year

Room rates are per room per night

ALEXANDER HOTEL

AT MERRION SQUARE,
DUBLIN 2

TEL: 01-607 3700 FAX: 01-661 5663
EMAIL: alexanderres@ocallaghanhotels.ie
WEB: www.ocallaghanhotels.ie

HOTEL U MAP 8 O 11

Contemporary style deluxe hotel ideally located in Dublin city centre beside Trinity College, 5 mins walk from museums, shops and business districts. 102 air-conditioned guestrooms and suites, Caravaggio's Restaurant, Winners Bar, gymnasium and extensive meeting facilities. Free private valet car parking. USA Toll Free Reservations 1800 569 9983 or on line at www.ocallaghanhotels.ie

Member of O'Callaghan Hotels

Room Rate from €215.00 to €340.00
£169.33 to £267.77

JOHN CLESHAM
GENERAL MANAGER

American Express
Diners
Mastercard
Visa

102 102

Inet

IRISH HOTELS FEDERATION

Open All Year

ANCHOR GUEST HOUSE

49 LOWER GARDINER STREET,
DUBLIN 1

TEL: 01-878 6913 FAX: 01-878 8038
EMAIL: gtcoyne@gpo.iol.ie
WEB: www.anchorguesthouse.com

GUESTHOUSE ★★★ MAP 8 O 11

The Anchor Guesthouse is located in the heart of the city centre. It is a tastefully refurbished Georgian house with a modern purpose built bedroom wing attached. Our location is a perfect base for city exploration. Temple Bar, Trinity College, Grafton Street, theatres, galleries and museums are but a stone's throw. We are 2 minutes walk from the central bus station, which has connections to the airport and ferry terminals.

B&B from €31.75 to €50.80
£25.01 to £40.01

JOAN & GERRY COYNE
PROPRIETORS

Mastercard
Visa

☺ Midweek specials from €95.25

22 22

IRISH HOTELS FEDERATION

Open All Year

ANGLESEA TOWN HOUSE

63 ANGLESEA ROAD,
BALLSBRIDGE,
DUBLIN 4

TEL: 01-668 3877 FAX: 01-668 3461

GUESTHOUSE ★★★★ MAP 8 O 11

This is a world-renowned guesthouse of national breakfast award fame. It has been featured on TV in both Ireland and the UK and has won entry in British, Irish, European and American travel guides and journals. It is a fine Edwardian residence of 7 en suite rooms with phone and TV, offering quiet elegance to discerning guests who wish to combine country-style charm with convenience to town. A warm welcome awaits you from your hostess Helen Kirrane and her family.

B&B from €60.00 to €70.00
£47.25 to £55.13

HELEN KIRRANE
OWNER

American Express
Mastercard
Visa

7 7

Closed 15 December - 08 January

B&B rates are per person sharing per night incl. Breakfast

ARDAGH HOUSE

NO.1 HIGHFIELD ROAD,
RATHGAR,
DUBLIN 6
TEL: 01-497 7068 FAX: 01-497 3991
EMAIL: enquiries@ardagh-house.ie
WEB: www.ardagh-house.ie

GUESTHOUSE ★★★ MAP 8 O 11

Having been recently totally refurbished, Ardagh House is conveniently situated in a premier residential area. This imposing turn of the century premises contains many of the gracious and spacious features of a fine detached residence of that era and yet incorporating modern creature comforts. Within easy distance of the city centre, RDS, etc. This fine property stands on approximately 1/2 acre with ample off street car parking and good gardens.

B&B from €35.00 to €64.00
£27.56 to £50.40

WILLIE AND MARY DOYLE
PROPRIETORS

Mastercard
Visa

19 19

Closed 23 - 27 December

ARLINGTON HOTEL

23/25 BACHELORS WALK,
O'CONNELL BRIDGE,
DUBLIN 1
TEL: 01-804 9100 FAX: 01-804 9152
EMAIL: info@arlington.ie
WEB: www.arlington.ie

HOTEL ★★★ MAP 8 O 11

The most central hotel in Dublin, overlooking the river Liffey at O'Connell Bridge. Dublin's top attractions and shopping districts on your doorstep. 115 en suite bedrooms, free secure underground parking, meeting room. Magnificent medieval Knightsbridge bar with live Irish music and dancing 7 nights a week all year round (free admission). Carvery lunch and à la carte bar menu available, candle light Knights bistro. Perfect base for business or pleasure.

B&B from €67.28 to €120.00
£52.98 to £94.49

PAUL KEENAN
GENERAL MANAGER

American Express
Mastercard
Visa

 Midweek specials from €170.14

115 115

Closed 24 - 26 December

ASHFIELD HOUSE

5 CLONSKEAGH ROAD,
DUBLIN 6
TEL: 01-260 3680 FAX: 01-260 4236
EMAIL: ashfieldhouse@holidayhound.com

GUESTHOUSE U MAP 8 O 11

One of Dublin's friendliest family run guesthouses. Providing comfort and service of a very high standard to the tourist and business sector. Rooms are en suite with TV, direct dial phones, tea/coffee facilities, hairdryer etc. A fax service is available. 10 mins from city centre, RDS, Lansdowne Road, Leopardstown Racecourse, ferry ports etc. Many top class pubs and restaurants adjacent to Ashfield House. We provide off street parking. There is an excellent bus service directly to city centre. Air coach direct to airport is a mere 5 min walk.

B&B from €52.00 to €76.00
£40.95 to £59.85

FRANK AND OLIVE TAYLOR

Mastercard
Visa

10 10

Closed 24 - 27 December

Room rates are per room per night

ASHLING HOTEL

PARKGATE STREET,
DUBLIN 8

TEL: 01-677 2324 FAX: 01-679 3783
EMAIL: info@ashlinghotel.ie
WEB: www.ashlinghotel.ie

HOTEL ★★★ MAP 8 O 11

Why choose us? Stylish refurbishment. Spacious en suite bedrooms, secure parking, conference/meeting rooms. Under 8 mins by taxi/bus to city cntr/Temple Bar. Lovely quaint pubs, Guinness Brewery, Phoenix Park, other attractions nearby. Easily found location by car/rail/bus. By car take city centre route & briefly follow River Liffey westward. Taxi/airlink bus from airport, Heuston Intercity rail station opposite. For onward journeys we are within easy access of all major roads.

Member of Best Western Hotels

B&B from €53.00 to €95.00
£41.74 to £74.82

ALAN MOODY
GENERAL MANAGER

American Express
Diners
Mastercard
Visa

☺ Midweek specials from €135.00

147 147

HOTELS
FEDERATION

Closed 24 - 26 December

ASTON HOTEL

7/9 ASTON QUAY,
DUBLIN 2

TEL: 01-677 9300 FAX: 01-677 9007
EMAIL: stay@aston-hotel.com
WEB: www.aston-hotel.com

HOTEL U MAP 8 O 11

A warm welcome awaits you at the Aston Hotel, located in Temple Bar and overlooking the River Liffey. Friendly staff and pleasant surroundings will make your stay a memorable one. All our 27 rooms are en suite and offer every guest comfort including direct dial phone, colour TV, hairdryer and tea/coffee making facilities. A leisurely stroll from the Aston brings you to all Dublin's top attractions and amenities and makes it an ideal base for exploring the capital.

B&B from €40.00 to €75.00
£31.50 to £59.07

ANN WALSH
MANAGER

American Express
Diners
Mastercard
Visa

27 27

HOTELS
FEDERATION

Closed 24 - 27 December

AUBURN GUESTHOUSE

OLD NAVAN ROAD, CASTLEKNOCK,
(AT AUBURN ROUNDABOUT),
DUBLIN 15

TEL: 01-822 3535 FAX: 01-822 3550
EMAIL: auburngh@iol.ie

GUESTHOUSE ★★★ MAP 8 O 11

Auburn - Excellent accommodation. Set on it's own grounds. Landscaped gardens and guest carpark. City centre 15 minutes, M50 adjacent, Dublin Airport 10 minutes. Ideal location for business or holiday. Blanchardstown Complex with shopping and many amenities 5 minutes. Numerous Golf Courses near by. Restaurants within walking distance.

Member of Premier Guesthouses

B&B from €35.55 to €44.44
£28.00 to £35.00

ELAINE COWLEY
MANAGERESS

American Express
Mastercard
Visa

7 7

Closed 23 December - 06 January

B&B rates are per person sharing per night incl. Breakfast

BAGGOT COURT

92 LOWER BAGGOT STREET,
DUBLIN 2

TEL: 01-661 2819 FAX: 01-661 0253
EMAIL: baggot@indigo.ie

GUESTHOUSE N   MAP 8 O 11

This beautifully refurbished house is situated in the heart of Georgian Dublin and only a 6 minute walk to the city centre. Ideally situated for theatres, museums and art galleries plus a wide selection of fine restaurants and traditional Irish pubs. Our professional and friendly staff pride themselves on providing luxurious accommodation with the personal service of a private residence.

B&B from €57.15 to €88.90
£45.01 to £70.01

ROXANNE MOONEY
MANAGER

American Express
Mastercard
Visa

☺   Midweek specials from €152.40

🛏🛁☎🖥T✳P🍴
11 11

Closed 23 December - 06 January

BARRY'S HOTEL

1-2 GREAT DENMARK STREET,
DUBLIN 1

TEL: 01-874 9407 FAX: 01-874 6508

HOTEL ★★   MAP 8 O 11

Barry's Hotel is one of Dublin's oldest hotels built in the later part of Georgian Period. Situated 300 yds off O'Connell Street. Barry's unique ambience friendly service assure visitors whether on business or pleasure the warmest of welcomes and special attention. The hotel is within walking distance of the Abbey and Gate Theatres, National Wax Museum, Croke Park and principal shopping districts and major tourist attractions.

B&B from €50.80 to €57.15
£40.00 to £45.00

SINEAD FAHY
MANAGER

Mastercard
Visa

🛏🛁🖥TCCM♫S a/c 🍴
32 32

Closed 24 - 27 December

BELGRAVE GUESTHOUSE

8-10 BELGRAVE SQUARE,
RATHMINES,
DUBLIN 6

TEL: 01-496 3760 FAX: 01-497 9243

GUESTHOUSE ★★★   MAP 8 O 11

The Belgrave consists of three interconnecting early Victorian buildings overlooking a well matured square. While retaining all the character and charm of its era, the Belgrave has all the conveniences of a modern 3*** guesthouse, each room is en suite and has colour TV, direct dial telephone, tea making facilities. Private car park. Ideally located. We look forward to hosting you and according you a warm welcome for which we are renowned. AA ◆◆◆.

B&B from €57.14 to €88.88
£45.00 to £70.00

PAUL AND MARY O'REILLY
OWNERS

Mastercard
Visa

🛏🛁☎🖥TCCM✳P7🍴Inet
24 24

Closed 22 December - 02 January

Room rates are per room per night

BELVEDERE HOTEL

GREAT DENMARK STREET,
DUBLIN 1

TEL: 01-874 1413 FAX: 01-872 8631

HOTEL R   MAP 8 O 11

Situated only three minutes walking distance from O'Connell Street, it is the ideal base for shopping and taking in the sights of this famous historic city. This area includes the National Wax Museum, major theatres, cinemas, sporting and concert venues, including the Point Theatre where most major acts perform. We are also the most convenient hotel to the new Croke Park, the main venue for all Gaelic Games.

B&B from €50.80 to €57.15
£40.00 to £45.00

MARION HENEGHAN
MANAGER

American Express
Diners
Mastercard
Visa

40   40

Closed 24 - 28 December

BERKELEY COURT

LANSDOWNE ROAD,
BALLSBRIDGE,
DUBLIN 4

TEL: 01-660 1711 FAX: 01-661 7238
EMAIL: berkeleycourt@jurysdoyle.com
WEB: www.jurysdoyle.com

HOTEL ★★★★★   MAP 8 O 11

Luxury, tradition and charm distinguish The Berkeley Court and add a touch of eminence to everything about it. This is why this 5-star hotel is the natural host to international dignitaries and celebrities. Located in the heart of Dublin's fashionable embassy belt, the city is just a short walk away.

Member of Leading Hotels of the World
B&B from €98.50 to €196.00
£77.58 to £154.36

JOE RUSSELL
GENERAL MANAGER

American Express
Diners
Mastercard
Visa

188 188

Inet

Open All Year

BEWLEY'S HOTEL BALLSBRIDGE

MERRION ROAD,
BALLSBRIDGE,
DUBLIN 4

TEL: 01-668 1111 FAX: 01-668 1999
EMAIL: bb@BewleysHotels.com
WEB: www.BewleysHotels.com

HOTEL ★★★   MAP 8 O 11

A new stylish concept in a prime location on Merrion Road combining the past with the present. Accommodating you in style with over 220 deluxe bedrooms and 9 purpose built meeting rooms. Enjoy an exciting dining experience in O'Connell's Restaurant. Bewley's Hotels Book on-line www.BewleysHotels.com

Room Rate from €87.60 to €99.00
£68.99 to £77.97

CLIO O'GARA
GENERAL MANAGER

American Express
Diners
Mastercard
Visa

220 220

Closed 24 - 26 December

B&B rates are per person sharing per night incl. Breakfast

BEWLEY'S HOTEL NEWLANDS CROSS

NEWLANDS CROSS,
NAAS ROAD (N7),
DUBLIN 22
TEL: 01-464 0140 FAX: 01-464 0900
EMAIL: res@BewleysHotels.com
WEB: www.BewleysHotels.com

HOTEL ★★★ MAP 8 O 11

A unique blend of quality, value and flexibility for independent discerning guests. Located just off the N7, minutes from the M50, Dublin Airport and the city centre. Our large spacious family size rooms are fully equipped with all modern amenities. Our Bewley's Restaurant offers you a range of dining options, from traditional Irish breakfast to full table service à la carte. Real time on line reservations and availability at www.BewleysHotels.com

Room Rate from €69.84 to €75.00
£55.00 to £59.07

DAMIEN MOLLOY
GENERAL MANAGER

American Express
Diners
Mastercard
Visa

258 258

Closed 24 - 26 December

BEWLEY'S PRINCIPAL HOTEL

19/20 FLEET STREET,
TEMPLE BAR,
DUBLIN 2
TEL: 01-670 8122 FAX: 01-670 8103
EMAIL: bewleyshotel@eircom.net
WEB: www.bewleysprincipalhotel.com

HOTEL ★★★ MAP 8 O 11

Located in the heart of the city. We offer the finest traditions of quality and service from both Bewley's and Principal Hotels. Our location makes us an ideal base for both business or pleasure. Completely refurbished in early 2000. Some bedrooms have air conditioning, all are equipped to the highest standards. A warm welcome awaits you.

B&B from €50.00 to €100.00
£39.38 to £78.76

CAROL MCNAMARA
GENERAL MANAGER

American Express
Diners
Mastercard
Visa

☺ Midweek specials from €150.00

70 70

Closed 24 - 27 December

BLOOMS HOTEL

6 ANGLESEA STREET,
TEMPLE BAR,
DUBLIN 2
TEL: 01-671 5622 FAX: 01-671 5997
EMAIL: blooms@eircom.net
WEB: www.blooms.ie

HOTEL ★★★ MAP 8 O 11

Blooms Hotel is situated at the centre of Dublin's cultural and artistic heart - Temple Bar. The hotel itself is only a few minutes stroll from Grafton Street's shopping and most of the city's best sights. And for those who want to set the town alight, Blooms is on the doorstep of Dublin's most famous nightlife - not least of which is its own nightclub, Club M. Blooms Hotel is a perfect choice for partygoers but not for those planning an early night!

Room Rate from €88.00 to €200.00
£69.31 to £157.51

MARTIN KEANE
OWNER

American Express
Diners
Mastercard
Visa

86 86

Closed 22 - 27 December

Room rates are per room per night

BROOKS HOTEL

DRURY STREET,
DUBLIN 2

TEL: 01-670 4000 FAX: 01-670 4455
EMAIL: reservations@brookshotel.ie
WEB: www.sinnotthotels.com

HOTEL ★★★★ MAP 8 O 11

Located in the fashionable heart of Dublin City, 3 mins from Grafton St, Temple Bar, Dublin Castle & Trinity College. Brooks is a designer/boutique hotel with high standards throughout, appealing in particular to the discerning international traveller. With superbly appointed air conditioned accommodation, the Butter Lane Bar, residents drawing room, Francesca's Restaurant & the Markets meeting room, Brooks is designed to cater for the sophisticated visitor. Secure parking available opposite the hotel.

B&B from € 108.00 to € 127.00
£85.06 to £100.02

ANNE MCKIERNAN
GENERAL MANAGER

American Express
Diners
Mastercard
Visa

72 72

Inet FAX

IRISH HOTELS FEDERATION

Open All Year

BROWNES TOWNHOUSE & BRASSERIE

22 ST. STEPHENS GREEN,
DUBLIN 2

TEL: 01-638 3939 FAX: 01-638 3900
EMAIL: info@brownesdublin.com
WEB: www.brownesdublin.com

GUESTHOUSE ★★★★ MAP 12 O 11

Overlooking St. Stephen's Green, Brownes Brasserie and Townhouse has the most superb location in Dublin. Brownes - a rare find, striking the perfect balance between traditional comfort and a relaxed contemporary atmosphere. With 12 luxury rooms, it has all of the intimacy, warmth & character of a privately run townhouse, yet corporate guests have the convenience of ISDN, direct personal telephone and fax lines and cable TV and air conditioning.

Member of Manor House Hotels
Room Rate from € 159.00 to €508.00
£125.22 to £400.08

BARRY CANNY
PROPRIETOR

American Express
Diners
Mastercard
Visa

12 12

FAX

IRISH HOTELS FEDERATION

Closed 24 December - 03 January

BURLINGTON

UPPER LEESON STREET,
DUBLIN 4

TEL: 01-660 5222 FAX: 01-660 8496
EMAIL: burlington@jurysdoyle.com
WEB: www.jurysdoyle.com

HOTEL ★★★★ MAP 8 O 11

The Burlington is a Dublin institution, always at the heart of the action and central to the whole whirl of Dublin life. Its lively bars and restaurants and friendly open charm conspire to create an atmosphere that is hard to forget. Ireland's largest conference hotel, it is centrally located - just a 5-minute stroll to the city centre.

B&B from € 86.00 to € 157.00
£67.73 to £123.65

JOHN CLIFTON
GENERAL MANAGER

American Express
Diners
Mastercard
Visa

504 504

Inet FAX

IRISH HOTELS FEDERATION

Open All Year

B&B rates are per person sharing per night incl. Breakfast

BUSWELLS HOTEL

23/27 MOLESWORTH STREET,
DUBLIN 2

TEL: 01-614 6500 FAX: 01-676 2090
EMAIL: buswells@quinn-hotels.com
WEB: www.quinnhotels.com

HOTEL U   MAP 8 O 11

One of Dublin's best kept secrets. This elegant Georgian Building provides the highest standards in a relaxing environment. A haven for discerning traveller. Just minutes walk from St. Stephen's Green and Grafton Street.Our dedicated business suite and dry leisure suite are our newest facilities we have to offer you.

Member of Quinn Hotels

B&B from €63.50 to €109.00
£50.01 to £85.84

PAUL GALLAGHER
GENERAL MANAGER

American Express
Diners
Mastercard
Visa

Closed 24 - 26 December

BUTLERS TOWN HOUSE

44 LANSDOWNE ROAD,
BALLSBRIDGE,
DUBLIN 4

TEL: 01-667 4022 FAX: 01-667 3960
EMAIL: info@butlers-hotel.com
WEB: www.butlers-hotel.com

GUESTHOUSE ★★★★   MAP 8 O 11

An oasis of country tranquillity in the heart of Dublin, Butlers Town House is an experience as opposed to a visit. Opened in March 1997, fully restored to reflect its former glory, but with all modern comforts from air-conditioning to modem points. Butlers Town House is renowned for its elegance and premier guest service. Private secure car park available.

Member of Manor House Hotels

B&B from €95.00 to €107.00
£74.82 to £84.27

ADRIAN D HARKINS
GENERAL MANAGER

American Express
Diners
Mastercard
Visa

Closed 23 - 26 December

CAMDEN COURT HOTEL

CAMDEN STREET,
DUBLIN 2

TEL: 01-475 9666 FAX: 01-475 9677
EMAIL: sales@camdencourthotel.com
WEB: www.camdencourthotel.com

HOTEL ★★★   MAP 8 O 11

The Camden Court Hotel is situated in the heart of Dublin within a 10 minute walk of Grafton Street. The hotel comprises of 246 well-appointed bedrooms all en suite with hairdryer, direct dial phone, colour TV, trouser press and tea/coffee making facilities. We also provide excellent conference facilities, restaurant and themed bar. Our state of the art leisure centre consists of a 16m swimming pool, sauna, steamroom, jacuzzi, solarium and a fully equipped gym. Secure carparking.

B&B from €82.50 to €127.00
£64.97 to £100.02

DARIN MAGUIRE
ASSISTANT GENERAL MANAGER

American Express
Diners
Mastercard
Visa

Closed 24 December - 02 January

Room rates are per room per night

CAMDEN DE LUXE HOTEL

84/87 CAMDEN STREET LOWER,
DUBLIN 2

TEL: 01-478 0808 FAX: 01-475 0713
EMAIL: info@camden-deluxe.ie
WEB: www.camden-deluxe.ie

HOTEL ★★   MAP 8 O 11

The Camden De Luxe Hotel, situated in the heart of Dublin's City Centre, is just a short walk from the bustling shopping area of Grafton Street and the lively nightlife quarter of Temple Bar which boasts dozens of restaurants, bars and live music. The hotel is sited on the old Theatre De Luxe and has recently been tastefully renovated and comprises of 34 en suite rooms, Planet Murphy Bar and Restaurant and also offers corporate facilities.

B&B from €90.00 to €155.00
£70.88 to £122.07

JUSTINE POWER
MANAGER

American Express
Diners
Mastercard
Visa

🛏️🔌☎️📺T♿️🅰️🌡️
34   34

Closed 24 - 27 December

CASSIDYS HOTEL

CAVENDISH ROW,
UPPER O'CONNELL ST.,
DUBLIN 1

TEL: 01-878 0555 FAX: 01-878 0687
EMAIL: rese@cassidys.iol.ie
WEB: www.cassidyshotel.com

HOTEL ★★★   MAP 8 O 11

A little gem in the heart of the city. Cassidys is a modern 88 bedroomed townhouse hotel located opposite the famous Gate Theatre in the city centre. Cassidys is a short walk from numerous museums, theatres, bars and shopping districts. The warm and welcoming atmosphere of Groomes Bar lends a traditional air to Cassidys and fine dining is assured in the stylish surroundings of Restaurant 6. Limited parking for guests. Conference facilities available.

B&B from €60.00 to €105.00
£47.25 to £82.69

MARTIN CASSIDY
GENERAL MANAGER

American Express
Diners
Mastercard
Visa

·/🍴

☺️   Midweek specials Sun-Thurs
€55.00pps B&B per night

🛏️🔌☎️📺TC CMPS🅰️🌡️
88   88

Closed 23 - 27 December

CASTLE HOTEL

2-4 GARDINER ROW,
DUBLIN 1

TEL: 01-874 6949 FAX: 01-872 7674
EMAIL: hotels@indigo.ie

HOTEL ★★   MAP 8 O 11

Elegant Georgian hotel close to Dublin's main shopping district, renowned for its friendly service. One of Dublin's oldest hotels. Authentically restored the décor and furnishings offer modern comfort combined with olde world features: crystal chandeliers, antique mirrors, marble fireplaces and period staircases. The individually decorated rooms offer private bathroom, satellite TV, direct dial phone and beverage making facilities. The hotel has an intimate residents bar and private parking.

Member of Castle Hotel Group
B&B from €45.00 to €58.00
£35.44 to £45.68

YVONNE EVANS
MANAGERESS

Mastercard
Visa

☺️   Midweek specials from €140.00

🛏️🔌☎️📺TC♿️PS🅰️🌡️
38   38

Closed 24 - 27 December

B&B rates are per person sharing per night incl. Breakfast

CEDAR LODGE

98 MERRION ROAD,
DUBLIN 4

TEL: 01-668 4410 FAX: 01-668 4533
EMAIL: info@cedarlodge.ie
WEB: www.cedarlodge.ie

GUESTHOUSE ★★★★ MAP 8 O 11

Cedar Lodge the luxurious alternative to a hotel. Modern comforts and Edwardian style combine to create a truly unique experience. Our beautifully furnished en suite bedrooms are of international standard. This jewel among guesthouses is located in Leafy Ballsbridge, adjacent to RDS, the British Embassy and the Four Seasons Hotel. 10 minutes from the city centre, close to airport and ferry ports. Private car park. AA Premier Selected ◆◆◆◆◆, RAC ◆◆◆◆◆.

B&B from €45.00 to €82.00
£35.44 to £64.58

GERARD & MARY DOODY
OWNERS

American Express
Mastercard
Visa

☺ Midweek specials from €150.00

16   16

Closed 23 - 28 December

CELTIC LODGE GUESTHOUSE

81/82 TALBOT STREET,,
DUBLIN 1

TEL: 01-677 9955 FAX: 01-878 8698
EMAIL: celticguesthouse@eircom.net

GUESTHOUSE P MAP 8 O 11

This gracious Victorian residence is in the heart of the city centre adjacent to the bus and train stations and 15 minutes from the airport. A stroll from our door is the vibrant Temple Bar district with its numerous pubs, restaurants & clubs. Trinity College, Christchurch Cathedral, Dublin Castle & a number of theatres are within a stones throw. All room en suite & finished to a very high standard with internal phone system, cable TV & tea/coffee making facilities. Next door a traditional bar with Irish Music seven nights a week, free. Traditional restaurant opening shortly.

B&B from €38.00 to €51.00
£29.93 to £40.16

NOEL TYNAN
DIRECTOR

Mastercard
Visa

☺ Midweek specials from €95.25

29   29

Open All Year

CENTRAL HOTEL

1-5 EXCHEQUER STREET,
DUBLIN 2

TEL: 01-679 7302 FAX: 01-679 7303
EMAIL: reservations@centralhotel.ie
WEB: www.centralhotel.ie

HOTEL ★★★ MAP 8 O 11

City centre location. Award winning Library bar, Exchequer bar and recently refurbished restaurant.Temple Bar, Dublin's Left Bank, one block away. Trinity College, Grafton Street and Christchurch 5 mins from hotel. Rooms en suite include, DD phones, voicemail, hairdryers, tea/coffee making facilities, multi-channel TV. 8 private meeting rooms. Secure parking available nearby.

Member of Best Western Hotels

B&B from €69.84 to €101.58
£55.00 to £80.00

GUY THOMPSON
OPERATIONS DIRECTOR

American Express
Diners
Mastercard
Visa

70   70

Inet

Closed 24 - 27 December

Room rates are per room per night

CHARLEVILLE LODGE

268-272 NORTH CIRCULAR ROAD,
PHIBSBOROUGH,
DUBLIN 7
TEL: 01-838 6633 FAX: 01-838 5854
EMAIL: charleville@indigo.ie
WEB: www.charlevillelodge.ie

GUESTHOUSE ★★★ MAP 8 O 11

Charleville Lodge, (former home of Lord Charleville), is an elegant terrace of Victorian houses located mins. from the city centre, Trinity College & Temple Bar, en route to Dublin Airport and car ferry. The luxurious en suite bedrooms have direct dial phones and colour TV. Rated ◆◆◆◆ by AA and RAC we are holders of the Sparkling Diamond award. Our car park is for guest use and is complimentary. Let us make your arrangements with local golf clubs. Visit our website.

Member of Premier Guesthouses
B&B from € 35.00 to € 75.00
£27.56 to £59.07

VAL & ANNE STENSON
OWNERS

American Express
Diners
Mastercard
Visa

☺ Midweek specials from €99.00

30 28

Closed 20 - 26 December

CHIEF O'NEILL'S HOTEL

SMITHFIELD VILLAGE,
DUBLIN 7
TEL: 01-817 3838 FAX: 01-817 3839
EMAIL: reservations@chiefoneills.com
WEB: www.chiefoneills.com

HOTEL U MAP 8 O 11

Chief O'Neill's Hotel is dedicated to the memory of Francis O'Neill, Chicago Chief of Police & one of the most important individual collectors of Irish traditional music this century. Its theme is Irish traditional music expressed through Ireland's finest contemporary design. Each of the 73 en suite luxury rooms is equipped with a CD/Hi-Fi system, multi-channel TV, direct dial phone & tea/coffee facility. Restaurants & visitor attractions surround the hotel. The Jervis St shopping centre, O'Connell St are within walking distance.

Room Rate from € 180.00 to € 380.00
£141.74 to £299.22

SALLY A BUCKLEY
GENERAL MANAGER

American Express
Diners
Mastercard
Visa

73 73

Inet

Closed 24 - 26 December

CLARA HOUSE

23 LEINSTER ROAD,
RATHMINES,
DUBLIN 6
TEL: 01-497 5904 FAX: 01-497 5904
EMAIL: clarahouse@eircom.net

GUESTHOUSE ★★★ MAP 8 O 11

Clara House is a beautifully maintained listed Georgian house with many original features skillfully combined with modern day comforts. Each bedroom has en suite bathroom, remote control colour TV, direct dial telephone, radio/alarm clock, tea/coffee making facilities, hair dryer and trouser press. Clara House is a mile from downtown with bus stops 100 metres away. Bus stop for Ballsbridge/RDS is 200 metres. Secure parking at rear of house.

B&B from € 44.00 to € 57.00
£34.65 to £44.88

PHIL & PAUL REID
PROPRIETORS

Mastercard
Visa

13 13

Open All Year

B&B rates are per person sharing per night incl. Breakfast

CLARENCE HOTEL

6-8 WELLINGTON QUAY,
DUBLIN 2

TEL: 01-407 0800 FAX: 01-407 0820
EMAIL: reservations@theclarence.ie
WEB: www.theclarence.ie

HOTEL U   MAP 8 O 11

Located on the River Liffer, The Clarence Hotel was built in 1852 and was transformed into a boutique hotel in 1996. Many of the hotel's original features have been revived and a unique balance between old and new has been achieved. It's 50 bedrooms and suites, are individually designed in contemporary elegant style. A treatment room is available together with Valet Parking, a first for Dublin City. The Tea Room Restaurant and Octagon bar provide a social focus for The Clarence and Dublin City.

Member of Leading Small Hotels of the World

Room Rate from €285.00 to €305.00
£224.46 to £240.21

ROBERT VAN EERDE
GENERAL MANAGER

American Express
Diners
Mastercard
Visa

50   50

IRISH HOTELS FEDERATION

Closed 24 - 26 December

CLARION HOTEL DUBLIN IFSC

INTERNATIONAL FINANCIAL
SERVICES CENTRE,
DUBLIN 1

TEL: 01-433 8800 FAX: 01-433 8801
EMAIL: info@clarionhotelifsc.com
WEB: www.clarionhotelifsc.com

HOTEL N   MAP 8 O 11

New to City Centre the latest in stylish contemporary hotels in a cosmopolitan ambience. Bedrooms are comfortably appointed with modern features. Enjoy a choice of eating experiences - European Cuisine in our Sinergie Restaurant, an exciting twist of Eastern fare in Kudos Bar, and International style coffee bar. Well equipped meeting rooms for small and large conferences. Unwind at Sanovitae Health and Fitness Club including 18m indoor swimming pool, which is complimentary to guests.

Member of Choice Hotels International

B&B from €82.00 to €120.00
£64.58 to £94.51

BRENDAN CURTIS

American Express
Diners
Mastercard
Visa

☺ Weekend specials from €165.00

147   147

alc   Inet

Closed 24 - 27 December

CLARION STEPHENS HALL HOTEL AND SUITES

THE EARLSFORT CENTRE,
LOWER LEESON STREET,
DUBLIN 2

TEL: 01-638 1111 FAX: 01-638 1122
EMAIL: stephens@premgroup.com
WEB: www.premgroup.com

HOTEL ★★★   MAP 8 O 11

Deluxe all suite accommodation in the heart of Dublin city. Each suite consists of bedroom, bathroom, living room and kitchen facilities including fax machine, modem point and CD players. Visit our new restaurant Romanza, where you can enjoy authentic Italian and European cuisine. Free underground car parking available to all guests. Toll Free USA for Clarion Hotels: 1800 252 7466.

Member of Choice Hotels Ireland

Room Rate from €83.00 to €123.00
£65.37 to £96.87

JIM MURPHY
MANAGING DIRECTOR

American Express
Diners
Mastercard
Visa

☺ Weekend specials from €165.00

33   33

Inet   FAX

IRISH HOTELS FEDERATION

Open All Year

Room rates are per room per night

CLIFDEN GUESTHOUSE

32 GARDINER PLACE,
DUBLIN 1

TEL: 01-874 6364 FAX: 01-874 6122
EMAIL: bnb@indigo.ie
WEB: www.clifdenhouse.com

GUESTHOUSE ★★★ MAP 8 O 11

A refurbished city centre Georgian home. Our private car park provides security for guest's cars, even after check-out. All rooms have shower, WC, WHB, TV, direct dial phone and tea making facilities. We cater for single, twin, double, triple and family occupancies. Convenient to airport, ferryports, Bus Aras (bus station) and DART. We are only 5 minutes walk from O'Connell Street. AA and RAC approved.

Room Rate from €60.00 to €140.00
£47.25 to £110.26

JACK & MARY LALOR

Mastercard
Visa

☺ Midweek specials from €105.00

14 14

Open All Year

CLIFTON COURT HOTEL

O'CONNELL BRIDGE,
DUBLIN 1

TEL: 01-874 3535 FAX: 01-878 6698
EMAIL: cliftoncourt@eircom.net
WEB: www.cliftoncourthotel.com

HOTEL ★★ MAP 8 O 11

Situated in the city centre overlooking the River Liffey at O'Connell Bridge. Beside Dublin's two premier shopping streets. Abbey Theatre, Point Depot, DART/train stations and Bus Aras (airport shuttle bus) are within 3 minutes walk. Our bedrooms are equipped with TV, tea/coffee facilities and are all en suite.

B&B from €64.00 to €71.00
£50.40 to £55.92

MO HALPIN
MANAGER

American Express
Mastercard
Visa

30 30

Closed 24 - 27 December

CLONTARF CASTLE HOTEL

CLONTARF,
DUBLIN 3

TEL: 01-833 2321 FAX: 01-833 0418
EMAIL: info@clontarfcastle.ie
WEB: www.clontarfcastle.ie

HOTEL ★★★★ MAP 8 O 11

This historic castle, dating back to 1172, is today a luxurious 4**** deluxe, 111 room hotel. Ideally situated only 10 minutes from the city centre and 15 minutes from the airport. With superb facilities including uniquely designed rooms equipped with all the modern facilities. Templar's Bistro specialising in modern international cuisine, 2 unique bars, state of the art conference and banqueting facilities and stunning lobby. Complimentary carparking.

B&B from €82.50 to €145.00
£64.97 to £114.20

ENDA O'MEARA
MANAGING DIRECTOR

American Express
Diners
Mastercard
Visa

111 111

Closed 24 - 25 December

B&B rates are per person sharing per night incl. Breakfast

COMFORT INN, TALBOT STREET

95-98 TALBOT STREET,
DUBLIN 1

TEL: 01-874 9202 FAX: 01-874 9672
EMAIL: info@talbot.premgroup.ie
WEB: www.comfort-inn-dublin.com

GUESTHOUSE ★★★ MAP 8 O 11

Talbot Street boasts the perfect location, just 2 minutes walk from O'Connell Street. In the surrounding area, you will find many shops, restaurants, pubs, theatres and nightclubs. Temple Bar and Trinity College are just a short stroll away. All rooms are en suite, with colourful modern decor. Full Irish Breakfast available every morning.

Member of Choice Hotels Ireland

Room Rate from € 75.00 to € 190.00
£59.06 to £149.61

JOANNA DOYLE
MANAGER

American Express
Diners
Mastercard
Visa

48   48

Closed 24 - 27 December

CONRAD DUBLIN

EARLSFORT TERRACE,
DUBLIN 2

TEL: 01-602 8900 FAX: 01-676 5424
EMAIL: info@conraddublin.ie
WEB: www.conraddublin.com

HOTEL ★★★★★ MAP 8 O 11

In the heart of the city providing unsurpassed hospitality to all visitors lies the Conrad Dublin. 191 luxurious guestrooms including 9 suites with colour TV, ergonomic workstation, DD phone, air conditioning, minibars, fluffy bathrobes and 24-hour room service. Dining is available in the Plurabelle Restaurant and the hotel is home to one of the most traditional Irish pubs in town, Alfie Byrnes. Fitness centre also available. At the Conrad Dublin service is the secret.

Room Rate from € 205.00 to € 380.00
£161.45 to £299.27

MICHAEL GOVERNEY
GENERAL MANAGER

American Express
Diners
Mastercard
Visa

191   191

FAX

Open All Year

DAVENPORT HOTEL

AT MERRION SQUARE,
DUBLIN 2

TEL: 01-607 3500 FAX: 01-661 5663
EMAIL: davenportres@ocallaghanhotels.ie
WEB: www.davenporthotel.ie

HOTEL U MAP 8 O 11

This elegant deluxe hotel is located at Merrion Square in Dublin City centre, beside Trinity College and just a 5 minute walk from the principal business, shopping and cultural districts. Fully air-conditioned with 115 deluxe guestrooms, discreet drawing room bar, fine dining restaurant and extensive meeting facilities, it offers an oasis of tranquillity in the heart of Dublin. Free private valet car parking. USA Toll Free Reservations 1800 569 9983 or on line at www.ocallaghanhotels.ie

Member of O'Callaghan Hotels

Room Rate from € 215.00 to € 395.00
£169.33 to £311.09

KEVIN DENNER
GENERAL MANAGER

American Express
Diners
Mastercard
Visa

115   115

Inet

Open All Year

Room rates are per room per night

DERGVALE HOTEL

4 GARDINER PLACE,
DUBLIN 1

TEL: 01-874 4753 FAX: 01-874 8276
EMAIL: dergvale@indigo.ie
WEB: www.dergvale.com

HOTEL ★★ MAP 8 O 11

The Dergvale Hotel is located within walking distance of all principal shopping areas, cinemas, museums, Trinity College, Dublin Castle and airport bus. Luxury bedrooms with showers en suite, colour TV and direct dial telephone. Fully licensed. A courteous and efficient staff are on hand to make your stay an enjoyable one. The hotel is under the personal supervision of Gerard and Nancy Nolan.

B&B from €38.00 to €57.00
£29.93 to £44.89

GERARD NOLAN
OWNER

American Express
Mastercard
Visa

🛏️ 🛁 ☎️ 🖥️ T C 🛏️ aid
20   17

HOTELS
IRISH FEDERATION

Closed 24 December - 07 January

DONNYBROOK HALL

6 BELMONT AVENUE,
DONNYBROOK,
DUBLIN 4

TEL: 01-269 1633 FAX: 01-269 2649

WEB: www.donnybrookhall.com

GUESTHOUSE ★★★ MAP 8 O 11

Situated in the fashionable Donnybrook district of Dublin, this beautifully restored Victorian residence retains many original features. Each of our en suite rooms are of international standard and are individually designed in elegant style. This guesthouse is ideally located just a short walk from the cultural, commercial and entertinament heart of the city. Nearby is the RDS, RTE, UCD, Lansdowne Road, St. Stephens Green and Trinity College.

B&B from €40.00 to €70.00
£31.50 to £55.13

DOROTHY GLENNON
OWNER

American Express
Mastercard
Visa

🛏️ 🛁 ☎️ 🖥️ T C ✳️ ∪ 🍴 🍷

Open All Year

DONNYBROOK LODGE

131 STILLORGAN ROAD,
DONNYBROOK,
DUBLIN 4

TEL: 01-283 7333 FAX: 01-260 4770

GUESTHOUSE ★★★ MAP 8 O 11

Relax in comfortable surroundings in the heart of Dublin's most exclusive area. Ideally situated close to city centre, ferryports and adjacent to RDS, Lansdowne, UCD and RTE. A short stroll from a host of restaurants and entertainment. Recently refurbished, our well-appointed rooms feature en suites, direct dial phone and TV. Private parking available. Enjoy a leisurely breakfast in our elegant dining room, overlooking gardens. A relaxed atmosphere and warm welcome awaits you.

B&B from €34.92 to €60.32
£27.50 to £47.50

PAT BUTLER

Mastercard
Visa

🛏️ 🛁 ☎️ 🖥️ T C ✳️ P 🍷
7   7

HOTELS
IRISH FEDERATION

Open All Year

B&B rates are per person sharing per night incl. Breakfast

DRURY COURT HOTEL

28-30 LOWER STEPHEN STREET,
DUBLIN 2

TEL: 01-475 1988 FAX: 01-478 5730
EMAIL: druryct@indigo.ie
WEB: www.drurycourthotel.com

HOTEL ★★★ MAP 8 O 11

Located in the heart of Dublin, beside Stephen's Green and Grafton Street. Convenient to the hotel are theatres, galleries, museums, Trinity College and Temple Bar. The Hotel comprises 32 luxurious bedrooms all en suite with direct dial phone, computer lines, multi-channel TV/Radio and tea/coffee facilities. There is also a restaurant and lively bar. The hotel is adjacent to secure public car parking. Just perfect for the leisure or business visitor.

Member of MinOtel Ireland Hotel Group

B&B from €58.00 to €108.00
£45.68 to £85.06

PAUL HAND
GENERAL MANAGER

American Express
Diners
Mastercard
Visa

🛏️ 📶 ☎️ 🍴 📺 T C ➰ CM ∪ ♪ S 🔲 alc
32 32
🔲 Inet

HOTELS
FEDERATION

Closed 23 - 27 December

EGAN'S GUESTHOUSE

7/9 IONA PARK,
GLASNEVIN,
DUBLIN 9

TEL: 01-830 3611 FAX: 01-830 3312
EMAIL: info@eganshouse.com
WEB: www.eganshouse.com

GUESTHOUSE ★★★ MAP 8 O 11

Egan's House is an elegant family run Edwardian house in a quiet area but only 1.7k from Dublin's city centre and bustling night-life. All 23 guestrooms are en suite with TV, telephone, hairdryer and tea/coffee facility. Internet access and free car parking are available. Dublin airport is just 10 minutes by taxi and the car ferry is also close by, as is Croke Park, the Point Depot, RDS and championship golf courses.

Member of Premier Guesthouses

B&B from €44.00 to €57.00
£34.65 to £44.89

MONICA & PAT FINN
PROPRIETORS

Mastercard
Visa

😊 Midweek specials from €40.00

🛏️ 📶 ☎️ 📺 T C ➰ CM ❄️ P ♀ ⚡
23 23

HOTELS
FEDERATION

Closed 23 December - 05 January

EGLINTON MANOR

83 EGLINTON ROAD,
DONNYBROOK,
DUBLIN 4

TEL: 01-269 3273 FAX: 01-269 7527

GUESTHOUSE ★★★★ MAP 8 O 11

This gracious red-bricked Victorian Old House which has just been refurbished to the highest standard is situated in the very elegant suburb of Donnybrook. It is very close to the city centre and the RDS. All rooms have a bathroom and tea/coffee makers, TV, radio, and direct dial telephones. Private free car parking. 4**** premises with lovely garden. 48 hours is our cancellation policy.

B&B from €63.49 to €76.19
€50.00 to €60.00

ROSALEEN CAHILL O'BRIEN

American Express
Mastercard
Visa

🛏️ 📶 🔲 T 🔲 C CM ❄️ ♪ ♫ ⚡ FAX
7 7

HOTELS
FEDERATION

Open All Year

Room rates are per room per night

FERRYVIEW HOUSE

96 CLONTARF ROAD,
CLONTARF,
DUBLIN 3

TEL: 01-833 5893 FAX: 01-853 2141
EMAIL: ferryview@oceanfree.net
WEB: www.ferryviewhouse.com

GUESTHOUSE ★★★ MAP 8 O 11

Ferryview House is located in the exclusive coastal suburb of Clontarf, 2.5 miles from the city centre on a regular bus route. The recently totally refurbished family run guesthouse is also selected ◆◆◆◆ with the Automobile Association. The House is close to Dublin port, the Point Theatre, East Point Business Park (2km) and airport 15 minutes. Local facilities include restaurants, coastal walks, Clontarf Rugby Club, tennis and 3 golf clubs.

B&B from €40.00 to €57.00
£31.50 to £44.89

MARGARET ALLISTER

Mastercard
Visa

8 8

Closed 22 December - 01 January

FITZSIMONS HOTEL

21-22 WELLINGTON QUAY,
TEMPLE BAR,
DUBLIN 2

TEL: 01-677 9315 FAX: 01-677 9387
EMAIL: info@fitzsimons-hotel.com
WEB: www.fitzsimonshotel.com

HOTEL ★★ MAP 8 O 11

The Fitzsimons Hotel situated on the banks of the River Liffey beside the new Millenium Bridge, in the heart of the City's thriving left bank - Temple Bar. It's location offers the visitor doorstep access to this vibrant, colourful, exciting locale and all it has to offer. Theatres, Galleries, Studios, Bars, Restaurants, live music venues and alternative shops. Home to Dublins top entertainment venue with 3 floors of fun Fitzsimons Bar, Restaurant and the Ballroom Nite Club.

B&B from €55.00 to €100.00
£43.32 to £78.76

DARINA HOWARD
MANAGER

American Express
Mastercard
Visa

26 26

Closed 24 - 26 December

FITZWILLIAM

41 UPPER FITZWILLIAM STREET,
DUBLIN 2

TEL: 01-662 5155 FAX: 01-676 7488
EMAIL: fitzwilliamguesthouse@eircom.net

GUESTHOUSE ★★★ MAP 8 O 11

Centrally located in the heart of elegant Georgian Dublin, minutes walk from St. Stephen's Green, National Concert Hall and Galleries. Enjoy the charm of this spacious town house. Rooms with en suite facilities, colour TV, direct dial telephone, clock/radios and hair dryers. Overnight car parking available. Relax at our excellent restaurant. Our friendly staff will ensure your stay is a relaxed and memorable one.

B&B from €50.80 to €70.00
£40.00 to £55.12

DECLAN CARNEY
MANAGER

American Express
Diners
Mastercard
Visa

12 12

Closed 21 December - 04 January

B&B rates are per person sharing per night incl. Breakfast

FITZWILLIAM HOTEL

ST. STEPHEN'S GREEN,
DUBLIN 2

TEL: 01-478 7000 FAX: 01-478 7878
EMAIL: enq@fitzwilliamhotel.com
WEB: www.fitzwilliamhotel.com

HOTEL U MAP 8 O 11

A modern classic uniquely positioned on St. Stephen's Green, paces away from Grafton Street, Ireland's premier shopping location. Understated luxury, a fresh approach and impeccable service make it the perfect retreat for business and pleasure travelers. Dine in the highly acclaimed Restaurant Peacock Alley or the Fashionable Citron. Facilities include 3 conference rooms, free car parking for residents & Ireland's largest roof garden. Voted by CondÈ Nast Traveller Magazine as one of the Top 21 Hottest Hotels in the World.

Member of Summit Hotels

Room Rate from €275.00 to €635.00
£216.58 to £500.10

JOHN KAVANAGH
GENERAL MANAGER

American Express
Diners
Mastercard
Visa

130 130

Inet FAX

IRISH HOTELS FEDERATION

Open All Year

FORTE TRAVELODGE

AUBURN AVENUE ROUNDABOUT,
NAVAN ROAD, CASTLEKNOCK,
DUBLIN 15

TEL: 1800-709709 FAX: 01-820 2151

WEB: www.travelodge.co.uk

HOTEL U MAP 8 O 11

Situated on the N3 route only 5 miles from Dublin City Centre, just off the M50 Dublin ring road and mins from the Airport, this superb hotel offers comfortable yet affordable accommodation. Each room is large enough to sleep up to three adults, a child under 12 and a baby in a cot. Price is fixed per room regardless of the number of occupants. Each room has en suite bathroom, colour satellite TV including Sky Sports and Sky Movies and direct dial phone. Sited next to Little Chef restaurant. Freephone from UK 0800 850 950.

Room Rate from €79.95 to €89.95
£62.97 to £70.84

SIMON PERKINS

American Express
Diners
Mastercard
Visa

100 100

Open All Year

FOUR SEASONS HOTEL DUBLIN

SIMMONSCOURT ROAD,
BALLSBRIDGE,
DUBLIN 4

TEL: 01-665 4000 FAX: 01-665 4099

WEB: www.fourseasons.com

HOTEL ★★★★★ MAP 8 O 11

The charms of Irish tradition and hospitality combine to provide the stage for Four Seasons Hotel Dublin. Set within the showgrounds of the historic Royal Dublin Society, the hotel brings together 259 exceptional guestrooms and suites with the finest facilities for business and relaxation. Residential in style, the hotel features 15,000 sq ft of meeting and banquet space, fine dining in Seasons Restaurant and an 11,000 sq ft full service spa.

Room Rate from €375.00 to €495.00
£295.28 to £389.77

JOHN BRENNAN
GENERAL MANAGER

American Express
Diners
Mastercard
Visa

259 259

alc Inet FAX

IRISH HOTELS FEDERATION

Open All Year

Room rates are per room per night

GEORGE FREDERIC HANDEL HOTEL

16-18 FISHAMBLE STREET,
CHRISTCHURCH, TEMPLE BAR,
DUBLIN 8
TEL: 01-670 9400 FAX: 01-670 9410
EMAIL: info@handelshotel.com
WEB: www.handelshotel.com

HOTEL U MAP 8 O 11

Our secret is out! Centrally located, while situated in the heart of Dublin's vibrant Temple Bar area, the George Frederic Handel Hotel is also within easy walking distance of the city's main tourist attractions and financial districts. We offer a high standard of accommodation combined with a warm Irish welcome - all at a great price. Live online booking system at www.handelshotel.com

B&B from €44.45 to €95.25
£35.00 to £75.00.

SHANE WALSH
OPERATIONS MANAGER

American Express
Diners
Mastercard
Visa

40 40

IRISH HOTELS FEDERATION

Closed 24 - 27 December

GEORGIAN COURT GUESTHOUSE

77-79 LOWER GARDINER STREET,
DUBLIN 1
TEL: 01-855 7872 FAX: 01-855 5715
EMAIL: georgiancourt@eircom.net

GUESTHOUSE U MAP 8 O 11

Situated in the centre of Dublin City, 200m from O'Connell Street, Dublin's main shopping street, 50m from the city centre bus station. The 41 bus direct from Dublin Airport stops outside our door. 150m to Connolly rail station. 10 mins walk to Temple Bar. Secure car park available. Built in 1805 and located in a fine Georgian terrace. All rooms are en suite, colour TV, tea/coffee facilities, internal phones, hairdryer, electric iron available.

B&B from €44.00 to €63.00
£34.65 to £49.62

EILEEN CONROY
OWNER

Mastercard
Visa

45 45

IRISH HOTELS FEDERATION

Closed 24 - 27 December

GEORGIAN HOTEL

18-22 BAGGOT STREET LOWER,
DUBLIN 2
TEL: 01-634 5000 FAX: 01-634 5100
EMAIL: info@georgianhotel.ie

HOTEL ★★★ MAP 8 O 11

This very comfortable 200 year old house with new extension in the heart of Georgian Dublin, next to St. Stephen's Green and a 5 minute walk to the major sites including Trinity College, galleries, museums, cathedrals, theatres and to fashionable shopping streets and pubs. Bathrooms en suite, TV, ISDN. Perfect location for business or holiday travellers and offers all the amenities of an exclusive hotel. Private car park.

B&B from €57.00 to €105.00
£44.89 to £82.69

ANNETTE O'SULLIVAN
MANAGING DIRECTOR

American Express
Diners
Mastercard
Visa

47 47

FAX

IRISH HOTELS FEDERATION

Open All Year

B&B rates are per person sharing per night incl. Breakfast

GLEN GUESTHOUSE

84 LOWER GARDINER STREET,
DUBLIN 1

TEL: 01-855 1374 FAX: 01-855 2506
EMAIL: theglen@eircom.net
WEB: homepage.eircom.net/~theglen

GUESTHOUSE ★★★ MAP 8 O 11

The Glen is a beautifully restored and maintained guesthouse. Located in the heart of Dublin City, adjacent to shops, theatres, cinemas, galleries, museums and Dublin's famous night spots. Close to bus and train stations en route to airport. Rooms en suite, TV, direct dial phones, tea and coffee facilities in all rooms.

B&B from € 29.00 to € 50.00
£22.84 to £39.38

JOHN MURRAY
MANAGER

Mastercard
Visa

12   12

Open All Year

GLENOGRA HOUSE

64 MERRION ROAD,
BALLSBRIDGE,
DUBLIN 4

TEL: 01-668 3661 FAX: 01-668 3698
EMAIL: glenogra@indigo.ie
WEB: www.glenogra.com

GUESTHOUSE ★★★★ MAP 8 O 11

Located opposite the RDS and Four Seasons Hotel, close to city centre, bus, rail, embassies, restaurants, car ferries. Glenogra provides luxury and elegance in a personalised, family run environment. The cosy drawing room is perfect for a restoring afternoon tea. En suite bedrooms are decorated in harmony with a period residence, are all non-smoking with phone, TV, coffee making facilities. Private car parking. AA, RAC ♦♦♦♦♦.

Member of Premier Guesthouses
Room Rate from € 88.00 to € 98.00
£69.31 to £77.18

CHERRY AND SEAMUS MCNAMEE
PROPRIETORS

American Express
Mastercard
Visa

12   12

IRISH HOTELS FEDERATION

Closed 20 December - 07 January

GRAFTON CAPITAL HOTEL

STEPHENS STREET LOWER,
DUBLIN 2

TEL: 01-648 1100 FAX: 01-648 1122
EMAIL: info@graftoncapital-hotel.com
WEB: www.capital-hotels.com

HOTEL ★★★ MAP 8 O 11

Nestling in the heart of Dublin's most fashionable & cultural areas, your first experience of the Grafton Capital Hotel is that of its traditional Georgian townhouse façade. Thereafter, guests will enjoy the luxury of its superbly appointed accommodation, affording a wealth of comforts for the discerning guest. Make the most of this prime central location - Grafton St, St Stephens Green and the colourful Temple Bar area, are all a short stroll from the hotel. Restaurants, Cafés Bars and a host of visitor attractions all nearby.

Member of Capital Hotels
B&B from € 76.50 to € 107.50
£60.25 to £84.66

EIMEAR DOWD
GENERAL MANAGER

American Express
Diners
Mastercard
Visa

75   75

inet

IRISH HOTELS FEDERATION

Closed 24 - 26 December

Room rates are per room per night

GRAFTON HOUSE

26-27 SOUTH GREAT GEORGES STREET,
DUBLIN 2

TEL: 01-679 2041 FAX: 01-677 9715
EMAIL: graftonguesthouse@eircom.net

GUESTHOUSE ★★★ MAP 8 O 11

This charming 3*** guesthouse ideally located in the heart of the city within 2 minutes walking distance of Dublin's premier shopping centre Grafton Street, St. Stephen's Green, Trinity College and Dublin Castle. All bedrooms newly decorated with bathroom/shower, direct dial telephone, TV, hairdryers, tea and coffee making facilities. Public car parking close by in enclosed car parks. Grafton House is the ideal location for business or holidays.

B&B from €44.44 to €63.49
£35.00 to £50.00

BRIDGET COLLINS

Mastercard

Visa

16 16

Closed 23 - 30 December

GRESHAM HOTEL

23 UPPER O'CONNELL STREET,
DUBLIN 1

TEL: 01-874 6881 FAX: 01-878 7175
EMAIL: info@gresham-hotels.com
WEB: www.gresham-hotels.com

HOTEL ★★★★ MAP 8 O 11

Situated on Dublin's main thoroughfare, The Gresham provides the ultimate in luxury & service, convenient to the capital's theatres, galleries & shopping malls. Elegant & eminently traditional, The Gresham offers 288 luxury bedrooms including 6 penthouse suites. Two conference centres with 26 air-conditioned meeting rooms & a fitness suite complement the spacious ground floor facilities, which feature the Aberdeen Restaurant, Toddy's Bar & the Gresham Lounge. Multi-storey car park €6/day.

B&B from €114.28 to €177.76
£90.00 to £140.00

SHAY LIVINGSTONE
GENERAL MANAGER

American Express

Diners

Mastercard

Visa

Weekend 2 B&B €200.00 pps

288 288

Open All Year

HARCOURT HOTEL

60 HARCOURT STREET,
DUBLIN 2

TEL: 01-478 3677 FAX: 01-475 2013
EMAIL: reservations@harcourthotel.ie
WEB: www.harcourthotel.ie

HOTEL ★★★ MAP 8 O 11

Centrally located close to Grafton Street and St. Stephen's Green, convenient to the city's theatres, museums and tourist attractions. Our elegantly refurbished bedrooms are fully equipped and include tea/coffee making facilities. Once the home of George Bernard Shaw, now the home of traditional Irish music.

Member of Holiday Ireland Hotels
B&B from €50.80 to €114.00
£40.01 to £89.78

SALLY MCGILL
GENERAL MANAGER

American Express

Diners

Mastercard

Visa

Midweek specials from €177.80

46 46

Open All Year

B&B rates are per person sharing per night incl. Breakfast

HARDING HOTEL

COPPER ALLEY,
FISHAMBLE STREET,
DUBLIN 2

TEL: 01-679 6500 FAX: 01-679 6504
EMAIL: harding.hotel@usitworld.com
WEB: www.hardinghotel.ie

HOTEL ★★ MAP 8 O 11

Harding Hotel is a stylish city centre hotel located within Dublin's thriving left bank, Temple Bar. This historic area with its cobbled streets offers the visitor a variety of shops, restaurants, pubs and theatres. All 53 rooms are equipped to the highest standard with direct dial phone, TV, hairdryer and tea/coffee making facilities. The lively Darkey Kelly's Bar & Restaurant is the perfect setting for business or pleasure.

Member of USIT Accommodation Centres

Room Rate from €60.00 to €92.00
£47.25 to £72.45

EDEL KINSELLA
MANAGER

American Express
Mastercard
Visa

53 53

Closed 23 - 27 December

HARRINGTON HALL

70 HARCOURT STREET,
DUBLIN 2

TEL: 01-475 3497 FAX: 01-475 4544
EMAIL: harringtonhall@eircom.net
WEB: www.harringtonhall.com

GUESTHOUSE ★★★★ MAP 8 O 11

Harrington Hall with its secure private parking in the heart of Georgian Dublin, provides the perfect location for holiday and business visitors alike to enjoy the surrounding galleries, museums, cathedrals, theatres, fashionable shopping streets, restaurants and pubs. All rooms are equipped to today's exacting standards with en suite, direct dial phone, hospitality tray, trouser press and multi channel TV, access to fax facilities, e-mail and internet. All floors are serviced by elevator.

B&B from €82.50 to €125.00
£64.97 to £98.45

HENRY KING
PROPRIETOR

American Express
Mastercard
Visa

😊 Midweek specials from €200.00

28 28

Closed 23 December - 01 January

HARVEY'S GUEST HOUSE

11 UPPER GARDINER STREET,
DUBLIN 1

TEL: 01-874 8384 FAX: 01-874 5510
EMAIL: harveysguesthse@iol.ie
WEB: www.harveysguesthouse.com

GUESTHOUSE ★★★ MAP 8 O 11

This fully restored family run Georgian guesthouse provides a friendly atmosphere. Located in the heart of Dublin City and only 500m from O'Connell Bridge and Temple Bar. Conveniently reached by the No 41 airport bus, first stop on our street by the church. Our en suite facilities include bath/shower and hairdryers. Our car park is free. All rooms have TV and telephone.

B&B from €35.00 to €60.00
£21.00 to £36.00

EILISH FLOOD
PROPRIETOR

Mastercard
Visa

13 13

Closed 23 - 27 December

Room rates are per room per night

HAZELBROOK HOUSE

85 LOWER GARDINER STREET,
DUBLIN 1

TEL: 01-836 5003 FAX: 01-855 0310
EMAIL: hazelbrook@eircom.net
WEB: homepage.eircom.net/~hazelbrook/

GUESTHOUSE U MAP 8 O 11

Hazelbrook House offers superb accommodation with 34 en suite rooms including family rooms. All have remote control TV, iron, tea/coffee facilities and hairdryer. We provide a good Irish breakfast, cater for vegetarians and childrens special needs. Fax/phone on premises. For tourists there are attractions nearby: Trinity College, St Stephens Green and Dublin's trendy Temple Bar area. Our staff are always friendly and, most important, a warm welcome is assured.

B&B from €50.80 to €57.15
£40.01 to £45.01

DOLORES BURNETT
MANAGER

Mastercard
Visa

34 34

Closed 23 - 28 December

HEDIGAN'S

TULLYALLAN HOUSE,
14 HOLLYBROOK PARK, CLONTARF,
DUBLIN 3

TEL: 01 853 1663 FAX: 01-833 3337
EMAIL: hedigans@indigo.ie

GUESTHOUSE ★★★ MAP 8 O 11

Hedigan's is a late Victorian listed residence in Clontarf located 15 mins from the airport, Dublin Port, Point Theatre 5 mins, city centre 10 mins. Local facilities include 3 golf courses, beach and Stann's Rose Gardens. This elegant house offers a choice of single, double and twin luxurious en suite rooms. Also available is a gracious drawing room and gardens. RAC Highly Acclaimed. AA Selected ◆◆◆◆.

B&B from €38.00 to €57.00
£29.93 to £44.89

MATT HEDIGAN
PROPRIETOR

Mastercard
Visa

9 9

IRISH
HOTELS
FEDERATION

Closed 22 December - 10 January

HERBERT PARK HOTEL

BALLSBRIDGE,
DUBLIN 4

TEL: 01-667 2200 FAX: 01-667 2595
EMAIL: reservations@herbertparkhotel.ie
WEB: www.herbertparkhotel.ie

HOTEL ★★★★ MAP 8 O 11

Ideally located in Ballsbridge five minutes from the city centre, adjacent to the RDS with spectacular views over 48 acre Herbert Park. All 153 rooms are fully air-conditioned and appointed to the highest international standards. The award winning Pavillion Restaurant overlooks Herbert Park and plays host to live jazz each Sunday during Buffet Luncheon. Facilities include cardiovascular gym, meeting rooms, complimentary car parking. The hotel has been awarded 75% and two rosettes by the Automobile Association.

Member of UTELL International
B&B from €156.50 to €175.00
£123.25 to £137.82

EWAN PLENDERLEITH
GENERAL MANAGER

American Express
Diners
Mastercard
Visa

153 153

P aid Inet FAX

IRISH
HOTELS
FEDERATION

Open All Year

B&B rates are per person sharing per night incl. Breakfast

HIBERNIAN HOTEL

EASTMORELAND PLACE,
BALLSBRIDGE,
DUBLIN 4

TEL: 01-668 7666 FAX: 01-660 2655
EMAIL: info@hibernianhotel.com
WEB: www.hibernianhotel.com

HOTEL U MAP 8 O 11

The Hibernian Hotel, a splendid city centre Victorian building. Bedrooms are elegant & luxurious offering every modern facility complete with Neutrogena® toiletries. Guests can enjoy gourmet delights in the hotel's restaurant. AA Courtesy & Care Award 1999/hotel of the year 1997 from Small Luxury Hotels. Close to museums, theatres, concert halls & Grafton Street. Sister property of McCausland Hotel, Belfast and Woodstock Hotel, Ennis (Near Shannon) Co. Clare. GDS Acc Code:LX.UK Toll free:00 800 525 48000

Member of Small Luxury Hotels of the World

Room Rate from € 139.67 to €241.25
£110.00 to £190.00

TUATHAL BREHENY
GENERAL MANAGER

American Express
Diners
Mastercard
Visa

😊 Weekend specials from €165.07

40 40

HOTELS

Closed 24 - 26 December

HILTON DUBLIN

CHARLEMONT PLACE,
DUBLIN 2

TEL: 01-402 9988 FAX: 01-402 9966
EMAIL: reservations_dublin@hilton.com
WEB: www.dublin.hilton.com

HOTEL U MAP 8 O 11

Overlooking the Grand Canal, the welcoming Hilton Dublin is within walking distance of the main shopping and cultural centre. The Hilton features 189 en suite, well equipped rooms. For that little something extra you can try one of our club rooms, featuring soft bathrobes, mouth-watering chocolates, internet access via the television. Sample our culinary delights in the beautiful surroundings of the Waterfront Restaurant or try Champions Sports Bar. Car parking is available.

Room Rate from € 184.00 to €286.00
£144.91 to £225.24

PATRICK STAPLETON
GENERAL MANAGER

American Express
Diners
Mastercard
Visa

😊 Weekend specials from €176.00

189 189

inet

HOTELS

Open All Year

HOLIDAY INN DUBLIN CITY CENTRE

99-107 PEARSE STREET,
DUBLIN 2

TEL: 01-670 3666 FAX: 01-670 3636
EMAIL: info@holidayinndublin.ie
WEB: www.holidayinndublin.ie

HOTEL ★★★ MAP 8 O 11

Ireland's first Holiday Inn, located in the heart of the city centre, within walking distance of Lansdowne Road, RDS, The Point, Shelbourne Park. 92 superb en suite rooms with satellite TV and fax/modem line. Executive rooms, disabled and designated non-smoking rooms also available. Each room has either a king bed or two queen beds. Residents Gym. Esther Keogh's Traditional Irish Pub. Function rooms and conference facilities for up to 200 people. Secure private paid underground hotel car park.

B&B from €57.14 to €94.60
£45.00 to £74.50

JOHN R. MORAN
GENERAL MANAGER

American Express
Diners
Mastercard
Visa

92 92

HOTELS

Open All Year

Room rates are per room per night

HOTEL ISAACS

STORE STREET,
DUBLIN 1

TEL: 01-855 0067 FAX: 01-836 5390
EMAIL: hotel@isaacs.ie
WEB: www.isaacs.ie

HOTEL ★★★ MAP 8 O 11

Situated in the heart of Dublin City, 5 mins by foot from O'Connell Street Bridge, Hotel Isaacs, a converted wine-ware house, is the perfect location for the visitor to Dublin, at the perfect price, close to the shopping & financial centre. All rooms are tastefully furnished & are en suite with telephone, TV, tea/coffee making facilities & iron/ironing board. The restaurant, Il Vignardo, serves great tasting Italian food 7 days a week. Nearby overnight parking available at special rates.

B&B from €55.00 to €95.00
£43.32 to £74.82

EVELYN HANNIGAN
GENERAL MANAGER

American Express
Mastercard
Visa

☺ Weekend specials from €140.00

58 58

HOTELS
FEDERATION

Closed 23 - 27 December

HOTEL ST. GEORGE

7 PARNELL SQUARE,
DUBLIN 1

TEL: 01-874 5611 FAX: 01-874 5582
EMAIL: hotels@indigo.ie
WEB: indigo.ie/~hotels

HOTEL U MAP 8 O 11

The historical Hotel St. George is located on Parnell Square at the top of O'Connell Street, Dublin's principal thoroughfare. Within walking distance of the Abbey and the Gate Theatre, Municipal Art Gallery, Dublin's Writers Museum, principal shopping district and other major tourist attractions. Each bedroom is en suite, individually decorated, every modern comfort, including direct dial phone, colour TV and tea/coffee making facilities. Private car park.

B&B from €57.15 to €69.85
£45.01 to £55.01

JIM STAUNTON
PROPRIETOR

Mastercard
Visa

53 53

Closed 24 - 27 December

JACKSON COURT HOTEL

29/30 HARCOURT STREET,
DUBLIN 2

TEL: 01-475 8777 FAX: 01-475 8793
EMAIL: info@jackson-court.ie

HOTEL ★★ MAP 8 O 11

Minutes walk from Grafton Street, Stephens Green and most of Dublin's historic landmarks. Enjoy the combination of local Dubliners and visitors from abroad in our hotel, busy bar and Dublin's hottest night spot, Copper Face Jacks. Rates include full Irish breakfast, night club admission, service and taxes. We look forward to welcoming you!

B&B from €60.32 to €60.32
£47.51 to £47.51

LESLEY-ANNE HAYES
MANAGER

American Express
Diners
Mastercard
Visa

☺ Midweek specials from €133.35

26 26

HOTELS
FEDERATION

Closed 24 - 27 December

B&B rates are per person sharing per night incl. Breakfast

JURYS BALLSBRIDGE HOTEL

PEMBROKE ROAD,
BALLSBRIDGE,
DUBLIN 4

TEL: 01-660 5000 FAX: 01-660 5540
EMAIL: ballsbridge@jurysdoyle.com
WEB: www.jurysdoyle.com

HOTEL ★★★★★ MAP 8 O 11

One of Dublin's top international business hotels, Jurys Ballsbridge is renowned for its genial charm. Luxury accommodation, excellent restaurants and bars, a superb leisure centre and all the charms of the capital close at hand.

TOWERS

LANSDOWNE ROAD, DUBLIN 4
TEL: 01-667 0033 FAX: 01-660 5540
EMAIL: towers@jurysdoyle.com

5 Star Superior hotel adjacent to Jurys Ballsbridge Hotel.

B&B from €86.00 to €202.00
£67.73 to £159.06

RICHARD BOURKE
GENERAL MANAGER

American Express
Diners
Mastercard
Visa

394 394

Open All Year

JURYS GREEN ISLE HOTEL

NAAS ROAD,
DUBLIN 22

TEL: 01-459 3406 FAX: 01-459 2178
EMAIL: greenisle@jurysdoyle.com
WEB: www.jurysdoyle.com

HOTEL ★★★ MAP 8 O 11

Located on the main route from Dublin to the South, the friendly hub of a thriving Dublin South West, Jurys Green Isle is situated away from the hustle and bustle but within comfortable striking distance. Generous rooms, a welcoming bar and restaurant make it the perfect refuge for either the business or leisure guest.

B&B from €61.00 to €96.00
£48.04 to £75.61

JIM FLYNN
GENERAL MANAGER

American Express
Diners
Mastercard
Visa

90 90

Open All Year

JURYS INN CHRISTCHURCH

CHRISTCHURCH PLACE,
DUBLIN 8

TEL: 01-454 0000 FAX: 01-454 0012
EMAIL: jurysinnchristchurch@jurysdoyle.com
WEB: www.jurysdoyle.com

HOTEL ★★★ MAP 8 O 11

Located in Dublin's oldest quarter in the heart of the city just opposite the historical Christchurch Cathedral, Jurys Inn Christchurch is within easy strolling distance of voguish Temple Bar, St Patrick's Cathedral, Trinity College and fashionable Grafton Street.

Room Rate from €91.00 to €96.00
£71.67 to £75.61

BOBBY FITZPATRICK
GENERAL MANAGER

American Express
Diners
Mastercard
Visa

182 182

Closed 24 - 26 December

Room rates are per room per night

JURYS INN CUSTOM HOUSE

CUSTOM HOUSE QUAY,
DUBLIN 1

TEL: 01-607 5000 FAX: 01-829 0400
EMAIL: jurysinncustomhouse@jurysdoyle.com
WEB: www.jurysdoyle.com

HOTEL ★★★ MAP 8 O 11

Virtually in the shadow of Gandon's magnificent Custom House, from which it's named, Jurys Inn Custom House is centrally and attractively located along the river in the International Financial Services Centre. Within easy walking distance are all of the city's main shopping districts and cultural attractions.

Room Rate from €91.00 to €96.00
£71.67 to £75.61

EDWARD STEPHENSON
GENERAL MANAGER

American Express
Diners
Mastercard
Visa

239 239

Closed 24 - 26 December

JURYS MONTROSE HOTEL

STILLORGAN ROAD,
DUBLIN 4

TEL: 01-269 3311 FAX: 01-269 1164
EMAIL: montrose@jurysdoyle.com
WEB: www.jurysdoyle.com

HOTEL ★★★ MAP 8 O 11

On the main route into the city from Dublin's southside, overlooking the luscious ground of University College Dublin, Jurys Montrose Hotel is just a 10-minute drive from the city centre. Noted for the lively atmosphere and local flavour of its bars and restaurants, its popular appeal is enduring.

B&B from €61.00 to €96.00
£48.04 to £75.61

CONOR O'KANE
GENERAL MANAGER

American Express
Diners
Mastercard
Visa

179 179

Open All Year

JURYS SKYLON HOTEL

UPPER DRUMCONDRA ROAD,
DUBLIN 9

TEL: 01-837 9121 FAX: 01-837 2778
EMAIL: skylon@jurysdoyle.com
WEB: www.jurysdoyle.com

HOTEL ★★★ MAP 8 O 11

A smart hotel on the northern approach, ten minutes from the airport and five from the city centre, Jurys Skylon Hotel has just the right blend of style and informality to make your stay special. Its restaurant and bar are welcoming and just as popular in the neighbourhood as with guests.

B&B from €61.00 to €96.00
£48.04 to £75.61

LOUIS LANGAN
GENERAL MANAGER

American Express
Diners
Mastercard
Visa

88 88

Open All Year

B&B rates are per person sharing per night incl. Breakfast

JURYS TARA HOTEL

MERRION ROAD,
DUBLIN 4

TEL: 01-269 4666 FAX: 01-269 1027
EMAIL: tara@jurysdoyle.com
WEB: www.jurysdoyle.com

HOTEL ★★★ MAP 8 O 11

Along the curve of Dublin Bay with
perfect views of the sea and shore,
Jurys Tara Hotel is perfectly situated
between the city, which is two miles
away, and the charming southside
villages of Blackrock, Sandycove and
Dalkey. A spacious modern hotel, it
provides the features and services to
make your stay a pleasant one.

B&B from €61.00 to €96.20
£48.04 to £75.76

MELISSA HYNES
GENERAL MANAGER

American Express
Diners
Mastercard
Visa

113 113

Open All Year

KELLYS HOTEL

SOUTH GREAT GEORGES STREET,
DUBLIN 2

TEL: 01-677 9277 FAX: 01-671 3216
EMAIL: kellyhtl@iol.ie
WEB: www.kellyshtl.com

HOTEL U MAP 8 O 11

Situated in the heart of Dublin beside
fashionable Grafton Street. A few
minutes walk to Trinity College.
Temple Bar and many of Dublin's
famous pubs and restaurants are on
our doorstep. Places of historical,
cultural and literary interest are close
by. Kelly's is a budget hotel of
unbeatable value for a city centre
location. There is no service charge
and our prices include breakfast.
Frommers recommended. Parking
available in adjacent public multi-
storey carpark (for fee).

B&B from €44.00 to €51.00
£34.65 to £40.17

TERRY MOSER
GENERAL MANAGER

American Express
Mastercard
Visa

23 21

Closed 20 - 26 December

KILRONAN GUESTHOUSE

70 ADELAIDE ROAD,
DUBLIN 2

TEL: 01-475 5266 FAX: 01-478 2841
EMAIL: info@dublinn.com
WEB: www.dublinn.com

GUESTHOUSE ★★★ MAP 8 O 11

This exclusive AA RAC ◆◆◆◆
recommended Georgian House is in a
secluded setting, walking distance
from St. Stephen's Green, Trinity
College, National Concert Hall, Dublin
Castle, Cathedrals, St. Patrick's,
Christchurch and most of Dublin's
historic landmarks. Well appointed
bedrooms with private shower, direct
dial phone, TV, hairdryers, tea/coffee
facilities and quality orthopedic beds.
Commended by New York Times,
Beth Byrant, Michelin Guide, Fodors,
Frommer & Karen Browns.

Member of Premier Guesthouses
B&B from €44.00 to €76.00
£34.65 to £59.85

ROSE & TERRY MASTERSON
OWNERS

American Express
Diners
Mastercard
Visa

10 10

Open All Year

Room rates are per room per night

KINGSWOOD COUNTRY HOUSE

OLD KINGSWOOD,
NAAS ROAD, CLONDALKIN,
DUBLIN 22
TEL: 01-459 2428 FAX: 01-459 2207
EMAIL: kingswoodhse@eircom.net

GUESTHOUSE ★★★ MAP 8 O 11

A warm and welcoming Country House nestling within beautiful walled gardens. Strategically located 3km from the M50 at the beginning of the N7(Naas Road) the gateway to the West and South West. Enjoy the intimate atmosphere of the restaurant which features open fires and sophisticated Irish dishes with a French influence. The seven tastefully decorated bedrooms are all en suite with TV, direct dial phone. Recommended - Egon Ronay, Good Hotel Guide, RAC, AA ♦♦♦♦.

B&B from €50.80 to €63.50
£40.01 to £50.01

SHEILA O'BRYNE
MANAGERESS

American Express
Diners
Mastercard
Visa

🏨 📞 ☎ 🖵 T C CM❋U P 7 Y alc
7 7

IRISH HOTELS FEDERATION

Closed 25 - 27 December

LANSDOWNE HOTEL

27-29 PEMBROKE ROAD,
BALLSBRIDGE,
DUBLIN 4
TEL: 01-668 2522 FAX: 01-668 5585
EMAIL: lanhotel@iol.ie
WEB: www.lansdownehotel.com

HOTEL ★★★ MAP 8 O 11

The Lansdowne Hotel is a 3*** Georgian hotel just minutes walk from city centre. We combine olde world charm with modern facilities. Ideally located, with Lansdowne Stadium, RDS, Point Theatre and Dublin's business district just a short stroll. You can relax and enjoy fine Irish cuisine in our Celtic Restaurant or savour the local atmosphere in our Den Bar while enjoying mouth-watering food from our bar menu. We have a fully equipped conference and banqueting hall. Private car park.

Member of MinOtel Ireland Hotel Group
B&B from €50.00 to €88.00
£39.38 to £69.31

MARGARET ENGLISH
ASSISTANT MANAGER

American Express
Diners
Mastercard
Visa

🏨 📞 ☎ 🖵 T C CMP S 🅰 alc
40 40

IRISH HOTELS FEDERATION

Closed 23 - 27 December

LANSDOWNE MANOR

46-48 LANSDOWNE ROAD,
BALLSBRIDGE,
DUBLIN 4
TEL: 01-668 8848 FAX: 01-668 8873
EMAIL: lansdownemanor@eircom.net
WEB: www.lansdownemanor.ie

GUESTHOUSE ★★★★ MAP 8 O 11

Located in Ballsbridge, Lansdowne Manor is the ideal base for attending rugby matches at Lansdowne Road, conferences at the RDS (Royal Dublin Society) and 15 minutes walk from city centre. Lansdowne Manor comprises two early Victorian mansions which maintain the elegance of their original era. Rooms range from single to executive, each with en suite, DD phone, writing desk, trouser press, hairdryer and multi channel TV. Laundry services, private meeting room and secretarial services are available. AA Selected premises ♦♦♦♦.

Room Rate from €65.00 to €90.00
£51.19 to £70.88

BRENDA O'FLYNN-MOODY
GENERAL MANAGER

American Express
Diners
Mastercard
Visa

🏨 📞 ☎ 🖵 T C P S Inet FAX
21 21

IRISH HOTELS FEDERATION

Closed 23 December - 02 January

B&B rates are per person sharing per night incl. Breakfast

LE MERIDIEN SHELBOURNE

27 ST. STEPHEN'S GREEN, DUBLIN 2

TEL: 01-663 4500 FAX: 01-661 6006
EMAIL: shelbourneinfo@lemeridien-hotels.com
WEB: www.shelbourne.ie

HOTEL ★★★★★ MAP 8 O 11

Ireland's most distinguished address, provides the ultimate in luxury and service. In the heart of Dublin, overlooking St. Stephen's Green, within walking distance of shopping areas and Dublin's social and cultural life. The hotel has 190 rooms, 2 bars and 2 restaurants. The Lord Mayor's Lounge is a must for afternoon tea. The Shelbourne Club offers exclusive surroundings with fantastic choice of equipment, 18m pool, sauna, steam room, jacuzzi and top class cardiovascular equipment. Strictly over 18s only.
WAP: wap.shelbourne.ie

B&B from € 105.00 to € 325.00
£82.69 to £255.96

JEAN RICOUX
GENERAL MANAGER

American Express
Diners
Mastercard
Visa

190 190
alc Inet

Open All Year

LONGFIELDS

9/10 FITZWILLIAM STREET LOWER, DUBLIN 2

TEL: 01-676 1367 FAX: 01-676 1542
EMAIL: info@longfields.ie
WEB: www.longfields.ie

HOTEL ★★★ MAP 8 O 11

Longfield's, a charming and intimate hotel in the heart of Ireland's capital where, with its award winning No. 10 Restaurant, one can relax in oppulence reminiscent of times past. Avid followers of good food guides and well known accommodation publications will have noted numerous accolades bestowed upon this renowned residence. Its central location and its impeccable service make it a must for discerning travellers.

Member of Manor House Hotels
B&B from € 75.00 to € 125.00
£59.07 to £98.43

CHRIS VOS
GENERAL MANAGER

American Express
Diners
Mastercard
Visa

26 26

Closed 24 - 27 December

LYNAM'S HOTEL

63/64 O'CONNELL STREET, DUBLIN 1

TEL: 01-888 0886 FAX: 01-888 0890
EMAIL: lynams.hotel@indigo.ie
WEB: www.lynams-hotel.com

HOTEL U MAP 12 O 11

A boutique style 42 bedroom hotel located on O'Connell Street, close to the GPO and all of Dublin's many attractions. Decorated with elegance and individuality. All rooms are en suite, have direct dial phones and data port. 2 comfortable lounges are provided for guest use and our restaurant offers modern style cuisine. Lynam's Hotel is under the personal management of its owner Mr Gerard Lynam.

B&B from € 57.00 to € 82.50
£44.89 to £64.97

GERARD LYNAM

American Express
Diners
Mastercard
Visa

☺ Midweek specials from €135.00

41 41

Closed 24 - 28 December

Room rates are per room per night

LYNDON GUESTHOUSE

26 GARDINER PLACE,
DUBLIN 1

TEL: 01-878 6950 FAX: 01-878 7420
EMAIL: lyndonh@gofree.indigo.ie

GUESTHOUSE ★★ MAP 8 O 11

Lyndon House is an extremely popular, beautifully restored, modernly designed, Georgian guesthouse. It is excellently located in the heart of Dublin's City Centre off Parnell Square at the top of O'Connell Street & is on 41/41c airport bus route. It is family run, so emphasis is on good value, warm atmosphere and friendly service. Rooms are bathroom en suite, with TV, internal telephone and hospitality tray. Highly Acclaimed AA ♦♦.

B&B from €32.00 to €45.00
£25.20 to £35.44

MICHAEL MOLONEY
DIRECTOR

Mastercard

Visa

9   9   T C

IRISH HOTELS FEDERATION

Open All Year

MAPLE HOTEL

75 LOWER GARDINER STREET,
DUBLIN 1

TEL: 01-874 0225 FAX: 01-874 5239

WEB: www.focus-irl.com/maplehotel

HOTEL ★★ MAP 8 O 11

The Maple Hotel is situated in the heart of the city, just off O'Connell Street, beside all theatres, cinemas, main railway, bus and DART stations with a direct bus link to Dublin Airport. The hotel is owned and run by the Sharkey Family who have been welcoming guests here for over 38 years. All luxurious bedrooms en suite, colour TV, direct dial phones, hair dryer, coffee/tea facilities. Private car parking.

B&B from €41.90 to €57.14
£33.00 to £45.00

THE SHARKEY FAMILY

Mastercard

Visa

12   12   T P S

IRISH HOTELS FEDERATION

Closed 23 December - 14 January

MARIAN GUEST HOUSE

21 UPPER GARDINER STREET,
DUBLIN 1

TEL: 01-874 4129

GUESTHOUSE ★ MAP 8 O 11

Situated in Georgian Dublin, just off Mountjoy Square and five minutes walk from city centre and all principal shopping areas, cinemas, theatres, museums. All our rooms are tastefully decorated, with central heating and all usual amenities are available. There are tea/coffee making facilities. The Marian is family run and you are sure to get a warm welcome. On the 41 bus route from Dublin Airport. Open all year.

B&B from €27.00 to €30.00
£21.26 to £23.63

CATHRINE MCELROY
OWNER

Mastercard

Visa

6   6   C P

IRISH HOTELS FEDERATION

Open All Year

B&B rates are per person sharing per night incl. Breakfast

MERCER HOTEL

MERCER STREET LOWER,
DUBLIN 2

TEL: 01-478 2179 FAX: 01-478 0328
EMAIL: stay@mercerhotel.ie
WEB: www.mercerhotel.ie

HOTEL ★★★ MAP 8 O 11

Luxury boutique style hotel situated in a prime city centre location next to Grafton Street & St. Stephens Green, an ideal base to explore Dublin's main historical sights, theatres, trendy bars and restaurants. 31 superbly appointed en suite rooms. Discreetly blended into the décor is a full complement of modern amenities including individually controlled air conditioning, TV/Video, CD player, trouser press, fax, modem points, DD phone, hairdryer. Conference and restaurant facilities.

Member of Mercer Accommodation Group

Room Rate from € 165.00 to € 203.00
£129.95 to £159.88

CAROLINE FAHY
GENERAL MANAGER

American Express
Diners
Mastercard
Visa

31 31

Inet FAX

IRISH HOTELS FEDERATION

Closed 24 - 27 December

MERRION HALL

54 MERRION ROAD,
BALLSBRIDGE,
DUBLIN 4

TEL: 01-668 1426 FAX: 01-668 4280
EMAIL: merrionhall@iol.ie
WEB: www.halpinsprivatehotels.com

GUESTHOUSE ★★★★ MAP 8 O 11

The 4**** Award-winning Merrion Hall offers an elegant combination of Edwardian grace, fine food and modern comforts, all one expects of a private hotel, aircon suites, executive facilities, jacuzzis, 4-poster beds, private carpark & gardens. Adjacent to RDS & Four Seasons Hotel, close to city centre, airport and car ferry terminals by DART or bus. Accolades, AA ♦♦♦♦♦, RAC Property of Year, Times, Bestloved Hotels, Johansens. Sister property of adjoining Blakes, Aberdeen Lodge & Halpins Hotel, Co. Clare. USA toll free 1800 617 3178. UK free phone 0800 096 4748.

Member of Charming Hotels

B&B from € 45.00 to € 90.00
£35.44 to £70.88

PAT HALPIN
PROPRIETOR

American Express
Diners
Mastercard
Visa

30 30

Inet FAX

IRISH HOTELS FEDERATION

Open All Year

MERRION HOTEL

UPPER MERRION STREET,
DUBLIN 2

TEL: 01-603 0600 FAX: 01-603 0700
EMAIL: info@merrionhotel.com
WEB: www.merrionhotel.com

HOTEL ★★★★★ MAP 8 O 11

The Merrion Hotel, Dublin's most stylish 5***** hotel is situated in the city centre opposite Government Buildings on Upper Merrion Street. This hotel brings new standards of excellence to Ireland's capital by the nature of the discreet but friendly service offered to guests. With the meticulous restoration of four grade 1 listed Georgian town houses, the Merrion provides 145 beautifully appointed guest rooms and suites, many overlooking magnificent 18th century gardens.

Member of Leading Hotels of the World

Room Rate from € 280.00 to € 415.00
£220.48 to £326.77

PETER MACCANN
GENERAL MANAGER

American Express
Diners
Mastercard
Visa

145 145

alc Inet FAX

IRISH HOTELS FEDERATION

Open All Year

Room rates are per room per night

MERRION SQUARE MANOR

NO 31 MERRION SQUARE NORTH,
DUBLIN 2

TEL: 01-662 8551 FAX: 01-662 8556
EMAIL: merrionmanor@eircom.net
WEB: www.merrionsquaremanor.com

GUESTHOUSE ★★★ MAP 8 O 11

Merrion Square Manor is situated overlooking Dublin's most gracious Georgian square. Located a 5 minute stroll from the city centre this beautiful house has been tastefully restored and extends the welcome of Georgian days gone by. Bedrooms are individually designed and decorated, all are en suite and have been appointed to the highest standards. Private parking available. AA selected premises ◆◆◆◆.

Room Rate from €65.00 to €150.00
£51.19 to £118.12

ANNA O'MARA
MANAGER

American Express
Diners
Mastercard
Visa

🛏🔥☎🖥TC☕
18 18

Closed 22 December - 03 January

MESPIL HOTEL

MESPIL ROAD,
DUBLIN 4

TEL: 01-667 1222 FAX: 01-667 1244
EMAIL: mespil@leehotels.ie
WEB: www.leehotels.ie

HOTEL ★★★ MAP 8 O 11

On the leafy banks of the Grand Canal, the Mespil offers an ideal city centre location. The emphasis throughout is on space and comfort and the modern stylish decor is reflected in Glaze Restaurant and the Terrace Bar. All 256 en suite rooms are bright, spacious and tastefully furnished. The Mespil provides the perfect base, close to all shopping and cultural amenities and offering excellent value for money. Private car parking.

Member of Lee Hotels

Room Rate from €120.63 to €180.00
£95.00 to £141.76

MARTIN HOLOHAN
GENERAL MANAGER

American Express
Diners
Mastercard
Visa

Inet

🛏🔥☎🖥⬆TC☕CMP🔒alc♿
256 256

Closed 22 - 27 December

MONT CLARE HOTEL

MERRION SQUARE,
DUBLIN 2

TEL: 01-607 3800 FAX: 01-661 5663
EMAIL: montclareres@ocallaghanhotels.ie
WEB: www.ocallaghanhotels.ie

HOTEL ★★★ MAP 8 O 11

The Mont Clare features 74 luxurious fully air conditioned bedrooms, traditional lounge bar, Goldsmith's Restaurant, convention facilities and free private valet parking. Overlooking Merrion Square the Mont Clare Hotel is the ideal city centre location, just a few minutes walk to all major attractions including Trinity College, museums, theatres, exhibition centres and shopping areas. Reservations via UTELL International Worldwide. USA Toll Free Reservations 1800 5699983. On-line bookings: www.ocallaghanhotels.ie

Member of O'Callaghan Hotels

Room Rate from €149.00 to €230.00
£117.35 to £181.14

LARRY BOWE
GENERAL MANAGER

American Express
Diners
Mastercard
Visa

Inet

🛏🔥☎🖥⬆T☕CM🏠P🔒alc♿
74 74

Open All Year

B&B rates are per person sharing per night incl. Breakfast

MORGAN HOTEL

**10 FLEET STREET,
TEMPLE BAR,
DUBLIN 2**
TEL: 01-679 3939 FAX: 01-679 3946
EMAIL: sales@themorgan.com
WEB: www.themorgan.com

HOTEL U   MAP 8 O 11

The Morgan is a boutique contemporary style hotel with great emphasis on aesthetic detail. The rooms provide the ultimate in comfort and luxury for the discerning traveller. All rooms are equipped with TV/video, mini-hifi, voicemail and ISDN lines. Located in the vibrant Temple Bar area, The Morgan is in close proximity to theatres, shops, restaurants and the financial district of Dublin.

Member of Design & Planet Hotels

Room Rate from € 165.00 to € 480.00
£129.93 to £377.96

SANDRA DOYLE
GENERAL MANAGER

American Express
Diners
Mastercard
Visa

61 61

Closed 24 - 26 December

MORRISON

**LOWER ORMOND QUAY,
DUBLIN 1**
TEL: 01-887 2400 FAX: 01-878 3185
EMAIL: info@morrisonhotel.ie
WEB: www.morrisonhotel.ie

HOTEL ★★★★   MAP 8 O 11

One of the most luxurious and sophisticated hotels in Dublin, the Morrison is in the heart of the city overlooking the River Liffey. The 84 superior rooms, 6 stunning suites and the uniquely designed penthouse are decorated in a style which combines the use of natural Irish materials. Features include Halo Restaurant, offering modern European style cooking, the Morrison Bar and Café Bar and Lobo, a late night club.

Member of Sterling Hotels & Resorts

B&B from € 124.00 to € 190.50
£97.66 to £150.03

ANTHONY KENNA
GENERAL MANAGER

American Express
Diners
Mastercard
Visa

91 91

Closed 24 - 27 December

MOUNT HERBERT HOTEL

**HERBERT ROAD,
LANSDOWNE ROAD,
DUBLIN 4**
TEL: 01-668 4321 FAX: 01-660 7077
EMAIL: info@mountherberthotel.ie
WEB: www.mountherberthotel.ie

HOTEL U   MAP 8 O 11

This Gracious Victorian residence is 5 mins south of the city centre in Ballsbridge, Dublin's most exclusive area, where most diplomatic embassies are based. Facilities include 185 modern bedrooms, restaurant, licensed bar, coffee bar, sauna, gift shop, conference centre, private car park and picturesque gardens. The Loughran Family has been welcoming guests for over 45 years and it is renowned for its superb value and its warm and friendly atmosphere.

B&B from € 59.50 to € 90.00
£46.86 to £70.88

MICHELLE SWEENEY
MANAGER

American Express
Diners
Mastercard
Visa

☺ Midweek specials from €140.00

185 185

Open All Year

Room rates are per room per night

NORTH STAR HOTEL

AMIENS STREET,
DUBLIN 1

TEL: 01-836 3136 FAX: 01-836 3561
EMAIL: norths@regencyhotels.com
WEB: www.regencyhotels.com

HOTEL ★★★ MAP 8 O 11

City centre location directly opposite I.F.S.C., beside Connolly Rail Station & Busarus. Trinity College, St Stephen's Green, main shopping areas & Temple Bar all within walking distance. 90 newly appointed, air-cond. executive bedrooms with 2 luxurious suites. Rooms are en suite with colour TV, DD phone, hairdryer & trouser press. The hotel has been enhanced by a new reception, lobby & restaurant and has excellent meeting facilities with ISDN lines & video conferencing. We have a fully equipped gym with sauna/ changing rooms. 24hr supervised car park.

B&B from €76.20 to €101.60
£60.01 to £80.02

DAVID KIELY
GENERAL MANAGER

American Express
Diners
Mastercard
Visa

☺ Weekend specials from €100.33

125 125

Inet

HOTELS
FEDERATION

Open All Year

NORTHUMBERLAND LODGE

68 NORTHUMBERLAND ROAD,
BALLSBRIDGE,
DUBLIN 4

TEL: 01-660 5270 FAX: 01-668 8679
EMAIL: info@northumberlandlodge.com
WEB: www.northumberlandlodge.com

GUESTHOUSE ★★★ MAP 8 O 11

Luxurious Victorian house, built in the 1850s, situated in the prestigious embassy belt of Ballsbridge, Dublin 4. Close to the RDS, Shelbourne Park, bus and Dart station city centre. We offer executive accommodation - fully equipped rooms with multi channel TV, DD phone, hairdryer, etc. Secure car parking. A friendly welcome and service is guaranteed.

B&B from €50.79 to €101.58
£40.00 to £80.00

AVRIL MORDAUNT

Mastercard
Visa

8 8

Open All Year

NUMBER 31

31 LEESON CLOSE,
DUBLIN 2

TEL: 01-676 5011 FAX: 01-676 2929
EMAIL: number31@iol.ie
WEB: www.number31.ie

GUESTHOUSE ★★★★ MAP 8 O 11

An award winning guest house right in the heart of Georgian Dublin. The former home of Ireland's leading architect Sam Stephenson just a few minutes walk from St. Stephen's Green and galleries. An oasis of tranquillity and greenery, where guests are encouraged to come back and relax and feel at home at any time of the day. Vast breakfasts in the dining room or in a sunny plant filled conservatory. Recommended by the Good Hotel Guide, Egon Ronay, Bridgestone 100 Best Places, Fodors.

B&B from €70.00 to €120.00
£55.13 to £94.51

DEIRDRE & NOEL COMER

American Express
Mastercard
Visa

18 18

Open All Year

B&B rates are per person sharing per night incl. Breakfast

OLD DUBLINER GUESTHOUSE

62 AMIENS STREET,
DUBLIN 1

TEL: 01-855 5666 FAX: 01-855 5677
EMAIL: info@olddubliner.ie
WEB: www.olddubliner.com

GUESTHOUSE ★★★ MAP 8 O 11

The Old Dubliner is a listed Georgian town house that has been completely refurbished to a high standard. All rooms are en suite with TV, phone, hairdryers and tea/coffee making facilities. Situated in the heart of the city close to Connolly station and central bus station, 10 minutes walk from O'Connell St. and vibrant Temple Bar. Convenient to Point Theatre. Secure car park (limited availability). Our professional and friendly service will ensure a memorable stay.

B&B from €40.00 to €60.00
£31.50 to £47.25

JOHN O'NEILL

Mastercard
Visa

14   14

IRISH HOTELS FEDERATION

Closed 24 December - 02 January

ORMOND QUAY HOTEL

7-11 UPPER ORMOND QUAY,
DUBLIN 7

TEL: 01-872 1811 FAX: 01-872 1362
EMAIL: ormondqh@indigo.ie
WEB: www.ormondquayhotel.com

HOTEL U MAP 8 O 11

Overlooking the River Liffey and just minutes from Dublin's vibrant Temple Bar and bustling O'Connell St. The Ormond Quay Hotel is one of the city's best known. Alongside our 60 fully equipped en suite rooms, excellent conference and meeting facilities, food and entertainment in our acclaimed Sirens Bar and the unique Grosvenor Room art gallery. The Ormond Quay Hotel can proudly boast a friendly and welcoming atmosphere right at the heart of it.

B&B from €35.00 to €95.00
£27.56 to £74.81

VERONICA TIMLIN
GENERAL MANAGER

American Express
Mastercard
Visa

60   60

IRISH HOTELS FEDERATION

Open All Year

ORWELL LODGE HOTEL

77A ORWELL ROAD,
RATHGAR,
DUBLIN 6

TEL: 01-497 7256 FAX: 01-497 9913

WEB: www.orwelllodgehotel.ie

HOTEL ★ MAP 8 O 11

The Orwell is a comfortable hotel situated in the leafy garden suburb of Rathgar dating back to the elegant Victorian era. It enjoys a fine reputation for convivial atmosphere and good quality food of an international flavour. Under the personal management of Michael Lynch with friendly qualified staff who ensure that your visit is enjoyable. We serve breakfast, lunch, dinner and bar food. Family and corporate functions are catered for. Off street parking available.

B&B from €63.00 to €91.00
£49.62 to £71.67

MICHAEL LYNCH
OWNER

American Express
Diners
Mastercard
Visa

10   10

IRISH HOTELS FEDERATION

Closed 23 - 27 December

Room rates are per room per night

O'SHEAS HOTEL

19 TALBOT STREET,
DUBLIN 1

TEL: 01-836 5670 FAX: 01-836 5214
EMAIL: osheashotel@eircom.net

HOTEL ★ MAP 8 O 11

O'Sheas Hotel offers a warm and friendly atmosphere and is close to the shopping and cultural centre of Dublin. Its bar and lounge typify everyday life in Ireland offering traditional music seven nights a week. Guests can enjoy a wide and varied menu at pub prices in our cosy restaurant. Accommodation is en suite with satellite television and we are eager to look after your every need.

B&B from €38.10 to €50.80
£30.00 to £40.00

JOHN MCCORMACK
MANAGER

American Express
Diners
Mastercard
Visa

34 34

Closed 25 December

OTHELLO HOUSE

74 LOWER GARDINER STREET,
DUBLIN 1

TEL: 01-855 4271 FAX: 01-855 7460
EMAIL: othello1@eircom.net

GUESTHOUSE ★★ MAP 8 O 11

Othello is 150m from Abbey Theatre, 200m from Dublin's main O'Connell Street, 50m from central bus station. Number 41 bus direct from Dublin Airport stops outside door. 150m to Connolly Railway Station, 1 mile to ferry terminal, 800m to Point Theatre. Lock up secure car park. All rooms en suite with TV, telephone, tea/coffee making facilities. Trinity College, National Museum, National Library all within walking distance.

B&B from €40.00 to €50.00
£31.50 to £39.38

JOHN GALLOWAY
MANAGER

American Express
Diners
Mastercard
Visa

22 22

Closed 23 - 26 December

PALMERSTOWN LODGE

PALMERSTOWN VILLAGE,
DUBLIN 20

TEL: 01-623 5494 FAX: 01-623 6214
EMAIL: info@palmerstownlodge.com
WEB: www.palmerstownlodge.com

GUESTHOUSE ★★★ MAP 8 O 11

Prime location adjacent to all amenities and facilities this superb purpose-built property adjoins the N4/M50 motorway. Minutes from the city centre and a mere 12 minutes drive to the airport we offer all the features and standards of a luxury hotel. Each elegant en suite bedroom has individual temperature control, ambient lighting, automated door locking system, phone, TV, etc. Separate tea/coffee and iron/trouser press facilities. Private car park. Golf Packages available.

B&B from €38.00 to €57.00
£29.93 to £44.89

GERRY O'CONNOR
OWNER

Mastercard
Visa

19 19

Open All Year

B&B rates are per person sharing per night incl. Breakfast

General Tourist Information

❈

Population
The population of the Republic of Ireland (26 counties) is over 3.5 million. Dublin is the largest City with over one million inhabitants, Cork the second largest City and Limerick, Capital of the Shannon Region, is the third.

❈

Language
Almost everyone in Ireland speaks English. The country is bilingual, English and Irish (the Gaelic language) are spoken, especially in the West.

❈

Weather
Influenced by the Gulf Stream, Ireland has a mild temperate climate with summer temperatures generally ranging from 14 to 16 degree Celsius (60-70 degree Fahrenheit). The temperatures in Spring and Autumn are generally around 10 degree Celsius (50 degree Fahrenheit) and in Winter between 4 and 7 degrees Celsius (30-40 degree Fahrenheit).

❈

Electrical Voltage
The standard electrical supply is 230 volts AC (50 cycles); plugs are flat, with three pins. If required, small travel transformers should be purchased before departure to Ireland.

❈

Shopping
All shops are generally open from 09.00 to 17.30 Monday to Saturday. Many small local shops, and grocery shops in villages and small towns open daily until 22.00. Shopping centres normally have one or two late night openings each week. Some shopping centres are also open on Sundays.

Room rates are per room per night

PEMBROKE TOWNHOUSE

90 PEMBROKE ROAD,
BALLSBRIDGE,
DUBLIN 4

TEL: 01-660 0277 FAX: 01-660 0291
EMAIL: info@pembroketownhouse.ie
WEB: www.pembroketownhouse.ie

GUESTHOUSE ★★★★ MAP 8 O 11

A superb example of classic 18th century Georgian elegance perfectly located in the heart of Dublin's business district. Our aim has been to merge traditional Georgian elegance with contemporary style to create a townhouse with its own unique, welcoming personality. Each of our en suite bedrooms is individually designed to the highest standard. Gourmet and traditional Irish breakfast is served in our bright, refreshing dining room. Private secure car parking to rear. Use of local Leisure Centre.

Member of C.M.V.

B&B from €52.00 to €108.00
£40.95 to £85.06

CLEMENT GLEESON
GENERAL MANAGER

American Express
Diners
Mastercard
Visa

48 48

PHOENIX PARK HOUSE

38-39 PARKGATE STREET,
DUBLIN 8

TEL: 01-677 2870 FAX: 01-679 9769
EMAIL: info@dublinguesthouse.com
WEB: www.dublinguesthouse.com

GUESTHOUSE ★★ MAP 8 O 11

This friendly AA listed family run guesthouse directly beside the Phoenix Park with its many facilities is ideally located 2 minutes walk from Heuston Station with direct bus service to ferry ports, Dublin Airport, Connolly Train Station and central bus station. Close to the Guinness Brewery, Whiskey Corner, the re-located National Museum and Kilmainham Museum of Modern Art, the popular Temple Bar and numerous pubs and restaurants. Secure car parking available nearby.

B&B from €30.00 to €55.00
£23.63 to £43.31

MARY SMITH & EMER SMITH
PROPRIETORS

American Express
Diners
Mastercard
Visa

25 25

PLAZA HOTEL

BELGARD ROAD,
TALLAGHT,
DUBLIN 24

TEL: 01-462 4200 FAX: 01-462 4600
EMAIL: reservations@plazahotel.ie
WEB: www.plazahotel.ie

HOTEL ★★★★ MAP 8 O 11

120 bedrooms, 2 suites. Convenient location on Belgard Road, just off the M50 motorway, 5 miles from the city centre. Secure underground car parking. Extensive conference & banqueting facilities for up to 220 people. Floor one serving food from 9.00am - 10.00pm Mon-Sat. Obar1 music bar. The Playhouse Nightclub. Grumpy McClafferty's traditional pub. 20 minutes from Dublin Airport.

Room Rate from €90.00 to €160.00
£70.88 to £126.00

CHARLES COSTELLOE
GENERAL MANAGER

American Express
Diners
Mastercard
Visa

122 122

B&B rates are per person sharing per night incl. Breakfast

PORTOBELLO HOTEL & BAR

33 SOUTH RICHMOND STREET, DUBLIN 2

TEL: 01-475 2715 FAX: 01-478 5010
EMAIL: portobellohotel@indigo.ie

HOTEL U   MAP 8 O 11

This landmark building is located in the heart of Dublin City along the Grand Canal. First opened in 1793, the Portobello Hotel boasts a long tradition in hospitality and this new revival combines to provide all guests with comfortable accommodation, good food and a traditional Irish pub.

B&B from € 57.00 to € 63.50
£44.89 to £50.01

URSULA FOX
MANAGER

American Express
Diners
Mastercard
Visa

22 22
FAX

HOTELS
FEDERATION

Open All Year

QUALITY CHARLEVILLE HOTEL AND SUITES

LOWER RATHMINES ROAD, DUBLIN 6

TEL: 01-406 6100 FAX: 01-406 6200
EMAIL: info@charlevillehotel.com
WEB: www.qualitycharlevillehotel.com

HOTEL ★★★   MAP 8 O 11

Ideally located for business or leisure, situated in the popular suburb of Rathmines Village, only a 15 min walk to Dublin's famous Grafton St, museums, galleries and theatres. Most rooms are suites offering sittingroom, kitchenette, separate bedrooms and bathroom. All equipped with fax machine, voice mail, CD player and modem point. Carmines Restaurant has an extensive European menu, also there is a multi-level themed bar. Free underground parking for residents.

Member of Choice Hotels Ireland

Room Rate from € 85.50 to € 101.50
£67.34 to £79.94

ANN BYRNE
GENERAL MANAGER

American Express
Diners
Mastercard
Visa

51 51
Inet FAX

HOTELS
FEDERATION

Open All Year

QUALITY HOTEL & SUITES

NAAS ROAD, CO. DUBLIN

TEL: 01-458 7000 FAX: 01-458 7019
EMAIL: info@qualitycitywest.com
WEB: www.premgroup.com

HOTEL P   MAP 8 O 11

Located just 8 miles from Dublin City Centre and 20 minutes drive to Dublin Airport on the main N7 Dublin-Cork Route. A unique concept in hotel and suite accommodation, the hotel is comprised of 7 separate units. In addition to spacious bedrooms, the hotel offers one and two bedroom suites. Each suite offers the independence of a lounge, dining area and kitchenette. Free carparking for hotel guests plus hotel restaurant.

Member of Choice Hotels International

Room Rate from € 127.00 to € 165.00
£100.02 to £129.95

EVELYN HARAN
GENERAL MANAGER

American Express
Diners
Mastercard
Visa

☺ Midweek specials from €152.00

144 144

Closed 24 - 28 December

Room rates are per room per night

RAGLAN LODGE

10 RAGLAN ROAD,
BALLSBRIDGE,
DUBLIN 4

TEL: 01-660 6697 FAX: 01-660 6781

GUESTHOUSE ★★★★ MAP 8 O 11

Raglan Lodge is a magnificent Victorian residence dating from 1861. It is just ten minutes from the heart of Dublin in a most peaceful location. There are seven guest rooms, all of which have bathrooms en suite, colour TV, radio/alarm, telephone and tea/coffee facilities. Several of the rooms are noteworthy for their fine proportions and high ceilings. National winner of the Galtee Irish Breakfast Award. Secure car parking facilities. Recommended by RAC, AA and Egon Ronay. Also, received breakfast award in Georgina Campbell's Jameson Guide 2001.

B&B from €63.50 to €82.55
£50.01 to £65.01

HELEN MORAN
PROPRIETRESS

American Express
Diners
Mastercard
Visa

7 7

IRISH HOTELS FEDERATION

Closed 20 December - 07 January

RATHMINES CAPITAL HOTEL

LOWER RATHMINES ROAD,
DUBLIN 6

TEL: 01-496 6966 FAX: 01-491 0603
EMAIL: info@rathminescapital-hotel.com
WEB: www.capital-hotels.com

HOTEL ★★★ MAP 8 O 11

Enjoy the best of both worlds, Dublin city 5 minutes by car, whilst guests travelling to/from all major cities nationwide, enjoy easy & direct access from the M50 link road. Regular bus service to the city nearby. Free on site car parking. Relax in comfortable, spacious accommodation, where a genuinely warm welcome awaits. Experience our stylish cosmopolitan "Savannah" café bar, or explore this lively district with its many bars, restaurants, shops & cafés. RDS exhibition centre, Lansdowne Rd sporting ground & Harolds Cross dog racing- all nearby.

Member of Capital Hotels
B&B from €73.00 to €80.00
£57.49 to £63.01

FRANCES DEMPSEY
GENERAL MANAGER

American Express
Diners
Mastercard
Visa

54 54

IRISH HOTELS FEDERATION

Closed 24 - 26 December

RED COW MORAN HOTEL

RED COW COMPLEX,
NAAS ROAD,
DUBLIN 22

TEL: 01-459 3650 FAX: 01-459 1588
EMAIL: reservations@morangroup.ie
WEB: www.redcowhotel.com

HOTEL ★★★★ MAP 8 O 11

4**** Red Cow Moran Hotel combines classic elegance with modern design, situated at the Gateway to the Provinces, convenient to city centre, 15 mins from Dublin Airport. Bedrooms are fully air-conditioned with colour teletext TV, direct dial phones/fax, hairdryer, trouser press & tea/coffee facilities. The complex boasts a choice of lively bars and features two superb restaurants and a carvery restaurant, conference facilities, babysitting service on request. Night Club. Free carparking. AA 4****. A Moran Hotel.

B&B from €55.00 to €120.00
£43.32 to £94.51

TOM & SHEILA MORAN
PROPRIETORS

American Express
Diners
Mastercard
Visa

123 123

Inet FAX

IRISH HOTELS FEDERATION

Closed 24 - 26 December

B&B rates are per person sharing per night incl. Breakfast

REGENCY AIRPORT HOTEL

SWORDS ROAD,
WHITEHALL,
DUBLIN 9
TEL: 01-837 3544 FAX: 01-836 7121
EMAIL: regency@regencyhotels.com
WEB: www.regencyhotels.com

HOTEL ★★★ MAP 8 O 11

The Regency Hotel is located 3km
north of Dublin's city centre on main
route to Dublin's International Airport
and Northern Ireland. All rooms are
en suite with colour TV, DD phone
and tea/coffee making facilities. The
hotel incorporates 70 executive rooms
with hairdryers and trouser press as
standard. The hotel features the
Shanard Restaurant, the Appian
Lounge and its own theatre. Rooks
Theme Restaurant is renowned for its
steaks, chicken and pasta dishes with
seating for 200. The hotel has ample
parking.

B&B from €76.20 to €114.30
£60.01 to £90.02

BRIAN MCGETTIGAN
GENERAL MANAGER

American Express
Diners
Mastercard
Visa

☺ Weekend specials from €100.33

212 212

Open All Year

ROYAL DUBLIN HOTEL

O'CONNELL STREET,
DUBLIN 1

TEL: 01-873 3666 FAX: 01-873 3120
EMAIL: enq@royaldublin.com
WEB: www.royaldublin.com

HOTEL ★★★ MAP 8 O 11

Located in the heart of the city on
Dublin's most famous street,
O'Connell Street. Perfect base from
which to explore shops, theatres,
museums and galleries. Guest rooms
include hairdryer, tea/coffee making
facilities, direct dial telephone and all
are en suite. Relax in the elegant
Georgian Room or enjoy the lively
Raffles Bar. Excellent food available
all day in the Café Royale Brasserie.
Secure car park available.

Member of Best Western Hotels
Room Rate from €140.00 to €175.00
£110.26 to £137.82

DARRAGH BRADY
GENERAL MANAGER

American Express
Diners
Mastercard
Visa

117 117

inet

Closed 24 - 26 December

SACHS HOTEL

19-29 MOREHAMPTON ROAD,
DONNYBROOK,
DUBLIN 4
TEL: 01-668 0995 FAX: 01-668 6147

HOTEL ★★ MAP 8 O 11

Set in a quiet exclusive south city
location, yet only a short stroll from
the heart of Dublin. A unique blend of
Georgian excellence and modern
amenities. You will feel the warmth of
our welcome and the charm of the
traditional decor. Spacious bedrooms
individually designed and with en
suite, colour TV and direct dial phone.
Extensive conference and banqueting
facilities.

B&B from €53.96 to €95.23
£42.50 to £75.00

ANN BYRNE
MANAGER

American Express
Diners
Mastercard
Visa

20 20

Open All Year

Room rates are per room per night

SCHOOL HOUSE HOTEL

2-8 NORTHUMBERLAND ROAD,
BALLSBRIDGE,
DUBLIN 4

TEL: 01-667 5014 FAX: 01-667 5015

HOTEL ★★★★ MAP 8 O 11

Situated in the heart of one of Dublin's most fashionable districts the hotel offers superb accommodation, good food and lively pub. All 31 bedrooms are furnished to the highest international standard, catering for both business and leisure visitors to the capital. Located just a short walk from the commercial, cultural and entertainment heart of the city, the School House Hotel is poised to become one of the city's leading new hotels.

B&B from €70.00 to €122.00
£55.13 to £96.08

BERTIE KELLY
GENERAL MANAGER

American Express
Diners
Mastercard
Visa

2 nights special B&B from €170.00 p.p.s.

31 31

IRISH HOTELS FEDERATION

Closed 24 - 27 December

SHELDON PARK HOTEL & LEISURE CENTRE

KYLEMORE ROAD,
DUBLIN 12

TEL: 01-460 1055 FAX: 01-460 1880
EMAIL: info@sheldonpark.ie
WEB: www.sheldonpark.ie

HOTEL ★★★ MAP 8 O 11

Warm and friendly, the Sheldon Park Hotel is ideally situated just 20 mins from Dublin Airport and 20 mins from the city centre. Just off the M50, we offer easy access to Ireland's most scenic country routes. Spend a relaxing day in our leisure centre, complete with swimming pool, sauna and jacuzzi and finish with a meal in our bistro style restaurant followed by live entertainment.

B&B from €70.00 to €150.00
£55.12 to £118.12

DONNACHA ROCHE
GENERAL MANAGER

American Express
Diners
Mastercard
Visa

72 72

IRISH HOTELS FEDERATION

Closed 24 - 26 December

ST. AIDEN'S GUESTHOUSE

32 BRIGHTON ROAD,
RATHGAR,
DUBLIN 6

TEL: 01-490 2011 FAX: 01-492 0234
EMAIL: staidens@eircom.net

GUESTHOUSE ★★★ MAP 8 O 11

St. Aiden's charming family-run guesthouse is modernised to the highest standard of comfort and elegance while preserving its early Victorian character. Located in one of Dublin's most prestigious areas. 15 mins from city centre on an excellent bus route, 10 mins from the M50 with its links to the airport and national routes, private parking at rear. Hospitality tray and books are provided in lovely drawing room. Under the personal care of Maura O'Carroll and recommended AA ♦♦♦.

B&B from €38.00 to €50.00
£29.93 to £39.38

MAURA O'CARROLL
PROPRIETRESS

Mastercard
Visa

8 8

IRISH HOTELS FEDERATION

Open All Year

B&B rates are per person sharing per night incl. Breakfast

ST. ANDREWS

1 LAMBAY ROAD,
DRUMCONDRA,
DUBLIN 9

TEL: 01-837 4684 FAX: 01-857 0446
EMAIL: andrew@dublinn.com
WEB: www.dublinn.com/andrew

GUESTHOUSE ★★★ MAP 8 O 11

Welcome to St Andrews, situated 10 mins from city centre, airport & car ferry. Refurbished to a Bord Failte high standard, we offer a variety of en suite rooms with direct dial phone, multi-channel TV, hairdryer. Hospitality trolley is provided in guests' lounge. Excellent base for exploring the famed attractions of Dublin - Temple Bar, Grafton St, Trinity College, museums, theatres, galleries, etc. Recommended by AA and RAC. Recently awarded the Sparkling Diamond accolade by RAC.

Member of Premier Guesthouses

B&B from €35.00 to €50.00
£27.56 to £39.38

EILEEN LYNCH
OWNER

Mastercard
Visa

13 13

Open All Year

STAUNTONS ON THE GREEN

83 ST. STEPHEN'S GREEN,
DUBLIN 2

TEL: 01-478 2300 FAX: 01-478 2263
EMAIL: hotels@indigo.ie
WEB: http://indigo.ie/~hotels

GUESTHOUSE ★★★ MAP 8 O 11

Large Georgian house overlooking St. Stephen's Green, own private gardens. All rooms are en suite and fully equipped with direct dial telephone, TV and tea/coffee welcoming trays, trouser press and hairdryer. It is close to museums, galleries, Grafton Street shopping area and many other major tourist attractions. Stauntons On the Green occupies one of Dublin's most prestigious locations, close to many corporate headquarters and government buildings.

B&B from €70.00 to €83.00
£55.12 to £65.36

JOANNE NORMAN

American Express
Diners
Mastercard
Visa

30 30

Closed 24 - 27 December

STEPHENS GREEN HOTEL

ST. STEPHEN'S GREEN,
DUBLIN 2

TEL: 01-607 3600 FAX: 01-661 5663
EMAIL: stephensgreenres@ocallaghanhotels.ie
WEB: www.ocallaghanhotels.ie

HOTEL ★★★★ MAP 8 O 11

A shoppers haven, this de luxe boutique hotel is just a 2 minute walk from Grafton Street shops and cafés. The hotel is a splendid craft of Georgian elegance and contemporary style with a four storey glass atrium overlooking St. Stephen's Green. 64 luxurious air conditioned guestrooms and 11 suites, restaurant, traditional bar, gymnasium and business centre. Car parking. USA Toll Free Reservations 1800 569 9983 or on line at www.ocallaghanhotels.ie

Member of O'Callaghan Hotels

Room Rate from €220.00 to €355.00
£173.26 to £279.59

SALLY HUGHES
GENERAL MANAGER

American Express
Diners
Mastercard
Visa

75 75

Inet

Open All Year

Room rates are per room per night

TAVISTOCK HOUSE

64 RANELAGH ROAD,
RANELAGH,
DUBLIN 6
TEL: 01-498 8000 FAX: 01-498 8000
EMAIL: info@tavistockhouse.com
WEB: www.tavistockhouse.com

GUESTHOUSE ★★★ MAP 8 O 11

Magnificent Victorian house, tastefully converted retaining all its original plasterwork - very homely. Situated on the city side of Ranelagh Village, on the corner of Ranelagh / Northbrook Roads. We are only 7 mins walk from Stephen's Green in the heart of Dublin, near Helen Dillon's world famous garden. All rooms have colour TV, direct dial phone, hair dryer and tea/coffee making facilities. Private parking. There is a wide variety of restaurants locally. Internet facilities.

B&B from € 38.00 to € 90.00
£29.93 to £70.88

MAUREEN & BRIAN CUSACK
CO-OWNERS

American Express
Mastercard
Visa

6   6

Open All Year

TEMPLE BAR HOTEL

FLEET STREET,
TEMPLE BAR,
DUBLIN 2
TEL: 01-677 3333 FAX: 01-677 3088
EMAIL: templeb@iol.ie
WEB: www.towerhotelgroup.ie

HOTEL ★★★ MAP 8 O 11

A Tower Group Hotel - situated in the heart of Dublin's Temple Bar, in close proximity to theatres, shops and restaurants, the Temple Bar Hotel features 129 en suite bedrooms fully equipped with modern facilities, restaurant, Conference and meeting room facilities for up to 70 people. The Temple Bar Hotel is within easy access of train stations, airport and Dublin port, there is a multi storey car park nearby.

Member of Tower Hotel Group
B&B from € 76.20 to € 107.95
£60.01 to £85.02

DEIRDRE POWER
GENERAL MANAGER

American Express
Diners
Mastercard
Visa

129 129

Closed 24 - 27 December

TRINITY CAPITAL HOTEL

PEARSE STREET,
DUBLIN 2
TEL: 01-648 1000 FAX: 01-648 1010
EMAIL: info@trinitycapital-hotel.com
WEB: www.capital-hotels.com

HOTEL ★★★ MAP 8 O 11

Enjoy Dublin city on your doorstep. With a prime central location close to Grafton St, Temple bar & several places of interest, guests will enjoy the classic contemporary style of this new hotel. Relax in superb accommodation & enjoy our mediterranean style dining menu. Choose the mellow lobby bar for a selection of wines & coffees or the ultimate three-level, themed nightclub adjacent, "Fireworks". Residents avail of complimentary admission to all 13 leading Capital bars.'

Member of Capital Hotels
B&B from € 76.50 to € 107.50
£60.00 to £84.50

JOSEPHINE PEPPER

American Express
Diners
Mastercard
Visa

81   81

Inet

Closed 24 - 26 December

B&B rates are per person sharing per night incl. Breakfast

TRINITY LODGE

12 SOUTH FREDERICK STREET,
DUBLIN 2

TEL: 01-679 5044 FAX: 01-679 5223
EMAIL: trinitylodge@eircom.net

GUESTHOUSE ★★★ MAP 8 O 11

Situated in the heart of Dublin, Trinity Lodge offers superb en suite accommodation in a traditional Georgian townhouse. You will find all of Dublin's business, shopping and historic centres right on our doorstep and you are just steps away from Grafton Street, Trinity College and vibrant Temple Bar. Each room, from our singles to our 650 sq' suites, is equipped with air conditioning, personal safe, satellite TV, radio alarm, tea/coffee facilities and trouser press.

B&B from €70.00 to €215.00
£55.13 to £169.33

PETER MURPHY
MANAGING DIRECTOR

American Express
Diners
Mastercard
Visa

10 10

Open All Year

UPPERCROSS HOUSE

26-30 UPPER RATHMINES ROAD,
DUBLIN 6

TEL: 01-497 5486 FAX: 01-497 5361
EMAIL: uppercrosshotel@ireland.com
WEB: www.uppercrosshousehotel.com

HOTEL ★★★ MAP 8 O 11

Uppercross House is a hotel providing 49 bedrooms of the highest standard of comfort. All with direct dial phone, TV, tea/coffee maker, central heating and all en suite. Uppercross House has its own secure parking and is ideally situated in Dublin's south side 2km from St. Stephen's Green and R.D.S., with excellent public transport from directly outside the door. A fully licensed restaurant and bar opens nightly with a warm and friendly atmosphere.

B&B from €50.00 to €75.00
£39.38 to £59.07

DAVID MAHON
PROPRIETOR

American Express
Diners
Mastercard
Visa

49 49

Closed 23 - 30 December

WATERLOO HOUSE

8-10 WATERLOO ROAD,
BALLSBRIDGE,
DUBLIN 4

TEL: 01-660 1888 FAX: 01-667 1955
EMAIL: waterloohouse@eircom.net
WEB: www.waterloohouse.ie

GUESTHOUSE ★★★★ MAP 8 O 11

A warm welcome awaits you at this luxury guesthouse, in the heart of Georgian Dublin. It comprises 2 Georgian houses, refurbished to superb standard, retaining original features, offer unique atmosphere, style, elegance. Minutes from; RDS, St. Stephen's Green, Grafton Street, city centre. Delicious breakfast is served in dining room, overlooking conservatory & gardens. Lift & carpark. Recommended: Bridgestone 100 Best Places, Alister Sawday's, Michelin Guide and AA ◆◆◆◆.

B&B from €41.27 to €88.90
£32.50 to £70.01

EVELYN CORCORAN
PROPRIETOR

Mastercard
Visa

17 17

Closed 23 - 28 December

Room rates are per room per night

WATERLOO LODGE

23 WATERLOO ROAD,
BALLSBRIDGE,
DUBLIN 4

TEL: 01-668 5380 FAX: 01-668 5786
EMAIL: info@waterloolodge.com
WEB: www.waterloolodge.com

GUESTHOUSE ★★★ MAP 8 O 11

Waterloo Lodge is centrally located in Ballsbridge on the south side of Dublin City. Just minutes walk from the city centre, Stephen's Green, Temple Bar, museums, theatres, restaurants and pubs with a bus route outside our door. Our rooms are en suite, tastefully decorated, have direct dial phone, cable TV and hairdryer. Most are non-smoking. Fax and email facilities are available. We assure you of a warm welcome and a pleasant stay.

B&B from €37.50 to €70.00
£29.53 to £55.13

CATHAL DALY
OWNER

Mastercard
Visa

10 10

IRISH HOTELS FEDERATION

Closed 24 - 26 December

WEST COUNTY HOTEL

CHAPELIZOD,
DUBLIN 20

TEL: 01-626 4011 FAX: 01-623 1378

HOTEL ★★ MAP 8 O 11

The West County Hotel, an established family run hotel, located in the picturesque village of Chapelizod. Situated just off the N4 & close to the M50 motorway, which makes it convenient to both Dublin Airport (10 miles) and Dublin city centre (4 miles). Our hotel comprises 50 en suite bedrooms, which are fully equipped with TV, DD phone, tea/coffee making facilities, ironing board and hairdryer. Food is served all day. A warm and friendly welcome awaits you at the West County Hotel.

B&B from €58.00 to €70.00
£45.68 to £55.13

EAMON FENNELLY
HEAD OF SALES & MARKETING

American Express
Diners
Mastercard
Visa

50 50

IRISH HOTELS FEDERATION

Closed 24 - 26 December

WESTBURY

GRAFTON STREET,
DUBLIN 2

TEL: 01-679 1122 FAX: 01-679 7078
EMAIL: westbury@jurysdoyle.com
WEB: www.jurysdoyle.com

HOTEL ★★★★★ MAP 8 O 11

Smartly set just off Grafton Street in the very heart of the city, The Westbury can best be described as a truly international 5-star hotel; sophisticated, stylish and at the glamorous hub of Dublin life. Luxury, impeccable service, smart contemporary surroundings with the city at your feet.

Member of Leading Hotels of the World
B&B from €124.00 to €224.50
£97.66 to £176.81

PARAIC DOYLE
GENERAL MANAGER

American Express
Diners
Mastercard
Visa

204 204

Inet FAX

IRISH HOTELS FEDERATION

Open All Year

B&B rates are per person sharing per night incl. Breakfast

WESTIN DUBLIN

AT COLLEGE GREEN,
DUBLIN 2

TEL: 01-645 1000 FAX: 01-645 1234
EMAIL: reservations.dublin@westin.com
WEB: www.westin.com

HOTEL N   MAP 8 O 11

Situated in the best city location. Ideal for business and leisure travellers. Offering an ambience of warmth and Irish hospitality with the international level of service and amenities that are uniquely Westin. The Exchange Restaurant offers a blend of local and international dishes. The Mint Bar, creatively transformed from the original bank's vaults. The Atrium Lounge housed in the former bank building, with its magnificent glass roof. The Banking Hall, dating from 1863, has been timelessly restored to its original 19th century splendour.

Room Rate from €223.00 to €336.00
£175.60 to £264.57

ENDA M MULLIN
GENERAL MANAGER

American Express
Diners
Mastercard
Visa

163 163

Open All Year

GLANDORE HOUSE

GLANDORE PARK, LWR MOUNTTOWN,
ROAD, DUN LAOGHAIRE,
CO. DUBLIN

TEL: 01-280 3143 FAX: 01-280 2675
EMAIL: info@glandorehouse.com
WEB: www.glandorehouse.com

GUESTHOUSE ★★★   MAP 8 P 11

Staying at Glandore House allows visitors to take a step back into a more gracious era while at the same time offering the most modern guesthouse facilities. All rooms are en suite with TV, direct dial phone, tea/coffee facilities. Trouser press/ironing centre. A 6 person lift and off street car parking is also available. Situated 5 minutes drive from Dun Laoghaire Ferry Terminal, DART Station and bus terminals, therefore offering easy accessibility to the city centre and surrounding areas.

B&B from €38.00 to €57.00
£29.93 to £44.89

GRAINNE JACKMAN
MANAGER

Mastercard
Visa

12 12

Closed 22 December - 03 January

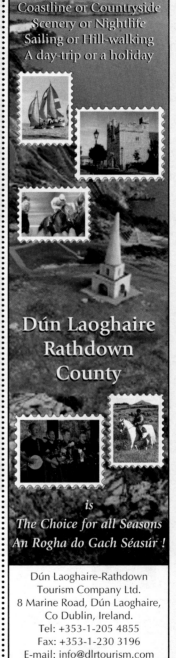

Coastline or Countryside
Scenery or Nightlife
Sailing or Hill-walking
A day-trip or a holiday

Dún Laoghaire Rathdown County

is
The Choice for all Seasons
An Rogha do Gach Séasúr !

Dún Laoghaire-Rathdown
Tourism Company Ltd.
8 Marine Road, Dún Laoghaire,
Co Dublin, Ireland.
Tel: +353-1-205 4855
Fax: +353-1-230 3196
E-mail: info@dlrtourism.com
www.dlrtourism.com

Room rates are per room per night

GRESHAM ROYAL MARINE

MARINE ROAD,
DUN LAOGHAIRE,
CO. DUBLIN

TEL: 01-280 1911 FAX: 01-280 1089

EMAIL: info@gresham-royalmarinehotel.com
WEB: www.gresham-hotels.com

HOTEL ★★★ MAP 8 O 11

This elegant 19th century hotel, with panoramic views of Dublin Bay and the picturesque port of Dun Laoghaire, is set in its own landscaped gardens and features 103 bedrooms, including 8 Victorian four-poster suites. The elegant Bay Lounge, Toddy's Bar, and the Powerscourt Room Restaurant provide the ideal location to unwind. Only 20 mins to city centre by rapid rail or bus. Excellent conference facilities. Complimentary car parking. AA, RAC and Egon Ronay recommended.

B&B from €85.00 to €230.00
£66.93 to £181.14

PAUL MCCRACKEN
GENERAL MANAGER

American Express
Diners
Mastercard
Visa

103 103

IRISH HOTELS FEDERATION

Open All Year

KINGSTON HOTEL

ADELAIDE ST., (OFF GEORGES ST.),
DUN LAOGHAIRE,
CO. DUBLIN

TEL: 01-280 1810 FAX: 01-280 1237

EMAIL: reserv@kingstonhotel.com
WEB: www.kingstonhotel.com

HOTEL ★★ MAP 8 O 11

A delightful 38 bedroomed hotel with panoramic views of Dublin Bay, approximately 15 minutes from city centre. Beside ferryport and DART line. Situated convenient to R.D.S., Point Depot, Lansdowne Road and Leopardstown Racecourse. All rooms are en suite with direct dial phone, TV, tea/coffee making facilities. A family run hotel serving food all day in our lounge/bar and our Haddington Bistro opened nightly.

Member of MinOtel Ireland Hotel Group
B&B from €60.00 to €62.50
£47.25 to £49.22

JAMES J WALSH

American Express
Diners
Mastercard
Visa

 Weekend specials from €100.00

38 38

IRISH HOTELS FEDERATION

Closed 25 December

BAILY COURT HOTEL

MAIN STREET,
HOWTH,
CO. DUBLIN

TEL: 01-832 2691 FAX: 01-832 3730

EMAIL: info@bailycourthotel.com
WEB: www.bailycourthotel.com

HOTEL ★★ MAP 12 P 11

Located in the heart of the beautiful fishing village of Howth with 20 en suite rooms with TV, direct dial phone and tea/coffee making facilities. The city centre is 25 minutes away by DART and Dublin Airport 12km. A carvery lunch is served daily. Local amenities include golf, fishing and hill walking.

Member of Logis of Ireland
B&B from €51.00 to €58.00
£40.17 to £45.68

TOM MURPHY
MANAGER

American Express
Mastercard
Visa

20 20

Closed 24 - 26 December

B&B rates are per person sharing per night incl. Breakfast

DEER PARK HOTEL AND GOLF COURSES

**HOWTH,
CO. DUBLIN**

TEL: 01-832 2624 FAX: 01-839 2405
EMAIL: sales@deerpark.iol.ie
WEB: www.deerpark-hotel.ie

HOTEL ★★★ MAP 12 P 11

14km from Dublin City/Airport on a quiet hillside overlooking the bay, Deer Park enjoys spectacular elevated sea views. Featuring Ireland's largest golf complex (5 courses), 18m swimming pool, sauna and steam room and two all-weather tennis courts. Whether on a golfing holiday or a visit to Dublin you will find Deer Park the ideal choice.

Member of Coast and Country Hotels

B&B from €73.00 to €84.00
£57.49 to £66.16

DAVID & ANTOINETTE TIGHE
MANAGERS

American Express
Diners
Mastercard
Visa

Weekend specials from €147.00

80 80

Closed 23 - 27 December

KING SITRIC FISH RESTAURANT & ACCOMMODATION

**EAST PIER,
HOWTH,
CO. DUBLIN**

TEL: 01-832 5235 FAX: 01-839 2442
EMAIL: info@kingsitric.ie
WEB: www.kingsitric.com

GUESTHOUSE ★★★★ MAP 8 P 11

Est. 1971, Aidan and Joan MacManus have earned an international reputation for fresh seafood in their harbour-side restaurant in the picturesque fishing village of Howth. Now with 8 guest rooms, all with sea views. Wine lovers will enjoy browsing in the atmospheric wine cellar. For leisure pursuits, Howth is the perfect location for golfing, walking and sailing. Dublin City is 20 mins by DART; Dublin Airport 20 mins driving.

Member of Ireland's Blue Book

B&B from €60.00 to €95.25
£47.25 to £75.02

AIDAN AND JOAN MACMANUS

American Express
Mastercard
Visa

Weekend specials from €155.00

8 8

Closed 21 January - 04 February

COURT HOTEL

**KILLINEY BAY,
CO. DUBLIN**

TEL: 01-285 1622 FAX: 01-285 2085
EMAIL: book@killineycourt.ie
WEB: www.killineycourt.ie

HOTEL ★★★ MAP 8 P 10

Like a jewel in the crown, the Court Hotel, a Victorian mansion situated in Killiney, a magnificent seascape setting, south of Dublin. Features 86 en suite rooms, choice of Restaurants (Egon Ronay recommended). Cocktail Bar/Conservatory & Lounge - perfect place to relax and unwind in comfort. International state of the art conference centre with simultaneous interpreting equipment. Close to Leopardstown Racecourse and several golf courses. 100m to DART train serving Dublin, Howth & Bray.

Member of Choice Hotels International

B&B from €77.00 to €105.00
£60.64 to £82.69

JOHN O'DOWD
MANAGING DIRECTOR

American Express
Diners
Mastercard
Visa

Weekend specials from €138.00

86 86

Open All Year

Room rates are per room per night

FITZPATRICK CASTLE DUBLIN

KILLINEY,
CO. DUBLIN

TEL: 01-230 5400 FAX: 01-230 5466
EMAIL: dublin@fitzpatricks.com
WEB: www.fitzpatrickhotels.com

HOTEL ★★★★ MAP 8 P 10

Located in scenic Killiney with panoramic views of Dublin Bay Fitzpatrick Castle is ideally located 20 mins from Dublin City centre and close to the beauty of Wicklow County. Comprising of 113 newly refurbished Castle style rooms and suites, it boasts the renowned PJ's Restaurant, intimate Library Bar/Lounge, excellent health and fitness facilities and 22m pool. Our conference centre and banqueting suites cater for 4 to 400 people with state of the art communications and conference equipment.

B&B from €113.00 to €125.50
£88.98 to £98.82

EOIN O'SULLIVAN
GENERAL MANAGER

American Express
Diners
Mastercard
Visa

113 113

IRISH HOTELS FEDERATION

Closed 24 - 26 December

BECKETTS COUNTRY HOUSE HOTEL

COOLDRINAGH HOUSE,
LEIXLIP,
CO. KILDARE/DUBLIN

TEL: 01-624 7040 FAX: 01-624 7072
EMAIL: becketts@eircom.net

HOTEL ★★★ MAP 8 N 11

Becketts is situated in a quiet scenic area just off the N4 motorway at the Leixlip roundabout close to Dublin's new outer ring with easy access to Dublin Airport and all major road networks. Once home to the mother of Samuel Beckett the completely refurbished Cooldrinagh House is now home to Becketts. There are 4 suites and 6 luxury bedrooms and an elegant restaurant with a reputation for superb cuisine and full bar facilities.

B&B from €60.00 to €72.50
£47.25 to £57.10

JOHN O'BYRNE
MANAGING DIRECTOR

American Express
Diners
Mastercard
Visa

10 10

IRISH HOTELS FEDERATION

Open All Year

FINNSTOWN COUNTRY HOUSE HOTEL

NEWCASTLE ROAD,
LUCAN,
CO. DUBLIN

TEL: 01-601 0700 FAX: 01-628 1088
EMAIL: manager@finnstown-hotel.ie
WEB: www.finnstown-hotel.ie

HOTEL ★★★ MAP 8 N 11

One of County Dublin's, finest country house hotels. Set in 45 acres of private grounds it offers privacy, peace and seclusion yet is only twenty minutes drive from the bustling city centre of Dublin. If it's good old-fashioned hospitality you're after, great food and drink, a relaxed atmosphere and stylish surroundings, you're in the right place! Leisure facilities include an 18 hole-putting course, gym, turkish bath, tennis court and in-door heated swimming pool.

Member of Grand Heritage
B&B from €57.14 to €107.93
£45.00 to £85.00

PAULA SMITH
GENERAL MANAGER

American Express
Diners
Mastercard
Visa

☺ Weekend specials from €197.00

53 53

IRISH HOTELS FEDERATION

Open All Year

B&B rates are per person sharing per night incl. Breakfast

SPA HOTEL

**LUCAN,
CO. DUBLIN**

TEL: 01-628 0494 FAX: 01-628 0841
EMAIL: info@lucanspahotel.ie
WEB: www.lucanspahotel.ie

HOTEL ★★ MAP 8 N 11

Situated on the N4, the gateway to the West, and 6km from M50, this elegant hotel is ideally located for convenience, comfort and is exceptionally well appointed with central heating, direct dial phone, colour TV, tea/coffee facilities and ironing board. Our restaurant offers a choice of 3 menus and superb wines. Ideal for conference and weddings alike.

Member of MinOtel Ireland Hotel Group
B&B from €58.00 to €70.00
£45.68 to £55.13

FRANK COLGAN
DIRECTOR

American Express
Diners
Mastercard
Visa

70 70

Closed 25 December

CARRIAGE HOUSE

**LUSK (NEAR AIRPORT),
CO. DUBLIN**

TEL: 01-843 8857 FAX: 01-843 8933
EMAIL: carrhous@iol.ie
WEB: www.iol.ie/~carrhous

GUESTHOUSE U MAP 12 O 12

Carriage House is a family run, warm and friendly guesthouse conveniently situated 10 minutes from Dublin Airport, 20 minutes from city. On main Dublin bus route (33). Relax in our indoor heated swimming pool and sauna. Charming award winning gardens and putting green. All rooms en suite with direct dial phone and colour TV. Tea/coffee making facilities and secure car parking. Semi finalist in Leverclean accommodation awards. Breakfast menu.

B&B from €35.00 to €42.00
£27.56 to £33.08

ROBERT & GEMMA MCAULEY
PROPRIETORS

Mastercard
Visa

14 14

Open All Year

GRAND HOTEL

**MALAHIDE,
CO. DUBLIN**

TEL: 01-845 0000 FAX: 01-816 8025
EMAIL: booking@thegrand.ie
WEB: www.thegrand.ie

HOTEL ★★★★ MAP 12 O 12

The Grand Hotel is situated by the sea in the village of Malahide. Just 10 minutes drive from Dublin Airport and 20 minutes from the city centre, the hotel is ideally situated for guests staying for business or leisure. The conference and business centre is one of Ireland's largest and most successful. All 150 bedrooms have tea/coffee making facilities and fax/modem lines. Most bedrooms have spectacular sea views. Leisure centre includes a 21 metre swimming pool, jacuzzi and fully equipped gymnasium.

B&B from €85.00 to €155.00
£66.94 to £122.07

MATTHEW RYAN
MANAGING DIRECTOR

American Express
Diners
Mastercard
Visa

150 150

Closed 25 - 27 December

Room rates are per room per night

ISLAND VIEW HOTEL

COAST ROAD,
MALAHIDE,
CO. DUBLIN
TEL: 01-845 0099 FAX: 01-845 1498
EMAIL: info@islandviewhotel.ie
WEB: www.islandviewhotel.ie

HOTEL ★★ MAP 12 O 12

Island View Hotel is ideally located for comfort and convenience and just a 10 minute drive from Dublin Airport. Our rooms are all en suite and fully equipped with modern facilities. Oscar Taylors Restaurant is an exclusive 150 seater restaurant with a panoramic view of Lambay Island and Malahide coastline. The restaurant is noted for its excellent cuisine. The menu is extensive and moderately priced.

B&B from € 50.00 to € 65.00
£39.38 to £51.19

PHILIP DARBY
HOTEL MANAGER

American Express
Diners
Mastercard
Visa

10 10

Open All Year

PORTMARNOCK HOTEL & GOLF LINKS

STRAND ROAD,
PORTMARNOCK,
CO. DUBLIN
TEL: 01-846 0611 FAX: 01-846 2442
EMAIL: reservations@portmarnock.com
WEB: www.portmarnock.com

HOTEL ★★★★ MAP 12 O 11

Once the home of the Jameson whiskey family, the Portmarnock Hotel and Golf Links is in a prime location reaching down to the sea, with views over the 18-hole Bernhard Langer designed links golf course. The 19th century character of the ancestral home is retained in the wood panelled walls, marble fireplaces and ornate ceilings of the Jameson Bar. Located just 15 minutes from Dublin Airport and 25 minutes from the city centre.

Member of Summit Hotels
B&B from € 100.00 to € 190.00
£78.76 to £149.64

SHANE COOKMAN
GENERAL MANAGER

American Express
Diners
Mastercard
Visa

Weekend specials from €190.00

103 103

Open All Year

WHITE SANDS HOTEL

COAST ROAD,
PORTMARNOCK,
CO. DUBLIN
TEL: 01-846 0003 FAX: 01-846 0420
EMAIL: sandshotel@eircom.net
WEB: www.whitesandshotel.ie

HOTEL ★★★ MAP 12 O 11

Ideally located facing the velvet strand. It is a 3*** family run Hotel. 10 minutes from Dublin Airport and 25 minutes from the City Centre with an abundance of golf courses nearby. The Hotel consists of 32 en suite tastefully decorated bedrooms, many with panoramic sea views. The Kingsford Smith Restaurant serves contemporary food with Irish flair. Carvery served daily. Private Function & Meeting rooms and the renowned Tamango Nightclub. Extensive Car Parking. Cead Mile Failte.

B&B from € 69.85 to € 101.60
£55.01 to £80.02

GEORGINA HIGGINS
GENERAL MANAGER

American Express
Diners
Mastercard
Visa

Midweek 2 B&B &1 Dinner from €139.70

32 32

Closed 24 - 26 December

B&B rates are per person sharing per night incl. Breakfast

CITYWEST HOTEL CONFERENCE, LEISURE & GOLF RESORT

SAGGART,
CO. DUBLIN

TEL: 01-401 0500 FAX: 01-458 8565
EMAIL: info@citywesthotel.com
WEB: www.citywesthotel.com

HOTEL ★★★★   MAP 8 N 11

Nestling peacefully in its own private estate located close to Dublin City Centre and Airport, this luxury 332 bedroom hotel boasts a 5***** Leisure Club with 20m pool, two on-site 18 hole Golf Courses and extensive conference facilities, including a new Convention Centre (total capacity 6,500 delegates). The Terrace Restaurant, fashionable Grill Room and Carvery offer fine dining, whilst the lively lounges and bars are a popular meeting place for locals and visitors alike. Ample complimentary parking.

B&B from €60.31 to €111.10
£47.50 to £87.50

JOHN GLYNN
CHIEF EXECUTIVE

American Express
Diners
Mastercard
Visa

332 332

Open All Year

REDBANK HOUSE GUESTHOUSE & RESTAURANT

6 & 7 CHURCH STREET,
SKERRIES,
CO. DUBLIN

TEL: 01-849 0439 FAX: 01-849 1598
EMAIL: redbank@eircom.net
WEB: www.redbank.ie

GUESTHOUSE ★★★   MAP 12 P 12

Enjoy the extended hospitality of the McCoy's in Redbank House. The world famous seafood restaurant is the dining room of Redbank House. The seven en suite rooms have the McCoys sense of style and elegance. The area is particularly rich in golf courses and a wide variety of leisure activities includes sea fishing, boat trips, sailing and horse riding. The Chef Proprietor Terry McCoy cooks the catch of the day landed at Skerries Pier specialising in the world famous Dublin Bay prawns.

Member of Logis of Ireland
B&B from €50.00 to €55.00
£39.38 to £43.32

TERRY MCCOY
PROPRIETOR

American Express
Diners
Mastercard
Visa

7 7

Closed 24 - 27 December

REDBANK LODGE & RESTAURANT

12 CONVENT LANE,
SKERRIES,
CO. DUBLIN

TEL: 01-849 1005 FAX: 01-849 1598
EMAIL: redbank@eircom.net
WEB: www.guesthousesireland.com

GUESTHOUSE ★★★   MAP 12 P 12

Situated in the picturesque fishing port of Skerries, North County Dublin. Each of the five en suite double bedrooms are elegantly decorated with direct dial telephone and TV. Adjacent to the award winning Redbank Restaurant, with its famous reputation for superb cuisine (fish dishes our speciality) and a well stocked wine cellar. With easy access to Dublin City & Dublin Airport as well as enjoying local attractions such as Ardgillan Demesne, the nearby Boyne Valley & Newgrange.

Member of Logis of Ireland
B&B from €39.00 to €45.00
£30.71 to £35.44

TERRY MCCOY
OWNER

American Express
Diners
Mastercard
Visa

5 5

Closed 24 - 28 December

Room rates are per room per night

MARINE HOTEL

SUTTON CROSS,
DUBLIN 13

TEL: 01-839 0000 FAX: 01-839 0442
EMAIL: info@marinehotel.ie
WEB: www.marinehotel.ie

HOTEL ★★★ MAP 12 P 11

The Marine Hotel 3*** (AA***) overlooks the north shore of Dublin Bay. The two acres of lawn sweep down to the sea shore. All bedrooms are en suite and have trouser press, TV, Direct Dial phone and tea/coffee facilities. The city centre is 6km away and the airport 25 minutes drive. Close by is the DART rapid rail system. The hotel has a heated indoor swimming pool and sauna. Nearby are the Royal Dublin and Portmarnock championship golf courses.

B&B from € 76.00 to € 117.00
£59.85 to £92.14

SHEILA BAIRD
GENERAL MANAGER

American Express
Diners
Mastercard
Visa

48 48

Closed 25 - 27 December

CARNEGIE COURT HOTEL

NORTH STREET,
SWORDS,
CO. DUBLIN

TEL: 01-840 4384 FAX: 01-840 4505
EMAIL: info@carnegiecourt.com

HOTEL P MAP 12 O 12

The Carnegie Court is a new hotel perfectly located, 5 mins from Dublin Airport, 20 minutes to the city centre and situated in the historic village of Swords. The hotel comprises of 36 air-conditioned, en suite rooms, each appointed with TV, DD phone, tea/coffee facilities and all the latest communication technology. Enjoy and relax in our spacious restaurant and uniquely designed bars. We also provide modern conference and banqueting facilities and extensive car parking.

B&B from € 44.44 to € 101.58
£35.00 to £80.00

SHARON CAFFREY
HOTEL OPERATIONS MANAGER

American Express
Diners
Mastercard
Visa

☺ Weekend specials from €126.00

36 36

Closed 24 - 28 December

FORTE TRAVELODGE

PINNOCK HILL,
SWORDS,
CO. DUBLIN

TEL: 1800-709709 FAX: 01-840 9235

WEB: www.travelodge.co.uk

HOTEL U MAP 8 O 11

Situated only 12.8km from Dublin City centre on the Dublin to Belfast road and minutes from the airport, this superb modern hotel offers comfortable yet affordable, accommodation. Each room is large enough to sleep up to three adults, a child under 12 and a baby in a cot. Excellent range of facilities, from en suite bathroom to colour TV including Sky Sports and Sky Movies. Unbeatable value for business or leisure. Sited next to Little Chef restaurant. From UK call free: 0800 850 950

Room Rate from € 79.95 to € 89.95
£62.97 to £70.84

STEPHANE PEJUS
MANAGER

American Express
Diners
Mastercard
Visa

100 100

Open All Year

B&B rates are per person sharing per night incl. Breakfast

GLENMORE HOUSE

AIRPORT ROAD,
NEVINSTOWN, SWORDS,
CO. DUBLIN
TEL: 01-840 3610 FAX: 01-840 4148
EMAIL: rebeccagibney@eircom.net
WEB: www.glenmorehouse.com

GUESTHOUSE ★★★ MAP 12 O 12

Ideally situated just 1km from Dublin Airport and 20 minutes from the city centre, on the main airport/city bus routes, Glenmore House is a spacious family-run guesthouse set in 2 acres of gardens, lawns and private secure carparks. All rooms are beautifully decorated with bathroom, phone, TV, tea/coffee facilities and hairdryer. The warmest of welcomes at a very reasonable cost for business and leisure alike.

B&B from €35.00 to €45.00
£27.56 to £35.44

REBECCA GIBNEY
PROPRIETOR

Mastercard
Visa

20 20

I R I S H
HOTELS
FEDERATION

Closed 23 - 28 December

ASHVIEW HOUSE

THE WARD,
ASHBOURNE ROAD,
CO. DUBLIN
TEL: 01-835 0499 FAX: 01-835 9716
EMAIL: ashviewhouse@holidayhound.com

GUESTHOUSE ★★ MAP 12 O 11

A family run warm and friendly 2** guesthouse with guest sitting room, snooker room, private car park and landscaped gardens, golf, horse riding and swimming nearby. Situated on the main Dublin/Derry Road, N2, 11km from Dublin City, 9km from Dublin Airport. Close to Fairyhouse Racecourse and Tattersalls Sales. Located 5km from Ashbourne it's an ideal touring centre for Newgrange, Slane Castle and the Boyne in Co. Meath. Clay pigeon shooting and fishing in the Boyne River.

B&B from €26.00 to €45.00
£20.48 to £35.44

JOSEPHINE FAY
PROPRIETOR

8 3

I R I S H
HOTELS
FEDERATION

Closed 20 - 31 December

BEAUFORT HOUSE

GHAN ROAD,
CARLINGFORD,
CO. LOUTH
TEL: 042-937 3879 FAX: 042-937 3878
EMAIL: michaelcaine@beauforthouse.net
WEB: www.beauforthouse.net

GUESTHOUSE ★★★ MAP 12 O 5

Beaufort House, AA ◆◆◆◆◆, a magnificent shoreside residence with glorious sea and mountain views in medieval Carlingford Village. Your hosts, Michael & Glynnis Caine, Bord Failte award winners of excellence, will ensure the highest standards. In-house activities include sailing school and yacht charter. Golfing arranged in any of five golf courses within 20 mins of Beaufort House. Helipad and private car parking. Dinner by prior arrangement. Small business conference facilities available.

B&B from €33.00 to €43.00
£25.99 to £33.86

MICHAEL & GLYNNIS CAINE

Mastercard
Visa

5 5

I R I S H
HOTELS
FEDERATION

Open All Year

Room rates are per room per night

MCKEVITT'S VILLAGE HOTEL

MARKET SQUARE,
CARLINGFORD,
CO. LOUTH

TEL: 042-937 3116 FAX: 042-937 3144

WEB: www.mckevittshotel.com

HOTEL ★★ MAP 12 O 15

McKevitts Village Hotel is family owned and personally supervised by Kay & Terry McKevitt. At the hotel, pride of place is taken in the personal attention given to guests by owners and staff. Carlingford is one of Ireland's oldest and most interesting medieval villages. Beautifully situated on the shores of Carlingford Lough and half way between Dublin and Belfast.

Member of Irish Family Hotels

B&B from €45.00 to €60.00
£35.44 to £47.25

TERRY & KAY MCKEVITT
OWNERS

Mastercard

Visa

13 13
alc

Open All Year

BELLINGHAM CASTLE HOTEL

CASTLEBELLINGHAM,
CO. LOUTH

TEL: 042-937 2176 FAX: 042-937 2766
EMAIL: bellinghamcastle@eircom.net
WEB: www.bellinghamcastle.com

HOTEL ★★ MAP 12 O 14

Bellingham Castle Hotel is situated close by the pleasant little village of Castlebellingham, Co.Louth, resting in countryside enveloped in history, legend and engaged in beautiful scenery. In the hotel itself, which is an elegant refurbished 17th century castle, you will find all the facilities of a modern hotel, harmonising beautifully with the antique decor and atmosphere of old world splendour.

B&B from €50.80 to €57.15
£40.01 to £45.01

PASCHAL KEENAN
MANAGER

American Express

Mastercard

Visa

19 19
alc

Closed 24 - 26 December

BOYNE VALLEY HOTEL & COUNTRY CLUB

DROGHEDA,
CO. LOUTH

TEL: 041-983 7737 FAX: 041-983 9188
EMAIL: reservations@boyne-valley-hotel.ie
WEB: www.boyne-valley-hotel.ie

HOTEL ★★★ MAP 12 O 13

Gracious country house on 16 acres of gardens and woodlands, beside historic town of Drogheda, south on the N1. 40km from Dublin and 32km airport. Cellar Bistro with daily supply of fresh fish. Nearby, historic sites of Newgrange, Dowth, Knowth and medieval abbeys Mellifont, Monasterboice and Slane. Leisure club with 20m pool, large gym etc. 2 tennis courts. 34 new bedrooms opening September 1st 2002.

B&B from €76.50 to €76.50
£60.25 to £60.25

MICHAEL MCNAMARA
PROPRIETOR/MANAGER

American Express

Diners

Mastercard

Visa

37 37

Inet FAX

Open All Year

B&B rates are per person sharing per night incl. Breakfast

WESTCOURT HOTEL

WEST STREET,
DROGHEDA,
CO. LOUTH

TEL: 041-983 0965 FAX: 041-983 0970
EMAIL: westcourthotel@eircom.net
WEB: www.westcourt.com

HOTEL ★★★ MAP 12 O 13

At the Westcourt Hotel, our visitors will find the highest standard of courtesy and efficiency coupled with luxurious surroundings in the heart of the historical town of Drogheda. Our bedrooms are all en suite and decorated with television, direct dial phone, tea/coffee making facilities. Our Syzygy Restaurant serving contemporary and traditional cuisine and Bridie Mac's original Irish bar have the finest food, drink, and atmosphere for you to enjoy. We pride ourselves on a highly personalised service and look forward to welcoming you.

B&B from € 60.00 to € 63.00
£47.25 to £49.62

VALERIE SHERLOCK
MANAGER

American Express
Diners
Mastercard
Visa

27 27

HOTELS FEDERATION

Closed 25 December

BALLYMASCANLON HOUSE HOTEL

DUNDALK,
CO. LOUTH

TEL: 042-937 1124 FAX: 042-937 1598
EMAIL: info@ballymascanlon.com
WEB: www.globalgolf.com/ballymascanlon

HOTEL ★★★ MAP 12 O 14

Ballymascanlon Hotel is a Victorian mansion set in 130 acre demesne on the scenic Cooley Peninsula. The hotel while retaining its old world ambience has recently had its facilities modernised. Our leisure centre incorporates a 20m deck level pool, leisure pool, sauna, jacuzzi, steam room, gymnasium and tennis courts. Our 18 hole Parkland golf course surrounding the hotel is both a pleasurable challenge to play and exhilarating to view.

B&B from € 70.00 to € 72.50
£55.13 to £57.10

OLIVER QUINN

American Express
Diners
Mastercard
Visa

☺ Weekend specials from €175.00

90 90

HOTELS FEDERATION

Closed 24 - 27 December

CARRICKDALE HOTEL & LEISURE COMPLEX

CARRICKCARNON,
RAVENSDALE, DUNDALK,
CO. LOUTH

TEL: 042-937 1397 FAX: 042-937 1740
EMAIL: manager@carrickdale.com
WEB: www.carrickdale.com

HOTEL ★★★ MAP 12 O 14

The Hotel, Conference, swimming and leisure complex is situated midway between Dublin and Belfast on the main N1 just 10km north of Dundalk, 8km south of Newry. Our 119 en suite rooms include our newly open 68 deluxe tower block, rooms containing 15 fully air-conditioned executive suites with mini bar facilities. Tastefully decorated bar and restaurant serving excellent food and wines. Ideal destination for touring Cooley, Carlingford and all of Northern Ireland's major tourist attractions.

B&B from € 57.50 to € 57.50
£45.29 to £45.28

JOHN MCPARLAND
PROPRIETOR

American Express
Diners
Mastercard
Visa

119 119

HOTELS FEDERATION

Closed 25 - 26 December

Room rates are per room per night

CLANBRASSIL HOTEL

CLANBRASSIL STREET,
DUNDALK,
CO. LOUTH
TEL: 042-933 4141 FAX: 042-932 8779
EMAIL: clanbrassilhotel@hotmail.com

HOTEL ★★ MAP 12 O 14

Ideally situated midway between the two capitals, Belfast and Dublin, in the heart of Dundalk Town, a heavenly location for shopaholics, with an abundance of superb shopping facilities. With six 18 hole golf courses within 10km drive, this area is a golf fanatics paradise. Carlingford Lough, the Mourne & Cooley Mountains, and the Boyne Valley are just a few of the many famous local tourist attractions waiting to be discovered.

B&B from €45.00 to €51.00
£35.44 to £40.16

ANITA MCCANN

American Express
Diners
Mastercard
Visa

☺ Weekend specials from €100.00

15 15

Closed 25 - 26 December

DERRYHALE HOTEL

CARRICK ROAD,
DUNDALK,
CO. LOUTH
TEL: 042-933 5471 FAX: 042-933 5471
EMAIL: info@minotel.iol.ie

HOTEL ★★ MAP 12 O 14

Midway between Dublin and Belfast, Derryhale Hotel is an ideal base for touring the north east of Ireland, Mountains of Mourne, Carlingford, Cooley Peninsula. Bedrooms contain TV and direct dial telephone. Good quality food is a tradition at the hotel. Derryhale Hotel has wedding and conference facilities. Activities close by include fishing, water skiing, sailing, beaches, horse riding and golf.

Member of MinOtel Ireland Hotel Group
Room Rate from €55.00 to €65.00
£43.31 to £51.18

LIAM SEXTON
MANAGING DIRECTOR

American Express
Diners
Mastercard
Visa

☺ Weekend specials from €115.00

19 19

Open All Year

FAIRWAYS HOTEL

DUBLIN ROAD,
DUNDALK,
CO. LOUTH
TEL: 042-932 1500 FAX: 042-932 1511
EMAIL: info@fairways.ie
WEB: www.fairways.ie

HOTEL ★★★ MAP 12 O 14

The Fairways Hotel and conference centre is situated 3 miles south of Dundalk, approximately one hour's drive from Dublin or Belfast, and five minutes from the seaside. Facilities include 101 tastefully furnished rooms, a new fully equipped conference and banqueting centre, catering for up to 1,000 delegates. Carvery/grill and Modi's Restaurant serving full meals and snacks throughout the day. Golf can be organised by the hotel on a choice of local golf courses.

B&B from €57.50 to €70.00
£45.29 to £55.13

BRIAN P. QUINN
MANAGING DIRECTOR

American Express
Diners
Mastercard
Visa

101 101

Closed 24 - 25 December

B&B rates are per person sharing per night incl. Breakfast

HOTEL IMPERIAL

PARK STREET,
DUNDALK,
CO. LOUTH

TEL: 042-933 2241 FAX: 042-933 7909

EMAIL: info@imperialhoteldundalk.com

HOTEL ★★ MAP 12 O 14

Built in the 70's this is a modern hotel of high standard. There is an excellent bar, also a coffee shop which is open from 8am - 10pm. Dining room open all day serving à la carte menu and dinner from 6pm - 10pm. Secure parking can be arranged nearby at no extra charge. Rooms being refurbished at the moment to a high standard.

B&B from €44.44 to €53.96
£35.00 to £42.50

PETER QUINN
MANAGING DIRECTOR

American Express
Diners
Mastercard
Visa

47 47

alc

HOTELS
FEDERATION

Closed 25 - 26 December

AISLING HOUSE

DUBLIN ROAD,
ASHBOURNE,
CO. MEATH

TEL: 01-835 0359 FAX: 01-835 1135

GUESTHOUSE ★★ MAP 12 O 12

Situated on one acre of landscaped gardens on the Dublin/Derry Road N2 a mile from Ashbourne Village, only 20 minutes from Dublin City centre and Airport, convenient to Fairyhouse Racecourse and Tattersalls sales. Rooms en suite with guest lounge, games room and private car park. Aisling House is an ideal base for business or holiday. Local amenities include golf, horse riding, clay pidgeon shooting and fishing in the Boyne River.

B&B from €38.00 to €44.00
£29.93 to £34.65

NUALA O'CONNELL
PROPRIETOR

Mastercard
Visa

9 9

Closed 24 - 28 December

ASHBOURNE HOUSE HOTEL

MAIN STREET,
ASHBOURNE,
CO. MEATH

TEL: 01-835 0167 FAX: 01-835 2095

EMAIL: ashhouse@indigo.ie

HOTEL ★ MAP 12 O 12

The Ashbourne House Hotel is situated only 12 miles from Dublin, on the main Dublin to Derry Road (N2), and is only a fifteen minute drive to Dublin Airport. This modern Hotel, combined with Old World Charm is a most popular choice for both tourists and business people. It has ample private car parking. It is convenient to Fairyhouse Racecourse and Tattersalls sales. Local amenities include numerous golf courses, horse riding and is close to many historic places of interest.

B&B from €39.00 to €49.00
£30.71 to £38.59

ANNE-MARIE LAMBE
MANAGER

Mastercard
Visa

10 5

HOTELS
FEDERATION

Open All Year

Room rates are per room per night

BROADMEADOW COUNTRY HOUSE & EQUESTRIAN CENTRE

BULLSTOWN,
ASHBOURNE,
CO. MEATH

TEL: 01-835 2823 FAX: 01-835 2819
EMAIL: info@irelandequestrian.com
WEB: www.irelandequestrian.com

GUESTHOUSE ★★★★ MAP 12 O 12

This exceptional family-run country house is located near Ashbourne Village, only 12km from Dublin Airport and 20km from the city centre. It is set in 100 acres of farmland with a modern purpose-built equestrian centre. All rooms en suite and designed for maximum guest comfort. Private car parking, tennis court and landscaped gardens. Surrounded by numerous golf courses and restaurants. Ideal location for both tourist and business people. Specialists in equestrian packages.

Member of Equestrian Holidays Ireland

B&B from €45.00 to €50.00
£35.44 to £39.38

SANDRA DUFF
MANAGER

Mastercard
Visa

🛏 ⬧ ☎ ◻ T C ➜ ❄ ⚲ U P ⬛
8   8

IRISH HOTELS FEDERATION

Closed 24 - 26 December

OLD DARNLEY LODGE HOTEL

MAIN STREET,
ATHBOY,
CO. MEATH

TEL: 046-32283 FAX: 046-32255
EMAIL: info@olddarnley.com
WEB: www.olddarnley.com

HOTEL CR MAP 11 M 12

This 19th century hotel has just recently been refurbished to the very highest standards. The hotel is a haven of tranquillity and is ideally located. Dublin and Athlone are only one hour's drive away. All bedrooms are en suite and offer a variety of services including, direct dial phone, multi channel TV, trouser press, hair dryers and tea/coffee making facilities. There are plenty of historic landmarks to see and plenty of activities to enjoy, including golf, fishing, boating, horse riding.

B&B from €52.50 to €55.00
£41.35 to £43.32

MARY MURPHY

American Express
Diners
Mastercard
Visa

✓🍽

🛏 ⬧ ☎ ◻ T C ➜ C M ❄ U ♫ P ⬛
14   14
S 🔒 alc

IRISH HOTELS FEDERATION

Open All Year

NEPTUNE BEACH HOTEL & LEISURE CLUB

BETTYSTOWN,
CO. MEATH

TEL: 041-982 7107 FAX: 041-982 7412
EMAIL: info@neptunebeach.ie
WEB: www.neptunebeach.ie

HOTEL U MAP 12 O 13

Located 25 mins north of Dublin Airport with a spectacular setting overlooking Bettystown Beach. All 38 rooms are elegantly furnished to provide the comfort and facilities expected of a leading hotel. Enjoy fine dining in the restaurant, afternoon tea in the cosy Winter Garden or a relaxing drink in the Neptune Bar. The leisure club facilities include 20m swimming pool, jacuzzi, sauna and fitness suite. Local golf courses: Laytown & Bettystown, Seapoint and Co. Louth.

B&B from €127.00 to €177.80
£100.00 to £140.00

DENIS J. REDDAN
PROPRIETOR

American Express
Mastercard
Visa

✓🍽

☺ Midweek specials from €151.00pps

🛏 ⬧ ☎ ◻ ➜ ❄ 🔍 🖥 ♫ P alc
38   38

IRISH HOTELS FEDERATION

Open All Year

B&B rates are per person sharing per night incl. Breakfast

Room rates are per room per night

HEADFORT ARMS HOTEL

KELLS,
CO. MEATH

TEL: 046-40063 FAX: 046-40587
EMAIL: headfortarms@eircom.net
WEB: www.headfortarms.com

HOTEL ★★ MAP 11 M 13

Situated in the historical town of Kells, it is 40km from Dublin on the main Derry/Donegal route. This traditional family hotel has 19 bedrooms, all have bath/shower, TV, video, etc. We at the Headfort offer a blend of homeliness, good taste and first class management. Conference facilities provided. Available locally: golf, fishing, tennis. Coffee shop / carvery open 7 days until 10pm. New contemporary "Vanilla Pod" Restaurant serving worldwide food. Open from 5.30pm - late, early bird menu available & Sunday lunch. Phone 046-40084 direct reservations.

B&B from €57.14 to €107.93
£45.00 to £85.00

VINCENT DUFF
GENERAL MANAGER

American Express
Mastercard
Visa

🛏🛎☎🖥📺Ⓣ🅲🍴CM❄♪⛵🅿🆂
19 19

🚪ⓐˡᶜ🖨

IRISH HOTELS FEDERATION

Closed 25 December

STATION HOUSE HOTEL

KILMESSAN,
CO. MEATH

TEL: 046-25239 FAX: 046-25588
EMAIL: stationhousehotel@eircom.net
WEB: www.thestationhousehotel.com

HOTEL U MAP 12 N 12

Step off the fast track into a relaxed rural setting where peace and tranquility exude. Set on 5 acres of gardens. This first class hotel offers many amenities we appreciate today along with much of yesterday's charm. The Signal Suite is unique with four poster bed and whirlpool bath. The award winning Signal Restaurant is open 7 days a week for lunch and dinner. A short drive from Dublin, Trim or Navan. It is a haven at the end of a journey.

B&B from €44.45 to €63.50
£35.01 to £50.01

CHRIS & THELMA SLATTERY
PROPRIETORS

American Express
Diners
Mastercard
Visa

🚩

🛏🛎☎🖥Ⓣ🅲CM❄♪🅿🆂ⓐˡᶜ
20 20

🖨 Inet

IRISH HOTELS FEDERATION

Open All Year

ARDBOYNE HOTEL

DUBLIN ROAD,
NAVAN,
CO. MEATH

TEL: 046-23119 FAX: 046-22355
EMAIL: ardboyne-sales@quinn-hotels.com
WEB: www.quinnhotels.com

HOTEL ★★★ MAP 12 N 13

Having been recently refurbished, the Ardboyne Hotel is the newest member of the Quinn Hotel Group and is enjoying its attractive facelift. Situated in its own pleasant grounds, the hotel is conveniently located on the outskirts of Navan and is the perfect base for visiting the many places of interest. Our restaurant offers delicious food in cosy surroundings and our function rooms will cater for every occasion from the grand and gracious to the private and intimate.

Member of Quinn Hotels
B&B from €58.00 to €62.00
£45.68 to £48.83

MICHAEL MCLAUGHLIN
GENERAL MANAGER

American Express
Diners
Mastercard
Visa

🚩

🛏🛎☎🖥Ⓣ🅲🍴CM❄♪🅿ⓐˡᶜ
29 29

🖨

IRISH HOTELS FEDERATION

Closed 24 - 26 December

B&B rates are per person sharing per night incl. Breakfast

MA DWYERS GUESTHOUSE

DUBLIN ROAD,
NAVAN,
CO. MEATH
TEL: 046-77992 FAX: 046-77995

GUESTHOUSE ★★★ MAP 12 N 13

Ma Dwyers newly opened guesthouse possesses many of the qualities of a high class hotel, along with a cosy homely feel which is so vitally important. 9 beautiful en suite rooms with a direct dial telephone, TV, hairdryer and tea/coffee facilities with fax and photocopying services available. Ideally located just minutes walk from the town centre and plenty of historic landmarks to see and activities to enjoy including golf, fishing, boating and horseriding.

B&B from €35.00 to €40.00
£27.56 to £31.50

MARY MURPHY

Mastercard
Visa

🛏️🐾☎️⬜🇹🇨⤴🐴⌣📐
 9   9

Closed 24 - 27 December

NEWGRANGE HOTEL

BRIDGE STREET,
NAVAN,
CO. MEATH
TEL: 046-74100 FAX: 046-73977
EMAIL: info@newgrangehotel.ie
WEB: www.newgrangehotel.ie

HOTEL ★★★ MAP 12 N 13

Newly built, grade A*** boutique style hotel, gothic in design, situated in the heart of Navan Town, offering the highest international standards. A warm Irish ambience awaits 30 mins from Dublin Airport. Renowned for high quality food, restaurant plus café, 2 theme bars, conference facilities 500. De luxe bedrooms, equipped with modern facilities, power showers, private car park. Newgrange burial tombs 20 minutes drive. 5 golf courses, horse racing, fishing, castles & gardens, local craft shops, N3 from Dublin.

B&B from €63.49 to €88.89
£50.00 to £70.01

NOEL J O'MAHONY
GENERAL MANAGER

American Express
Diners
Mastercard
Visa

☺ Weekend specials from €126.35

🛏️🐾☎️⬜🇹🇨⤴CM⌣♪PS
 36   36

🅰️alc 🖥️inet

IRISH HOTELS FEDERATION

Closed 25 - 26 December

CONYNGHAM ARMS HOTEL

SLANE,
CO. MEATH

TEL: 041-988 4444 FAX: 041-982 4205
EMAIL: enquiry@conynghamarms.com
WEB: www.conynghamarms.com

HOTEL ★★ MAP 12 N 13

Located in a lovely manor village built c. 1850, this traditional family hotel with 4 poster beds, where you can enjoy good food and friendly service, is an ideal base from which to tour the Boyne Valley - particularly the tomb of Knowth and Newgrange, various abbeys, and the birth place of Francis Ledwidge, all within 15 minutes drive. Available locally: 5 golf courses within 25km. Village Inn Hotels reservations: 353-1-295 8900.

Member of C.M.V.
B&B from €48.00 to €57.00
£37.79 to £44.88

GRAHAM & BERNIE CANNING
PROPRIETOR

Diners
Mastercard
Visa

🛏️🐾☎️⬜🇹🇨⤴CM❄⌣PS
 14   14

alc

IRISH HOTELS FEDERATION

Open All Year

Room rates are per room per night

HIGHFIELD HOUSE

MAUDLINS ROAD,
TRIM,
CO. MEATH
TEL: 046-36386 FAX: 046-38182
EMAIL: highfieldhouseaccom@eircom.net

GUESTHOUSE ★★ MAP 11 M 12

Highfield House guest accommodation is a beautiful period residence. Historical building dates back to the early 18th century. It is situated overlooking Trim Castle and the River Boyne just off the main Dublin Road. Inside there are seven spacious en suite guest rooms with colour TV, direct dial phone, coffee/tea facilities. Beautiful view from all rooms. 2 mins walking distance to town. Newgrange 30km. Dublin Airport 30 km. Babysitting service & laundry service. Private car parking. We pride ourselves on a highly personalised service and look forward to welcoming you.

B&B from €32.00 to €38.00
£25.20 to £29.92

EDWARD & GERALDINE DUIGNAN
PROPRIETORS

Mastercard
Visa

🛏️📶☎️🗑️T🅰️C❄️🛁🧴¹⁸🅟🏌️
7 7

IRISH HOTELS FEDERATION

Closed 22 December - 05 January

WELLINGTON COURT HOTEL

SUMMERHILL ROAD,
TRIM,
CO. MEATH
TEL: 046-31516 FAX: 046-36002
EMAIL: wellingtoncourt@eircom.net

HOTEL ★★ MAP 11 M 12

The Wellington Court Hotel is family owned and offers visitors a warm welcome and old fashioned courtesy along with excellent facilities. Our 18 rooms are all en suite with direct dial phone, colour TV, central heating. Also tea/coffee facilities. Superb accommodation, excellent food, set in Ireland's most historic surroundings with the magnificent medieval ruins of King John's Castle, one of the most enduring attractions in the area. Additional Tel. No.: 01-821 3311

B&B from €45.00 to €50.00
£35.44 to £39.38

M & C NALLY
PROPRIETORS

American Express
Mastercard
Visa

🛏️📶☎️🗑️T🅰️C CM🔍🛁🎵🅟S🅰️
18 18

🅰️🅗

IRISH HOTELS FEDERATION

Closed 25 - 26 December

ARKLOW BAY HOTEL

ARKLOW,
CO. WICKLOW

TEL: 0402-32309 FAX: 0402-32300
EMAIL: arklowbay@eircom.net
WEB: www.arklowbay.com

HOTEL ★★★ MAP 8 O 8

Nestled in the heart of Co. Wicklow, a warm welcome awaits your arrival. Set just outside scenic Arklow with panoramic views of The Garden of Ireland. State of the art Health and Leisure Centre recently opened. A lively bar, excellent cuisine, banqueting for 500 pax and extensive conference facilities in a range of suites. Enjoy golf, fishing, hovercrafting and quadracing, all available locally. Sister hotel to the Springhill Court in Kilkenny.

Member of Chara Hotel Group
B&B from €50.00 to €70.00
£39.38 to £55.13

ROBERT MCCARTHY
GENERAL MANAGER

American Express
Diners
Mastercard
Visa

🛏️📶☎️🗑️TC🔍CMCS❄️🛜🛁🎵
93 93
🎵🅟🅰️🅗🛜🧴

IRISH HOTELS FEDERATION

Open All Year

B&B rates are per person sharing per night incl. Breakfast

BRIDGE HOTEL

BRIDGE STREET,
ARKLOW,
CO. WICKLOW
TEL: 0402-31666 FAX: 0402-31666

HOTEL ★★ MAP 8 O 8

The Bridge Hotel is a family-run 15 bedroomed hotel situated at the bridge in Arklow beside the Avoca River and only 10 mins walk to the sea. Arklow has a strong seafaring heritage and is famous for its pottery. The town offers a great variety of holiday activities whether you swim, play golf, tennis, fish or walk. Arklow is an ideal base from which to see the beautiful scenery of Wicklow. Only 6.5km to Ballykissangel.

B&B from €35.00 to €42.00
£27.56 to £33.08

JIM HOEY
PROPRIETOR

Mastercard
Visa

🛏🔥☎🖵TCCMU♪PS🔲alc 🛎
15 14

HOTELS
IRISH
FEDERATION

Closed 25 December

CLOGGA BAY HOTEL

CLOGGA,
ARKLOW,
CO. WICKLOW
TEL: 0402-39299 FAX: 0402-91538

HOTEL ★★ MAP 8 O 8

Family owned and managed establishment situated 3km south of Arklow Town. Set on a 2 acre garden in the country by the sea, approx 60km from Rosslare and Dublin. A central location for touring Wicklow and Wexford. All rooms en suite with colour T.V. and direct dial telephone. Local attractions include golf, fishing and swimming. Our restaurant offers good traditional food.

B&B from €44.40 to €50.79
£35.00 to £40.00

FIOUNNUALA JAMESON
PROPRIETOR

American Express
Mastercard
Visa

🛏🔥☎🖵TCCM✳♪PS🔲alc
10 10

HOTELS
IRISH
FEDERATION

Open All Year

GLENART CASTLE HOTEL

GLENART CASTLE,
ARKLOW,
CO. WICKLOW
TEL: 0402-31031 FAX: 0402-31032
EMAIL: glenart@eircom.net

HOTEL U MAP 8 O 8

The Hidden Castle of Glenart set amidst 63 acres of gardens and woodlands. Built circa. 1750 by the Earls of Carysfort, situated in the heart of the Avoca Valley. Only an hour's drive from Dublin, via N11. Local attractions include fishing, shooting, hillwalking and horse riding. A short drive to Arklow and golf courses including Druid's Glen, Collattin, Woodenbridge and the Arklow Golf Course. Minutes away from the picturesque Ballykissangel (Avoca) Village.

B&B from €45.00 to €76.00
£35.44 to £59.85

DESMOND NAIK
DIRECTOR

American Express
Mastercard
Visa

🛏🔥☎🖵TCCM✳P alc 🛎
28 28

HOTELS
IRISH
FEDERATION

Open All Year

Room rates are per room per night

BALLYKNOCKEN COUNTRY HOUSE

GLENEALY,
ASHFORD,
CO. WICKLOW
TEL: 0404-44627 FAX: 0404-44696
EMAIL: cfulvio@ballyknocken.com
WEB: www.ballyknocken.com

GUESTHOUSE N MAP 8 P 9

An 1850's romantic farmhouse, elegantly furnished with antiques and family memorabilia. Charming bedrooms, some with iron beds and claw feet baths offer lovely views over gardens and forest. Relax by the Drawing Room's log fire before the splendid dinner using garden and local produce. Superb breakfasts. Near to Wicklow Mountains, Glendalough, Powerscourt. Excellent golf, e.g. Druid's Glen. Own walking programmes. Dublin 29 miles. Frommers recommended. AA ◆◆◆◆.

B&B from €38.00 to €45.00
£29.93 to £35.44

CATHERINE FULVIO
PROPRIETOR

Mastercard
Visa

☺ Midweek specials from €110.00

7 7

Closed 01 December - 01 March

BEL-AIR HOTEL

ASHFORD,
CO. WICKLOW
TEL: 0404-40109 FAX: 0404-40188
EMAIL: belairhotel@eircom.net
WEB: www.nci.ie

HOTEL U MAP 8 P 9

Bel-Air Hotel is a family run hotel and equestrian centre, situated in the centre of 81 hectares of farm and parkland. Managed by the Murphy Freeman family since 1937. The lovely gardens have a breathtaking view to the sea. The traditional family atmosphere and rich history makes the hotel a popular venue, good restaurant, rooms en suite with tea making facilities, T.V. and hairdryers. Bel Air Holiday village adjacent to hotel.

B&B from €44.44 to €57.14
£35.00 to £45.00

FIDELMA FREEMAN
OWNER

American Express
Diners
Mastercard
Visa

10 10

Closed 24 December - 10 January

CHESTER BEATTY INN

ASHFORD VILLAGE,
CO. WICKLOW
TEL: 0404-40206 FAX: 0404-49003
EMAIL: hotelchesterbeatty@eircom.net
WEB: www.hotelchesterbeatty.ie

HOTEL U MAP 8 P 9

The Chester Beatty Inn is in the village of Ashford on the main N11 road, 35 mins south of Dublin. Ideally situated for touring, golf (adjacent to Druids Glen and many other golf courses), fishing, hill walking and gardens (opposite Mount Usher Gardens, 15 mins from Powerscourt Gardens). Charming country inn style family run hotel comprising 12 luxury en suite rooms, award-winning restaurant, lounge and traditional Irish bar all with open log fires. Secure private car park.

Member of Logis of Ireland
B&B from €50.00 to €75.00
£39.37 to £59.07

KITTY & PAUL CAPRANI

American Express
Diners
Mastercard
Visa

12 12

Closed 24 - 26 December

B&B rates are per person sharing per night incl. Breakfast

CULLENMORE HOTEL

ASHFORD,
CO. WICKLOW

TEL: 0404-40187 FAX: 0404-40471
EMAIL: cullenmore@eircom.net
WEB: www.cullenmorehotel.com

HOTEL ★★ MAP 8 P 9

The Cullenmore Hotel is a pleasant, friendly, family run hotel, located near Ashford in the garden of Ireland. All bedrooms are modern, en suite, with two designed for wheelchair users. TV (satellite) and direct dial phone are standard throughout. Extensive bar food menu served all day. Ideal venue for a relaxing break. Very reasonable rates.

Room Rate from €60.00 to €80.00
£47.25 to £62.99

OLIVE & DIRK VAN DER FLIER

American Express
Diners
Mastercard
Visa

18 18

Closed 24 December - 03 January

BROOKLODGE

MACREDDIN VILLAGE,
(AUGHRIM),
CO. WICKLOW

TEL: 0402-36444 FAX: 0402-36580
EMAIL: brooklodge@macreddin.ie
WEB: www.brooklodge.com

HOTEL N MAP 8 O 8

Find paradise in the sublime Brooklodge, an AA /RAC**** countryhouse hotel in a spectacular Wicklow valley, yet only an hour from Dublin. Savour the sumptuous cuisine in the stunning Strawberry Tree Restaurant, which serves only free range, organic and wild foods. Relax in our charming waterside lounge or enjoy a perfect pint from our very own microbrewery. Unwind outdoors in our equestrian and archery, clay shooting and falconry centres.

Member of Manor House Hotels
B&B from €87.50 to €105.00
£68.91 to £82.69

FREDA WOLFE & EVAN DOYLE
HOSTS

American Express
Diners
Mastercard
Visa

 Weekend specials from €190.00

40 40

Open All Year

LAWLESS'S HOTEL

AUGHRIM,
CO. WICKLOW

TEL: 0402-36146 FAX: 0402-36384
EMAIL: reservations@lawlesshotel.com
WEB: www.lawlesshotel.com

HOTEL ★★★ MAP 8 O 8

Lawless's Hotel, established in 1787, is a charming family run hotel which has been tastefully renovated. The award-winning restaurant enjoys a well established reputation for fine cuisine. Approximately one hour from Dublin, nestling in the Wicklow Hills, there is a wide choice of excellent golf courses nearby as well as scenic hill-walking, pony treking and trout fishing in the adjacent river. Other accommodation available in hotel grounds.

Member of Irish Country Hotels
B&B from €55.00 to €66.00
£43.32 to £51.98

SEOIRSE & MAEVE O'TOOLE
PROPRIETORS

Diners
Mastercard
Visa

 Midweek specials from €150.00

14 14

Closed 24 - 26 December

Room rates are per room per night

VALE VIEW HOTEL

AVOCA,
CO. WICKLOW

TEL: 0402-35236 FAX: 0402-35144
EMAIL: valeview@indigo.ie
WEB: http://indigo.ie/-valeview/

HOTEL ★★ MAP 8 O 8

Family-run hotel noted for its hospitality. Situated overlooking the famous Vale of Avoca, with spectacular panoramic views. Two miles from Ballykissangel and one hour from Dublin. Surrounded by numerous scenic hill walks. Excellent golf courses nearby. All bedrooms en suite with Tea/Coffee making facilities, T.V., Phone. Function rooms to cater for different types of function, big or small. Extensive bar, à la carte & dinner menus. Large car park.

B&B from €40.00 to €70.00
£31.50 to £55.13

PETER AND MARY KING
PROPRIETORS

American Express
Diners
Mastercard
Visa

10 10

Closed 24 - 26 December

BEECHWOOD HOUSE

MANOR KILBRIDE,
BLESSINGTON,
CO. WICKLOW

TEL: 01-458 2802 FAX: 01-458 2802
EMAIL: amccann@beechwoodhouse.ie
WEB: www.beechwoodhouse.ie

GUESTHOUSE P MAP 8 N 10

A beautiful Country House set in 2 acres of mature gardens lying between Blessington Lakes and the Wicklow Mountains. Beechwood House is a house for all seasons, full of charm and a relaxed informal atmosphere with large bright guest rooms all en suite. Food is home cooked with vegetarian a house speciality. Activities locally include hill walking, golf, angling and water sports. All this and at the same time providing convenient access to Dublin City.

B&B from €32.00 to €64.00
£25.20 to £50.40

BARRY EDWARDS & ADRIENNE
MCCANN

Mastercard
Visa

6 6

Closed 24 December - 08 January

DOWNSHIRE HOUSE HOTEL

BLESSINGTON,
CO. WICKLOW

TEL: 045-865199 FAX: 045-865335
EMAIL: info@downshirehouse.com
WEB: www.downshirehouse.com

HOTEL ★★★ MAP 8 N 10

Downshire is a family run country hotel on Blessington's main street on route N81. Dublin 25km. Twenty five bedrooms all en suite, large garden, close to horse riding, fishing, hill walking, leisure centre on Blessington Lakes. Fresh food is supplied daily and cooked under highly qualified supervision. Ideal location for touring the Wicklow Mountains or Midlands. RAC*** Award and RAC Dining Award in recognition of the overall dining experience..

Member of Irish Family Hotels
B&B from €68.80 to €68.80
£54.18 to £54.18

JOAN FLYNN
MANAGER

Mastercard
Visa

25 25

Closed 20 December - 07 January

B&B rates are per person sharing per night incl. Breakfast

TULFARRIS HOTEL & GOLF RESORT

BLESSINGTON LAKES,
CO. WICKLOW

TEL: 045-867600 FAX: 045-867565
EMAIL: info@tulfarris.com
WEB: www.tulfarris.com

HOTEL ★★★★ MAP 8 N 10

Tulfarris Hotel and Golf Resort is located on the Wicklow/Kildare border, near Blessington, & within 50 minutes drive of Dublin City Centre & Airport. The 18th Century Tulfarris Estate is nestled between the spectacular Wicklow Mountains & Blessington Lakes. It has 80 en suite spacious bedrooms, and 5 luxurious suites with separate sitting rooms and private balconies. Our Balcony and Courtyard Bar Restaurants offer a choice of dining.We offer many leisure facilities including a spectacular 18 hole Championship Golf Course.

B&B from € 80.00 to € 138.00
£63.01 to £108.68

JIM & MAEVE HAYES
MANAGING DIRECTOR & PROP

American Express
Diners
Mastercard
Visa

Weekend specials from €189.00

80 80

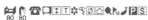

Open All Year

CROFTON BRAY HEAD INN

STRAND ROAD,
BRAY,
CO. WICKLOW
TEL: 01-286 7182 FAX: 01-286 7182

GUESTHOUSE ★★ MAP 8 P 10

This 130 year old building is situated on the seafront, under the Bray Head Mountain. A 10 minute walk away from an excellent commuter train to Dublin, but also ideally located for touring Wicklow - The Garden of Ireland. The Bray Head Inn has ample car-parking and is fully licensed. It has a lift, en suite bedrooms with TV and Telephone. Our very reasonable prices include full Irish Breakfast.

B&B from € 38.00 to € 38.00
£29.93 to £29.93

NANCY REGAN

Mastercard
Visa

30 30

Closed 01 October - 01 June

ESPLANADE HOTEL

SEAFRONT,
BRAY,
CO. WICKLOW
TEL: 01-286 2056 FAX: 01-286 6496
EMAIL: esplan@regencyhotels.com
WEB: www.regencyhotels.com

HOTEL ★★★ MAP 8 P 10

The Esplanade is on the seafront in Bray, at the gateway to beautiful County Wicklow, but only 30 minutes drive from Dublin City. This old Victorian hotel and Lacy's Restaurant oozes with character, charm and open turf fires. Our award winning chef creates the finest cullinery delights daily. Conference and banqueting facilities are available in a choice of rooms with capacity for 120 people. Leisure Centre with gym, sauna and 10 seater jacuzzi.

B&B from € 63.50 to € 95.25
£50.00 to £75.00

MAUREEN & JOHN O'CONNOR
GENERAL MANAGERS

American Express
Diners
Mastercard
Visa

Weekend Specials from €110.00
p.p.s

40 40

Closed 24 - 26 December

Room rates are per room per night

ROYAL HOTEL AND LEISURE CENTRE

MAIN STREET,
BRAY,
CO. WICKLOW
TEL: 01-286 2935 FAX: 01-286 7373
EMAIL: royal@regencyhotels.com
WEB: www.regencyhotels.com

HOTEL ★★★ MAP 8 P 10

Located in the coastal resort of Bray, ideally positioned at the gateway to the garden county of Ireland and yet only 30 minutes DART journey from Dublin City Centre. Leisure facilities include a pool, sauna, steamroom, whirlpool spa and jacuzzi. Other facilities include a Massage and Beauty Clinic and a creche. The hotel is established for conferences, weddings and corporate banquets. The Heritage Restaurant offers fine dining in luxurious surroundings and you can enjoy live musical entertainment most nights. 24 hour supervised car park.

B&B from € 101.60 to € 152.40
£80.02 to £120.02

MAUREEN MCGETTIGAN-O'CONNOR
GENERAL MANAGER

Diners
Mastercard
Visa

☺ Weekend specials from €100.33

90 90

Open All Year

WESTBOURNE HOTEL

QUINSBORO ROAD,
BRAY,
CO. WICKLOW
TEL: 01-286 2362 FAX: 01-286 8530

HOTEL ★★ MAP 8 P 10

The Westbourne Hotel is ideally located on the north east coast of the 'Garden of Ireland' in the charming town of Bray. Only minutes from exceptional scenery, beaches and has fast access to Dublin via the DART. Newly refurbished bedrooms en suite, direct dial phone, TV and tea/coffee making facilities. Dusty Millers Bar is a live music venue with music Wed-Sun. Clancy's Traditional Irish Bar, craic agus ceol. The Tube Nite Club open Thur-Sun. Food served all day.

B&B from € 45.00 to € 50.00
£35.44 to £39.38

SUSAN MC CARTHY
GENERAL MANAGER

Mastercard
Visa

13 13

Closed 25 - 26 December

WOODLAND COURT HOTEL

SOUTHERN CROSS,
BRAY,
CO. WICKLOW
TEL: 01-276 0258 FAX: 01-276 0298
EMAIL: info@woodlandscourthotel.com
WEB: www.woodlandscourthotel.com

HOTEL ★★★ MAP 8 P 10

Located just minutes from the N11 motorway and 12 miles from Dublin City Centre the Woodland Court Hotel has much to offer the tourist and business traveller. 65 well-appointed en suite rooms, state of the art conference/business centre and excellent value meals in our restaurant. An ideal venue for touring Dublin City and County Wicklow. Special group and business rates available on request.

Room Rate from € 65.00 to € 130.00
£51.19 to £102.38

NUALA KINSELLA
GENERAL MANAGER

American Express
Diners
Mastercard
Visa

65 65

Open All Year

B&B rates are per person sharing per night incl. Breakfast

RATHSALLAGH HOUSE, GOLF AND COUNTRY CLUB

DUNLAVIN,
CO. WICKLOW

TEL: 045-403112 FAX: 045-403343
EMAIL: info@rathsallagh.com
WEB: www.rathsallagh.com

GUESTHOUSE ★★★★ MAP 8 N 9

Winner of the prestigious Country House of the Year Award 2000 and a member of Ireland's Blue Book, Rathsallagh is a large 4**** Grade A country house converted from Queen Anne stables in 1798. Rathsallagh, with its own 18 hole Championship Golf Course, is set in a peaceful oasis of 530 acres of rolling parkland with thousands of mature trees, lakes and streams. On the west side of the Wicklow Mountains close to Punchestown and The Curragh Racecourses, yet only 1 hour from Dublin Airport.

Member of Ireland's Blue Book

B&B from € 115.00 to € 135.00
£90.57 to £106.32

THE O'FLYNN FAMILY PROPRIETORS

American Express
Diners
Mastercard
Visa

29   29

Inet

Closed 23 - 27 December

POWERSCOURT ARMS HOTEL

ENNISKERRY,
CO. WICKLOW

TEL: 01-282 8903 FAX: 01-286 4909

HOTEL ★ MAP 8 O 10

Powerscourt Arms Hotel owned by the McTernan Family. Snuggling in the foothills of the Wicklow Mountains the Powerscourt Arms is an ideal base for touring expeditions, it is an intimate family run hotel with 12 bedrooms furnished to include direct dial telephone en suite bathrooms and multi channel TV, ample car parking facilities. The restaurant seats up to 45 people, our lounge with strong features of American white ash, serves bar food daily. The public bar also has its own atmosphere complete with an open fire.

B&B from € 44.45 to € 50.80
£35.00 to £40.00

CHARLES MCTERNAN GENERAL MANAGER

Mastercard
Visa

12   12

Closed 24 - 25 December

SUMMERHILL HOUSE HOTEL

ENNISKERRY,
CO. WICKLOW

TEL: 01-286 7928 FAX: 01-286 7929
EMAIL: info@summerhillhousehotel.com

HOTEL ★★★ MAP 8 O 10

This charming hotel is just a short walk to the quaint village of Enniskerry, and the famous Powerscourt Gardens. Located on the N11, 19km south of Dublin City & 15km to Dunlaoire Ferryport. 57 spacious bedrooms, private free car parking, traditional Irish breakfast, hill walking & nature trails, local golf courses, family rooms (2 adults and 3 children). Enjoy a rare blend of the Wicklow countryside close to Dublin City.

Member of Logis of Ireland

B&B from € 50.00 to € 75.00
£39.38 to £59.07

EILEEN MURPHY GENERAL MANAGER

American Express
Mastercard
Visa

57   57

Open All Year

Room rates are per room per night

GLENVIEW HOTEL

GLEN-O-THE-DOWNS,
DELGANY,
CO. WICKLOW
TEL: 01-287 3399 FAX: 01-287 7511
EMAIL: glenview@iol.ie
WEB: www.glenviewhotel.com

HOTEL U   MAP 8 0 10

Set idyllically in the garden of Ireland, the newly accredited AA ♦♦♦♦ Glenview Hotel offers a relaxing atmosphere and discreet friendly service. The Woodlands Restaurant provides unrivalled views over the Glen in which to sample its widely acclaimed cuisine & service. The Conservatory Bar with live music and the state of the art leisure club complete the perfect base for a holiday. Golf, horse riding, shooting and hill walking are within easy reach of the hotel. 25 mins from Dublin. Ideal for conferences.

Member of Stafford Hotels

B&B from €88.88 to €114.30
£70.00 to £90.02

ANNE MARIE WHELAN
GENERAL MANAGER

American Express
Diners
Mastercard
Visa

☺ Weekend specials from €165.00

🛏 🔌 ☎ 🖥 📺 T C ⭢ C M ❋ 🔱 🖼 🔍
74 74
♘ ♪ 🅿 🆂 🔳 ⓐⓒ ♿ Inet

IRISH HOTELS FEDERATION

Closed 24 - 26 December

DERRYBAWN MOUNTAIN LODGE

DERRYBAWN,
LARAGH, GLENDALOUGH,
CO. WICKLOW
TEL: 0404-45644 FAX: 0404-45645
EMAIL: derrybawnlodge@eircom.net

GUESTHOUSE ★★★   MAP 8 0 9

Derrybawn Mountain Lodge is a family-run guesthouse, situated on the slopes of Derrybawn Mountain. A walkers paradise close by famous Wicklow Way. Tranquil setting, mountain views, all rooms have bath & shower en suite, direct dial phone, coffee/tea making facilities, hairdryer. Spacious dining and lounge area to relax. Enjoy National Park, Glenmalure, historic Glendalough and Clara Vale. Members of local mountain rescue team. Excellent fresh food & wine. A warm welcome awaits you.

B&B from €38.00 to €45.00
£29.93 to £35.44

TERESA KAVANAGH
PROPRIETOR

American Express
Mastercard
Visa

☺ Midweek specials from €105.00

🛏 🔌 ☎ 🖥 T C ⭢ C M ❋ 🅿 🆂 🍴 ⬤
8   8

IRISH HOTELS FEDERATION

Closed 24 - 27 December

GLENDALOUGH HOTEL

GLENDALOUGH,
CO. WICKLOW

TEL: 0404-45135 FAX: 0404-45142
EMAIL: info@glendaloughhotel.ie

HOTEL ★★★   MAP 8 0 9

The Glendalough Hotel, built in the early 1800s, is a family run hotel situated in the heart of Wicklow's most scenic valley and within the Glendalough National Park. The hotel has recently been extended offering 43 beautifully decorated en suite bedrooms with satellite TV and direct dial phone. The hotel's restaurant offers superb cuisine and wines in a tranquil environment overlooking the Glendasan River. The Tavern Bar serves good pub food and offers entertainment at weekends.

B&B from €62.00 to €85.00
£48.83 to £66.94

PATRICK CASEY

American Express
Diners
Mastercard
Visa

☺ Weekend specials from €125.00

🛏 🔌 ☎ 🖥 📺 T C ⭢ C M ❋ ♘ ♪ 🅿 🆂
43 43
ⓐⓒ ♿

IRISH HOTELS FEDERATION

Closed 06 January - 01 February

B&B rates are per person sharing per night incl. Breakfast

CHARLESLAND GOLF HOTEL & COUNTRY CLUB

CHARLESLAND,
GREYSTONES,
CO. WICKLOW
TEL: 01-287 8200 FAX: 01-287 0078
EMAIL: hotel@charlesland.com
WEB: www.charlesland.com

HOTEL ★★ MAP 8 P 10

Charlesland boasts 12 spacious en suite rooms. All rooms have remote control TV, DD phone and internet access, tea/coffee making facilities as well as spectacular views of the golf course and Irish sea. Food is our speciality and our menu is available all day. Ideal not only for the golfer but also for visitors touring the area.

B&B from €44.50 to €54.00
£35.05 to £42.53

PATRICK BRADSHAW
DIRECTOR OF GOLF

American Express
Mastercard
Visa

12 12   alc Inet

Open All Year

LA TOUCHE HOTEL

TRAFALGAR ROAD,
GREYSTONES,
CO. WICKLOW
TEL: 01-287 4401 FAX: 01-287 4504
EMAIL: enquiries@latouche.net
WEB: www.latouche.net

HOTEL ★★ MAP 8 P 10

Our hotel has a superb location overlooking the sea in the garden of Ireland. At our doorstep are Glendalough, Powerscourt and Mount Usher Gardens. All rooms are en suite with remote satellite TV, radio, tea/coffee facilities and DD phone. Our Captain's Lounge is the main meeting place for locals and visitors alike with a carvery and evening menu 7 days a week. The Waterfront Conference Centre caters for parties up to 500. Also available are Bennigans Fun Bar and Club Life Night Club.

B&B from €45.00 to €64.00
£35.44 to £50.40

DECLAN RYAN
GENERAL MANAGER

American Express
Mastercard
Visa

29 29   alc

IRISH
HOTELS
FEDERATION

Open All Year

COME PLAY ONE OF WICKLOW'S FINEST COURSES

GLEN
of the
DOWNS
GOLF CLUB

Coolnaskeagh, Delgany, Co. Wicklow.
Tel: (01) 2876240 / Fax: (01) 2870063

Truly Magnificent Panoramic Views of the Wicklow Mountains & the Irish Sea.

The entire course has been built to U.S.G.A. specifications. Golfers of all standards will find the course a challenge with its natural slopes and valleys combined with it's undulating greens and some 90 bunkers.

* 18 Hole Championship Parkland Course

* Located only 35 mins from Dublin

* New 15,000 sq. ft. pavillion with full Bar, Restaurant, Conferance Room & Golf Shop

* Golf clubs, buggies, caddy cars for hire

* Short game practice area

Green Fees: Until 31st March

**Mon - Fri £40 / Early Bird £30
Sat & Sun £50**

**Visitors Welcome
Everyday**

Room rates are per room per night

AVONBRAE GUESTHOUSE

RATHDRUM,
CO. WICKLOW

TEL: 0404-46198 FAX: 0404-46198
EMAIL: avonbrae@gofree.indigo.ie
WEB: www.avonbrae.com

GUESTHOUSE ★★★ MAP 8 O 9

A small, long established, family run guesthouse, nestling in the Wicklow Hills. We pride ourselves in our good food and personal attention and extend a warm welcome to first time guests and to the many who return again and again. Horse riding, trekking, fishing and excellent golf available locally. We specialise in hill walking holidays and to relax - our own indoor heated pool and games room.

B&B from €33.00 to €33.00
£25.99 to £25.99

PADDY GEOGHEGAN
PROPRIETOR

American Express
Mastercard
Visa

6 6

Closed 30 November - 28 February

HUNTER'S HOTEL

NEWRATH BRIDGE,
RATHNEW,
CO. WICKLOW

TEL: 0404-40106 FAX: 0404-40338
EMAIL: reception@hunters.ie
WEB: www.hunters.ie

HOTEL ★★★ MAP 8 P 9

One of Ireland's oldest coaching inns, its award winning gardens along River Vartry provide a haven from the world at large. Restaurant provides the very best of Irish food, fresh fish. Local amenities include golf, tennis, horseriding and fishing. Beautiful sandy beaches and sightseeing in the Garden of Ireland. Dublin 44.8km. Rosslare 115.2km. Off N11 at Rathnew or Ashford. Irish Country Houses and Restaurant Association. Refurbished 95-96. 1996 new Conference Room added.

Member of Ireland's Blue Book
B&B from €89.00 to €108.00
£70.09 to £85.06

GELLETLIE FAMILY
PROPRIETORS

Mastercard
Visa

16 16

Closed 24 - 26 December

TINAKILLY COUNTRY HOUSE AND RESTAURANT

WICKLOW,
(RATHNEW),
CO. WICKLOW

TEL: 0404-69274 FAX: 0404-67806
EMAIL: reservations@tinakilly.ie
WEB: www.tinakilly.ie

HOTEL ★★★★ MAP 8 P 9

This Victorian mansion was built for Captain Halpin, who laid the world's telegraph cables. The bedrooms, some with 4 posters, are furnished in period style and most overlook the Irish Sea. Award winning cuisine is prepared from garden vegetables, local fish and Wicklow lamb. The family welcome ensures a relaxing, memorable stay. Available locally - golf, horse riding, Powerscourt, Mount Usher Gardens and Wicklow Mountains. Dublin 46km. Awarded RAC Gold Ribbon for Excellence. Blue Book member.

Member of Small Luxury Hotels
B&B from €102.00 to €119.00
£80.33 to £93.72

JOSEPHINE & RAYMOND POWER
PROPRIETORS

American Express
Diners
Mastercard
Visa

51 51

Open All Year

B&B rates are per person sharing per night incl. Breakfast

GORMANSTOWN MANOR

FARM GUEST HOUSE,
NEAR WICKLOW TOWN (OFF N11),
CO. WICKLOW

TEL: 0404-69432 FAX: 0404-61832

EMAIL: gormanstownmanor@eircom.net
WEB: http://homepage.eircom.net/~gormanstownmanor

GUESTHOUSE ★★ MAP 8 P 9

A warm welcome awaits you at this charming family guesthouse. Bright spacious en-suite bedrooms. Peaceful relaxed atmosphere, spectacular surroundings. We have a golf driving range and an 18 hole golf pitch 'n' putt with a professional golf pro in attendance daily. Landscaped gardens, nature walks & superb personal services. Ideally located for golf and touring the Garden of Ireland. Breathtaking scenery, mountains, valleys, rivers, lakes & woodlands. Enjoy stunning sandy beaches of Brittas Bay, sailing, fishing, gardens, heritage, horseriding, polo, golf.

B&B from €38.00 to €57.00
£29.93 to £44.89

MARGARET MURPHY
PROPRIETOR

Mastercard
Visa

Midweek specials from €125.00

9 9

⊟ 👤 ☎ 🖵 T C C M ✿ ♪ P S

IRISH HOTELS FEDERATION

Open All Year

GRAND HOTEL

WICKLOW,
CO. WICKLOW

TEL: 0404-67337 FAX: 0404-69607

EMAIL: grandhotel@eircom.net
WEB: www.grandhotel.ie

HOTEL ★★★ MAP 8 P 9

This charming hotel is the perfect base for touring the beautiful Garden of Ireland. Situated in Wicklow Town, it is only a 40 minute drive from Dublin on the N11. Enjoy golf, fishing, hill walking, sandy beaches and sight seeing locally. 33 large, bright, comfortable bedrooms all en suite with direct dial telephone, multi channel TV and tea/coffee making facilities. Fine food served in the restaurant and bar all day. Lively lounge bar. Conference facilities.

B&B from €47.50 to €75.00
£37.41 to £59.07

JOHN SULLIVAN
GENERAL MANAGER

Mastercard
Visa

Weekend specials from €115.00

33 33

⊟ 👤 ☎ 🖵 ⊟ T C ♦ C M U ♪ P S ⊠

IRISH HOTELS FEDERATION

Open All Year

VALLEY HOTEL AND RESTAURANT

WOODENBRIDGE,
VALE OF AVOCA, ARKLOW,
CO. WICKLOW

TEL: 0402-35200 FAX: 0402-35542

HOTEL CR MAP 8 O 8

Quaint country family run hotel. Ideally located for touring County Wicklow. 1.5 miles from Ballykissangel. 1 hour to Dublin and Rosslare. Surrounded by woodlands and forest and gold miner stream running by hotel. Walking distance to Woodenbridge Golf Club. Our restaurant offers excellent food and our bars are lively with good atmosphere. Hill walking, fishing, beaches are all within minutes of the hotel.

B&B from €44.44 to €47.00
£35.00 to £37.02

DOREEN O'DONNELL
PROPRIETOR

American Express
Diners
Mastercard
Visa

10 10

⊟ 👤 ☎ 🖵 T C ♦ C M ♦ U ♪ ♫ P 📶

S ⊠

IRISH HOTELS FEDERATION

Open All Year

Room rates are per room per night

WOODENBRIDGE HOTEL

VALE OF AVOCA,
ARKLOW,
CO. WICKLOW
TEL: 0402-35146 FAX: 0402-35573
EMAIL: wbhotel@iol.ie
WEB: www.woodenbridgehotel.com

HOTEL ★★★ MAP 8 O 8

Family owned and run with 23 en suite bedrooms, rooms with balconies overlooking scenic 18 hole Woodenbridge Golf Course. Dating from 1608, the hotel is the oldest in Ireland. Our restaurant and bar serve the very best of food. Winner of tourism menu awards for 1998/'99. Bar food served all day. Horse riding, fishing, golfing, fine beaches and walking are all available locally. Near Avoca, film location for Ballykissangel. Adequate car parking.

B&B from €52.00 to €70.00
£40.95 to £55.13

ESTHER O'BRIEN & BILL O'BRIEN
PROPRIETORS

American Express
Mastercard
Visa

23 23

IRISH
HOTELS
FEDERATION

Closed 25 December

when driving in ireland

✳

ALWAYS DRIVE ON THE LEFT HAND SIDE OF THE ROAD

✳

ALWAYS GIVE WAY TO TRAFFIC FROM THE RIGHT AT ROUNDABOUTS

✳

KEEP YOUR DISTANCE FROM TRAFFIC IN FRONT OF YOU

✳

REFRAIN FROM USING MOBILE PHONES WHILST DRIVING

✳

ENJOY YOUR VISIT TO IRELAND – BUT BE VIGILANT

B&B rates are per person sharing per night incl. Breakfast

The East Coast and midlands of Ireland offers a great diversity in scenery and a wealth of attractions to the visitor. Whether you are walking in the Wicklow Mountains or the Slieve Blooms, exploring the Shannon or the Cooley Peninsula or just relaxing on the sandy beaches, this ancient Region has something for everybody. Catch the excitement of the Stradbally Steam Festival, the Wicklow Gardens Festival and the Mullingar Festival. In addition, there are many Summer Schools and other events, that take place throughout the Region.

MAJOR ATTRACTIONS

The Region is rich in archeological and historical sites of great interest, from the passage graves in the Boyne Valley, and the new Bru Na Boinne Visitor Centre, the early Christian settlements of Clonmacnoise and Glendalough to more recent wonders such as the Japanese Gardens at Tully; Wicklow Gaol, Wicklow Town; Avondale House in Rathdrum; Kilruddery House and Gardens, Bray; Russborough House in Blessington and Powerscourt Gardens and Waterfall, Enniskerry.

Other popular attractions include Newgrange Farm, Slane; Mosney; Crookstown Mill in Ballitore; Charleville Castle, Tullamore; Locke's Distillery, Kilbeggan; Athlone Castle Visitor Centre, Newtowncashel Heritage Centre and the designated Heritage towns of Athy, Kildare Town, Ardagh, Carlingford, Trim, Kells, Baltinglass, Abbeyleix and Tullamore; Heywood Gardens, Gash Gardens and Donaghmore Farm Museum in Co. Laois; Wineport Sailing Centre, Athlone; Holy Trinity Visitor Centre, Carlingford and the National Gardens Exhibition Centre, Kilquade. In addition, Corlea

Trackway Exhibition Centre, Kenagh, the County Museum Dundalk, Tullamore Dew Heritage Centre and Belvedere House, Garden and Park in Mullingar are also well worth a visit. Indeed there are many other interesting places to visit throughout the Region.

High quality golfing and equestrian facilities are widely available in the Region. Coarse, Game and Sea fishing is also available as is Cruising, Walking and other activities. There is a great variety of accommodation from the most luxurious of Hotels to the more modest family run unit and other types of accommodation, each in their own way offering superb service to the visitor.

Full details on all festivals and events, heritage and special interest activities from angling to walking in the East Coast and Midlands Region are available from the local Tourist Information Office or from East Coast and Midlands Tourism, Market House, Mullingar, Co. Westmeath.
Tel: (00 353) 044-48650
Fax: (00 353) 044-40413
E-mail: info@ecoast-midlandstourism.ie
Web site: www.ecoast-midlands.travel.ie

BREFFNI ARMS HOTEL

ARVAGH,
CO. CAVAN

TEL: 049-433 5127 FAX: 049-433 5799
EMAIL: breffniarms@hotmail.com
WEB: www.breffniarms.com

HOTEL N   MAP 11 K 14

The Breffni Arms is a 12 room en suite family-run licensed hotel and leisure centre. Ideally situated for a choice of golf courses, fishing, horse-riding and pitch & putt, etc. Facilities include 13m indoor swimming pool, sauna, steam room, jacuzzi and fitness room. All our rooms have TV, phone, computer point and tea/coffee making facilities.

B&B from €51.00 to €63.00
£40.17 to £49.62

EAMONN & PHILOMENA GRAY

Mastercard
Visa

12 12
Inet

Open All Year

BAILIE HOTEL

BAILIEBOROUGH,
CO. CAVAN

TEL: 042-966 5334 FAX: 042-966 6506
EMAIL: mulbarton@eircom.net

HOTEL ★★   MAP 11 M 14

Friendly family run hotel. Rooms en suite. TV, direct dial phone. Excellent reputation for good food. Carvery lunches served daily. Also à la carte and evening dinner. Food served all day in lounge. Coarse fishing close by. Golf course and mountain climbing also close by. Newly opened swimming pool and leisure centre in town. Ideal for a relaxing break.

B&B from €35.00 to €44.00
£27.56 to £34.65

KEVIN MURPHY
MANAGER

American Express
Mastercard
Visa

☺ Weekend specials from €85.00

18 18

Open All Year

LACKEN MILL HOUSE AND GARDENS

LACKEN LOWER,
BALLINAGH,
CO. CAVAN

TEL: 049-433 7592
EMAIL: info@lackenmillhouse.com
WEB: www.lackenmillhouse.com

GUESTHOUSE ★★★   MAP 11 K 14

Lacken Mill House, set amid 4 acres of mature woodlands, mill races, streams, developing gardens and 400m of River Erne frontage exudes exceptional beauty in natural surroundings. Fish the Erne on site or the myriad excellent local lakes. Enjoy sporting activities or relax in rural tranquillity. The stone built house offers Georgian elegance with open fires and all modern conveniences. Children welcome. Come and visit, you will return. 4 course table d'hôte meals 7.30 - 9.00pm, must be booked before 2pm. Wines available. Tel: 049 - 436 7933.

B&B from €36.00 to €39.00
£28.35 to £30.71

NAOMI BRENNAN/EAMON O'DONOGHUE

Mastercard
Visa

5 5

IRISH HOTELS FEDERATION

Closed 19 - 27 December

KEEPERS ARMS

BRIDGE STREET,
BAWNBOY, BALLYCONNELL,
CO. CAVAN
TEL: 049-952 3318 FAX: 049-952 3008
EMAIL: keepers@iol.ie
WEB: keepersarms@holidayhound.com

GUESTHOUSE ★★ MAP 11 K 15

Come taste our wares... in West Cavan. Enjoy the Shannon Erne Waterway on land or by water. Day or evening cruising, angling on our lakes and rivers, pet farms, Irish Music/Dancing Schools, horse riding, or try 18 Hole (Championship) golf all in our area. Explore to your heart's desire the maze of country roads adjoining the Cavan and Ulster Way. Delights on the Kingfisher Route with your bicycle. Unexpected pleasures await you in our peaceful & beautiful West Cavan.

B&B from €29.00 to €38.00
£22.84 to £29.92

SHEILA MCKIERNAN

Mastercard
Visa

11 11

aid

IRISH HOTELS FEDERATION

Closed 24 - 26 December

SLIEVE RUSSELL HOTEL, GOLF & COUNTRY CLUB

BALLYCONNELL,
CO. CAVAN
TEL: 049-952 6444 FAX: 049-952 6474
EMAIL: slieve-russell@quinn-hotels.com
WEB: www.quinnhotels.com

HOTEL ★★★★ MAP 11 K 15

The Slieve Russell Hotel, Golf and Country Club offers a unique experience in relaxation and leisure to our guests. Enjoy excellent cuisine, professional and friendly service and a range of leisure facilities. The 18 hole PGA championship golf course ensures a challenging game, whilst beginners will enjoy the 9 hole par 3 course. Country Club facilities include: a 20m leisure pool, saunas, steamroom, jacuzzi, fitness suite, tennis, snooker, hair/beauty salon, creche and games room.

Member of Quinn Hotels
B&B from €95.00 to €147.00
£74.82 to £115.77

SHEILA GRAY
GENERAL MANAGER

American Express
Diners
Mastercard
Visa

159 159

IRISH HOTELS FEDERATION

Open All Year

HOTEL KILMORE

DUBLIN ROAD,
CAVAN
TEL: 049-433 2288 FAX: 049-433 2458
EMAIL: kilmore-sales@quinn-hotels.com
WEB: www.quinnhotels.com

HOTEL ★★★ MAP 11 L 14

The Hotel Kilmore is ideally located in the heart of Ireland's Lakeland District. Recently refurbished, the hotel offers 39 luxuriously appointed rooms. Renowned for fine cuisine, our AA Rosette Annalee Restaurant boasts a wide selection of dishes including local fish and game, complemented by an extensive wine list. Ideal venue for conferences and private functions. The Hotel Kilmore is the perfect base for a business visit or to enjoy the varied leisure pursuits in the area.

Member of Quinn Hotels
B&B from €55.00 to €60.00
£43.32 to £47.25

JIM BURKE
GENERAL MANAGER

American Express
Diners
Mastercard
Visa

39 39

aid inet

IRISH HOTELS FEDERATION

Closed 24 - 26 December

Room rates are per room per night

CABRA CASTLE HOTEL

KINGSCOURT,
CO. CAVAN

TEL: 042-966 7030 FAX: 042-966 7039
EMAIL: cabrach@iol.ie
WEB: www.cabracastle.com

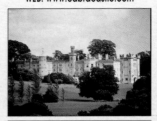

HOTEL ★★★★ MAP 11 M 14

Follow in the footsteps of Oliver Cromwell and James II, and treat yourself to a stay in a castle. Cabra Castle stands on 88 acres of gardens and parkland, with its own nine hole golf course. The bar and restaurant offer views over countryside famous for its lakes and fishing, as well as Dun a Ri Forest Park. An ideal venue for that holiday, specialising in golfing and equestrian holidays. Member of: Manor House Hotels Tel: 01-295 8900, GDS Access Code: UI Toll Free 1-800-44-UTELL.

Member of Manor House Hotels

B&B from €58.00 to €102.00
£45.67 to £80.33

HOWARD CORSCADDEN
MANAGER

American Express
Mastercard
Visa

80 80

IRISH HOTELS FEDERATION

Closed 23 - 27 December

PARK HOTEL

VIRGINIA,
CO. CAVAN

TEL: 049-854 6100 FAX: 049-854 7203
EMAIL: virginiapark@eircom.net
WEB: www.bichotels.com

HOTEL ★★★ MAP 11 L 13

Beautifully restored hotel set in its own 100 acre historic estate. Located on the shores of Lough Ramor and nestled among some of the country's most beautifully landscaped gardens. Guests can avail of our 9 hole golf course, 15 miles of walking trails and excellent fishing locally. Dine in the beautiful surroundings of our AA award winning restaurant. Our conference facilities can cater for up to 100 delegates.

B&B from €60.00 to €100.00
£47.25 to £78.76

FRANK CLEVELAND

American Express
Mastercard
Visa

☺ Golden Years midweek break 3 Dinners, B&B from €165.00

25 25

IRISH HOTELS FEDERATION

Open All Year

SHARKEYS HOTEL

MAIN STREET,
VIRGINIA,
CO. CAVAN

TEL: 049-854 7561 FAX: 049-854 7761
EMAIL: sharkeys@destination-ireland.com
WEB: www.destination-ireland.com/sharkeys

HOTEL ★★ MAP 11 L 13

Egon Ronay award winning family run hotel, situated in the heart of Virginia, 80km from Dublin, on the main route to Donegal. It is furnished to the highest standards, direct dial phone, TV in all rooms. Enjoy a day's fishing or travelling around the lake region and return to relax in the comfort of our restaurant and sample some of the delights of our award winning chef. It has both à la carte and dinner menus, carvery and extensive bar menu. Food served all day. 9 hole golf course 5 minutes walk.

B&B from €50.00 to €55.00
£39.38 to £43.32

PAT AND GORETTI SHARKEY
PROPRIETORS

Mastercard
Visa

☺ Weekend specials from €100.00

13 13

IRISH HOTELS FEDERATION

Open All Year

TONLEGEE HOUSE AND RESTAURANT

ATHY,
CO. KILDARE

TEL: 0507-31473 FAX: 0507-31473
EMAIL: marjorie@tonlegeehouse.com
WEB: www.tonlegeehouse.com

GUESTHOUSE ★★★★ MAP 7 M 9

Tonlegee House is situated on its own grounds, just outside Athy and only an hour from the bustle of Dublin. Our guests' relaxation is assured in the tranquil comfort of this lovingly restored Georgian Country House and Restaurant. With its antique furnishings and open fires it is an ideal place to stay for either an activity filled or leisurely break. Recommended by the Bridgestone Guide's Best 100 Places to Stay in Ireland.

Member of Premier Guesthouses

B&B from €55.00 to €55.00
£43.32 to £43.32

MARJORIE MOLLOY
PROPRIETOR

American Express
Mastercard
Visa

🛏🏃☎🖥Ⓣ©❋Ⓟ🔋alc
12 12

Closed 01 - 14 November

ARDENODE HOTEL

BALLYMORE EUSTACE,
CO. KILDARE

TEL: 045-864198 FAX: 045-864139
EMAIL: info@ardenodehotel.com
WEB: www.ardenodehotel.com

HOTEL U MAP 8 N 10

Situated on the borders of Counties Wicklow and Kildare and just 20km from Dublin City, this hotel is a perfect base for touring. The Ardenode is a family run country house hotel, set in 7 acres of scenic gardens where personal attention, a warm welcome and friendly service awaits you. Enjoy fine dining in our gourmet restaurant. Relax in the scenic Garden Lounge. Conference facilities and banqueting rooms available.

B&B from €47.63 to €127.00
£37.50 to £100.00

THE BROWNE SISTERS
MANAGERS

American Express
Mastercard
Visa

🛏🏃☎🖥Ⓣ©CM❋🔍Ⓠ∪🖊Ⓟ🔋
17 17

alc 🛒 Inet

IRISH HOTELS FEDERATION

Closed 24 - 26 December

KILKEA CASTLE

CASTLEDERMOT,
CO. KILDARE

TEL: 0503-45156 FAX: 0503-45187
EMAIL: kilkea@iol.ie
WEB: www.kilkeacastle.ie

HOTEL ★★★★ MAP 7 M 8

Kilkea Castle is the oldest inhabited Castle in Ireland. Built in 1180, offering the best in modern comfort while the charm and elegance of the past has been retained. The facilities include de luxe accommodation, a fine dining room, d'Lacy's Restaurant, restful bar/lounge area, full banqueting and conference facilities and full on site leisure centre with an indoor heated swimming pool, sauna, jacuzzi, steamroom and fully equipped gym. 18 hole golf course encircles the Castle.

B&B from €90.00 to €140.00
£70.88 to £110.26

PAUL CORRIDAN
GENERAL MANAGER

American Express
Diners
Mastercard
Visa

🛏🏃☎🖥⬆CM🔍Ⓠ∪🔟🖊Ⓟ
36 36

🔋alc

IRISH HOTELS FEDERATION

Closed 23 - 27 December

Room rates are per room per night

STANDHOUSE HOTEL LEISURE & CONFERENCE CENTRE

CURRAGH RACECOURSE,
CURRAGH (THE),
CO. KILDARE

TEL: 045-436177 FAX: 045-436180
EMAIL: reservations@strandhousehotel.com
WEB: www.strandhousehotel.com

HOTEL U MAP 7 M 10

Standhouse Hotel has a tradition which dates back to 1700. Situated beside the Curragh Racecourse it has become synonymous with The Classics. The premises has been restored to its former elegance and offers the discerning guest a fine selection of quality restaurants, bars, leisure facilities, including 20 metre pool, state of the art gym, jacuzzi, steam room, sauna and plunge pool. Conference facilities cater for 2 to 500 delegates.

B&B from €76.20 to €101.60
£60.01 to £80.02

PAT KENNY
GENERAL MANAGER

American Express
Diners
Mastercard
Visa

63 63

Closed 25 - 26 December

CURRAGH LODGE HOTEL

DUBLIN ROAD,
KILDARE TOWN,
CO. KILDARE

TEL: 045-522144 FAX: 045-521247

HOTEL ★★ MAP 7 M 10

The Curragh Lodge Hotel is situated in Kildare Town on the N7 from Dublin going south. Steeped in history, Kildare is a must for tourists not only for its heritage but for its other attractions such as the Japanese Gardens and the Irish National Stud and Horse Museum. The Curragh Lodge Hotel offers excellent accommodation, food, drink, service and entertainment. Minutes away from the classic Curragh Racecourse and midway between Belfast and Cork. It is an ideal stopover.

B&B from €51.00 to €76.00
£40.17 to £59.85

OWEN BLAKE
MANAGER

Mastercard
Visa

20 20

Closed 25 Decemebr

AMBASSADOR HOTEL

KILL,
CO. KILDARE

TEL: 045-877064 FAX: 045-877515
EMAIL: ambassador-sales@quinn-hotels.com
WEB: www.quinnhotels.com

HOTEL ★★★ MAP 8 N 10

Situated just 20km from Dublin City, this 36 bedroomed hotel is ideally located for those travelling from the south or west. Our restaurants boast excellent cuisine and our bar provides music 4 nights per week. Local amenities include 3 race courses, The Curragh, Naas and Punchestown, four golf courses, Goffs Horse Sales, (just across the road) and plenty of horse riding. The Ambassador has something for everybody.

Member of Quinn Hotels
B&B from €55.00 to €70.00
£43.32 to £55.13

RITA GLEESON
GENERAL MANAGER

American Express
Diners
Mastercard
Visa

36 36

Open All Year

LEIXLIP HOUSE HOTEL

CAPTAIN'S HILL,
LEIXLIP,
CO. KILDARE
TEL: 01-624 2268 FAX: 01-624 4177
EMAIL: info@leixliphouse.com
WEB: www.leixliphouse.com

HOTEL ★★★   MAP 8 N 11

A most elegant Georgian house hotel built in 1772. Leixlip House is a mere 20 mins drive from Dublin City centre. The hotel has been lovingly restored and offers the discerning guest the highest standards of comfort and hospitality. It can cater for conferences of up to 70 people and our banqueting facilities can comfortably accommodate 120 people. Our signature restaurant The Bradaun has been awarded several accolades and offers varied and interesting menus & wine lists.

Member of The Small Hotel Company
B&B from € 70.00 to € 95.00
£55.13 to £74.82

CHRISTIAN SCHMELTER
GENERAL MANAGER

American Express
Diners
Mastercard
Visa

15   15

Open All Year

GLENROYAL HOTEL, LEISURE CLUB & CONFERENCE CENTRE

STRAFFAN ROAD,
MAYNOOTH,
CO. KILDARE
TEL: 01-629 0909 FAX: 01-629 0919
EMAIL: hotel@glenroyal.ie
WEB: www.glenroyal.ie

HOTEL ★★★   MAP 8 N 11

Premier 3*** hotel offering the finest in accommodation and leisure facilities. 20 mins from Dublin close to the M4. Leisure facilities include 20m pool, gym, sauna, jacuzzi and steamroom. Conferences from 2 - 400 and banquets up to 250 can be catered for. We are ideally located for those interested in golf and racing with the K Club and Carton close by. For racing, Naas, The Curragh and Punchestown are easily accessible. After an exhausting day relax in Nancy Spain's Bar where good food is served throughout the day.

B&B from € 69.00 to € 75.00
£54.34 to £59.07

HELEN COURTNEY
GENERAL MANAGER

American Express
Diners
Mastercard
Visa

Weekend specials from €130.00

52   52

Closed 25 December

ONE VISIT...

Three Different Worlds

Visit
St. Fiachra's Garden

World famous
Japanese Gardens

Guided Tours of
Irish National Stud

Tully, Kildare Town,
Co. Kildare, Ireland.
Email: japanesegardens@eircom.net
website: www.irish-national-stud.ie

Opening Hours
12th Feb - 12th Nov.
9.30 am to 6.00 pm
7 days per week

STRAFFAN COURT HOTEL

STRAFFAN ROAD,
MAYNOOTH,
CO. KILDARE
TEL: 01-628 5002 FAX: 01-628 9781
EMAIL: bookings@straffancourthotel.com
WEB: www.straffancourthotel.com

HOTEL N   MAP 8 N 11

The Straffan Court Hotel is a family owned and managed hotel situated in the heart of County Kildare. Ideally positioned close to the M4 and M50. 20 mins from the city centre. Our location is ideal for those interested in golf, racing, and all equestrian activities. Only a 5 min drive from the prestigious K Club - an 18-hole championship golf course designed by Arnold Palmer and venue for the Ryder Cup in 2006. It is an ideal haven for the golf enthusiast. Many golf courses nearby.

Room Rate from €107.93 to €139.67
£85.00 to £110.00

LINDA MC PHILLIPS

American Express
Diners
Mastercard
Visa

21 21

HOTELS

Closed 24 - 28 December

HAZEL HOTEL

DUBLIN ROAD,
MONASTEREVIN,
CO. KILDARE
TEL: 045-525373 FAX: 045-525810
EMAIL: sales@hazelhotel.com
WEB: www.hazelhotel.com

HOTEL ★★   MAP 7 N 10

The Hazel Hotel is a family run country hotel on the main Dublin/Cork/Limerick road (N7). All bedrooms have bath/shower, colour TV and international direct dial telephone. The hotel's restaurant has extensive à la carte and table d'hôte menus. Ample car parking. Entertainment is provided. Ideal base for going to the Curragh, Naas or Punchestown racecourses. Several golf courses close by. National Stud and Japanese Gardens only 7 miles from hotel. No service charge.

Member of Logis of Ireland
B&B from €50.00 to €63.49
£39.38 to £50.00

MARGARET KELLY
PROPRIETOR

American Express
Diners
Mastercard
Visa

22 22

FAX

HOTELS

Closed 25 - 26 December

HARBOUR HOTEL & RESTAURANT

LIMERICK ROAD,
NAAS,
CO. KILDARE
TEL: 045-879145 FAX: 045-874002

HOTEL ★★   MAP 8 N 10

Looking after the needs of our guests and providing quality service is a priorty in this family run hotel. All rooms have colour TV, direct dial telephone, hair dryer and teasmade. We offer superb home cooked food, extensive à la carte and table d'hôte menus and excellent wine list. Relax and enjoy a drink in our comfortable lounge. Conveniently situated to Dublin City, ferry, airport, Punchestown, The Curragh and Mondello.

B&B from €44.50 to €57.00
£35.03 to £44.88

MARY MONAGHAN
PROPRIETOR

American Express
Diners
Mastercard
Visa

10 10

HOTELS

Closed 25 - 31 December

ANNAGH LODGE GUESTHOUSE

NAAS ROAD,
NEWBRIDGE,
CO. KILDARE
TEL: 045-433518 FAX: 045-433538
EMAIL: annaghlodge@eircom.net
WEB: www.annaghlodge.ie

GUESTHOUSE ★★★ MAP 7 M 10

New purpose-built guesthouse in peaceful setting, ideally located beside all town amenities, including hotels, restaurants and leisure centres. Facilities include private parking and sauna. Annagh Lodge provides the highest standard of comfort in superior rooms with all modern conveniences combined with excellent service. Dublin and the airport are 30 mins drive. Curragh, Naas and Punchestown racecourses, 8 golf courses and fishing are a short drive. Access for wheelchairs.

Member of Best Guest
B&B from €40.00 to €65.00
£31.50 to £51.19

DERNA WALLACE
PROPRIETOR

Mastercard
Visa

9   9

HOTELS
FEDERATION

Closed 23 December - 02 January

EYRE POWELL HOTEL

MAIN STREET,
NEWBRIDGE,
CO. KILDARE
TEL: 045-438822 FAX: 045-438828
EMAIL: epowel@indigo.ie

HOTEL N MAP 7 M 10

The Eyre Powell Hotel is a 33 bedroom hotel situated in the heart of Newbridge. Its rooms are well appointed and all en suite with DD phone, TV and trouser press. The Charlotte Room Restaurant can cater for up to 60 pax while a pre dinner drink can be enjoyed in Jacobs Well Bar. Conference facilities available for groups of 10 to 120 people.

B&B from €50.80 to €76.20
£40.01 to £60.01

GERRY LAVIN
GENERAL MANAGER

American Express
Diners
Mastercard
Visa

33   33

HOTELS
FEDERATION

Closed 24 - 27 December

GABLES GUESTHOUSE & LEISURE CENTRE

RYSTON,
NEWBRIDGE,
CO. KILDARE
TEL: 045-435330 FAX: 045-435355
EMAIL: gablesguesthse@ireland.com

GUESTHOUSE ★★★ MAP 7 M 10

Set on the banks of the Liffey, our family run guesthouse has 10 bedrooms with bath/shower, multi channel TV, direct dial telephone, hairdryer and teas maid. Our leisure centre includes a 14 metre indoor swimming pool, jacuzzi, steam room, sauna and fully equipped gymnasium. Horse racing, golfing and fishing are well catered for locally. A warm and friendly welcome awaits you at the Gables. Brochures available on request.

B&B from €38.00 to €57.00
£29.93 to £44.89

RAY CRIBBIN
PROPRIETOR

Mastercard
Visa

10   10

Closed 23 December - 02 January

Room rates are per room per night

KEADEEN HOTEL

NEWBRIDGE,
CO. KILDARE

TEL: 045-431666 FAX: 045-434402
EMAIL: keadeen@iol.ie
WEB: www.keadeenhotel.kildare.ie

HOTEL ★★★★ MAP 7 M 10

On 9 acres of award winning landscaped gardens, adjacent to the primary Dublin/Cork/Limerick road. This newly refurbished 4**** hotel containing The Keadeen Health and Fitness Club is 40km from Dublin, 2km from the Curragh Racecourse and is accessible off the M7. Our 55 luxurious en suite bedrooms are equipped to International Standards with 22 extra luxurious rooms opening in April, 2002. Extensive Conference and Banqueting facilities available.

B&B from €77.00 to €140.00
£60.64 to £110.26

ROSE O'LOUGHLIN
PROPRIETOR

American Express
Diners
Mastercard
Visa

 Weekend specials available

55 55

Closed 24 - 27 December

K CLUB

AT STRAFFAN,
CO. KILDARE

TEL: 01-601 7200 FAX: 01-601 7299
EMAIL: resortsales@kclub.ie
WEB: www.kclub.ie

HOTEL ★★★★★ MAP 8 N 11

Ireland's only AA 5 Red Star hotel, located 30 minutes from Dublin Airport, invites you to sample its pleasures. Leisure facilities include an 18 hole championship golf course designed by Arnold Palmer, home to the Smurfit European Open and venue for the Ryder Cup in 2006. In addition, both river and coarse fishing are available with full health & leisure club and sporting activities. Meeting and private dining facilities also available. Member of Ireland's Blue Book.

Member of Preferred Hotels & Resorts WW

Room Rate from €270.00 to €485.00
£212.60 to £381.89

RAY CARROLL
CHIEF EXECUTIVE

American Express
Diners
Mastercard
Visa

45 45

Open All Year

ABBEYLEIX MANOR HOTEL

ABBEYLEIX,
CO. LAOIS

TEL: 0502-30111 FAX: 0502-30220
EMAIL: info@abbeyleixmanorhotel.com
WEB: www.abbeyleixmanorhotel.com

HOTEL ★★★ MAP 7 L 8

Already making a name for itself for its high standard of service, the recently opened Abbeyleix Manor Hotel with its fabulous bar and restaurant, is the perfect stop-off point halfway between Dublin and Cork on the N8. All the luxury bedrooms are en suite and food is available all day. Abbeyleix's friendly, rural atmosphere will revive the most jaded traveller and with golf, fishing and walking available locally, there is plenty to see and do.

B&B from €55.00 to €70.00
£43.32 to £55.13

DONAL CRONIN
MANAGER

American Express
Diners
Mastercard
Visa

23 23

Inet FAX

Closed 25 - 26 December

CASTLE ARMS HOTEL

THE SQUARE,
DURROW,
CO. LAOIS
TEL: 0502-36117 FAX: 0502-36566

HOTEL ★ MAP 7 L 8

The Castle Arms Hotel is a family run hotel situated in the award winning picturesque village of Durrow. We are situated one and a half hours from Dublin, two hours from Cork and three hours from Belfast. Our reputation is for good food, service and friendliness. Local amenities include fishing, Granstown Lake is described as being the best Coarse fishing lake in Europe. Trout can be fished from the local Rivers Erkina and Nore, horse trekking and many golf courses within easy reach.

B&B from €35.00 to €40.00
£27.56 to £31.50

SEOSAMH MURPHY
GENERAL MANAGER

American Express
Mastercard
Visa

10 10

Open All Year

CASTLE DURROW

DURROW,
CO. LAOIS
TEL: 0502-36555 FAX: 0502-36559
EMAIL: info@castledurrow.com
WEB: www.castledurrow.com

HOTEL P MAP 7 L 8

Lord, Lady or Mistress?? Crisp linen, soft velvet, smokey leather and tall Georgian windows. Break away and enjoy the contemporary style and comfort that characterises Castle Durrow. Each room is individually fashioned and lavishly spacious, all with views of the estate and its restored gardens. Fine fusion dining, outdoor activities, conference and wedding facilities - only 90 minutes from Dublin on the main Cork Road (N8), Co. Laois. Escape to Castle Durrow ...... without leaving it all behind.

B&B from €62.00 to €110.00
£48.83 to £86.62

DAVID & LAURA STARNES
MANAGERS

American Express
Diners
Mastercard
Visa

24 24

Open All Year

KILLESHIN HOTEL

PORTLAOISE,
CO. LAOIS
TEL: 0502-21663 FAX: 0502-21976
EMAIL: killeshinhotel@eircom.net

HOTEL ★★★ MAP 7 L 9

Centrally located just off the M7 approximately one and a half hours south of Dublin, you will find the ideal location for your weekend break. The Killeshin Hotel is the ideal stopover for the tourist or traveller. The location, cuisine and ambience together with our friendly relaxed style will ensure a memorable stay. Leisure centre which comprises 20 metre swimming pool, steam room, sauna, jacuzzi and state of the art gymnasium are now open.

B&B from €55.00 to €55.00
£43.32 to £43.32

P.J. MC CANN
GROUP GENERAL MANAGER

American Express
Diners
Mastercard
Visa

44 44

Open All Year

O'LOUGHLIN'S HOTEL

MAIN STREET,
PORTLAOISE,
CO. LAOIS
TEL: 0502-21305 FAX: 0502-60883
EMAIL: oloughlins@eircom.net

HOTEL ★★ MAP 7 L 9

O'Loughlin's Hotel is situated in the heart of Portlaoise Town. It has been completely refurbished by new owners Declan & Elizabeth O'Loughlin. There are 14 en suite bedrooms beautifully decorated with charm, character and comfort. The hotel provides entertainment 3 nights a week in the exclusive Club 23. Food is served all day from 8am to 9pm. There is an excellent lunch and an à la carte menu. Guests are assured of personal attention and a warm welcome from owners, management and staff.

B&B from €47.50 to €55.00
£37.41 to £43.32

DECLAN & ELIZABETH O'LOUGHLIN
OWNERS

Mastercard
Visa

14 14

IRISH HOTELS FEDERATION

Closed 25 December

RICHMOND INN GUESTHOUSE

CLONDRA,
CO. LONGFORD
TEL: 043-26126 FAX: 043-26126
EMAIL: therichmondinn@eircom.net

GUESTHOUSE U MAP 11 J 13

A family run guesthouse and pub in the picturesque village of Clondra. 9km from Longford Town. The Richmond Inn occupies a prime position in this pretty village, standing on the banks of the Royal Canal overlooking the harbour. Your hosts are Des & Frances McPartland who assure their patrons of a warm welcome and fine home cooking. All rooms are en suite with TV, direct dial phone, tea/coffee making facilities. Local amenities include fishing, horse riding, golf, walking and cycling.

B&B from €29.20 to €36.20
£23.00 to £28.51

DES AND FRANCES MCPARTLAND
OWNERS

Mastercard
Visa

5 5

IRISH HOTELS FEDERATION

Open All Year

LONGFORD ARMS HOTEL

MAIN STREET,
LONGFORD
TEL: 043-46296 FAX: 043-46244
EMAIL: longfordarms@eircom.net
WEB: www.longfordarms.ie

HOTEL ★★★ MAP 11 J 13

Ideally located in the heart of the midlands, this comfortable hotel, newly renovated to exacting standards has a vibrant and relaxing atmosphere. The hotel boasts a state of the art conference centre, new health and leisure centre, excellent restaurant and award winning coffee shop where you can be assured of fine food, service and a warm welcome in relaxing convivial surroundings. Available locally: 18 hole golf course, angling, equestrian centre and watersports on the Shannon.

B&B from €65.00 to €85.00
£51.19 to £66.93

DENISE BATT
MANAGER

American Express
Diners
Mastercard
Visa

Weekend specials from €99.00

60 60

IRISH HOTELS FEDERATION

Closed 24 - 26 December

NUREMORE HOTEL & COUNTRY CLUB

**CARRICKMACROSS,
CO. MONAGHAN**

TEL: 042-966 1438 FAX: 042-966 1853
EMAIL: nuremore@eircom.net
WEB: www.nuremore-hotel.ie

HOTEL ★★★★ MAP 12 N 14

Set in tranquil and beautiful surroundings, amidst a championship 18-hole golf course, the Nuremore offers unrivalled standards of service and sporting, leisure and conference facilities. The Country Club boasts an 18m swimming pool, whirlpool, sauna, steam-room, gymnasium, tennis courts and a beauty treatment centre. There are a wide range of spacious rooms and demi-suites on offer and our award-winning restaurant serves superb cuisine in idyllic surroundings. 1.5 hours from Dublin.

*B&B from €100.00 to €150.00
£78.76 to £118.13*

JULIE GILHOOLY
PROPRIETOR

American Express
Diners
Mastercard
Visa

69 69

Open All Year

GLENCARN HOTEL AND LEISURE CENTRE

**MONAGHAN ROAD,
CASTLEBLAYNEY,
CO. MONAGHAN**

TEL: 042-974 6666 FAX: 042-974 6521

HOTEL ★★★ MAP 11 M 15

Situated on the main Dublin route to the North West. This hotel has 27 bedrooms all en suite, with direct dial telephone, TV (family rooms available). Beside Lough Muckno Forest Park, great for fishing, water skiing, boating or a leisurely stroll. The Glencarn has established its name for quality food and efficient service. Music in the Temple Bar & night club. Our leisure centre boasts a jacuzzi, steam rooms, changing rooms, plunge pool, childrens pool, 21 meter swimming pool, gym.

*B&B from €50.00 to €61.00
£39.38 to £48.03*

PATRICK MCFADDEN
GENERAL MANAGER

American Express
Diners
Mastercard
Visa

 Weekend specials from €122.00

27 27

Closed 24 - 25 December

FOUR SEASONS HOTEL & LEISURE CLUB

**COOLSHANNAGH,
MONAGHAN**

TEL: 047-81888 FAX: 047-83131
EMAIL: info@4seasonshotel.ie
WEB: www.4seasonshotel.ie

HOTEL ★★★ MAP 11 M 16

Elegance without extravagance!! Enjoy the excellent service, warmth and luxury of this family run hotel. Relax by the turf fire in the Still Bar or savour the food in the informal setting of the Range Restaurant. For an alternative option we offer fine dining in our new restaurant, Avenue. The rooms have all modern facilities and residents have unlimited use of our leisure facilities, 18m pool, jacuzzi, steamroom, sauna and gym. Also available massage and sunbed. Available locally: 18-hole golf course, angling, equestrian centre and water sports.

*B&B from €57.00 to €95.00
£44.88 to £74.82*

FRANK MCKENNA
MANAGING DIRECTOR

American Express
Diners
Mastercard
Visa

44 44

Closed 25 - 26 December

Room rates are per room per night

HILLGROVE HOTEL

OLD ARMAGH ROAD,
MONAGHAN

TEL: 047-81288 FAX: 047-84951
EMAIL: hillgrove@quinn-hotels.com
WEB: www.quinnhotels.com

HOTEL U   MAP 11 M 16

This hotel combines comfort and genuine Irish hospitality, only 2 hours from Dublin, it offers 44 superbly appointed rooms, comfortable surroundings and a delightful restaurant. On the boundaries of the ecclesiastical capital of Ireland, the ancient seat of the Kings, the Hillgrove is perfectly situated for those who enjoy the rich tapestry of local history. There is a variety of activities offered by Monaghan, the most northerly town in the Lakeland Region.

Member of Quinn Hotels
B&B from €54.00 to €67.00
£42.53 to £52.77

ROSS MEALIFF
GENERAL MANAGER

American Express
Diners
Mastercard
Visa

44 44

Closed 24 - 27 December

BROSNA LODGE HOTEL

BANAGHER-ON-THE-SHANNON,
CO. OFFALY

TEL: 0509-51350 FAX: 0509-51521
EMAIL: della@iolfree.ie
WEB: www.brosnalodge.com

HOTEL ★★   MAP 7 J 10

A family owned country hotel, close to the River Shannon, welcomes guests with superb hospitality and relaxed elegance. Mature gardens surround the hotel. With unique peat bogs, mountains, the Shannon and Clonmacnois, you will delight in this gentle little known part of Ireland. Fishing, golf, pony trekking, nature and historical tours arranged locally. Enjoy beautiful food in our restaurant, The Fields and drinks in Pat's Olde Bar. Courtesy of Choice Programme.

B&B from €35.45 to €40.63
£27.92 to £32.00

PAT & DELLA HORAN
PROPRIETORS

American Express
Diners
Mastercard
Visa

☺ Weekend specials from €95.00

14 14

Closed 25 - 26 December

COUNTY ARMS HOTEL

RAILWAY ROAD,
BIRR,
CO. OFFALY

TEL: 0509-20791 FAX: 0509-21234
EMAIL: countyarmshotel@eircom.net

HOTEL ★★★   MAP 7 J 9

One of the finest examples of late Georgian architecture (C.1810), its well preserved interior features are outstanding. The atmosphere is warm, cosy & peaceful. Our hotel gardens and glasshouses provide fresh herbs, fruit and vegetables for our various menus. All our recently renovated bedrooms have private bathroom, telephone, colour TV & tea maker. 2 rooms adapted with facilities for disabled. Locally available golf, horseriding, fishing, tennis & heated indoor pool.

Member of MinOtel Ireland Hotel Group
B&B from €50.00 to €70.00
£39.38 to £55.13

WILLIE & GENE LOUGHNANE
OWNERS

American Express
Diners
Mastercard
Visa

☺ Weekens specials from €125.00

24 24

Closed 24 - 28 December

DOOLYS HOTEL

EMMET SQUARE,
BIRR,
CO. OFFALY
TEL: 0509-20032 FAX: 0509-21332
EMAIL: doolyshotel@esatclear.ie
WEB: www.doolyshotel.com

HOTEL ★★★ MAP 7 J 9

An historic 250 year old coaching inn, this 3*** Bord Failte and AA hotel has been modernised to a very high standard of comfort and elegance. All bedrooms en suite, tastefully decorated with colour TV, video, radio, direct dial phone, tea/coffee making facilities. The Emmet Restaurant offers superbly cooked international dishes and is complemented by our modern Coachouse Grill and Bistro where you can obtain hot meals all day.

B&B from €47.00 to €47.00
£37.00 to £37.00

SHARON GRANT/JO DUIGNAN
PROPRIETOR/GENERAL MANAGER

American Express
Diners
Mastercard
Visa

☺ Weekend specials from €121.00

18 18

Closed 25 December

KINNITTY CASTLE DEMESNE

KINNITTY,
BIRR,
CO. OFFALY
TEL: 0509-37318 FAX: 0509-37284
EMAIL: kinnittycastle@eircom.net
WEB: www.kinnittycastle.com

HOTEL U MAP 7 J 9

The luxuriously refurbished Castle is situated 1.5 hrs from Dublin, Galway and Limerick, 37 magnificent en suite rooms, stately reception rooms in the main castle and excellent restaurant with gourmet food and fine wines. Conference & banqueting facilities are available. Moneyguyneen House on the estate with 12 en suite bedrooms is refurbished to exceptional country house standards. Facilities include an equestrian centre, clay pigeon shooting, falconry, walking, gym, golf and fishing nearby.

B&B from €120.00 to €165.00
£94.49 to £129.92

FEARGHAL O'SULLIVAN
GENERAL MANAGER

American Express
Diners
Mastercard
Visa

☺ Weekend specials from €222.00pp

49 49

Open All Year

Clonmacnoise & West Offaly Railway

Enjoy a guided rail tour of the bog - the only one of its kind in the world
Tel: 0905 74114
Web: www.bnm.ie
Opening Hours: April - Early October

Ireland's Historic Science Centre, Birr Castle Demesne

World famous gardens and telescope. Home to Irelands Historic Science Centre
Tel: 0509 20336
Web: www.birrcastle.com
Opening Hours: Year Round

Tullamore Dew Heritage Centre

Visit Tullamore Dew Heritage Centre and enjoy the audio visual tour of Tullamores distilling history and tasting of Tullamore Dew Whiskey or Irish Mist Liquer
Tel: 0506 25015
Web: www.tullamore–dew.org
Opening Hours: Year Round

Room rates are per room per night

MALTINGS GUESTHOUSE

CASTLE STREET,
BIRR,
CO. OFFALY
TEL: 0509-21345 FAX: 0509-22073
EMAIL: themaltingsbirr@eircom.net

GUESTHOUSE ★★★ MAP 7 J 9

Secluded on a picturesque riverside setting beside Birr Castle, in the centre of Ireland's finest Georgian town. Built circa 1810 to store malt, for Guinness, and converted in 1994 to a 13 bedroom guesthouse with full bar and restaurant. All bedrooms are comfortably furnished with bath/shower en suite, colour TV and phones.

B&B from €29.00 to €32.00
£22.84 to £25.20

MAEVE GARRY
MANAGERESS

Mastercard
Visa

☺ Weekend specials from €77.00

🛏️🐾📞🅣🅣🅲🚲CM❄️☝️🤝🅿️🔒alc
13 13

Open All Year

SPINNERS TOWN HOUSE

CASTLE ST,
BIRR,
CO. OFFALY
TEL: 0509-21673 FAX: 0509-21672
EMAIL: spinners@indigo.ie
WEB: www.spinners-townhouse.com

GUESTHOUSE ★★ MAP 7 J 9

With an outlook over the majestic walls of Birr Castle, the townhouse offers a modern revival of Georgian architecture and style. An enclosed courtyard garden and 13 spacious stylish bedrooms, thoughtfully designed for comfort and relaxation offering an hospitable oasis for the weary traveller. En suite rooms, direct dial phone and tour guide on request, French/German spoken. Our Bistro internationally renowned for food and wine...A complete hospitality package.

B&B from €32.00 to €45.00
£25.20 to £35.44

LIAM F MALONEY
MANAGING DIRECTOR

American Express
Diners
Mastercard
Visa

☺ Midweek specials from €84.00

🛏️🐾📞🅣🅐🅒🚲CM❄️☝️🤝🆂🆈alc
13 13

Inet FAX

Open All Year

BRIDGE HOUSE HOTEL & LEISURE CLUB

TULLAMORE,
CO. OFFALY
TEL: 0506-22000 FAX: 0506-25690
EMAIL: info@bridgehouse.com
WEB: www.bridgehouse.com

HOTEL ★★★ MAP 7 K 10

The famous Bridge House, now a luxury 72 room hotel and leisure complex in the heart of Tullamore. Magnificent award winning bar, restaurant & coffee shop, we are justifiably proud of our great tradition of hospitality, good food and service. The leisure complex, indoor swimming pool, spa pool, sauna, jacuzzi, gym and indoor world club golf driving range and simulator, two championship golf courses within 5 min. and only 45 mins from 2006 Ryder Cup Venue, The K Club. Shopping centre and numerous attractions and activities locally.

B&B from €75.00 to €95.00
£59.07 to £74.82

COLM MCCABE
MANAGER

American Express
Mastercard
Visa

✓1

🛏️🐾📞🅣🅣🅲🚲CM❄️🏌️🎱🖥️
72 72
🔍🗝️🤝🎵🅿️🆂🔒alc Inet FAX

Closed 24 - 26 December

MOORHILL HOUSE HOTEL

MOORHILL,
CLARA ROAD, TULLAMORE,
CO. OFFALY
TEL: 0506-21395 FAX: 0506-52424
EMAIL: info@moorhill.ie
WEB: www.moorhill.ie

HOTEL U MAP 7 K 10

Moorhill is a unique experience in the best possible ways. Combining the classic quality of a Victorian country house with the informal ambience of a modern hotel. In Moorhill, we have placed particular emphasis on marrying the elegant surroundings and atmosphere of the hotel with a warm Irish welcome and friendly efficient service. Centrally located and ideal for a relaxing break from daily life or to conduct business at a quiet & efficient pace.

B&B from €45.00 to €50.00
£35.44 to £39.38

DAVID AND ALAN DUFFY

American Express
Mastercard
Visa

10 10

IRISH
HOTELS
FEDERATION

Closed 24 - 26 December

SEA DEW GUESTHOUSE

CLONMINCH ROAD,
TULLAMORE,
CO. OFFALY
TEL: 0506-52054 FAX: 0506-52054

GUESTHOUSE ★★★ MAP 7 K 10

Set in a mature garden of trees, Sea Dew is a purpose built guesthouse, providing guests with a high standard of comfort, located only 5 minutes walk from the town centre. The conservatory breakfast room will give you a bright start to the day, where there is an excellent selection of fresh produce. All bedrooms are spacious with en suite facilities, TV and direct dial telephones. Golfing, fishing, horse riding and shooting are available nearby. Access for wheelchairs.

B&B from €38.00 to €38.00
£29.93 to £29.93

CLAIRE & FRANK GILSENAN
PROPRIETORS

Mastercard
Visa

12 12

IRISH
HOTELS
FEDERATION

Closed 23 December - 02 January

GLENDEER
Award Winning Open Farm

Take a break at Glendeers 6 Acres Open Farm, sign posted on the N6, just west of Athlone. Stretch your legs along the unspoilt nature walk where old horse drawn farm machinery can be viewed. Feed the pet animals which include deer, Vietnamese pot belly pigs, emu, ostrich, ponies, donkeys, Jersey cows, Jacob sheep, Anglo Nubian goats, peacocks and other rare birds and domestic fowl. A coffee shop, souvenir, craft & tuck shop, with soft drinks, ice cream, sweets etc., picnic area, playground and toilet facilities are also provided. The farm has been designed so that visitors can mingle with all the pet animals. Groups catered for with guided tour by arrangement, also suitable for birthday parties.

Opening Times for the Open Farm
Easter Sunday and remaining weekends
for the month of April
Open every day from the
1st May – end of September
Monday – Saturday 10 a.m. – 6 p.m.
Sunday 12 p.m. – 6 p.m.

For further information contact
The O'Connell Family
Glendeer Fram,
Drum, Athlone
Co. Roscommon
Phone: 0902 37147
E-mail: glendeer@glendeer.com
Web: www.glendeer.com

Room rates are per room per night

TULLAMORE COURT HOTEL

TULLAMORE,
CO. OFFALY

TEL: 0506-46666 FAX: 0506-46677
EMAIL: info@tullamorecourthotel.ie
WEB: www.tullamorecourthotel.ie

HOTEL U   MAP 7 K 10

The Tullamore Court Hotel, Conference and Leisure Centre has brought a new style and sophistication to the midlands since its opening in 1997. Its contemporary design, furnishing and warm bright colour scheme creates an atmosphere of luxury, elegance and style. Situated on the outskirts of Tullamore, the hotel is within easy reach of all parts of Ireland making it the ideal central location for your conference or short break.

B&B from € 100.00 to € 145.00
£78.76 to £114.20

JOE O'BRIEN
MANAGING DIRECTOR

American Express
Diners
Mastercard
Visa

Weekend specials from €140.00

72 72

Closed 24 - 26 December

CREGGAN COURT HOTEL

KILMARTIN N6 CENTRE,
N6 ROUNDABOUT, ATHLONE,
CO. WESTMEATH

TEL: 0902-77777 FAX: 0902-77111
EMAIL: info@creggancourt.com
WEB: www.creggancourt.com

HOTEL N   MAP 7 J 11

The Creggan Court Hotel located just off the N6 in Athlone, midway between Dublin & Galway. The ideal base to explore Clonmacnois, Ely O'Carroll country and the Shannon Basin, Athlone a golfer's paradise, surrounded by local championship golf courses including Glasson Golf Club. The Creggan Court Hotel offers spacious en suite family rooms, direct dial ISDN lines. Casual dining in our Granary Bar & Restaurant or a romantic dinner for two in our Lemon Tree Restaurant.

B&B from € 44.45 to € 57.15
£35.00 to £45.00

PATRICIA FLYNN
GENERAL MANAGER

American Express
Diners
Mastercard
Visa

73 73

Closed 25 - 26 December

HODSON BAY HOTEL

ATHLONE,
CO. WESTMEATH

TEL: 0902-80500 FAX: 0902-80520
EMAIL: info@hodsonbayhotel.com
WEB: www.hodsonbayhotel.com

HOTEL ★★★   MAP 11 J 11

Located on the lakeshore of Lough Ree, commanding breathtaking views of the neighbouring golf club and surrounding countryside. Offering sandy beaches and a modern marina with cruiser berthing, summer season daily lake cruise. The purpose built conference centre, leisure complex and award-winning bar and two rosette AA fish restaurant combine to make the hotel one of the finest in Ireland. Exit Athlone bypass, take the N61 Roscommon Road.

B&B from € 50.00 to € 94.00
£39.38 to £74.03

MICHAEL DUCIE
DIRECTOR/GENERAL MANAGER

American Express
Diners
Mastercard
Visa

Weekend specials from €100.00

133 133

Open All Year

ROYAL HOEY HOTEL

ATHLONE,
CO. WESTMEATH

TEL: 0902-72924 FAX: 0902-75194

HOTEL ★★ MAP 11 J 11

The Royal Hoey hotel offers comfort and cuisine. Today, the Royal is a modern hotel with all the services and comforts associated with today's travellers' needs. There are 38 luxuriously appointed bedrooms, colour TV, telephone, passenger lift to all floors, secure car parking, fully licensed bar and function room. Excellent restaurant. Fast food coffee dock. Restful lounge space, where you can relax and enjoy a slower pace of life.

B&B from €50.79 to €59.68
£40.00 to £47.00

MARY HOEY
PROPRIETOR

American Express
Diners
Mastercard
Visa

38 38

IRISH HOTELS FEDERATION

Closed 25 - 27 December

SHAMROCK LODGE HOTEL AND CONFERENCE CENTRE

CLONOWN ROAD,
ATHLONE,
CO. WESTMEATH

TEL: 0902-92601 FAX: 0902-92737
EMAIL: info@shamrocklodgehotel.ie
WEB: www.shamrocklodgehotel.ie

HOTEL U MAP 11 J 11

Extensive landscaped gardens form a tranquil setting for this elegant manor style country house. The hotel is situated in the heart of Ireland, just 5 minutes walk from Athlone Town centre, making it the ideal location for conferences or as a touring base for the rest of Ireland. Our superbly appointed en suite bedrooms are equipped with all modern facilities while still retaining their old world charm.

B&B from €50.79 to €69.84
£40.00 to £55.00

PADDY MCCAUL
PROPRIETOR

American Express
Diners
Mastercard
Visa

 Midweek special 3 B&B & 2 Dinner from €190.00

27 27

IRISH HOTELS FEDERATION

Closed 24 - 26 December

Room rates are per room per night

AUSTIN FRIAR HOTEL

AUSTIN FRIARS STREET,
MULLINGAR,
CO. WESTMEATH

TEL: 044-45777 FAX: 044-45880

EMAIL: reception@austin-friar.com
WEB: www.austin-friar.com

HOTEL U MAP 11 L 12

Offering warm hospitality in the best of Irish tradition, the Austin Friar Hotel provides a range of modern facilities and a dedicated professional and friendly service. Unique in its structural design, the hotel was built in an elliptical shape and features a central atrium. All rooms are en suite with interiors of warm natural colour and soft furnishing giving a modern, sophisticated appearance. Austins, the Californian-style restaurant, is the ideal place to enjoy good food.

B&B from €45.00 to €80.00
£35.44 to £63.01

MARGARET HARDMAN
GENERAL MANAGER

American Express
Diners
Mastercard
Visa

19 19

HOTELS
IRISH
FEDERATION

Closed 24 - 26 December

BLOOMFIELD HOUSE HOTEL & LEISURE CLUB

BELVEDERE, TULLAMORE ROAD,
MULLINGAR,
CO. WESTMEATH

TEL: 044-40894 FAX: 044-43767

EMAIL: reservation@bloomfieldhouse.com
WEB: www.bloomfieldhouse.com

HOTEL ★★★ MAP 11 L 12

Situated 2 miles south of Mullingar on the shores of Lough Ennell, Bloomfield House is the perfect place to unwind and relax. Only 1 hour from Dublin, the hotel can boast 65 en suite rooms, a lake-view bar and restaurant and a full leisure centre including massage, aromatherapy and beauty therapies. It is adjacent to Mullingar Golf Club and Belvedere House & Gardens and a full range of activities can be arranged, from equestrian to fishing. Email: sales@bloomfieldhouse.com for further details.

B&B from €77.00 to €110.00
£60.64 to £86.63

SEAMUS LAFFAN
GENERAL MANAGER

American Express
Diners
Mastercard
Visa

Weekend specials from €170.00

65 65

HOTELS
IRISH
FEDERATION

Closed 24 - 26 December

GREVILLE ARMS HOTEL

MULLINGAR,
CO. WESTMEATH

TEL: 044-48563 FAX: 044-48052

EMAIL: grevillearmshotel@eircom.net
WEB: www.grevillearms.com

HOTEL ★★★ MAP 11 L 12

In the heart of Mullingar town, the Greville Arms is a home from home where customers and their comfort is our main concern. Bedrooms all en suite with colour TV and DD phone. The Greville Restaurant is renowned for its cuisine and fine wines. No visit to Mullingar would be complete without a visit to our Ulysses Bar with its life sized wax figure of James Joyce and other memorabilia.

B&B from €65.00 to €85.00
£51.19 to £66.94

JOHN COCHRANE
GENERAL MANAGER

American Express
Diners
Mastercard
Visa

Weekend specials from €120.00

39 39

HOTELS
IRISH
FEDERATION

Closed 25 December

AN TINTAIN GUESTHOUSE

MAIN STREET,
MULTYFARNHAM,
CO. WESTMEATH
TEL: 044-71411 FAX: 044-71434
EMAIL: antintain@ireland.com
WEB: www.allirishaccommodation.net/antintain

GUESTHOUSE ★★★ MAP 11 K 12

Situated in a picturesque riverside setting with listed forge, in the quaint village of Multyfarnham. Behind the old world frontage lies a modern, luxurious, purpose built 3* guesthouse and restaurant, furnished to the highest standards, complete with TV, direct dial phone and hairdryer, all rooms en suite. Enjoy a relaxing drink and candlelit dining in our renowned fully licensed restaurant. Located in the heart of the country we are an ideal base for touring.

Member of Premier Guesthouses

B&B from € 34.90 to € 38.00
£27.49 to £29.93

JACK & CAROLINE SLEATOR

Mastercard
Visa

Closed 23 December - 27 December

---

when driving in ireland

✳

ALWAYS DRIVE ON THE LEFT HAND SIDE OF THE ROAD

✳

ALWAYS GIVE WAY TO TRAFFIC FROM THE RIGHT AT ROUNDABOUTS

✳

KEEP YOUR DISTANCE FROM TRAFFIC IN FRONT OF YOU

✳

REFRAIN FROM USING MOBILE PHONES WHILST DRIVING

✳

ENJOY YOUR VISIT TO IRELAND – BUT BE VIGILANT

Room rates are per room per night

SOUTH EAST
The Sunny South East - Coast and County

This year take time, time for you; time to share with those for whom you care.

And there is no better place on earth - convenient, full of interest and with that special appeal - than the Sunny South East of Ireland. Enjoy it at any time, especially in the 'Secret Season', when its many interest points and charms will be revealed at their most relaxed best. Many attractions – of the more than 60 - are open and welcoming. Restaurants and hotels provide really keen offers. Everywhere you will discover for yourself that elusive yet tangible difference that has made this Region grow so much in popularity during the last few years.

For this is now one of the best loved holiday regions even among Irish people themselves. It combines the tranquil elegance of historic, old towns and villages with the classic splendour of mediaeval Kilkenny, Viking Wexford and regal Waterford, the Crystal City and regional capital.

The enchanting coastline, with its necklace of small, intimate, fishing villages, interspaced by safe, sandy beaches – many have been awarded the coveted Blue Flag Status – coupled with the mild, warm climate, all conspire to give substance to the region's age old title - The Sunny South East.

Inland, the deep and ancient river valleys of the Blackwater, Barrow, Nore, Slaney and Suir rivers still retain the dim echo and the more than 60 historic sites and attractions, ranging from forts, abbeys, museums and centres which collectively tell the colourful story of invaders and traders, merchants and early missionaries that once walked this land.

Our five great rivers, rich in fish and wild life, have carved a patchwork of fertile valleys and plains through Carlow, Kilkenny South Tipperary, Waterford and Wexford as they meander their majestic, unhurried way to the Celtic Sea.

There is so much to do in the South East. Golf - our greatest activity - is to be enjoyed on over 30 courses, both links and parkland: equestrian fans and race goers, greyhounds followers and anglers will each enjoy, in their own way, the wide-open spaces that beckon everywhere. Walkers and cyclists appreciate the wide range - and lengths – of waymarked walks. The well signposted touring routes for motorist are also an attraction with a growing band of devotees.

If you have not yet enjoyed the South East take time to do so this year. You will find a special welcome awaits you.

Call into any of our tourist offices and pick up a wide range of literature to help you plan and secure the best possible pleasure from your visit.

For all details contact   South East Tourism,
41 The Quay, Waterford
Tel 051 875823 Fax 051 877388
or visit any of our offices at Carlow Kilkenny Wexford or Rosslare

Guinness Enniscorthy Strawberry Fair,
Enniscorthy, Co. Wexford.
June
Waterford Spraoi & International Rhythm
Festival, Co. Waterford.
July
Kilkenny Arts Week, Kilkenny.
August
Wexford Opera Festival,
Wexford.
October

Event details correct at time of going to press

BALLYVERGAL HOUSE

**DUBLIN ROAD,
CARLOW**

**TEL: 0503-43634 FAX: 0503-40386
EMAIL: ballyvergal@indigo.ie**

GUESTHOUSE ★★★ MAP 7 M 8

A large family run guesthouse conveniently located just outside Carlow Town on the Dublin Road (N9), adjacent to Carlow's 18 hole championship golf course. We offer our guests en suite rooms with TV, direct dial phone and hairdryer, a large residents' lounge and extensive private car parking. Most importantly you are assured of a warm friendly welcome. We are ideally located for golf (Carlow, Mount Wolseley, Kilkea Castle, Mount Juliet), angling, shooting, horseriding, and pitch & putt.

B&B from €27.00 to €35.00
£21.26 to £27.56

CON & ITA MARTIN
PROPRIETORS

American Express
Mastercard
Visa

🛏🤵☎🖥T🅐🅒❄♒🎵🄿🄢♿
10 10

IRISH HOTELS FEDERATION

Closed 22 - 31 December

BARROWVILLE TOWN HOUSE

**KILKENNY ROAD,
CARLOW TOWN,
CO. CARLOW**

TEL: 0503-43324 FAX: 0503-41953

WEB: www.barrowvillehouse.com

GUESTHOUSE ★★★ MAP 7 M 8

A period listed residence in own grounds, 3 minutes walk to town centre. Well appointed rooms with all facilities. Antique furnishing. Traditional or buffet breakfast served in conservatory overlooking the gardens. Ideal location for golf, at Carlow, Kilkea, Mt Wolseley, touring SE, Glendalough, Kilkenny, Waterford and visiting various gardens. Recommended by AA RAC Bridgestone 100 Best Jameson Guide. Guesthouse of the year 2000 and other good guide books. German spoken.

Member of Premier Guesthouses of Ireland
B&B from €32.50 to €35.00
£25.60 to £27.56

RANDAL & MARIE DEMPSEY
PROPRIETORS

American Express
Mastercard
Visa

🛏🤵☎🖥T❄♒🄿🄢♿
7 7

IRISH HOTELS FEDERATION

Open All Year

CARLOW GUESTHOUSE

**GREEN LANE,
DUBLIN ROAD,
CARLOW**

TEL: 0503-36033 FAX: 0503-36034
EMAIL: carlowguesthouse@eircom.net
WEB: www.carlowguesthouse.com

GUESTHOUSE ★★★ MAP 7 M 8

Located on the N9, 5 minute walk from town centre approaching from Dublin. Our property is secluded on its own grounds with private gardens and car parks. Carlow Guest House offers an ideal setting to tour the South East during the day while enjoying Carlow's bustling nightlife in the evening including a wide selection of restaurants, music venues, etc to satisfy every taste. Room facilities include TV, trouser press, hair dryer, tea/coffee, and telephone. Welcome to Carlow "The Celtic County".

Member of Premier Guesthouses
B&B from €28.57 to €50.80
£22.50 to £40.01

GER MCCORMACK

Mastercard
Visa

🛏🤵☎🖥T◆CM❄♒🄿🄢♿
9 9

IRISH HOTELS FEDERATION

Open All Year

Room rates are per room per night

DOLMEN HOTEL AND RIVER COURT LODGES

KILKENNY ROAD,
CARLOW

TEL: 0503-42002 FAX: 0503-42375
EMAIL: reservations@dolmenhotel.ie
WEB: www.dolmenhotel.ie

HOTEL ★★★ MAP 7 M 8

Nestled along the scenic banks of the River Barrow and set in 20 acres of landscaped beauty is the Dolmen Hotel, 1.5km from Carlow. Fishing, golf, shooting and horseriding are just some of the sporting facilities surrounding the hotel. With 40 beautifully appointed rooms including 3 luxury suites with en suite, TV, direct dial phone, trouser press and hairdryer. Our 1 bedroomed lodges are ideal for the sporting enthusiast. One of the largest conference and banqueting facilities in the South East.

B&B from € 50.00 to € 75.00
£39.38 to £59.07

PADRAIG BLIGHE
GENERAL MANAGER

American Express
Diners
Mastercard
Visa

40 40

aic Inet

IRISH HOTELS FEDERATION

Closed 25 December

REDSETTER GUESTHOUSE

14 DUBLIN STREET,
CARLOW

TEL: 0503-41848 FAX: 0503-42837

GUESTHOUSE ★★ MAP 7 M 8

Redsetter Guesthouse is situated in Carlow's town centre. A delightful 17 bedroom tastefully furnished residence (14 ensuite), it offers you the essence of comfort, hospitality and security (a large lock-up car park). An ideal base for touring the south east with very good public transport available. Local attractions include a variety of resturants, Irish music, golf, angling, horseriding, swimming, museum and historical sites.

B&B from € 30.00 to € 34.00
£23.62 to £26.77

GAVIN FEELEY
OWNER

Mastercard
Visa

17 14

Closed 24 - 26 December

SEVEN OAKS HOTEL

ATHY ROAD,
CARLOW

TEL: 0503-31308 FAX: 0503-32155
EMAIL: sevenoak@eircom.net
WEB: www.sevenoakshotel.com

HOTEL ★★★ MAP 7 M 8

Ideally located just 3 mins walk to Carlow town centre also bus/train station. We specialise in the best of Irish foods in our Tudor Bar carvery and intimate T.D. Molloy's Restaurant. Individually designed rooms, combining a selection of executive suites. Rooms are accessible by lift. Fully equipped conference facilities, with professional and friendly staff make the Seven Oaks Hotel an ideal venue for all such occasions whether large or small. Work out in our fully equipped Greekbank Health and Leisure Club with 20m Swimming Pool, Gym, Sauna & Steam Room.

B&B from € 57.14 to € 69.84
£45.00 to £55.00

MICHAEL MURPHY
MANAGER/DIRECTOR

American Express
Diners
Mastercard
Visa

Special offers apply

60 60

P aic

IRISH HOTELS FEDERATION

Closed 25 December

B&B rates are per person sharing per night incl. Breakfast

LORD BAGENAL INN

MAIN STREET,
LEIGHLINBRIDGE,
CO. CARLOW

TEL: 0503-21668 FAX: 0503-22629
EMAIL: info@lordbagenal.com
WEB: www.lordbagenal.com

HOTEL ★★★ MAP 7 M 8

Situated in the heritage village of Leighlinbridge along the River Barrow, with private marina and gardens, we are ideally located to explore the South East. Our en suite bedrooms are luxuriously furnished to the highest standards. Award winning restaurant reputed for fine food and excellent wines. Locals and visitors frequent our bar where carvery lunch and bar food are served daily. Children always welcome. Weddings, conferences, banquets catered for. Gold Medal Entente Florale Floral Pride.

B&B from €50.80 to €76.20
£40.00 to £60.00

JAMES & MARY KEHOE

American Express
Diners
Mastercard
Visa

12 12

Closed 25 - 26 December

MOUNT WOLSELEY HOTEL, GOLF AND COUNTRY CLUB

TULLOW,
CO. CARLOW

TEL: 0503-51674 FAX: 0503-52123
EMAIL: wolseley@iol.ie
WEB: www.mountwolseley.ie

HOTEL U MAP 8 N 8

Sensitive restoration of existing buildings, some dating back to the first half of the last century, coupled with additional construction work, have combined to provide a hotel with conference facilities, health centre, including 20m pool and accommodation of exceptional standards with timeless elegance at Mount Wolseley Hotel, Golf and Country Club. The hotel itself an architectural delight, offers panoramic views of the golf course, featuring bars, lounges, restaurant and function rooms.

B&B from €55.00 to €90.00
£43.31 to £70.88

STEPHEN ANDERSON
HOTEL MANAGER

Mastercard
Visa

40 40

Closed 25 December

AVALON INN

THE SQUARE,
CASTLECOMER,
CO. KILKENNY

TEL: 056-41302 FAX: 056-41963
EMAIL: avalinn@eircom.net

GUESTHOUSE ★★★ MAP 7 L 7

The Avalon Inn, a Georgian building, set in the quiet town of Castlecomer, 16km from Kilkenny. A rural setting with quiet woodland walks nearby. The area has good trout and salmon fishing. 1km away there is a 9 hole golf course. There are many excellent golf courses nearby. Staying in Castlecomer offers you the best of both worlds with Kilkenny 15 minutes away and at your doorstep fishing, golfing, horseriding and leisurely walks.

B&B from €33.00 to €36.50
£25.99 to £28.74

PAT KEARNS
DIRECTOR

Mastercard
Visa

Midweek specials from €82.00

5 5

Closed 23 - 26 December

WATERSIDE

THE QUAY,
GRAIGUENAMANAGH,
CO. KILKENNY

TEL: 0503-24246 FAX: 0503-24733

EMAIL: info@waterside.iol.ie
WEB: www.watersideguesthouse.com

GUESTHOUSE ★★★ MAP 7 M 7

A beautifully restored 19th century cornstore with feature wooden beams and imposing granite exterior. Riverside location, all rooms have a view of the River Barrow. Excellent base for boating, fishing, hillwalking. 16km from Mount Juliet for golf. Nearby 13th century Duiske Abbey. 27km from historical Kilkenny. Superb restaurant features continental cuisine & international flavour wine list. Relaxed & friendly approach. Perfect for small groups. Guided hillwalking for groups.

B&B from €35.00 to €50.00
£27.56 to £39.38

BRIAN & BRIGID ROBERTS
MANAGERS

Mastercard

Visa

10 10

Open All Year

BAMBRICKS TROYSGATE HOUSE

KILKENNY CITY,
KILKENNY

TEL: 056-51000 FAX: 056-51200
EMAIL: troysgate@eircom.net

GUESTHOUSE U MAP 7 L 7

Troysgate House formerly the Jailhouse of the old walled-in medieval City of Kilkenny. Conveniently located in the heart of the city. 17 en suite rooms. Angling, swimming, horse riding nearby. Kilkenny Golf Course 1km away. It is an historic and charming old world inn which has retained its character while serving the needs of the modern world. Troysgate House incorporates Bambrick's renowned traditional pub which truly has an atmosphere all of its own.

B&B from €25.00 to €60.00
£19.69 to £47.25

PAT LYNCH
MANAGER

Mastercard

Visa

17 17

Open All Year

BERKELEY HOUSE

5 LOWER PATRICK STREET,
KILKENNY

TEL: 056-64848 FAX: 056-64829
EMAIL: berkeleyhouse@eircom.net

GUESTHOUSE ★★★ MAP 7 L 7

A warm and genuine welcome awaits you here at this charming owner operated period residence, uniquely situated in the very heart of medieval Kilkenny City. Berkeley House boasts ample private car parking, 9 spacious & tastefully decorated rooms, all en suite with multi channel TV, direct dial phone & tea/coffee facilities. We pride ourselves with a dedicated and professional team and ensure that every effort will be made to make your stay with us a most enjoyable one.

B&B from €35.00 to €59.00
£27.56 to £46.47

DECLAN CURTIS
MANAGER

Mastercard

Visa

☺ Midweek specials from €39.00

9 9

Closed 22 - 26 December

B&B rates are per person sharing per night incl. Breakfast

BRANNIGANS GLENDINE INN

CASTLECOMER ROAD,
KILKENNY

TEL: 056-21069 FAX: 056-70714
EMAIL: branigan@iol.ie

GUESTHOUSE R MAP 7 L 7

The Glendine Inn has been a licensed tavern for over 200 years. It consists of 7 bedrooms (all en suite), a residents' lounge and dining room on 1st floor. Downstairs there are lounge and public bars serving snack or bar lunches. We are ideally located for golf (course 200m away), the railway station and the historic city of Kilkenny only 1.5km away. We assure you of a friendly welcome.

B&B from €28.00 to €42.00
£22.05 to £33.08

MICHAEL BRANNIGAN
PROPRIETOR

American Express
Diners
Mastercard
Visa

7 7

Open All Year

BUTLER HOUSE

PATRICK STREET,
KILKENNY

TEL: 056-65707 FAX: 056-65626
EMAIL: res@butler.ie
WEB: www.butler.ie

GUESTHOUSE ★★★ MAP 7 L 7

Sweeping staircases, magnificent plastered ceilings, marble fireplaces and a walled garden are all features of this notable Georgian townhouse. Although secluded and quiet, Butler House is located in the heart of the city, close to the castle. The house was restored by the Irish State Design Agency in the early 1970s. The combination of contemporary design and period elegance provides an interesting and unique experience. Suites and superior rooms available. Conference/ function facilities and private car park available. AA ◆◆◆◆.

B&B from €55.00 to €100.00
£43.32 to £78.76

GABRIELLE HICKEY
MANAGER (ACTING)

American Express
Diners
Mastercard
Visa

☺ Midweek specials from €145.00

13 13

Inet

Closed 24 - 29 December

CLUB HOUSE HOTEL

PATRICK STREET,
KILKENNY

TEL: 056-21994 FAX: 056-71920
EMAIL: clubhse@iol.ie
WEB: www.clubhousehotel.com

HOTEL ★★ MAP 7 L 7

Situated uniquely in a cultural and artistic centre and against the background of Kilkenny's beautiful medieval city, the magnificent 18th century Club House Hotel maintains a 200 year old tradition of effortless comfort, hospitality and efficiency. The en suite rooms are decorated in both modern and period style with complimentary beverages, TV, hairdryer and phone. Food is locally sourced, cooked and presented to highest standards. Victors Bar old world charm and luxury.

Member of MinOtel Ireland Hotel Group
B&B from €44.50 to €95.00
£35.05 to £74.82

JAMES P. BRENNAN
MANAGING DIRECTOR

American Express
Diners
Mastercard
Visa

☺ Weekend specials from €125.00

28 28

Closed 24 - 27 December

Room rates are per room per night

FANAD HOUSE

CASTLE ROAD,
KILKENNY

TEL: 056-64126 FAX: 056-56001
EMAIL: fanadhouse@hotmail.com

GUESTHOUSE N   MAP 7 L 7

Overlooking Kilkenny Castle Park, Fanad House is a five minute walk from the city centre. The newly built guesthouse offers all en suite rooms with complimentary beverages, multi-channel TV, hairdryer and direct dial phone. Extensive breakfast menu available. Private and secure parking provided. An ideal base for exploring the medieval city. We are adjacent to Kilkenny Tennis Club. Owner operated is your guarantee for an enjoyable stay.

B&B from €40.00 to €57.00
£31.50 to £44.89

PAT WALLACE
PROPRIETOR

Mastercard

Visa

8   8

Open All Year

HIBERNIAN HOTEL

1 ORMONDE STREET,
KILKENNY CITY,
KILKENNY

TEL: 056-71888 FAX: 056-71877
EMAIL: info@hibernian.iol.ie
WEB: www.kilkennyhibernianhotel.com

HOTEL U   MAP 7 L 7

Kilkenny's finest boutique hotel. Nestled in the Shadow of Kilkenny Castle, the Hibernian Hotel is a national treasure. The overall result is one of atmosphere, elegance and comfort, combined with a service that is hospitable, friendly and above all professional. Offering 42 luxury bedrooms, incorporating Junior Suites and Penthouses, the Classic Hibernian Bar, the City's leading Contemporary Bar - Morrisons and one of the regions leading restaurants - Jacobs Cottage. With secure off street parking, ideal for the smaller incentive meeting. Owner operated.

Member of Best Loved Hotels

B&B from €69.83 to €113.00
£55.00 to £88.99

DAVID LAWLOR
GENERAL MANAGER/DIRECTOR

American Express

Diners

Mastercard

Visa

42   42

Closed 24 - 25 December

HOTEL KILKENNY

COLLEGE ROAD,
KILKENNY

TEL: 056-62000 FAX: 056-65984
EMAIL: kilkenny@griffingroup.ie
WEB: www.griffingroup.ie

HOTEL ★★★   MAP 7 L 7

Hotel Kilkenny is situated in picturesque landscaped gardens, less than 10 minutes walk from medieval Kilkenny City. Facilities include 103 completely refurbished rooms, the wonderful Broom's Bistro, relaxing Rosehill Bar and the superb 5 star Active Health + Fitness Club with 20m pool and spa area, excellent gymnasium, beauty treatment rooms and hairdressing salon. Excellent conference facilities available for 4-400 delegates. Why resort to less?

B&B from €64.00 to €114.00
£50.40 to £89.77

RICHARD BUTLER
GENERAL MANAGER

American Express

Diners

Mastercard

Visa

103 103

Open All Year

B&B rates are per person sharing per night incl. Breakfast

KILFORD ARMS

JOHN STREET, KILKENNY

TEL: 056-61018 FAX: 056-61018
EMAIL: kilfordarms@indigo.ie
WEB: www.travel-ireland.com/irl/kilford.htm

GUESTHOUSE U   MAP 7 L 7

The Kilford Arms is 50 yards from the bus/rail station and still in the city centre, offering you 3 luxury bars, luxury accommodation, entertainment nightly and a beautiful traditional Irish restaurant. Bar food is available all day. Late bar every night, games room. A new purpose built car park and state of the art nite club called Club Life all under one roof at a price hard to beat.

B&B from € 35.00 to € 65.00
£27.56 to £51.19

PIUS PHELAN
OWNER

Mastercard

Visa

Midweek specials from €100.00

50 50

Open All Year

KILKENNY HOUSE

FRESHFORD ROAD, KILKENNY

TEL: 056-70711 FAX: 056-70698
EMAIL: kilkennyhouse@iol.free.ie

GUESTHOUSE ★★★   MAP 7 L 7

Located 1km from the city on the northside's R693 near St. Lukes Hosptial. Set in 2 acres of mature gardens with ample private car parking. A full Irish and buffet breakfast is served in the conservatory. All rooms are en suite with tea/coffee facilities, TV, hairdryer, pine furniture, oak floors. Guests have privacy and peace with their own entrance, stairs and siting room. Owner operated, guarantees "Rest for the tired".

B&B from € 30.00 to € 35.00
£23.62 to £27.56

MICHELENE AND TED DORE
PROPRIETORS

Mastercard

Visa

10 10

Closed 21 - 28 December

KILKENNY ORMONDE HOTEL

ORMONDE STREET, KILKENNY

TEL: 056-23900 FAX: 056-23977
EMAIL: info@kilkennyormonde.com
WEB: www.kilkennyormonde.com

HOTEL ★★★★   MAP 7 L 7

The new Kilkenny Ormonde Hotel, RAC 4**** accredited, is designed to compliment its famous sister hotel, the Aghadoe Heights in Killarney, bringing the same level of service and excellence to Kilkenny City. The Kilkenny Ormonde is centrally located just off High Street and is adjacent to a secure 24 hour car park. With 118 large superior rooms, a conference centre with 10 meeting rooms and extensive leisure club, the Kilkenny Ormonde is ideal for both the leisure and corporate traveller.

B&B from € 107.93 to € 120.62
£85.00 to £95.00

PATRICK CURRAN
GENERAL MANAGER/DIRECTOR

American Express

Diners

Mastercard

Visa

118 118

Closed 24 - 26 December

Room rates are per room per night

KILKENNY RIVER COURT

THE BRIDGE,
JOHN STREET,
KILKENNY

TEL: 056-23388 FAX: 056-23389

EMAIL: reservations@kilrivercourt.com
WEB: www.kilrivercourt.com

HOTEL U MAP 7 L 7

Award winning RAC/AA 4**** hotel, leisure club and conference centre. City centre location, stunning views of Kilkenny Castle and the river Nore. Ideal as a conference venue or simply sheer relaxation. Leisure facilities, which include swimming, pool, sauna, geyser pool, jacuzzi fully equipped gymnasium and beauty salon. Bridge House - dedicated conference and business centre. Limited free carparking. Within easy access of Dublin, Waterford and Cork.

B&B from €88.88 to €320.00
£70.00 to £252.02

PETER WILSON
GENERAL MANAGER

American Express
Diners
Mastercard
Visa

90 90

Closed 25 - 26 December

LACKEN HOUSE

DUBLIN ROAD,
KILKENNY

TEL: 056-61085 FAX: 056-62435

EMAIL: info@lackenhouse.ie
WEB: www.lackenhouse.ie

GUESTHOUSE ★★★ MAP 7 L 7

Stay at Lacken House and enjoy high quality accommodation, superb food and a friendly welcome. We are a family run guest house, situated in Kilkenny City, where you can enjoy exploring the medieval city. Superior & standard bedrooms available, all bedrooms are en suite with colour TV, tea/coffee facilities. Private car parking available for all residents. Our house features the home cooking of our award winning chefs, where fresh food is cooked to perfection. Full bar service is also available.

Member of Logis of Ireland
B&B from €51.00 to €95.00
£40.16 to £74.81

JACKIE & TREVOR TONER
OWNERS

American Express
Mastercard
Visa

11 11

Closed 07 - 21 January

LANGTON HOUSE HOTEL

69 JOHN STREET,
KILKENNY

TEL: 056-65133 FAX: 056-63693

EMAIL: langtons@oceanfree.net
WEB: www.langtons.ie

HOTEL ★★★ MAP 7 L 7

Langton's Kilkenny, award-winning bar and restaurant; it has won National Pub of the Year 4 times. Now open, a wonderful new hotel extension with a 'five star' finish and the same standards of excellence that have made Langton's famous. Complete with executive, penthouse and art deco rooms the new Langton's Hotel completes the award-winning picture.

B&B from €57.14 to €95.23
£45.00 to £75.00

EAMONN LANGTON
PROPRIETOR

American Express
Diners
Mastercard
Visa

☺ Weekend specials from €120

26 26

Closed 25 - 26 December

B&B rates are per person sharing per night incl. Breakfast

LAURELS

COLLEGE ROAD,
KILKENNY

TEL: 056-61501 FAX: 056-71334
EMAIL: laurels@eircom.net
WEB: www.thelaurelskilkenny.com

GUESTHOUSE N MAP 7 L 7

Purpose built townhouse 6-10 minutes walk from city centre and castle. Private car parking. All rooms en-suite (some with whirlpool baths & super king sized beds). TV, Hairdryer, Tea/Coffee in all rooms. Some of the comments in Visitors Book: "Absolutely Wonderful", "Best B&B we had in Ireland", "First class & recommendable", "What more could one ask for, and a whirlpool bath too", "Wonderful".

B&B from €29.00 to €39.00
£22.84 to £30.71

BRIAN AND BETTY MCHENRY

Mastercard
Visa

🛏️🐾☎️🖥️TC🍴CM✳️🔱♪PS⚡
8   8

Inet FAX

IRISH HOTELS FEDERATION

Open All Year

METROPOLE HOTEL

HIGH STREET,
KILKENNY

TEL: 056-63778 FAX: 056-70232

HOTEL ★ MAP 7 L 7

The Metropole Hotel is situated in the heart of Kilkenny City. Occupies a dominant position in Kilkenny's main shopping area (High Street). Within walking distance of all the city's medieval buildings e.g. Kilkenny Castle, Roth House and St. Canice's Cathedral. All bedrooms are en suite with multi channel TV, direct dial telephone and tea/coffee facilities. Live entertainment. Bord Failte approved.

B&B from €25.00 to €45.00
£19.69 to £35.44

ROBERT DELANEY
PROPRIETOR

Mastercard
Visa

✓

🛏️🐾☎️🖥️TC🍴♪PS🔳aic
12 12

IRISH HOTELS FEDERATION

Open All Year

NEWPARK HOTEL

CASTLECOMER ROAD,
KILKENNY

TEL: 056-60500 FAX: 056-60555
EMAIL: info@newparkhotel.com
WEB: www.newparkhotel.com

HOTEL ★★★ MAP 7 L 7

The recently refurbished Newpark Hotel (3***, AA***), set in 40 acres of parkland in Ireland's Medieval city. 111 bedrooms en suite with TV, hairdryer, phone and tea/coffee making facilities. The executive leisure centre includes a 52ft. pool, sauna, jacuzzi, steam room and gym. Gullivers Restaurant specialises in fine dining. The "Scott Dove Bar and Bistro" serves carvery lunch and a superb evening bar menu, with live entertainment most nights. State of the art conference and banqueting facilities.

Member of Best Western Hotels
B&B from €62.85 to €101.00
£49.50 to £79.53

DAVID O'SULLIVAN
GENERAL MANAGER

American Express
Diners
Mastercard
Visa

😊 Weekend specials from €177.00

🛏️🐾☎️🖥️🖥️TC🍴CM✳️🔱🔳U
111 111

♪♪PS🔳aic🔌🛁

IRISH HOTELS FEDERATION

Open All Year

O'MALLEYS GUESTHOUSE

ORMONDE ROAD,
KILKENNY CITY

TEL: 056-71003 FAX: 056-71577
EMAIL: o'malleys@eircom.net

GUESTHOUSE ★★ MAP 7 L 7

Situated on the Ormonde Road in Kilkenny City. The house itself is in a quiet court with private parking. All rooms are tastefully decorated, en suite, multi-channel TV, direct dial phone, tea/coffee facilities. Just one minutes walk to Kilkenny Castle, Design Centre, Rothe House, St Canice's Cathedral and lots of shops, pubs and restaurants. You are assured of a Cead Mile Failte.

B&B from €25.39 to €38.09
£20.00 to £30.00

CAROLINE & EIMER CROGHAN
MANAGERS

Mastercard

Visa

6   6

Closed 24 - 26 December

SPRINGHILL COURT HOTEL

WATERFORD ROAD,
KILKENNY

TEL: 056-21122 FAX: 056-61600
EMAIL: springhillcourt@eircom.net
WEB: www.springhillcourt.com

HOTEL ★★★ MAP 7 L 7

The Springhill Court Hotel is situated only minutes from Kilkenny's vibrant and lively city centre. We have completed major developments throughout the hotel. We now offer 86 spacious en suite bedrooms, a dedicated business centre and excellent cuisine in our Claddagh Dining Room. The Paddock Bar offers weekend entertainment. The hotel is an ideal base for touring the South East. Car parking available. Sister Hotel: The Arklow Bay Hotel & Leisure Club, Wicklow.

Member of Chara Hotel Group
B&B from €51.00 to €89.00
£40.17 to £70.09

JOHN HICKEY
GENERAL MANAGER

American Express

Diners

Mastercard

Visa

☺ Weekend specials from €127.00

86   86

S 🅰 ♿ ✦ ♿

IRISH HOTELS FEDERATION

Open All Year

ZUNI

26 PATRICK STREET,
KILKENNY

TEL: 056-23999 FAX: 056-56400
EMAIL: info@zuni.ie
WEB: www.zuni.ie

HOTEL U MAP 7 L 7

Zuni is a small, contemporary family run hotel and restaurant. We are located at 26 Patrick Street, Kilkenny City Centre. Ideally located for all Kilkenny's historic sights, great shopping, wonderful restaurants, bars and night clubs. Our restaurant at Zuni offers an unforgettable dining experience with excellent food prepared by our award winning chefs. Flawless friendly service in a relaxed atmosphere.

B&B from €40.00 to €75.00
£31.50 to £59.07

PAULA BYRNE & SANDRA MCDONALD
HOSTS

American Express

Mastercard

Visa

☺ Midweek specials from €115.00 pps
(2B&B 1D)

13   13

IRISH HOTELS FEDERATION

Closed 23 - 27 December

B&B rates are per person sharing per night incl. Breakfast

CARROLLS HOTEL

**KNOCKTOPHER,
CO. KILKENNY**

TEL: 056-68082 FAX: 056-68290
EMAIL: info@carrollshotel.com
WEB: www.carrollshotel.com

HOTEL ★★ MAP 7 L 6

Situated on the N10 between Kilkenny and Waterford. Enjoy the excellent service, warmth and luxury of our newly opened family-run hotel. All rooms en suite with TV and direct dial phone. Our Sionnach Sioc Restaurant has an excellent reputation for good food. The hotel provides live music 3 nights a week. Golfing, karting, fishing, horse riding and shooting are available nearby.

B&B from €45.00 to €90.00
£35.44 to £70.88

WILLIAM CARROLL
PROPRIETOR

American Express
Diners
Mastercard
Visa

10 10

Closed 24 - 26 December

RISING SUN

**MULLINAVAT,
VIA WATERFORD,
CO. KILKENNY**

TEL: 051-898173 FAX: 051-898435
EMAIL: therisingsun@eircom.net
WEB: www.therisingsun.ie

GUESTHOUSE ★★★ MAP 4 L 6

A family run guesthouse, 12.8km from Waterford City on the main Waterford - Dublin Road. It has 10 luxurious bedrooms all en suite with D/D telephone and TV. The Rising Sun Guesthouse is an ideal base for sports enthusiasts, surrounded by some beautiful golf courses within 15-30 minutes drive. The old world charm of stone and timberwork sets the tone of comfort and relaxation in the bar and lounge. Traditional home cooked lunches and bar food served daily. Full à la carte menu and wine list.

B&B from €35.00 to €45.00
£27.56 to £35.44

CLAIRE PHELAN
MANAGER

American Express
Mastercard
Visa

10 10

Closed 24 - 28 December

MOUNT JULIET ESTATE

**THOMASTOWN,
CO. KILKENNY**

TEL: 056-73000 FAX: 056-73019
EMAIL: info@mountjuliet.ie
WEB: www.mountjuliet.com

HOTEL ★★★★ MAP 7 L 6

Celebrating 12 years as one of the most prestigious hotels in Europe, 2001 saw the opening of the Sybaritic new Spa at Mount Juliet. Guests are also invited to enjoy fishing, clay shooting, archery and horse riding on this magnificent 1500 acre estate. With the WGC American Express Championship taking place on the estate's own Jack Nicklaus course in 2002 and a host of awards for both of the estate's restaurants, there has never been a better time to visit Mount Juliet.

Member of Small Luxury Hotels

Room Rate from €190.00 to €550.00
£149.64 to £433.08

RICHARD HUDSON
GENERAL MANAGER

American Express
Diners
Mastercard
Visa

59 59

Open All Year

Room rates are per room per night

CAHIR HOUSE HOTEL

THE SQUARE,
CAHIR,
CO. TIPPERARY
TEL: 052-42727 FAX: 052-42727
EMAIL: cahirhousehotel@eircom.net

HOTEL ★★★ MAP 3 J 6

At the crossroads to the South where the N8/N24 meet. We enjoy a town centre location. Visit the Rock of Cashel, Galtee and Comeragh Mountains, Cahir Castle, Swiss Cottage, Mitchelstown Caves, Lismore. Excellent fishing on the River Suir. Enjoy golf breaks, 7 courses locally to play. O'Briens Bar, food available all day. Butlers Pantry offers full à la carte and table d'hôte menus. Quality Irish produce. Enjoy beautiful, comfortable rooms, all en suite.

B&B from €45.00 to €55.00
£35.44 to £43.32

LIAM DUFFY M.I.H.C.I.

American Express
Mastercard
Visa

☺ Weekend specials from €95.00

40 40

Closed 24 - 26 December

KILCORAN LODGE HOTEL

CAHIR,
CO. TIPPERARY
TEL: 052-41288 FAX: 052-41994
EMAIL: kilcoran@eircom.net
WEB: www.tipp.ie/kilcoran.htm

HOTEL ★★★ MAP 3 J 6

Kilcoran, a former hunting lodge set in spacious grounds overlooking beautiful countryside. An ideal holiday base located equal distance (15 min drive) between Tipperary, Cashel, Clonmel and Mitchelstown and 45 mins drive from Cork, Kilkenny and Limerick on the main Cork-Dublin road. The hotel has the charm of bygone days yet all the modern facilities of a 3 star hotel. Guests have free access to Shapes leisure centre with indoor pool etc. Golf, hillwalking, fishing, etc. locally.

B&B from €49.52 to €107.93
£39.00 to £85.00

JACQUELINE MULLEN
MANAGING DIRECTOR

American Express
Diners
Mastercard
Visa

22 22

Open All Year

AULBER HOUSE

DEERPARK,
CASHEL,
CO. TIPPERARY
TEL: 062-63713
EMAIL: beralley@eircom.net

GUESTHOUSE N MAP 3 J 6

Aulber House - newly built luxury guesthouse. Ideally located on the outskirts of the historic town of Cashel. Home away from home. Perfect base for touring the South. Beautiful views of the Rock of Cashel and Hoare Abbey from some rooms and lobby. All rooms are spacious with en suite, power showers, direct dial phones, TV, hairdryers and computer modems. Non smoking bedrooms and dining room. Golf and angling facilities available locally.

B&B from €32.00 to €40.00
£25.20 to £31.50

BERNICE & SEAN ALLEY

☺ Midweek specials from €83.00

12 12

Closed 24 - 28 December

B&B rates are per person sharing per night incl. Breakfast

BAILEYS OF CASHEL

MAIN STREET,
CASHEL,
CO. TIPPERARY
TEL: 062-61937 FAX: 062-62038
EMAIL: info@baileys-ireland.com
WEB: www.baileys-ireland.com

GUESTHOUSE ★★★ MAP 3 J 6

Baileys is a beautifully restored listed Georgian House ideally situated right in the town centre with private parking available. With en suite bedrooms individually and tastefully decorated, Baileys is perfect for an overnight stop or a relaxing weekend stay. The fully licenced Cellar Restaurant, with its open fire and cosy atmosphere, is a wonderful place to enjoy excellent food and wine with friendly and attentive service. A.A. rated 4 ♦♦♦♦

B&B from €38.10 to €44.45
£30.00 to £35.00

PHIL DELANEY
MANAGER

American Express
Diners
Mastercard
Visa

🛏️🅿️ ☎️🖥️T∪♪🅿️🄰alc
8   8

IRISH HOTELS FEDERATION

Closed 24 - 28 December

CASHEL PALACE HOTEL

MAIN STREET,
CASHEL,
CO. TIPPERARY
TEL: 062-62707 FAX: 062-61521
EMAIL: reception@cashel-palace.ie
WEB: www.cashel-palace.ie

HOTEL ★★★★ MAP 3 J 6

Built in 1730 as an Archbishop's Palace, the Cashel Palace has been restored as a hotel, complemented by tranquil walled gardens and a private walk to the famous Rock of Cashel. Our 23 bedrooms are all en suite with TV, phone, trouser press. Our Bishop's Buttery Restaurant is open for lunch and dinner, while the Guinness Bar is open for light snacks daily, both offering modern Irish cuisine at affordable prices. Sunday lunch served in our Palace Suite.

B&B from €55.00 to €137.50
£43.31 to £108.27

SUSAN & PATRICK MURPHY
PROPRIETORS

American Express
Diners
Mastercard
Visa

⛳♪♪🍴

🛏️🅿️ ☎️🖥️🚻TC🍷CM❄️∪♪🅿️S
23 23
🄰alc

IRISH HOTELS FEDERATION

Closed 24 - 26 December

DUNDRUM HOUSE HOTEL

DUNDRUM,
CASHEL,
CO. TIPPERARY
TEL: 062-71116 FAX: 062-71366
EMAIL: dundrumh@iol.ie
WEB: www.dundrumhousehotel.com

HOTEL ★★★ MAP 3 J 7

A Haven of peace and tranquillity, the hotel is surrounded by the manicured fairways of its own 18 hole championship course designed by Philip Walton. The Country Club features the Venue Clubhouse Bar/Restaurant, state of the art Health & Leisure centre with 20m deck level indoor pool, gym, jacuzzi, sauna. Beauty treatments by appointment. Elegant guest bedroom with antiques, and penthouse suites. Rossmore Restaurant is renowned for fine foods and wines.

Member of C.M.V.
B&B from €70.00 to €114.00
£55.11 to £89.76

AUSTIN & MARY CROWE
PROPRIETORS

American Express
Diners
Mastercard
Visa

⛳♪

☺ Weekend specials from €152.00

🛏️🅿️ ☎️🖥️🚻TC🍷CM❄️🍷🏠🔟
86 86
♪♪🎵🅿️S🄰alc

IRISH HOTELS FEDERATION

Open All Year

Room rates are per room per night

LEGENDS TOWNHOUSE & RESTAURANT

THE KILN,
CASHEL,
CO. TIPPERARY
TEL: 062-61292
EMAIL: info@legendsguesthouse.com
WEB: www.legendsguesthouse.com

GUESTHOUSE ★★★ MAP 3 J 5

Legends Townhouse and Restaurant, graded AA ♦♦♦♦ is uniquely situated at the foot of the Rock of Cashel. Awarded Bridgestone 100 Best Places To Stay & 100 Best Restaurants In Ireland. A warm welcome, friendly & attentive service will help you unwind & relax. Enjoy excellent cuisine in our own restaurant, fine wines & a good night's rest before waking to an extensive breakfast selection served in the shadow of 'The Rock'. An ideal base for touring Waterford, Kilkenny, Cork & Limerick. Local amenities: 18 hole golf, pony trekking, guided walks, craft centres.

B&B from € 29.00 to € 57.00
£22.84 to £44.89

ROSEMARY & MICHAEL O'NEILL

Mastercard
Visa

☺ Weekend specials from €95.00

🛏 🐾 ☎ 🖵 T C ❄ ♲ ♪ ♫ 🄿 🄶 ald ♨
7 7

IRISH HOTELS FEDERATION

Closed 17 February - 12 March

BRIGHTON HOUSE

1 BRIGHTON PLACE,
CLONMEL,
CO. TIPPERARY
TEL: 052-23665 FAX: 052-25210
EMAIL: brighton@iol.ie
WEB: www.tipp.ie/brighton.htm

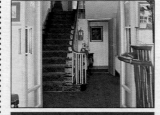

GUESTHOUSE ★★ MAP 3 K 5

Family run 3 storey Georgian guest house, with a hotel ambience and antique furnishings. Clonmel Town centre - the largest inland town in Ireland bridging Rosslare Harbour (132km) with Killarney (160km) and the South West. Host to Fleadh Cheoil na hEireann 1993/94. Visit Rock of Cashel, Mitchelstown Caves, Cahir Castle etc. Golf, fishing and pony trekking arranged locally. All rooms direct dial phones, TV, radio, hairdryer and tea/coffee making facilities.

B&B from € 31.75 to € 38.10
£25.01 to £30.01

BERNIE MORRIS
PROPRIETOR

Mastercard
Visa

🛏 🐾 ☎ 🖵 T P S ♨
6 5

IRISH HOTELS FEDERATION

Closed 24 - 29 December

CLONMEL ARMS HOTEL

CLONMEL,
CO. TIPPERARY

TEL: 052-21233 FAX: 052-21526
EMAIL: theclonmelarms@eircom.net
WEB: www.tipp.ie/clonmelarms.htm

HOTEL ★★★ MAP 3 K 5

Town centre hotel ideally situated either for business or pleasure. All 30 rooms en suite, direct dial telephone and colour TV. Full conference facilities available. The Paddock Restaurant open until 9.30pm each day provides the perfect setting for your personal or business requirements. The Paddock Bar is ideal for a quite drink or alternatively a lively night out with the Paddock music sessions every weekend. Food in the Paddock is served daily.

B&B from € 57.15 to € 76.20
£45.00 to £60.00

NEILUS MCDONNELL
MANAGER

American Express
Diners
Mastercard
Visa

🛏 🐾 ☎ 🖵 ⬆ T C ➤ C M ♲ ♪ ♫ P S
30 30
🄿 ald ♨

IRISH HOTELS FEDERATION

Closed 25 December

B&B rates are per person sharing per night incl. Breakfast

FENNESSY'S HOTEL

GLADSTONE STREET,
CLONMEL,
CO. TIPPERARY
TEL: 052-23680 FAX: 052-23783

HOTEL ★★ MAP 3 K 5

Established old hotel. This beautiful Georgian building is newly restored and refurbished. Right in the centre of Clonmel, it is easily located by spotting from afar the green steeple of the town's main church, opposite which it stands. All bedrooms have direct dial phone, large TV, hair dryer, en suite, some with jacuzzi. Family run hotel. Elegant and antique decor throughout. After your visit, you will wish to return.

B&B from €32.00 to €45.00
£25.20 to £35.44

RICHARD AND ESTHER FENNESSY
PROPRIETORS

Mastercard
Visa

10   10

Open All Year

HEARNS HOTEL

PARNELL STREET,
CLONMEL,
CO. TIPPERARY
TEL: 052-21611 FAX: 052-21135

HOTEL ★★ MAP 3 K 5

Situated in the centre of Clonmel Town, the historical Bianconi House, is ideal as a touring base for Cahir Castle, Rock of Cashel, Holycross Abbey, The Vee, Mitchelstown Caves and seaside resorts of Tramore and Clonea. All bedrooms are fully en suite with direct dial phone and TV. Ample parking, relaxing bar, live entertainment at weekends. Also available is our new restaurant, which serves continental food, new nightclub and attractive conference facilities.

B&B from €50.00 to €57.00
£39.38 to £44.89

J J HEALY
GENERAL MANAGER

American Express
Diners
Mastercard
Visa

25   25

alc

Closed 25 - 26 December

HOTEL MINELLA & LEISURE CENTRE

CLONMEL,
CO. TIPPERARY

TEL: 052-22388 FAX: 052-24381
EMAIL: hotelminella@eircom.net
WEB: www.hotelminella.ie

HOTEL ★★★ MAP 3 K 5

Country house hotel set in landscaped grounds along the River Suir. Hotel Minella prides itself in its exceptional service & hospitality. Rooms throughout are elegantly furnished, 5 suites with jacuzzis, 3 with 4-poster beds & private steam rooms. The Award Winning Leisure Centre is a favourite with its guests: 20 meter pool, Gym, Outdoor Canadian Hot Tub, Steam Room, Massage & Therapy Rooms. Tennis court. AA Rosette Restaurant. Conference room for 500. Family owned. An ideal venue for touring the South East.

B&B from €75.00 to €110.00
£59.07 to £86.63

ELIZABETH NALLEN
MANAGING DIRECTOR

American Express
Diners
Mastercard
Visa

☺ Weekend specials from €165.00

70   70

Closed 23 - 29 December

Room rates are per room per night

MULCAHYS

47 GLADSTONE STREET,
CLONMEL,
CO. TIPPERARY
TEL: 052-25054 FAX: 052-24544
EMAIL: mulcahys@eircom.net
WEB: www.mulcahys.ie

GUESTHOUSE ★★ MAP 3 K 5

Mulcahys is run by the Higgins family. Our bedrooms are tastefully designed, all en suite with tea/coffee making facilities, multi channel TV and hairdryer. The carvery opens for lunch from 12pm and our "East Lane" menu is served from 6pm which includes lobsters and oysters from our fish tank. "Dance the night away" at our award winning nightclub "Dannos". Some of Ireland's best golf courses are within easy reach of Clonmel and the River Suir has been described as an "anglers paradise".

B&B from € 35.00 to € 50.00
£27.56 to £39.37

ROS DONAGHUE

American Express
Mastercard
Visa

10 10

Closed 24 December - 02 January

RAHEEN HOUSE HOTEL

RAHEEN ROAD,
CLONMEL,
CO. TIPPERARY
TEL: 052-22140 FAX: 052-27528

WEB: www.tipp.ie/raheen.htm

HOTEL U MAP 3 K 5

Raheen Country House Hotel, a beautiful old Georgian house dating back to 1832, is situated within its own 3.5 acres of beautifully tended gardens at the foot of the Comeragh Mountains. It's riverside location provides a tranquil countryside setting for a relaxing break, yet is only five minutes walk from the centre of Clonmel.

B&B from € 57.50 to € 57.50
£45.00 to £45.00

STEPHEN WEIR/ELIZABETH DAY
MANAGER/PROPRIETOR

Mastercard
Visa

☺ Weekend specials from €133.32

14 14

Open All Year

RECTORY HOUSE HOTEL

DUNDRUM,
CO. TIPPERARY

TEL: 062-71266 FAX: 062-71115
EMAIL: rectoryh@iol.ie
WEB: www.rectoryhousehotel.com

HOTEL ★★★ MAP 3 I 7

The Rectory House Hotel is a family run hotel standing amidst its tree lined grounds. It is a gracious country house providing an ideal haven for the country lover. Comfort and tranquillity are offered to our guests in tastefully decorated rooms en suite. Our candlelit restaurant and conservatory provides home cooking. Member of The Best Western International Group. 1km from 18-hole golf course.

Member of Best Western Hotels
B&B from € 45.00 to € 57.00
£35.44 to £44.88

JAMES SHEILS
PROPRIETOR

Mastercard
Visa

10 10

alc

Closed 23 - 27 December

B&B rates are per person sharing per night incl. Breakfast

AHERLOW HOUSE HOTEL

GLEN OF AHERLOW,
CO. TIPPERARY

TEL: 062-56153 FAX: 062-56212
EMAIL: aherlow@iol.ie
WEB: www.aherlowhouse.ie

HOTEL ★★★ MAP 3 I 6

Aherlow House Hotel and 4**** de luxe holiday homes. The Lodges are set in the middle of a coniferous forest just 4 miles from Tipperary Town. Originally a hunting lodge now converted into an exquisitely furnished hotel. Aherlow House welcomes you to its peaceful atmosphere, enhanced by a fine reputation for hospitality, excellent cuisine and good wines. Overlooks the Glen of Aherlow and has beautiful views of the Galtee Mountains. Activities can be arranged.

B&B from €62.00 to €82.00
£48.83 to £64.58

FRANCES FOGARTY
MANAGER

American Express
Diners
Mastercard
Visa

🛏 🛎 ☎ ⊺ Ⓣ C ➔ CM ❄ U ♪ Ⓟ Ⓢ
30   30
🖵 alc ☕
IRISH HOTELS FEDERATION
Open All Year

GLEN HOTEL

GLEN OF AHERLOW,
CO. TIPPERARY

TEL: 062-56146 FAX: 062-56152

HOTEL ★★ MAP 3 I 6

The Glen Hotel set in the shadows of the majestic Galtee Mountains, amidst the splendour of the Aherlow Valley is just 5 miles from Tipperary Town. To relax, dream, reminisce or plan - this is the ideal haven. Our bedrooms are all en suite and have been recently tastefully redecorated. This family operated hotel has built up a fine reputation for excellent cuisine and offers friendly and efficient service. Hill walking, horse riding, fishing and golf.

B&B from €42.00 to €55.00
£33.08 to £43.32

MARGOT AND JAMES COUGHLAN
PROPRIETORS

American Express
Diners
Mastercard
Visa

✅🍽

🛏 🛎 ☎ ⊺ Ⓣ C ➔ CM ❄ U ♪ Ⓟ Ⓢ
24   24
🖵 alc ☕
IRISH HOTELS FEDERATION
Open All Year

HORSE AND JOCKEY INN

HORSE AND JOCKEY,
(NEAR CASHEL),
CO. TIPPERARY

TEL: 0504-44192 FAX: 0504-44747
EMAIL: horseandjockeyinn@eircom.net
WEB: www.horseandjockeyinn.com

HOTEL ★★★ MAP 7 J 7

The Horse and Jockey Inn, located at the heartland of County Tipperary, midway between Cork and Dublin on the N8 holds great association with people from sporting, cultural and political walks of life. Our modern refurbishment includes spacious lounge and bar facilities, a high quality restaurant, de luxe accommodation and a modern conference centre. Experience the atmosphere that's steeped in tradition and share with us the real Ireland, in the comfort of our new inn.

B&B from €60.00 to €65.00
£47.25 to £51.19

TOM EGAN
PROPRIETOR

American Express
Diners
Mastercard
Visa

🛏 🛎 ☎ ⊺ Ⓣ C CM ❄ U ♪ Ⓟ alc ☕
29   29
Inet FAX
IRISH HOTELS FEDERATION
Open All Year

Room rates are per room per night

ARDAGH HOUSE

KILLENAULE,
CO. TIPPERARY

TEL: 052-56224 FAX: 052-56224
EMAIL: ahouse@iol.ie

GUESTHOUSE ★ MAP 3 K 7

Fully licensed family guesthouse, piano lounge bar, residents' lounge, rooms en suite, home cooking. Set in the shadow of romantic Slievenamon, in the area of the Derrynaflan Chalice, the famous Coolmore Stud, in the heart of the Golden Vale. Near Holycross Abbey, Cashel and Kilkenny. Central for hunting, fishing, shooting, golf, horse riding and less strenuous walks through the hills of Killenaule. Finally, just one hour from the sea.

B&B from €26.00 to €29.00
£20.48 to £22.84

KATHLEEN & DAVID CORMACK
PROPRIETORS

Mastercard
Visa

6   6

IRISH HOTELS FEDERATION

Closed 25 December

ACH NA SHEEN GUESTHOUSE

CLONMEL ROAD,
TIPPERARY,
CO. TIPPERARY

TEL: 062-51298 FAX: 062-80467
EMAIL: gernoonan@eircom.net

GUESTHOUSE ★★ MAP 3 I 6

Family run guesthouse, 5 minutes from the town centre with a spacious sunlounge and diningroom overlooking gardens and the beautiful Galtee Mountains. Our 10 rooms, 7 are en suite, are all equipped with TV and tea/coffee making facilities on request.
Ach-na-Sheen is adjacent to the picturesque Glen of Aherlow where fishing and hill walking can be arranged. Golf can be enjoyed at any one of 3 nearby championship courses. Ger & Sylvia Noonan offer you the utmost in Irish hospitality.

B&B from €30.00 to €40.00
£23.63 to £31.50

GER & SYLVIA NOONAN
PROPRIETORS

Mastercard
Visa

9   7

IRISH HOTELS FEDERATION

Closed 01 December - 01 January

BALLYGLASS COUNTRY HOUSE HOTEL

GLEN OF AHERLOW ROAD,
BALLYGLASS,
TIPPERARY TOWN

TEL: 062-52104 FAX: 062-52229
EMAIL: ballyglasshouse@eircom.net

HOTEL ★ MAP 3 I 6

Family run Ballyglass Country House Hotel is set in its own grounds. The hotel is very comfortable with all facilities. There is a fine restaurant serving the best of local produce. The Forge Bar is adjacent to the hotel for that quiet drink. We are just 2 miles from Tipperary Town at the entrance to the Glen of Aherlow where there are an abundance of superb walks.

B&B from €35.55 to €36.82
£28.00 to £29.00

JOAN AND BILL BYRNE
PROPRIETORS

American Express
Mastercard
Visa

☺   Weekend specials from €76.18

10   10

IRISH HOTELS FEDERATION

Closed 24 - 25 December

B&B rates are per person sharing per night incl. Breakfast

ROYAL HOTEL

BRIDGE STREET,
TIPPERARY TOWN,
CO. TIPPERARY
TEL: 062-33244 FAX: 062-33596
EMAIL: royalht@iol.ie

HOTEL ★★ MAP 3 I 6

Situated in Tipperary Town, a familiar meeting place serving excellent food from 8am to 10pm daily, using finest quality local produce, tastefully decorated rooms with all amenities. Just a few minutes from Tipperary Race Course, 3 outstanding golf clubs (special arrangements & packages available to the hotel for Tipperary, Dundrum & Ballykisteen clubs). Sport & Leisure Complex 3 mins from the hotel. The Excell Theatre within a short walking distance. So if its business or pleasure, a warm welcome awaits you.

B&B from €38.09 to €57.15
£30.00 to £45.00

KAREN BYRNES & EOIN O'SULLIVAN
HOSTS

American Express
Diners
Mastercard
Visa

16 16

alc

IRISH HOTELS FEDERATION

Closed 24 - 26 December

CLIFF HOUSE HOTEL

ARDMORE,
CO. WATERFORD
TEL: 024-94106 FAX: 024-94496
EMAIL: thecliffhousehotel@eircom.net
WEB: www.cliffhotelardmore.com

HOTEL ★★ MAP 3 K 3

Located in Ardmore which is renowned for its famous Round Tower and St. Declan's Well. This is a family owned hotel with a warm friendly atmosphere. Enjoy locally produced food in tranquil surroundings with spectacular views of the sea from both the Waterfront Restaurant and Bar and all the en suite bedrooms.

B&B from €41.50 to €54.00
£32.68 to £42.53

JOHN AND MARGARET FOLEY
PROPRIETORS

Mastercard
Visa

13 13

Closed 01 November - 28 February

NEWTOWN FARM GUESTHOUSE

GRANGE,
ARDMORE, VIA YOUGHAL,
CO. WATERFORD
TEL: 024-94143 FAX: 024-94054
EMAIL: newtownfarm@eircom.net
WEB: www.newtownfarm.com

GUESTHOUSE ★★★ MAP 3 K 3

Family-run farm guesthouse in scenic location, surrounded by its own farmlands with dairying as the main enterprise, with views of the Atlantic Ocean, hills and cliff walks. All bedrooms en suite with tea/coffee making facilities, TV, DD phone and hairdryer. Grange is 6 minutes from the beach and Ardmore Round Tower and Cathedral, built in the 12th century, raises its heights to 97 feet. 2 hours drive from Port of Rosslare. Signposted on N25 turn left at Flemings Pub, 200m.

Member of Premier Guesthouses
B&B from €29.00 to €35.00
£22.84 to £27.56

TERESA O'CONNOR
PROPRIETOR

Mastercard
Visa

☺ Midweek specials from €95.00

7 7

7 Inet

IRISH HOTELS FEDERATION

Closed 20 December - 10 January

Room rates are per room per night

ROUND TOWER HOTEL

COLLEGE ROAD,
ARDMORE,
CO. WATERFORD

TEL: 024-94494 FAX: 024-94254
EMAIL: rth@eircom.net

HOTEL U   MAP 3 K 3

Situated within walking distance of Ardmore's award-winning beach, the Round Tower Hotel offers 10 well appointed en suite bedrooms. Fresh local produce feature prominently on both the bar and restaurant menus. The ancient monastic settlement of St. Declan & the Round Tower are situated behind the hotel. Ardmore also boasts some world famous cliff walks and breathtaking scenery. Ardmore is 21kms from Dungarvan & a 2 hour drive from the port of Rosslare on the Primary N25 route.

B&B from €40.00 to €45.00
£31.50 to £35.44

AIDAN QUIRKE
PROPRIETOR

Mastercard
Visa

Closed 01 November - 28 February

HANORAS COTTAGE

NIRE VALLEY,
BALLYMACARBRY,
CO. WATERFORD

TEL: 052-36134 FAX: 052-36540
EMAIL: hanorascottage@eircom.net
WEB: www.hanorascottage.com

GUESTHOUSE ★★★★   MAP 3 K 5

A haven of peace and tranquillity in the Comeragh Mountains, Hanoras Cottage has everything for discerning guests. Relax in the sheer bliss of an adult only house with the soothing sounds of the Nire River running by. Spacious rooms with jacuzzi tubs. Superior rooms for that special occasion! Enjoy excellent cuisine from our Ballymaloe school chefs who cater for all diets. AA & RAC ◆◆◆◆◆ awards. Walking, golf, horse-riding and just relaxing!

B&B from €65.00 to €85.00
£51.19 to £66.94

SEAMUS & MARY WALL
PROPRIETORS

Mastercard
Visa

Closed 20 - 28 December

RICHMOND HOUSE

CAPPOQUIN,
CO. WATERFORD

TEL: 058-54278 FAX: 058-54988
EMAIL: info@richmondhouse.net
WEB: www.richmond.house.net

GUESTHOUSE ★★★★   MAP 3 J 4

Delightful 18th century Georgian Countryhouse and fully licenced award winning restaurant set in private grounds. Relax in total peace and tranquillity in front of log fires. Each room is a perfect blend of Georgian splendour combined with all modern comforts for the discerning guest. AA ◆◆◆◆◆. Recommended in the Bridgestone Guides; 100 Best Places to Stay and 100 Best Restaurants in Ireland. Recent Winner of the Gilbeys Gold Medal Award for Excellence.

B&B from €64.00 to €108.00
£50.40 to £85.06

PAUL & CLAIRE DEEVY
PROPRIETORS

American Express
Diners
Mastercard
Visa

Closed 23 December - 20 January

B&B rates are per person sharing per night incl. Breakfast

THREE RIVERS GUEST HOUSE

CHEEKPOINT,
CO. WATERFORD

TEL: 051-382520 FAX: 051-382542
EMAIL: mail@threerivers.ie
WEB: www.threerivers.ie

GUESTHOUSE ★★★ MAP 4 M 5

AA Selected ♦♦♦ guesthouse overlooking scenic Waterford Estuary. Situated on the outskirts of the historic village, Cheekpoint, with its award winning pubs and seafood restaurants. Sample the delights of breakfast in our Estuary View dining room or relax over coffee in our spacious lounge. Ideal base for touring the sunny South East, close to Waterford, Dunmore East, Tramore and 2km from Faithlegg Golf Course. All rooms en suite with direct dial phone.

Member of Premier Guesthouses

B&B from €34.00 to €45.00
£26.78 to £35.44

TIM & AINE HAIER

American Express
Mastercard
Visa

Midweek specials from €92.00
excl. July/Aug.

14   14

Closed 20 December - 7 January

BARNAWEE BRIDGE GUESTHOUSE

KILMINION,
DUNGARVAN,
CO. WATERFORD
TEL: 058-42074

WEB: www.waterford-accomodation.com/barnawee.htm

GUESTHOUSE N MAP 3 K 4

Our newly built guesthouse with fabulous sea and mountain views near all local amenities including three 18 hole golf courses, indoor swimming, sea angling, tennis, fishing and bird watching. Also various country side walks. Rooms are very spacious all with en suite and all modern facilities available to all our customers. The making for a very enjoyable stay. Telephone 087 / 086-262 0269.

B&B from €32.00 to €45.00
£25.20 to £35.44

MICHELLE DWANE/GARY TREEN
PROPRIETORS

Mastercard
Visa

Midweek specials from €70.00

6   6

Open All Year

CLONEA STRAND HOTEL, GOLF & LEISURE

CLONEA,
DUNGARVAN,
CO. WATERFORD
TEL: 058-42416 FAX: 058-42880
EMAIL: info@clonea.com
WEB: www.clonea.com

HOTEL ★★★ MAP 3 K 4

Clonea Strand Hotel overlooking Clonea Beach. Family run by John and Ann McGrath. All rooms en suite with tea/coffee making facilities, hair-dryer and colour TV. Indoor leisure centre with heated pool, jacuzzi, sauna, Turkish bath, gymnasium and ten pin bowling alley. Situated close by is our 18 hole golf course bordering on the Atlantic Ocean with a scenic background of Dungarvan Bay and Comeragh Mountains. Our Bay Restaurant specialises in locally caught seafood.

B&B from €42.00 to €82.00
£33.08 to £64.58

MARK KNOWLES
GEN.MGR.GROUP/MARKETING

American Express
Diners
Mastercard
Visa

58   58

Open All Year

Room rates are per room per night

LAWLORS HOTEL

BRIDGE STREET,
DUNGARVAN,
CO. WATERFORD
TEL: 058-41122 FAX: 058-41000
EMAIL: info@lawlors-hotel.ie
WEB: www.lawlors-hotel.ie

HOTEL ★★★ MAP 3 K 4

Lawlors Hotel is family run with 89 bedrooms, all en suite with tea/coffee making facilities, TV and direct dial phone. Lawlors is the ideal choice for your stay in the beautiful West Waterford countryside. Conferences, Weddings, Parties, Seminars are especially catered for. Good food is a speciality at Lawlors and the friendly atmosphere of Dungarvan Town is brought to life in the Old Worlde bar surroundings.

B&B from €41.00 to €70.00
£32.29 to £55.12

MICHAEL BURKE
PROPRIETOR

American Express
Diners
Mastercard
Visa

89 89

Closed 25 December

PARK HOTEL

DUNGARVAN,
CO. WATERFORD
TEL: 058-42899 FAX: 058-42969
EMAIL: photel@indigo.ie

HOTEL ★★★ MAP 3 K 4

Overlooking the Colligan River Estuary, owned and run by the Flynn Family, whose experience in the hotel business is your best guarantee of an enjoyable and memorable stay. The hotel's spacious and comfortable bedrooms have been furnished with flair and imagination. All have private bathroom, direct dial telephone, 16 channel satellite TV. The hotel's leisure centre has a 20m swimming pool, sauna, steam room & gym.

B&B from €48.25 to €62.22
£38.00 to £49.00

PIERCE FLYNN
MANAGER

American Express
Diners
Mastercard
Visa

29 29

Open All Year

POWERSFIELD HOUSE

BALLINAMUCK,
DUNGARVAN,
CO. WATERFORD
TEL: 058-45594 FAX: 058-45550
EMAIL: powersfieldhouse@cablesurf.com
WEB: www.powersfield.com

GUESTHOUSE N MAP 3 K 4

Powersfield House is situated just outside Dungarvan on the R672. Ideally located for the three 18-hole Golf Courses and beautiful beaches. The bedrooms are individually decorated using antique furniture, crisp linens and fresh flowers. Dinner is served on Thursday, Friday and Saturday nights in our restaurant. Advance booking advised. Wine and beer license.

Member of Premier Guesthouses
B&B from €41.00 to €51.00
£32.29 to £40.17

EUNICE & EDMUND POWER

Mastercard
Visa

6 6

Open All Year

B&B rates are per person sharing per night incl. Breakfast

SEAVIEW

WINDGAP,
N25/YOUGHAL ROAD, DUNGARVAN,
CO. WATERFORD

TEL: 058-41583 FAX: 058-41679

EMAIL: faheyn@gofree.indigo.ie
WEB: www.amireland.com/seaview/

GUESTHOUSE ★★★ MAP 3 K 4

Want your vacation to never stop being a vacation? Enjoy breakfast overlooking the sea? Play one of Dungarvans three 18 hole golf courses or take a bus tour of the area and let someone else do the driving. How about dinner, entertained by traditional Irish musicians, at the nearby Marine Bar? Make every ounce of your vacation count. Try Seaview on N25 5km west of Dungarvan. Fax and e-mail facilities available. Continental and Full Irish breakfast served. Laundry service available.

B&B from €25.00 to €30.00
£19.69 to £23.62

NORA & MARTIN & MEALLA FAHEY

Mastercard
Visa

⌂ ♪ ☎ ⌷ T C CM✲ʊ J P ⚐ S ⚏
8   8

Open All Year

HAVEN HOTEL

DUNMORE EAST,
CO. WATERFORD

TEL: 051-383150 FAX: 051-383488

EMAIL: info@thehavenhotel.com
WEB: www.thehavenhotel.com

HOTEL ★★ MAP 4 M 5

The Haven Hotel is family owned and managed. Situated in Dunmore East, one of Ireland's most beautiful seaside resorts. The restaurant is renowned for its first class food and specialises in prime rib beef, steaks and locally caught seafood. The Haven is an ideal location for day trips to the many surrounding golf clubs. Children are also made especially welcome with our motto being - the children of today are the customers of tomorrow.

B&B from €50.00 to €65.00
£39.38 to £51.19

JEAN & JOHN KELLY
MANAGERS/OWNERS

Mastercard
Visa

⌂ ♪ ☎ ⌷ /AC ⤶ CM✲ʊ J P S
24   24
⚐ ⓐⓛⓒ ☕

Closed 30 October - 03 March

OCEAN HOTEL

DUNMORE EAST,
CO. WATERFORD

TEL: 051-383136 FAX: 051-383576

EMAIL: oceanhotel@ireland.com

HOTEL ★★ MAP 4 M 5

The Ocean Hotel 15 minutes drive from Waterford City, is situated in one of Ireland's most picturesque villages. The Jewel of the sunny South East. We offer you the personal attention & service, only a family run hotel can provide. Our extensive à la carte menu is available in both dining room and bar with a strong emphasis on seafood dishes. Our menu is reasonably priced. Golf packages arranged. Our new Alfred D Snow Bar is air conditioned with decor depicting a nautical theme. Entertainment in the bar most nights during the summer and Saturday nights all year around.

B&B from €44.45 to €57.15
£35.01 to £45.01

BRENDAN GALLAGHER
PROPRIETOR

American Express
Diners
Mastercard
Visa

✓

⌂ ♪ ☎ ⌷ T C ⤶ CMʊ J ♪P ⚐ ⓐⓛⓒ
12   12

Closed 25 December

Room rates are per room per night

FAITHLEGG HOUSE HOTEL

FAITHLEGG,
CO. WATERFORD

TEL: 051-382000 FAX: 051-382010
EMAIL: faithleg@iol.ie
WEB: www.faithlegg.com

HOTEL U   MAP 4 M 5

A Tower Group Hotel - Faithlegg House Hotel is located on the already renowned 18-hole championship golf course, overlooking the Estuary of the River Suir. This elegantly restored Country House Hotel incorporates 82 bedrooms, including 14 master rooms in the original house; a unique fitness, health and beauty club featuring a 17m pool; plus comprehensive meeting, conference and event management facilities. RAC ♦♦♦♦ recommended.

Member of Tower Hotel Group

B&B from €95.25 to €165.00
£75.02 to £129.95

MADGE BARRY
GENERAL MANAGER

American Express
Diners
Mastercard
Visa

☺ Weekend specials from €177.75

82 82

Closed 23 - 27 December

LISMORE HOTEL

MAIN STREET,
LISMORE,
CO. WATERFORD

TEL: 058-54555 FAX: 058-53068

WEB: www.trailblazers.ie/lismorehotel

HOTEL ★★   MAP 3 J 4

Situated in the heart of historical Lismore, on the Munster Blackwater River, this newly refurbished hotel is the ideal location for a relaxing break. Take a walk back through time and enjoy Lismore with its majestic castle and gardens, historical cathedral and peaceful river walks. Horse riding, fishing and golf are all available locally. Our warm and friendly staff await your arrival and we look forward to serving you in our award winning restaurant.

B&B from €38.50 to €55.00
£30.31 to £43.30

JAMES KELLY
MANAGER

Mastercard
Visa

☺ Weekend specials from €80.00

19 19

Closed 25 December

BELAIR GUEST HOUSE

RACECOURSE ROAD,
TRAMORE,
CO. WATERFORD

TEL: 051-381605 FAX: 051-386688

GUESTHOUSE ★★   MAP 4 L 5

Belair is a beautiful Georgian house built in 1797 featuring delightful enclosed gardens. The house, which overlooks Tramore Bay and miles of sandy beach, has been newly refurbished throughout. All rooms en suite, TV, phone, tea/coffee facilities. It is quiet and peaceful for that restful break and offers safe parking. Fishing, tennis, horseriding, surfing, golfing and Splashworld all at hand. Waterford Crystal and six excellent golf courses within an eight mile radius.

B&B from €31.74 to €44.44
£25.00 to £35.00

MARY CURRAN
MANAGER

Mastercard
Visa

6 6

Closed 31 October - 15 March

B&B rates are per person sharing per night incl. Breakfast

GRAND HOTEL

TRAMORE,
CO. WATERFORD

TEL: 051-381414 FAX: 051-386428
EMAIL: thegrandhotel@eircom.net
WEB: www.grand-hotel.ie

HOTEL ★★★ MAP 4 L 5

The Grand Hotel opened it's doors in 1790 and for more than two hundred years it's name has been synonymous with the grace and style of the era. It overlooks the golden strands of Tramore which are probably the most enchanting and the most popular of the Atlantic coast resorts. The 83 newly refurbished bedrooms have bathrooms en suite, DD phones, multi channel TV, tea/coffee facilities and hair dryers.

B&B from €44.45 to €57.15
£35.01 to £45.01

SEAN WALSH
GENERAL MANAGER

American Express
Diners
Mastercard
Visa

Weekend specials from €101.60

83   83

Open All Year

MAJESTIC HOTEL

TRAMORE,
CO. WATERFORD

TEL: 051-381761 FAX: 051-381766
EMAIL: info@majestic-hotel.ie
WEB: www.majestic-hotel.ie

HOTEL ★★★ MAP 4 L 5

A warm welcome awaits you at the family owned and managed Majestic Hotel, overlooking Tramore Bay and its famous 3 miles of sandy beach. Only 10km from Waterford City. All 60 bedrooms are en suite with TV, phone, hairdryer & tea/coffee facilities. Full leisure facilities available to guests at Splashworld Health and Fitness Club near hotel. Special golf packages on south east sunshine circuit. Les Routiers Gold Key Award 1999.

Member of Les Routiers Ireland
B&B from €45.00 to €60.00
£35.44 to £47.25

ANNETTE & DANNY DEVINE
PROPRIETORS

American Express
Mastercard
Visa

Weekend specials from €102.00

60   60

Open All Year

O'SHEA'S HOTEL

STRAND STREET,
TRAMORE,
CO. WATERFORD

TEL: 051-381246 FAX: 051-390144
EMAIL: info@osheas-hotel.com
WEB: www.osheas-hotel.com

HOTEL ★★ MAP 4 L 5

O'Shea's is an intimate family run hotel, newly refurbished and extended, situated beside Tramore's famous 5km safe sandy beach and just a few minutes from Splashworld. Sample our seafood and steak restaurant, full bar food menu also available. Entertainment every night during Summer. Golfing holiday packages are our speciality - we will organise your tee times at any of the surrounding golf courses. We look forward to meeting you.

B&B from €35.00 to €65.00
£27.56 to £51.19

NOREEN & JOE O'SHEA
PROPRIETORS

American Express
Diners
Mastercard
Visa

Weekend specials from €110.00

30   30

Closed 22 - 31 December

Room rates are per room per night

SANDS HOTEL

STRAND ROAD,
TRAMORE,
CO. WATERFORD

TEL: 051-381355 FAX: 051-393869

HOTEL N MAP 4 L 5

The Sands Hotel, newly refurbished and extended. All rooms en suite, TV, direct dial telephone, tea/coffee facilities. Situated in the heart of Tramore's tourist area, a minutes walk from the beach and Splashworld. A choice of 3 bars with entertainment to suit all ages. Carvery lunches, evening grill menu, full bar food menu. Friendly atmosphere and homely welcome.

B&B from €44.00 to €57.00
£34.65 to £44.88

PAUL CUSACK GEN. MANAGER
FREDDIE PIPER OWNER

Mastercard
Visa

20 20

Closed 24 - 31 December

ARLINGTON LODGE COUNTRY HOUSE & RESTAURANT

JOHN'S HILL,
WATERFORD

TEL: 051-878584 FAX: 051-878127
EMAIL: info@arlingtonlodge.com
WEB: www.arlingtonlodge.com

GUESTHOUSE ★★★★ MAP 4 L 5

Newly opened, the former Bishop's house has been lovingly restored to provide all the amenities of a luxury 4**** country house. Each deluxe bedroom has a unique style, whilst the elegance of the Robert Paul Restaurant perfectly reflects the superb quality of the finest cuisine. For a short break, a memorable wedding, special occasion or intimate retreat for a business meeting, Arlington Lodge is the perfect venue, an oasis in the heart of Waterford City. AA♦♦♦♦.

B&B from €57.50 to €115.00
£45.28 to £90.57

MAURICE KELLER
MANAGER/PROPRIETOR

American Express
Mastercard
Visa

Special offers available

20 20

inet

HOTELS
FEDERATION

Closed 24 - 27 December

BELFRY HOTEL

CONDUIT LANE,
WATERFORD

TEL: 051-844800 FAX: 051-844814
EMAIL: info@belfryhotel.ie
WEB: www.belfryhotel.ie

HOTEL ★★★ MAP 4 L 5

This new, family-run hotel is a wonderful blend of modern and traditional design, creating a warm and welcoming atmosphere. The hotel offers its guests a combination of comfort, excellent food, service and friendly hospitality. With its luxurious bedrooms, the delightful Riada Restaurant, stylish Chapter House bar and great city centre location, the Reid family invites you to enjoy every minute of your stay at the Belfry Hotel.

B&B from €47.00 to €89.00
£37.02 to £70.09

SHARON REID
GENERAL MANAGER

American Express
Mastercard
Visa

Weekend specials from €100.00

49 49

inet

HOTELS
FEDERATION

Closed 24 - 26 December

B&B rates are per person sharing per night incl. Breakfast

BRIDGE HOTEL

**NO 1 THE QUAY,
WATERFORD**

TEL: 051-877222 FAX: 051-877229
EMAIL: info@bridgehotelwaterford.com
WEB: www.bridgehotelwaterford.com

HOTEL ★★★ MAP 4 L 5

Whether your stay in Waterford's Viking City is one of business or pleasure, you will quickly find that the Bridge Hotel, situated in the heart of this vibrant and exciting city, is exactly where you will want to stay. This 100 en suite bedroom hotel offers the finest traditions of quality & service expected from a modern 3*** hotel. Our restaurants specialise in local seafood & succulent steaks. Relax & enjoy a drink in our Timbertoes Bar. 2 minutes walk from bus & rail.

Member of MinOtel Ireland Hotel Group

B&B from € 48.25 to € 82.53
£38.00 to £65.00

BRIDGET & JIM TREACY
PROPRIETORS

American Express
Diners
Mastercard
Visa

Weekend specials from €113.00

100 100

Closed 24 - 26 December

COACH HOUSE

**BUTLERSTOWN CASTLE,
BUTLERSTOWN, CORK ROAD,
WATERFORD**

TEL: 051-384656 FAX: 051-384751
EMAIL: coachhse@iol.ie
WEB: homepages.iol.ie/~coachhse

GUESTHOUSE ★★★ MAP 4 L 5

Surround yourself with comfort in this elegantly restored 19th century house. Situated 3 miles from Waterford City (Waterford Crystal 5 mins away) in an historic, tranquil, romantic setting (13th century castle in grounds). All rooms en suite. Private sauna available. 5 golf courses within 6 miles radius. Excellent pubs, restaurants nearby. 3*** Irish Tourist Board, AA ♦♦♦♦, Michelin recommended, Best Magazine's No.1 in Ireland. 'Crackling log fires and personal attention'.

B&B from € 35.50 to € 44.50
£27.96 to £35.05

DES O'KEEFFE
PROPRIETOR

American Express
Diners
Mastercard
Visa

7 7

Closed 20 December - 20 January

DIAMOND HILL COUNTRY HOUSE

**SLIEVERUE,
WATERFORD**

TEL: 051-832855 FAX: 051-832254
EMAIL: diamondhill29@hotmail.com
WEB: www.diamondhillhouse.com

GUESTHOUSE ★★★ MAP 4 L 5

Situated 1.2km from Waterford City off the Rosslare Waterford Road N25. A long established guesthouse of considerable charm and friendliness, set in its own national award winning gardens. The house has been extensively refurbished incorporating family heirlooms and antiques resulting in a countryside oasis, a haven of luxury and tranquility, yet only mins from the bustling city of Waterford. Recommended by Frommers, Foders, Michelin, AA, RAC. Member of Premier Guesthouses.

Member of Premier Guesthouses

B&B from € 32.00 to € 40.00
£25.20 to £31.50

MARJORIE SMITH LEHANE
OWNER

Mastercard
Visa

18 18

Closed 25 - 26 December

Room rates are per room per night

DOOLEY'S HOTEL

THE QUAY,
WATERFORD

TEL: 051-873531 FAX: 051-870262
EMAIL: hotel@dooleys-hotel.ie
WEB: www.dooleys-hotel.ie

HOTEL ★★★ MAP 4 L 5

The waters of the River Suir swirl and eddy past the door of this renowned hotel, which is situated on The Quay in Waterford. With its high level of comfort and good service Dooley's is an ideal choice for a centrally located hotel, close to all amenities, culture and business centres. This family run hotel caters for the corporate/leisure traveller. The hotel has a purpose-built conference centre with full facilities - The Rita Nolan Conference and Banqueting Suite. Enjoy the style and comfort of our new Ship Restaurant and Dry Dock Bar.

Member of Holiday Ireland Hotels
B&B from €51.00 to €76.00
£40.17 to £59.85

JUNE DARRER
PROPRIETOR/MANAGER

American Express
Diners
Mastercard
Visa

113 113

Inet

Closed 25 - 27 December

FORTE TRAVELODGE

CORK ROAD (N25),
WATERFORD

TEL: 1800-709709 FAX: 051-358890

WEB: www.travelodge.co.uk

HOTEL U MAP 4 L O5

Situated on the N25 primary route from Rosslare Harbour to Cork, 1 mile from Waterford City and minutes from the Waterford Crystal Factory, this superb hotel offers comfortable yet affordable accommodation. Each room can sleep up to 3 adults, a child under 12 years and a baby in a cot. Price is fixed per room regardless of the number of occupants. Each room is en suite, has colour TV, Sky Sports and Movies. Sited next to Little Chef Restaurant. Freephone from UK: 0800 850 950.

Room Rate from €59.95 to €69.95
£47.22 to £55.09

MAURA BUTLER

American Express
Diners
Mastercard
Visa

32 32

Inet

Open All Year

GRANVILLE HOTEL

MEAGHER QUAY,
WATERFORD

TEL: 051-305555 FAX: 051-305566
EMAIL: stay@granville-hotel.ie
WEB: www.granville-hotel.ie

HOTEL ★★★ MAP 4 L 5

Waterford's most prestigious city centre hotel RAC**** overlooking the River Suir. This family run hotel is one of Ireland's oldest with significant historical connections. Justly proud of the Granville's heritage, owners Liam and Ann Cusack today vigourously pursue the Granville's long tradition of hospitality, friendliness and comfort. It has been elegantly refurbished, retaining its old world Georgian character. Award winning Bianconi Restaurant, Thomas Francis Meagher Bar.

Member of Best Western Hotels
B&B from €70.00 to €95.00
£55.13 to £74.82

LIAM AND ANN CUSACK
MANAGERS/PROPRIETORS

American Express
Diners
Mastercard
Visa

98 98

Inet

Closed 25 - 27 December

B&B rates are per person sharing per night incl. Breakfast

IVORY'S HOTEL

TRAMORE ROAD,
WATERFORD

TEL: 051-358888 FAX: 051-358899
EMAIL: info@ivorys-hotel.ie
WEB: www.ivorys-hotel.ie

HOTEL ★★★ MAP 4 L 5

A friendly, family-run hotel, Ivory's Hotel is Waterford's best value. Ideally located adjacent to Waterford Crystal Factory & city centre. Each en suite room combines the convenience of direct dial phone, multi-channel TV with welcoming tea/coffee making facilities, in comfortable surroundings. The hotel boasts Una's Signature Restaurant, emphasising the best fresh local produce. Unwind in McGinty's Pub Carvery & allow us to arrange golf, fishing. Secure car-park. Groups welcome.

B&B from €45.00 to €75.00
£35.44 to £59.07

DECLAN & NATALIE IVORY
MANAGING PROPRIETORS

American Express
Diners
Mastercard
Visa

Weekend specials from €100.00

40 40

Open All Year

JURYS WATERFORD HOTEL

FERRYBANK,
WATERFORD

TEL: 051-832111 FAX: 051-832863
EMAIL: waterford@jurysdoyle.com
WEB: www.jurysdoyle.com

HOTEL ★★★ MAP 4 L 5

The hotel is set in its own grounds on 38 lush acres overlooking the River Suir and the city - a short walk away. An air of space and light pervades everywhere. Spacious, comfortable rooms, good dining and a superb leisure centre ensure a very pleasant stay.

B&B from €63.00 to €96.00
£49.62 to £75.61

STAN POWER
GENERAL MANAGER

American Express
Diners
Mastercard
Visa

98 98

Closed 24 - 28 December

O'GRADY'S RESTAURANT & GUESTHOUSE

CORK ROAD,
WATERFORD

TEL: 051-378851 FAX: 051-374062
EMAIL: info@ogradyshotel.com
WEB: www.ogradyshotel.com

GUESTHOUSE U MAP 4 L 5

O'Gradys Restaurant and Guesthouse is ideally located on the main Cork Road (N25), adjacent to the Waterford Crystal factory and city centre. Family-run by Euro Toque chef Cornelius and his wife Sue; they offer the excellent combination of reasonably priced accommodation and a superb licensed Michelin recommended restaurant which specialises in fresh local seafood. Private off street parking. 4 championship golf courses nearby. Tennis, horseriding and fishing. French and Gaelic spoken.

B&B from €40.00 to €45.00
£31.50 to £35.44

CORNELIUS AND SUE
PROPRIETORS

American Express
Diners
Mastercard
Visa

9 9

Closed 23 December - 02 January

Room rates are per room per night

QUALITY HOTEL WATERFORD

CANADA STREET,
WATERFORD

TEL: 051-856600 FAX: 051-856605
EMAIL: marinagm@gofree.indigo.ie
WEB: www.choicehotelsireland.ie

HOTEL U MAP 4 L 5

The Marina Hotel is located on the waterfront just 2 mins from the city centre. The hotel which has a distinctive art deco style, incorporates superbly designed rooms. All rooms are en suite with multi-channel TV, direct dial phone, hairdryer, trouser press and tea/coffee making facilities. The Waterfront Bar & Bistro Restaurant offer an excellent choice of dishes. Guests have complimentary use of a secure indoor carpark, sauna.

Member of Choice Hotels Ireland

B&B from €45.00 to €85.00
£35.44 to £66.94

DECLAN MEAGHER
GENERAL MANAGER

American Express
Diners
Mastercard
Visa

80 80
a|c Inet

Open All Year

RHU GLEN COUNTRY CLUB HOTEL

LUFFANY,
SLIEVERUE,
WATERFORD

TEL: 051-832242 FAX: 051-832242
EMAIL: rhuglennhotel@ireland.com

HOTEL ★★ MAP 4 L 5

Built within its own grounds with parking for cars, coaches etc. the hotel is family run. Situated on the N25 Rosslare to Waterford Road, convenient to ferries, it offers a superb location whether your pleasure be golfing, fishing, or simply exploring the South East. All rooms are en suite with direct dial phone and multi-channel TV. The restaurant is renowned for its service of fine food. Relax and enjoy our lounge bars and ballroom with live entertainment provided by Ireland's top artistes.

B&B from €38.00 to €51.00
£29.93 to £40.17

LIAM MOONEY
PROPRIETOR

American Express
Diners
Mastercard
Visa

☺ Weekend specials from €100

19 19
a|c

Closed 24 - 25 December

RICE GUESTHOUSE
BATTERBERRY'S BAR

35 & 36 BARRACK STREET,
WATERFORD

TEL: 051-371606 FAX: 051-357013
EMAIL: ricegh@eircom.net

GUESTHOUSE U MAP 4 L 5

We are situated next to Mount Sion Christian Brothers school which Blessed Edmund Ignatius Rice founded in 1802. Tours of the shrine and museum may be arranged, so the name Rice Guesthouse. 21 en suite rooms have cable TV and direct dial phone. Ideally situated to the main shopping centre, Waterford Crystal and train and bus station. Ideal base for touring the South East or golf breaks. Tee times can be arranged and afterwards enjoy live entertainment most nights in our lounge.

B&B from €39.00 to €47.50
£30.71 to £37.41

JOHN & OLIVE O'DRISCOLL

Mastercard
Visa

21 21

Open All Year

B&B rates are per person sharing per night incl. Breakfast

ST. ALBANS GUESTHOUSE

CORK ROAD,
WATERFORD

TEL: 051-358171 FAX: 051-358171
EMAIL: stalbansbandb@yahoo.com
WEB: www.hotelbnb.com

GUESTHOUSE ★★ MAP 4 L 5

St. Albans is a well established family run guesthouse. Ideally located minutes walk from Waterford City Centre and Waterford Crystal. Our very spacious superbly appointed rooms are all en suite with multi-channel TV, tea/coffee facilities and hairdryer. Secure parking at rear of premises. 4 championship golf courses in vicinity. Horse riding 3km. Tennis courts, swimming pool 2 minutes. Several local beaches and breathtaking scenery. Bus and train station a short distance. Freephone: U.K.: 0800 912 3910 USA: 0877 207 3910

B&B from €32.00 to €38.00
£25.20 to £29.93

TOM & HELEN MULLALLY
PROPRIETORS

Mastercard
Visa

8   8

IRISH
HOTELS
FEDERATION

Closed 18 - 28 December

TOWER HOTEL & LEISURE CENTRE

THE MALL,
WATERFORD

TEL: 051-875801 FAX: 051-870129
EMAIL: towerw@iol.ie
WEB: www.towerhotelgroup.ie

HOTEL ★★★ MAP 4 L 5

A Tower Group Hotel - with its riverside location in the heart of Waterford City and 140 guest bedrooms with every modern amenity, the Tower Hotel is the largest hotel in the South East region and the flagship hotel of the Tower Group. Facilities include: Two new restaurants - traditional Carvery and continental style Bistro; Riverside Bar; Leisure & Fitness centre with 20m pool and private guest car park.

Member of Tower Hotel Group
B&B from €46.00 to €96.00
£36.23 to £75.61

PAUL MCDAID
GENERAL MANAGER

American Express
Diners
Mastercard
Visa

☺ Weekend specials from €109.00

140 140

IRISH
HOTELS
FEDERATION

Closed 24 - 28 December

WATERFORD CASTLE HOTEL & GOLF CLUB

THE ISLAND,
BALLINAKILL,
WATERFORD

TEL: 051-878203 FAX: 051-879316
EMAIL: info@waterfordcastle.com
WEB: www.waterfordcastle.com

HOTEL U MAP 4 L 5

Waterford Castle Hotel & Country Club is uniquely situated on a 310 acre island overlooking the estuary of the River Suir, 3 miles from Waterford City. Access to the island is by a chain linked car ferry. Highest standards of comfort, tastefully furnished with antiques and open fireplaces. The 15th century Castle combines gracious living of an elegant past with every modern comfort, service and convenience. Own 18 hole championship golf course, set in a peaceful oasis of beautiful parkland with nature plantations.

Room Rate from €180.00 to €420.00
£141.76 to £330.78

GILLIAN BUTLER
GENERAL MANAGER

American Express
Diners
Mastercard
Visa

19   19

IRISH
HOTELS
FEDERATION

Open All Year

Room rates are per room per night

WOODLANDS HOTEL

DUNMORE ROAD,
WATERFORD

TEL: 051-304574 FAX: 051-304575
EMAIL: woodhl@iol.ie
WEB: www.woodlandshotel.ie

HOTEL ★★★ MAP 4 L 5

Woodlands Hotel is located 3 miles from Waterford City Centre and yet has all the facilities of a countryside hotel with open spaces, a river view and parking for 150 cars. The hotel facilities include 46 en suite rooms with all modern amenities, a split level bar designed to generate a great pub atmosphere. Our restaurant offers the very best cuisine in an intimate setting, state of the art leisure centre plus full conference and banqueting facilities.

B&B from €57.15 to €120.65
£45.01 to £95.02

PAULINE HAYES

American Express
Diners
Mastercard
Visa

😊 Specials available

46 46

IRISH HOTELS FEDERATION

Closed 25 - 27 December

DUNBRODY COUNTRY HOUSE HOTEL & RESTAURANT

ARTHURSTOWN,
CO. WEXFORD

TEL: 051-389600 FAX: 051-389601
EMAIL: info@dunbrodyhouse.com
WEB: www.dunbrodyhouse.com

HOTEL ★★★★ MAP 4 M 5

Dunbrody Country House Hotel is regarded as one of Ireland's top country retreats. Offering award-winning cuisine and luxurious surroundings Dunbrody is recommended by all good guides. "Country House of the Year 2001" from Georgina Campbell, Dunbrody is also a member of Small Luxury Hotels of the World. Come and enjoy the unique ambience that is Dunbrody House. Breakfast every day until noon.

Member of Ireland's Blue Book
B&B from €95.00 to €180.00
£74.82 to £141.76

KEVIN & CATHERINE DUNDON
OWNERS

American Express
Diners
Mastercard
Visa

19 19

IRISH HOTELS FEDERATION

Closed 22 - 27 December

BAYVIEW HOTEL

COURTOWN HARBOUR,
GOREY,
CO. WEXFORD

TEL: 055-25307 FAX: 055-25576
EMAIL: bayview@iol.ie
WEB: www.bayview.ie

HOTEL ★★ MAP 8 O 7

The Bayview is owned and run by the McGarry Family. The hotel is overlooking the marina at Courtown Harbour. It is renowned for its good food and friendly atmosphere. All rooms are en suite with TV, video channel and direct dial telephone. Self catering apartments in hotel. Enjoy the Tennis Centre free to guests. Courtown's 18 hole golf course 2km. It is an ideal setting for weddings and parties. Nearby is the Courtown superb indoor 25m pool.

B&B from €52.00 to €57.00
£40.95 to £44.89

BRIAN MCGARRY
MANAGER

American Express
Mastercard
Visa

13 13

IRISH HOTELS FEDERATION

Closed 01 November - 01 March

B&B rates are per person sharing per night incl. Breakfast

COURTOWN HOTEL

COURTOWN HARBOUR,
GOREY,
CO. WEXFORD
TEL: 055-25210 FAX: 055-25304
EMAIL: courtownhotel@indigo.ie

HOTEL P   MAP 8 O 7

The family run Courtown Hotel & Leisure Centre is renowned for its friendly atmosphere and excellent cuisine. Featuring the A.A award winning "Bradley's" Restaurant and a selection of lounge bars. All rooms are en suite with T.V. and direct dial telephone. Residents enjoy complimentary use of our leisure facilities which include an indoor heated swimming pool, sauna, jacuzzi & steam room. Weddings and parties a speciality

B&B from €44.50 to €57.00
£35.03 to £44.88

SANDRA MELIA
PROPRIETOR

American Express
Diners
Mastercard
Visa

22 22

Closed 01 November - 10 March

HARBOUR HOUSE GUESTHOUSE

COURTOWN HARBOUR,
COURTOWN, GOREY,
CO. WEXFORD
TEL: 055-25117 FAX: 055-25117
EMAIL: stay@harbourhouseguesthouse.com
WEB: www.harbourhouseguesthouse.com

GUESTHOUSE ★★   MAP 8 O 7

Harbour House just off the main Rosslare/Dublin N11 route and only 6.4km from Gorey is ideally located in the renowned seaside resort of Courtown Harbour. Harbour House is the ideal base for both business and holiday travellers and is central to all amenities and only three minutes from Courtown's sandy beaches. All rooms are en suite. Own private car park. Your holiday here is under the personal supervision of the O'Gorman Family.

B&B from €32.00 to €38.00
£25.20 to £29.92

DONAL & MARGARET O'GORMAN
PROPRIETORS

American Express
Diners
Mastercard
Visa

10 10

Closed 31 October - 10 April

HOTEL CURRACLOE

CURRACLOE,
CO. WEXFORD

TEL: 053-37308 FAX: 053-37587
EMAIL: hotelcurracloe@eircom.net
WEB: www.hotelcurracloe.com

HOTEL N   MAP 4 O 6

Hotel Curracloe is ideally situated, only five miles from Wexford Town, minutes from Blue/Green Flag beaches and central to golfing, angling, bird-watching, hill walking and horse riding amenities. Our 29 rooms are en suite with modern facilities and our award-winning Blake Restaurant and Tavern Pub serve the best of home produce. The Brent Banqueting Room will cater for every special occasion. Our friendly staff will ensure that Hotel Curracloe is the perfect base for your leisure time in the sunny South East.

B&B from €34.90 to €51.00
£27.49 to £40.17

ANDREW WOODHEAD-DIXON
GENERAL MANAGER

Mastercard
Visa

29 29

Open All Year

Room rates are per room per night

LEMONGROVE HOUSE

BLACKSTOOPS,
ENNISCORTHY,
CO. WEXFORD
TEL: 054-36115 FAX: 054-36115
EMAIL: lemongrovehouse@iolfree.ie

GUESTHOUSE ★★★ MAP 4 N 6

Spacious luxury home 1km north of Enniscorthy just off roundabout on Dublin/Rosslare Road (N11). Lemongrove House is set in mature gardens with private parking. All rooms en suite with direct dial phone, TV, hairdryer and tea/coffee making facilities. Recommended by Guide du Routard, AA, and other leading guides. Within walking distance of a choice of restaurants, pubs and new pool and leisure centre. Locally we have beaches, golf, horseriding, walking and quad track.

B&B from €26.00 to €32.00
£20.48 to £25.20

COLM & ANN MCGIBNEY
OWNERS

Mastercard

Visa

6 6

Open All Year

MURPHY - FLOODS HOTEL

MARKET SQUARE,
ENNISCORTHY,
CO. WEXFORD
TEL: 054-33413 FAX: 054-33413
EMAIL: mfhotel@indigo.ie
WEB: www.murphyfloods.com

HOTEL ★★ MAP 4 N 6

Overlooking Market Square of historic 6th century Enniscorthy Town on Slaney salmon river. Package rates for golf breaks, midweek and weekends. Elegant restaurant, in Georgian style, presents menus of quality and variety. Room service, excellent bar food, packed lunches available, cots provided, night porter service. Central for touring lovely Slaney Valley and sunny South East. Rosslare Ferry 43km, Waterford 56km, Dublin 120km, Shannon 240km. 1km from National 1798 Centre.

B&B from €40.00 to €60.00
£31.50 to £47.25

MICHAEL J WALL
PROPRIETOR

American Express

Diners

Mastercard

Visa

☺ Weekend specials from €90.00

19 17

IRISH
HOTELS
FEDERATION

Closed 24 - 28 December

PINES COUNTRY HOUSE HOTEL

CAMOLIN,
ENNISCORTHY,
CO. WEXFORD
TEL: 054-83600 FAX: 054-83588
EMAIL: thepines@eircom.net
WEB: www.pinescountryhousehotel.com

HOTEL ★★ MAP 4 N 6

This delightful family run business is a must to relax or up the fitness level with a state of the art gym, sauna steam, on site pony trekking, sea fishing, boat hire. Mediterranean cuisine. Nearby golf. Beaches, Courtown, Curraghcloe. Historic Ferns Heritage Park, hill walking and bird watching. Sunbed. Bouncy Castle and Slide. Local nightclubs, singing lounges and restaurants.

B&B from €31.74 to €48.25
£25.00 to £38.00

FRANK MURHILL
DIRECTOR MANAGER

Mastercard

Visa

11 11

IRISH
HOTELS
FEDERATION

Open All Year

B&B rates are per person sharing per night incl. Breakfast

RIVERSIDE PARK HOTEL

THE PROMENADE,
ENNISCORTHY,
CO. WEXFORD
TEL: 054-37800 FAX: 054-37900
EMAIL: riversideparkhotel@eircom.net
WEB: www.riversideparkhotel.com

HOTEL ★★★ MAP 4 N 6

Located on the banks of the picturesque River Slaney, the Riverside Park Hotel is a welcome addition to the bustling market town of Enniscorthy. Comprising 60 delightfully furnished rooms offering every modern convenience. Two spacious bars, The Moorings Restaurant and our exciting Tex-Mex experience, The Alamo. 30 mins drive from Rosslare, the hotel is the perfect base for touring historic Vinegar Hill and the "Sunny South East's" myriad visitor attractions, golf courses & sandy beaches.

B&B from €67.00 to €77.00
£52.76 to £60.63

JIM MAHER
GENERAL MANAGER

American Express
Diners
Mastercard
Visa

☺ Weekend specials from €170.00

60 60

Closed 24 - 26 December

TREACYS HOTEL

TEMPLESHANNON,
ENNISCORTHY,
CO. WEXFORD
TEL: 054-37798 FAX: 054-37733
EMAIL: info@treacyshotel.com
WEB: www.treacyshotel.com

HOTEL ★★★ MAP 4 N 6

Situated in the heart of Enniscorthy, It is the ideal spot for excitement and relaxation. Whether it's sport, entertainment, fine dining or a festive night life you want, look no further. The Bagenal Harvey Restaurant serves outstanding cuisine both à la carte and table d'hôte. Artistically presented, guests can choose from our award-winning Temple Bar or enjoy late night entertainment at Benedicts superpub. You can trust Treacys Hotel to provide you with the luxury and service our guests have come to expect. We will make your stay a memorable one.

B&B from €50.00 to €62.00
£39.38 to £48.83

ANTON & YVONNE TREACY

American Express
Diners
Mastercard
Visa

48 48

Closed 24 - 26 December

HORSE AND HOUND INN

BALLINABOOLA,
FOULKSMILLS,
CO. WEXFORD
TEL: 051-428323 FAX: 051-428471
EMAIL: mur40@iol.ie

GUESTHOUSE ★★★ MAP 4 N 5

The Horse and Hound Inn, Ballinaboola, Co. Wexford is owned and run by the Murphy Family. Situated six miles from New Ross on the N25 from Rosslare. It is a convenient venue for a meal and a rest. Best Irish produce is used in preparing specialities of fish and beef dishes. There are twelve bedrooms should you wish to stay. Catering for all needs - from private parties, weddings to conferences.

B&B from €40.00 to €45.00
£31.50 to £35.44

CHRISTY MURPHY

Mastercard
Visa

12 12

Open All Year

Room rates are per room per night

ASHDOWN PARK HOTEL CONFERENCE & LEISURE CENTRE

COACH ROAD,
GOREY,
CO. WEXFORD
TEL: 055-80500 FAX: 055-80777
EMAIL: info@ashdownparkhotel.com
WEB: www.ashdownparkhotel.com

HOTEL P MAP 8 O 7

This stylish new hotel has been designed to a superior 3*** standard. 60 highly comfortable bedrooms, including 6 suites offer all modern conveniences. Enjoy a drink by the cosy fire in the lounge followed by a splendid dinner in the elegant restaurant. The magnificent leisure centre sports a swimming pool, jacuzzi, children's pool, gym, sauna and solarium. Centrally located close to Dublin and Rosslare, Ashdown Park is ideally located for touring Counties Wexford / Wicklow.

B&B from €65.00 to €95.00
£51.18 to £74.81

MATT O'CONNOR
GENERAL MANAGER

American Express
Diners
Mastercard
Visa

60 60

Closed 24 - 26 December

MARLFIELD HOUSE HOTEL

GOREY,
CO. WEXFORD

TEL: 055-21124 FAX: 055-21572
EMAIL: info@marlfieldhouse.ie
WEB: www.marlfieldhouse.com

HOTEL ★★★★ MAP 8 O 7

This Regency period house is set amidst 36 acres of grounds and is filled with beautiful antiques. The Bowe family opened its doors to guests in 1978 and has gained an outstanding reputation since. The kitchen garden provides the produce for its award winning conservatory dining room. Member of Relais et Châteaux and Ireland's Blue Book, AA Red Star and RAC Gold Ribbon Hotel.

Member of Relais & Châteaux
B&B from €111.00 to €120.00
£87.42 to £94.49

MARY BOWE
PROPRIETOR

American Express
Diners
Mastercard
Visa

20 20

alc

IRISH HOTELS FEDERATION

Closed 15 December - 25 January

HOTEL SALTEES

KILMORE QUAY,
CO. WEXFORD

TEL: 053-29601 FAX: 053-29602

HOTEL ★★ MAP 4 N 5

Hotel Saltees is situated in the picturesque fishing village of Kilmore Quay. Renowned for its thatched cottages and maritime flavour, it is located just 22km from Wexford Town and 19km from the international port of Rosslare. Offering excellent value accommodation, with all rooms en suite, TV, telephone and all well designed to cater for families. The Coningbeg Seafood Restaurant, specialises in serving the freshest seafood. Shore and deep-sea fishing available locally.

B&B from €36.00 to €45.00
£28.35 to £35.44

TOMMY AND NED BYRNE
PROPRIETORS

Mastercard
Visa

Weekend specials from €108.00

10 10

IRISH HOTELS FEDERATION

Closed 25 December

B&B rates are per person sharing per night incl. Breakfast

QUAY HOUSE

KILMORE QUAY,
CO. WEXFORD

TEL: 053-29988 FAX: 053-29808
EMAIL: quayplaice@eircom.net
WEB: www.quayhouseguesthouse.com

GUESTHOUSE ★★★ MAP 4 N 5

3*** Guesthouse. AA Selected ♦♦♦. Quay House is located in the centre of Kilmore Quay; famous for its thatched cottages, marina, sea angling, nature trails and walks along the Wexford Coast. Quay House offers you a stay that will bring you back again and again. Good food and wine served in our restaurant Quay Plaice. All inclusive mini breaks available excluding July & August. Private car park to rear.

B&B from €35.00 to €38.00
£27.56 to £29.93

SIOBHAN MCDONNELL
PROPRIETOR

Mastercard
Visa

🐋

🛏🐾☎🖥C🐕☀♂🅿🆂🆈alc🪑
10 10

Closed 20 December - 04 February

CLARION BRANDON HOUSE HOTEL & LEISURE CENTRE

NEW ROSS,
CO. WEXFORD

TEL: 051-421703 FAX: 051-421567
EMAIL: brandonhouse@eircom.net
WEB: www.brandonhousehotel.ie

HOTEL ★★★ MAP 4 M 6

A de luxe country manor house set in landscaped grounds with panoramic views overlooking the River Barrow. Dine in the AA award winning restaurant or relax in the Library Bar. All rooms are elegantly furnished. Luxurious health & leisure club with 20m pool, sauna, steam room, jacuzzi, fully equipped gym, kiddies pool, hydro therapy grotto and thalasso treatment room. Nearby golf, angling, beaches, horseriding & gardens. An ideal base for touring the sunny South East.

Member of Choice Hotels Ireland
B&B from €63.00 to €97.00
£49.62 to £76.39

GRACE MCPHILLIPS
GENERAL MANAGER

American Express
Diners
Mastercard
Visa

✓🍴

☺ Weekend specials from €138.00

🛏🐾☎🖥T🗚C🐕CM☀❄🏠U
♪🅹🅿🆂🆊alc🪑 Inet
61 61

Closed 24 - 25 December

CREACON LODGE HOTEL

CREACON,
NEW ROSS,
CO. WEXFORD

TEL: 051-421897 FAX: 051-422560
EMAIL: info@creaconlodge.com
WEB: www.creaconlodge.com

HOTEL ★★★ MAP 4 M 6

Set amidst the peace and tranquillity of the countryside. 45 minutes drive from Rosslare, 2 hours from Dublin and only a short scenic drive to the Hook Peninsula and JFK Park. Relax and enjoy our beautiful gardens, comfy sofas and log fires and sample the delights of our award winning restaurant and bar. All bedrooms are en suite with DD phone, colour TV. Local amenities include golf, angling, horse-riding water sports and sandy beaches. The Dunbrody Famine Ship is not to be missed.

B&B from €44.00 to €64.00
£34.65 to £50.40

JOSEPHINE FLOOD

Mastercard
Visa

☺ Weekend specials from €114.00

🛏🐾☎🖥T🗚C🐕CM☀♂U🅿🆊alc
10 10

Closed 23 - 28 December

Room rates are per room per night

CEDAR LODGE HOTEL & RESTAURANT

CARRIGBYRNE,
NEWBAWN, (NEAR NEW ROSS),
CO. WEXFORD
TEL: 051-428386 FAX: 051-428222
EMAIL: cedarlodge@eircom.net
WEB: www.prideofeirehotels.com

HOTEL ★★★ MAP 4 N 6

Charming 3*** country hotel located in a picturesque setting, 30 minutes drive from Rosslare Port on the N25 New Ross Road. All bedrooms en suite with direct dial phone and TV. The restaurant which concentrates on freshly prepared produce, is noted for its good food. Recommended by Michelin, Good Hotel Guide, RAC. Forest walks nearby. Golf, horse riding, JF Kennedy Park, county museum, heritage park and sandy beaches within easy driving distance. The Cedar Lodge is a de luxe hotel - a cut above the rest.

B&B from €70.00 to €90.00
£55.13 to £70.88

TOM MARTIN
PROPRIETOR

American Express
Diners
Mastercard
Visa

🛏 🐾 ☎ 🖥 T CM✱P🔒 alc
28 28

IRISH HOTELS FEDERATION

Closed 20 December - 01 February

CHURCHTOWN HOUSE

TAGOAT,
ROSSLARE,
CO. WEXFORD
TEL: 053-32555 FAX: 053-32577
EMAIL: churchtown.rosslare@indigo.ie
WEB: www.churchtown-rosslare.com

GUESTHOUSE ★★★★ MAP 4 O 5

AA Guesthouse of the Year 1998, and RAC Little Gem 2001. Churchtown is a period house c.1703 where peace and tranquillity together with country house hospitality combine with modern comforts to make it 'A SPECIAL PLACE TO STAY'. A rural setting in mature gardens, 0.5 mile off the N25 and 5 mins from Rosslare Ferryport/Strand. Explore Wexford's 'Land of Living History', gardens, golf, beaches, birdwatching, fishing and riding. Evening meals served Tues-Sat. Please pre-book.

Member of Manor House Hotels
B&B from €65.00 to €95.00
£51.19 to £74.82

AUSTIN AND PATRICIA CODY
OWNERS

American Express
Mastercard
Visa

🛏 🐾 ☎ 🖥 T ✱ ↺ 🍴 💲
14 14

IRISH HOTELS FEDERATION

Closed 30 November - 01 March

CROSBIE CEDARS HOTEL

ROSSLARE,
CO. WEXFORD

TEL: 053-32124 FAX: 053-32243
EMAIL: info@crosbiecedars.iol.ie
WEB: www.crosbiecedarshotel.com

HOTEL ★★★ MAP 4 O 5

The Crosbie Cedars Hotel is an AA*** de luxe hotel situated in the heart of Rosslare. The hotel provides elegant and tastefully designed en suite rooms, restaurant and bars, ensuring a comfortable and relaxing stay for all. A haven of outstanding quality, offering true Irish warmth and hospitality. Ideal, golf centre within easy reach of 3 excellent courses, Rosslare, St. Helens and Wexford. Golf rates and packages available.

B&B from €42.00 to €64.00
£33.08 to £50.40

LIZ SINNOTT
GENERAL MANAGER

American Express
Diners
Mastercard
Visa

🛏 🐾 ☎ 🖥 ↕ T 🌙 C ↺ CM✱↺🎵
34 34
P S Q alc

IRISH HOTELS FEDERATION

Closed 24 - 26 December

B&B rates are per person sharing per night incl. Breakfast

DANBY LODGE HOTEL

ROSSLARE ROAD,
KILLINICK, ROSSLARE,
CO. WEXFORD

TEL: 053-58191 FAX: 053-58191
EMAIL: danby@eircom.net

HOTEL U   MAP 405

Nestling in the heart of South County Wexford, Danby Lodge Hotel has rightfully earned for itself a reputation for excellence in cuisine and accommodation. Once the home of the painter Francis Danby, 1793-1861, this hotel bears all the hallmarks of a charming country residence. Conveniently located on main Rosslare to Wexford Road (N25). Danby Lodge Hotel offers the visitor a quiet country getaway yet just minutes drive from the port of Rosslare and the town of Wexford. RAC and AA recommended.

Room Rate from €65.00 to €115.00
£51.19 to £90.57

RAYMOND PARLE
OWNER

American Express
Diners
Mastercard
Visa

☺ Midweek specials available

24   24

Closed 22 - 30 December

KELLY'S RESORT HOTEL

ROSSLARE,
CO. WEXFORD

TEL: 053-32114 FAX: 053-32222
EMAIL: kellyhot@iol.ie
WEB: www.kellys.ie

HOTEL ★★★★   MAP 405

Since 1895 the Kelly Family have created a truly fine resort hotel. Good food, wine and nightly entertainment are very much part of the tradition. Amenities include tennis, squash, snooker, bowls, croquet and an excellent choice of local golf courses. Pamper and relax in our Health & Beauty Centre. 7-day break (July/August): 5-day midweek & 2-day weekend (Spring/Autumn). Special Activity Midweeks in Spring & Autumn - wine tasting, cooking demonstrations, gardening, painting, etc.

B&B from €70.00 to €105.00
£55.00 to £83.00

WILLIAM J KELLY
MANAGER/DIRECTOR

American Express
Mastercard
Visa

☺ Special Autumn & Spring Offer, 5 days full board from €500.00 + 10% s.c

99   99

Closed 09 December - 22 February

AILSA LODGE

ROSSLARE HARBOUR,
CO. WEXFORD

TEL: 053-33230 FAX: 053-33581
EMAIL: ailsalodge@eircom.net
WEB: www.ailsalodge.com

GUESTHOUSE ★★   MAP 405

Ailsa Lodge a family run guesthouse in the town of Rosslare Harbour. Positioned in a quiet location with private grounds and spacious parking, it overlooks the Irish Sea, the beach and the ferryport. 5 minutes walk from the bus/rail/ferry terminal. All rooms en suite with TV and direct dial phone. Early breakfasts served. A short walk from all shops, pubs and restaurants. Excellent beaches, fishing, walks and golf courses locally.

B&B from €26.00 to €33.00
£20.48 to £25.99

DOMINIC SHEIL
PROPRIETOR

Mastercard
Visa

7   7

Closed 22 - 31 December

Room rates are per room per night

CORAL GABLES

TAGOAT,
ROSSLARE HARBOUR,
CO. WEXFORD
TEL: 053-31213 FAX: 053-31414
EMAIL: coralgables@eircom.net
WEB: www.coralgablesguesthouse.com

GUESTHOUSE ★★ MAP 405

Coral Gables is situated on a hilltop in quiet secluded surroundings overlooking the Wexford/Rosslare N25, just 3km from the ferry. Good food and friendly atmosphere provides the perfect stopover for visitors arriving and departing through Rosslare Port or for golfing, fishing, horseriding or relaxing on our safe sandy beaches. Our guesthouse has 15 en suite rooms with direct dial phone, tea/coffee facilities, hairdryer, TV, central heating, private car parking. TV lounge.

B&B from €30.00 to €40.00
£23.63 to £31.50

SARAH & PAUL HASLAM
PROPRIETORS

Mastercard

Visa

15 15

Open All Year

EURO LODGE

ROSSLARE HARBOUR,
CO. WEXFORD.
TEL: 053-33118 FAX: 053-33120
EMAIL: eurolodge@eircom.net
WEB: www.wexford-online.com/eurolodge

GUESTHOUSE ★★★ MAP 405

Euro Lodge offers luxury accommodation, conveniently located only 600m from Rosslare Ferryport. All our rooms have bathroom en suite with colour TV, phone, tea/coffee facilities. Twin and family rooms available. An ideal location to stay while touring the South East. Close to all amenities. With two 18 hole golf courses, sandy beaches, fishing, horse riding and leisure centre nearby. Ample private car parking. Ideal for coach parties.

Room Rate from €65.00 to €65.00
£51.19 to £51.19

HELEN SINNOTT
MANAGER

Mastercard

Visa

20 20

Closed 01 November - 28 February

FERRYPORT HOUSE

ROSSLARE HARBOUR,
CO. WEXFORD
TEL: 053-33933 FAX: 053-33033
EMAIL: thh@iol.ie
WEB: www.tuskarhousehotel.com

GUESTHOUSE ★★★ MAP 405

A new luxury guesthouse conveniently located close to Rosslare Ferryport (400m). The last guesthouse when leaving Ireland and the first on your return. It has 17 en suite bedrooms with direct dial phone, colour TV, central heating, tea/coffee making facilities, hairdryer and private car parking. Local amenities include golf, fishing, horse riding and safe sandy beaches.

B&B from €25.00 to €45.00
£19.69 to £35.44

BILLY & PATRICA ROCHE
PROPRIETORS

Mastercard

Visa

17 17

Open All Year

B&B rates are per person sharing per night incl. Breakfast

HOTEL ROSSLARE

ROSSLARE HARBOUR,
CO. WEXFORD

TEL: 053-33110 FAX: 053-33386
EMAIL: info@hotelrosslare.ie
WEB: www.hotelrosslare.ie

HOTEL ★★★ MAP 4 0 5

Hotel Rosslare, the longest established hotel in Rosslare Harbour, enjoys spectacular views over the harbour and Europort. Enjoy a meal in the Anchorage Bistro overlooking the bay or spend some time in the historic Portholes Bar. Relax in our en suite rooms, most with sea views, direct dial phone, satellite TV and tea/coffee making facilities. Superbly located, we are only a short drive from 6 golf courses, magnificent beaches, angling, horse riding and Wexford Town.

B&B from € 37.00 to € 62.00
£29.13 to £48.81

AILEEN BOYD
GENERAL MANAGER

American Express
Diners
Mastercard
Visa

25 25

IRISH
HOTELS
FEDERATION

Closed 24 - 25 December

ROSSLARE GREAT SOUTHERN HOTEL

ROSSLARE HARBOUR,
CO. WEXFORD

TEL: 053-33233 FAX: 053-33543
EMAIL: res@rosslare-gsh.ie
WEB: www.greatsouthernhotels.com

HOTEL ★★★ MAP 4 0 5

In Rosslare, a favourite resort, the Great Southern Hotel provides a warm welcome with traditional hospitality. The hotel is beautifully situated on a clifftop overlooking Rosslare Harbour. All rooms are en suite with direct dial phone, TV, radio, hairdryer, in-house movie channel and tea/coffee facilities. Enjoy the leisure centre with indoor swimming pool, jacuzzi, steam room, the comfortable lounges and excellent food of the Mariner's Restaurant. Central reservations Tel: 01-214 4800 or UTELL.

Room Rate from € 140.00 to € 150.00
£110.24 to £118.11

ROISIN BUCKLEY
GENERAL MANAGER

American Express
Diners
Mastercard
Visa

☺ Weekend specials from €120.00

99 99

IRISH
HOTELS
FEDERATION

Closed 02 January - 02 February

ST. MARTINS

ST. MARTINS ROAD,
ROSSLARE HARBOUR,
CO. WEXFORD

TEL: 053-33133 FAX: 053-33133
EMAIL: info@saintmartins.com
WEB: www.saintmartins.com

GUESTHOUSE ★★★ MAP 4 0 5

St Martins Guesthouse is situated only 500 metres from Rosslare Europort providing the ideal base for ferry and train travel but also for touring the South East. Local activities include golf, horse-riding, angling and watersports as well as visitor attractions such as Yola Farmstead and the Heritage Park. All rooms are en suite with TV, tea/coffee making facilities, direct dial phone and hairdryer. Some rooms also available with 4 poster beds.

B&B from € 25.00 to € 37.00
£19.69 to £29.14

ORLA ROCHE/PATRICK PEARE
HOSTS

Mastercard
Visa

7   7

IRISH
HOTELS
FEDERATION

Closed 24 - 27 December

Room rates are per room per night

TUSKAR HOUSE HOTEL

ROSSLARE HARBOUR,
CO. WEXFORD

TEL: 053-33363 FAX: 053-33033
EMAIL: thh@iol.ie
WEB: www.tuskarhousehotel.com

HOTEL ★★★ MAP 4 O 5

Family run hotel enjoying panoramic views of Rosslare Bay, just 219m from ferry and train terminals. It has all en suite bedrooms with telephone, TV, central heating and some with balconies. Dinner served nightly until 11pm and Sunday lunch 12.30 to 2.30, with local seafood a speciality. Regular entertainment in the lively Punters Bar. Local amenities include: golf, fishing, horse riding and safe beaches. Michelin recommended.

B&B from €38.00 to €60.00
£29.93 to £47.25

ORLA ROCHE
GENERAL MANAGER

American Express
Diners
Mastercard
Visa

Weekend specials from €99.00

30 30

Closed 25 - 26 December

FAYTHE GUEST HOUSE

THE FAYTHE,
SWAN VIEW,
WEXFORD

TEL: 053-22249 FAX: 053-21680
EMAIL: faythhse@iol.ie
WEB: www.faytheguesthouse.com

GUESTHOUSE ★★★ MAP 4 O 6

Family run guesthouse in quiet part of town centre, is built on the grounds of a former castle of which one wall remains today. All rooms refurbished recently, some overlook our gardens and Wexford Harbour. Due to all improvements we are now graded to 3***. All rooms have bathroom en suite, colour TV, direct dial phone, clock radio and tea/coffee making facilities. Rosslare Ferry Port is only 15 minutes drive (early breakfast on request). We also have a large private car park.

B&B from €26.00 to €40.00
£20.48 to £31.50

DAMIAN AND SIOBHAN LYNCH
PROPRIETORS

Mastercard
Visa

10 10

Closed 24 - 30 December

FERRYCARRIG HOTEL

FERRYCARRIG BRIDGE,
WEXFORD

TEL: 053-20999 FAX: 053-20982
EMAIL: ferrycarrig@griffingroup.ie
WEB: www.griffingroup.ie

HOTEL ★★★★ MAP 4 N 6

Ferrycarrig Hotel boasts one of the most inspiring locations of any hotel in Ireland, with sweeping views across the River Slaney Estuary. Facilities include 103 bedrooms and suites, two award winning waterfront restaurants - including Tides Gourmet Restaurant, the most unusual Drydock Bar, an excellent conference centre and the superb 5***** Active Health and Fitness club with 20m pool and spa area. The hotel is part owner of St. Helen's Bay Golf Course.

B&B from €63.50 to €133.00
£50.01 to £104.75

MARK BROWNE
GENERAL MANAGER

American Express
Diners
Mastercard
Visa

103 103

Open All Year

B&B rates are per person sharing per night incl. Breakfast

RIVERBANK HOUSE HOTEL

THE BRIDGE,
WEXFORD

TEL: 053-23611 FAX: 053-23342
EMAIL: river@indigo.ie
WEB: www.riverbankhousehotel.com

HOTEL ★★★ MAP 4 0 6

The Riverbank House Hotel commands magnificent views of the old Viking town, the River Slaney and the miles of golden beach surrounding Wexford. The hotel boasts an excellent à la carte menu, delicious bar food together with an exciting wine list. Benefiting from its own private car park, the hotel offers easy access to five of the best golf courses in the South East, sea angling sites & shooting - ensuring that whatever your stay, business or leisure, it will be most enjoyable.

B&B from €45.00 to €77.00
£35.44 to £60.64

COLM CAMPBELL
GENERAL MANAGER

American Express
Diners
Mastercard
Visa

17 17

Closed 25 December

SAINT GEORGE

GEORGE STREET,
WEXFORD

TEL: 053-43474 FAX: 053-24814
EMAIL: stgeorge@eircom.net

GUESTHOUSE ★★ MAP 4 0 6

You are sure of a warm welcome here at the Saint George, a family-run guesthouse in the centre of Wexford Town, the heart of the sunny South East. We are close to all amenities and provide a private lock-up car park. All our bedrooms have bathroom en suite. They are equipped with direct dial phone, colour TV, hairdryer, tea/coffee making facilities. All rooms are non smoking, but there is a smoking lounge available. Only 15 minutes drive from Rosslare Ferry Port. Early breakfast on request.

B&B from €30.00 to €35.00
£23.63 to £27.56

KAYME SCALLAN
PROPRIETOR

Mastercard
Visa

9 9

Closed 10 December - 29 January

TALBOT HOTEL CONFERENCE AND LEISURE CENTRE

TRINITY STREET,
WEXFORD

TEL: 053-22566 FAX: 053-23377
EMAIL: talbotwx@eircom.net
WEB: www.talbothotel.ie

HOTEL ★★★ MAP 4 0 6

Located in the heart of Wexford Town is the Talbot Hotel Conference & Leisure Centre. Our Quay Leisure Centre offers extensive leisure facilities for the fitness enthusiast and for those who just want pure pampering. Award winning Slaney Restaurant offers fresh Wexford fayre and an extensive wine list. Evening entertainment in the Trinity Bar at weekends. Bedrooms are fully equipped with direct dial phone, satellite TV and are tastefully decorated for your comfort and relaxation.

Member of Select Hotels of Ireland

B&B from €67.00 to €75.00
£52.76 to £59.06

URSULA SINNOTT
GENERAL MANAGER

American Express
Diners
Mastercard
Visa

☺ Weekend specials from €154.91

99 99

Open All Year

Room rates are per room per night

WESTGATE HOUSE

WESTGATE,
WEXFORD

TEL: 053-22167 FAX: 053-22167
EMAIL: westgate@wexmail.com
WEB: www.wexford-online.com/westgate

GUESTHOUSE ★★ MAP 4 O 6

Westgate House stands in a charming, traditional area across the road from the famed Selskar Abbey and Westgate Castle. It is an historic house formerly Westgate Hotel in 1812. It has been refurbished in period style with taste and elegance, with beautifully furnished bedrooms which create a sense of ease and timelessness. Matching this, it offers full modern amenities. Situated in the exciting town centre with superb shops, pubs and restaurants. A secure lock-up car park is provided.

B&B from €32.00 to €32.00
£25.20 to £25.20

M & D ALLEN
OWNERS

Mastercard
Visa

🏨 📺 T C ❄ J P 🔑
10 10

IRISH HOTELS FEDERATION

Closed 23 - 27 December

WHITES HOTEL

GEORGE STREET,
WEXFORD

TEL: 053-22311 FAX: 053-45000
EMAIL: info@whiteshotel.iol.ie
WEB: www.wexfordirl.com/accommodation/whites/

HOTEL ★★★ MAP 4 O 6

Est. 1779, this charming 3*** hotel is centrally located in the historic and picturesque town of Wexford. The hotel's facilities include a health & fitness club, Harpers superb brasserie restaurant offering the finest local and international dishes for lunch & dinner and the immensely popular Harpers Bar where carvery lunches and bar food is served daily and which is open late Thurs-Sun. The hotel is 5 mins walk from the bus and train station and only 20 mins drive from Rosslare Europort.

Member of Best Western Hotels
B&B from €51.00 to €64.00
£40.17 to £50.40

MICHAEL CONNOLLY
GENERAL MANAGER

American Express
Diners
Mastercard
Visa

✓ 🍸

☺ Midweek 3 D B&B from €115.00

🏨 📞 📺 T C ❄ CM 🖥 J P 🔑
82 82

álc

IRISH HOTELS FEDERATION

Open All Year

WHITFORD HOUSE HOTEL

NEW LINE ROAD,
WEXFORD

TEL: 053-43444 FAX: 053-46399
EMAIL: whitford@indigo.ie
WEB: www.whitford.ie

HOTEL ★★★ MAP 4 N 5

One of the leading family run tourist establishments in the South East. Footprints award winning restaurant receives constant accolades for excellence, presentation and value. Seafood a speciality. Standard and Superior de luxe accommodation. Entertainment at weekends. Unwind in our indoor swimming pool (Mar/mid Nov) or serve an ace on our tennis court. For younger members we boast a children's playground. Locally there is golf, fishing, horse riding and excellent beaches. AA, RAC and Michelin recommended.

B&B from €57.00 to €83.00
£44.89 to £65.37

KAY WHITTY
PROPRIETOR

American Express
Mastercard
Visa

✓

☺ Weekend specials from €140.00

🏨 📞 T C ❄ CM ☀ 🎾 U
36 36

J P S 🔑 álc 🔑 inet

IRISH HOTELS FEDERATION

Closed 23 December - 03 January

B&B rates are per person sharing per night incl. Breakfast

SOUTH WEST
The spectacular South West

Located in the south-west corner of Ireland, the Cork and Kerry region offers its visitors a great diversity of scenery, culture and leisure activities. Cork and Kerry claims some of the most varied and spectacular scenery in the country.

The Queenstown Story, Cobh, Co. Cork

Natural attractions abound, from the West Cork coast, the Beara and Dingle peninsulas and the Ring of Kerry to the Lakes of Killarney and the Bandon, Lee and Blackwater valleys.

With its remarkable charm, bumpy bridges, hilly streets and distinctive continental air the city of Cork will not fail, like the rest of the Region, to captivate and welcome all visitors, young and old. Cobh, situated on the southern short of the Great Island, lies in one of the world's largest natural harbours. The Queenstown Story in Cobh tells the story of emigration and the history of sail and steam in Cork Harbour. Cobh was the last port of call for the ill-fated Titanic.

The coast road from Kinsale to Skibbereen passes through many attractive villages and towns giving breath-taking views of the south west coastline. Kinsale, a town which has retained its old world charm and character is firmly established as one of Ireland's leading gourmet centres. Passing onto Clonakilty, Ireland's 1999 national Tidy Towns winners, one of Cork's many picturesque and colourful towns. There are many amenities in the area, with places of interest to visit, sporting and leisure activities and festivals.

The unspoilt coastal and inland waters of Cork and Kerry offer numerous water sports, from fishing to sailing, diving and windsurfing.

The Ring of Kerry is a journey through some of the country's most outstanding scenery. It is not only one of great natural beauty - it is enhanced by the influence of both ancient folklore and local traditions. With its three famous lakes and great mountain ranges Killarney has been

the inspiration of poets and painters over many centuries. A spectacular attraction is the Skellig Experience Centre at Valentia Island which imaginatively tells the story of the history of the Skelligs.

The Dingle Peninsula has some of the most intersting antiquities, historic sites and varied scenery in the whole country. Dingle, the most westerly town in Europe is an excellent centre for the visitor. It still retains much of its old-world atmosphere with its many shops and restaurants.

For further information contact:
Cork Kerry Tourism, Aras Failte,
Grand Parade, Cork.
Tel. (021) 273251. Fax. (021) 273504
email: user@cktourism.ie

Killarney Tourist Office, Beech Road,
Killarney, Co. Kerry.
Tel. (064) 31633. Fax (064) 34506.

The Skellig Experience Visitor
Centre, Valentia Island, Co. Kerry

SEA VIEW GUEST HOUSE

CLUIN VILLAGE,
ALLIHIES, BEARA,
CO. CORK

TEL: 027-73004 FAX: 027-73211
EMAIL: seaviewg@iol.ie
WEB: www.seaviewallihies.com

GUESTHOUSE ★★★ MAP 1 C 2

Sea View Guest House is a family run concern in the remote and unspoilt Beara Peninsula. All bedrooms are en suite with TV and telephone. Situated in the village of Allihies it is within walking distance of a beach, playground and tennis court. The nearby hills afford excellent opportunities for walking, offering breathtaking views. Traditional Irish music and a friendly welcome can be found in the village pubs.

Member of Premier Guesthouses

B&B from €26.67 to €31.75
£21.00 to £25.01

JOHN AND MARY O'SULLIVAN
PROPRIETORS

Mastercard
Visa

10 10

Closed 31 October - 01 March

BAYVIEW HOTEL

BALLYCOTTON,
CO. CORK

TEL: 021-464 6746 FAX: 021-464 6075
EMAIL: info@bayviewhotel.net
WEB: www.bayviewhotel.net

HOTEL ★★★★ MAP 3 J 3

The Bayview Hotel is a luxury 35 bedroom hotel, magnificently situated overlooking Ballycotton Bay and fishing harbour. Private gardens with steps lead to the sea and bathing spot. The Capricho Restaurant produces innovative Irish cuisine and was awarded 2 rosettes by the AA. There are 6 superb golf courses in the area, sea angling, heritage centres and many other activities available. GDS Access Code: UI Toll Free 1-800-44-UTELL

Member of Manor House Hotels

B&B from €78.50 to €96.00
£61.82 to £75.61

STEPHEN BELTON
GENERAL MANAGER

American Express
Diners
Mastercard
Visa

35 35

Closed 31 October - 31 March

SPANISH POINT SEAFOOD RESTAURANT & GUEST HOUSE

BALLYCOTTON,
CO. CORK

TEL: 021-464 6177 FAX: 021-464 6179
EMAIL: spanishp@indigo.ie

GUESTHOUSE ★★★ MAP 3 J 3

Spanish Point Seafood Restaurant & Guest accommodation is situated on a cliff face overlooking Ballycotton Bay. The conservatory restaurant specialises in seafood which is caught from our own trawler. Mary Tattan, Chef/Owner, trained at Ballymaloe Cookery School. We have recently built on a new lounge and sun deck for our residents and guests to enjoy. Local cliff walk and beaches to be enjoyed.

B&B from €39.00 to €39.00
£30.71 to £30.71

MARY TATTAN
CHEF/OWNER

Diners
Mastercard
Visa

5 5

Closed 02 January - 13 March

B&B rates are per person sharing per night incl. Breakfast

BALLYLICKEY MANOR HOUSE

BALLYLICKEY,
BANTRY BAY,
CO. CORK

TEL: 027-50071 FAX: 027-50124
EMAIL: ballymh@eircom.net
WEB: www.ballylickeymanorhouse.com

GUESTHOUSE ★★★★ MAP 2 E 2

Overlooking beautiful Bantry Bay in 4 hectares of parkland and ornamental gardens, bordered by the Ouvane River, Ballylickey, a 17th century manor house together with cottages around the swimming pool, offers both standard and luxury suite accommodation, an outdoor heated swimming pool, private fishing, 2 golf courses (3 and 8km) and riding nearby. Ballylickey is a member of the Irish Country House and Restaurant Association and of Relais and Châteaux International.

Member of Ireland's Blue Book
B&B from € 102.00 to € 171.00
£80.33 to £134.67

MR AND MRS GRAVES
OWNERS

American Express
Diners
Mastercard
Visa

11 11

Closed 15 November - 15 March

SEA VIEW HOUSE HOTEL

BALLYLICKEY,
BANTRY,
CO. CORK

TEL: 027-50073 FAX: 027-51555
EMAIL: seaviewhousehotel@eircom.net
WEB: www.cmvhotel.com

HOTEL ★★★★ MAP 2 E 2

Delightful country house hotel and restaurant, set back in extensive grounds on main Bantry/Glengarriff Road. All bedrooms en suite, D.D. telephone and colour TV. Ideal for touring West Cork and Kerry. Two golf courses nearby. Recommended Egon Ronay, Good Hotel Guide etc. For the restaurant, AA Rosettes and Bord Failte Awards of Excellence. Seafood a speciality. Member of Manor House Hotels. A wing of new superior rooms was added in Winter 2000 and also a conservatory to the dining room.

Member of Manor House Hotels
B&B from € 65.00 to € 120.00
£51.18 to £94.49

KATHLEEN O'SULLIVAN
PROPRIETOR

American Express
Diners
Mastercard
Visa

☺ Special offers on request

25 25

Closed 15 November - 15 March

ABBEY HOTEL

BALLYVOURNEY,
CO. CORK

TEL: 026-45324 FAX: 026-45449
EMAIL: abbeyhotel@eircom.net
WEB: www.theabbeyhotel.net

HOTEL U MAP 2 F 3

Family run hotel nestles in the valley of the Sullane River among the Cork and Kerry Mountains on the N22. It combines a friendly atmosphere and excellent catering. An ideal base for touring Kerry and Cork. A wide range of activities are available to you at the hotel including fishing, mountaineering, nature walks and golfing. 39 bedrooms with private facilities, direct dial phone & colour TV. Within 20 minutes drive are two 18 hole golf courses and trout fishing on the Sullane River.

B&B from € 32.00 to € 45.00
£25.20 to £35.44

CORNELIUS CREEDON
PROPRIETOR

American Express
Diners
Mastercard
Visa

39 39

Closed 01 November - 16 March

Room rates are per room per night

BALTIMORE BAY GUEST HOUSE

THE WATERFRONT,
BALTIMORE,
CO. CORK

TEL: 028-20600 FAX: 028-20495
EMAIL: baltimorebay@youenjacob.com
WEB: www.youenjacob.com

GUESTHOUSE ★★★ MAP 2 E 1

Baltimore Bay Guest House is a superbly appointed new guesthouse with 8 spacious bedrooms. 5 bedrooms have a magnificent view on the sea. Two restaurants are attached to the guesthouse, La Jolie Brise budget restaurant, Egon Ronay listed, and Chez Youen, Egon Ronay Best Irish Fish Restaurant of the Year in 1994 and listed as one of the best places to stay in Ireland. Sawday Guide. Guide du Routard. Youen & Mary Jacob and sons, Proprietors. Sailing facilities.

B&B from €32.00 to €52.00
£25.20 to £40.95

YOUEN & MARY JACOB
OWNER-MANAGERS

American Express
Mastercard
Visa

🛏️ 🍴 ☎️ 🖥️ T C CM ♩ S ▯ alc 🍷
8   8

IRISH HOTELS FEDERATION

Open All Year

BALTIMORE HARBOUR HOTEL & LEISURE CENTRE

BALTIMORE,
CO. CORK

TEL: 028-20361 FAX: 028-20466
EMAIL: info@bhrhotel.ie
WEB: www.bhrhotel.ie

HOTEL ★★★ MAP 2 E 1

The hotel is situated overlooking the Harbour & Islands in the charming coastal village of Baltimore. It is the ideal haven from which to explore the beauty and wonders of West Cork and the sea and to enjoy the many varied activities available locally, including sailing, golfing, angling, diving, horse-riding, walking, cycling and of course the Islands. We are especially suited for families and offer children's entertainment during peak season. Enjoy our superb indoor leisure centre. Newly refurbished bedrooms.

B&B from €55.00 to €80.00
£43.32 to £63.01

ANTHONY PALMER
GENERAL MANAGER

American Express
Diners
Mastercard
Visa

😊 Weekend specials from €115.00

🛏️ 🍴 ☎️ 🖥️ 🚻 T C 🅿️ CM ❄️ 🔔 📶 U
♩ ♫ P S ▯ alc 🍷
64   64

IRISH HOTELS FEDERATION

Closed 01 January - 01 February

CASEY'S OF BALTIMORE

BALTIMORE,
CO. CORK

TEL: 028-20197 FAX: 028-20509
EMAIL: caseys@eircom.net
WEB: www.caseysofbaltimore.com

HOTEL ★★★ MAP 2 E 1

A warm welcome awaits you at Casey's of Baltimore. Situated at the entrance to Baltimore with its lovely views overlooking the bay, this superb family run hotel is the perfect place to spend some time. All rooms feature en suite bathrooms, satellite TV, tea/coffee facility, direct dial phone, hairdryer and trouser press. The traditional pub and restaurant feature natural stone and wood decor, a spectacular view, extensive menu - seafood is our speciality. Activities can be arranged.

Member of Coast and Country Hotels
B&B from €55.00 to €66.00
£43.32 to £51.98

ANN & MICHAEL CASEY
OWNERS

American Express
Diners
Mastercard
Visa

😊 Midweek specials from €114.00

🛏️ 🍴 ☎️ 🖥️ T C 🅿️ CM U ♩ ♫ P S 🍷
alc 🍷 Inet
14   14

IRISH HOTELS FEDERATION

Closed 04 - 18 October

B&B rates are per person sharing per night incl. Breakfast

MUNSTER ARMS HOTEL

OLIVER PLUNKETT STREET,
BANDON,
CO. CORK
TEL: 023-41562 FAX: 023-41562
EMAIL: info@munsterarmshotel.com
WEB: www.munsterarmshotel.com

HOTEL ★★★   MAP 2 G 2

Set at the gateway to West Cork, 30 high quality en suite bedrooms with tea/coffee facilities, direct dial telephone, remote control T.V. radio and hairdryer. Set in beautiful scenic West Cork accessible by the N71 route from Cork City. Renowned for its homely atmosphere and superb quality. Ideal touring base and easily accessible to Kinsale, Cork City, Blarney, Killarney and West Cork. Relax and be pampered! Guests of the Munster Arms Hotel may use the leisure facilities at the local Bandon Leisure Centre for a nominal fee payable direct to the leisure centre.

B&B from €42.00 to €50.00
£33.08 to £39.38

JOHN COLLINS/DON O'SULLIVAN

American Express
Diners
Mastercard
Visa

30 30

Closed 25 - 26 December

ATLANTA HOUSE

MAIN STREET,
BANTRY,
CO. CORK
TEL: 027-50237 FAX: 027-50237
EMAIL: atlantaguesthouse@eircom.net
WEB: www.atlantaguesthouse.com

GUESTHOUSE ★★★   MAP 2 E 2

Atlanta House is a long established family run guesthouse situated in the centre of Bantry. It is an ideal base from which to tour West Cork and Kerry if you are walking, cycling or driving. Golf, fishing and horseriding are all close by. Rooms are en suite with TV, D.D phone & tea/coffee making facilities. We assure you of a warm welcome and we look forward to seeing you in Bantry.

B&B from €25.00 to €28.00
£19.69 to £22.05

RONNIE & ESTHER O'DRISCOLL
OWNERS

American Express
Mastercard
Visa

9 9

Closed 20 - 31 December

BANTRY BAY HOTEL

WOLFE TONE SQUARE,
BANTRY,
CO. CORK
TEL: 027-50062 FAX: 027-50261
EMAIL: bantrybay@eircom.net
WEB: www.bantrybayhotel.com

HOTEL ★★   MAP 2 E 2

The Bantry Bay has been operated by the O'Callaghan family for over 50 years in the centre of historic Bantry. Extensively renovated since 1995, the premises consists of a choice of family, tourist and commercial accommodation. All rooms are en suite with TV, DD phone, teamaker and hairdryer. They are complimented by our beautiful maritime theme bar and restaurant. Carvery in operation daily. Guests assured of a hearty O'Callaghan welcome.

B&B from €46.09 to €48.88
£36.30 to £38.50

VIVIAN O'CALLAGHAN SNR/JNR
PROPRIETOR/MANAGER

American Express
Diners
Mastercard
Visa

14 14

Closed 24 - 27 December

Room rates are per room per night

VICKERY'S INN

NEW STREET,
BANTRY,
CO. CORK
TEL: 027-50006 FAX: 027-20002
EMAIL: vickerys_inn@westcork.com
WEB: www.westcork.com/vickerys-inn

GUESTHOUSE ★ MAP 2 E 2

Originally a coaching inn established 1850. All bedrooms en suite with TV, telephones, tea/coffee making facilities. Extensive menus available. Guide du Routard recommended. Ideally situated to explore the scenic West Cork/Kerry region. Golf, horseriding, river, lake and seafishing close by. Internet access available.

B&B from €31.00 to €35.00
£24.41 to £27.56

HAZEL VICKERY
PROPRIETOR

American Express
Diners
Mastercard
Visa

13 13

Closed 23 - 29 December

WESTLODGE HOTEL

BANTRY,
CO. CORK
TEL: 027-50360 FAX: 027-50438
EMAIL: reservations@westlodgehotel.ie
WEB: www.westlodgehotel.ie

HOTEL ★★★ MAP 2 E 2

3*** hotel beautifully situated in the scenic surroundings of Bantry Bay. Super health and leisure centre including indoor heated swimming pool, children's pool, toddlers pool, sauna, steam room, jacuzzi, gym, aerobics, squash. Outdoor amenities include tennis, pitch & putt, wooden walks. The Westlodge specialise in family holidays with organised activities during June, July & August. A warm and friendly welcome awaits you at the Westlodge. Self-catering cottages available.

B&B from €57.00 to €83.00
£44.89 to £65.37

EILEEN M O'SHEA MIHCI
GENERAL MANAGER

American Express
Diners
Mastercard
Visa

Weekend specials from €114.00

90 90

Closed 23 - 28 December

ASHLEE LODGE

TOWER,
BLARNEY,
CO. CORK
TEL: 021-438 5346 FAX: 021-438 5726
EMAIL: info@ashleelodge.com
WEB: www.ashleelodge.com

GUESTHOUSE P MAP 2 H 3

Situated just outside Blarney, Ashlee Lodge offers superior accommodation for the discerning guest. Ideal for visiting Blarney Castle and Blarney Woollen Mills and just 10 mins drive from Cork City. Luxurious ground floor rooms and suites boast air conditioning, king size beds, widescreen TV/CD units and whirlpool baths. Relax in our sauna and Canadian hot tub. Experience our renowned gourmet breakfast. Superb gardens and private car park. French and German spoken.

B&B from €50.00 to €82.00
£39.38 to £64.58

ANNE & JOHN O'LEARY
PROPRIETORS

American Express
Mastercard
Visa

Autumn/Spring specials

8 8

Open All Year

B&B rates are per person sharing per night incl. Breakfast

BLARNEY CASTLE HOTEL

**BLARNEY,
CO. CORK**

TEL: 021-438 5116 FAX: 021-438 5542
EMAIL: info@blarney-castle-hotel.com
WEB: www.blarney-castle-hotel.com

HOTEL ★★ MAP 2 H 3

Established in 1837, still run by the Forrest family. Picturesque inn on unique village green, 5 miles from Cork City. Superbly appointed bedrooms, unspoilt traditional bar and restaurant specialising in finest local produce. Killarney, Kenmare, Kinsale, Cobh, West Cork, Waterford and numerous golf courses all an easy drive. Immediately to the left the magnificent gardens of Blarney Castle guarding that famous stone, to the right Blarney Woollen Mills. Private car park for hotel guests. Quality entertainment nightly in the village.

B&B from €45.00 to €55.00
£35.44 to £43.32

**IAN FORREST
MANAGER**

American Express
Diners
Mastercard
Visa

☺ Weekend specials from €100.00

🛏🐾☎📷🗄T🅲➡CM◡♪♫P🅂🅰
10 10

alc 🖥 inet

IRISH
HOTELS
FEDERATION

Closed 25 - 26 December

BLARNEY PARK HOTEL

**BLARNEY,
CO. CORK**

TEL: 021-438 5281 FAX: 021-438 1506
EMAIL: info@blarneypark.com
WEB: www.blarneypark.com

HOTEL ★★★ MAP 2 H 3

Located in the heart of picturesque Blarney, famous for its castle and stone, this modern hotel enjoys a relaxed atmosphere and offers a wide range of facilities, and award winning leisure centre (and 40 - meter slide). You can truly unwind after a hard day discovering Cork and the majestic Lee Valley. Well situated to visit Blarney Woollen Mills, or for day trips to the Ring of Kerry and Waterford Crystal. Children will love our supervised playroom. Callsave 1850 50 30 10.

B&B from €75.00 to €90.00
£59.07 to £70.88

**AIDEN GRIMES
GENERAL MANAGER**

American Express
Diners
Mastercard
Visa

🏌🎾

🛏🐾☎📷🗄T🅰🅲➡CM❄🈁
91 91

🖼🔍◡🎣P🅂🅰alc inet

IRISH
HOTELS
FEDERATION

Closed 23 - 26 December

CHRISTY'S HOTEL

**BLARNEY,
CO. CORK**

TEL: 021-438 5011 FAX: 021-438 5350
EMAIL: christys@blarney.ie
WEB: www.christyshotel.com

HOTEL ★★★ MAP 2 H 3

Christy's 3★★★ Hotel with 45 beautifully appointed superior rooms and 3 executive suites. Many of the bedrooms have spectacular views of the famous Blarney Castle. All rooms have been tastefully decorated in the traditional style. Christy's has all day dining in our self service restaurant and evening dining in our new Grill Bar. The hotel boasts one of the finest fitness centres in the area. Located within the old Mill buildings in the famous Blarney Woollen Mills complex. Within the complex you can enjoy a relaxing drink and experience some Irish hospitality in Christy's Pub.

B&B from €75.00 to €95.00
£59.07 to £74.82

DECLAN MORIARTY

American Express
Diners
Mastercard
Visa

🛏🐾☎📷🗄T🅲➡CM🖼🈁🎣◡
48 48

♪P🅂🅰alc 🖥

IRISH
HOTELS
FEDERATION

Closed 24 - 26 December

Room rates are per room per night

SUNSET RIDGE HOTEL

KILLEENS,
BLARNEY,
CO. CORK

TEL: 021-438 5271 FAX: 021-438 5565

EMAIL: sunsetridge@holidayhound.com
WEB: www.holidayhound.com/sunsetridge

HOTEL ★ MAP 2 H 3

Situated on main Cork/Limerick road, Cork City 4.8km / Blarney Village 3.2km. All rooms en suite, TV, direct dial phone. Fully licensed bar, complimentary entertainment Wed/Sat/Sun, bar food available. Our restaurant offers a selection of lunch, dinner and à la carte menus daily. Local amenities include horse riding, golf and fishing. A scenic nature trail walk links our hotel with Blarney Village. Special rates for group bookings. Bus tours catered for.

B&B from €35.00 to €46.00
£27.56 to £36.23

DENIS CRONIN
MANAGER

American Express
Diners
Mastercard
Visa

28 28

a/c

IRISH HOTELS FEDERATION

Closed 25 - 26 December

WATERLOO INN

WATERLOO,
BLARNEY,
CO. CORK

TEL: 021-438 5113 FAX: 021-438 2829

EMAIL: waterlooinn@eircom.net
WEB: www.blarneybandb.com

GUESTHOUSE ★★ MAP 2 H 3

Enjoy a holiday in an old country inn located just 1.5 miles from Blarney Castle and 6 miles from Cork City. Set in a peaceful location this riverside inn offers comfortable rooms with tea/coffee making facilities. Relax in our conservatory, have a drink in the bar or walk up to the old round tower of Waterloo. All leisure activities nearby (golf, horse riding etc). This is an ideal centre to tour the South of Ireland. Secure parking available.

B&B from €28.00 to €32.00
£22.05 to £25.20

PATRICIA DORAN/MARY DUGGAN
PROPRIETORS

Mastercard
Visa

5 3

Closed 15 November - 15 February

CARRIGALINE COURT HOTEL

CARRIGALINE,
CO. CORK

TEL: 021-485 2100 FAX: 021-437 1103

EMAIL: carrigcourt@eircom.net
WEB: www.carrigcourt.com

HOTEL U MAP 3 H 3

A well established luxury hotel situated only minutes from the city centre, airport and ferryport. RAC **** hotel. All rooms offer the very best in the modern comforts. ISDN phone, satellite TV and radio as standard. Superb dining guaranteed in the Kingfisher Restaurant. An Carrig leisure centre, luxurious and stress-free facilities include a 20m pool. Golf arranged at Cork's best courses. Local facilities include sailing, hill walking and a host of other events in this beautiful area.

B&B from €80.00 to €95.00
£63.01 to £74.82

JOHN O'FLYNN
GENERAL MANAGER

American Express
Diners
Mastercard
Visa

☺ Weekend specials from €120.00

52 52

IRISH HOTELS FEDERATION

Closed 25 December

B&B rates are per person sharing per night incl. Breakfast

FERNHILL GOLF & COUNTRY CLUB

FERNHILL,
CARRIGALINE,
CO. CORK
TEL: 021-4372 226 FAX: 021-4371 011
EMAIL: fernhill@iol.ie
WEB: www.fernhillgolfhotel.com

GUESTHOUSE ★★★ MAP 3 H 3

Fernhill Golf & Country is the ideal venue for your relaxing holiday; 18 hole golf course (free to residents), indoor swimming pool, sauna, tennis, horse riding and fishing. 10 mins from Cork City and Airport, 5 mins from Ringaskiddy Ferries, 30 mins from Kinsale. All rooms en suite, TV, direct dial phone, tea/coffee making facilities, full bar and restaurant all day in clubhouse. Music at weekends.

B&B from €44.00 to €71.00
£34.65 to £55.91

MICHAEL BOWES
OWNER

American Express
Diners
Mastercard
Visa

18 18

Closed 20 December - 02 January

GLENWOOD HOUSE

BALLINREA ROAD,
CARRIGALINE,
CORK
TEL: 021-437 3878 FAX: 021-437 3878
EMAIL: glenwoodhouse@eircom.net
WEB: www.glenwoodhotel.com

GUESTHOUSE ★★★★ MAP 3 H 3

Glenwood House is a purpose built, self contained Guesthouse, designed with all guest requirements in mind. The rooms are large and spacious, offering similar facilities to those of quality hotels, firm orthopedic beds, heated towel rails, complimentary beverages, trouser press, satelite TV, power shower and many more. Located close to Ringaskiddy Ferry Port (5mins), Cork City (7mins), Kinsale (15mins), Crosshaven (5mins), Airport (5mins). We offer secure car parking, and have facilities to look after disabled guests. All accommodation is of hotel quality.

Member of Premier Guesthouses
B&B from €50.00 to €65.00
£39.38 to £51.19

CATHERINE MAYE
PROPRIETOR

Mastercard
Visa

16 16

Inet FAX

Closed 25 - 31 December

CASTLE

CASTLETOWNSHEND,
CO. CORK
TEL: 028-36100 FAX: 028-36166
EMAIL: castle_townshend@hotmail.com

GUESTHOUSE ★ MAP 2 F 1

18th century Townshend family home overlooking Castlehaven Harbour. Set in own grounds at waters edge with access to small beach and woods. Most bedrooms en suite on second floor with excellent sea views. Panelled hall/sitting room with TV and open fire. Breakfast in elegant dining room. Mary Ann's Restaurant close by. Ideal for touring Cork and Kerry. Also self catering apartments and cottages. For illustrated brochure please apply.

B&B from €35.00 to €65.00
£27.56 to £51.19

MRS COCHRANE-TOWNSHEND

Mastercard
Visa

7 6

Closed 15 December - 15 January

Room rates are per room per night

DEERPARK HOTEL

LIMERICK ROAD,
CHARLEVILLE,
CO. CORK
TEL: 063-81581 FAX: 063-81581
EMAIL: info@deerparkhotel.com
WEB: www.charleville.com

HOTEL ★★ MAP 2 G 5

The Deerpark Hotel is the ideal centre for your stay in North Cork, South Limerick, South Tipperary area. Convenient to Blarney, Cork, Adare, Shannon and the Glen of Aherlow. Horse riding, bicycle hire, fishing, pitch & putt special green fees at one of Munster's finest inland 27 hole courses (18 & 9) are all available locally to our guests. Extensive à la carte menu throughout the day. Site on 9 acres with mature gardens. The Sheehan Family welcome you to the Deerpark Hotel.

Room Rate from €50.00 to €89.00
£39.38 to £70.09

ROSARIO & MARK SHEEHAN
PROPRIETORS

Mastercard
Visa

20 20

alc

IRISH HOTELS FEDERATION

Open All Year

DUNMORE HOUSE HOTEL

MUCKROSS,
CLONAKILTY,
CO. CORK
TEL: 023-33352 FAX: 023-34686
EMAIL: dunmorehousehotel@eircom.net
WEB: www.dunmorehousehotel.com

HOTEL ★★★ MAP 2 G 2

Situated on the South West coast of Ireland, Dunmore House Hotel is family owned. Rooms are beautifully decorated, all with spectacular views of the Atlantic Ocean. Sample a true taste of West Cork with our home-cooked local produce and seafood. Private foreshore available for sea angling. Green fees at the on-site golf club are free to residents. Wheelchair access throughout hotel. Interesting collection of local and modern Irish art.

Member of Green Book of Ireland

B&B from €60.00 to €80.00
£47.25 to £63.01

DERRY & MARY O'DONOVAN
PROPRIETORS

American Express
Diners
Mastercard
Visa

☺ Midweek specials from €180.00

23 23

alc

IRISH HOTELS FEDERATION

Closed 01 February - 01 March

EMMET HOTEL

EMMET SQUARE,
CLONAKILTY,
CO. CORK
TEL: 023-33394 FAX: 023-35058
EMAIL: emmethotel@eircom.net
WEB: www.emmethotel.com

HOTEL U MAP 2 G 2

Ideally located in a Georgian square within two minutes walk of the main street and a five minute drive to beautiful beaches. The Emmet offers old fashioned courtesy with a very friendly ambience. Our restaurant has established itself as having the best food in West Cork using fresh organic seasonal produce. Leisure centre, golf, riding and angling available locally. New patio garden, serving food and drink daily during the summer months. Also, barbeque facilities for parties up to 40 max.

B&B from €44.43 to €57.13
£34.99 to £44.99

TONY & MARIE O'KEEFFE
MANAGER

American Express
Diners
Mastercard
Visa

20 20

S alc

Open All Year

B&B rates are per person sharing per night incl. Breakfast

FERNHILL HOUSE HOTEL

CLONAKILTY,
CO. CORK

TEL: 023-33258 FAX: 023-34003
EMAIL: info@fernhillhousehotel.com
WEB: www.fernhillhousehotel.com

HOTEL ★★ MAP 2 G 2

Fernhill House is a family run old Georgian style hotel located on picturesque grounds 0.8km from Clonakilty. All bedrooms en suite with tea/coffee making facilities, phone, TV and hairdryer. Conference and function facilities available, Par 3 golf 18 hole Pitch & Putt course. Our hotel offers an intimate homely atmosphere, excellent food and a comfortable bar. Holiday with us and enjoy scenic West Cork from centrally situated Fernhill House Hotel. Use of local leisure facility available.

B&B from €45.00 to €50.00
£35.44 to £39.38

MICHAEL & TERESA O'NEILL
PROPRIETORS

American Express
Diners
Mastercard
Visa

11 11

Closed 23 December - 01 January

LODGE & SPA AT INCHYDONEY ISLAND

CLONAKILTY,
CO. CORK

TEL: 023-33143 FAX: 023-35229
EMAIL: reservations@inchydoneyisland.com
WEB: www.inchydoneyisland.com

HOTEL ★★★★ MAP 2 G 2

Situated on the idyllic island of Inchydoney, between two EU blue flag beaches, the hotel offers de luxe rooms, a fully equipped thalassotherapy (seawater) spa, restaurant, Dunes Pub and function and meeting facilities. Within a short distance guests can enjoy sailing, golf at the Old Head of Kinsale, riding and deep sea fishing. The style of cooking in the Gulfstream Restaurant reflects the wide availability of fresh seafoods and organically grown vegetables.

Member of Concorde Hotels

B&B from €129.25 to €156.75
£101.79 to £123.45

MICHAEL KNOX-JOHNSTON

American Express
Diners
Mastercard
Visa

67 67

Open All Year

Clonakilty ...

Seeing is Believing

**Discover Our Clonakilty
An ideal holiday
destination and base from
which to tour West Cork**

10 Miles of Sandy Beaches

**For Further Information:
Please Contact:
Clonakilty and District
Chamber of Tourism**

"In existence to care for you"

Callsave 1850 230 730
Tel: 00 353 23 35047
E-mail: tourism@clonakilty.ie
Website: www.clonakilty.ie

Room rates are per room per night

O'DONOVAN'S HOTEL

PEARSE STREET,
CLONAKILTY,
WEST CORK
TEL: 023-33250 FAX: 023-33250
EMAIL: odhotel@iol.ie
WEB: www.odonovanshotel.com

HOTEL ★ MAP 2 G 2

Charles Stewart Parnell, Marconi and Gen Michael Collins found time to stop here. This fifth generation, family run hotel is located in the heart of Clonakilty Town. Abounding in history, the old world charm has been retained whilst still providing the guest with facilities such as bath/shower en suite, TV etc. Our restaurant provides snacks and full meals and is open to non-residents. Ideal for conferences, private functions, meetings etc., with lock up car park.

B&B from € 45.00 to € 52.00
£35.44 to £40.95

O'DONOVAN FAMILY
PROPRIETORS

American Express
Mastercard
Visa

26 26

Open All Year

QUALITY HOTEL AND LEISURE CENTRE

CLONAKILTY,
CO. CORK

TEL: 023-35400 FAX: 023-35404
EMAIL: qualityhotel@eircom.net
WEB: www.qualityhotelclon.com

HOTEL ★★★ MAP 2 G 2

Clonakilty is a thriving and busy attractive town with a wealth of musical and artistic cultural activities. Excellent visitor attractions include model railway village, Lisselan Gardens plus access to superb sandy beaches, which makes Clonakilty the perfect gateway to West Cork. The new hotel complex with award winning leisure centre, 5 executive holiday homes, Lannigans Restaurant & Oscars Bar is completed with a 3 screen multiplex cinema. Your value for money choice.

Member of Choice Hotels Ireland
B&B from € 38.00 to € 70.00
£29.93 to £55.13

DAVID HENRY
GENERAL MANAGER

American Express
Diners
Mastercard
Visa

☺ Weekend specials from €100.00

58 58

Closed 24 - 27 December

BELLA VISTA HOUSE HOTEL

BISHOP'S ROAD,
COBH,
CO. CORK

TEL: 021-481 2450 FAX: 021-481 2215
EMAIL: bellavis@indigo.ie
WEB: http://indigo.ie/~bellavis

HOTEL ★★ MAP 3 I 3

Bella Vista Hotel is a family business set in a beautiful Victorian villa. Situated on an elevated site just above the picturesque town of Cobh with tremendous views of Cork Harbour. All 17 rooms + 1 family suite are decorated to a very high standard with DD phone, tea/coffee making facilities, full bar facilities for guest use only and on site private parking. Just two mins walk to town centre and central to main railway line & Fota Wildlife Park. The hotel is located within 15 minutes drive of no fewer than 5 golf courses, with Fota Golf Course just 2 mins drive.

B&B from € 32.00 to € 44.50
£25.20 to £35.05

KEVIN MURPHY
PROPRIETOR

American Express
Mastercard
Visa

18 18

Open All Year

B&B rates are per person sharing per night incl. Breakfast

COMMODORE HOTEL

COBH,
CO. CORK

TEL: 021-481 1277 FAX: 021-481 1672
EMAIL: commodorehotel@eircom.net
WEB: www.commodorehotel.ie

HOTEL ★★ MAP 313

The Commodore Hotel newly refurbished, owned by the O'Shea family for 30 years overlooks Cork Harbour. 25 minutes from city centre. Facilities: indoor pool, snooker, entertainment, roof garden. Available locally free golf and pitch & putt. Ideal for visiting Fota, Blarney, The Jameson and Queenstown Heritage Centres. All 42 rooms have full facilities, 21 overlook Cork Harbour. Ringaskiddy Ferryport 15 mins via river car ferry.

Member of Logis of Ireland
B&B from €40.00 to €95.00
£31.50 to £74.82

PATRICK O'SHEA
GENERAL MANAGER

American Express
Diners
Mastercard
Visa

Weekend specials from €108.00

42 42

Closed 24 - 27 December

WATERSEDGE HOTEL

YACHT CLUB QUAY,
COBH,
CO. CORK

TEL: 021-481 5566 FAX: 021-481 2011
EMAIL: watersedge@eircom.net
WEB: www.watersedgehotel.ie

HOTEL ★★★ MAP 313

Situated on the waterfront overlooking Cork Harbour. All rooms en suite with satellite TV, tea making facilities, direct dial phone, modem, hairdryer, trouser press. Our restaurant, Jacobs Ladder, is renowned for its seafood, steaks, ambience and friendly staff. Local activities and sightseeing include Cobh Heritage Centre (next door), Cathedral, Titanic Trail, Fota Wildlife Park, golf, sailing, angling, tennis, horseriding. Ideal touring base for Cork City, Kinsale & Blarney.

B&B from €50.00 to €127.00
£40.00 to £100.00

MARGARET & MIKE WHELAN
PROPRIETORS

American Express
Diners
Mastercard
Visa

19 19

Closed 23 - 28 December

Titanic Trail
Cobh, Co. Cork

Explore Cobh's Fascinating history and the towns' direct links with Titanic! The original Titanic Trail guided walking tour takes place every day all year.

Leaving at **11am daily** from the Commodore Hotel this famous tour is educational, interesting and fun. Cost is €6 (£4.75) which includes a complimentary glass of stout. Duration is approximately 75 minutes.

Afternoon Trails can also be arranged. Groups welcome. Night time Ghost Walk also available for groups seeking mystery and fun.

Contact: Michael Martin
Author and Creator Titanic Trail

Tel: + 353 (21) 4815211
Mobile: +353 (87) 276 7218
Email: info@titanic-trail.com
URL www.titanic-trail.com

Room rates are per room per night

AIRPORT LODGE

FARMERS CROSS, KINSALE ROAD,
CORK AIRPORT,
CO. CORK

TEL: 021-431 6920 FAX: 087-5249 8100
EMAIL: airlodge@indigo.ie
WEB: www.corkairportlodge.com

GUESTHOUSE U MAP 2 H 3

Located at the gates of Cork Airport, 15 minutes drive from Ringaskiddy Ferryport and adjacent to all major roads around Cork City, we are ideal as a first/last night stop. Cork City is only 8km away, Kinsale 30km. We have extensive free car parking and provide a welcome break before you continue your journey.

Room Rate from €45.00 to €80.00
£35.44 to £63.01

MARY & MAURICE BERGIN
PROPRIETORS

Mastercard
Visa

5   5

IRISH HOTELS FEDERATION

Closed 24 - 29 December

GREAT SOUTHERN HOTEL

CORK AIRPORT,
CO. CORK

TEL: 021-494 7500 FAX: 021-494 7501
EMAIL: res@corkairport-gsh.com
WEB: www.greatsouthernhotels.com

HOTEL P MAP 2 H 3

The Great Southern Hotel Cork Airport is a stylish contemporary hotel conveniently located within walking distance of the terminal at Cork Airport. With a wide range of meeting rooms, a business centre and a leisure centre with gymnasium, steam room and jacuzzi, it is the perfect base for business meetings or for first or last night stays. Bookable worldwide through UTELL International or Central Reservations: 01-214 4800.

Room Rate from €140.00 to €150.00
£110.24 to £118.11

PAT CUSSEN
GENERAL MANAGER

American Express
Diners
Mastercard
Visa

81   81

inet FAX

IRISH HOTELS FEDERATION

Closed 24 - 26 December

ACHILL HOUSE

WESTERN ROAD,
CORK CITY

TEL: 021-427 9447 FAX: 021-427 9447
EMAIL: info@achillhouse.com
WEB: www.achillhouse.com

GUESTHOUSE ★★★ MAP 2 H 3

Stay in luxury, comfort and style at Achill House. This elegant period house is ideally located in the heart of Cork City centre and opposite UCC. All rooms have de luxe en suite bathrooms with optional jacuzzi. An extensive breakfast menu caters for all tastes from hearty Irish breakfast to lighter options. Achill House is convenient to ferry, airport and bus termini, the perfect base for exploring Cork and Kerry. A warm and relaxed atmosphere awaits you whether on business or pleasure.

B&B from €35.00 to €55.00
£27.56 to £43.32

HELENA MCSWEENEY
PROPRIETOR

Mastercard
Visa

☺ Room only from €50.00 - €75.00

6   6

IRISH HOTELS FEDERATION

Open All Year

B&B rates are per person sharing per night incl. Breakfast

ACORN HOUSE

14 ST. PATRICK'S HILL,
CORK

TEL: 021-450 2474 FAX: 021-450 2474
EMAIL: info@acornhouse-cork.com
WEB: www.acornhouse-cork.com

GUESTHOUSE ★★★ MAP 2 H 3

Acorn House is a comfortable refurbished listed Georgian house of architectural merit dating back to 1810. It is a 3 minute walk to St. Patrick Street, Cork City's principal thoroughfare with theatres and excellent choice of restaurants. 5 minutes walk to bus and rail stations; 15 minutes drive to airport and car ferry. Rooms en suite with TV, phone and tea/coffee facilities. Michelin and Stilwell recommended. Children over 12 welcome.

B&B from €32.00 to €45.00
£25.20 to £35.44

JACKIE BOLES
PROPRIETOR

Mastercard
Visa

9   9

HOTELS
FEDERATION

Closed 22 December - 10 January

AMBASSADOR HOTEL

MILITARY HILL,
ST. LUKES,
CORK

TEL: 021-455 1996 FAX: 021-455 1997
EMAIL: info@ambassadorhotel.ie
WEB: www.ambassadorhotel.ie

HOTEL U MAP 2 H 3

Located on a hilltop, the Ambassador Hotel commands spectacular views over Cork City and Harbour. 60 spacious bedrooms luxuriously decorated to the highest standards. A gourmet award-winning "Season's Restaurant", Cocktail Bar, Embassy Bar, Conference Centre and Banqueting facilities, all combine to ensure a memorable stay.

Member of Best Western Hotels

B&B from €45.00 to €88.00
£35.44 to £69.31

DUDLEY FITZELL

American Express
Diners
Mastercard
Visa

60   60

HOTELS
FEDERATION

Closed 24 - 26 December

Room rates are per room per night

ANTOINE HOUSE

**WESTERN ROAD,
CORK**

TEL: 021-427 3494 FAX: 021-427 3092
EMAIL: info@antoinehouse.com
WEB: www.antoinehouse.com

GUESTHOUSE ★★ MAP 2 H 3

Located at gateway to West Cork and Kerry for business or pleasure. An ideal base from which to explore, less than one mile from city centre and in close proximity to airport, train, ferry, Blarney and Fota. All rooms en suite with direct dial phones, Satellite TV, hairdryer, tea/coffee facilities. Private lock up car park at rear, golf, shooting, fishing, horse-riding, flying can be arranged. Children welcome. Frommers recommended and AA listed.

B&B from €30.00 to €50.00
£23.63 to £39.38

KEVIN CROSS
PROPRIETOR

American Express
Diners
Mastercard
Visa

10 10

Open All Year

ARBUTUS LODGE HOTEL

**MONTENOTTE,
CORK**

TEL: 021-450 1237 FAX: 021-450 2893
EMAIL: info@arbutuslodge.net
WEB: www.arbutuslodge.net

HOTEL ★★★ MAP 2 H 3

Elegant townhouse built in the late 18th century, set in its own gardens, overlooking the River Lee and Cork City. There are 16 rooms all individually decorated. An imaginative fusion of French influence and Irish produce combined with an impressive wine list ensures that Arbutus Lodge has one of the best restaurants in Ireland. There is a delightful bar and patio where meals are served all day and also a traditional bar where there is traditional music at weekends. The hotel is family owned and John and family look forward to meeting you.

B&B from €60.00 to €82.50
£47.25 to £64.97

CARMODY FAMILY

American Express
Diners
Mastercard
Visa

☺ Weekend specials from €135.00

16 16

Closed 23 - 28 December

ASHLEY HOTEL

**COBURG STREET,
CORK**

TEL: 021-450 1518 FAX: 021-450 1178
EMAIL: ashleyhotel@eircom.net
WEB: www.ashleyhotel.com

HOTEL U MAP 2 H 3

The Ashley Hotel is family-owned, run by Anita Coughlan and her enthusiastic staff, with all the benefits of the city centre location to shops and other attractions. It is the perfect place to relax and have fun. The Ashley has plenty to offer you with a secure lock-up car park, 27 rooms with bathroom en suite, tea/coffee making facilities and direct dial phone with a lively bar and restaurant.

B&B from €51.00 to €64.00
£40.17 to £50.40

ANITA COUGHLAN

American Express
Diners
Mastercard
Visa

27 27

Open All Year

B&B rates are per person sharing per night incl. Breakfast

BLARNEY STONE

WESTERN ROAD,
CORK CITY

TEL: 021-427 0083 FAX: 021-427 0471
EMAIL: bsgh@eircom.net
WEB: www.blarney-stone-guesthouse.com

GUESTHOUSE P   MAP 2 H 3

This newly refurbished Victorian residence has character and charm and offers you luxurious accommodation in the heart of the city. Situated opposite University College and within close proximity to a selection of restaurants, bars and entertainment places. Also ideally located for ferry, airport, train and bus. All rooms are tastefully decorated to the highest standard with de luxe en suite optional jacuzzi, TV, DD phone, tea/coffee making facilities. A warm and friendly atmosphere awaits you.

B&B from €31.74 to €63.50
£25.00 to £50.00

ANGELA HARTNETT

Mastercard
Visa

🛏️🐾☎️💻TCCM✣♪PS⬆️inet
8 8

Open All Year

BRAZIER'S WESTPOINT HOUSE

WESTERN ROAD,
(OPP. UCC),
CORK

TEL: 021-427 5526 FAX: 021-425 1955
EMAIL: info@braziersguesthouse.com
WEB: www.braziersguesthouse.com

GUESTHOUSE U   MAP 2 H 3

A warm welcome and friendly service awaits you at the family run Brazier's Westpoint House which is located less than 10 minutes walk from Cork City centre and opposite University College Cork. Tastefully decorated, all rooms are en suite with colour TV, direct dial phone, hairdryers, tea/coffee facilities and we have a private lock-up carpark at the rear. An ideal base to visit Cork and tour the beautiful South West. AA approved.

B&B from €32.00 to €38.00
£25.20 to £29.93

JOY BRAZIER
PROPRIETOR

American Express
Mastercard
Visa

🛏️🐾☎️💻C✋CM✣P⬆️
8 8

IRISH
HOTELS
FEDERATION

Closed 23 December - 06 January

Room rates are per room per night

BROOKFIELD HOTEL

BROOKFIELD HOLIDAY VILLAGE, COLLEGE ROAD, CORK

TEL: 021-480 4700 FAX: 021-480 4793

HOTEL ★★★ MAP 2 H 3

Brookfield Hotel, College Road is just 1 mile from Cork City centre. Set on 10 acres of rolling parkland, it is truly a rural setting. *24 bright, modern bedrooms. *Family rooms. *Interconnecting rooms. *Complimentary use of our leisure and fitness centre which incorporates 25m indoor pool. Kiddies pool, water slide, saunas, steam room, spa jacuzzi, outdoor hot tub, massage, gym, sunbeds, outdoor tennis courts.

B&B from €50.00 to €95.00
£39.38 to £74.82

MIRIAM RYAN
RESERVATIONS MANAGER

American Express
Mastercard
Visa

🛏 🛋 ☎ ⬛🔆🍽 Ⓣ Ⓐ Ⓒ ⚡CMCS✲✧
📺🏠🏊♨Ⓤ♪Ⓟ ald 🛍
24 24

CLARION HOTEL & SUITES CORK

MORRISON'S QUAY, CORK

TEL: 021-427 5858 FAX: 021-427 5833
EMAIL: morisons@iol.ie
WEB: www.choicehotelscork.com

HOTEL ★★★ MAP 2 H 3

Clarion Hotel & Suites Cork is situated in the heart of the business and shopping district. Less than a 5 minute walk from Patrick St., Cork's vibrant main thoroughfare. This contemporary styled hotel meets all accommodation requirements for the individual traveller as well as for the family holiday.

Member of Choice Hotels Ireland

Room Rate from €82.55 to €215.90
£65.01 to £170.04

FRANK CASHMAN
GENERAL MANAGER

American Express
Diners
Mastercard
Visa

✔

☺ Weekend specials from €125.73

🛏 🛋 ☎ ⬛🔆 Ⓣ Ⓒ ⚡CM Ⓤ♪ⓅⓈ 🛍
56 56
ald 🖥 Inet FAX

IRISH HOTELS FEDERATION

COMMONS INN

NEW MALLOW ROAD, CORK

TEL: 021-421 0300 FAX: 021-421 0333
EMAIL: info@commonsinn.com
WEB: www.commonsinn.com

HOTEL ★★★ MAP 3 H 3

Close to Cork City, on the main Cork to Blarney road, this family run hotel contains the popular Commons bar, C Restaurant and the Roebuck Room function centre. All rooms contain two queen sized beds and are priced per room. Enjoy carvery lunch in the bar or dinner in one of Cork's best restaurants. Whether you're in Cork on business or for pleasure we are at your service.

Room Rate from €63.50 to €90.00
£50.01 to £70.88

ASHLEY O'NEILL
ACCOMMODATION MANAGER

American Express
Diners
Mastercard
Visa

🛏 🛋 ☎ ⬛Ⓒ CM✲♪Ⓟ 🛍 ald 🖥 Inet
40 40
FAX

B&B rates are per person sharing per night incl. Breakfast

CRAWFORD HOUSE

WESTERN ROAD,
CORK

TEL: 021-427 9000 FAX: 021-427 9927
EMAIL: crawford@indigo.ie
WEB: www.crawfordguesthouse.com

GUESTHOUSE ★★★ MAP 3 H 3

One of Cork's finest guesthouse's offering bed & breakfast in a contemporary setting. All the bedrooms provide comfort and luxury with oak-wood furniture and orthopaedic 6ft king size beds. De luxe en suites include jacuzzi baths and power showers. Fax/modem points in all rooms. Located directly across from University College Cork. 10 min. walk city centre. Private lock up car park. AA ◆◆◆◆ & RAC ◆◆◆◆ and Sparkling Diamond award 2001.

B&B from €38.00 to €57.00
£29.92 to £44.88

CECILIA O'LEARY
MANAGER

American Express
Mastercard
Visa

🛏🕯☎🖥C M P⚡ Inet FAX
12 12

IRISH HOTELS FEDERATION

Closed 23 - 27 December

D'ARCYS

7 SIDNEY PLACE,
WELLINGTON ROAD,
CORK

TEL: 021-450 4658 FAX: 021-450 2791
EMAIL: accommodation@darcysguesthouse.com
WEB: www.darcysguesthouse.com

GUESTHOUSE ★ MAP 2 H 3

Not until you enter 7 Sidney Place do you realise what a large building it is. High ceilings and large spacious rooms. The front rooms have views over the city. Rooms are uncluttered, calm, cool places, very peaceful in the centre of the city. Children are welcome. Breakfast is not to be missed. Try freshly squeezed fruit juices, smoked salmon and scrambled eggs and home made preserves.

B&B from €40.00 to €45.00
£31.50 to £35.44

CLARE D'ARCY
PROPRIETOR

American Express
Diners
Mastercard
Visa

🛏🕯☎C⚡
6 2

IRISH HOTELS FEDERATION

Closed 23 - 27 December

FOTA HOUSE & GARDENS

LOCATION

Located 8 miles east of Cork City, just off the main Cork - Waterford Road, (N25). Take exit for Cobh, and continue 1 mile. Entrance is shared with Fota Wildlife Park. Access also by train. Car parking is available on site.

FACILITIES

The facilities at Fota include Tours, a Café, Retail Outlet and an evening corporate banqueting centre. The banqueting facility at Fota House has a maximum capacity for 70 people in the largest room and a number of smaller rooms with varying capacities. A Marquee Service in the gardens is available (Full details on request).

OPEN DAILY-7 DAYS.
Admission Charge Applies

CARRIGTWOHILL, CO. CORK
Tel: 00 353 21 4815543
Fax: 00 353 21 4815541
Email: info@fotahouse.com
Web: www.fotahouse.com

Room rates are per room per night

DOUGHCLOYNE HOTEL

DOUGHCLOYNE,
CORK CITY

TEL: 021-431 2535 FAX: 021-431 6086
EMAIL: dough1@iol.ie

HOTEL ★★★ MAP 2 H 3

The Doughcloyne Hotel is situated 2 miles from the city centre, close to the University Hospital in Wilton and Cork Airport, South Link N28 exit Doughcloyne Sarsfields Road roundabout. Our restaurant presents bonne cuisine with friendly service. The lounge bar is noted for its lunch-time barfood and live music at the weekends. Guests have complimentary use of Brookfield Leisure Centre with a 25m swimming pool located near by.

B&B from €39.00 to €51.00
£30.71 to £40.17

DAVID HARNEY
GENERAL MANAGER

American Express
Diners
Mastercard
Visa

☺ Weekend specials from €89.00

🛏 🐾 ☎ 🖵 🇹🇨 CMP🄰abc 🍴
50 50

Closed 24 December - 02 January

EAGLE LODGE GUEST HOUSE

1 WILLOWBROOK,
WESTERN ROAD,
CORK

TEL: 021-427 7380 FAX: 021-427 6432
EMAIL: eaglelodgecork@eircom.net
WEB: www.eaglelodge.net

GUESTHOUSE ★★★ MAP 2 H 3

Eagle Lodge is a 10 minute walk from city centre and close to bus and train stations. All rooms en suite with TV, tea/coffee making facilities, hair dryer and ironing facilities. An ideal base from which to tour West Cork and Kerry. Situated opposite University College. Eagle Lodge is within a short walk of many traditional Irish pubs and a variety of restaurants to suit all tastes.

B&B from €28.00 to €50.00
£22.05 to £39.38

NORA MURRAY
PROPRIETOR

American Express
Diners
Mastercard
Visa

☺ 3 nights B&B from €85.00

🛏 🐾 🖵 🇨 🅹 🄿🅂 🍴
7 7

HOTELS
FEDERATION

Open All Year

FAIRY LAWN

WESTERN ROAD,
CORK

TEL: 021-454 3444 FAX: 021-454 4337
EMAIL: fairylawn@holidayhound.com
WEB: www.holidayhound.com/fairylawn.htm

GUESTHOUSE ★★★ MAP 3 H 3

Fairy Lawn, newly restored & beautifully extended, this luxury guesthouse, with open fires, is tastefully decorated throughout. Bedrooms provide comfort with orthopaedic 6 ft beds (optional), satellite TV. DD phones, hairdryers and hospitality trays. Deluxe en suites with power showers. This family-run guesthouse, where a warm welcome awaits you & breakfast is not to be missed. Opposite UCC. Close to City Centre with ample private car parking to the front. AA ◆◆◆◆. RAC ◆◆◆◆ & Sparkling Diamond Award 2000 & 2001. Ideal touring base for South of Ireland.

B&B from €32.00 to €45.00
£25.20 to £35.44

TONY & JOAN MCGRATH
PROPRIETORS

Mastercard
Visa

🛏 🐾 ☎ 🖵 🇹🅄 🅹🄿🅂 🍴
14 14

HOTELS
FEDERATION

Open All Year

B&B rates are per person sharing per night incl. Breakfast

FORTE TRAVELODGE

BLACKASH,
KINSALE ROAD,
CORK

TEL: 1800-709709 FAX: 021-431 0723

WEB: www.travelodge.co.uk

HOTEL U MAP 3 H 3

Situated a couple of miles from Cork City centre, minutes from the Airport and on the direct routes to/from the car ferry, beautiful Kinsale and West Cork, this superb modern hotel offers comfortable yet affordable accommodation. Each room is large enough to sleep up to three adults, a child under 12 and a baby in a cot. Excellent range of facilities from en suite bathroom to colour TV including Sky Sports and Sky Movies. Sited next to Little Chef Restaurant. Freephone from UK 0800 850 950.

Room Rate from €54.95 to €69.95
£43.28 to £55.09

CAROLINE WALSH
MANAGER

American Express
Diners
Mastercard
Visa

40 40

Open All Year

GARNISH HOUSE

WESTERN ROAD,
CORK

TEL: 021-427 5111 FAX: 021-427 3872
EMAIL: garnish@iol.ie
WEB: www.garnish.ie

GUESTHOUSE ★★★ MAP 3 H 3

A stay in Garnish House is a memorable one. Tastefully appointed rooms, with optional en suite jacuzzi and our extensive gourmet breakfast is certain to please. 24 hr reception for enquiries. Situated opposite UCC. Convenient to ferry, airport, bus terminal and city centre. Ideal base to visit Southern Ireland. Open all year. Recommended by AA 4♦♦♦♦, RAC 4♦♦♦♦ and Bridgestone Best Places to Stay, AA awards Sparkling Diamond & Warm Welcome. Suites & studios accommodation also available.

B&B from €40.00 to €64.00
£31.50 to £50.40

JOHANNA LUCEY
MANAGERESS

American Express
Diners
Mastercard
Visa

14 14

Open All Year

GRESHAM METROPOLE

MACCURTAIN STREET,
CORK

TEL: 021-450 8122 FAX: 021-450 6450
EMAIL: info@gresham-metropole.com
WEB: www.gresham-hotels.com

HOTEL ★★★ MAP 3 H 3

Located in Cork City, the Gresham Metropole has been recently refurbished to the highest international standards. The hotel features the Riverview Restaurant, Met Bar and Waterside café. 11 state of the art conference rooms all with modern amenities & natual daylight. The superb leisure centre includes three main pool areas, a whirlpool spa, sauna, steam room, aerobics studio and gym. Complimentary secure parking for guests.

B&B from €95.00 to €175.00
£74.81 to £137.80

JOE KEARNEY
GENERAL MANAGER

American Express
Diners
Mastercard
Visa

☺ Weekend specials from €125.00

113 113

Open All Year

Room rates are per room per night

HAYFIELD MANOR HOTEL

PERROTT AVENUE,
COLLEGE ROAD,
CORK

TEL: 021-484 5900 FAX: 021-431 6839
EMAIL: enquiries@hayfieldmanor.ie
WEB: www.hayfieldmanor.ie

HOTEL ★★★★★ MAP 2 H 3

Cork's premier 5***** hotel pleasantly secluded 7km from Cork International Airport and 1km from Cork City. Luxurious guest rooms, drawing rooms and library. Private health spa including indoor pool and treatment rooms. Hayfield Manor retains a country house atmosphere with every luxury the modern traveller could wish for. Conference facilities for up to 80 delegates.

Member of Small Luxury Hotels of the World

B&B from €160.00 to €200.00
£126.01 to £157.51

MARGARET NAUGHTON
GENERAL MANAGER

American Express
Diners
Mastercard
Visa

Weekend specials from €255.00

87 87

Open All Year

HOTEL ISAACS

48 MAC CURTAIN STREET,
CORK

TEL: 021-450 0011 FAX: 021-450 6355
EMAIL: cork@isaacs.ie
WEB: www.isaacs.ie

HOTEL ★★★ MAP 3 H 3

A homely city centre hotel set in its own courtyard garden and Greene's Restaurant even overlooks a waterfall! Our comfortable en suite rooms with an Irish literary theme have phone, TV, tea/coffee making facilities and hairdryers. We are 5-10 minutes from all amenities (commercial or leisure) including bus and train stations with nearby limited free carparking. Hotel Isaacs Cork is simply an oasis within Cork City centre.

B&B from €45.00 to €80.00
£35.44 to £63.01

PAULA LYNCH
GENERAL MANAGER

American Express
Mastercard
Visa

Weekend specials from €130.00

36 36

Closed 23 - 26 December

IMPERIAL HOTEL

SOUTH MALL,
CORK

TEL: 021-427 4040 FAX: 021-427 5375
EMAIL: info@imperialhotelcork.ie
WEB: www.imperialhotelcork.ie

HOTEL ★★★ MAP 3 H 3

Located in the heart of the business and shopping district, this historic city centre hotel was acquired by Flynn Hotels in 1998. Since then the Imperial has undergone extensive renovations. South's Bar is one of the most popular in Cork and the new French style coffee shop is a must for all visitors. Conference facilities for up to 450 delegates. Secure car parking for residents.

Room Rate from €100.00 to €113.00
£78.74 to £88.98

JOHN VILLIERS-TUTHILL
GENERAL MANAGER

American Express
Diners
Mastercard
Visa

88 88

Closed 24 - 27 December

B&B rates are per person sharing per night incl. Breakfast

JOHN BARLEYCORN HOTEL

RIVERSTOWN,
GLANMIRE,
CORK

TEL: 021-482 1499 FAX: 021-482 1221
EMAIL: johnbarleycorn@eircom.net

HOTEL ★★ MAP 3 H 3

This fine 18th century residence retains all the atmosphere and charm of a rustic coach stop. Nestling in its own grounds of river and trees, just a short 6km jaunt from Cork City, just off the R639 (alternative Cork/Dublin Road). Ideal base for trips to Blarney, Kinsale, Fota and Cobh Heritage Centre. We welcome all guests with enthusiasm and attention. A Village Inn Hotel, Central reservations tel: 01-295 8900, fax: 01-295 8940.

Member of Village Inn Hotels

B&B from €38.09 to €44.44
£30.00 to £35.00

OLIVIA LOFTUS
MANAGERESS

American Express
Diners
Mastercard
Visa

17 17

Closed 24 - 25 December

JURYS CORK HOTEL

WESTERN ROAD,
CORK

TEL: 021-427 6622 FAX: 021-427 4477
EMAIL: cork@jurysdoyle.com
WEB: www.jurysdoyle.com

HOTEL ★★★★ MAP 2 H 3

Quite simply the finest hotel in Cork with a genteel southern charisma all its own. Set on the banks of the Lee in the heart of the city, smart shopping and prime business districts are within a few minutes walk. Top-class international facilities are complemented by the warmth and friendliness for which "Corkonians" are noted.

B&B from €63.00 to €125.50
£49.62 to £98.84

FERGAL SOMERS
GENERAL MANAGER

American Express
Diners
Mastercard
Visa

185 185

Closed 24 - 26 December

JURYS INN CORK

ANDERSON'S QUAY,
CORK

TEL: 021-427 6444 FAX: 021-427 6144
EMAIL: jurysinncork@jurysdoyle.com
WEB: www.jurysdoyle.com

HOTEL ★★★ MAP 2 H 3

Jurys Inn Cork enjoys a superb location right in the heart of Cork City, overlooking the River Lee. Vibrant business and shopping districts and a host of restaurants, bars, museums and galleries are literally within a few minutes walk. An excellent base to explore city or the very stunning Co. Cork countryside.

Room Rate from €75.00 to €122.00
£59.07 to £96.07

JULIEANN BRENNAN
GENERAL MANAGER

American Express
Diners
Mastercard
Visa

133 133

Closed 24 - 27 December

Room rates are per room per night

KILLARNEY GUEST HOUSE

WESTERN ROAD,
(OPP. UCC),
CORK

TEL: 021-427 0290 FAX: 021-427 1010
EMAIL: killarneyhouse@iol.ie
WEB: www.killarneyguesthouse.com

GUESTHOUSE ★★★ MAP 2 H 3

This charming guesthouse is renowned for its unique blend of comfort, style and hospitality. Its sumptuous breakfast menu includes a buffet table laden with fresh produce and home baking. All rooms are en suite with optional jacuzzi bath. A close walk to the city centre and opposite the University College Cork. Large lock up car park for your security. AA acclaimed and RAC 4 ♦♦♦♦ Award 2002.

B&B from €35.00 to €50.00
£27.50 to £40.00

MARGARET O'LEARY
MANAGERESS

American Express
Mastercard
Visa

🛏📞💻TC CMP⚓
19 19

IRISH HOTELS FEDERATION

Closed 23 - 26 December

KINGSLEY HOTEL

VICTORIA CROSS,
CORK

TEL: 021-480 0500 FAX: 021-480 0527
EMAIL: resv@kingsleyhotel.com
WEB: www.kingsleyhotel.com

HOTEL U MAP 2 H 3

This de luxe Hotel is nestled on the River Lee, located only minutes from Cork's Airport. State of the art facilities, an elegant atmosphere and tranquil surroundings. The Sabrona Lounge and Library with open fires are havens of tranquillity. Otters Brasserie is a creative dining experience. Poachers Bar is a distinctly different hotel bar. For business clients a customised business centre and conference facilities. The Kingsley Club allows guests unwind at leisure.

B&B from €70.88 to €127.00
£55.82 to £100.02

MICHAEL ROCHE
GENERAL MANAGER

American Express
Diners
Mastercard
Visa

😊 Weekend specials from €154.00

🛏📞💻TC CM❄🍴🅿🏠U
57 57
♪🅿📞🔒alc⚓ Inet FAX

IRISH HOTELS FEDERATION

Open All Year

LANCASTER LODGE

WESTERN ROAD,
CORK

TEL: 021-425 1125 FAX: 021-425 1126
EMAIL: info@lancasterlodge.com
WEB: www.lancasterlodge.com

GUESTHOUSE ★★★★ MAP 2 H 3

Lancaster Lodge is a purpose-built 39 roomed en suite guesthouse including two luxury suites with jacuzzi baths. Located alongside Jurys Hotel and only five minutes from the city centre, the guesthouse provides free private parking, 24-hour reception, an extensive breakfast menu, spacious rooms including wheelchair facilities and lift to each floor. For comfort and convenience Lancaster Lodge awaits you.

B&B from €45.00 to €85.00
£35.44 to £66.94

SUSAN LEAHY
MANAGERESS

American Express
Diners
Mastercard
Visa

🛏📞💻TC⚓UPS⚓ Inet
39 39

IRISH HOTELS FEDERATION

Closed 23 - 25 December

B&B rates are per person sharing per night incl. Breakfast

LOTAMORE HOUSE

TIVOLI,
CORK

TEL: 021-482 2344 FAX: 021-482 2219
EMAIL: lotamore@iol.ie

GUESTHOUSE ★★★★ MAP 3 H 3

A beautiful house with 20 en suite rooms, 4****, and all the amenities of a hotel. 9 mins drive from the city centre but having a quiet location surrounded by 4 acres. Cobh Heritage Centre, Fota Island, many golf courses. Blarney, Kinsale within easy reach. Situated 3 mins from the Lee Tunnel. Ideally situated for travelling to the airport, ferry terminals, West Cork, Killarney and the Ring of Kerry.

B&B from €39.00 to €45.00
£30.71 to £35.44

MAIREAD HARTY
PROPRIETOR/MANAGER

American Express
Mastercard
Visa

2 Nights B&B €78.00

20   20

Closed 20 December - 07 January

LOUGH MAHON HOUSE

TIVOLI,
CORK

TEL: 021-450 2142 FAX: 021-450 1804
EMAIL: info@loughmahon.com
WEB: www.loughmahon.com

GUESTHOUSE ★★★ MAP 3 H 3

Family run comfortable Georgian house with private parking. Convenient to city centre, bus and rail station. En suite bedrooms are decorated to a high standard with every comfort for our guests. TV, direct dial phone, tea/coffee maker, hair dryer, trouser press and ironing facilities available. Near to Fota Wildlife Park, Cobh Heritage Centre, golf clubs and fishing. Ideal base for trips to Blarney Castle, Kinsale and Killarney. 2 mins Lee Tunnel.

Member of Premier Guesthouses
B&B from €32.00 to €44.50
£25.20 to £35.05

MARGOT MEAGHER
PROPRIETOR

American Express
Mastercard
Visa

6   6

Closed 23 - 28 December

MARYBOROUGH HOUSE HOTEL

MARYBOROUGH HILL,
DOUGLAS,
CORK

TEL: 021-436 5555 FAX: 021-436 5662
EMAIL: maryboro@indigo.ie
WEB: www.maryborough.com

HOTEL ★★★★ MAP 3 H 3

Distinctive, delightful and different. Maryborough is set on 24 acres of listed gardens and woodland, located only 10 minutes from Cork City. This charming 18th century house with its creatively designed extension features exquisite conference, banqueting and leisure facilities. 79 spacious rooms, some with balconies overlooking the magnificent gardens and orchards. Zing's Restaurant, in contemporary relaxed design is an exciting mix of modern flavour's and styles. 4 mins from Lee Tunnel. Wheelchair friendly.

B&B from €70.00 to €115.00
£55.13 to £90.57

JUSTIN MCCARTHY
GENERAL MANAGER

American Express
Diners
Mastercard
Visa

Weekend specials from €140.00

79 · 79

Closed 24 - 27 December

Room rates are per room per night

QUALITY HOTEL CORK

JOHN REDMOND STREET,
CORK

TEL: 021-455 1793 FAX: 021-455 1665
EMAIL: qualshan@indigo.ie
WEB: www.choicehotelscork.com

HOTEL U   MAP 2 H 3

Quality Hotel Cork is situated in the shadow of the famous Shandon Bells. Less than a 5 minute walk from Patrick Street, Cork's vibrant main thoroughfare, this modern hotel combines its rich heritage with all the conveniences expected by today's corporate and leisure guests. Bells Bar and Bistro offers an exciting and creative dining experience. Limited car parking available. A superb venue for conferences and meetings.

Member of Choice Hotels Ireland

B&B from €44.45 to €76.20
£35.01 to £60.01

SHANE MCSHORTALL
GENERAL MANAGER

American Express
Diners
Mastercard
Visa

😊 Weekend specials from €125.73

64 64

Closed 24 - 27 December

REDCLYFFE GUEST HOUSE

WESTERN ROAD,
CORK

TEL: 021-427 3220 FAX: 021-427 8382
EMAIL: redclyffe@eircom.net

GUESTHOUSE ★★   MAP 2 H 3

Redclyffe is a charming Victorian red brick guesthouse, family run and decorated to the highest standard. Opposite University, museum, consultants clinic and Jury's hotel. 13 luxurious bedrooms, all en suite with direct dial phone, satellite TV, hairdryer & tea/coffee making facilities. 10 minutes walk to city centre, No 8 bus at door. Easy drive to airport & car ferry. AA approved. Spacious car park front & rear. Be assured of a warm welcome.

B&B from €30.00 to €45.00
£23.63 to £35.44

MICHAEL & MAURA SHEEHAN
PROPRIETORS

American Express
Diners
Mastercard
Visa

13 13

Open All Year

ROCHESTOWN PARK HOTEL

ROCHESTOWN ROAD,
DOUGLAS,
CORK

TEL: 021-489 2233 FAX: 021-489 2178
EMAIL: info@rochestownpark.com
WEB: www.rochestownpark.com

HOTEL ★★★★   MAP 3 H 3

The Rochestown Park Hotel is a manor style hotel set in mature gardens. Facilities include an award winning leisure centre and Ireland's Premier Thalasso Therapy Centre. A large proportion of our 114 bedrooms (48 additional rooms opening March 2002) are air-conditioned and overlook our gardens and Mahon Golf Club. We cater for weekend breaks, conferences, meetings, as well as groups, families and weddings.

B&B from €50.00 to €88.00
£39.37 to £69.29

LIAM LALLY
GENERAL MANAGER

American Express
Diners
Mastercard
Visa

114 114

Closed 24 - 26 December

B&B rates are per person sharing per night incl. Breakfast

ROSERIE VILLA GUEST HOUSE

MARDYKE WALK,
OFF WESTERN ROAD,
CORK

TEL: 021-427 2958 FAX: 021-427 4087
EMAIL: info@roserievilla.com
WEB: www.roserievilla.com

GUESTHOUSE ★★★ MAP 2 H 3

Roserie Villa is a 10 minute walk from city centre and close to bus and train stations. 16 en suite bedrooms with direct dial telephone, TV, tea/coffee making facilities, hairdryer and ironing facilities. An ideal base for the busy executive or holiday maker to explore the south west. Airport and ferry 15 minutes drive. Golf, tennis, cricket, fishing nearby and just minutes from university college.

B&B from €35.00 to €50.00
£27.56 to £39.37

PADDY MURPHY
PROPRIETOR

American Express
Mastercard
Visa

16 16

Open All Year

SAINT KILDA GUESTHOUSE

WESTERN ROAD,
CORK

TEL: 021-427 3095 FAX: 021-427 5015
EMAIL: gerald@stkildas.com
WEB: www.stkildas.com

GUESTHOUSE ★★★ MAP 2 H 3

Exclusive overnight accommodation just 10 minutes walk to city centre. Directly opposite university with long-established tennis and cricket clubs at rear. Magnificent swimming and leisure centre nearby. Killarney 1 hour, Kinsale 30 minutes, airport and Blarney Castle 20 minutes. Registered with RAC and recommended by Frommers, Stilwells and Lonely Planet guides. A short pleasant drive to numerous golf courses including Old Head of Kinsale, Fota Island, Lee Valley and Monkstown.

B&B from €32.00 to €50.00
£25.20 to £39.38

GERALD COLLINS
PROPRIETOR

Mastercard
Visa

20 20

Closed 17 December - 9 January

SEVEN NORTH MALL

7 NORTH MALL,
CORK

TEL: 021-439 7191 FAX: 021-430 0811
EMAIL: sevennorthmall@eircom.net

GUESTHOUSE ★★★★ MAP 2 H 3

Comfortable 240 year old listed house on tree lined mall, facing south, overlooking River Lee. Adjacent to all sites including theatres, art galleries, Shandon, the University and some of Ireland's best restaurants. Individually decorated en suite bedrooms include direct dial telephone, cable TV, trouser press and hair dryer. Small conference room, private car park and accommodation for disabled guests. Children over 12 welcome. ITB Graded 4★★★★.

B&B from €45.00 to €60.00
£35.44 to £47.25

ANGELA HEGARTY
PROPRIETOR

Mastercard
Visa

7 7

IRISH
HOTELS
FEDERATION

Closed 16 December - 06 January

Room rates are per room per night

SILVERSPRINGS MORAN HOTEL

TIVOLI,
CORK

TEL: 021-450 7533 FAX: 021-450 7641
EMAIL: silversprings@morangroup.ie
WEB: www.morangroup.ie

HOTEL ★★★★ MAP 3 H 3

4**** hotel set in sylvan terraced grounds overlooking the River Lee and Cork city. Each of the 109 deluxe bedrooms has cable TV, trouser press and tea/coffee maker. The hotel restaurant has a relaxed atmosphere and exciting well priced menu. The adjoining Gallery Lounge is an art themed modern trendy café. Enjoy Thadys Quills Bar with its regular entertainment. Full leisure facilities including 25m pool. Excellent base for touring Cork's many visitor attractions. 4 championship golf courses nearby. 7 miles from Cork airport. Free parking. A Moran hotel.

B&B from €55.00 to €100.00
£43.32 to £78.76

TOM & SHEILA MORAN
PROPRIETORS

American Express
Diners
Mastercard
Visa

109 109

Closed 25 - 26 December

VICTORIA HOTEL

PATRICK STREET,
COOK STREET,
CORK

TEL: 021-427 8788 FAX: 021-427 8790
EMAIL: vicgeneral@eircom.net
WEB: www.thevictoriahotel.com

HOTEL ★★ MAP 3 H 3

The Victoria Hotel is situated in Cork City Centre. All rooms have bath & shower, direct dial phone, TV and hair dryer. Family suites available. Built in 1810, it was frequented by European Royalty and was home to some of our own great political leaders, including Charles Stewart Parnell who made his major speeches from its upper balcony. James Joyce recounts his stay in one of his novels.

Member of MinOtel Hotel Group
B&B from €38.09 to €76.18
£30.00 to £60.00

KING FAMILY

American Express
Mastercard
Visa

29 29

Open All Year

VICTORIA LODGE

VICTORIA CROSS,
CORK

TEL: 021-454 2233 FAX: 021-454 2572

GUESTHOUSE ★★★★ MAP 2 H 3

This newly renovated monastery located just minutes from city centre, yet standing in mature gardens, has 28 luxury bedrooms with private bath and shower, colour TV, orthopaedic beds, computerised fire detection, direct dial telephone, central heating, tea making facilities, secure car parking, lift to each floor. Convenient to tennis village, golf clubs, museum and fishing facilities. Light snacks, cold meals and drinks served.

B&B from €38.10 to €40.65
£30.00 to £32.01

DEIRDRE MC CARTHY
MANAGER

American Express
Mastercard
Visa

28 28

Closed 24 - 29 December

B&B rates are per person sharing per night incl. Breakfast

VIENNA WOODS HOTEL

GLANMIRE,
CORK

TEL: 021-482 1146 FAX: 021-482 1120
EMAIL: vienna@iol.ie
WEB: www.viennawoodshotel.com

HOTEL ★★★ MAP 3 H 3

50 bedroom luxury hotel, formerly an 18th century mansion home. Set on 20 acres of mature woodland yet minutes drive from Cork City. "Golfers Paradise" directly adjacent to Cork's premier courses (booked exclusively by the world media coverage for Murphy's Irish Open). Extensive conference and banqueting facilities with plenty of private parking.

B&B from €40.00 to €60.00
£31.50 to £47.25

JOHN GATELY/DARINA O'DRISCOLL
PROPRIETORS

American Express
Diners
Mastercard
Visa

🛏️ ♨️ ☎️ 🖥️ T C CM ✂️ 🎵 P
50 50
S ♿ alc ☕ Inet

IRISH HOTELS FEDERATION

Closed 24 - 26 December

WHISPERING PINES HOTEL

CROSSHAVEN,
CO. CORK

TEL: 021-483 1843 FAX: 021-483 1679
EMAIL: reservations@whisperingpineshotel.com
WEB: www.whisperingpineshotel.com

HOTEL ★★ MAP 3 I 3

Whispering Pines, personally run by the Twomey Family is a charming hotel sheltered by surrounding woodland & overlooking the Owenabue River. In this idyllic setting one can enjoy good company, quality homecooked food & a host of amenities to ensure your stay is a restful & memorable experience. All rooms with direct dial phone, tea/coffee facilities & TV. Our 3 angling boats fish daily from April-Oct. Ideal base for touring Cork/Kerry Region. Cork Airport 12kms & Cork City 19km. AA approved.

B&B from €30.00 to €50.00
£23.63 to £39.38

NORMA TWOMEY
PROPRIETOR

American Express
Diners
Mastercard
Visa

🛏️ ♨️ ☎️ T C CM ✂️ P S ♿
15 15
☕

IRISH HOTELS FEDERATION

Closed 01 December - 01 January

DUN-MHUIRE HOUSE

KILBARRY ROAD,
DUNMANWAY,
CO. CORK

TEL: 023-45162 FAX: 023-45162
EMAIL: hayesdunmhuire@eircom.net

GUESTHOUSE ★★★ MAP 2 F 2

An exclusive family run guesthouse, situated in the heart of West Cork. It has a lot to offer the holiday maker who will appreciate its relaxed atmosphere and high standards. Ideal base to tour Cork and Kerry. Luxury bedrooms with full bathroom, TV, tea/coffee making facility and DD phone. Breakfast menu includes freshly squeezed juices. Smoked salmon and fresh fish in season with our home made breads. Local amenities include: swimming, golf, tennis, fishing and pony riding. Scenic walks nearby.

Member of Premier Guesthouses
B&B from €31.74 to €44.00
£25.00 to £34.65

CARMEL & LIAM HAYES
PROPRIETORS

Mastercard
Visa

🛏️ ♨️ ☎️ T C CM ✂️ P S ♿
6 6
alc ☕

IRISH HOTELS FEDERATION

Closed 24 - 26 December

Room rates are per room per night

CASTLEHYDE HOTEL

CASTLEHYDE,
FERMOY,
CO. CORK
TEL: 025-31865 FAX: 025-31485
EMAIL: cashyde@iol.ie
WEB: www.castlehydehotel.com

HOTEL U MAP 3 1 4

Country house hotel accommodation in a fully restored Georgian house and courtyard. Gracious hospitality in gracious surroundings. Only 35 minutes from Cork, a world apart from its bustle! All outdoor pursuits catered for. Heated outdoor pool. Exquisite cuisine served in Mermaids Restaurant, perfect peace in the library. The ideal base in the beautiful North Cork region, be it for leisure or for business.

Member of Best Loved Hotels of The World

B&B from €72.50 to €95.00
£57.09 to £74.82

HELEN & ERIK SPEEKENBRINK

American Express
Diners
Mastercard
Visa

🛏🏧☎️⏹TC❄️↻∪ᏢS🔒alc
14 14

Open All Year

GLANWORTH MILL COUNTRY INN

GLANWORTH,
CO. CORK
TEL: 025-38555 FAX: 025-38560
EMAIL: glanworth@iol.ie
WEB: www.glanworth.com

GUESTHOUSE ★★★★ MAP 3 1 4

A water mill, a Norman castle, a river, an ancient bridge, gorgeous rooms, a gourmet restaurant, tea rooms, library, craft shop, courtyard garden, leisure garden and river walk... you'll find it here at Glanworth Mill. Unwind in this 1790 water mill with its sense of history & love of literature. There is a wealth of activities nearby - fishing, horse-riding, golf, hill walking, historic trails & houses & gardens to visit. Hidden Gem Award 2000. Golden Plate 2001. All in the lush Blackwater Valley of North Cork.

B&B from €57.00 to €64.00
£44.89 to £50.40

LYNNE GLASSCOE & EMELYN HEAPS

American Express
Diners
Mastercard
Visa

🛏🏧☎️TCCM❄️∪Ꮲ🔒alc☕
10 10

Closed 24 December -04 January

CASEY'S HOTEL

THE VILLAGE,
GLENGARRIFF,
CO. CORK
TEL: 027-63010 FAX: 027-63072
EMAIL: caseyshotel@yahoo.com

HOTEL ★★ MAP 1 D 2

Casey's Hotel has been run by the same family since 1884. Recently refurbished to cater for the expectations of the modern traveller. All rooms en suite with direct dial phones and TV. The hotel offers personal, friendly service with old fashioned courtesy, private car park and gardens. Casey's Hotel is the perfect base for day trips to Barley Cove, Gougane Barra, Killarney and the Ring of Kerry. Come and discover the unspoilt beauty of the Beara Peninsula. Hill walking tours arranged.

B&B from €35.50 to €47.00
£27.96 to £37.02

DONAL & EILEEN DEASY
OWNERS

American Express
Diners
Mastercard
Visa

🛏🏧☎️⏹TC❄️🎵Ᏼ🔒alc☕
19 19

Closed 15 November - 01 March

B&B rates are per person sharing per night incl. Breakfast

GLENGARRIFF ECCLES HOTEL

**GLENGARRIFF,
CO. CORK**

TEL: 027-63003 FAX: 027-63319
EMAIL: eccleshotel@iol.ie
WEB: www.eccleshotel.com

HOTEL ★★★ MAP 2 D 2

Located in beautiful Bantry Bay, the Glengarriff Eccles Hotel is one of the oldest established hotels in Ireland. The hotel boasts 66 recently refurbished en suite bedrooms, restaurant (where seafood is a speciality), bar and function room. Situated directly opposite the world famous Garnish Island, the hotel is ideally located to explore the beauty of the Beara peninsula.

B&B from €40.00 to €65.00
£31.50 to £51.19

THOS O'BRIEN
GENERAL MANAGER

American Express
Mastercard
Visa

66 66

Open All Year

GOUGANE BARRA HOTEL

**GOUGANE BARRA,
BALLINGEARY,
CO. CORK**

TEL: 026-47069 FAX: 026-47226
EMAIL: gouganebarrahotel@eircom.net
WEB: www.cork-guide.ie

HOTEL ★★ MAP 2 E 3

Situated on its own grounds overlooking Gougane Barra Lake, the source of the River Lee. Most bedrooms enjoy fine views of the lake, glens and hills beyond. Ideally situated for touring the beauty spots of Cork and Kerry, 72km west of Cork City and Airport. A walk along the banks of the Lee through the forest park which covers 162 hectares, will take you through varied scenery of mystic beauty. We are members of CMV marketing group. GDS Access Code UI Toll Free: 1-800-44-UTELL

Member of Coast and Country Hotels

B&B from €50.00 to €56.00
£39.38 to £44.10

BREDA & CHRISTOPHER LUCEY

American Express
Diners
Mastercard
Visa

28 28

Closed 15 October - 19 April

CREEDON'S HOTEL

**INCHIGEELA,
MACROOM,
CO. CORK**

TEL: 026-49012 FAX: 026-49265

HOTEL ★ MAP 2 F 3

The story of Creedon Hotel is one of great continuity and change. At the hub of the village, it has been a family hotel for 3 generations. The simplicity and comfort reflects the natural, relaxed atmosphere of an inn where the spirit is renewed in tranquil surroundings and where people always come first. It is ideal for small group getaways where the complicated luxuries of modern life are replaced by simplicity. Experience the real 'Hidden Ireland'.

Member of Irish Family Hotels

B&B from €32.00 to €32.00
£25.20 to £25.20

JOSEPH & ANNE CREEDON
PROPRIETORS

Mastercard
Visa

12 8

Open All Year

Room rates are per room per night

INNISHANNON HOUSE HOTEL

INNISHANNON,
CO. CORK

TEL: 021-477 5121 FAX: 021-477 5609

EMAIL: info@innishannon-hotel.ie
WEB: www.innishannon-hotel.ie

HOTEL ★★★ MAP 2 G 2

The most romantic hotel in Ireland built in 1720 in the Petit Chateau style on the banks of the river Bandon, close to Kinsale. All rooms en suite with TV, DD phone, radio, etc. Award winning restaurant (AA**, RAC, Egon Ronay) serving fresh fish and lobster. Superb wine cellar, stunning views, boating and free salmon and trout fishing from the grounds. Horse-riding and golf nearby. GDS code: UI Toll Free 1-800-44 UTELL.

Member of Manor House Hotels

B&B from €58.00 to €121.00
£45.68 to £95.30

PETER CURRAN
DIRECTOR/GENERAL MANAGER

American Express
Diners
Mastercard
Visa

13 13

Closed 24 - 27 December

ACTONS HOTEL

PIER ROAD,
KINSALE,
CO. CORK

TEL: 021-477 2135 FAX: 021-477 2231

EMAIL: info@actonshotelkinsale.com
WEB: www.actonshotelkinsale.com

HOTEL ★★★ MAP 2 H 2

Located in landscaped gardens overlooking Kinsale's beautiful harbour. Renowned for its cuisine and friendly atmosphere, Actons also features an award-winning restaurant (Kinsale Good Food Circle Member), Bar/Bistro and Leisure Centre. Located in the historic town of Kinsale with restaurants, pubs, cafés, art & craft shops etc. Activities nearby: golfing, fishing, sailing, walking, historical sites.

B&B from €63.00 to €120.00
£49.62 to £94.51

JACK WALSH
GENERAL MANAGER

American Express
Diners
Mastercard
Visa

76 76

Open All Year

BLINDGATE HOUSE

BLINDGATE,
KINSALE,
CO. CORK

TEL: 021-477 7858 FAX: 021-477 7868

EMAIL: info@blindgatehouse.com
WEB: www.blindgatehouse.com

GUESTHOUSE ★★★★ MAP 2 H 2

Overlooking the town, Blindgate House caters for the discerning traveller, combining traditional Irish hospitality with modern facilities and imaginative cuisine. All rooms are ensuite, airy and bright and have satellite TV, telephone, fax and modem connections. Our kitchen is run to an extremely high standard, using fresh local produce and breakfast is quite a treat. No better way to start the day! There is a large private car park adjacent to the house and a south facing quiet garden for relaxing. We promise to make your stay a memorable one.

Room Rate from €127.00 to €153.00
£100.02 to £120.50

MAEVE COAKLEY

American Express
Diners
Mastercard
Visa

11 11

Closed 23 December - 01 March

B&B rates are per person sharing per night incl. Breakfast

CAPTAINS QUARTERS

5 DENIS QUAY,
KINSALE,
CO. CORK
TEL: 021-477 4549 FAX: 021-477 4944
EMAIL: captquarters@eircom.net
WEB: www.captains-kinsale.com

GUESTHOUSE ★★★ MAP 2 H 2

This Georgian period townhouse is situated close to the yacht club marina and in easy walking distance of all restaurants and town centre amenities. It offers quality accommodation in a maritime ambience. The spacious and tranquil lounge overlooks the harbour. The wheelchair accessible groundfloor rooms (1 twin / 1 single, sharing shower / toilet) are also very convenient for the elderly. TV, direct dial phone, tea/coffee making facilities, hairdryer in all rooms. German and French spoken.

B&B from €25.00 to €39.00
£19.69 to £30.71

BERNY & CAPT. RUDI TEICHMANN
CO-OWNERS

Mastercard
Visa

6   4

IRISH HOTELS FEDERATION

Closed 28 January - 27 March

COTTAGE LOFT

6 MAIN STREET,
KINSALE,
CO. CORK
TEL: 021-477 2803 FAX: 021-477 2803

GUESTHOUSE ★★ MAP 2 H 2

Located in the heart of Kinsale, the 200 year old town house has an old world charm. Decorated in rich deep tones giving a warm and welcoming ambience. All rooms are en suite with direct dial telephone and TV. Tea & Coffee making facilities in all rooms. Our restaurant, a member of Kinsale's Good Food Circle is noted for its excellent cuisine. All Michael's dishes are created using the finest and freshest ingredients available locally.

B&B from €29.00 to €35.00
£22.84 to £27.56

MICHAEL & CAROLANNE BUCKLEY
OWNERS

American Express
Mastercard
Visa

☺ Weekend specials from €78.00

6   6

IRISH HOTELS FEDERATION

Closed 23 - 27 December

HARBOUR LODGE

SCILLY,
KINSALE,
CO. CORK
TEL: 021-477 2376 FAX: 021-477 2675
EMAIL: relax@harbourlodge.com
WEB: www.harbourlodge.com

GUESTHOUSE ★★★★ MAP 2 H 2

Harbour Lodge has been refurbished and upgraded to make it one of the finest guesthouses on the coast. Comfort, personal service, charm and sophistication in a relaxed ambience complement the spacious rooms and huge beds with fine linen. The sweeping view of Kinsale bay, the spectacular Orangerie and terrace is quite unique. The private parking is our competitions envy. Staff and management are here for our guest 24 hours.

B&B from €78.00 to €92.00
£61.42 to £72.44

RAOUL DE GENDRE
PROPRIETORS

American Express
Diners
Mastercard
Visa

☺ Off season packages available

8   8

Open All Year

Room rates are per room per night

JIM EDWARDS

MARKET QUAY,
KINSALE,
CO. CORK

TEL: 021-477 2541 FAX: 021-477 3228

GUESTHOUSE ★★ MAP 2 H 2

All rooms are en suite with TV, tea/coffee facilities, telephone and all tastefully decorated. Situated in the heart of the town means easy access to all the lively bars and entertainment of the town. The guest house boasts an excellent seafood restaurant (fully licenced) which is a member of the Kinsale Good Food Circle and ensures a gourmet breakfast.

B&B from €35.00 to €45.00
£27.56 to £35.44

JIM EDWARDS

American Express
Mastercard
Visa

🏨👤☎🖥©CM♪🎱alc☕
6   6

Open All Year

KIERANS FOLKHOUSE INN

GUARDWELL,
KINSALE,
CO. CORK

TEL: 021-477 2382 FAX: 021-477 4085
EMAIL: folkhse@indigo.ie

GUESTHOUSE ★★★ MAP 2 H 2

A charming 250 year old, award winning Country Inn, managed by Denis and Geraldine Kieran for the past 13 years, awarded the Irish "Inn of the Year". 27 en-suite rooms, the Bacchus Niteclub and the Spanish themed "Cordoba" Bar which was awarded the "Dining Pub of the Year 2000" & features live music nightly. Shrimps Seafood Bistro is one of the newest members of the Kinsale Good Food Circle. It's an attractive restaurant featuring a unique stained glass wall & contemporary paintings, including works by artist Geraldine.

Member of Logis of Ireland
B&B from €38.00 to €50.00
£29.93 to £39.38

GERALDINE & DENIS KIERAN
OWNERS

American Express
Mastercard
Visa

🏨👤☎🖥TC🚿CM♪🎵🎱alc☕
27   27

Closed 25 December

KILCAW HOUSE

KINSALE,
SITUATED ON R600,
CO. CORK

TEL: 021-477 4155 FAX: 021-477 4755
EMAIL: info@kilcawhouse.com
WEB: www.kilcawhouse.com

GUESTHOUSE ★★★ MAP 2 H 2

A family run guesthouse on the outskirts of Kinsale with safe off the road parking and wonderful country views. It is built with a traditional flair yet is modern and luxurious. The bedrooms are spacious, furnished in antique pine, en suite with TV, phone and tea/coffee making facilities. Just a 20 minute drive from Airport and Ferry. An ideal base for touring Blarney, Cobh and Old Head of Kinsale.

B&B from €28.00 to €38.00
£22.04 to £29.92

HENRY & CHRISTINA MITCHELL
OWNERS

American Express
Mastercard
Visa

🏨👤☎🖥©🌸✸J P☕
7   7

Open All Year

B&B rates are per person sharing per night incl. Breakfast

LONG QUAY HOUSE

LONG QUAY,
KINSALE,
CO. CORK

TEL: 021-477 3201 FAX: 021-477 4563
EMAIL: longquayhouse@eircom.net

GUESTHOUSE ★★★ MAP 2 H 2

Long Quay House is a Georgian residence which typifies its era with rooms of splendid dimensions, furnished to afford the greatest possible guest comfort. Bedrooms are en suite (majority with bath), TV, direct dial phone, tea making facilities and hair dryer. Located centrally overlooking inner harbour, yacht marina and within walking distance of all Kinsale's gourmet restaurants and many tourist attractions. Sea angling trips by local skippers arranged. AA recognised establishment ◆◆◆◆.

B&B from €31.75 to €50.75
£25.01 to £39.97

JIM & PETER DEASY
HOSTS

Mastercard
Visa

🏨 🛏 ☎ 🖥 C 🍴 CM ♪ S 🔌 Inet
7   7

Closed 15 November - 27 December

OLD BANK HOUSE

11 PEARSE STREET,
NEXT TO POST OFFICE, KINSALE,
CO. CORK

TEL: 021-477 4075 FAX: 021-477 4296
EMAIL: oldbank@indigo.ie
WEB: www.oldbankhousekinsale.com

GUESTHOUSE ★★★★ MAP 2 H 2

The Old Bank House is a Georgian residence of great character & charm providing luxurious accommodation in the historic harbour town of Kinsale. Each bedroom has super King or Twin beds, antique furniture and original art, whilst bathrooms are beautifully appointed with tub and shower, top quality toiletries and Egyptian cotton towels and bathrobes. Gourmet breakfast by award winning Master Chef Michael Riese. Golf friendly and tee times arranged. Voted one of the "Top 100 Places to Stay in Ireland" every year since 1990. RAC ◆◆◆◆ AA ◆◆◆◆.

Room Rate from €155.00 to €230.00
£122.07 to £181.14

MICHAEL & MARIE RIESE
PROPRIETORS

American Express
Mastercard
Visa

🏨 🛏 ☎ 🖥 T U 🍴
17   17

IRISH
HOTELS
FEDERATION

Closed 23 - 26 December

QUAYSIDE HOUSE

PIER ROAD,
KINSALE,
CO. CORK

TEL: 021-477 2188 FAX: 021-477 2664
EMAIL: quaysidehouse@eircom.net

GUESTHOUSE ★★★ MAP 2 H 2

A family run guesthouse ideally located in a picturesque setting overlooking the Kinsale Harbour adjacent to town centre, yachting marina and all amenities. All bedrooms are en suite with direct dial telephone, TV and tea/coffee making facilities. Kinsale's famous gourmet restaurants are all within walking distance and Kinsale's golf club is just a five minute drive. Sea angling trips can be arranged.

B&B from €26.00 to €52.00
£20.48 to £40.95

MARY COTTER

Mastercard
Visa

🏨 🛏 ☎ 🖥 C 🍴 ❄ U ♪ 🔌
6   6

IRISH
HOTELS
FEDERATION

Open All Year

Room rates are per room per night

TIERNEYS GUEST HOUSE

MAIN STREET,
KINSALE,
CO. CORK
TEL: 021-477 2205 FAX: 021-477 4363
EMAIL: mtierney@indigo.ie
WEB: www.tierneys-kinsale.com

GUESTHOUSE ★★ MAP 2 H 2

Tierney's Guest House. A well established guest house perfectly situated in the heart of magnificent award winning Kinsale. Our guest house offers all amenities, TV, en suite, hair dryers, tea/coffee on request. Tastefully decorated and a warm welcome guaranteed. Stay in Tierney's and be in the centre of Kinsale and enjoy the Gourmet Restaurants, various bars & music lounges, breathtaking scenery, water sports, golf etc.

B&B from €33.00 to €33.00
£25.99 to £25.99

MAUREEN TIERNEY
OWNER

American Express
Mastercard
Visa

9   9

IRISH HOTELS FEDERATION

Closed 23 - 28 December

TRIDENT HOTEL

WORLD'S END,
KINSALE,
CO. CORK
TEL: 021-477 2301 FAX: 021-477 4173
EMAIL: info@tridenthotel.com
WEB: www.tridenthotel.com

HOTEL ★★★ MAP 2 H 2

The hotel enjoys a superb waterfront location. All rooms are en suite, many with sea views. Award winning Savannah Waterfront Restaurant is a member of the 'Good Food Circle', the popular Wharf Tavern provides bar food daily & weekend entertainment in summer. Leisure facilities include sauna, gym, steam room & jacuzzi. Conference & Banqueting facilities for large & small groups. Golf, sailing, fishing, tours & cruises available locally. Private parking & wheelchair access.

B&B from €55.00 to €110.00
£43.32 to £86.63

HAL McELROY
MANAGING DIRECTOR

American Express
Diners
Mastercard
Visa

Midweek specials from €172.00 (3 B&B & 2D)

58   58

IRISH HOTELS FEDERATION

Closed 24 - 27 December

WHITE HOUSE

PEARSE ST. & THE GLEN,
KINSALE,
CO. CORK
TEL: 021-477 2125 FAX: 021-477 2045
EMAIL: whitehse@indigo.ie
WEB: www.whitehouse-kinsale.ie

GUESTHOUSE ★★★ MAP 2 H 2

The White House epitomises Kinsale hospitality with 3*** accommodation, Chelsea's Bistro, Le Restaurant D'Antibes and a thoroughly modern bar where all the old values of guest satisfaction, comfort and value for money prevail. We have welcomed both visitors and locals since the 1850s and from its earliest days has enjoyed a reputation for fine food, drinks of good cheer and indulgent service. Today we pride ourselves on enhancing that tradition. A member of Kinsale's Good Food Circle.

Member of Premier Guesthouses
B&B from €44.45 to €76.00
£35.01 to £59.85

MICHAEL & ROSE FRAWLEY
PROPRIETORS

American Express
Diners
Mastercard
Visa

Weekend specials from €125.00

10   10

IRISH HOTELS FEDERATION

Closed 24 - 25 December

B&B rates are per person sharing per night incl. Breakfast

WHITE LADY HOTEL

LOWER O'CONNELL ST,
KINSALE,
CO. CORK
TEL: 021-477 2737 FAX: 021-477 4641
EMAIL: wlady@indigo.ie

HOTEL ★★ MAP 2 H 2

Looking after your needs and making you feel at home is the priority in this 10 bedroom hotel. All rooms have en suite facilities, TV and direct dial phone. Our restaurant provides you with a very varied and reasonably priced menu, while it also offers a selection of fresh seafood. Our on-site nite club ensures a lively atmosphere at weekends. Golf, horse riding and sea angling trips can be arranged at your request.

B&B from €45.00 to €60.00
£35.44 to £47.25

ANTHONY COLLINS/ROMAN MINIHANE
OWNERS

American Express
Mastercard
Visa

10 10

IRISH HOTELS FEDERATION

Closed 24 - 26 December

CASTLE HOTEL & LEISURE CENTRE

MAIN STREET,
MACROOM,
CO. CORK
TEL: 026-41074 FAX: 026-41505
EMAIL: castlehotel@eircom.net
WEB: www.castlehotel.ie

HOTEL ★★★ MAP 2 F 3

Experience an intimate welcome to the spectacular south west from the Buckley family, proprietors for fifty years. Our exciting new development (open Easter 2002) includes new superior rooms, our refurbished award-winning New Restaurant (AA Rosette 92-01), spacious bar, extended foyer and reception area, continental style café and conference and banqueting centre. Relax in our health and leisure centre or enjoy free pitch & putt and half-price green fees on Macroom's 18 hole golf course.

Member of Irish Country Hotels
B&B from €55.00 to €66.00
£43.32 to £51.98

DON & GERARD BUCKLEY
PROPRIETORS

American Express
Diners
Mastercard
Visa

 3 B&B, 2 dinners, 2 golf from €190.00

42 42

IRISH HOTELS FEDERATION

Closed 24 - 28 December

COOLCOWER HOUSE

COOLCOWER,
MACROOM,
CO. CORK
TEL: 026-41695 FAX: 026-42119
EMAIL: coolcowe@gofree.indigo.ie

GUESTHOUSE ★★ MAP 2 F 3

Coolcower House is a large country residence on picturesque grounds. The house is ideally located within easy driving distance of all the tourist attractions in the Cork-Kerry region including Killarney, Kenmare, Kinsale, Blarney and Bantry. Located on the river's edge for coarse fishing and boating. Also outdoor tennis court. Restaurant offers the best of home produce on its à la carte and dinner menus. Fully licensed bar. TV's and Tea/Coffee making facilities also direct dial telephones in all bedrooms.

B&B from €31.75 to €33.00
£25.01 to £25.99

EVELYN CASEY

Mastercard
Visa

Midweek specials from €82.53

12 12

IRISH HOTELS FEDERATION

Closed 14 December - 06 March

Room rates are per room per night

VICTORIA HOTEL

THE SQUARE,
MACROOM,
CO. CORK
TEL: 026-41082 FAX: 026-42148
EMAIL: hotelvictoria@eircom.net
WEB: www.thevictoria-hotel.com

HOTEL ★★ MAP 2 F 3

Situated in the centre of Macroom Town, the Victoria is a small friendly hotel, family owned and managed. An ideal base for your visit to the beautiful Lee Valley or the scenic south west. Local amenities include fishing, local 18 hole golf course, hiking, walking and horse riding. All our rooms are en suite with telephone, TV and tea/coffee facilities. À la carte and full dinner menu available. Bar meals served all day.

B&B from €33.01 to €66.02
£26.00 to £51.99

ENDA LINEHAN
MANAGERESS

American Express
Mastercard
Visa

 Midweek specials from €35.00

🏨 👜 ☎ ❏ T C 🛏 CM ♪ 🎵 P S 🏧
16 16

HOTELS

Closed 24 - 26 December

CORTIGAN HOUSE

GOLF COURSE ROAD,
MALLOW,
CO. CORK
TEL: 022-22770 FAX: 022-22732
EMAIL: info@cortiganhouse.com
WEB: www.cortiganhouse.com

GUESTHOUSE ★★★ MAP 2 G 4

A warm welcome awaits you at our 18th century home, overlooking Mallow Castle & River Blackwater, renowned for salmon & trout angling. Just a 25 minute drive from Cork City & Blarney. Cortigan House is ideally based for touring Kinsale, Killarney and South West. We are adjacent to Mallow Golf Club and within easy drive of ten other courses. 5 min walk to excellent restaurants, traditional pubs and genealogy centre. Recommended by Le Guide du Routard. AA selected ♦♦♦♦.

B&B from €30.00 to €45.00
£23.63 to £35.44

LIONEL & SHEILA BUCKLEY
PROPRIETORS

American Express
Mastercard
Visa

🏨 👜 ☎ ❏ T C 🛏 ❄ ♨ U 🅿 🛏
9 9

HOTELS

Closed 01 December - 01 February

HIBERNIAN HOTEL AND LEISURE CENTRE

MAIN STREET,
MALLOW,
CO. CORK
TEL: 022-21588 FAX: 022-22632
EMAIL: info@hibhotel.com
WEB: www.hibhotel.com

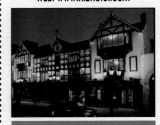

HOTEL ★★★ MAP 2 G 4

The Hibernian Hotel is a family owned hotel located at the heart of the Munster region, within easy access of Cork, Killarney and Blarney. The hotel has a beautiful Tudor style frontage and the interior is also tastefully decorated and the open fires create a very homely atmosphere. All rooms are en suite, fitted and equipped to modern-day standards. A choice of three restaurants and two bars provide excellent variety. Leisure facilities available from 1st April 2002.

B&B from €47.00 to €54.00
£37.02 to £42.53

CATHERINE GYVES
GENERAL MANAGER

American Express
Diners
Mastercard
Visa

🏨 👜 ☎ ❏ T C 🛏 CM ♨ 🏊 U ♪ 🎵
53 53

HOTELS

Closed 25 - 26 December

B&B rates are per person sharing per night incl. Breakfast

LONGUEVILLE HOUSE & PRESIDENTS' RESTAURANT

MALLOW, CO. CORK

TEL: 022-47156 FAX: 022-47459
EMAIL: info@longuevillehouse.ie
WEB: www.longuevillehouse.ie

HOTEL ★★★★ MAP 2 G 4

Longueville stands on a wooded eminence in a 500 acre private estate, overlooking the Blackwater Valley, itself famous for its game fishing and private walks. The aim at Longueville is peace and relaxation and for guests to partake only of its own fresh produce, superbly prepared by William O'Callaghan. Longueville is an ideal base for touring the scenic south-west, to laze by the fire in the drawing room, or to enjoy the peace and serenity of the estate. Member of Relais et Châteaux and Ireland's Blue Book.

Member of Ireland's Blue Book

B&B from €84.00 to €168.00
£66.16 to £132.31

WILLIAM O'CALLAGHAN
CHEF/PROPRIETOR

American Express
Diners
Mastercard
Visa

20   20

ⓐlc

Closed 04 November - 08 March

MALLOW PARK HOTEL

MALLOW, CO. CORK

TEL: 022-21527 FAX: 022-51222
EMAIL: info@mallowparkhotel.com
WEB: www.mallowparkhotel.com

HOTEL ★★ MAP 2 G 4

The Mallow Park Hotel, situated in the centre of Mallow, is decorated to the highest standard with a warm and welcoming foyer lounge, Carvery, bistro, and An Síbín traditional bar which provides the best of music entertainment every weekend, plus a hotel owned private car park. The Ballroom provides a great location for weddings, anniversaries and birthday parties. Conferences, fishing, walking or golf tours catered for. Mallow is an ideal location for touring the South West, Cork & the Ring of Kerry.

B&B from €38.10 to €50.80
£30.00 to £40.00

SEAN GLEESON
GENERAL MANAGER

American Express
Mastercard
Visa

20   20

ⓐlc

Closed 25 December

SPRINGFORT HALL HOTEL

MALLOW, CO. CORK

TEL: 022-21278 FAX: 022-21557
EMAIL: stay@springfort-hall.com
WEB: www.springfort-hall.com

HOTEL ★★★ MAP 2 G 4

Springfort Hall 18th century Georgian manor house, owned by the Walsh Family. Highly recommended restaurant, fully licensed bar, bedrooms en suite, coloured TV and direct outside dial. 6km from Mallow off the Limerick Road, N20. Ideal for touring the South West, Blarney, Killarney, Ring of Kerry. Local amenities, 18-hole golf course, horse riding, angling on River Blackwater. Gulliver Central Reservations.

B&B from €51.00 to €76.00
£40.17 to £59.85

WALSH FAMILY
PROPRIETORS

American Express
Diners
Mastercard
Visa

49   49

ⓐlc

Closed 23 - 29 December

Room rates are per room per night

BARNABROW COUNTRY HOUSE

CLOYNE,
MIDLETON,
EAST CORK

TEL: 021-465 2534 FAX: 021-465 2534
EMAIL: barnabrow@eircom.net
WEB: www.barnabrowhouse.com

GUESTHOUSE ★★★ MAP 313

17th century family-run country house set in 35 acres of parkland adjacent to the historic village of Cloyne (580AD). The house has been extensively refurbished to offer a perfect blend of old world charm & new world comfort. Trinity Rooms, our new restaurant, provides a unique venue for that special celebration. This is the perfect setting to relax and soak up an atmosphere of peaceful unhurried living with log fires and candlelit dinners. Nearby: Ballymaloe & Stephen Pearse.

B&B from €50.00 to €75.00
£39.38 to £59.06

GERALDINE O'BRIEN
PROPRIETOR

Diners
Mastercard
Visa

19 19

Closed 24 - 28 December

MIDLETON PARK HOTEL

OLD CORK ROAD,
MIDLETON,
CO. CORK

TEL: 021-463 5100 FAX: 021-463 5101
EMAIL: info@midletonpark.com
WEB: www.midletonpark.com

HOTEL ★★★ MAP 313

Completely refurbished & upgraded, the 75 bedroom Midleton Park & Leisure Centre is located on the N25, 10 miles east of Cork City. Convenient to the industrial, financial & commercial centres of the region & adjacent to Blue Flag Beaches, championship golf courses, heritage centres, Titanic trail, wildlife safari park & historic castles. Tastefully designed bedrooms, award winning restaurant, state of the art leisure centre including several treatment rooms all combine to help you relax, soak up the atmosphere and enjoy an unforgettable visit.

B&B from €50.00 to €100.00
£39.38 to £78.76

ANTHONY SAVAGE
RESIDENT MANAGER

American Express
Diners
Mastercard
Visa

75 75

Closed 25 December

FIR GROVE HOTEL

CAHIR HILL,
MITCHELSTOWN,
CO. CORK

TEL: 025-24111 FAX: 025-84541

HOTEL ★★ MAP 315

The Fir Grove Hotel is a modern hotel, set in its own grounds beneath the Galtee Mountains. Situated on the main Cork/Dublin Road, we are central to most of Munster's large towns and cities. We have a restaurant that serves good local food with a friendly service. All bedrooms are en suite with central heating and TV. Local facilities include golf, fishing, hill walks and pony trekking.

B&B from €40.00 to €45.00
£31.50 to £35.44

PAT & BRENDA TANGNEY
PROPRIETORS

American Express
Diners
Mastercard
Visa

15 15

Open All Year

B&B rates are per person sharing per night incl. Breakfast

CELTIC ROSS HOTEL CONFERENCE & LEISURE CENTRE

ROSSCARBERY,
WEST CORK

TEL: 023-48722 FAX: 023-48723
EMAIL: info@celticrosshotel.com
WEB: www.celticrosshotel.com

HOTEL ★★★ MAP 2 F 1

Nestled in Rosscarbery Bay, the Celtic Ross Hotel is a place for those who want more than just a hotel. It is distinguished by its tower, which hosts a 5,000 year old 40ft tall bog yew. Facilities include 67 guest rooms, many overlooking the bay, Druids Restaurant, Library Bar and tower, Old Forge Pub & Eaterie with regular entertainment. Full leisure centre including heated pool, bubble pool, steam room, sauna and fully equipped gym. Reservations: 1850-272737. Email: reservations@celticross.com

B&B from €50.78 to €82.53
£40.00 to £65.00

NOLLAIG HURLEY
GENERAL MANAGER

American Express
Diners
Mastercard
Visa

67 67

Open All Year

COLLA HOUSE HOTEL

COLLA,
SCHULL,
CO. CORK

TEL: 028-28105 FAX: 028-28497
EMAIL: collahousehotels@eircom.net
WEB: www.cork-guide.ie

HOTEL ★ MAP 2 D 1

An attractive family run hotel situated in a magnificent position overlooking the sea, with panoramic views of the Atlantic Ocean, Cape Clear and Carbery's Hundred Isles. It is surrounded by its own pitch & putt course running direct to the sea. Colla House also has its own horse-riding school on its grounds. All bedrooms en suite with direct dial telephone and TV. Local amenities include 18 hole golf course, deep sea angling and boat trips to islands.

B&B from €35.00 to €50.00
£27.56 to £39.38

MARTIN O'DONOVAN
PROPRIETOR

American Express
Diners
Mastercard
Visa

10 10

Open All Year

Room rates are per room per night

EAST END HOTEL

EAST END,
SCHULL,
CO. CORK
TEL: 028-28101 FAX: 028-27889
EMAIL: eastendhotel@eircom.net
WEB: www.eastendhotel.com

HOTEL ★★ MAP 2 D 1

A family run hotel overlooking Schull Harbour and within walking distance of the numerous amenities in this cosmopolitan village. The hotel's kitchen uses fresh produce and provides quality food all day. TV and DD phone in all rooms. Dine alfresco in our patio garden. We especially welcome families with young children.

Member of Irish Family Hotels

B&B from €34.92 to €47.62
£27.50 to £37.50

VAL DUFFY
MANAGER

American Express
Diners
Mastercard
Visa

15 15

Closed 23 - 27 December

BALLYMALOE HOUSE

SHANAGARRY,
MIDLETON,
CO. CORK
TEL: 021-465 2531 FAX: 021-465 2021
EMAIL: res@ballymaloe.ie
WEB: www.ballymaloe.ie

GUESTHOUSE ★★★★ MAP 3 I 3

A large country house on a 400 acre farm. Home and locally grown produce is served in the award winning restaurant. Small golf course, tennis court and outdoor pool. Sea and river fishing and riding can be arranged. The Allen Family also run a craft, kitchen shop and the café at the Art Gallery. Take the N25 from Cork City for approx 13 miles. Go right at roundabout towards Ballycotton. Ballymaloe House is 2 miles beyond Cloyne.

Member of Ireland's Blue Book

B&B from €90.00 to €130.00
£70.88 to £102.38

MYRTLE ALLEN
PROPRIETOR

American Express
Diners
Mastercard
Visa

32 32

Closed 22 - 27 December

GARRYVOE HOTEL

SHANAGARRY,
MIDLETON,
CO. CORK
TEL: 021-464 6718 FAX: 021-464 6824
EMAIL: garryvoehotel@eircom.net
WEB: www.bayviewhotel.net

HOTEL ★★ MAP 3 J 3

The coastal location overlooking 5 miles on one of Ireland's finest beaches, is the ideal holiday destination. The celebrated restaurant offers the very best of cuisine with fresh seafood a speciality. Activities include tennis, 6 golf courses in the area, Irish heritage, Fota Wildlife Park and many more. The Garryvoe Hotel will introduce an additional 36 bedrooms, conference rooms and leisure facilities towards the end of 2002.

Member of C.M.V. Hotels

B&B from €55.00 to €66.00
£43.32 to £51.98

CARMEL & JOHN O'BRIEN
PROPRIETORS

American Express
Diners
Mastercard
Visa

19 19

Closed 25 December

B&B rates are per person sharing per night incl. Breakfast

ELDON HOTEL

**BRIDGE STREET,
SKIBBEREEN,
WEST CORK**

TEL: 028-22000 FAX: 028-22191
EMAIL: welcome@eldon-hotel.ie
WEB: www.eldon-hotel.com

HOTEL U   MAP 2 E 1

Our aim is to provide the best of the simple things in life, good food, good drink and good company. Michael Collins found these when he visited the Eldon in the 1920's, our guests say they still find them today! Extracts of Collins' love letters to Kitty Kiernan and photos of his visits to the Eldon can be found in our new Porch Bar.

B&B from €35.50 to €80.00
£27.96 to £63.01

ARTHUR LITTLE/LYDIA O'FARRELL
MANAGERS

Diners
Mastercard
Visa

☺ Weekend specials from €96.50

19 19

🖳 inet

IRISH
HOTELS
FEDERATION

Closed 23 - 29 December

The Donkey Sanctuary

Visit The Donkey Sanctuary for a little peace and tranquillity.

We have taken into care 1,800 donkeys – many rescued from neglect.

We are at Liscarroll, near Mallow, Co. Cork.

Open Monday to Friday
9am to 4:30pm
Weekends and Bank Holidays
10am to 5pm
ADMISSION AND PARKING FREE

The Donkey Sanctuary, Knockardbane, Liscarroll, Mallow, Co. Cork.
Tel: (022) 48398
UK Registered Charity No. 264818
Web: www.thedonkeysanctuary.org.uk

Whether for business or pleasure West Cork is A Place Apart!

Call us now for your free **West Cork Holiday brochure**, and your free **West Cork Golf brochure** on callsave 1850 250 999 or 028 22812

West Cork Tourism, U.D.C. Offices, North Street, Skibbereen. Email: wctc@indigo.ie

Skibbereen Heritage Centre

The Lough Hyne Visitor Centre

The Great Famine Commemoration Exhibition

 Old Gasworks Building
Upper Bridge Street
Skibbereen, West Cork
Tel: 028 40900
Fax: 028 40957

Email: info@skibbheritage.com
Website: www.skibbheritage.com

Open March to October,
Tue-Sat, 7 days high season,
Winter by appointment.

Room rates are per room per night

WEST CORK HOTEL

ILEN STREET,
SKIBBEREEN,
CO. CORK

TEL: 028-21277 FAX: 028-22333

EMAIL: info@westcorkhotel.com
WEB: www.westcorkhotel.com

HOTEL ★★★ MAP 2 E 1

The West Cork Hotel offers one of the warmest welcomes you will find in Ireland, and combines old-fashioned courtesy with the comfort of tastefully decorated and well-equipped accommodation. Guests can enjoy the friendly bar atmosphere or dine in the elegant restaurant. However long your stay the West Cork Hotel is the perfect base from which to discover and explore the glorious surroundings and activities available in West Cork.

B&B from €48.00 to €76.00
£37.80 to £59.85

JOHN MURPHY
GENERAL MANAGER

American Express
Diners
Mastercard
Visa

Midweek specials from €197.00

30 30

Closed 22 - 27 December

AHERNE'S TOWNHOUSE & SEAFOOD RESTAURANT

163 NORTH MAIN STREET,
YOUGHAL,
CO. CORK

TEL: 024-92424 FAX: 024-93633

EMAIL: ahernes@eircom.net
WEB: www.ahernes.com

GUESTHOUSE ★★★★ MAP 3 J 3

Open turf fires and the warmest of welcomes await you in this family run hotel in the historic walled port of Youghal. Our rooms exude comfort and luxury, stylishly furnished with antiques and paintings. Our restaurant and bar food menus specialise in the freshest of locally landed seafood. Youghal is on the N25, 35 mins from Cork Airport and is a golfer's paradise. There are 18 golf courses within 1 hours drive. Find us in Ireland's Blue Book and other leading guides. Old Head of Kinsale 80 mins drive.

Member of Ireland's Blue Book
B&B from €70.00 to €102.00
£55.13 to £80.32

THE FITZGIBBON FAMILY

American Express
Diners
Mastercard
Visa

Weekend specials from €180.00

12 12

Closed 24 December - 03 January

DEVONSHIRE ARMS HOTEL & RESTAURANT

PEARSE SQUARE,
YOUGHAL,
CO. CORK

TEL: 024-92827 FAX: 024-92900

EMAIL: reservations@dev.arms.ie

HOTEL ★★ MAP 3 J 3

Luxurious old world family run hotel. Centrally located in the town of Youghal with Blue Flag Beach, 18 hole golf course, riding and historical walking tours. All bedrooms individually decorated, TV, direct dial telephone, hair dryer and valet cleaning unit service. Our restaurant (AA2 Rosettes) offers fresh seafood and a wide range of dishes to suit all tastes, also à la carte bar menu. Half an hour from Cork, two hour drive from Rosslare N25.

B&B from €45.40 to €50.80
£35.76 to £40.01

STEPHEN & HELEN O'SULLIVAN
PROPRIETORS

American Express
Diners
Mastercard
Visa

10 10

Closed 24 - 31 December

B&B rates are per person sharing per night incl. Breakfast

WALTER RALEIGH HOTEL

O'BRIEN PLACE,
YOUGHAL,
CO. CORK

TEL: 024-92011 FAX: 024-93560
EMAIL: info@walter-raleigh.com
WEB: www.walter-raleigh.com

HOTEL ★★ MAP 3 J 3

Newly refurbished, the hotel is ideally located on the main Cork to Waterford Road (N25). Overlooking Youghal Harbour and its famous five-mile Blue Flag beach. Renowned attractions such as the Jameson Distillery of Midleton, the Queenstown Experience of Cobh and the Castle of Blarney are all within easy reach of the hotel.

B&B from €38.00 to €58.00
£29.93 to £45.68

JOHN MURRAY
GENERAL MANAGER

American Express
Diners
Mastercard
Visa

38 38

Open All Year

CLIFF HOUSE HOTEL

CLIFF ROAD,
BALLYBUNION,
CO. KERRY

TEL: 068-27777 FAX: 068-27783
EMAIL: cliffhousehotel@eircom.net

HOTEL ★★★ MAP 5 D 6

Overlooking Ballybunion's sandy beaches, the modern 3*** Cliff House Hotel, with 45 deluxe guest bedrooms, is a golfers paradise. The region boasts 7 championship golf courses. Ballybunion's famous links are no more than a four-iron away, while Tralee, Killarney, Lahinch and Waterville golf clubs are all within easy reach. Every aspect of your golfing vacation is catered for - concession green fees are available at Ballybunion and tee times can be reserved for you.

Member of Holiday Ireland Hotels
B&B from €45.00 to €127.00
£35.43 to £100.00

KEVIN O' CALLAGHAN
DIRECTOR

American Express
Diners
Mastercard
Visa

45 45

Closed 24 - 26 December

EAGLE LODGE

BALLYBUNION,
CO. KERRY

TEL: 068-27224

GUESTHOUSE U MAP 5 D 6

Owner managed, delightful guesthouse situated in town centre. All bedrooms with bathrooms and central heating throughout. A beautiful lounge and private car park for guests. Local amenities include two championship golf courses, sea fishing, tennis, pitch and putt, swimming and boating. Extra value reduced green fees at Ballybunion Golf Club. Cliff walks and surfing also available.

B&B from €32.00 to €50.00
£25.20 to £39.38

MILDRED GLEASURE

8 8

Open All Year

Room rates are per room per night

HARTY COSTELLO TOWN HOUSE

MAIN STREET,
BALLYBUNION,
CO. KERRY
TEL: 068-27129 FAX: 068-27489
EMAIL: hartycostello@eircom.net

GUESTHOUSE ★★★★ MAP 5 D 6

8 luxury bedrooms en suite, in a Townhouse style, all modern conveniences. Elegant dining with traditional high standards of fresh food and wine in our Seafood Restaurant and Bar. Table d'hôte and extensive à la carte menus available. Local amenities, two championship golf links, cliff walks, hot seaweed baths, fishing, four golden beaches and bird watching. Ideal base for golfers or touring and horse riding.

B&B from €44.50 to €63.50
£35.05 to £50.01

DAVNET & JACKIE HOURIGAN
OWNERS

American Express
Mastercard
Visa

Weekend specials from €108.00

8 8

Closed 30 October - 01 April

MANOR INN

DOON ROAD,
BALLYBUNION,
CO. KERRY
TEL: 068-27577 FAX: 068-27757
EMAIL: drao@eircom.net
WEB: www.ballybunion-manorinn.com

GUESTHOUSE ★★★ MAP 5 D 6

The purpose built Manor Inn offers luxury accommodation overlooking the Atlantic at the mouth of the Shannon River. 1km from town centre, 2kms from world famous Ballybunion Golf Club. Bedrooms all en suite, TV, alarm radio, DD phone, computer port in bedroom, hairdryer, tea/coffee facilities and central heating. Antique bedroom a feature. Private car parking. Local amenities: 2, 18 hole links courses, concession green fees available, seaweed bath, sea angling, pony trekking, surfing, swimming, cliff walking and Shannon Ferry.

B&B from €30.00 to €58.00
£23.63 to £45.68

THE MANAGEMENT

American Express
Mastercard
Visa

9 9

Closed 15 November - 14 March

MARINE LINKS HOTEL

SANDHILL ROAD,
BALLYBUNION,
CO. KERRY
TEL: 068-27139 FAX: 068-27666
EMAIL: marinelinkshotel@eircom.net
WEB: www.marinelinksballybunion.com

HOTEL ★★ MAP 5 D 6

A small intimate owner-managed hotel with 10 rooms overlooking the mouth of the Shannon which welcomes golfers and holidaymakers from all over the world who enjoy the local amenities of golf, Blue Flag sandy beaches, hot seaweed baths, cliff walks, fishing, cycling and pony trekking. The restaurant is recognised in the area for fine dining with a table d'hôte and extensive à la carte menu served nightly.

B&B from €41.91 to €57.15
£33.01 to £45.01

MICHAEL NAGLE
PROPRIETOR

American Express
Diners
Mastercard
Visa

10 10

Closed 31 October - 01 March

B&B rates are per person sharing per night incl. Breakfast

TEACH DE BROC

LINK ROAD,
BALLYBUNION,
CO. KERRY
TEL: 068-27581 FAX: 068-27919
EMAIL: teachdebroc@eircom.net
WEB: www.ballybuniongolf.com

GUESTHOUSE ★★★★ MAP 5 D 6

Tea to tee in 2 minutes, is a reality when you stay at the golfers haven of Teach De Broc, located directly opposite entrance gates to World Famous Ballybunion Golf Club. Enjoy the personal attention that this 4**** country house has to offer, with full breakfast served from dawn to facilitate early tee times to a glass of wine in our residents lounge with fellow golfers in the evening. Your hosts Aoife and Seamus together with their valued staff will ensure that your stay at this golfers haven is memorable. Concession green fees available.

B&B from €50.00 to €80.00
£39.38 to £63.01

SEAMUS AND AOIFE BROCK OWNERS

Mastercard
Visa

10 10

Closed 15 December - 15 March

DERRYNANE HOTEL

CAHERDANIEL,
RING OF KERRY,
CO. KERRY
TEL: 066-947 5136 FAX: 066-947 5160
EMAIL: info@derrynane.com
WEB: www.derrynane.com

HOTEL ★★★ MAP 1 C 2

Amidst the most spectacular scenery in Ireland, halfway round the famous Ring of Kerry (on the N70) lies the Derrynane 3*** Hotel with 75 en suite bedrooms. Facilities include 15m outdoor heated pool, steamroom, sauna, gym and tennis court. We are surrounded by beautiful beaches and hills, lovely walks and Derrynane House and National Park. Deep sea angling, lake fishing, golf, horseriding, seasports, boat trips to Skellig Rock all within a short distance. Newly published hotel walking guide to the area.

Member of Best Western Hotels
B&B from €50.00 to €70.00
£39.38 to £55.12

MARY O'CONNOR MANAGER/DIRECTOR

American Express
Diners
Mastercard
Visa

Midweek specials from €115.00

75 75

Closed 15 October - 15 April

Room rates are per room per night

SCARRIFF INN

CAHERDANIEL,
CO. KERRY

TEL: 066-947 5132 FAX: 066-947 5425
EMAIL: scarriff1@aol.com
WEB: www.caherdaniel.net

GUESTHOUSE ★★ MAP 1 C 3

This family-run guesthouse overlooks
the best view in Ireland, with majestic
views of Derrynane, Kenmare and
Bantry Bay, situated halfway round
the Ring of Kerry. All our rooms have
sea views. Dine in our seafood
restaurant and enjoy outstanding
cuisine as recommended by Sir
Andrew Lloyd Webber or relax in our
Vista Bar and enjoy scenery and
ambience. The area is varied in
activities, the Kerry Way, several
beautiful beaches within walking
distance. Day trips to Skellig Rocks.

B&B from €25.00 to €35.00
£19.69 to £27.56

KATIE O'CARROLL
PROPRIETOR

American Express
Mastercard
Visa

Weekend specials from €75.00

6 6

Closed 30 October - 05 March

BARNAGH BRIDGE
COUNTRY GUEST HOUSE

CAMP,
TRALEE,
CO. KERRY

TEL: 066-713 0145 FAX: 066-713 0299
EMAIL: bbguest@eircom.net
WEB: www.barnaghbridge.com

GUESTHOUSE ★★★ MAP 1 C 5

A welcoming haven, Barnagh Bridge
nestles between mountains and sea
on the Dingle Peninsula. Our unique
guesthouse is set in landscaped
grounds with conservatory and dining
room overlooking Tralee Bay. Family
run with superb breakfasts including
home baking and morning special.
Ideal location for touring Dingle
Peninsula and Ring of Kerry. Local
golfing and walking. AA, RAC ◆◆◆◆,
Frommers and other guides listed.
Leave N86 at Camp, follow Conor
Pass Road R560 for 1 mile.

Member of Premier Guesthouses
B&B from €20.00 to €40.00
£15.75 to £31.50

HEATHER WILLIAMS
HOST

American Express
Mastercard
Visa

5 5

Closed 31 October - 01 March

ARD-NA-SIDHE

CARAGH LAKE,
KILLORGLIN,
CO. KERRY

TEL: 066-976 9105 FAX: 066-976 9282
EMAIL: sales@kih.liebherr.com
WEB: www.iol.ie/khl

HOTEL ★★★★ MAP 1 D 4

20 bedroom 4**** de luxe Victorian
mansion delightfully located in its
own park on Caragh Lake. Highest
standards of comfort. Tastefully
furnished with antiques and open
fireplaces. Luxurious lounges and
restaurant. Free boating, fishing and
facilities of sister hotels - Hotel Europe
and Hotel Dunloe Castle - available to
guests. 10 major golf courses
nearby. Special green fees. Central
Reservations Tel: 064-31900 Fax:
064-32118.

Room Rate from €215.00 to €309.00
£169.30 to £243.31

KATHLEEN DOWLING

American Express
Diners
Mastercard
Visa

20 20

Closed 01 October - 30 April

B&B rates are per person sharing per night incl. Breakfast

CARAGH LODGE

**CARAGH LAKE,
CO. KERRY**

TEL: 066-976 9115 FAX: 066-976 9316
EMAIL: caraghl@iol.ie
WEB: www.caraghlodge.com

GUESTHOUSE ★★★★ MAP 1 D 4

A Victorian fishing lodge standing in 7.5 acres of parkland containing many rare and subtropical trees and shrubs. Winner of the National Garden Award. The gardens sweep down to Caragh Lake, ideal for trout fishing. The lounges and dining room are very comfortably furnished and overlook the gardens and lake. Excellent cuisine includes local lamb and wild salmon. Golf and beaches within 5 minutes.

Member of Ireland's Blue Book

B&B from €80.00 to €138.00
£63.01 to £108.68

MARY GAUNT
OWNER

American Express
Diners
Mastercard
Visa

🚻 🏠 ☎ T ✳ 🌸 ⚲ U ♫ P 🅿 alc
14   14

Closed 16 October - 12 April

CRUTCH'S HILLVILLE HOUSE HOTEL

**CONOR PASS ROAD, CASTLEGREGORY,
DINGLE PENINSULA,
CO. KERRY**

TEL: 066-713 8118 FAX: 066-713 8159
EMAIL: macshome@iol.ie

HOTEL ★★ MAP 1 C 5

Delightful country house owned and managed by Ron & Sandra. Situated near Fermoyle Beach on Kerry's scenic Dingle Peninsula. Close to the highest mountain pass in Ireland - The Conor Pass, Slea Head, Dingle & Killarney. The Fermoyle Room Restaurant offers traditional home cooking using fresh local produce, vegetarians, special diets catered for on request. A friendly country house atmosphere, generously sized rooms, some with four poster beds & sea views, cosy bar and open fires - golf, surfing, horse riding, walks, island trips all nearby.

Member of Coast and Country Hotels

B&B from €48.00 to €57.00
£37.80 to £44.89

RON & SANDRA
PROPRIETORS

American Express
Diners
Mastercard
Visa

☺   3 B&B and 3 Dinners €215

🚻 🏠 ☎ T C ✉ CM ✳ U ♫ P ⚑ 7 S 🅿
19   19

alc Inet FAX

Open All Year

Room rates are per room per night

O'CONNOR'S GUESTHOUSE

**CLOGHANE,
DINGLE PENINSULA,
CO. KERRY**
TEL: 066-713 8113 FAX: 066-713 8270
EMAIL: oconnorsguesthouse@eircom.net
WEB: www.oconnorsguesthouse.freeservers.com

GUESTHOUSE ★★ MAP 1 B 5

A long established, spacious country home with spectacular views of sea and mountains, overlooking Brandon Bay and within easy reach of Dingle on the Dingle Way. Private car park, guest lounge, open fire, home cooked meals, pub and a warm welcome are just some of the things awaiting our guests.

**B&B from €28.00 to €35.00
£22.05 to £27.56**

MICHEAL & ELIZABETH O'DOWD
OWNERS

Mastercard

Visa

☺ Week partial board from €285.00

🛏🐾 T A C 🌙 C M ❄ U J P 🄰 ald 🛍
9   9

Closed 01 November - 28 February

ALPINE HOUSE

**MAIL ROAD,
DINGLE,
CO. KERRY**
TEL: 066-915 1250 FAX: 066-915 1966
EMAIL: alpinedingle@eircom.net
WEB: www.alpineguesthouse.com

GUESTHOUSE ★★★ MAP 1 B 4

Superb guesthouse run by the O'Shea Family. AA ◆◆◆◆ and RAC ◆◆◆◆ highly acclaimed. Elegant en suite bedrooms with TV, direct dial phone, hairdryers, central heating and tea/coffee facilities. Spacious dining room with choice of breakfast. Delightful guest lounge. 2 minutes walk to town centre, restaurants, harbour and bus stop. Local amenities include Slea Head Drive and Blasket Islands, also pony trekking, angling and boat trips to Fungi the dolphin.

**B&B from €26.00 to €40.00
£20.48 to £31.50**

PAUL O'SHEA
MANAGER

American Express

Mastercard

Visa

🛏🐾☎ T C ❄ U J P S 🛍
10 10

Open All Year

BAMBURY'S GUEST HOUSE

**MAIL ROAD,
DINGLE,
CO. KERRY**
TEL: 066-915 1244 FAX: 066-915 1786
EMAIL: bamburysguesthouse@eircom.net
WEB: www.bamburysguesthouse.com

GUESTHOUSE ★★★ MAP 1 B 4

AA selected ◆◆◆◆, new house, excellent location, 2 minutes walk to town centre. Offering peaceful accommodation in spacious, double, twin or triple rooms all with en suite, direct dial telephone and satellite TV. Attractive guest lounge to relax in. Private car parking, choice of breakfast in spacious dining room. Local attractions, Dingle Peninsula, horse riding, angling and golf on local 18 hole golf links. Reduced green fees can be arranged. Listed in all leading guides.

**B&B from €27.00 to €46.00
£21.26 to £36.23**

BERNIE BAMBURY
PROPRIETOR

Mastercard

Visa

🛏🐾☎ U P
12 12

Open All Year

B&B rates are per person sharing per night incl. Breakfast

BARR NA SRAIDE INN

UPPER MAIN STREET,
DINGLE,
CO. KERRY

TEL: 066-915 1331 FAX: 066-915 1446

EMAIL: barrnasraide@eircom.net
WEB: http://homepage.eircom.net/~barrnasraide/

GUESTHOUSE ★★★ MAP 1 B 4

Family run bar/guesthouse. Located in the town centre. The Barr na Sraide Inn has been recently refurbished to a very high standard. An extensive menu awaits our guests for breakfast. End each day with a relaxing drink in our comfortable bar amongst the locals. Private enclosed car park. Ideal base for your stay in the South West. Golf, fishing, sailing, cycling, horse riding and trips to Fungi the dolphin available nearby.

B&B from €40.00 to €55.00
£31.50 to £43.32

PATRICIA GEANEY

Mastercard
Visa

22 22

IRISH HOTELS FEDERATION

Closed 17 - 26 December

BENNERS HOTEL

MAIN STREET,
DINGLE,
CO. KERRY

TEL: 066-915 1638 FAX: 066-915 1412

EMAIL: benners@eircom.net
WEB: www.bennershotel.com

HOTEL ★★★ MAP 1 B 4

A 300 year old hotel with young ideas. Benners is a timeless part of Kerry's proud holiday tradition. It is part of the emotional experience that lingers on… long after a visit to the magnificent Dingle Peninsula. Benners is synonymous with excellence in comfort and cuisine, specialising in a daily fresh Atlantic catch. Our rooms are all en suite with antique furniture, hairdryer, TV, direct dial phone and tea/coffee facilities. Open all year. Special weekend and midweek packages available.

Member of Manor House Hotels

B&B from €79.00 to €102.00
£62.22 to £80.33

PAT GALVIN
GENERAL MANAGER

American Express
Diners
Mastercard
Visa

51 51

IRISH HOTELS FEDERATION

Closed 25 - 26 December

Room rates are per room per night

BOLAND'S GUESTHOUSE

GOAT STREET,
DINGLE,
CO. KERRY
TEL: 066-915 1426
EMAIL: bolanddingle@eircom.net
WEB: http://homepage.eircom.net/~bolanddingle

GUESTHOUSE ★★ MAP 1 B 4

A warm welcome awaits you in our family run guesthouse. Situated in Dingle Town with panoramic views of Dingle Bay. All our rooms are en suite with direct dial phones, TV, hairdryers, tea/coffee making facilities. Full breakfast menu in our conservatory dining room. Relax and enjoy the magnificent views of Dingle Bay from our guest lounge.

B&B from €25.39 to €38.09
£20.00 to £30.00

BREDA BOLAND
OWNER

Mastercard

Visa

7 7

Closed 01 December - 31 January

CAPTAINS HOUSE

THE MALL,
DINGLE,
CO. KERRY
TEL: 066-915 1531 FAX: 066-915 1079
EMAIL: captigh@eircom.net
WEB: http://homepage.eircom.net/~captigh/

GUESTHOUSE ★★★ MAP 1 B 4

A welcome awaits you at the Captains House situated in Dingle Town. Approached by foot bridge over the Mall Stream and through award winning gardens our three star family run guest house is tastefully furnished with items collected on the Captains voyages. All rooms are en suite with direct dial telephones and TV. A breakfast menu featuring home made bread and preserves is served in the conservatory overlooking the garden.

B&B from €40.00 to €45.00
£31.50 to £35.44

MARY & JIM MILHENCH
PROPRIETORS

American Express

Diners

Mastercard

Visa

8 8

Closed 01 December - 16 March

CLEEVAUN COUNTRY HOUSE

LADYS CROSS,
MILLTOWN, DINGLE,
CO. KERRY
TEL: 066-915 1108 FAX: 066-915 2228
EMAIL: cleevaun@iol.ie
WEB: www.cleevaun.com

GUESTHOUSE ★★★ MAP 1 B 4

Galtee Regional Breakfast Winner 1994. Cleevaun is set in landscaped gardens overlooking Dingle Bay, 1 mile from Dingle Town. Rooms with private bathrooms, TVs, hairdryers, tea/coffee facilities. Relax and enjoy the magnificent views of Dingle Bay from our breakfast room while you choose from our award winning menu. Often described as an oasis of peace and tranquillity. Cleevaun is commended by AA, RAC, and Karen Browne. Local amenities golf, walking, pony trekking.

B&B from €32.00 to €44.00
£25.20 to £34.65

CHARLOTTE CLUSKEY
HOST

Mastercard

Visa

8 8

IRISH
HOTELS
FEDERATION

Closed 15 November - 15 March

B&B rates are per person sharing per night incl. Breakfast

COASTLINE GUESTHOUSE

THE WOOD,
DINGLE,
CO. KERRY
TEL: 066-915 2494 FAX: 066-915 2493
EMAIL: coastlinedingle@eircom.net
WEB: www.coastlinedingle.com

GUESTHOUSE ★★★ MAP 1 B 4

Beautiful new guesthouse on the water's edge of Dingle Bay. All rooms are en suite with direct dial phone, TV, hairdryer, tea/coffee making facilities and many have panoramic views of the harbour. Ground floor rooms available. Enjoy our excellent breakfast and relax in our sitting room in the evening and watch the fishing fleet return with their catch. Private car park. 5 minutes walk to town centre. Ideal base to enjoy all Dingle has to offer - excellent restaurants and pubs.

B&B from €28.00 to €38.00
£22.05 to £29.93

VIVIENNE O'SHEA
PROPRIETOR

Mastercard

Visa

🛏🛴☎🖥T❄♪PS🍽
6   6

IRISH
HOTELS
FEDERATION

Closed 18 November - 31 January

CONNORS

DYKEGATE STREET,
DINGLE,
CO. KERRY
TEL: 066-915 1598 FAX: 066-915 2376

GUESTHOUSE ★★ MAP 1 B 4

Welcome to our newly refurbished guesthouse. All rooms en suite with TV, clock radio, hairdryer, direct dial phone, tea/coffee making facilities, central heating, orthopaedic beds. We are situated in the heart of Dingle Town. Within walking distance to all restaurants and pubs. Recommended Guide Du Routard, Rick Steves Guide to Ireland and Stilwells Guide. Breakfast menu available in our spacious dining room. Packed lunches available on request.

B&B from €26.00 to €35.00
£20.48 to £27.56

CAROL CONNOR

American Express

Mastercard

Visa

🛏🛴🖥T©♪🍽
15   15

Closed 22 - 26 December

Room rates are per room per night

DINGLE SKELLIG HOTEL

DINGLE,
CO. KERRY

TEL: 066-915 0200 FAX: 066-915 1501
EMAIL: dsk@iol.ie
WEB: www.dingleskellig.com

HOTEL ★★★★ MAP 1 B 4

Renowned hotel situated on the beautiful harbour of Dingle Bay. Luxurious leisure club & pool; jacuzzi, geyser pool, children's pool, steamroom, gymnasium. Ki-massage, reflexology & aromatherapy. Fungi Kids Club and Creche available weekends and holidays. Excellent cuisine specialising in locally caught seafood. Established conference & banqueting centre with stunning views for up to 250 people. Reduced green fees & guaranteed tee times (including weekends) at Ceann Sibeal.

B&B from €60.00 to €135.00
£47.25 to £106.32

PHILIP GAVIN
GENERAL MANAGER

American Express
Diners
Mastercard
Visa

☺ Weekend specials from €135.00

 112 112

I R I S H
HOTELS
FEDERATION

Closed 23 - 27 December

DOYLES SEAFOOD BAR & TOWN HOUSE

JOHN STREET,
DINGLE,
CO. KERRY

TEL: 066-915 1174 FAX: 066-915 1816
EMAIL: cdoyles@iol.ie
WEB: www.doylesofdingle.com

GUESTHOUSE ★★★★ MAP 1 B 4

The Townhouse has the most delightful rooms in Dingle. 8 spacious bedrooms with full bathrooms have recently been refurbished in a most comfortable style. Satelite TV, phone, trouser press/iron, tea/coffee facilities. The restaurant has an old range, sugan chairs. Natural stone and wood combination gives Doyle's a cosy country atmosphere. Lobster our speciality, is chosen from a tank in the bar. The menu consists only of fresh food & is chosen on a daily basis from the fish landed by the Dingle boats.

Member of Ireland's Blue Book
B&B from €39.00 to €57.00
£30.71 to £44.89

SEAN CLUSKEY
HOST

Diners
Mastercard
Visa

 8 8

I R I S H
HOTELS
FEDERATION

Closed 15 November - 14 February

EMLAGH HOUSE

DINGLE,
CO. KERRY

TEL: 066-915 2345 FAX: 066-915 2369
EMAIL: info@emlaghhouse.com
WEB: www.emlaghhouse.com

GUESTHOUSE N MAP 1 B 4

Welcome to Emlagh House, our Georgian style family-run home, overlooking Dingle Harbour. Here you will certainly relax in our calm and gracious surroundings. Spacious rooms are individually decorated on the theme of native Irish wild flowers. All rooms have large en suites, separate shower/bath, DD phone, TV and video, radio/CD, ironing board/trouser press and PC outlets. A short stroll will bring you to the heart of Dingle town to sample its delights. Golf Courses & Sea fishing nearby.

B&B from €90.00 to €105.00
£70.87 to £82.68

GRAINNE & MARION KAVANAGH

Mastercard
Visa

11 11

I R I S H
HOTELS
FEDERATION

Closed 30 November - 28 December

B&B rates are per person sharing per night incl. Breakfast

GORMANS CLIFFTOP HOUSE AND RESTAURANT

GLAISE BHEAG, BALLYDAVID,
DINGLE PENINSULA, TRALEE,
CO. KERRY
TEL: 066-915 5162 FAX: 066-915 5162
EMAIL: gormans@eircom.net
WEB: www.gormans-clifftophouse.com

GUESTHOUSE ★★★★ MAP 1 B 5

A welcoming cliff top refuge on the western edge of the Dingle Peninsula. All rooms pay homage to the landscape, offering breathtaking views of the Ocean and Mountains. Our emphasis is on comfort, mini suites boasting king size beds and jacuzzi baths. Downstairs guests can gather around the fire to read or chat, dine handsomely in our fully licensed restaurant. AA ♦♦♦♦ premier select. Les Routiers "Hidden Gem Ireland" 2001.

Member of Best Loved Hotels of The World

B&B from €50.00 to €75.00
£39.38 to £59.07

VINCENT AND SILE O'GORMAIN PROPRIETORS

Mastercard
Visa

☺ Midweek specials from €125.00

🛏🐕☎📺T☐C❄♪U⏧P🅿alc
9   9

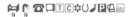

IRISH HOTELS FEDERATION

Closed 10 January - 01 March

GREENMOUNT HOUSE

UPPER JOHN STREET,
DINGLE,
CO. KERRY
TEL: 066-915 1414 FAX: 066-915 1974
EMAIL: mary@greenmounthouse.com
WEB: www.greenmounthouse.com

GUESTHOUSE ★★★★ MAP 1 B 4

Greenmount House is the proud recipient of the 1997 RAC Guest House of the Year for Ireland. A charming 4**** country house yet centrally located. Spacious lounges to relax in and take advantage of its magnificent scenic location overlooking Dingle Town & Harbour. Each bedroom has private bathroom TV/radio & direct dial phone. Award winning buffet breakfasts served in conservatory with commanding views of Dingle. Luxurious, peaceful retreat. Recognised by all leading guides.

B&B from €35.00 to €62.50
£27.56 to £49.22

JOHN & MARY CURRAN OWNERS

Mastercard
Visa

🛏🐕☎📺T☐❄P🚗
7   7

IRISH HOTELS FEDERATION

Closed 10 - 27 December

Room rates are per room per night

HEATON'S GUESTHOUSE

THE WOOD,
DINGLE,
CO. KERRY

TEL: 066-915 2288 FAX: 066-915 2324
EMAIL: heatons@iol.ie
WEB: www.heatonsdingle.com

GUESTHOUSE ★★★★ MAP 1 B 4

Superb 4**** family run guesthouse situated on the shore of Dingle Bay with spectacular views, 5 minutes walk from the town. All rooms are en suite (pressure shower and bath), with TV, DD phone and tea/coffee welcome tray. Breakfast is our speciality. Luxury junior-suites and deluxe rooms recently opened (rates available on request). Local amenities include golf, sailing, fishing, surfing, cycling, walking, horse riding and the renowned gourmet restaurants.

B&B from €35.00 to €55.00
£27.56 to £43.32

NUALA & CAMERON HEATON
PROPRIETORS

Mastercard
Visa

16   16

Open All Year

MILLTOWN HOUSE

MILLTOWN,
DINGLE,
CO. KERRY

TEL: 066-915 1372 FAX: 066-915 1095
EMAIL: milltown@indigo.ie
WEB: http://indigo.ie/~milltown/

GUESTHOUSE ★★★★ MAP 1 B 4

Award winning family run Milltown House is ideally located overlooking Dingle Bay and Town from our private gardens. All rooms which retain the character of the 130 year old house are en suite, have tea/coffee making facilities, direct dial phone, TVs, trouser press and hairdryer. Some rooms are wheelchair friendly. Assistance in planning your day. One of the most scenic and quiet locations in the town area, walking less than 15 minutes, driving 2 minutes!

B&B from €42.00 to €64.00
£33.08 to £50.40

TARA KERRY

American Express
Mastercard
Visa

10   10

Closed 30 November - 31 January

OLD PIER

AN FHEOTHANACH,
BALLYDAVID, DINGLE,
CO. KERRY

TEL: 066-915 5242
EMAIL: info@oldpier.com
WEB: www.oldpier.com

GUESTHOUSE ★★★ MAP 1 B 4

Situated in the heart of the West Kerry Gaeltacht on the Dingle Peninsula overlooking beautiful Smerwick Harbour and the Atlantic Ocean. This family run establishment offers 3*** accommodation with beautiful sea and mountain vistas. The Old Pier Restaurant offers a broad range of locally caught seafood, prime steak and meat dishes. Adjacent activities include 18 hole golf course, deep sea angling, mountain walking and archaeology sites. A warm welcome awaits you.

B&B from €26.00 to €51.00
£20.48 to £40.17

JACQUI & PADRAIG O CONNOR

Mastercard
Visa

☺   Discount for stays of 2 nights

6   6

Open All Year

B&B rates are per person sharing per night incl. Breakfast

PAX HOUSE

UPPER JOHN STREET,
DINGLE,
CO. KERRY
TEL: 066-915 1518 FAX: 066-915 2461
EMAIL: paxhouse@iol.ie
WEB: www.pax-house.com

GUESTHOUSE ★★★★ MAP 1 B 4

Pax House is a family-run guesthouse dedicated to the comfort of you the visitor. Situated 1km from Dingle town centre, commanding spectacular views of the bay and harbour, its the ideal base for all your holiday activities: golf, angling, hill-walking, sightseeing, dining and drinking out. Breakfast is a major event, with fish, meats, cheese, homemade breads, preserves and yoghurt. We offer guests, charm, tranquillity unequalled hospitality. AA ◆◆◆◆◆. Voted top ten places to stay in Ireland.

Member of Premier Guesthouses

B&B from €45.00 to €80.00
£35.44 to £63.01

RON & JOAN BROSNAN WRIGHT
OWNERS

Mastercard
Visa

🏠 ⛹ ☎ T C M ❄ ♪ P 🖨 FAX
12 12

IRISH HOTELS FEDERATION

Closed 01 December - 31 January

SMERWICK HARBOUR HOTEL

BALLYFERRITER,
DINGLE,
CO. KERRY
TEL: 066-915 6470 FAX: 066-915 6473
EMAIL: info@smerwickhotel.com
WEB: www.smerwickhotel.com

HOTEL ★★★ MAP 1 B 5

Smerwick Harbour Hotel, Seafood Restaurant with its old world bar, is located a short distance from Dingle town. Our local 18 hole golf course is on your doorstep, 4km away, reduced green fees for guests. All rooms en suite (family rooms also). Spacious lounge. Enjoy excellent cuisine in our seafood restaurant, specialising in local seafood and char grilled steaks. Quality barfood also available. Old world ambience, as featured on our web site. The best sandy beaches in Ireland nearby. New elevator installed. Groups & weddings catered for.

B&B from €38.00 to €64.00
£29.93 to £50.40

FIONNBAR WALSH
MANAGER

American Express
Mastercard
Visa

🙂 Weekend specials from €102.00

🏠 ⛹ ☎ ↕ T C ♿ CM ❄ ♪ ♪ P
32 32

S 🚗 aid

IRISH HOTELS FEDERATION

Open All Year

Room rates are per room per night

TOWERS HOTEL

GLENBEIGH,
CO. KERRY

TEL: 066-976 8212 FAX: 066-976 8260
EMAIL: towershotel@eircom.net
WEB: www.towershotel.com

HOTEL ★★★ MAP 1 C 4

The family run Towers Hotel, on the Ring of Kerry, is an ideal place to relax and enjoy the splendours of Kerry. The hotel is a short distance from sandy beaches and dramatic mountains. Paradise for golfers, walkers, fishermen and anyone interested in the Kerry landscape. The Towers internationally known restaurant is renowned for its excellent seafood and distinguished atmosphere. Its traditional pub provides a chance to mingle with the people of Glenbeigh in a real Kerry atmosphere.

Member of Coast and Country Hotels

B&B from €50.00 to €61.00
£39.38 to £48.04

DOLORES SWEENEY
PROPRIETOR

American Express
Mastercard
Visa

28 28

Closed 01 December - 28 March

GLENCAR HOUSE HOTEL

GLENCAR,
CO. KERRY

TEL: 066-976 0102 FAX: 066-976 0167
EMAIL: info@glencarhouse.com
WEB: www.glencarhouse.com

HOTEL ★★ MAP 1 C 4

The Glencar House Hotel, built in 1732, lies framed by the McGillycuddy Reeks Mountains and is 2km from Caragh Lake. Declared an area of Special Conservation in 1997, it is the perfect base for a relaxing or activity holiday. Local golf courses include Dooks, Beaufort and Killarney. Traditional Irish cuisine is served in our restaurant. Salmon and trout fishing is available on the Caragh Fishery and boats are for hire on Caragh Lake. All bedrooms have private bath/shower and TV.

Member of Great Fishing Houses of Ireland

B&B from €50.00 to €70.00
£39.38 to £55.13

KEVIN FACTOR
MANAGER

American Express
Diners
Mastercard
Visa

Week partial board from €495.00

18 18

HOTELS
FEDERATION

Closed 16 October - 23 February

ASHBERRY LODGE

SNEEM ROAD,
N70, KENMARE,
CO. KERRY

TEL: 064-42720
EMAIL: ashberry@iolfree.ie
WEB: www.kenmare.com/ashberry

GUESTHOUSE ★★★ MAP 1 D 3

Welcome to our new family-run guesthouse which offers friendly comfortable accommodation with spacious en suite bedrooms, central heating, excellent showers, colour TV, direct dial phones and a breakfast menu. We are situated on the Ring of Kerry Road, N70, which is within a short walking distance to the town centre. It is an ideal homebase to tour the Ring of Beara, Ring of Kerry, Gap of Dunloe, Healy's Pass, and much more! Also available are two 18 hole golf courses.

B&B from €27.50 to €32.50
£21.66 to £25.60

FRANCIE & REGINA MURPHY

Mastercard
Visa

8 8

HOTELS
FEDERATION

Open All Year

B&B rates are per person sharing per night incl. Breakfast

BRASS LANTERN

OLD RAILWAY ROAD,
KENMARE,
CO. KERRY
TEL: 064-42601 FAX: 064-42600
EMAIL: thebrasslantern@eircom.net
WEB: www.kenmare-insight.com/brasslantern

GUESTHOUSE ★★★ MAP 1 D 3

We are ideally located on a quiet residential road 2 minutes walk from Kenmare centre. The house has been designed to ensure our guests enjoy a comfortable and peaceful stay. Spacious bedrooms with en suite facilities, telephone and TV. Ground floor rooms perfect for anyone who has difficulty with stairs. Tea and coffee available throughout the day. Relax in front of a glowing fire with a book from our library. Plan activities with the help of our guide books, maps and local knowledge.

B&B from €25.00 to €45.00
£19.69 to £35.44

PADRAIG JONES
MANAGER

Mastercard

Visa

🛏️🏃☎️🖥️©🚶🏊Ⓟ🆂 Inet

IRISH HOTELS FEDERATION

Open All Year

DAVITTS

HENRY STREET,
KENMARE,
CO. KERRY
TEL: 064-42741 FAX: 064-42756
EMAIL: davittskenmare@eircom.net
WEB: www.davitts-kenmare.com

GUESTHOUSE ★★★ MAP 1 D 3

If you are looking for luxury accommodation in the heart of Kenmare, then Davitt's is the guesthouse for you. Bar/bistro, restaurant downstairs serving excellent food throughout the year. Family run premises that offers everything for a perfect holiday under one roof. All our luxury bedrooms are en suite with satellite TV, DD phones (pc compatible) and hairdryers. The rooms are sited at the back of the building guaranteeing a restful night in spacious, beautifully decorated rooms.

B&B from €31.75 to €38.10
£25.01 to £30.01

DONAL & MARY CREMIN
PROPRIETORS

American Express

Mastercard

Visa

✓

🛏️🏃☎️🖥️ⓉⒸCM🎵🎶Ⓟ🆐Inet
11 11

Closed 24 - 27 December

DROMQUINNA MANOR HOTEL

BLACKWATER BRIDGE P.O.,
KENMARE,
CO. KERRY
TEL: 064-41657 FAX: 064-41791
EMAIL: info@dromquinna.com
WEB: www.dromquinna.com

HOTEL ★★★ MAP 1 D 3

Breathtaking south facing views, of sea, islands and mountains. 29 delightful rooms, four-posters, suites & Ireland's only Tree House. Conservatory dining room, Intl cuisine, informal atmosphere. Coach House Annexe with 18 charming rooms including family rooms. 40 acres of grounds, marina, jetty, slipway, small beach. Amenities: Water Sports, Children's Playground, Boathouse Restaurant. Golf Courses: Ring of Kerry 3 minutes, Kenmare 5 minutes. Well placed for sight seeing in Kerry.

B&B from €69.85 to €127.00
£55.01 to £100.02

MIKE & SUE ROBERTSON
PROPRIETORS

American Express

Diners

Mastercard

Visa

🛏️🏃☎️🖥️Ⓣ🅰️Ⓒ🍴CM❄️🎣🚶Ⓟ
29 29 🏇🆐⛵

Closed 31 October - 01 March

Room rates are per room per night

FOLEYS SHAMROCK

HENRY STREET,
KENMARE,
CO. KERRY
TEL: 064-42162 FAX: 064-41799
EMAIL: foleyest@iol.ie
WEB: www.foleyskenmare.com

GUESTHOUSE ★★★ MAP 1 D 3

Foleys is situated in Kenmare, Kerry Heritage town, ten very comfortable centrally heated en suite rooms with colour TV, phone & tea making facilities. Our chef owned restaurant & pub bistro serves Irish & international cuisine. Traditional sessions in the pub. Foleys is within walking distance of Kenmare 18 hole golf course, horse riding & fishing trips can be arranged. One of Ireland's Best - Fodors. Also recognised by Routard & Michelin.

B&B from € 30.00 to € 50.00
£23.63 to £39.38

MARGARET FOLEY
OWNER/MANAGER

Mastercard

Visa

🛏🚶🕾📺TⒸ☺♫🔊alc 🖥 inet
10 10

Open All Year

KENMARE BAY HOTEL

KENMARE,
CO. KERRY
TEL: 064-41300 FAX: 064-41541
EMAIL: kenmare@leehotels.ie
WEB: www.leehotels.ie

HOTEL ★★★ MAP 1 D 3

We offer a quiet hospitality with panoramic views of both the Cork and Kerry Mountains. By day you can choose from golfing, walking, fishing, touring and cycling; by night we offer quality cuisine followed by traditional Irish music in our lounge. Located in 6 acres of parkland, we are only half a km from Ireland's most colourful heritage town - Kenmare.

Member of Lee Hotels
B&B from € 38.00 to € 50.00
£29.93 to £39.38

TERRY O'DOHERTY
GENERAL MANAGER

Diners

Mastercard

Visa

🛏🚶🕾📺TⒸ🐾CM♫PS🔊alc 🖥
136 136

IRISH HOTELS FEDERATION

Closed 04 November - 28 March

LANSDOWNE ARMS HOTEL

WILLIAM STREET,
KENMARE,
CO. KERRY
TEL: 064-41368 FAX: 064-41114
EMAIL: info@lansdownearms.com
WEB: www.lansdownearms.com

HOTEL ★★★ MAP 1 D 3

Ideally situated in Kenmare adjacent to Kenmare Golf Club. Try a relaxing drink in the Shelbourne Bar or join in the craic in Moeran's with its open log fire. Irish Traditional music every night 1st of June to 30th September - every Friday and Saturday night all year round! Choose from freshest locally sourced meat and fish in our elegant restaurant and select from an extensive wine list. All bedrooms finished to the highest standard.

B&B from € 63.50 to € 76.20
£50.00 to £60.00

RICHARD VOKE, OWNER
PATRICK GEOGHEGAN, MANAGER

American Express

Diners

Mastercard

Visa

🛏🚶🕾📺CCM♫PS🔊alc 🖥
26 26

IRISH HOTELS FEDERATION

Open All Year

B&B rates are per person sharing per night incl. Breakfast

LODGE

KILLOWEN ROAD,
KENMARE,
CO. KERRY

TEL: 064-41512 FAX: 064-42724
EMAIL: thelodgekenmare@eircom.net
WEB: www.thelodgekenmare.com

GUESTHOUSE ★★★★ MAP 1 D 3

Newly-built luxury guesthouse situated directly opposite Kenmare's 18 hole golf course. Within 3 minutes walk of some of the finest restaurants in Ireland. All rooms are elegantly furnished with kingsize beds and en suite bathrooms. The rooms are very well appointed with DD phone, TV, controllable central heating and safes. An ideal location for the active, with walking, horseriding and fishing nearby. 4 of the bedrooms are on ground level with one especially equipped for wheelchair use.

B&B from €45.00 to €55.00
£35.44 to £43.31

ROSEMARIE QUILL
PROPRIETOR

Mastercard

Visa

10 10

Closed 07 November - 17 March

O'DONNABHAIN'S

HENRY STREET,
KENMARE,
CO. KERRY

TEL: 064-42106 FAX: 064-42321
EMAIL: info@odonnabhain-kenmare.com
WEB: www.odonnabhain-kenmare.com

GUESTHOUSE ★★★ MAP 1 D 3

Conviently located in the centre of Kenmare Town, providing affordable accommodation with lashings of old world charm. Spacious en suite rooms (direct dial phone, TV 6 channels, parking), some with king size beds, finished with the comfort of the guests in mind. Rooms are located away from the bar, so as to ensure no sleepless nights, quietness in the centre of town. Ideal base to discover the South's attractions.

B&B from €30.00 to €48.00
£23.63 to £37.80

JEREMIAH FOLEY
OWNER

Mastercard

Visa

10 10

Open All Year

PARK HOTEL KENMARE

KENMARE,
CO. KERRY

TEL: 064-41200 FAX: 064-41402
EMAIL: info@parkkenmare.com
WEB: www.parkkenmare.com

HOTEL ★★★★★ MAP 1 D 3

Standing proudly amidst some of Irelands most breathtaking scenery, the limestone building, dating from 1897 welcomes guests with renowned warmth. A deluxe base from which to tour the famous Ring of Kerry, Ring of Beara or simply enjoy the intimacy of your accommodations. The dining room overlooking Kenmare Bay is regarded as one of Ireland's most respected offering the finest cuisine and an extensive wine list from around the world. Privately owned and managed a most pleasant stay is assured.

Member of Ireland's Blue Book
B&B from €176.00 to €349.00
£138.61 to £274.86

FRANCIS BRENNAN
PROPRIETOR

American Express

Diners

Mastercard

Visa

47 47

Closed 02 January - 10 April

Room rates are per room per night

RIVERSDALE HOUSE HOTEL

KENMARE,
CO. KERRY

TEL: 064-41299 FAX: 064-41075
EMAIL: riversdale@eircom.net
WEB: www.kenmare.com/riversdale

HOTEL ★★★ MAP 1 D 3

Located on the scenic shores of Kenmare Bay and backed by the McGillycuddy Reeks and Caha Mountains the hotel is the ideal choice to tour the famous Ring of Kerry and beautiful West Cork. Recently refurbished, the hotel boasts 4 luxurious suites, each with panoramic views of the scenery beyond our seven acre garden. Our Waterfront Restaurant is renowned for its fine cuisine while local activities include an 18 hole golf course, deep sea angling, hill walking, cycling and water-skiing.

Member of Best Western Hotels

B&B from €45.00 to €75.00
£35.44 to €59.07

PEGGY O'SULLIVAN
PROPRIETOR

American Express
Diners
Mastercard
Visa

64 64

HOTELS FEDERATION

Closed 06 November - 22 March

ROSEGARDEN GUESTHOUSE

SNEEM RD (N70),
KENMARE,
CO. KERRY

TEL: 064-42288 FAX: 064-42305
EMAIL: rosegard@iol.ie
WEB: www.euroka.com/rosegarden

GUESTHOUSE ★★★ MAP 1 D 3

The Rosegarden Guesthouse and Restaurant is situated within walking distance of Kenmare Town, Ring of Kerry (N70). Set in 1 acre of landscaped garden with 350 roses. Private car park. All rooms en suite, power showers, centrally heated. Restaurant open from 6.30 pm. Menu includes lamb, steaks, salmon, stuffed crab, mussels and wine list. Enjoy our peaceful and relaxed ambience. We are looking forward to your visit. Ask for our 3 and 7 day specials.

B&B from €28.00 to €35.00
£22.05 to £27.56

INGRID & PETER RINGLEVER

American Express
Diners
Mastercard
Visa

3 Day special B&B&D €140-150

8 8

HOTELS FEDERATION

Closed 01 November - 31 March

SEA SHORE FARM

TUBRID,
KENMARE,
CO. KERRY

TEL: 064-41270 FAX: 064-41270
EMAIL: seashore@eircom.net
WEB: http://homepage.eircom.net/~seashore

GUESTHOUSE ★★★ MAP 1 D 3

Our setting on the Bay is uniquely peaceful and private yet only 1 mile from town. Our farm extends to the shore affording unspoilt field walks in natural habitat with plentiful bird/wildlife. Large en suite rooms with panoramic seascapes, king beds, phone, tea facilities, etc. AA ◆◆◆◆ Selected, Recommended Guide du Routard, Los Angeles Times. Sign posted 300m from Kenmare by Esso Station - junction N71/N70 Killarney/Ring of Kerry Sneem Road.

B&B from €38.00 to €57.00
£29.93 to £44.89

MARY PATRICIA O'SULLIVAN
PROPRIETOR

Mastercard
Visa

6 6

HOTELS FEDERATION

Closed 01 November - 28 February

B&B rates are per person sharing per night incl. Breakfast

SHEEN FALLS LODGE

KENMARE,
CO. KERRY

TEL: 064-41600 FAX: 064-41386
EMAIL: info@sheenfallslodge.ie
WEB: www.sheenfallslodge.ie

HOTEL ★★★★★ MAP 1 D 3

The lodge presides over a dramatic
300 acre estate above the Sheen
Waterfalls and the Kenmare Bay.
Superb dining is available in either La
Cascade Restaurant or Oscars Bistro.
Facilities on the estate include
horseriding, tennis, clay shooting,
salmon fishing, heli-pad and two 18
hole golf courses nearby; within the
lodge, health and fitness centre,
swimming pool, library, billiard room,
wine cellar and conference facilities
available for up to 120 delegates.

Member of Relais & Châteaux

Room Rate from €240.00 to €380.00
£189.02 to £299.27

ADRIAAN BARTELS
GENERAL MANAGER

American Express
Diners
Mastercard
Visa

☺ Weekend specials from €300.00

61 61

IRISH HOTELS FEDERATION

Closed 02 January - 01 February

19TH GREEN

LACKABANE,
FOSSA, KILLARNEY,
CO. KERRY

TEL: 064-32868 FAX: 064-32637
EMAIL: 19thgreen@eircom.net
WEB: www.19thgreen-bb.com

GUESTHOUSE ★★★ MAP 2 E 4

Family run guesthouse 3km from
Killarney Town. Ring of Kerry Road;
adjacent to Killarney's 3 x 18 hole
championship courses. Ideal for
golfers playing Killarney, Beaufort,
Dooks, Waterville, Tralee or
Ballybunion. All tee times arranged.
Putting green for guests' use. Tours
arranged: Gap of Dunloe, Ring of
Kerry and Dingle Peninsula. All rooms
en suite with direct dial phone and
TV. Whether you are sightseeing,
fishing, rambling or golfing, the 19th
Green will suit you to a tee.

B&B from €30.00 to €45.00
£23.63 to £35.44

TIMOTHY AND BRIDGET FOLEY
PROPRIETORS

Mastercard
Visa

10 10

IRISH HOTELS FEDERATION

Closed 01 November - 01 March

ABBEY LODGE

MUCKROSS ROAD,
KILLARNEY,
CO. KERRY

TEL: 064-34193 FAX: 064-35877
EMAIL: abbeylodgekly@eircom.net

GUESTHOUSE ★★★★ MAP 2 E 4

Abbey Lodge, newly refurbished to a
very high standard with all rooms en
suite, TV, tea/coffee, direct dial phone
and central heating, is located on the
Muckross Road (N71) a three minute
walk to town centre. Private car park
for guests. The King family invites you
to experience the delights of Killarney
and Kerry from this ideal location
where genuine recommendations for
tours and sightseeing is gladly
provided. Cead Mile Failte.

B&B from €32.00 to €51.00
£25.20 to £40.17

JOHN G KING
OWNER

Mastercard
Visa

15 15

Closed 20 - 28 December

Room rates are per room per night

AGHADOE HEIGHTS HOTEL

LAKES OF KILLARNEY,
KILLARNEY,
CO. KERRY
TEL: 064-31766 FAX: 064-31345
EMAIL: info@aghadoeheights.com
WEB: www.aghadoeheights.com

HOTEL ★★★★★ MAP 2 E 4

Perched on the hill of Aghadoe, overlooking Killarney's lakes & mountains this luxury ***** hotel embraces each guest in a gracious & elegant setting. The exquisite & spacious guest rooms offer balconies, DVD players, air cond., spectacular views & access to private leisure facilities. The hotel's reputation for excellence is reflected in the award winning cuisine & service of Fredrick's Restaurant, holder of the AA Triple Rosette Award since 1993. Our efficient & courteous staff will ensure a memorable and exceptional stay.

Member of Preferred Hotels & Resorts Worldwide

B&B from €129.00 to €164.00
£101.60 to £129.14

PAT & MARIE CHAWKE
GENERAL MANAGERS

American Express
Diners
Mastercard
Visa

69 69

Open All Year

AISLING HOUSE

COUNTESS ROAD,
KILLARNEY,
CO. KERRY
TEL: 064-31112 FAX: 064-30079
EMAIL: aislinghouse@eircom.net

GUESTHOUSE ★★★ MAP 2 E 4

Aisling House located in peaceful surroundings just 800 meters off Muckross Road and 8 minutes walk from the centre of Killarney. All bedrooms are en suite, with tea/coffee facilities, TV and central heating. There is private car park and garden for guests. Aisling House is well within walking distance of Killarney National Park, Ross Castle and Muckross House. Tours of the Ring of Kerry/Dingle may be arranged. Nearby facilities include golf, horse riding, angling.

Member of Premier Guesthouses

B&B from €23.00 to €32.00
£18.11 to £25.20

PADDY O'DONOGHUE
OWNER

Mastercard
Visa

10 10

Closed 20 - 27 December

ARBUTUS HOTEL

COLLEGE STREET,
KILLARNEY,
CO. KERRY
TEL: 064-31037 FAX: 064-34033
EMAIL: arbutushotel@eircom.net
WEB: www.arbutuskillarney.com

HOTEL ★★★ MAP 2 E 4

To get a taste of the real Ireland, stay at a family run hotel with turf fires, good food, personal service with spacious rooms en suite. Oak panelled bar where the best Guinness is filled while traditional music weaves its magic through the air. If you're coming to sightsee, golf, fish or relax, the Arbutus is where you'll find a home away from home.

B&B from €50.00 to €95.00
£39.38 to £74.82

SEAN BUCKLEY
PROPRIETOR

Diners
Mastercard
Visa

☺ 2 B&B 1 Dinner from €130.00

36 36

inet FAX

Open All Year

B&B rates are per person sharing per night incl. Breakfast

ASHVILLE GUESTHOUSE

ROCK ROAD,
KILLARNEY,
CO. KERRY

TEL: 064-36405 FAX: 064-36778
EMAIL: ashvillehouse@eircom.net
WEB: www.ashvillekillarney.com

GUESTHOUSE ★★★ MAP 2 E 4

Ashville is a spacious family run guesthouse, 2 mins walk from town centre, on main Tralee Road (N22). Private car park. Comfortably furnished en suite rooms include orthopaedic beds, direct dial phone, multi channel TV, hairdryer. Sample our varied breakfast menu. Convenient to Killarney National Park, pony trekking, golf and fishing. Ideal touring base for Ring of Kerry, Dingle and Beara. Declan and Elma assure you of a warm welcome at Ashville. Awarded AA ◆◆◆, RAC ◆◆◆◆.

B&B from €26.00 to €38.00
£20.48 to £29.93

DECLAN & ELMA WALSH
PROPRIETORS

American Express
Mastercard
Visa

12 12

Closed 18 - 30 December

BEAUFIELD HOUSE

PARK ROAD,
KILLARNEY,
CO. KERRY

TEL: 064-34440 FAX: 064-34663

GUESTHOUSE ★★★ MAP 2 E 4

Beaufield House is a family run guesthouse, 2km from Killarney Town Centre on main Cork Road (N22). 14 modern centrally heated bedrooms all with bath/shower en suite, direct dial telephone, radio and TV. Spacious visitors' lounge. Relax and enjoy local amenities which include golf, fishing, Killarney's famous lakes, mountains, National Park, tour the Ring of Kerry and Dingle Peninsula. You will be made welcome when you stay at Beaufield House.

Member of Premier Guesthouses
B&B from €25.00 to €38.00
£19.69 to £29.93

MOYA BOWE
PROPRIETOR

Diners
Mastercard
Visa

14 14

Closed 12 - 29 December

Room rates are per room per night

BROOK LODGE HOTEL

HIGH STREET,
KILLARNEY,
CO. KERRY
TEL: 064-31800 FAX: 064-35001
EMAIL: brooklodgekillarney@eircom.net
WEB: www.brooklodgekillarney.com

HOTEL ★★★ MAP 2 E 4

Brook Lodge Hotel is a new hotel, family-run, situated in the heart of Killarney Town, set back from the street on over an acre of landscaped garden with private parking. Our large and tastefully decorated bedrooms are all en suite, including tea/coffee, direct dial phone, hairdryer, multichannel TV. Wheelchair facilities. Lift. Excellent cuisine in Brook Restaurant with wine licence and residents' bar.

B&B from €45.00 to €70.00
£35.44 to £55.13

JOAN COUNIHAN
OWNER

American Express
Diners
Mastercard
Visa

18 18

inet

IRISH HOTELS FEDERATION

Closed 01 November - 14 March

CASTLE OAKS

MUCKROSS ROAD,
KILLARNEY,
CO. KERRY
TEL: 064-34154 FAX: 064-36980
EMAIL: info@killarneyoaks.com
WEB: www.killarneyoaks.com

GUESTHOUSE ★★★ MAP 2 E 4

At the gateway to Killarney National Park and only minutes from the lively town centre, you are always assured of a warm and friendly welcome at this luxury, family-run guesthouse. Enjoy the comfort of the spacious rooms, including large family rooms, all en suite with direct dial phone, colour TV, hair dryer and power shower; or relax in the guest lounge with our complimentary tea/coffee whilst absorbing breathtaking views of Killarney's lakes and mountains. Private parking.

B&B from €35.55 to €44.44
£28.00 to £35.00

EAMON & VALERIE COURTNEY
PROPRIETORS

Mastercard
Visa

16 16

IRISH HOTELS FEDERATION

Closed 10 - 27 December

CASTLELODGE GUESTHOUSE

MUCKROSS ROAD,
KILLARNEY,
CO. KERRY
TEL: 064-31545 FAX: 064-32325
EMAIL: castlelodge@eircom.net
WEB: http://homepage.eircom.net/~castlelodge/

GUESTHOUSE U MAP 2 E 4

Conveniently located, just two minutes walk from Killarney Town Centre. Open all year round, our Guesthouse offers very friendly staff, a homely atmosphere and easy access to all the major attractions and magnificent scenery in Killarney. Good restaurants and Live Music will be recommended, come and see the sights, hear the Music and taste the atmosphere.

B&B from €26.00 to €45.00
£20.48 to £35.44

TONY O'SHEA

American Express
Diners
Mastercard
Visa

25 25

Open All Year

B&B rates are per person sharing per night incl. Breakfast

CASTLEROSSE HOTEL & LEISURE CENTRE

KILLARNEY,
CO. KERRY

TEL: 064-31144 FAX: 064-31031
EMAIL: castler@iol.ie
WEB: www.towerhotelgroup.ie

HOTEL ★★★ MAP 2 E 4

A Tower Group Hotel - situated right on the lakeside, between the golf course and the National Park and a little over a mile from Killarney Town Centre, the Castlerosse commands magnificent views of the lakes and mountains, especially from the restaurant and panoramic bar. The impressive range of leisure facilities, including an on site golf course, Leisure centre with 20m swimming pool and 2 floodlit tennis courts makes the Castlerosse the perfect location for a holiday or leisure break.

Member of Tower Hotel Group
B&B from €45.00 to €75.00
£35.44 to £59.07

DANNY BOWE
GENERAL MANAGER

American Express
Diners
Mastercard
Visa

Weekend specials from €105.00

Closed 03 November - 14 March

COFFEY'S LOCH LEIN HOUSE HOTEL

GOLF COURSE ROAD,
FOSSA, KILLARNEY,
CO. KERRY

TEL: 064-31260 FAX: 064-36151
EMAIL: ecoffey@indigo.ie
WEB: www.lochlein.com

HOTEL N MAP 2 E 4

Superb family run hotel, uniquely situated by the shores of Killarney's Lower Lake. Magnificent views of lakes & mountains. Ideally located on the Ring of Kerry/Dingle roads, near the Gap of Dunloe. Tours personally arranged. Nearby four 18 hole championship golf courses, horseriding & fishing.
While you will be surprised by the delightful new building, you will be pleased that the hospitality, grade A service & relaxed atmosphere have not changed. A warm welcome awaits you here.

B&B from €30.00 to €80.00
£23.63 to £63.01

EITHNE COFFEY
PROPRIETOR

American Express
Diners
Mastercard
Visa

Closed 01 November - 15 March

Room rates are per room per night

DARBY O'GILLS COUNTRY HOUSE HOTEL

LISSIVIGEEN,
MALLOW ROAD, KILLARNEY,
CO. KERRY
TEL: 064-34168 FAX: 064-36794
EMAIL: darbyogill@eircom.net
WEB: www.darbyogillshotel.com

HOTEL U MAP 2 E 4

Darby O'Gills Country House Hotel is a charming family run hotel set in quiet rural setting just on the edge of Killarney Town. Our location is ideal for touring the wonders of Kerry and Cork, playing golf, fishing, hillwalking or just plain relaxing. Killarney Town centre is only a five minute drive. We are a family friendly hotel and personal attention is guaranteed. Open all year with excellent rates offering great value.

Member of MinOtel Ireland Hotel Group

B&B from €40.00 to €65.00
£30.00 to £50.00

PAT & JOAN GILL & FAMILY

American Express
Diners
Mastercard
Visa

25 25

Open All Year

DROMHALL HOTEL

MUCKROSS ROAD,
KILLARNEY,
CO. KERRY
TEL: 064-39300 FAX: 064-34242
EMAIL: info@dromhall.com
WEB: www.dromhall.com

HOTEL U MAP 2 E 4

Killarney's famous mountain scenes provide a magnificent backdrop for the Dromhall Hotel. Located 5 minutes walk from town the hotel offers the comfort and service one associates with a first class hotel while retaining the friendliness and welcome of a family run hotel. From the moment you enter the elegant marbled lobby the scene is set for a special experience. Banquet and conference facilities for up to 300. Award winning Kaynes Bistro. Full leisure centre.

B&B from €45.00 to €70.00
£35.44 to £55.13

BERNADETTE RANDLES
MANAGING DIRECTOR

American Express
Diners
Mastercard
Visa

Weekend specials from €99.00

68 68

Closed 22 - 27 December

EARLS COURT HOUSE

WOODLAWN JUNCTION,
MUCKROSS ROAD, KILLARNEY,
CO. KERRY
TEL: 064-34009 FAX: 064-34366
EMAIL: info@killarney-earlscourt.ie
WEB: www.killarney-earlscourt.ie

GUESTHOUSE ★★★★ MAP 2 E 4

A family run 4**** magical hideaway, 5 mins walk to town centre. 'Small Hotel of the Year for Ireland' 1998 and RAC Little Gem Award 2000. Country house ambience rich in tradition - antiques, paintings, open fires, fresh flowers, home baking & Irish hospitality. Spacious bedrooms are graced with antiques & soft furnishings, king beds, full bathroom, modem, and balconies. Suites with four poster beds. Breakfast is special - a feast offering tempting choices. Private parking. AA♦♦♦♦♦

B&B from €45.00 to €64.00
£35.44 to £50.40

EMER & RAY MOYNIHAN
OWNERS

Mastercard
Visa

11 11

Closed 30 November - 01 February

B&B rates are per person sharing per night incl. Breakfast

EVISTON HOUSE HOTEL

NEW STREET,
KILLARNEY,
CO. KERRY
TEL: 064-31640 FAX: 064-33685
EMAIL: evishtl@eircom.net
WEB: www.killarney-hotel.com

HOTEL ★★★ MAP 2 E 4

Eviston House Hotel is located in the centre of Killarney yet only a few minutes away from the National Park and championship golf courses. All our luxurious bedrooms are complete with private bathroom, direct dial telephone, tea/coffee facilities, hair dryer and satellite TV. The elegant Colleen Bawn Restaurant offers fine food in intimate surroundings. Afterwards visit our famous pub, the Danny Mann, for the best in traditional music and great 'craic'.

Member of Best Western Hotels

B&B from €38.00 to €75.00
£29.93 to £59.07

EDWARD EVISTON
PROPRIETOR

American Express
Diners
Mastercard
Visa

☺ Weekend specials from €100.00

🛏🏸☎🖥🚻T🅲🍴CM◡♫P🅿S
75 75

🍷alc 🖥 Inet

IRISH
HOTELS
FEDERATION

Open All Year

FAILTE HOTEL

COLLEGE STREET,
KILLARNEY,
CO. KERRY
TEL: 064-33404 FAX: 064-36599
EMAIL: failtehotel@eircom.net
WEB: www.kerry-insight.com

HOTEL ★★ MAP 2 E 4

The Failte Hotel, recently refurbished to a very high standard, is owned and managed by the O'Callaghan family. Sons Dermot and Donal run the award winning restaurant. It is internationally known for its high standard of cuisine. Paudie supervises the award winning bar. It is situated in the town centre, adjacent to railway station, new factory outlet, shopping complex. Also close by are many local cabarets & night clubs. Local amenities include golfing, fishing, walking.

B&B from €38.00 to €57.00
£29.93 to £44.89

DERMOT & EILEEN O'CALLAGHAN
PROPRIETORS

American Express
Mastercard
Visa

🛏🏸☎🖥T🅲CM◡♫🚻alc🛒
12 12

IRISH
HOTELS
FEDERATION

Closed 24 - 26 December

Room rates are per room per night

FOLEY'S TOWNHOUSE

23 HIGH STREET,
KILLARNEY,
CO. KERRY
TEL: 064-31217 FAX: 064-34683

GUESTHOUSE ★★★★ MAP 2 E 4

Originally a 19th Century Coaching Inn, this old house has hosted generations of travellers. Newly refurbished, this is a 4**** family-run town centre located guesthouse. Luxury bedrooms are individually designed for comfort complete with every modern amenity. Downstairs is our award-winning seafood and steak restaurant. Chef/owner Carol provides meals from fresh local produce. Choose from approx 200 wines. Personal supervision. Private parking. Awarded AA ♦♦♦♦♦, RAC highly acclaimed.

B&B from €58.75 to €62.95
£46.27 to £49.58

CAROL HARTNETT
PROPRIETOR
American Express
Mastercard
Visa

28 28

Closed 06 November - 16 March

FRIARS GLEN

MANGERTON ROAD,
MUCKROSS, KILLARNEY,
CO. KERRY
TEL: 064-37500 FAX: 064-37388
EMAIL: fullerj@indigo.ie
WEB: www.indigo.ie/~fullerj

GUESTHOUSE ★★★★ MAP 2 E 4

This 4**** Guesthouse, built in a traditional style, offers a haven of peace and tranquility; set in it's own 28 acres of wood and pastureland and located in the heart of Killarney National Park. Reception rooms have a rustic feel, with a warm and friendly atmosphere, finished in stone and wood with open fires and antiques. Bedrooms & bathrooms are finished to the highest standards. The dining room, patio & garden have a terrific mountain view. An ideal base in the South West. Highly recommended by Michelin and Michele Erdvig.

B&B from €35.00 to €55.00
£27.56 to £43.32

MARY & JOHN FULLER
PROPRIETORS
Mastercard
Visa

10 10

Closed 31 October - 01 March

FUCHSIA HOUSE

MUCKROSS ROAD,
KILLARNEY,
CO. KERRY
TEL: 064-33743 FAX: 064-36588
EMAIL: fuchsiahouse@eircom.net
WEB: www.fuchsiahouse.com

GUESTHOUSE ★★★★ MAP 2 E 4

We invite you to enjoy the affordable luxury of Fuchsia House which is set well back from the road in mature, leafy gardens yet is only 7 minutes walk from Killarney Town Centre. Purpose built to combine the amenities of a modern 4**** guest-house with the elegance of an earlier age, Fuchsia House offers spacious rooms with orthopaedic beds dressed in crisp cotton & linen, private bath with power shower, direct dial phone. Conservatory. Irish & vegetarian menu. Winner 1999 "Best Guesthouse" in Killarney Looking Good Competition. RAC Sparkling Diamond Award.

B&B from €35.00 to €52.00
£27.56 to £40.95

MARY TREACY
OWNER
Mastercard
Visa

8 8

Closed 05 November - 28 February

B&B rates are per person sharing per night incl. Breakfast

GLEANN FIA COUNTRY HOUSE

DEERPARK,
KILLARNEY,
CO. KERRY
TEL: 064-35035 FAX: 064-35000
EMAIL: info@gleannfia.com
WEB: www.gleannfia.com

GUESTHOUSE R   MAP 2 E 4

Set in a secluded 30 acre wooded river valley, 1 mile from Killarney - Gleann Fia is the perfect holiday setting. Our Victorian style country house offers tasteful en suite rooms, each with phone & orthopaedic beds. Stroll along the river walk admiring the wild flowers & Autumn colours. Relax by the peat fire or in the conservatory. Wholesome breakfasts include freshly squeezed oranges, scrambled eggs with smoked salmon, fresh fish, country cheeses, homemade preserves. A professional & friendly homestyle service. 300yds from Killarney's Ring road N22.

B&B from €31.74 to €63.49
£25.00 to £50.00

CONOR & BRIDGET O'CONNELL
YOUR HOSTS

American Express
Mastercard
Visa

☺   Midweek specials High Season
€133.32

17 17

Closed 02 January - 28 February

GLENA GUESTHOUSE

MUCKROSS ROAD,
COLLEGE STREET, KILLARNEY,
CO. KERRY
TEL: 064-32705 FAX: 064-35611
EMAIL: glena@iol.ie
WEB: www.kerry-insight/glena.com

GUESTHOUSE ★★★   MAP 2 E 4

Glena House award-winning guesthouse, AA ♦♦♦♦, RAC acclaimed, Les Routier recommended. It's the simple things that make it right; in a great location, a bed to rest in, a shower/bath to invigorate, tea/coffee when you want. A bowl of ice for a bedroom drink, homebaking and a breakfast as individual as you are. Glena House where memories are made, 5 minutes walk from town centre. Parking.

B&B from €35.00 to €50.00
£27.56 to £39.38

MARINA & TIM BUCKLEY
OWNERS/MANAGERS

American Express
Diners
Mastercard
Visa

26 26

Closed 01 December - 15 March

GLENEAGLE HOTEL

KILLARNEY,
CO. KERRY

TEL: 064-36000 FAX: 064-32646
EMAIL: gleneagl@iol.ie
WEB: www.gleneagle-hotel.com

HOTEL ★★★   MAP 2 E 4

Ireland's leading leisure and conference/convention hotel, adjacent to Killarney's National Park with beautifully furnished rooms. Ireland's National Events Centre is ideally suited for conventions, conferences, exhibitions, sporting events, concerts and theatrical productions. Our award winning chefs will delight you in both our restaurants. We have a great line-up of entertainment all year round. Relax and unwind using our indoor/outdoor leisure facilities.

B&B from €55.00 to €109.00
£43.32 to £85.84

O'DONOGHUE FAMILY
PROPRIETORS

American Express
Diners
Mastercard
Visa

250 250

Open All Year

Room rates are per room per night

HOLIDAY INN KILLARNEY

MUCKROSS ROAD,
KILLARNEY,
CO. KERRY

TEL: 064-33000 FAX: 064-33001
EMAIL: resrevations@holidayinnkillarney.com
WEB: www.holidayinnkillarney.com

HOTEL ★★★ MAP 2 E 4

Holiday Inn Killarney enjoys a quiet but central location close to Killarney Town Centre. Its 24 suites and spacious en suite rooms are tastefully decorated to the highest standard. Our fully-equipped leisure centre is the perfect place to relax and unwind. Our Library Point Restaurant serves the finest of local cuisine while Saddlers Pub serves food daily and has entertainment nightly. A haven for all seasons!

B&B from €45.00 to €85.00
£35.44 to £66.93

DAVID HENNESSY
GENERAL MANAGER

American Express
Diners
Mastercard
Visa

104 104

Open All Year

HOTEL DUNLOE CASTLE

KILLARNEY,
CO. KERRY

TEL: 064-44111 FAX: 064-44583
EMAIL: sales@kih.liebherr.com
WEB: www.iol.ie/khl

HOTEL ★★★★★ MAP 2 E 4

110 bedroomed resort near Killarney, facing the famous Gap of Dunloe. Historical park and botanic gardens with ruins of castle. Elegant decor with many valuable antiques. Luxurious lounges, cocktail bar, gourmet restaurant. Extensive leisure facilities: pool, sauna, gym, riding, putting green, tennis, jogging track. 10 championship courses nearby. Sister hotels: Ard-na-Sidhe and Hotel Europe. Central Reservations: Tel: 064-31900, Fax: 064-32118.

Room Rate from €228.00 to €340.00
£179.56 to £267.77

MICHAEL BRENNAN
MANAGER

American Express
Diners
Mastercard
Visa

110 110

Closed 01 October - 15 April

HOTEL EUROPE

KILLARNEY,
CO. KERRY

TEL: 064-31900 FAX: 064-32118
EMAIL: sales@kih.liebherr.com
WEB: www.iol.ie/khl

HOTEL ★★★★★ MAP 2 E 4

De luxe resort known internationally for its spectacular location on the Lakes of Killarney. 205 spacious bedrooms and suites of highest standards, many with lake view. Elegant lounges, cocktail bar, Panorama Restaurant. Boutique. Health/fitness centre, 25m indoor pool, sauna, gym. Tennis, horseriding, fishing, boating, cycling. 10 championship courses nearby. Sister hotels: Hotel Dunloe Castle and Ard-na-Sidhe.

Room Rate from €228.00 to €268.00
£179.56 to £211.03

MALCOLM MCKENZIE-VASS

American Express
Diners
Mastercard
Visa

205 205

Closed 15 November - 15 March

B&B rates are per person sharing per night incl. Breakfast

HUSSEYS TOWNHOUSE & BAR

43 HIGH STREET,
KILLARNEY,
CO. KERRY
TEL: 064-37454 FAX: 064-33144
EMAIL: husseys@iol.ie
WEB: www.husseystownhouse.com

GUESTHOUSE ★★★ MAP 2 E 4

Centrally located, within walking distance of Killarney National Park, the principal shopping areas & the best restaurants in town. This family owned house offers peaceful accommodation in tastefully decorated rooms, equipped to a high standard. Enjoy a choice of breakfast in our delightful dining room, relax in our comfortable guest lounge or cosy friendly bar. For walkers, cyclists, golfers or touring Kerry this is the discerning traveller's perfect choice. Private parking.

B&B from €26.00 to €38.00
£20.48 to £29.93

GERALDINE O'LEARY
OWNER

American Express
Mastercard
Visa

🛏️ 🧑 ☎ 🖥️ ⛵ 🅿️ 🚗
5 5

Closed 31 October - 21 March

INTERNATIONAL BEST WESTERN HOTEL

KENMARE PLACE,
KILLARNEY,
CO. KERRY
TEL: 064-31816 FAX: 064-31837
EMAIL: inter@iol.ie
WEB: www.killarney-inter.com

HOTEL ★★★ MAP 2 E 4

A warm welcome awaits you at the International. This town centre hotel has been brought into the 21st Century with carefully planned refurbishment. 80 luxurious bedrooms - 10 with Jacuzzi en suite - all to make your stay a memorable one. Excellent cuisine served daily. Traditional music in our award winning Hannigans Pub. 100m from Killarney National Park. Killarney's three 18 hole championship golf courses nearby. Bus/Train Station 200m. Overall winner of 'Killarney Looking Good 2000' award.

Member of Best Western Hotels
B&B from €50.00 to €90.00
£39.38 to £70.88

TERENCE MULCAHY
GENERAL MANAGER

American Express
Diners
Mastercard
Visa

☺ Weekend specials from €100.00

🛏️ 🧑 ☎ 🖥️ ⬆️ 🇹 C ⬇️ CM ⛵ 🎵 Ⓢ ⬛
80 80

a|c 🖨️ Inet

Closed 22 - 29 December

INVERARAY FARM GUESTHOUSE

BEAUFORT,
KILLARNEY,
CO. KERRY
TEL: 064-44224 FAX: 064-44775
EMAIL: inver@indigo.ie
WEB: www.irishfarmholidays.com

GUESTHOUSE ★★ MAP 2 E 4

A luxury farm guesthouse in a quiet sylvan setting. Views of Killarney lakes, mountains and Gap of Dunloe. 9km west of Killarney, 1km off N72, left over bridge at Shop. Free private trout and salmon fishing on River Laune. Angling, walking and golfing tours arranged. Tea-room, playroom, playground and pony for children. Singing pubs, horse-riding locally. Home-baking, seafood and dinner a speciality with good, wholesome home cooking. Recommended Le Guide du Routard 2001.

B&B from €26.00 to €31.00
£20.48 to £24.41

EILEEN & NOEL SPILLANE
PROPRIETORS

🛏️ 🧑 ☎ 🇹 🐎 C ⬇️ CM ❄️ ⛵ 🅿️
9 9

Closed 30 November - 20 February

Room rates are per room per night

KATHLEENS COUNTRY HOUSE

TRALEE ROAD,
KILLARNEY,
CO. KERRY
TEL: 064-32810 FAX: 064-32340
EMAIL: info@kathleens.net
WEB: www.kathleens.net

GUESTHOUSE ★★★★ MAP 2 E 4

Set in 3 acres of mature gardens in peaceful rural surrounds, 3k from Killarney town. Friendliness and attentiveness make Kathleen's special. RAC Small Hotel of the Year for Ireland, AA ◆◆◆◆ amongst its many awards. Rooms furnished in antique pine with bath/power shower, tea/coffee facilities, hairdryer, telephone, orthopaedic beds. Ideal golf base. Original paintings adorn every wall. Non-smoking house. Easy to get to. Hard to leave!

B&B from €45.00 to €62.00
£35.44 to £48.82

KATHLEEN O'REGAN SHEPPARD
PROPRIETOR

American Express
Mastercard
Visa

17 17

Closed 01 November - 10 March

KILLARNEY AVENUE HOTEL

KENMARE PLACE,
KILLARNEY,
CO. KERRY
TEL: 064-32522 FAX: 064-33707
EMAIL: kavenue@odonoghue-ring-hotels.com
WEB: www.odonoghue-ring-hotels.com

HOTEL ★★★★ MAP 2 E 4

This boutique 4**** hotel has an idyllic setting in the heart of downtown Killarney. Well appointed air-conditioned guestrooms provide guests with every care and comfort. Druids Restaurant provides a perfect blend of local and classical cuisine. The Kenmare Rooms is a distinctly different hotel bar. Guests are welcome to use the leisure facilities of our sister hotel (Killarney Towers Hotel), 100m away. Underground garage parking available.

B&B from €70.00 to €150.00
£55.13 to £118.13

FRANK MC CARTHY
GENERAL MANAGER

American Express
Mastercard
Visa

66 66

Closed 01 December - 31 January

KILLARNEY COURT QUALITY HOTEL

TRALEE ROAD,
KILLARNEY,
CO. KERRY
TEL: 064-37070 FAX: 064-37060
EMAIL: stay@irishcourthotels.com
WEB: www.irishcourthotel.com

HOTEL ★★★ MAP 2 E 4

Opened in April '98 the Killarney Court Hotel is a 5 minute walk from Killarney Town Centre, only 15km from Kerry International Airport and close to 3 world famous golf courses. Our 100 en suite bedrooms boast a tasteful neo-gothic style decor. Enjoy a meal in our Seasons Restaurant with traditional Irish and international cuisine or a drink in McGillicuddys traditional Irish pub with its wonderful 'ceol, ol agus craic' atmosphere. We assure you your stay will be enjoyable.

Member of Irish Court Hotels
B&B from €45.00 to €110.00
£35.00 to £85.00

ROBERT LYNE
PROPRIETOR

American Express
Diners
Mastercard
Visa

96 96

Open All Year

B&B rates are per person sharing per night incl. Breakfast

KILLARNEY GREAT SOUTHERN HOTEL

KILLARNEY,
CO. KERRY

TEL: 064-31262 FAX: 064-31642
EMAIL: res@killarney-gsh.com
WEB: www.greatsouthernhotels.com

UNDER REFURBISHMENT · OPENING MAY 2002

HOTEL R MAP 2 E 4

Experience bygone charm with modern comfort set in scenic gardens in the heart of Killarney. This hotel has extensive leisure facilities - indoor heated swimming pool, sauna, steamroom, plunge pool, gym, jacuzzi, outdoor tennis courts and children's playground. Other facilities - hair & beauty salons, cocktail bar, main dining room and Peppers À la Carte Restaurant. Conference facilities for 800 delegates. Bookable worldwide through UTELL Intl or Central Res., Tel 01-214 4800.

Room Rate from €230.00 to €254.00
£181.11 to €200.00

CONOR HENNIGAN
GENERAL MANAGER

American Express
Diners
Mastercard
Visa

Weekend specials from €185.00

180 180

IRISH HOTELS FEDERATION

Closed 01 January - 30 April

KILLARNEY HEIGHTS HOTEL

CORK ROAD,
KILLARNEY,
CO. KERRY

TEL: 064-31158 FAX: 064-35198
EMAIL: khh@iol.ie

HOTEL U MAP 2 E 4

Situated 1km from Killarney Town Centre on the Cork Road, this beautiful 70 bedroomed hotel overlooks the majestic Torc & Mangerton Mountains. Open fires, olde world flagstone floors and pitch pine furnishings create a unique nostalgic atmosphere in the bars, restaurants and bistro. The hotel is easily accessed by mainline rail or by flying into Kerry Airport, just 14km away. The Killarney Heights Hotel, the perfect venue for the perfect holiday.

Member of Logis of Ireland
B&B from €53.50 to €76.50
£42.13 to €60.25

BERNARD O'RIORDAN

Diners
Mastercard
Visa

70 70

IRISH HOTELS FEDERATION

Closed 23 - 26 December

KILLARNEY LODGE

COUNTESS ROAD,
KILLARNEY,
CO. KERRY

TEL: 064-36499 FAX: 064-31070
EMAIL: klylodge@iol.ie
WEB: www.killarneylodge.net

GUESTHOUSE ★★★★ MAP 2 E 4

Killarney Lodge, a purpose built guesthouse set in private walled-in gardens, only 2 minutes walk from the town centre. The guesthouse provides private parking, spacious en suite air conditioned bedrooms with all modern amenities including wheelchair facilities. Enjoy an extensive breakfast menu in the spacious dining room and relax in comfortable lounges with open fires. The Lodge has already gained an outstanding reputation for quality of service, relaxed atmosphere and friendliness.

B&B from €40.00 to €60.00
£31.50 to €47.25

CATHERINE TREACY
OWNER

American Express
Diners
Mastercard
Visa

16 16

IRISH HOTELS FEDERATION

Closed 15 November - 14 February

Room rates are per room per night

CO. KERRY
KILLARNEY

KILLARNEY PARK HOTEL

KENMARE PLACE,
KILLARNEY,
CO. KERRY
TEL: 064-35555 FAX: 064-35266
EMAIL: info@killarneyparkhotel.ie
WEB: www.killarneyparkhotel.ie

HOTEL ★★★★★ MAP 2 E 4

Superbly located in the heart of Killarney Town, this family owned luxury hotel offers the quietness, intimacy and privacy associated with times past. In addition to a country house style lobby, library, drawing room and billiard room, the hotel also offers a magnificent 20m swimming pool, sauna, jacuzzi, outdoor hot tub, fitness suite and treatment room. Dining options include a candlelit dinner in the Park Restaurant or an appetising snack in the Garden Bar.

B&B from €110.00 to €167.50
£86.63 to £131.92

DONAGH DAVERN
GENERAL MANAGER
American Express
Diners
Mastercard
Visa

Weekend specials from €220.00

73 73

Closed 09 - 26 December

KILLARNEY PLAZA HOTEL

KENMARE PLACE,
KILLARNEY,
CO. KERRY
TEL: 064-38300 FAX: 064-33217
EMAIL: kplaza@odonoghue-ring-hotels.com
WEB: www.odonoghue-ring-hotels.com

UNDER CONSTRUCTION - OPENING MARCH 2002

HOTEL R MAP 2 E 4

This premier hotel enjoys a wonderful location in downtown Killarney and opens in 2002. All air-conditioned rooms have an atmosphere of tranquil, unhurried comfort and thoughtful colour schemes. A choice of restaurants and bars provide the perfect excuse to join us at this inviting address. Health and leisure facilities allow guests to unwind and relax with a hint of luxury. Underground garage parking available.

B&B from €90.00 to €220.00
£70.88 to £173.26

FRANK MCCARTHY
GENERAL MANAGER
American Express
Diners
Mastercard
Visa

167 167

Closed 01 December - 31 January

KILLARNEY ROYAL

COLLEGE STREET,
KILLARNEY,
CO. KERRY
TEL: 064-31853 FAX: 064-34001
EMAIL: royalhot@iol.ie
WEB: www.killarneyroyal.ie

HOTEL U MAP 2 E 4

Joe and Margaret Scally's charming Victorian townhouse is the older sister of their larger hotel, Hayfield Manor, Cork City. In the heart of Killarney, it is the perfect base for golfers and touring the South West Ireland. Each room has been individually designed, with air conditioning throughout, 24 hour personal service, elegant dining room and a local bar atmosphere. "Dedicated staff at this hotel give guests the sort of personal attention you would expect from a much smaller place." Alastair Sawday's Special Places to Stay in Ireland. RAC ****recommended

B&B from €63.53 to €158.83
£50.03 to £125.09

NICOLA DUGGAN
American Express
Diners
Mastercard
Visa

Weekend specials from €177.90

29 29

Closed 22 - 28 December

---

280 **SOUTH WEST**   B&B rates are per person sharing per night incl. Breakfast

KILLARNEY RYAN HOTEL & LEISURE CENTRE

CORK ROAD,
KILLARNEY,
CO. KERRY
TEL: 064-31555 FAX: 064-32438
EMAIL: ryan@indigo.ie
WEB: www.ryan-hotels.com

HOTEL ★★★   MAP 2 E 4

Just 2km from Killarney Town centre and ideally located for exploring Kerry, this hotel offers the perfect leisure break. Savour a meal in the Ross and Herbert Rooms, unwind in the Lobby Lounge or enjoy nightly entertainment in the bar. The extensive leisure centre features an 18m pool, steam rooms, sauna, jacuzzi and sports hall. An award winning creche and a children's activity programme during school holidays ensure a fun filled stay. Car park. AA, RAC and Egon Ronay recommended.

Room Rate from €114.00 to €152.00
£89.77 to £119.69

PAT GALVIN
GENERAL MANAGER

American Express
Diners
Mastercard
Visa

168 168

IRISH HOTELS FEDERATION

Closed 01 December - 31 January

KILLEEN HOUSE HOTEL

AGHADOE,
LAKES OF KILLARNEY,
CO. KERRY
TEL: 064-31711 FAX: 064-31811
EMAIL: charming@indigo.ie
WEB: www.killeenhousehotel.com

HOTEL ★★★   MAP 2 E 4

The Killeen House is truly a charming little hotel. With only 23 rooms, 8 of them deluxe, it is the ideal base for touring 'God's own country', the magical Kingdom of Kerry. With our DIY Golf Pub and an elegant award-winning dining room you are assured a memorable experience. Go on, do the smart thing and call us now! We look forward to extending the 'hospitality of the house' to you!

B&B from €67.50 to €100.00
£53.16 to £78.76

MICHAEL & GERALDINE ROSNEY
OWNERS

American Express
Diners
Mastercard
Visa

23 23

IRISH HOTELS FEDERATION

Closed 01 November - 31 March

KINGFISHER LODGE GUESTHOUSE

LEWIS ROAD,
KILLARNEY,
CO. KERRY
TEL: 064-37131 FAX: 064-39871
EMAIL: kingfisherguesthouse@eircom.net
WEB: www.kingfisherkillarney.com

GUESTHOUSE ★★★   MAP 2 E 4

A warm welcome awaits you at Kingfisher Lodge, a family run luxury Irish Tourist Board registered guesthouse, 3 minutes walk from Killarney Town Centre with its excellent pubs, restaurants, entertainment and shopping. Our spacious bedrooms are beautifully decorated with TV, direct dial phone and hairdryers. Relaxing guest lounge with tea/coffee facilities and channel TV. Varied breakfast menu. Private parking. Tackle, drying rooms available for anglers, walkers and golfers. Tours arranged.

B&B from €27.00 to €35.00
£21.26 to £27.56

ANN & DONAL CARROLL

Mastercard
Visa

9   9

IRISH HOTELS FEDERATION

Closed 14 December - 14 January

Room rates are per room per night

LAKE HOTEL

ON LAKE SHORE,
MUCKROSS ROAD, KILLARNEY,
CO. KERRY
TEL: 064-31035 FAX: 064-31902
EMAIL: lakehotel@eircom.net
WEB: www.lakehotel.com

HOTEL ★★★ MAP 2 E 4

The most beautiful location in Ireland. Set on Killarney's lake shore, open log fires, double height ceilings, relaxed and friendly atmosphere. Standard rooms, luxury lakeside suites with jacuzzi, balcony and some four poster beds, plus Roman and Medieval themed rooms with jacuzzi and double steam shower. Possibility of adult fitness centre in 2002 with outdoor hot tub on lake shore, sauna, steam room, exercise room. "A little bit of heaven on earth."

Member of Irish Family Hotels

B&B from €45.00 to €114.00
£35.44 to £89.78

TONY HUGGARD
MANAGING DIRECTOR

American Express
Diners
Mastercard
Visa

☺ Special half board rates

64 64

Closed 17 December - 07 February

LIME COURT

MUCKROSS ROAD,
KILLARNEY,
CO. KERRY
TEL: 064-34547 FAX: 064-34121
EMAIL: limecrt@iol.ie
WEB: www.lime-court.com

GUESTHOUSE ★★★ MAP 2 E 4

Lime Court has the perfect location, 3*** quality and superb standards. Just 5 minutes walk from town centre, easy off-street parking, on the main Ring of Kerry route and Muckross Road. Located beside 4 excellent pubs offering Irish music and good food. All room types available, singles, doubles, twins, triples and family rooms. All rooms are non-smoking. Lime Court is family-run, a second generation of caring for our guests.

B&B from €32.00 to €39.00
£25.20 to £30.71

GERALDINE & ALAN COURTNEY
OWNERS/MANAGERS

American Express
Mastercard
Visa

☺ 10% discount on 3 or more nights
(excl.Jul/Aug & Bank Hols)

16 16

Closed 10 November - 10 February

LINDEN HOUSE HOTEL

NEW ROAD,
KILLARNEY,
CO. KERRY
TEL: 064-31379 FAX: 064-31196

HOTEL ★★ MAP 2 E 4

Situated in a quiet tree lined avenue 2 minutes walk from the town centre. Linden House is under the personal supervision of Peter and Ann Knoblauch. The Linden Restaurant has an enviable reputation for good food prepared by owner chef. Year after year, guests return to Linden House, ample proof that you, too, will be made welcome and comfortable during your stay in beautiful Killarney.

B&B from €35.00 to €43.00
£27.56 to £33.87

ANN & PETER KNOBLAUCH
OWNERS/CHEF

Mastercard
Visa

☺ 3 nights B&B & 2 Dinners from
€140.00 to €170.00 pps

20 19

IRISH
HOTELS
FEDERATION

Closed 15 November - 01 February

B&B rates are per person sharing per night incl. Breakfast

MCSWEENEY ARMS HOTEL

COLLEGE STREET,
KILLARNEY,
CO. KERRY
TEL: 064-31211 FAX: 064-34553
EMAIL: sales@mcsweeneyarms.com
WEB: www.mcsweeneyarms.com

HOTEL ★★★ MAP 2 E 4

The McSweeney Arms Hotel is situated in the heart of Killarney Town. Small, cosy and run to a very high standard by your hosts Tony and Pauline McSweeney. There are 28 bedrooms with private bathroom, direct dial telephone, colour TV and hairdryer. Our bar and restaurant caters for all tastes with emphasis on traditional Irish food. Local amenities are four 18 hole championship golf courses also two 9 hole courses and the Killarney National Park.

B&B from €55.00 to €85.00
£43.32 to £66.94

TONY MCSWEENEY
PROPRIETOR

American Express
Diners
Mastercard
Visa

28 28

Closed 20 December - 05 February

MOUNTAIN VIEW GUEST HOUSE

MUCKROSS ROAD,
KILLARNEY,
CO. KERRY
TEL: 064-33293 FAX: 064-37295
EMAIL: tguerin@indigo.ie

GUESTHOUSE ★★ MAP 2 E 4

Mountain View Guest House offers the highest standard of accommodation by friendly and efficient staff. All rooms are en suite with direct dial phone, tea/coffee making facilities, multi channel televisions and hairdryers. Mountain View Guest House is located only 6 minutes walk from Killarney Town Centre and 3 minutes from the Gleneagle Country Club on the famous Ring of Kerry scenic route close to Ross Castle, Ross Golf Club, Muckross House, Torc Waterfall.

B&B from €23.00 to €38.00
£18.11 to £29.93

TIMOTHY GUERIN
OWNER

American Express
Mastercard
Visa

6 6

Closed 10 November - 10 March

MUCKROSS PARK HOTEL

LAKES OF KILLARNEY,
MUCKROSS VILLAGE, KILLARNEY,
CO. KERRY
TEL: 064-31938 FAX: 064-31965
EMAIL: muckrossparkhotel@eircom.net
WEB: www.muckrosspark.com

HOTEL ★★★★ MAP 2 E 4

Muckross Park Hotel is set in the heart of Killarney's National Park, comprising 27 superior rooms, including suites. Molly Darcy's, our award winning, traditional Irish pub and restaurant is an experience not to be missed. Situated 4km outside Killarney, and adjacent to Muckross House and Abbey. Local amenities include golf, boating, fishing, horse riding and hillwalking.

B&B from €70.00 to €95.00
£55.13 to £74.82

PATRICIA SHANAHAN
GENERAL MANAGER

American Express
Diners
Mastercard
Visa

Weekend specials from €145.00

27 27

Closed 26 November - 01 February

OAKLAND HOUSE

CORK ROAD,
KILLARNEY,
CO. KERRY
TEL: 064-37286 FAX: 064-37991
EMAIL: oakland@eircom.net

GUESTHOUSE ★★ MAP 2 E 4

Oakland House is a new family run guesthouse on the main Cork Road. 1km from town centre, bus and train stations. All rooms en suite with TV, direct dial phone. Golf, fishing, pony trekking, leisure centres nearby. All scenic tours arranged. Guest lounge with tea/coffee making facilities. Launderette, supermarket, post office, bureau de change approximately 100 metres. Visa, Amex, MasterCard, vouchers. Personal attention and a warm welcome awaits you at Oakland House.

B&B from €26.00 to €28.00
£20.48 to £22.05

DAVID & NOREEN HEGARTY
PROPRIETORS

American Express
Mastercard
Visa

8 8

IRISH HOTELS FEDERATION

Closed 24 - 26 December

OLD WEIR LODGE

MUCKROSS ROAD,
KILLARNEY,
CO. KERRY
TEL: 064-35593 FAX: 064-35583
EMAIL: oldweirlodge@eircom.net
WEB: www.oldweirlodge.com

GUESTHOUSE ★★★★ MAP 2 E 4

A purpose built, family-run, Tudor designed, magnificent house, conveniently located 500m from the centre of Killarney Town, within 1km of Killarney National Park. Set in landscaped garden with 30 en suite king sized bedrooms, with bath and power shower, DD phone, orthopaedic beds, multi-channel TV, hairdryer, tea/coffee facilities. 2 spacious lounges, private parking, with home baking a speciality. Friendly, relaxed atmosphere ensures an enjoyable stay. Elevator or ground floor rooms.

B&B from €38.00 to €48.00
£29.93 to £37.80

MAUREEN & DERMOT O'DONOGHUE
PROPRIETORS

American Express
Diners
Mastercard
Visa

30 30

IRISH HOTELS FEDERATION

Closed 23 - 26 December

RANDLES COURT CLARION HOTEL

MUCKROSS ROAD,
KILLARNEY,
CO. KERRY
TEL: 064-35333 FAX: 064-35206
EMAIL: randles@iol.ie
WEB: www.randleshotels.com

HOTEL ★★★★ MAP 2 E 4

Family owned and managed the Randles Court Hotel offers the luxury of a 4* Deluxe Hotel, the elegance and charm of a county house, exquisite cuisine and an enviable location. Dating back to 1906 the hotel has been tastefully developed into a 49 bedroomed hotel located close to Killarney National Park, Golf Course and minutes walk from town. New conference room. Leisure Club 17m pool & resident beauty therapist. 4*RAC

Member of Choice Hotels Ireland
B&B from €59.00 to €100.00
£46.47 to £78.76

TOM RANDLES
GENERAL MANAGER

American Express
Diners
Mastercard
Visa

Weekend specials from €130.00

49 49

IRISH HOTELS FEDERATION

Closed 20 - 28 December

B&B rates are per person sharing per night incl. Breakfast

RIVERMERE	RIVERSIDE HOTEL	ROSS HOTEL

RIVERMERE

MUCKROSS ROAD,
KILLARNEY,
CO. KERRY
TEL: 064-37933 FAX: 064-37944
EMAIL: rivermereguesthouse@eircom.net

GUESTHOUSE ★★★★ MAP 2 E 4

Rivermere is a custom built, family run 4**** guesthouse within walking distance of Lakes and National Park and only 7 minutes walk from town centre. All rooms are spacious with TV, radio, direct dial phone, orthopaedic beds, bath, power showers, hairdryer. Rivermere is in a delightful setting and combines luxury with charm, elegance and serenity, walkers and golfers paradise. Drying room available. Private parking. Choose from our delicious breakfast menu. A warm welcome awaits you.

B&B from €33.00 to €55.00
£25.99 to £43.32

HANNAH & ANDREW KISSANE
PROPRIETORS

Mastercard
Visa

🏌

🛏🏃☎🖥TC❄♨♿JPS⬛
8   8

IRISH HOTELS FEDERATION

Closed 01 November - 08 March

RIVERSIDE HOTEL

MUCKROSS ROAD,
KILLARNEY,
CO. KERRY
TEL: 064-39200 FAX: 064-39202
EMAIL: stay@riversidehotelkillarney.com
WEB: www.irishcourthotel.com

HOTEL N MAP 2 E 4

On the Muckross Road, the main road to Killarney National Park and Lakes and just 5 minutes from town centre. The hotel offers 69 well appointed bedrooms with many overlooking the famous Flesk River against the back drop of the beautiful MacGillycuddy Reeks. Bedrooms are equipped with telephone, TV, hairdryer, tea/coffee making facilities, computer points and 24 hour room service menu. The Bacchus Restaurant provides traditional and international cuisine prepared by our award winning chefs with table d'hôte and à la carte menus available.

Member of Irish Court Hotels
B&B from €45.00 to €110.00
£35.00 to £85.00

ROBERT LYNE
PROPRIETOR

American Express
Diners
Mastercard
Visa

Inet

🛏🏃☎🖥TC♿CMJP⬛
69   69

IRISH HOTELS FEDERATION

Open All Year

ROSS HOTEL

KENMARE PLACE,
KILLARNEY,
CO. KERRY
TEL: 064-31855 FAX: 064-31139
EMAIL: ross@kph.iol.ie

HOTEL ★★★ MAP 2 E 4

A warm and friendly welcome awaits you at the family owned Ross Hotel, established since 1929. Located directly within the town of Killarney, this elegant hotel has a perfect combination of old world character, superb cuisine and friendly attentive service. Private car parking and leisure facilities are available at our sister hotel, the Killarney Park Hotel. We are pleased to arrange for you golf on Kerry's premier courses, fishing, horseriding or guided walks.

B&B from €50.00 to €65.00
£39.38 to £51.19

JANET & PADRAIG TREACY
PROPRIETORS

American Express
Diners
Mastercard
Visa

🏌

☺ Weekend specials from €115.00

🛏🏃☎🖥TC♿CMJP⬛
32   32

IRISH HOTELS FEDERATION

Closed 02 December - 28 February

Room rates are per room per night

SCOTTS GARDENS HOTEL

KILLARNEY,
CO. KERRY

TEL: 064-31060 FAX: 064-36656
EMAIL: scottskill@eircom.net
WEB: www.gleneagle-hotel.com

HOTEL ★★★ MAP 2 E 4

Newly refurbished town centre hotel with private carpark facilities. 52 3*** standard bedrooms with direct dial phone, hairdryer, satellite TV, tea/coffee facilities. Adjacent to shops, restaurants, pubs, churches and Killarney National Park. Tours, cruises, golf, and fishing arranged. Entertainment nightly July/August and on weekends during the rest of the year.

B&B from €45.00 to €80.00
£35.44 to £63.01

MAURICE EOIN O'DONOGHUE
PROPRIETOR

American Express
Diners
Mastercard
Visa

52 52

Closed 24 - 26 December

SLIEVE BLOOM MANOR GUESTHOUSE

MUCKROSS ROAD,
KILLARNEY,
CO. KERRY

TEL: 064-34237 FAX: 064-35055
EMAIL: slievebloomanor@eircom.net
WEB: www.slievebloomkillarney.com

GUESTHOUSE ★★★ MAP 2 E 4

This charming 3*** guesthouse has a premier location on Muckross Road only 7 minutes walk to Killarney Town and gateway to Killarney's world famous National Park and lakes. Rooms are tastefully furnished with all facilities, varied breakfast menu available, private parking and store for bicycles etc. Local amenities include superb golf at Killarney's 2 renowned courses, horse riding and fishing. Leisure centre close by. All tours arranged. Looking forward to your visit.

B&B from €25.00 to €33.00
£19.69 to £25.99

TERESA CLERY
PROPRIETOR

Mastercard
Visa

11 11

Closed 15 December - 01 February

TORC GREAT SOUTHERN HOTEL

KILLARNEY,
CO. KERRY

TEL: 064-31611 FAX: 064-31824
EMAIL: res@torc-gsh.com
WEB: www.greatsouthernhotels.com

HOTEL ★★★ MAP 2 E 4

A 3*** modern hotel situated in beautiful gardens, just 5 minutes from Killarney Town. 95 rooms, all en suite, with direct dial phone, hairdryer, radio, tea/coffee making facilities and colour TV. Leisure facilities include indoor heated swimming pool, steamroom, jacuzzi. Outdoor tennis courts. Superbly located for golfing at Killarney's championship courses. An ideal base from which to tour the Kerry region. Bookable worldwide through Utell International or Central Reservations 01-214 4800.

Room Rate from €136.00 to €150.00
£107.09 to £118.12

FREDA DARCY
GENERAL MANAGER

American Express
Diners
Mastercard
Visa

☺ Weekend specials from €115.00

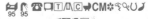
95 95

Closed 22 December - 07 January

B&B rates are per person sharing per night incl. Breakfast

TUSCAR LODGE

GOLF COURSE ROAD,
FOSSA, KILLARNEY,
CO. KERRY
TEL: 064-31978 FAX: 064-31978
EMAIL: tuscar.house@ireland.com

GUESTHOUSE ★★ MAP 2 E 4

Tuscar Lodge is a family run guesthouse. The proprietress Mrs Fitzgerald and her family always ensure that the guests have an enjoyable stay. Situated in scenic surroundings overlooking Loch Lein, with a magnificent view of the Magillycuddy Reeks. With its own car park, it is very central for touring the beauty spots of West Cork and Kerry. Pony trekking, boating, fishing and mountain climbing, all within easy range. Very near Killarney's three championship golf courses.

B&B from € 24.00 to € 33.00
£18.90 to £25.99

EILEEN FITZGERALD
PROPRIETOR

10 10

Closed 01 November - 28 February

VICTORIA HOUSE HOTEL

MUCKROSS ROAD,
KILLARNEY,
CO. KERRY
TEL: 064-35430 FAX: 064-35439
EMAIL: killarneylakes@eircom.net
WEB: www.victoriahousehotel.com

HOTEL N MAP 2 E 4

Set at the gateway to Killarney's National Park, this charming and cosy family owned and managed hotel offers the ambience of a country house, with first class personal and friendly staff. Attention to detail complements the elegantly furnished bedrooms and reception area. The restaurant maximises local produce with care and attention, where the menu changes in accordance with the seasons. Our hotel is a perfect base for exploring the sightseeing delights of Kerry and is the nearest located hotel to the I.N.E.C.

B&B from € 46.00 to € 70.00
£36.22 to £55.12

JOHN COURTNEY
PROPRIETOR

American Express
Diners
Mastercard
Visa

35 35

IRISH
HOTELS
FEDERATION

Closed 02 December - 01 February

WOODLAWN HOUSE

WOODLAWN ROAD,
KILLARNEY,
CO. KERRY
TEL: 064-37844 FAX: 064-36116
EMAIL: awrenn@eircom.net
WEB: www.kerry-insight.com/woodlawnhouse

GUESTHOUSE ★★★ MAP 2 E 4

Old style charm and hospitality. Family run. Relaxed atmosphere. All modern conveniences. Ideally located 5 minutes walk from town centre. Near leisure centre, lakes and golf courses. Tours arranged. Private parking. Decorated with natural pine wood. Orthopaedic beds dressed in white cotton and linen. Irish and vegetarian menus. Our wholesome breakfasts include freshly squeezed orange juice, homemade preserves and bread. Early bird breakfast also available. A warm welcome assured.

B&B from € 31.75 to € 50.79
£25.01 to £40.00

JAMES & ANNE WRENN

Mastercard
Visa

9 9

IRISH
HOTELS
FEDERATION

Closed 01 - 29 December

Room rates are per room per night

BIANCONI

KILLORGLIN,
RING OF KERRY,
CO. KERRY
TEL: 066-976 1146 FAX: 066-976 1950

GUESTHOUSE ★★★ MAP 1 D 4

Family run inn on the Ring of Kerry. Gateway to Dingle Peninsula, Killarney 18km. On the road to Glencar - famous for its scenery, lakes, hill walking and mountain climbing. Famous for its table. High standard of food in bar. Table d'hôte and à la carte available. 50 minutes to Waterville, Tralee & Ballybunion golf courses. 15 minutes to Dooks & Beaufort courses. 5 minutes to Killorglin Course. 15 mins to Killarney Course. Private access to Caragh Lake. Own boat. Mentioned by many guides.

B&B from € 44.45 to € 50.80
£35.01 to £40.01

RAY SHEEHY
OWNER

American Express
Diners
Mastercard
Visa

✓

🛏️ 🐕 ☎ 🖥️ T C ✏️ CM❄️✈️🎵🍺 alc
15. 15

IRISH
HOTELS
FEDERATION

Closed 23 - 29 December

CARRIG HOUSE

CARAGH LAKE,
KILLORGLIN,
CO. KERRY
TEL: 066-976 9100 FAX: 066-976 9166
EMAIL: info@carrighouse.com
WEB: www.carrighouse.com

GUESTHOUSE N MAP 1 D 4

Charming Victorian Manor on acres of woodlands and gardens (935 plant species) running down to the lake shore. Furnished in period style with antique furniture. Central to 12 superb golf courses, fishing, shooting, hillwalking or just lazing by the fireside with a good book. Critically acclaimed restaurant (open to non residents). Ideal for touring the Ring of Kerry, Dingle and Killarney. "Carrig is a lakeside dreamland with a stunning restaurant." (M Leland, Irish Examiner).

Member of Green Book of Ireland
B&B from € 62.00 to € 75.00
£48.81 to £59.07

FRANK & MARY SLATTERY
HOSTS/PROPRIETORS

Diners
Mastercard
Visa

✓

🛏️ 🐕 ☎ T ❄️🖥️ ✈️🎵P 🐕🍺 alc
16 16

IRISH
HOTELS
FEDERATION

Closed 01 December - 01 March

GROVE LODGE GUESTHOUSE

KILLARNEY ROAD,
KILLORGLIN,
CO. KERRY
TEL: 066-976 1157 FAX: 066-976 2330
EMAIL: info@grovelodge.com
WEB: www.grovelodge.com

GUESTHOUSE ★★★ MAP 1 D 4

Ideally located for all your holiday activities; golfing, fishing, hill walking, sightseeing, beaches, Ring of Kerry/Ring of Dingle, with local gourmet restaurants & pub entertainment. (5 min walk from town centre). We invite you to share your holiday with us in our newly refurbished, spacious & luxurious accommodation, situated on 3 acres of mature gardens & woodlands, fronted by the River Laune & McGillycuddy Reeks Mountains & savour our speciality gourmet breakfasts. RAC, AA ◆◆◆◆.

Member of Irish Premier Guesthouses
B&B from € 30.00 to € 55.00
£23.63 to £43.32

DELIA & FERGUS FOLEY
OWNERS & MANAGERS

American Express
Diners
Mastercard
Visa

✓

🛏️ 🐕 ☎ 🖥️ T C ✈️❄️✈️P 🍺
10 10

Closed 22 - 29 December

B&B rates are per person sharing per night incl. Breakfast

WESTFIELD HOUSE

KILLORGLIN,
CO. KERRY

TEL: 066-976 1909 FAX: 066-976 1996
EMAIL: westhse@iol.ie
WEB: www.westfieldhse.com

GUESTHOUSE ★★★ MAP 1 D 4

Westfield House is a family run guesthouse. All rooms are bright & spacious en suite, orthopaedic beds, direct dial telephone, TV, tea/coffee maker. Extra large family room available. We are situated on the Ring of Kerry in a quiet peaceful location only 5 minutes walk from town with panoramic views of MacGillycuddy Reeks. There are five 18 hole golf courses within 20 minutes drive. Recognised stop for many weary cyclists. Ideal location for the hillwalker and climber.

B&B from €32.00 to €32.00
£25.20 to £25.20

LEONARD CLIFFORD
PROPRIETOR

Mastercard

Visa

10 10

Closed 1 November - 16 March

LISTOWEL ARMS HOTEL

THE SQUARE,
LISTOWEL,
CO. KERRY

TEL: 068-21500 FAX: 068-22524
EMAIL: listowelarms@ireland.com

HOTEL ★★★ MAP 2 E 6

In a tranquil corner of Listowel's old square, the Listowel Arms Hotel is a haven of comfort and hospitality, an establishment with a proud tradition of fine food, and discreet service, a quite retreat, a warm and intimate meeting place. Famous for its annual race meeting, Listowel is an ideal location to explore the famous Ring of Kerry, Dingle Peninsula and Lakes of Kilarney. Tee times can be reserved at nearby world famous Ballybunion Golf Club along with Listowel Golf Club.

Member of Holiday Ireland Hotels
B&B from €45.00 to €127.00
£35.43 to £100.00

KEVIN O' CALLAGHAN
DIRECTOR

American Express

Mastercard

Visa

37 37
alc

Closed 24 - 26 December

MOORINGS

PORTMAGEE,
CO. KERRY

TEL: 066-947 7108 FAX: 066-947 7220
EMAIL: moorings@iol.ie
WEB: www.moorings.ie

GUESTHOUSE ★★★ MAP 1 B 3

The Moorings is a family owned guesthouse & restaurant overlooking the picturesque fishing port in Portmagee. Excellent cuisine, specialising in locally caught seafood. Adjacent to the Moorings is the Bridge Bar, also run by the family, where you can enjoy a wonderful night of music, song & dance. The Moorings is central to all local amenities including angling, diving, watersports, 18 hole golf course etc. Trips to Skellig Michael can be arranged. Recently awarded RAC ◆◆◆◆.

B&B from €31.74 to €44.44
£25.00 to £35.00

GERARD & PATRICIA KENNEDY
PROPRIETORS

Mastercard

Visa

14 14
Inet

Closed 01 November - 01 March

Room rates are per room per night

PARKNASILLA GREAT SOUTHERN HOTEL

SNEEM,
CO. KERRY

TEL: 064-45122 FAX: 064-45323
EMAIL: res@parknasilla-gsh.com
WEB: www.greatsouthernhotels.com

HOTEL ★★★★ MAP 1 C 3

Acknowledged as one of Ireland's finest hotels, Parknasilla is a 19th century house set in 300 acres of grounds. A classically individual hotel with 84 bedrooms equipped with every modern amenity. Leisure facilities include indoor heated swimming pool, sauna, steam room, jacuzzi, hydrotherapy baths, outdoor hot tub, pony trekking, clay pigeon shooting, archery, water skiing, private 9 hole golf course - special green fees for guests. Utell International or Central Reservations 01-214 4800

Room Rate from €230.00 to €250.00
£181.11 to £196.85

JIM FEENEY
GENERAL MANAGER

American Express
Diners
Mastercard
Visa

☺ Weekend specials from €195.00

84 84

Open All Year

TAHILLA COVE COUNTRY HOUSE

TAHILLA,
NEAR SNEEM,
CO. KERRY

TEL: 064-45204 FAX: 064-45104
EMAIL: tahillacove@eircom.net
WEB: www.tahillacove.com

GUESTHOUSE ★★★ MAP 1 D 3

Travel writers have described this family-run, fully licensed seashore guesthouse as the most idyllic spot in Ireland - the haunt of Irish/British dignitaries. Located on the Ring of Kerry seashore. 14 acre estate boasts mature gardens & private pier. Ideal place for a relaxing holiday/touring centre. Each room has en suite facilities, phone, TV, radio, hairdryer, iron and tea/coffee facilities. Log fires, superb views, home cooking. Take Sneem Road from Kenmare (N70).

B&B from €50.00 to €55.00
£39.38 to £43.32

JAMES/DEIRDRE/CHAS WATERHOUSE
OWNERS

American Express
Diners
Mastercard
Visa

9 9

Closed 15 October - 29 March

LANTERNS HOTEL

COAST ROAD,
TARBERT,
CO. KERRY

TEL: 068-36210 FAX: 068-36553

WEB: www.thelanternshotel.ie

HOTEL N MAP 5 E 7

The Lanterns Hotel is a superbly refurbished hotel overlooking the Shannon Estuary. An ideal tourist base we are central to world famous golf courses at Ballybunion, Adare, Killarney, Tralee and Lahinch. The Parsons Restaurant at the Lanterns Hotel has a reputation for excellent food and personal service. Under the personal supervision of owners Maurice and Maureen Fitzgerald.

B&B from €31.74 to €44.44
£25.00 to £35.00

MAUREEN FITZGERALD
OWNER

American Express
Mastercard
Visa

22 22

Inet

Open All Year

B&B rates are per person sharing per night incl. Breakfast

ABBEY GATE HOTEL

MAINE STREET,
TRALEE,
CO. KERRY
TEL: 066-712 9888 FAX: 066-712 9821
EMAIL: abbeygat@iol.ie
WEB: www.abbeygate-hotel.com

HOTEL ★★★ MAP 1 D 5

Welcome, the Abbey Gate Hotel is located in the heart of Tralee. All 100 rooms are spacious with full facilities. The Old Market Place Pub is Tralee's liveliest venue with great pub grub served all day and casual dining in our Bistro at night. Or try our fabulous Toscana Ristorante Italiano for the best in authentic Italian cuisine. The Abbey Gate Hotel is your gateway to the delights of Kerry.

B&B from €41.95 to €76.95
£33.04 to £60.60

PATRICK DILLON
GENERAL MANAGER

American Express
Diners
Mastercard
Visa

Weekend specials from €99.00

100 100

Closed 24 - 26 December

BALLYGARRY HOUSE HOTEL

KILLARNEY ROAD,
TRALEE,
CO. KERRY
TEL: 066-712 1233 FAX: 066-712 7630
EMAIL: ballygarry@eircom.net
WEB: www.ballygarry.com

HOTEL ★★★★ MAP 1 D 5

Ballygarry House Hotel invites you to relax by open fires and experience an air of wellbeing. Ideally situated for Kerry's magnificent golf courses, we can be found less than 1.5km from Tralee en route to Kerry Airport and Killarney (N22). This country house hotel boasts 46 luxurious rooms overlooking beautiful landscaped gardens. Our Riverside Restaurant offers modern and traditional cuisine in an intimate atmosphere. A warm welcome awaits you.

B&B from €65.00 to €95.00
£51.19 to £74.82

OWEN MCGILLICUDDY
PROPRIETOR

American Express
Mastercard
Visa

46 46

Closed 16 - 28 December

BALLYROE HEIGHTS HOTEL

BALLYROE,
TRALEE,
CO. KERRY
TEL: 066-712 6796 FAX: 066-712 5066
EMAIL: info@ballyroe.com
WEB: www.ballyroe.com

HOTEL ★★★ MAP 1 D 5

A modern luxurious hotel set in six and a half acres of woodland and sloping gardens. Situated 3km from Tralee Town it is the ideal base for touring, golfing or just relaxing. The views of the Sliabh Mish Mountains and Tralee Bay are breathtaking. Relax in our spectacular Summit Restaurant or Palace Bar while enjoying the view. All en suite bedrooms have satellite TV, hairdryer and tea/coffee making facilities.

B&B from €47.63 to €76.20
£37.50 to £60.00

MARK SULLIVAN
GENERAL MANAGER

American Express
Mastercard
Visa

Midweek specials from €146.00
(3 B&B, 2D)

25 25

Open All Year

Room rates are per room per night

BALLYSEEDE CASTLE HOTEL

BALLYSEEDY,
TRALEE,
CO. KERRY
TEL: 066-712 5799 FAX: 066-712 5287
EMAIL: ballyseede@eircom.net
WEB: www.ballyseedecastle.com

HOTEL ★★★ MAP 1 D 5

Ballyseede Castle Hotel is a casual, almost cosy 15th century castle on 35 hectares of parkland. The castle boasts a fine selection of continental cuisine as well as many traditional Irish dishes. Located on the main Tralee/Killarney Road within easy reach of Kerry's five magnificent golf courses, Ballybunion, Waterville, Killarney, Dooks and Barrow, the recently designed course for Tralee by Arnold Palmer. Ideally situated for touring the Ring of Kerry and Dingle Peninsula.

B&B from €90.00 to €130.00
£70.88 to £102.38

BART W O'CONNOR
MANAGING DIRECTOR

Diners

Mastercard

Visa

✓

12 12

HOTELS

Open All Year

BARROW COUNTRY HOUSE

WEST ARDFERT,
TRALEE,
CO. KERRY
TEL: 066-7136437 FAX: 066-7136402
EMAIL: info@barrowhouse.com
WEB: www.barrowhouse.com

GUESTHOUSE ★★★★ MAP 1 D 5

Built in 1723, Barrow Country House is located on Barrow Harbour next to the Slieve Mish Mountains and the Dingle Peninsula. This period house has been elegantly renovated and refurbised to provide a combination of luxurious suites and deluxe rooms. Each bedroom enjoys the comfort of modern day living in a unique and tranquil setting. Golf, angling, golden beaches, sailing, award winning restaurants and pubs close by. Former home of the Knight of Kerry.

B&B from €50.00 to €118.00
£39.37 to £92.91

LORRAINE WALSH
MANAGER

Mastercard

Visa

✓

☺ Special rates on request

16 16

HOTELS

Closed 20 December - 14 February

BRANDON COURT HOTEL

JAMES STREET,
TRALEE,
CO. KERRY
TEL: 066-712 9666 FAX: 066-712 9690
EMAIL: louise@brandonhotel.ie
WEB: www.brandonhotel.ie

HOTEL U MAP 1 D 5

The concept - quality at a fixed price. Bright, modern and spacious rooms, each with its own bathroom, colour TV, direct dial telephone and tea/coffee making facilities. The price remains fixed when a room is occupied by 1, 2 or 3 adults or up to 2 adults and 2 children. Bright, spacious public areas, cosy bar facilities and restaurant serving breakfast and light evening meals. Located in Tralee's old quarter, adjacent to Siamsa Tire, Aqua Dome and Kerry County Museum.

Room Rate from €69.85 to €139.70
£55.01 to £110.02

PETER MCDERMOTT
GENERAL MANAGER

American Express

Diners

Mastercard

Visa

✓

☺ Midweek specials from €133.35

49 49

Closed 01 October - 31 May

B&B rates are per person sharing per night incl. Breakfast

BRANDON HOTEL

PRINCES STREET,
TRALEE,
CO. KERRY
TEL: 066-712 3333 FAX: 066-712 5019
EMAIL: louise@brandonhotel.ie
WEB: www.brandonhotel.ie

HOTEL ★★★ MAP 1 D 5

This renowned, privately owned premises is located in the heart of Tralee Town, close to shopping and cultural interests. The hotel offers a wide range of accommodation - standard, superior and deluxe rooms - and a choice of bars and restaurants. It is also equipped with full leisure centre incorporating swimming pool, sauna and steamroom and has extensive conference facilities. The Brandon Hotel is easily reached by mainline rail or flying to Kerry County Airport just 10 miles away.

B&B from €44.45 to €127.00
£35.01 to £100.02

PETER MCDERMOTT
GENERAL MANAGER

American Express
Diners
Mastercard
Visa

☺ Weekend specials from €120.65

182 182

Closed 22 - 29 December

BROOK MANOR LODGE

FENIT ROAD,
TRALEE,
CO. KERRY
TEL: 066-712 0406 FAX: 066-712 7552
EMAIL: brookmanor@eircom.net

GUESTHOUSE ★★★★ MAP 1 D 5

A warm welcome awaits you at our new 4★★★★ luxurious, family-run lodge. Only minutes drive from Tralee, golden beaches and Arnold Palmer designed golf course. 30 minutes from Killarney. 40 minutes from Ballybunion. The Lodge is situated in acres of meadowlands and surrounded by a babbling brook. All our rooms are en suite with full facilities. Brook Manor Lodge is the ideal place for the perfect holiday.

Member of Premier Guesthouses
B&B from €38.09 to €63.49
£30.00 to £50.00

MARGARET & VINCENT O'SULLIVAN
OWNERS

American Express
Mastercard
Visa

8 8

Open All Year

GLENDUFF HOUSE

KIELDUFF,
TRALEE,
CO. KERRY
TEL: 066-713 7105 FAX: 066-713 7099
EMAIL: glenduffhouse@eircom.net
WEB: www.tralee-insight.com/glenduff

GUESTHOUSE ★★★ MAP 1 D 5

Enter the old world charm of the 19th century in our family run period house set on 6 acres with mature gardens. Refurbished to give the comforts of the modern day, yet keeping its original character with antiques & paintings. Personal attention assured. Relax & enjoy a drink in our friendly bar. Also self catering cottages in courtyard. Ideally situated for golf and sports amenities. From Tralee take route to racecourse off N21 at Clash Roundabout, continue for 4.5 miles.

Member of Premier Guesthouses
B&B from €34.00 to €54.00
£26.78 to £42.53

SHEILA SUGRUE
OWNER

Mastercard
Visa

5 5

Closed 01 November - 14 March

Room rates are per room per night

GRAND HOTEL

DENNY STREET,
TRALEE,
CO. KERRY
TEL: 066-712 1499 FAX: 066-712 2877
EMAIL: info@grandhoteltralee.com
WEB: www.grandhoteltralee.com

HOTEL ★★★ MAP 1 D 5

The Grand Hotel is a 3*** hotel situated in Tralee Town centre. Established in 1928, its open fires, ornate ceilings & mahogany furnishings offer guests old world charm in comfortable surroundings. All our rooms are equipped with direct dial phone, computer point, satellite TV and tea/coffee welcoming trays. Residents can avail of green fee reductions at Tralee Golf Club. Also reduced rates to the fabulous Aqua Dome Waterworld complex. Family rooms are available at discounted rates.

B&B from €45.00 to €85.00
£35.44 to £66.94

DICK BOYLE
GENERAL MANAGER

American Express
Diners
Mastercard
Visa

☺ Weekend special from €110.00

44 44

Closed 24 - 27 December

MEADOWLANDS HOTEL

OAKPARK,
TRALEE,
CO. KERRY
TEL: 066-718 0444 FAX: 066-718 0964
EMAIL: medlands@iol.ie
WEB: www.meadowlands-hotel.com

HOTEL ★★★★ MAP 1 D 5

A charming and intimate hotel, set in a tranquil corner of Tralee, on its own 3 acres with beautiful landscaped gardens. This small luxurious hotel comprises of 27 superbly appointed rooms including suites. Our gourmet restaurant specialises in the freshest of locally-caught seafood and shellfish cuisine. The Meadowlands is an ideal base for golfing enthusiasts and touring the Dingle Peninsula, Ring of Kerry, Killarney and West Cork. Experience an experience!

Member of MinOtel Ireland Hotel Group
B&B from €60.00 to €80.00
£47.25 to £63.01

JOHN PALMER
MANAGER

American Express
Diners
Mastercard
Visa

☺ Weekend specials from €140.00

27 27

Closed 24 - 26 December

OAKLEY HOUSE

BALLYMULLEN,
TRALEE,
CO. KERRY
TEL: 066-712 1727 FAX: 066-712 1727
EMAIL: info@oakleyguesthouse.com
WEB: www.oakleyguesthouse.com

GUESTHOUSE ★★ MAP 1 D 5

Spacious period house with old world charm and character. Situated on road to Dingle, Killorglin and Ring of Kerry. On N70 Road, turn right at Ballymullen Roundabout, right at next junction, situated on left. Situated on the outskirts of Tralee Town. Overlooking Slieve Mish Mountains. Ideal touring base. 8 minutes walk from town centre, National Folk Theatre, Medieval Experience. 10 minutes walk from Aqua Dome. Private car park. Convenient to beaches, angling, golf, horseriding and pony trekking. A cead mile failte awaits you.

B&B from €28.00 to €31.75
£22.05 to £25.01

MICHAEL & PHILOMENA BENNIS
PROPRIETORS

Mastercard
Visa

☺ Midweek specials from €80.00

7 7

Open All Year

B&B rates are per person sharing per night incl. Breakfast

QUALITY HOTEL TRALEE

CASTLE STREET,
TRALEE,
CO. KERRY
TEL: 066-712 1877 FAX: 066-712 2273
EMAIL: quality.benners@indigo.ie
WEB: www.choicehotelsireland.ie

HOTEL ★★★ MAP 1 D 5

Situated in the heart of bustling Tralee. Quality Hotel Tralee exudes an air of hospitality and vibrancy that appeals to young and old. All rooms are en suite with multi channel TV, DD phone, ironing and tea/coffee making facilities. Taste the popular delights of Lannigans Restaurant. Enjoy live entertainment in McDades Bar and dance away in the Courthouse Nite Club. 2 minutes from the train and bus station. 15 minutes from Kerry Airport.

Member of Choice Hotels Ireland

B&B from €45.00 to €70.00
£35.44 to £55.13

NANCY GALLAGHER
GENERAL MANAGER

American Express
Diners
Mastercard
Visa

45   45

HOTELS

Open All Year

TRALEE TOWNHOUSE

HIGH STREET,
TRALEE,
CO. KERRY
TEL: 066-718 1111 FAX: 066-718 1112
EMAIL: townhouse@iolfree.ie
WEB: www.traleetownhouse.com

GUESTHOUSE ★★★ MAP 1 D 5

Centrally located beside all of Tralee's visitor attractions; - Siamsa Tire, Aqua Dome, Tralee Superbowl, Geraldine Experience, Kerry County Museum, Blennerville Windmill, Steam Train and the new Tralee Marina. Local amenities include - for the golf enthusiast, the world renowned Tralee & Ballybunion Golf Courses are only a few miles away. 2 excellent 9 hole courses are within 1 mile of the town centre. Fishing, horse riding, hillwalking, sports centre with indoor pool, etc. 3*** AA.

B&B from €29.50 to €50.79
£23.23 to £40.00

ELEANOR COLLINS
MANAGER

Mastercard
Visa

19   19

HOTELS

Closed 24 - 28 December

BROOKHAVEN COUNTRY HOUSE

NEW LINE ROAD,
WATERVILLE,
CO. KERRY
TEL: 066-947 4431 FAX: 066-947 4724
EMAIL: brookhaven@esatclear.ie
WEB: www.euroka.com/brookhaven

GUESTHOUSE ★★★ MAP 1 B 3

AA ♦♦♦♦, RAC ♦♦♦♦, plus repeated sparkling diamond accolades. New purpose built guesthouse on the Ring of Kerry. Luxury spacious en suite rooms, with telephone, TV, hair dryer and hospitality tray. Rooms overlook the Atlantic Ocean and the Waterville Golf Course. Centrally located to all amenities e.g. golf, fishing (lake and sea), beaches, horse riding, walking, cycling, Skellig Islands and gourmet restaurants. Country house surrounded by landscaped colourful gardens.

B&B from €29.20 to €50.79
£23.00 to £40.00

MARY CLIFFORD
PROPRIETOR

5   5

HOTELS

Closed 01 January - 01 March

BUTLER ARMS HOTEL

WATERVILLE,
CO. KERRY

TEL: 066-947 4144 FAX: 066-947 4520
EMAIL: reservations@butlerarms.com
WEB: www.butlerarms.com

HOTEL ★★★ MAP 1 B 3

This charming hotel, on the scenic Ring of Kerry, has been run by 4 generations of the Huggard Family. Tastefully furnished bedrooms, many with magnificent seaviews, cosy lounges, award-winning restaurant specializing in local seafood (AA 2 Red Rosettes) and the Fishermens Bar with its cosmopolitan ambience. Only 1mile from Waterville's Championship Golf Links. Renowned salmon & seatrout fishing, sandy beaches, horseriding, hill-walking.

Member of Manor House Hotels

B&B from €79.00 to €111.00
£62.22 to £87.42

MARY & PETER HUGGARD
PROPRIETORS

American Express
Diners
Mastercard
Visa

☺ Weekend specials from €150.00

40 40

S alc Inet

HOTELS
FEDERATION

Closed 28 October - 28 March

LAKELANDS FARM GUESTHOUSE

LAKE ROAD,
WATERVILLE,
CO. KERRY

TEL: 066-947 4303 FAX: 066-947 4678
EMAIL: lakelands@eircom.net
WEB: www.kerrygems.ie/lakelands/

GUESTHOUSE ★★★ MAP 1 B 3

Luxury family run guesthouse in unique location set on 100 acre estate on the south shore of Europe's best free salmon and sea trout lake. Smoking and non smoking lounges. Comfortable spacious en-suite bedrooms with all mod cons, some with balcony or jacuzzi. Proprietor professional angler with 10 motor boats. Private pools on River Inny. Convenient to Waterville Golf Course. For the golf enthusiast we have a complimentary 250 yards practice range.

B&B from €30.00 to €40.00
£23.63 to £31.50

FRANK & ANNE DONNELLY
PROPRIETORS

Mastercard
Visa

☺ Week partial board from €420.00

10 10

HOTELS
FEDERATION

Closed 25 December

SMUGGLERS INN

CLIFF ROAD,
WATERVILLE,
CO. KERRY

TEL: 066-947 4330 FAX: 066-947 4422
EMAIL: thesmugglersinn@eircom.net
WEB: www.welcome.to/thesmugglersinn

GUESTHOUSE ★★★ MAP 1 B 3

The Smugglers Inn, a family run inn with old world charm and character, quiet location on 2km sandy beach. Adjacent to Waterville Golf Course, near lake and sea fishing facilities and sporting activities. Very high standard in our gourmet seafood restaurant, meals prepared by Harry Hunt, son Henry and daughter Lucy. Dining room under supervision of his wife Lucille. Comfortable en suite accommodation. Recommended by many good food guides. Breathtaking sea views and spectacular sunsets.

B&B from €38.00 to €57.00
£29.93 to £44.89

LUCILLE & HARRY HUNT
PROPRIETORS

American Express
Diners
Mastercard
Visa

14 14

Closed 31 October - 01 March

B&B rates are per person sharing per night incl. Breakfast

SHANNON
Romantic and Exciting

Your holiday in the Shannon Region can be as active or as placid as you choose. Whichever you choose, you are guaranteed relaxation and enjoyment. All the ingredients are there: the towering cliffs and golden beaches of Clare and North Kerry; the enigmatic rockscapes of the Burren; the gentle beauty of the rolling Slieve Bloom Mountains in South Offaly; Tipperary's fertile pastures and the woodland estates in the heart of County Limerick. And, of course, the mighty Shannon River, which has bestowed its riches on the surrounding countryside and glories in its beauty.

This is one of the few remaining places on earth where clean, unpolluted air is taken for granted.

You have the space to breathe, to refresh your spirit a universe away from frenetic and crowded cities.

There is a sense of timelessness aided by the many physical reminders of Ireland's turbulent past. Castles, forts and ancient churches, spanning centuries of history, abound. many have been lovingly restored.

At the famous Bunratty Castle, visitors can slip back in time and take part in a 15th century Mediaeval Banquet of romance and merriment. The Bunratty Folk Park, in the castle grounds, accurately recreates Irish village life at the turn of the century.

Sporting facilities, in contrast, are very much up to date. Imagine golfing in a magnificent, scenic setting or fishing some of the most productive and versatile fishing waters in Europe. Take to the saddle on horse-back and the countryside is yours.

If boating is your pleasure, the possibilities are, literally, limitless.

There are many elements to a really memorable holiday and the Shannon Region can provide them all. One of the most important is the feeling of being really welcome, of being valued. This intangible but very real feature of a Shannon holiday will be immediately evident in the sense of fun which you will encounter and an eagerness to treat you as an honoured guest.

In Ireland, enjoyment is an art form. Go to one of the many festivals in the Shannon Region and you will experience the art at its best. Entertainment, spontaneous or organised, is everywhere, so too is good food and good company. For further information contact: Tourist Information Office, Arthur's Quay, Limerick. Tel: 061 317522. Fax: 061 317939.
Visit our website: www.shannon-dev.ie/tourism

BALLYVAUGHAN LODGE

BALLYVAUGHAN,
CO. CLARE

TEL: 065-707 7292 FAX: 065-707 7287
EMAIL: ballyvau@iol.ie

GUESTHOUSE ★★★ MAP 6 F 10

Located in the heart of Ballyvaughan, a small fishing village overlooking Galway Bay. A custom built modern guesthouse, dedicated to the comfort and relaxation of our guests. Each room en suite having TV, direct dial phone, tea/coffee making facilities, etc. Allow us to plan your carefree days in the most unspoilt natural environment imaginable, the Burren, including Neolithic caves, sea fishing, hill walking, cycling, Cliffs of Moher and the Aran Islands.

B&B from €25.40 to €38.00
£20.01 to £29.93

PAULINE BURKE
OWNER

Mastercard

Visa

🛏🐾☎🖥TC🔌CM✳🕘♩P S⬥
10 10

HOTELS
FEDERATION

Closed 25 - 26 December

CAPPABHAILE HOUSE

BALLYVAUGHAN,
CO. CLARE

TEL: 065-707 7260 FAX: 065-707 7300
EMAIL: cappabhaile@oceanfree.net
WEB: www.cappabhaile.com

GUESTHOUSE ★★★ MAP 6 F 10

Relax, enjoy the peace & quiet, luxury & comfort and a warm family welcome at Cappabhaile House. All rooms generously sized with private bathrooms. We have scenic views of the Burren Mountains, Newtown Castle & Ailwee Cave. We have a private carpark, pitch & putt course, games room & the Burren Gallery, all FREE to our guests. Courtesy bus to facilitate hill walking, beaches, nature trails, pubs & restaurants. Perfect base for touring the Burren, Aran Islands, Galway and Connemara.

B&B from €26.00 to €39.00
£20.48 to £30.71

MARGARET & CONOR FAHY
PROPRIETORS

Mastercard

Visa

☺ Walks & Archaelogical tours from €50.00

🛏🐾☎🖥TC🔌CM✳🕘♩P
8   8

S ⬥ inet

HOTELS
FEDERATION

Closed 30 November - 01 March

DRUMCREEHY HOUSE

BALLYVAUGHAN,
CO. CLARE

TEL: 065-707 7377 FAX: 065-707 7379
EMAIL: B&B@drumcreehyhouse.com
WEB: www.drumcreehyhouse.com

GUESTHOUSE ★★★ MAP 6 F 10

Delightful country style house overlooking Galway Bay and the surrounding Burren landscape. Open fires, antique furnishings plus a friendly and personal service by conscientious hosts Armin and Bernadette help to make your stay both enjoyable and memorable. Tastefully decorated rooms, all en suite and equipped with TV and direct dial phone. Extensive breakfast menu and simple country style cooking in a relaxed and homely atmosphere. Ideally located for touring Clare, Kerry and Galway.

B&B from €28.00 to €38.00
£22.05 to £29.93

A & B MOLONEY-GREFKES
PROPRIETORS

Mastercard

Visa

🛏🐾☎🖥TC🔌CM✳🕘♩P T S⬥
10 10

HOTELS
FEDERATION

Open All Year

B&B rates are per person sharing per night incl. Breakfast

General Tourist Information

Banking

Banks are normally open from Monday to Friday 10.00 to 16.00. Many Banks stay open until 17.00 on Thursdays. Visitors are advised to change their bank notes at banks and Bureaux de Change to get the best exchange rate. Most credit cards, including all cards carrying the Eurocheque symbol, are accepted in hotels, restaurants, petrol stations and most shops. ATMs located at most banks accept major credit cards.

Medical Treatment

Citizens of the European Community are entitled to free hospital treatment in a public ward and should obtain an E111 form prior to departure. When necessary, this should be presented to the doctor or hospital visited, along with identification.
Visitors from other countries should check with their insurance agent or broker before travelling to establish their entitlement to recover additional medical expenses.

Public Holidays

The following are the public holidays in the Republic of Ireland (those in Northern Ireland differ slightly). Most companies and shops are closed on these days.

January 1st; March 17th; Friday before Easter; Monday after Easter; First Monday in May, June and August; Last Monday in October; Christmas Day; St. Stephen's Day

---

GREGANS CASTLE HOTEL

BALLYVAUGHAN,
CO. CLARE

TEL: 065-707 7005 FAX: 065-707 7111
EMAIL: res@gregans.ie
WEB: www.gregans.ie

HOTEL ★★★★ MAP 6 F 10

4**** luxury hotel amid splendid Burren mountain scenery, overlooking Galway Bay. Country house comforts, turf fires, tranquillity, no TV in rooms. Award winning gardens, food, service, accommodations. Individually designed superior rooms/suites. Nearby ocean swimming, horse riding, hillwalking. Golf at Lahinch. Halfway between Kerry and Connemara using ferry. RAC Blue Ribbon winner. AA Red Stars award. 1 hour to Shannon Airport. Excellence of private ownership for 26 years.

Member of Ireland's Blue Book
B&B from € 77.00 to € 98.00
£60.64 to £77.18

SIMON HADEN
MANAGER & DIRECTOR

American Express
Mastercard
Visa

☺ 3 days half board from €375.00pps

22 22

Closed 23 December - 13 February

HYLAND'S HOTEL

BALLYVAUGHAN,
CO. CLARE

TEL: 065-707 7037 FAX: 065-707 7131
EMAIL: hylandshotel@eircom.net
WEB: www.iol.ie/hotels

HOTEL ★★★ MAP 6 F 10

A charming family run hotel whose present owners are 7th and 8th generation proudly carrying on the tradition for hospitality and good food. Experience bygone charm with modern day facilities, open turf fires, informal bars and restaurants specialising in the finest local seafood. An ideal base for the golfing and walking enthusiasts, exploring the unique Burren landscape, visiting the Aran Islands, touring the unspoilt Clare, Connemara and Kerry countrysides, truly an artist's haven.

Member of Village Inn Hotels
B&B from € 48.00 to € 66.00
£37.80 to £51.98

MARIE GREENE
INN KEEPER

American Express
Diners
Mastercard
Visa

☺ Weekend specials from €110.00

30 30

Closed 15 December - 15 February

RUSHEEN LODGE

BALLYVAUGHAN,
CO. CLARE

TEL: 065-707 7092 FAX: 065-707 7152
EMAIL: rusheenl@iol.ie
WEB: www.rusheenlodge.com

GUESTHOUSE ★★★★ MAP 6 F 10

Guest House of the Year 2001-
Georgina Campbell Jameson guide,
RAC sparkling diamond, previous
winner RAC small hotel & guest
house of the year. Rusheen Lodge is
a 4****, AA ◆◆◆◆ and RAC ◆◆◆◆
highly acclaimed luxury guest house
nestling in the Burren mountains. The
Lodge provides elegant and tastefully
designed en suite bedrooms, suites,
dining room and residents' lounge
ensuring a comfortable and relaxing
stay. Excellent location for touring
Clare, Kerry and Connemara.

B&B from € 38.00 to € 44.00
£29.93 to £34.65

KAREN McGANN
PROPRIETOR

Mastercard
Visa

☺ Midweek specials from €102.00

🛏️📶☎️🖥️TC❄️☂️☺♪P S ⚓
8   8

IRISH HOTELS FEDERATION

Closed 30 November - 01 February

BUNRATTY CASTLE HOTEL AND CONFERENCE CENTRE

BUNRATTY,
CO. CLARE

TEL: 061-478700 FAX: 061-364891
EMAIL: info@bunrattycastlehotel.iol.ie
WEB: www.bunrattycastlehotel.com

HOTEL ★★★ MAP 6 G 7

The new Bunratty Castle Hotel is a
3*** Georgian hotel. Situated in the
centre of Bunratty Village overlooking
the historic Bunratty Castle and just
across the road from Ireland's oldest
pub, Durty Nellies. The rooms have
been tastefully decorated in the
traditional style. All rooms have air
conditioning, satellite TV and have
every modern comfort. Relax in
Kathleens Irish Pub and Restaurant
and enjoy great food. We welcome
you to experience the warmth and
hospitality here.

B&B from € 51.00 to € 83.00
£40.00 to £65.00

KATHLEEN McLOUGHLIN
DIRECTOR

American Express
Diners
Mastercard
Visa

🛏️📶☎️🖥️TC◀CM♻️☺♪🎵P
59   59

📠 a/c 🖥️ Inet

Closed 24 - 26 December

BUNRATTY GROVE

CASTLE ROAD,
BUNRATTY,
CO. CLARE

TEL: 061-369579 FAX: 061-369561
EMAIL: bunrattygrove@eircom.net
WEB: http://homepage.eircom.net/~bunrattygrove/

GUESTHOUSE ★★★ MAP 6 G 7

Bunratty Grove is a purpose built
luxurious guest house. This
guesthouse is located within 3
minutes drive from Bunratty Castle
and Folk Park and 10 minutes from
Shannon Airport. Fishing, golfing,
historical interests within a short
distance. Ideally located for tourists
arriving or departing Shannon Airport.
Bookings for Bunratty and Knappogue
Banquets taken on request. All rooms
en suite with multi-channel TV, hair
dryer, tea/coffee facilities and direct
dial phone.

B&B from € 30.00 to € 40.00
£23.63 to £31.50

PETER & PATSY GOLDEN
OWNERS

Mastercard
Visa

🛏️📶☎️🖥️TC❄️☺♪P ⚓
9   9

IRISH HOTELS FEDERATION

Closed 30 October - 01 April

B&B rates are per person sharing per night incl. Breakfast

BUNRATTY MANOR HOTEL

BUNRATTY,
CO. CLARE

TEL: 061-707984 FAX: 061-360588
EMAIL: bunrattymanor@eircom.net
WEB: www.bunrattymanor.net

HOTEL N   MAP 6 G 7

A Manor House hotel designed to reflect the ambience and comforts associated with elegant living. Beautiful gardens, superb classical Italian cuisine prepared by David (including vegetarian), renowned for friendliness, comfort, tranquillity and hospitality. Bunratty Village - excellent restaurants, fun pubs, the Castle and shopping - is two minutes walk! Within easy reach of eleven Championship golf courses and breathtaking scenery. Tea/coffee facilities, ice, TV and ISDN.

B&B from €49.00 to €59.00
£38.59 to £46.47

GERRY HUGHES
HOST

American Express

Diners

Mastercard

Visa

🛏️ ♿ ☎ 🖥️ T C ♦ ❄ 🌙 J P 🅿️ ⚡ Inet
14 14

HOTELS
IRISH FEDERATION

Closed 24 December - 01 March

BUNRATTY VIEW GUESTHOUSE

CRATLOE,
NEAR BUNRATTY,
CO. CLARE

TEL: 061-357352 FAX: 061-357491
EMAIL: bunrattyview@eircom.net

GUESTHOUSE ★★★   MAP 6 G 7

Bunratty View is a 3*** guesthouse located 10 minutes from Shannon Airport, 2 km from Bunratty Castle. Bedrooms have private bathroom, satellite TV, direct dial telephone, hair dryer, tea/coffee facilities, orthopaedic beds. Ideal for tourists arriving or departing Shannon Airport. Excellent location for touring Cliffs of Moher, Ailwee Caves, Lakes of Killaloe. Banquets for Bunratty and Knappogue booked on request. Recommended by leading guides for accommodation and hospitality.

B&B from €25.00 to €34.00
£19.69 to £26.78

JOE & MAURA BRODIE
PROPRIETORS

Mastercard

Visa

🙂 Midweek specials from €84.00

🛏️ ♿ ☎ 🖥️ T C ♦ CM ❄ 🌙 J P S ⚡
6 6

HOTELS
IRISH FEDERATION

Open All Year

BUNRATTY WOODS COUNTRY HOUSE

LOW ROAD,
BUNRATTY,
CO. CLARE

TEL: 061-369689 FAX: 061-369454
EMAIL: bunratty@iol.ie
WEB: www.iol.ie/~bunratty

GUESTHOUSE ★★★   MAP 6 G 7

Bunratty Woods is a 3*** luxurious guesthouse situated in the old grounds of Bunratty Castle (2 minutes drive) to Bunratty Castle and Folk Park and the renowned Durty Nellies Pub. All rooms are en suite with direct dial phone, TV, tea/coffee making facilities and hair dryer. Magnificent mountain views. Bunratty Woods is furnished with style and taste of a bygone era - featuring items such as a settle bed and a famine pot and many, many other items from yesteryear. Recommended by Frommer.

B&B from €32.00 to €35.00
£25.20 to £27.56

MAUREEN & PADDY O'DONOVAN
OWNERS

Diners

Mastercard

Visa

🛏️ ♿ ☎ 🖥️ T C ❄ 🌙 J P S ⚡
15 15

HOTELS
IRISH FEDERATION

Closed 30 November - 15 March

Room rates are per room per night

COURTYARD

BUNRATTY VILLAGE,
CO. CLARE

TEL: 061-361444 FAX: 061-364498
EMAIL: info@bunrattycourtyard.com
WEB: www.bunrattycourtyard.com

GUESTHOUSE P   MAP 6 G 7

The Courtyard is the ideal location for convenience and comfort when visiting the Mid West region. We are just two mins walk to a variety of shops, pubs and restaurants. Not forgetting Bunratty Castle and Folk Park. Shannon Airport is just a 10 min drive with regular bus and taxi service. For the golf enthusiast we have a variety of top class courses available locally.

B&B from €32.00 to €45.00
£25.20 to £35.44

MICHAEL & MARY WALSH
PROPRIETORS

American Express
Diners
Mastercard
Visa

11 11

Open All Year

CRATLOE LODGE

SETRIGHTS CROSS,
CRATLOE, NEAR BUNRATTY,
CO. CLARE

TEL: 061-357168

GUESTHOUSE ★★★   MAP 6 G 7

Cratloe Lodge is a 3*** luxury guesthouse purpose built to a high standard. Bedrooms are all en suite with satellite TV, direct dial phone and trouser press. Complimentary tea/coffee available on arrival. This guesthouse is located 10 minutes from Shannon Airport and 5 minutes from Bunratty Castle. Excellent location for those arriving or departing Shannon Airport. Ideal as starting point for touring Cliffs of Moher, Ailwee Caves and the Lakes of Killaloe.

B&B from €25.40 to €31.75
£20.01 to £25.01

TOM & MAURA GALVIN

Mastercard
Visa

7 7

Open All Year

FITZPATRICK BUNRATTY

BUNRATTY,
CO. CLARE

TEL: 061-361177 FAX: 061-471252
EMAIL: info@bunratty.fitzpatricks.com
WEB: www.fitzpatrickhotels.com

HOTEL U   MAP 6 G 7

Situated in wooded grounds in Bunratty Village against the backdrop of the medieval castle and folk park. Discover village life with lively pubs, colourful restaurants and shops. 4 miles from Shannon. Hotel facilities include excellent bar and restaurant, fitness centre and rooms with bath, satellite TV and direct dial phone. Four 18 hole championship golf courses within easy drive. Horse riding available locally. The ideal choice for your stay in the Mid West.

Room Rate from €152.36 to €241.25
£119.99 to £190.00

DENIS DEERY
GENERAL MANAGER

American Express
Diners
Mastercard
Visa

☺ Weekend specials from €100.30

115 115

IRISH
HOTELS
FEDERATION

Closed 24 - 26 December

B&B rates are per person sharing per night incl. Breakfast

ARAN VIEW HOUSE HOTEL & RESTAURANT

COAST ROAD,
DOOLIN,
CO. CLARE

TEL: 065-707 4061 FAX: 065-707 4540

EMAIL: bookings@aranview.com
WEB: www.aranview.com

HOTEL ★★★ MAP 5 E 9

A Georgian house built in 1736, has a unique position commanding panoramic views of the Aran Islands, the Burren region and the Cliffs of Moher. Situated on 100 acres of farmland, Aran View echoes spaciousness, comfort and atmosphere in its restaurant and bar. Menus are based on the best of local produce, fish being a speciality. All rooms with private bathroom, colour TV and direct dial phone. Visitors are assured of a warm and embracing welcome at the Aran View House Hotel.

B&B from €45.00 to €60.00
£35.44 to £47.25

THERESA & JOHN LINNANE
PROPRIETORS

American Express
Diners
Mastercard
Visa

☺ Weekend specials from €120.00

19 19

alc

IRISH
HOTELS
FEDERATION

Closed 31 October - 01 April

BALLINALACKEN CASTLE COUNTRY HOUSE & RESTAURANT

COAST ROAD,
DOOLIN,
CO. CLARE

TEL: 065-707 4025 FAX: 065-707 4025

EMAIL: ballinalackencastle@eircom.net
WEB: www.ballinalackencastle.com

HOTEL ★★★ MAP 5 E 9

A romantic peaceful oasis steeped in history and ambience offering the most spectacular views of the Cliffs of Moher, Aran Islands, Atlantic Ocean and Connemara Hills. Built in 1840 as the home of Lord O'Brien. Family members radiate a warm friendly welcome. Award winning chef Frank Sheedy (son-in-law) makes dining here an experience to remember. Peat and log fires add to the cosy atmosphere. Ideal base for exploring Clare. Recommended by Egon Ronay, Michelin, Fodor, Frommer, RAC. Charming Hotels of Ireland.

B&B from €50.00 to €100.00
£39.38 to £78.76

MARY AND DENIS O'CALLAGHAN
PROPRIETORS

American Express
Diners
Mastercard
Visa

✔

12 12

IRISH
HOTELS
FEDERATION

Closed 31 October - 19 April

CULLINAN'S RESTAURANT & GUESTHOUSE

DOOLIN,
CO. CLARE

TEL: 065-707 4183 FAX: 065-707 4239

EMAIL: cullinans@eircom.net
WEB: www.cullinansdoolin.com

GUESTHOUSE ★★★ MAP 5 E 9

Cullinan's Restaurant and Guesthouse, centrally located in the heart of Doolin provides spacious and elegant bedrooms, all en suite with tea/coffee making facilities, direct dial phone, hairdryers and a comfortable TV lounge. Idyllic setting with highly acclaimed restaurant overlooking the Aille River. Imaginative menus are carefully chosen by the chef/owner, specialising in the freshest of locally caught seafood. Natural stone and wood combined gives Cullinan's a cozy, comfortable atmosphere.

B&B from €25.00 to €35.00
£19.69 to £27.56

CAROL & JAMES CULLINAN
OWNERS

Mastercard
Visa

5 5

Closed 23 - 26 December

Room rates are per room per night

DOONMACFELIM HOUSE

DOOLIN,
CO. CLARE

TEL: 065-707 4503 FAX: 065-707 4129

WEB: www.kingsway.ie/doonmacfelim

GUESTHOUSE ★★★ MAP 5 E 9

Doonmacfelim House is a 3*** guesthouse, situated on our farm in the village of Doolin, famous for traditional Irish music. Excellent location for visiting Cliffs of Moher, boat to Aran Islands, visiting prehistoric ruins. Its geology, flora, caves, archaeology and history set it apart as a place of mystery and beauty. All rooms en suite, with hairdryers, direct dial telephone. Shannon Airport & Killimer Car Ferry 70km. Hard tennis court, rackets supplied.

B&B from €25.00 to €32.00
£19.69 to £25.20

MAJELLA & FRANK MOLONEY
OWNERS

Mastercard

Visa

🛏️🍴☎️TC🍴❄️🎣♨️🅿️
8   8

Closed 24 - 28 December

ARDILAUN GUESTHOUSE

GALWAY ROAD,
ENNIS,
CO. CLARE

TEL: 065-682 2311 FAX: 065-684 3989
EMAIL: purcells.ennis@eircom.net
WEB: www.ardilaun.com

GUESTHOUSE ★★★ MAP 6 F 8

Ardilaun is a modern, architect designed 3*** guesthouse overlooking the River Fergus and Ballyallia Lake amenity area. Most rooms enjoy panoramic views of the river and all are superbly decorated with en suite, phone, TV, hairdryer, tea and coffee facilities. Our gymnasium and sauna facility also overlook the river and are available to guests only. Ardilaun is just 2 mins drive to the fabulous new Ennis swimming pool. Situated 20 mins drive from Shannon airport on N18 and is an ideal touring base for Clare, Limerick and Galway.

B&B from €30.00 to €32.50
£23.63 to £25.59

ANNE PURCELL
PROPRIETRESS

Mastercard

Visa

🛏️🍴☎️🖥️TC🍴❄️🛁📷♨️🅿️
10   10
FAX

Closed 23 - 27 December

AUBURN LODGE QUALITY HOTEL

GALWAY ROAD,
ENNIS,
CO. CLARE

TEL: 065-682 1247 FAX: 065-682 1232
EMAIL: stay@irishcourthotels.com
WEB: www.irishcourthotels.com

HOTEL ★★★ MAP 6 F 8

Located in the historic town of Ennis, the 100 bedroom Auburn Lodge Hotel is the ideal base for the Golf or Fishing Holiday. Convenient to Lahinch, Shannon, Dromoland, Woodstock and Ennis. It offers a wide choice of rolling parkland or links courses - with golf to suit everyone. Within a few miles drive are the Cliffs of Moher, Scenic Burren, Ailwee Caves and Bunratty Castle and Folkpark. Enjoy nightly traditional music in Tailor Quigleys Pub and re-live the day's golf. Shannon International Airport 15km.

Member of Irish Court Hotel Group
B&B from €45.00 to €110.00
£35.44 to £86.63

SEAN LYNE
PROPRIETOR

American Express

Diners

Mastercard

Visa

🛏️🍴☎️🖥️TC🍴CM❄️♨️🎵🅿️S
100 100
♿🅰️ald🍴

Closed 25 December

B&B rates are per person sharing per night incl. Breakfast

BANNER LODGE

MARKET STREET,
ENNIS,
CO. CLARE
TEL: 065-682 4224 FAX: 065-682 1670
EMAIL: noelcarrennis@eircom.net
WEB: homepage.eircom.net/~bannerlodge

GUESTHOUSE ★★ MAP 6 F 8

Located in the heart of Ennis Town within easy reach of shops and restaurants. 10 miles from Shannon International Airport and within 30 minutes drive of all county tourist attractions. Downstairs Henry J's Bar provides nightly entertainment. All bedrooms are en suite with TV, phone and tea/coffee facilities. Local attractions include the Aran Islands, the Burren, Cliffs of Moher and Bunratty Castle.

B&B from €28.00 to €32.00
£22.05 to £25.20

NOEL CARR

| Mastercard |
| Visa |

8 8

Closed 23 - 31 December

CILL EOIN HOUSE

KILDYSERT CROSS,
CLARE ROAD, ENNIS,
CO. CLARE
TEL: 065-684 1668 FAX: 065-684 1669
EMAIL: cilleoin@iol.ie
WEB: www.euroka.com/cilleoin

GUESTHOUSE ★★★ MAP 6 F 8

Cill Eoin, named after the nearby 13th century Abbey, is a 3*** guesthouse on the main tourist route to the west coast of Clare, with its unparalleled beauty in the scenery of the desolate Burren and the majestic vistas, that are the Cliffs of Moher. Golf, with a links and three courses nearby, is abundantly available. Horse riding, fishing and many other pastimes are well provided for in the area. Call and see us soon, you will feel at home.

B&B from €30.00 to €35.00
£23.63 to £27.56

PAT & BRIDGET GLYNN LUCEY

| American Express |
| Diners |
| Mastercard |
| Visa |

14 14

IRISH
HOTELS
FEDERATION

Closed 24 December - 08 January

Room rates are per room per night

FOUNTAIN COURT

LAHINCH ROAD,
ENNIS,
CO. CLARE
TEL: 065-682 9845 FAX: 065-684 5030
EMAIL: kyran@fountain-court.com
WEB: www.fountain-court.com

GUESTHOUSE ★★★ MAP 6 F 8

Peaceful rural setting yet only 4 minutes drive to Ennis. Superb bedrooms with king sized beds, TV, tea making facilities, Hi Fi bath and power shower. Family run with delicious breakfasts. Beautiful reception rooms and the personal service of the owners make Fountain Court the ideal base to tour the Burren National Park, Cliffs of Moher and Bunratty Castle and Folk Park. Golf, fishing and horse riding all within easy reach. Shannon Airport 15km. Fax & Internet access from all rooms.

Member of Premier Guesthouses

B&B from €30.00 to €45.00
£23.63 to £35.44

KYRAN & BREED CARR

Mastercard
Visa

☺ Midweek specials from €95.00

🛏 👤 ☎ 🖥 T/AC ✴ U J P S Y alc ▭
12 12

Inet FAX

IRISH HOTELS FEDERATION

Closed 20 December - 07 January

GLENCAR GUESTHOUSE

GALWAY ROAD,
ENNIS,
CO. CLARE
TEL: 065-682 2348 FAX: 065-682 2885
EMAIL: glencar.ennis@eircom.net
WEB: http://glencar.ennis.ie

GUESTHOUSE ★★★ MAP 6 F 8

Glencar Guesthouse is a newly-refurbished 12 bedroomed 3*** accommodation. Situated on the N18 (Galway Road), 1km from Ennis Town and 20m from Auburn Lodge Hotel. Shannon Airport 20 minutes drive. Glencar is an ideal base for golfing, cycling, fishing or walking holidays. Special attractions: Bunratty Castle, Cliffs of Moher, the Burren and the Ailwee Caves all easily accessible. Ennis is the home of traditional Irish music.

B&B from €25.40 to €31.75
£20.01 to £25.01

PETER & LIZ HOULIHAN

Mastercard
Visa

🛏 👤 ☎ 🖥 T C ✴ CM U J P S ▭ Inet
12 12

IRISH HOTELS FEDERATION

Closed 23 December - 01 Febuary

MAGOWNA HOUSE HOTEL

INCH,
KILMALEY, ENNIS,
CO. CLARE
TEL: 065-683 9009 FAX: 065-683 9258
EMAIL: info@magowna.com
WEB: www.magowna.com

HOTEL ★★★ MAP 6 F 8

We are a beautifully located, family managed, country house hotel with extensive gardens and lovely views. Ideal for an active or purely relaxing break. Close to excellent golf courses, angling and walks. (Mid-Clare Way 1.5km) Shannon Airport, Cliffs of Moher, the Burren, Doolin, Bunratty Castle, Killimer Car Ferry to Kerry within easy reach. Conference room (capacity 200). Enjoy hospitality, comfort, good food and a genuine welcome in the heart of County Clare.

Member of Irish Family Hotels

B&B from €42.00 to €48.00
£33.08 to £37.80

GAY MURPHY
PROPRIETOR

American Express
Diners
Mastercard
Visa

☺ Weekend specials from €105.00

🛏 👤 ☎ 🖥 T C CM ✴ U J P 🍴 S 🏴
10 10

alc ▭

IRISH HOTELS FEDERATION

Closed 24 - 26 December

B&B rates are per person sharing per night incl. Breakfast

OLD GROUND HOTEL

O'CONNELL STREET,
ENNIS,
CO. CLARE
TEL: 065-682 8127 FAX: 065-682 8112
EMAIL: oghotel@iol.ie
WEB: www.flynnhotels.com

HOTEL ★★★ MAP 6 F 8

Ivy clad manor house dates to the 18th century. The hotel offers 83 de luxe rooms and superior suites. Our elegant formal dining room is renowned for excellent cuisine. Visit our recently opened Town Hall Café. The hotel is located in the heart of Ennis, 20 minutes drive from Shannon Airport, close to the Cliffs of Moher, the Burren, Bunratty Castle and many superb challenging golf courses. GDS Access LX.

Member of Flynn Hotels

B&B from € 48.00 to € 90.00
£37.80 to £70.88

ALLEN FLYNN, MANAGING DIR
MARY GLEESON, GEN MANAGER

American Express
Diners
Mastercard
Visa

☺ Weekend specials from €107.95

83 83

Closed 24 - 26 December

QUEENS HOTEL

ABBEY STREET,
ENNIS,
CO. CLARE
TEL: 065-682 8963 FAX: 065-682 8628
EMAIL: stay@irishcourthotels.com
WEB: www.irishcourthotels.com

HOTEL ★★★ MAP 6 F 8

The Queen's Town Centre Hotel is an ideal base for touring Bunratty Castle and Folk Park, Cliffs of Moher and the Burren. All bedrooms are en suite, with satellite TV, video, radio, phone, hairdryer, tea/coffee. Overlooking the 13th century Franciscan Abbey from which Ennis takes its origin. Adjoins the famous Cruise's Pub and Restaurant built circa 1658. Renowned for its authentic old world charm, superb home cooked Fayre and traditional music nightly. Shannon International Airport 15km.

Member of Irish Court Hotels

B&B from € 45.00 to € 110.00
£35.00 to £85.00

MAURICE WALSH
GENERAL MANAGER

American Express
Diners
Mastercard
Visa

50 50

Closed 25 December

TEMPLE GATE HOTEL

THE SQUARE,
ENNIS,
CO. CLARE
TEL: 065-682 3300 FAX: 065-682 3322
EMAIL: info@templegatehotel.com
WEB: www.templegatehotel.com

HOTEL ★★★ MAP 6 F 8

Resting on the site of a 19th century convent, the Gothic style combines with luxurious charm in this town house hotel. Sharing the grounds with the Clare Museum and set back from the centre of historic, yet progressive, Information Age town of Ennis. Exceptional bedrooms, AA Rosettes for JM's Bistro 5 consecutive years and acclaimed bar menu in James Joyce award-winning Preachers Pub. Near Shannon Airport, Bunratty Castle & Lahinch Golf Course.

B&B from € 60.00 to € 105.00
£47.25 to £82.69

VERA & JOHN MADDEN
PROPRIETORS

American Express
Diners
Mastercard
Visa

70 70

Closed 24 - 27 December

Room rates are per room per night

WESTBROOK HOUSE

GALWAY ROAD,
ENNIS,
CO. CLARE

TEL: 065-684 0173 FAX: 065-686 7777
EMAIL: westbrook.ennis@eircom.net
WEB: www.westbrookhouse.net

GUESTHOUSE ★★★ MAP 6 F 8

Westbrook House is a recently built luxury Guesthouse in Ennis. All rooms are fitted to exceptionally high standards. Within walking distance of the centre of historic Ennis, with its friendly traditional pubs and fantastic shopping. Ideal base for golfing holidays, special discounts with local golf courses. A short drive to the majestic Cliffs of Moher, the Burren or Bunratty Castle and Folk Park. Only 15 minutes from Shannon Airport.

B&B from €32.00 to €40.00
£25.20 to £31.50

SHEELAGH & DOMHNALL LYNCH
PROPRIETORS

Mastercard

Visa

10 10

Closed 23 - 26 December

WOODSTOCK HOTEL

SHANAWAY ROAD,
ENNIS (NEAR SHANNON),
CO. CLARE

TEL: 065-684 6600 FAX: 065-684 6611
EMAIL: info@woodstockhotel.com
WEB: www.woodstockhotel.com

HOTEL ★★★★ MAP 6 F 8

Woodstock Hotel is an exclusive property in a magnificent setting. The hotel offers 67 luxury bedrooms complete with Neutrogena® toiletries. Conference facilities for up to 200 and banqueting for up to 200 also. Contemporary dishes and a relaxing drink can be enjoyed in Spikes Brasserie & Bar. Facilities include 18 hole golf course, health and fitness spa - with swimming pool, gym, jacuzzi, sauna and steam room. Sister property of Hibernian Hotel, Dublin and McCausland Hotel, Belfast. GDS Access LX. UK Toll free: 00 800 525 48000.

Member of Small Luxury Hotels of the World
B&B from €64.76 to €136.50
£51.00 to £107.50

SIOBHAN MAHER
GENERAL MANAGER

American Express

Diners

Mastercard

Visa

Weekend specials from €168.88

67 67

Closed 24 - 26 December

FALLS HOTEL

ENNISTYMON,
CO. CLARE

TEL: 065-707 1004 FAX: 065-707 1367
EMAIL: falls@iol.ie
WEB: www.fallshotel.net

HOTEL ★★★ MAP 5 E 9

A superior 3*** hotel, its manor entrance gives a welcoming warmth leading to 130 spacious en suite bedrooms. The grounds extend to 50 acres of gardens, woodland and glen with river walks and woodland pathways which offer a haven of peace and tranquillity. An ideal base to explore the Burren, Cliffs of Moher, Ailwee Caves. For the sportsman there is the world famous Lahinch Golf Club close by.

B&B from €48.00 to €60.00
£37.80 to £47.25

DAN & EILEEN McCARTHY
PROPRIETORS

American Express

Diners

Mastercard

Visa

Weekend specials from €100.00

130 130

Open All Year

B&B rates are per person sharing per night incl. Breakfast

GROVEMOUNT HOUSE

LAHINCH ROAD,
ENNISTYMON,
CO. CLARE
TEL: 065-707 1431 FAX: 065-707 1823
EMAIL: grovmnt@gofree.indigo.ie

GUESTHOUSE ★★★ MAP 5 E 9

Grovemount House is a family run Guesthouse situated on the outskirts of Ennistymon town. From here you can access with ease the renowned Cliffs of Moher and the spectacular and unique Burren. Just 5mins drive away is Lahinch championship golf links and blue flag beach. Whatever is your pleasure: fishing, golfing, sightseeing, horse-riding or the best Traditional Music, enjoy and then return to luxurious tranquility in Grovemount House.

Member of Premier Guesthouses

B&B from €26.00 to €32.00
£20.48 to £25.20

SHEILA LINNANE
OWNER

Mastercard
Visa

☺ Midweek specials from €65.00

🛏🔥☎📇Ⓣ🅐🅒➡CM✳♨♪🅿🆂
8 8

IRISH HOTELS FEDERATION

Closed 29 October - 30 April

HALPIN'S TOWNHOUSE HOTEL

ERIN STREET,
KILKEE,
CO. CLARE
TEL: 065-905 6032 FAX: 065-905 6317
EMAIL: halpins@iol.ie
WEB: www.halpinsprivatehotels.com

HOTEL ★★★ MAP 5 D 7

Highly acclaimed 3*** town house hotel. Combination of old world charm, fine food, vintage wines & modern comforts - overlooking old Victorian Kilkee, near Shannon Airport & Killimer car ferry. Ideal base for touring - Cliffs of Moher, Bunratty, the Burren & Loop drive. Nearby golf courses- Lahinch, Doonbeg & Ballybunion. Accolades- RAC, AA, Times, Best Loved Hotels, Johansens. Sister property of Aberdeen Lodge and Merrion Hall. USA toll free 1800 617 3178. UK free phone 0800 096 4748.

Member of Green Book of Ireland

B&B from €35.00 to €60.00
£27.56 to £47.25

PAT HALPIN
PROPRIETOR

American Express
Diners
Mastercard
Visa

☺ Midweek specials from €115.00

🛏🔥☎📇Ⓣ🅒➡CM✳♨♪🅿🆂🅐
12 12
🅐🅒

IRISH HOTELS FEDERATION

Closed 15 November - 15 March

KILKEE BAY HOTEL

KILRUSH ROAD,
KILKEE,
CO. CLARE
TEL: 065-906 0060 FAX: 065-906 0062
EMAIL: info@kilkee-bay.com
WEB: www.kilkee-bay.com

HOTEL ★★★ MAP 5 D 7

A superb location - 3 minutes walk from Kilkee's renowned Blue Flag beach and town centre. This modern hotel has 41 spacious en suite bedrooms with direct dial phone, tea/coffee facilities and TV. On site tennis court, multiplex cinema, nite club, bar and seafood bistro. The perfect base for touring the Cliffs of Moher, Burren and Ailwee Caves. Shannon Airport/Limerick City within an hour's drive. Reduced rates at local dolphin watching, golf, diving centre, thalassotherapy, pony trekking and waterworld.

B&B from €31.74 to €50.79
£25.00 to £40.00

TONY LYNCH
GENERAL MANAGER

American Express
Mastercard
Visa

☺ Weekend specials from €95.23

🛏🔥☎📇Ⓣ🅐🅢🅒➡CMCS♨🔍
41 41
♨♪🎵🅿🆂🅐🅐🅒

IRISH HOTELS FEDERATION

Closed 03 January - 10 March

Room rates are per room per night

STRAND GUEST HOUSE

THE STRAND LINE,
KILKEE,
CO. CLARE

TEL: 065-905 6177 FAX: 065-905 6177
EMAIL: thestrandkilkee@eircom.net
WEB: www.clareguesthouse.com

GUESTHOUSE ★★★ MAP 5 O 7

Situated on the seafront in Kilkee, one of the most westerly seaside resorts in Europe. Kilkee is built around a 1.5km beach, considered one of the best and safest bathing places in the west with breathtaking coastal walks. The Strand makes an ideal touring base - visit the Burren, Cliffs of Moher, Ailwee Caves. For golf enthusiasts there is a local 18 hole course, Kilrush 13km, Lahinch 42km or Ballybunion 40km (via car ferry). Restaurant fully licenced, specialises in local seafood.

B&B from €30.00 to €45.00
£23.63 to £35.44

JOHNNY & CAROLINE REDMOND

Mastercard
Visa

6 6

Open All Year

THOMOND GUESTHOUSE & KILKEE THALASSOTHERAPY CENTRE

GRATTAN STREET,
KILKEE,
CO. CLARE

TEL: 065-905 6742 FAX: 065-905 6762
EMAIL: mulcahype@eircom.net
WEB: www.kilkeethalasso.com

GUESTHOUSE ★★★ MAP 5 D 7

Thomond Guesthouse is a magnificent new premises with 5 en suite rooms coupled with Kilkee Thalassotherapy Centre, offering natural seaweed baths, algae body wraps, beauty salon and other thalassotherapy treatments. Non-smoking. Children over 16 welcome. Ideal get-away for those looking for a totally unique and relaxing break. Situated in beautiful Kilkee with golfing (18), scuba diving, deep sea angling, dolphin watching, swimming, pony trekking and spectacular cliff walks, all within walking distance. Specials available. Private Car Parking.

B&B from €32.00 to €45.00
£25.20 to £35.55

EILEEN MULCAHY
PROPRIETOR

Mastercard
Visa

5 5

Closed 31 January - 28 February

KINCORA HALL HOTEL

KILLALOE,
CO. CLARE

TEL: 061-376000 FAX: 061-376665
EMAIL: kincora@iol.ie

HOTEL ★★★ MAP 6 H 8

Beautifully situated, overlooking our own picturesque Harbour & Yachting Marina on the shores of Lough Derg. This friendly, family run hotel exudes a warmth from the minute you enter and view the blazing open hearth fire, and the welcoming smile of the reception staff, you are assured of a memorable visit. Peaceful, relaxing, luxurious bedrooms with modern day facilities-many with views of Shannon. Enjoy lunch time carvery and candlelight dining. Scenic walks & nature trails, fishing, horseriding, watersports & golf, all within minutes. Conference facilities are available.

B&B from €65.00 to €90.00
£51.19 to £70.88

MATT SHERLOCK
GENERAL MANAGER

American Express
Diners
Mastercard
Visa

Midweek only - 2 B&Bs & 1 Dinner from €140.00

30 30

Closed 25 December

B&B rates are per person sharing per night incl. Breakfast

AILLWEE CAVE

In The West. In The Burren.
Ireland's premier showcave.

Add to the holiday experience by taking a stroll underground with one of our expert guides.

Ballyvaughan, Co. Clare. Tel: (065) 7077067

KILLIMER TARBERT FERRIES

Shannon Ferry Ltd.

When touring Ireland's Shannon Region remember that a 20 minute journey by ferry will take you from Tarbert in County Kerry across the Shannon estuary to Killimer in County Clare, or vice versa, saving you 137km (85 miles) from ferry terminal to terminal. The ferry leaves Killimer every hour on the hour and Tarbert every hour on the half hour.

No reservations are necessary and you buy your ticket onboard.

From Killimer, County Clare		Sailing Times	
Departure on the hour		First	Last
April to September	Weekdays	07.00H	21.00H
	Sundays	09.00H	21.00H
October to March	Weekdays	07.00H	19.00H
	Sundays	10.00H	19.00H

From Tarbert, County Kerry		Sailing Times	
Departure on the half hour		First	Last
April to September	Weekdays	07.30H	21.30H
	Sundays	09.30H	21.30H
October to March	Weekdays	07.30H	19.30H
	Sundays	10.30H	19.30H

Over 30 sailings a day • Sailings everyday of the year except Christmas Day •
The direct route to and from Kerry and Clare • Visitor Centre • Shop • Restaurant • Bridging the Best of Ireland's West

Telephone: 065–905 3124. Facsimile 065-905 3125. Email: enquiries@shannonferries.com Web: shannonferries.com

LAKESIDE HOTEL & LEISURE CENTRE

KILLALOE,
CO. CLARE

TEL: 061-376122 FAX: 061-376431
EMAIL: lakesidehotelkilaloe@eircom.net
WEB: www.lakesidekillaloe.com

HOTEL ★★★ MAP 6 H 8

On the banks of the River Shannon, overlooking Lough Derg, the Lakeside is the ideal base for touring Counties Clare, Limerick and Tipperary. Enjoy our fabulous indoor leisure centre with its 40 metre water-slide, swimming pools, sauna and steam rooms, jacuzzi, gym, snooker and creche rooms. Our 3*** hotel has 46 en suite bedrooms, including 10 superior family suites. Fully licensed restaurant and conference facilities available.

Member of Coast and Country Hotels

B&B from €55.00 to €75.00
£43.32 to £59.07

CHRISTOPHER BYRNES
GENERAL MANAGER

American Express
Diners
Mastercard
Visa

🛏️🍴☎️🖥️T🐎C♿CMCS❄️🎣🖨️
🖥️☕🏊‍♂️♪🅿️S🔋a/c ⌨️

HOTELS

Closed 23 - 26 December

LANTERN HOUSE

OGONNELLOE,
KILLALOE,
CO. CLARE

TEL: 061-923034 FAX: 061-923139
EMAIL: phil@lanternhouse.com
WEB: www.lanternhouse.com

GUESTHOUSE ★★★ MAP 6 H 8

Ideally situated overlooking Lough Derg in a beautiful part of East Clare, 6 miles north of historic Killaloe and 45 minutes drive from Shannon Airport. Our en suite rooms are non-smoking, have semi-orthopaedic beds, direct dial phone. TV and radio, residents' lounge, homely atmosphere and safe car parking. Enjoy the wonderful views from our fully licenced restaurant. Owner chef. Local activities include golf, watersports, fishing, pony trekking and walking.

B&B from €32.00 to €32.00
£25.20 to £25.20

ELIZABETH COPPEN/PHILIP HOGAN
OWNERS

American Express
Mastercard
Visa

🛏️🍴☎️🖥️T❄️♿♪🅿️🔋a/c

Closed 01 November - 03 March

TINARANA HOUSE HOTEL AND HEALTH RESORT

SCARRIFF ROAD,
KILLALOE,
CO. CLARE

TEL: 061-376966 FAX: 061-375369
EMAIL: info@tinaranahouse.com
WEB: www.tinaranahouse.com

HOTEL P MAP 6 H 8

Tinarana House, a majestic Victorian mansion, on the shores of Lough Derg amidst 300 acres of parklands in a stress free zone. A perfect envoirnment for rest and relaxation. What makes a visit to Tinarana special is its association with East Clinic in Killaloe with hydrotherapy and world renowed German, Swiss, Austrian and American treatments supervised by medical doctors and trained personnel. At Tinarana we offer body wraps, massage, reflexology, Reiki, facials and skincare treatments.

B&B from €70.00 to €96.00
£55.12 to £75.60

DEIRDRE DALY
GENERAL MANAGER

American Express
Diners
Mastercard
Visa

🛏️🍴☎️🖥️T❄️🖥️📷♪🅿️S🖐️a/c ⌨️ inet

Closed 24 December - 03 January

B&B rates are per person sharing per night incl. Breakfast

WATERMAN'S LODGE COUNTRY HOUSE HOTEL

BALLINA,
KILLALOE,
CO. CLARE
TEL: 061-376333 FAX: 061-375445
EMAIL: info@watermanslodge.ie
WEB: www.watermanslodge.ie

HOTEL ★★★ MAP 6 H 8

Perched on a hill overlooking the River Shannon, Watermans Lodge Country House Hotel offers with simplicity and taste, the attractions of high ceilings and large comfy beds and open fires. Less that 2 hours from Dublin and Cork it is an ideal venue for business and pleasure (only 15 minutes from Limerick). It boasts one of the finest restaurants in Killaloe - The Courtyard and a relaxing bar - The Derg Lounge. Fishing, golf, shooting all on our doorstep.

Member of C.M.V.
B&B from €69.88 to €95.20
£55.03 to £74.98

JOHN DOWNES
MANAGER

American Express
Mastercard
Visa

☺ W/end specials, subject to availability from €135.00

🔟 10 àlc Inet

HOTELS FEDERATION

Closed 24 - 25 December

CENTRAL GUESTHOUSE

46 HENRY STREET,
KILRUSH,
CO. CLARE
TEL: 065-905 1332 FAX: 065-905 1332
EMAIL: centralguesthouse@eircom.net
WEB: http://kilrushcentral.port5.com

GUESTHOUSE ★★★ MAP 5 E 7

Family run attractive Georgian town house on N67 route (Kilrush-Heritage town). Close to Shannon Airport - Killimer / Tarbert Car Ferry - Cliffs of Moher - the Burren and Loop Head Drive. Major golf courses nearby - Kilrush/Kilkee/Doonbeg/Lahinch/Ballybunion. Attractive woodlands with walled gardens and walks. Marina within walking distance, boat trips to Scattery Island. Also, Dolphin watching on Shannon River. Close to all restaurants and amenities.

Member of Premier Guesthouses of Ireland
B&B from €25.00 to €38.00
£19.69 to £29.93

SEAN & MARY COTTER
PROPRIETORS

Mastercard
Visa

☺ Midweek specials negotiable

6 6

HOTELS FEDERATION

Open All Year

ATLANTIC HOTEL

MAIN STREET,
LAHINCH,
CO. CLARE
TEL: 065-708 1049 FAX: 065-708 1029
EMAIL: atlantichotel@eircom.net

HOTEL ★★★ MAP 5 E 9

The Atlantic Hotel is a family run hotel where comfort and friendliness is our priorty. Intimate dining room offering the very best in local seafood. All rooms are en suite and have direct dial phone, TV, hairdryer and tea/coffee making facilities. 51km from Shannon Airport, 5 minutes from the famous Lahinch championship golf courses, Cliffs of Moher and the Burren. Recently refurbished and upgraded, this charming little hotel has much to offer our special guests. A warm welcom awaits you.

B&B from €48.00 to €54.00
£37.79 to £42.51

ALAN LOGUE
YOUR HOST

Diners
Mastercard
Visa

14 14 àlc

HOTELS FEDERATION

Closed 02 November - 01 March

Room rates are per room per night

DOUGH MOR LODGE

STATION ROAD,
LAHINCH,
CO. CLARE

TEL: 065-708 2063 FAX: 065-707 1384
EMAIL: dough@gofree.indigo.ie

GUESTHOUSE ★★★ MAP 5 E 9

Purpose-built family run guesthouse with residents' lounge and dining room. Private car parking and large garden. You can see Lahinch's famous golflinks from the house. Tee times can be booked and arranged for guests. This is an ideal location for golfing, touring the Burren or visiting the Cliffs of Moher. The beach is within 5 mins walk. Lahinch Sea World has a fine heated indoor swimming pool. The ideal place to unwind and enjoy your holiday.

B&B from €30.00 to €40.00
£23.63 to £31.50

JIM FOLEY

Mastercard
Visa

🏨 ⟨ ☎ ▯ T C 🍴 ❄ ∪ ♪ P 🍽
6 6

Closed 31 October - 31 March

GREENBRIER INN GUESTHOUSE

LAHINCH,
CO. CLARE

TEL: 065-708 1242 FAX: 065-708 1247
EMAIL: gbrier@indigo.ie
WEB: www.greenbrierinn.com

GUESTHOUSE ★★★ MAP 5 E 9

Luxurious 3*** guesthouse, overlooking Lahinch Golf Links and the Atlantic Ocean. Situated 300 yards from Lahinch Village with its excellent restaurants, pubs and shops. All rooms are en suite with antique style pine furnishings, pressurised showers, orthopaedic beds, DD phones, multi-channel TV, tea/coffee making facilities. An excellent base from which to visit the Cliffs of Moher, play the famous Lahinch Golf Links or the spectacular Greg Norman designed Doonbeg Golf Links 18 miles away. "Come & enjoy our home while away from your own".

Member of Premier Guesthouses of Ireland

B&B from €32.00 to €70.00
£25.20 to £55.13

MARGARET & VICTOR MULCAHY
PROPRIETORS

Mastercard
Visa

🏨 ⟨ ☎ ▯ T C 🍴 ❄ ∪ ♪ P S 🛏
14 14

IRISH HOTELS FEDERATION

Closed 08 January - 07 March

MOY HOUSE

LAHINCH,
CO. CLARE

TEL: 065-708 2800 FAX: 065-708 2500
EMAIL: moyhouse@eircom.net
WEB: www.moyhouse.com

GUESTHOUSE ★★★★ MAP 5 E 9

Moy House prevails over the breathtaking seascape of Lahinch Bay, set on 15 acres of grounds, adorned by mature woodland and a picturesque river. Major restoration has transformed this 18th century country house in keeping with present day expectations of superior standards, yet preserving its unique character style and period ambience. Personal attention and the relaxation of a sanctuary, yet minutes away from the many amenities available, are the hallmarks that distinguish us.

Member of Ireland's Blue Book

B&B from €95.00 to €114.50
£74.81 to £90.16

BERNADETTE MERRY
GENERAL MANAGER

American Express
Mastercard
Visa

🏨 ⟨ ☎ ▯ T ❄ ∪ P 🛎 Inet FAX
8 8

IRISH HOTELS FEDERATION

Closed 23 - 27 December

B&B rates are per person sharing per night incl. Breakfast

QUALITY ABERDEEN ARMS HOTEL

LAHINCH,
CO. CLARE

TEL: 065-708 1100 FAX: 065-708 1228
EMAIL: aberdeenarms@eircom.net
WEB: www.aberdeenarms.ie

UNDER REFURBISHMENT - OPENING MARCH 2002

HOTEL ★★★ MAP 5 E 9

A haven for the discerning traveller who will appreciate its relaxed and friendly atmosphere. Mackensies Restaurant offers excellent cuisine. The Aberdeen Grill serves imaginative and tempting fair. Lahinch's Golden Strand and Golf Course are about 5 minutes from the hotel which is just 51.2km from Shannon Airport on the beautiful Clare Coast. Whatever your preference, golf, fishing, horse riding, sightseeing all are within easy reach.

Member of Choice Hotels Ireland

B&B from €31.50 to €69.50
£24.81 to £54.74

BRIAN HEGARTY
GENERAL MANAGER

American Express
Diners
Mastercard
Visa

55 55

Closed 22 - 28 December

SANCTA MARIA HOTEL

LAHINCH,
CO. CLARE

TEL: 065-708 1041 FAX: 065-708 1529
EMAIL: sanctamaria01@eircom.net

HOTEL ★★ MAP 5 E 9

The McInerney Family have welcomed holiday makers to the Sancta Maria for over 40 years. Many of the attractive bedrooms overlook the famous Lahinch Golf Links and golden beach, which are within 100 metres of the hotel. Our restaurant specialises in fresh produce and special emphasis is placed on local seafoods and home baking. The Sancta Maria is the ideal base for touring the Burren or visiting the Cliffs of Moher and Aran Islands.

B&B from €34.28 to €41.90
£27.00 to £33.00

THOMAS MCINERNEY
PROPRIETOR

Mastercard
Visa

Weekend specials from €87.61

24 24

Closed 1 November - 1 March

SHAMROCK INN HOTEL

MAIN STREET,
LAHINCH,
CO. CLARE

TEL: 065-708 1700 FAX: 065-708 1029
EMAIL: atlantichotel@eircom.net

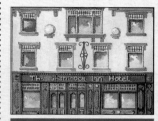

HOTEL ★★ MAP 5 E 9

Situated right in the heart of charming Lahinch. All tastefully decorated rooms have direct dial phone, TV, hairdryer and tea/coffee making facilities. Our restaurant is renowed for its warm and intimate atmosphere offering a choice of excellent cuisine, catering for all tastes. Delicious home cooked bar food is served daily and by night the bar comes to life with the sound of music. Whatever your interest, golf, fishing or horseriding, we can arrange it for you.

B&B from €48.00 to €54.00
£37.79 to £42.51

ALAN LOGUE
YOUR HOST

Diners
Mastercard
Visa

10 10

Closed 24 - 26 December

Room rates are per room per night

LISCANNOR BAY HOTEL

LISCANNOR,
CO. CLARE

TEL: 065-708 6000 FAX: 065-708 1713
EMAIL: info@liscannorbayhotel.com
WEB: www.liscannorbayhotel.com

HOTEL ★★★ MAP 5 E 9

The Liscannor Bay Hotel is situated in the picturesque village of Liscannor, nestling between the rugged Burren, the Cliffs of Moher and Lahinch. The hotel offers panoramic views of the Atlantic Ocean. The elegant bedrooms are an invitation to relax and unwind. Fresh fish from the bay, succulent "Burren" lamb and locally grown organic vegetables are combined by our award winning chefs to create a memorable dining experience. Lahinch 18-hole golf course is 1km. 25m leisure complex is 3km away.

B&B from €35.00 to €100.00
£27.56 to £78.76

BRIAN J O'HIGGINS

American Express
Diners
Mastercard
Visa

Weekend specials from €99.00

49 49

Closed 01 November - 15 March

CARRIGANN HOTEL

LISDOONVARNA,
CO. CLARE

TEL: 065-707 4036 FAX: 065-707 4567
EMAIL: carrigannhotel@eircom.net
WEB: www.gateway-to-the-burren.com

HOTEL ★★★ MAP 5 E 9

Quiet, friendly and relaxing family run hotel, set in its own landscaped grounds, just two minutes from village centre. Our restaurant, with views of the gardens, is the place to relax and enjoy fresh local produce expertly cooked and served. Perfect base for touring the Burren, Clare, Galway, Limerick. Burren walking holiday specialists - own maps/notes. One hour Shannon Airport. Ground floor rooms. Private parking.

Member of Logis of Ireland
B&B from €39.00 to €50.00
£30.71 to £39.38

MARY & GERARD HOWARD
PROPRIETORS

Mastercard
Visa

20 20

Closed 01 November - 28 February

KINCORA HOUSE AND GALLERY RESTAURANT

LISDOONVARNA,
CO. CLARE

TEL: 065-707 4300 FAX: 065-707 4490
EMAIL: kincorahotel@eircom.net
WEB: www.kincora-hotel.com

GUESTHOUSE ★★★ MAP 5 E 9

Relax in peace and tranquillity in our award winning Country Inn, where the Drennan Family offers a warm welcome to our guests. A landmark building since 1860, the house exudes charm, character and a lovely ambience. Enjoy fine food and fine art in our Gallery Restaurant, which is set in beautiful gardens. Relax in our old atmospheric pub with open turf fires. Ideal base, for the Burren, near the Cliffs of Moher and Lahinch Golf Course. Painting holidays a speciality. AA ◆◆◆◆ RAC ◆◆◆◆.

Member of Les Routiers Ireland
B&B from €35.00 to €57.00
£27.56 to £44.89

DOREEN & DIARMUID DRENNAN
PROPRIETORS

Mastercard
Visa

14 14

Closed 31 October - 01 March

B&B rates are per person sharing per night incl. Breakfast

RATHBAUN HOTEL

LISDOONVARNA,
CO. CLARE

TEL: 065-707 4009 FAX: 065-707 4009
EMAIL: rathbaunhotel@eircom.net
WEB: www.rathbaunhotel.com

HOTEL ★★ MAP 5 E 9

Rathbaun Hotel on the main street in the centre of Lisdoonvarna is a unique hotel for special guests. Quality accommodation, excellent food, genuinely friendly, efficient and personal service and brilliant value for money are the hallmarks of our hotel. We are also renowned for our bar music and unusual gift shop. We offer maps and helpful information on the Burren area to all our guests. Cead mile failte.

B&B from €23.00 to €38.00
£18.11 to £29.93

JOHN CONNOLLY
OWNER

Mastercard

Visa

🙂 Midweek specials from €68.00

12 12

Closed 08 October - 30 April

SHEEDY'S COUNTRY HOUSE HOTEL

LISDOONVARNA,
CO. CLARE

TEL: 065-707 4026 FAX: 065-707 4555
EMAIL: enquiries@sheedyscountryhouse.com
WEB: www.sheedyscountryhouse.com

HOTEL ★★★ MAP 5 E 9

Sheedys Country House offers a wonderfully idyllic escape, award winning cuisine and an unrivalled location on the edge of the Burren. Each of the 11 beautifully appointed guest rooms and suites have been individually designed with comfort in mind. Our restaurant is recognised very favourably in "The Good Food Guide" and holds 2 AA Rosettes. Recommended by the New York Times. Close to Doolin, Lahinch and 1 hour from Shannon.

Member of Irish Country Hotels
B&B from €50.80 to €83.00
£40.01 to £65.37

JOHN AND MARTINA SHEEDY

Mastercard

Visa

11 11

Closed 10 October - 01 April

BAY VIEW GUESTHOUSE

SPANISH POINT,
MILTOWN MALBAY,
CO. CLARE

TEL: 065-708 4006

GUESTHOUSE ★★★ MAP 5 E 8

A family run guesthouse overlooking the Atlantic Ocean. All rooms en suite with TV, DD phone, hair dryer and tea/coffee facilities. Also, guest private lounge. Nearby beaches, angling, golf, watersports, pubs and restaurants. Ideal for touring the Burren, Cliffs of Moher, etc. Private car park and walk to rocky shore.

B&B from €25.39 to €29.20
£20.00 to £23.00

ANN LAHIFF
PROPRIETOR

8 8

Closed 20 - 28 December

Room rates are per room per night

BELLBRIDGE HOUSE HOTEL

SPANISH POINT,
MILTOWN MALBAY,
CO. CLARE

TEL: 065-708 4038 FAX: 065-708 4830

EMAIL: bellbridge@eircom.net
WEB: www.westireland.com/bellbridge

HOTEL ★★★ MAP 5 E 8

Situated on the West Clare Coastline, this new hotel offers excellent accommodation and cuisine. Adjacent to Spanish Point Golf Course, sandy beaches, horse riding, fishing, tennis and water sports. Ideal base for touring the Burren, Cliffs of Moher, Aillwee Caves, Bunratty Castle and Folk Park. A family run hotel with friendly and efficient staff whose aim is to make your stay enjoyable and memorable. All rooms have hairdryer, tea/coffee making facilities, DD phone and colour TV. World famous Lahinch and Doonbeg Golf Courses are within a 10 min drive.

B&B from €38.00 to €51.00
£29.93 to £40.17

DEREK LOGUE
PROPRIETOR

American Express
Mastercard
Visa

59 59

Open All Year

BURKES ARMADA HOTEL

SPANISH POINT,
MILTOWN MALBAY,
CO. CLARE

TEL: 065-708 4110 FAX: 065-708 4632

EMAIL: info@burkesarmadahotel.com
WEB: www.burkesarmadahotel.com

HOTEL ★★★ MAP 5 E 8

The redeveloped Burkes Armada Hotel commands a superb oceanfront setting in the beautiful seaside resort of Spanish Point. All rooms are furnished to a very high standard with suites and superior rooms available. The Cape Restaurant offers exceptional cuisine under the attention of an award winning cullinary team, in contemporary modern surroundings with private bar area. Hotel also offers private garden area, fitness room, reading room, with holiday packages available. Also extensive conference and banqueting facilities.

Member of MinOtel Ireland Hotel Group
B&B from €30.00 to €65.00
£23.63 to £51.19

JOHN J.BURKE
GENERAL MANAGER

Mastercard
Visa

61 61

Open All Year

MOUNTSHANNON HOTEL

MOUNTSHANNON,
CO. CLARE

TEL: 061-927162 FAX: 061-927272

EMAIL: info@mountshannon-hotel.ie

HOTEL ★★ MAP 6 H 9

The Mountshannon Hotel, situated in the rural and peaceful village of Mountshannon, offers you first class accommodation in friendly surroundings. All bedrooms are en suite with direct dial phone, TV, tea/coffee making facilities and hairdryer. Our continental style restaurant, which is known for excellent and reasonably priced cuisine, overlooks our garden and Lough Derg. Private car park. Mountshannon Harbour is four minutes walk away. Fishing, pony trekking and golf are available.

Member of Irish Family Hotels
B&B from €31.74 to €44.44
£25.00 to £35.00

PAULINE AND MICHAEL MADDEN
DIRECTOR/OWNER

American Express
Mastercard
Visa

14 14

Closed 25 December

B&B rates are per person sharing per night incl. Breakfast

DROMOLAND CASTLE

NEWMARKET-ON-FERGUS,
CO. CLARE

TEL: 061-368144 FAX: 061-363355
EMAIL: sales@dromoland.ie
WEB: www.dromoland.ie

HOTEL ★★★★★ MAP 6 G 8

Located 13km from Shannon Airport. Stately halls, elegant public areas & beautifully furnished guest rooms are steeped in a timeless atmosphere that is unique to Dromoland. The international reputation for excellence is reflected in the award-winning cuisine in the castle's Earl of Thomond & The Fig Tree Restaurant in the Dromoland Golf & Country Club. A meticulously maintained 18-hole golf course, fishing, horse-riding, clay shooting, health & beauty clinic & much more.

Member of Preferred Hotels & Resorts WW

Room Rate from €194.00 to €469.00
£152.79 to £369.37

MARK NOLAN
GENERAL MANAGER

American Express
Diners
Mastercard
Visa

100 100

Open All Year

GOLF VIEW

LATOON, QUIN ROAD,
NEWMARKET-ON-FERGUS,
CO. CLARE

TEL: 061-368095 FAX: 065-682 8624
EMAIL: mhogangolfviewbandb@eircom.net
WEB: www.clarelive.com/golfview

GUESTHOUSE ★★★ MAP 6 G 8

New purpose built family run 3*** guesthouse, overlooking Dromoland Castle and Clare Inn Golf Course, one hundred metres off N18 on Quin Road at the entrance to the Clare Inn Hotel. Non smoking en suite rooms on the ground floor with phone, multi-channel TV and hair dryers. Local tourist attractions include Bunratty and Knappogue Castles, many 18 hole golf courses and horse riding schools. Castle banquets can be arranged. Shannon Airport 10 minutes. Private car park.

B&B from €32.00 to €40.00
£25.20 to £31.50

MAUREEN HOGAN
PROPRIETOR

Mastercard
Visa

6 6

Closed 20 - 28 December

HUNTERS LODGE

THE SQUARE,
NEWMARKET-ON-FERGUS,
CO. CLARE

TEL: 061-368577 FAX: 061-368057

GUESTHOUSE ★★★ MAP 6 G 8

Ideally situated for visitors arriving or departing from Shannon Airport (12km). We offer 6 comfortable bedrooms en suite with telephone and TV. Our olde worlde pub and restaurant specialises in good quality fresh food served in a relaxed atmosphere with a friendly and efficient service. Local tourist attractions include Bunratty Folk Park, castle banquets and many 18 hole golf courses. Ideal stopover for touring Co. Clare or commencing your trip to the west of Ireland.

B&B from €31.75 to €35.00
£25.01 to £27.56

ROBERT & KATHLEEN HEALY
PROPRIETORS

American Express
Diners
Mastercard
Visa

6 6

Open All Year

Room rates are per room per night

OAK WOOD ARMS HOTEL

SHANNON,
CO. CLARE

TEL: 061-361500 FAX: 061-361414
EMAIL: reservations@oakwoodarms.com
WEB: www.oakwoodarms.com

HOTEL ★★★ MAP 6 G 7

Located on the Airport Road, the recently refurbished Oak Wood Arms Hotel is convenient to Bunratty, the Aviation Park, Shannon Free Zone, golf club and town centre. Setting the standard on quality, the Oak Wood Arms has just completed renovations to the award winning "Sophies Lounge", maintaining it's standard of excellence. Experience our superior bedrooms, many air-conditioned, our new private fitness centre and our Chef Aidan McCarthy's excellent menu.

B&B from €55.00 to €100.00
£43.32 to £78.76

VICTOR O'SULLIVAN
MANAGING DIRECTOR

American Express
Diners
Mastercard
Visa

😊 Weekend specials from €95.00

100 100

Closed 24 - 26 December

QUALITY HOTEL SHANNON

BALLYCASEY,
SHANNON,
CO. CLARE

TEL: 061-364588 FAX: 061-364045
EMAIL: sales@qualityshannon.com
WEB: www.choicehotelsireland.ie

HOTEL U MAP 6 G 7

The Quality Hotel Shannon, located 4 miles from Shannon International Airport, opened in June 1999. This hotel has 54 en suite bedrooms, all complete with direct dial phone and multi channel TV. The Old Lodge Bar serves food all day. Carvery Luncheon is also available. Lannigans Restaurant, open until late every evening. Located on the main Limerick Road (N19), this hotel is the perfect place to explore all Ireland has to offer.

B&B from €50.00 to €120.00
£39.38 to £94.49

SEAN GRAHAM
GENERAL MANAGER

American Express
Diners
Mastercard
Visa

54 54

Closed 24 - 25 December

SHANNON GREAT SOUTHERN HOTEL

SHANNON AIRPORT,
SHANNON,
CO. CLARE

TEL: 061-471122 FAX: 061-471982
EMAIL: res@shannon-gsh.ie
WEB: www.greatsouthernhotels.com

HOTEL ★★★ MAP 6 G 7

Shannon Great Southern is a hotel with exceptional style and comfort within walking distance of the terminal building at Shannon Airport. All 115 rooms are en suite with direct dial phone, TV, tea/coffee making facilities, hairdryer and trouser press. Leisure facilities include a gym and steam room. Bookable worldwide through Utell International or central reservations 01-2144800.

Room Rate from €145.00 to €145.00
£114.18 to £114.18

CLODAGH CUSSEN
GENERAL MANAGER

American Express
Diners
Mastercard
Visa

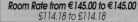

115 115

Closed 24 - 26 December

B&B rates are per person sharing per night incl. Breakfast

LEENS HOTEL

MAIN STREET,
ABBEYFEALE,
CO. LIMERICK
TEL: 068-31121 FAX: 068-32550
EMAIL: leenshotelabbeyfeale@eircom.net

HOTEL ★★ MAP 5 E 6

Leens Hotel is located in the Square, Abbeyfeale in the heart of West Limerick. It has been recently refurbished to the highest standard and is under the personal supervision of Maurice and Olive Sheehan. It has 19 new bedrooms, tastefully finished to a very high standard. There is a carvery lunch served daily and a wide selection of barfood available throughout the day. There is a very warm atmosphere in the Oak Bar and a very intimate restaurant offering the best in local produce.

B&B from €32.00 to €51.00
£25.20 to £40.17

OLIVE AND MAURICE SHEEHAN

American Express
Mastercard
Visa

19 19

Closed 24 - 26 December

ADARE MANOR HOTEL & GOLF RESORT

ADARE,
CO. LIMERICK
TEL: 061-396566 FAX: 061-396124
EMAIL: reservations@adaremanor.com
WEB: www.adaremanor.com

HOTEL ★★★★★ MAP 6 G 7

Located 20 miles from Shannon Airport. Adare Manor Hotel & Golf Resort, set on the banks of the River Maigue, boasts splendour in its luxuriously finished rooms. The Oak Room Restaurant provides haute cuisine laced with Irish charm. Indoor facilities include heated pool, fitness centre, sauna and massage therapy. Outdoor pursuits include fishing, horseriding, clay pigeon shooting and the Robert Trent Jones Senior championship golf course. New clubhouse with state of the art conference centre.

Member of Small Luxury Hotels

Room Rate from €210.00 to €670.00
£165.39 to £527.67

FERGHAL PURCELL
MANAGING DIRECTOR

American Express
Diners
Mastercard
Visa

74 74

Open All Year

CARRABAWN HOUSE

KILLARNEY ROAD (N21),
ADARE,
CO. LIMERICK
TEL: 061-396067 FAX: 061-396925
EMAIL: carrabaw@indigo.ie
WEB: www.carrabawnhouseadare.com

GUESTHOUSE ★★★ MAP 6 G 7

Beside Adare Manor Golf Course, multi recommended Carrabawn Guesthouse is a luxury establishment situated in the picturesque village of Adare, renowned for its Tidy Town awards. The Lohan Family offer you first class accommodation in friendly surroundings and assure you a most memorable stay. Colour TV, direct dial phone, tea/coffee making facilities and hairdryer in all rooms. Only 30 mins Shannon Airport / Bunratty Folk Park. Equestrian centre 1km, golf courses too numerous to mention.

Member of Premier Guesthouses

B&B from €30.00 to €45.00
£23.63 to £35.44

BRIDGET LOHAN
PROPRIETOR

Mastercard
Visa

7 7

Closed 24 - 26 December

Room rates are per room per night

DUNRAVEN ARMS HOTEL

ADARE,
CO. LIMERICK

TEL: 061-396633 FAX: 061-396541
EMAIL: reservations@dunravenhotel.com
WEB: www.dunravenhotel.com

HOTEL ★★★★ MAP 6 G 7

Established in 1792 a 4**** old world hotel surrounded by ornate thatched cottages, in Ireland's prettiest village. Each bedroom, including twelve suites, is beautifully appointed with antique furniture, dressing room and bathroom en suite. Award-winning restaurant, AA Three Red Rosettes. Leisure centre comprised of a 17m pool, steam room and gym studio. Equestrian and golf holidays a speciality. 30 mins from Shannon Airport. GDS Access Code UI Toll Free 1-800-44 UTELL

Member of Manor House Hotels
B&B from €96.02 to €120.00
£75.62 to £94.51

LOUIS MURPHY
PROPRIETOR

American Express
Diners
Mastercard
Visa

76 76

Open All Year

FITZGERALDS WOODLANDS HOUSE HOTEL AND LEISURE CLUB

KNOCKANES,
ADARE,
CO. LIMERICK

TEL: 061-605100 FAX: 061-396073
EMAIL: reception@woodlands-hotel.ie
WEB: www.woodlands-hotel.ie

HOTEL ★★★ MAP 6 G 7

Luxurious 94 bedroom hotel located in the Splendour of Adare, Co. Limerick on its own grounds of 44 acres. Superior and Executive Suites available boasting Jacuzzi baths. Award winning Brennan Room Restaurant, Timmy Mac's Traditional Bar and Bistro, Trad sessions and storytelling. Reva's Hair, Beauty & Relaxation Spa boasting Balneotherapy & Yonka. State of the art Health & Leisure Club. Golf & Pamper Packages a speciality. Excellent Wedding and Conference Facilities.

Member of Village Inn Hotels
B&B from €53.50 to €108.00
£42.13 to £85.06

DICK, MARY & DAVID FITZGERALD
HOSTS

American Express
Diners
Mastercard
Visa

 Weekend specials from €114.00

94 94

Closed 24 - 25 December

CASTLE OAKS HOUSE HOTEL & COUNTRY CLUB

CASTLECONNELL,
CO. LIMERICK

TEL: 061-377666 FAX: 061-377717
EMAIL: info@castle-oaks.com
WEB: www.castle-oaks.com

HOTEL ★★★ MAP 6 H 7

The Castle Oaks House Hotel and its superb country club leisure centre, including indoor pool, are set on a 26 acre estate on the banks of the River Shannon. All our lavishly furnished bedrooms are en suite. Our luxurious suites contain jacuzzis. The Castle Oaks is renowned for its superb cuisine and ambience. We welcome you to experience the warmth and hospitality of our Georgian mansion. Fishing and golfing available locally. Logis of Ireland member. Tel: 01-668 9743.

Member of Logis of Ireland
B&B from €52.50 to €65.00
£41.35 to £51.19

DELPHINE BLANCHET/BRIAN DUNNE
HOSTS

American Express
Diners
Mastercard
Visa

20 20

Closed 24 - 26 December

B&B rates are per person sharing per night incl. Breakfast

ALEXANDRA GUEST HOUSE

5-6 O'CONNELL AVENUE, LIMERICK

TEL: 061-318472 FAX: 061-400433
EMAIL: info@alexandra.iol.ie

GUESTHOUSE ★★   MAP 6 H 7

Elegant Victorian house, 5 minutes walk to the heart of the city centre and located on the Angela's Ashes trail. Many beautifuly architecturally renowed churches nearby. Comfortable spacious rooms, en suite with multi channel TV, direct dial phone. Relaxing guest lounge with tea/coffee facilities provided. Conveniently located for bus and rail stations and 20 minutes drive to Shannon and Bunratty. We can organise a taxi to pick up and drop off at Shannon etc. Multi guide recommendations.

B&B from €31.74 to €38.09
£25.00 to £30.00

AGNES DONOVAN
GENERAL MANAGER

Mastercard

Visa

10   7

Closed 23 December - 06 January

CASTLETROY PARK HOTEL

DUBLIN ROAD, LIMERICK

TEL: 061-335566 FAX: 061-331117
EMAIL: sales@castletroy-park.ie
WEB: www.castletroy-park.ie

HOTEL ★★★★   MAP 6 H 7

Limerick's finest 4★★★★ hotel, the Castletroy Park Hotel, stands on 14 acres of beautifully landscaped gardens overlooking the Clare Hills, 3.2km from Limerick City. Our traditionally styled hotel offers McLaughlin's fine dining restaurant, the Merry Pedlar Irish pub and an outstanding health and fitness club. The 101 rooms and 6 suites have been furnished and equipped to the highest international standards, ideally suited to today's discerning traveller.

B&B from €64.00 to €110.00
£50.40 to £86.63

DARAGH O'NEILL
GENERAL MANAGER

American Express

Diners

Mastercard

Visa

Weekend specials from €166.00

107 107

Open All Year

Visit Limerick's Hunt Museum

The Custom House, Limerick City

The Hunt Museum exhibits one of Ireland's greatest private collections of art and antiquities. The Collection reflects our Celtic past and also includes masterworks by da Vinci, Yeats and Renoir. Donated to the 'people of Ireland' by John and Gertrude Hunt, this generous gift ranks as one of the most outstanding in the nation's history.

Visitors can explore the collection and the lives of the collectors in the elegant 18th Century Custom House which provides an ideal setting for an enjoyable visit. A friendly welcome is assured and guided tours are available.

The museum gift shop showcases a wide range of local and international crafts and gifts. Our riverside restaurant looks out over the majestic Shannon.

The Gallery at the Hunt Museum features a year round programme of events and temporary exhibitions.

Full wheelchair access
Opening Times:
Monday to Saturday: 10.00am to 5.00pm
Sunday: 2.00pm to 5.00pm
The Hunt Museum • The Custom House
Rutland Street • Limerick
Telephone: +353-61-312833 • Facsimile: +353-61-312834
Email: info@huntmuseum.com

Room rates are per room per night

CLIFTON HOUSE GUEST HOUSE

ENNIS ROAD,
LIMERICK

TEL: 061-451166 FAX: 061-451224
EMAIL: cliftonhouse@eircom.net

GUESTHOUSE ★★★ MAP 6 H 7

Set in 1 acre of landscape gardens. All sixteen rooms en suite, with multi-channel TV, trouser press, hair dryers, direct dial telephone. Complimentary tea/coffee available in our spacious TV lounge. We are situated on the main Limerick/ Shannon Road. Within 15 minutes walk of city centre. 22 space car park. AA listed. Friendly welcome awaits you.

B&B from €32.00 to €32.00
£25.20 to £25.20

MICHAEL & MARY POWELL
PROPRIETOR

| Mastercard |
| Visa |

16 16

IRISH HOTELS FEDERATION

Closed 21 December - 02 January

CLONMACKEN HOUSE GUEST HOUSE

CLONMACKEN,
OFF ENNIS ROAD (AT IVANS),
LIMERICK

TEL: 061-327007 FAX: 061-327785
EMAIL: clonmac@indigo.ie
WEB: www.euroka.com/limerick/clonmacken

GUESTHOUSE ★★★ MAP 6 H 7

A purpose built, family run guest house, built to the highest standards, with multi-channel TV, direct dial phone, tea/coffee making facilities and hair dryer in each of its ten en suite superbly decorated bedrooms. Limerick City and King John's Castle are 5 minutes drive, Bunratty and Shannon Airport are situated nearby. Golf outings, coach tours, car hire & Bunratty Banquet can be arranged. Private secure car parking on our own 1 acre site. Home to the Cranberries and Frank McCourt.

Member of Premier Guesthouses
B&B from €32.00 to €32.00
£25.20 to £25.20

BRID AND GERRY MCDONALD
PROPRIETORS

| American Express |
| Diners |
| Mastercard |
| Visa |

10 10

IRISH HOTELS FEDERATION

Closed 21 December - 02 January

CRUISES HOUSE

DENMARK STREET,
LIMERICK

TEL: 061-315320 FAX: 061-316995
EMAIL: cruiseshouse@eircom.net

GUESTHOUSE ★★★ MAP 6 H 7

Limerick's largest guesthouse, situated in the heart of the city centre. Offering luxurious en suite accommodation with direct dial phone, satellite TV, tea/coffee making facilities and hairdryer in each room. Convenient to Limerick's finest restaurants, pubs and shops. Additional facilities include a business meeting room. Reception services - fax, photocoping and bureau de change available.

Member of Premier Guesthouses
B&B from €25.39 to €38.10
£20.00 to £30.01

CAROLE KELLY
MANAGER

| American Express |
| Diners |
| Mastercard |
| Visa |

29 29

Closed 24 December - 02 January

B&B rates are per person sharing per night incl. Breakfast

FORTE TRAVELODGE

COONAGH ROUNDABOUT,
ENNIS ROAD,
LIMERICK

TEL: 1800-709709 FAX: 061-454991

WEB: www.travelodge.co.uk

HOTEL N MAP 6 H 7

This superb modern hotel offers comfortable yet affordable, accommodation. Each room is large enough to sleep up to three adults, a child under 12 and a baby in a cot. Excellent range of facilities, from en suite bathroom to colour TV including Sky Sports and Sky Movies. Unbeatable value for business or leisure. From UK call free: 0800 850950 or from Ireland Freephone 1800 709709.

Room Rate from €59.95 to €69.95
£47.22 to £55.09

AISLING RYAN

American Express
Diners
Mastercard
Visa

🛏️ 🐾 ☎️ 🖥️ T C M P 🍴 🧺 alc

40 40

Open All Year

GLENTWORTH HOTEL

GLENTWORTH STREET,
LIMERICK

TEL: 061-413822 FAX: 061-413073
EMAIL: glentworthhotel@oceanfree.net

HOTEL R MAP 6 H 7

The Glentworth Hotel established in 1878 and situated in the city centre is the perfect location for entertainment & shopping. Our hotel features 42 newly refurbished en suite rooms with multi channel TV, hairdryer, tea/coffee facilities & trouser press. Superb restaurant, coffee shop, lounge bar, banqueting & conference facilities. 5 mins walk from bus/train, 25 mins from Shannon and private lock-up carpark. The Glentworth where people matter - Limerick's friendliest hotel.

Member of UTELL / Robert Reid
B&B from €40.00 to €70.00
£31.50 to £55.13

JEREMIAH FLYNN
DIRECTOR/GENERAL MANAGER

American Express
Diners
Mastercard
Visa

😊 Weekend specials from €110.00

🛏️ 🐾 ☎️ 🖥️ T C 🍴 CM 🛍️ 🖐️ ♪ ♫

42 42

P S 🅿️ alc 🧺 ft Inet FAX

IRISH
HOTELS
FEDERATION

Open All Year

GREENHILLS HOTEL
CONFERENCE/LEISURE

ENNIS ROAD,
LIMERICK

TEL: 061-453033 FAX: 061-453307
EMAIL: info@greenhillsgroup.com
WEB: www.greenhillsgroup.com

HOTEL ★★★ MAP 6 H 7

This hotel is set in 3.5 acres of gardens, is 5 minutes from Limerick City, 15 minutes from Shannon International Airport. Enjoy our popular theme bar the Jockey Club, award winning Bay Leaf Restaurant. Lamb a speciality - hotel's own farm. Also Brasserie Grill and residents' lounge. Super leisure centre, 18m swimming pool. Local amenities include horseriding, bowling and golf. Due in 2002, major refurbishment of hotel, incorporating new conference centre for 600 delegates, 5 syndicate rooms and a new themed restaurant.

B&B from €58.00 to €76.00
£45.68 to £59.85

MARK CARROLL
GENERAL MANAGER

American Express
Diners
Mastercard
Visa

✓ 🍴

😊 Weekend specials from €115.00

🛏️ 🐾 ☎️ 🖥️ T C 🍴 CM 🖐️ 🏊 🛍️ 🖐️

♪ 🎵 🎹 🅿️ alc 🧺 ft

IRISH
HOTELS
FEDERATION

Closed 25 - 26 December

Room rates are per room per night

GRESHAM ARDHU

ENNIS ROAD,
LIMERICK

TEL: 061-453922 FAX: 061-326333
EMAIL: info@gresham-hotels.com
WEB: www.gresham-hotels.com

HOTEL ★★★ MAP 6 H 7

Formely known as The Limerick Ryan Hotel, the original hotel dates back to 1780. Restored to enhance the original architecture, this hotel combines the grace and spaciousness of an earlier age with the comforts of today. 179 en suite bedrooms, 2 suites, the award winning Ardhu Restaurant, gymnasium, superior meeting rooms, Toddy's Bar, Cocktail Bar, business centre and complimentary car parking. 2km from the city and 15 minutes from Shannon Airport. AA, RAC and Egon Ronay recommended.

B&B from €50.80 to €92.07
£40.00 to £72.50

DERMOT FEHILY
GENERAL MANAGER

American Express
Diners
Mastercard
Visa

☺ Weekend specials from €100.33

181 181

HOTELS

Open All Year

HANRATTY'S HOTEL

5 GLENTWORTH STREET,
LIMERICK

TEL: 061-410999 FAX: 061-411077

HOTEL ★★ MAP 6 H 7

Compact, cosy and convenient, our 22 en suite rooms are decorated to a high standard to ensure comfort. Each room has TV, hairdryer and tea/coffee facilities and direct dial phone. Hanrattys, being Limerick's oldest hotel, retains its character in a modern world. Traditional bar with music most nights. City centre location, near all facilities. Overnight lock-up carpark.

Member of Irish Family Hotels
B&B from €32.00 to €41.27
£25.20 to £32.50

JOHN LIKELY
PROPRIETOR

American Express
Diners
Mastercard
Visa

22 22

HOTELS

Closed 24 - 26 December

JURYS INN LIMERICK

LOWER MALLOW STREET,
LIMERICK

TEL: 061-207000 FAX: 061-400966
EMAIL: jurysinnlimerick@jurysdoyle.com
WEB: www.jurysdoyle.com

HOTEL ★★★ MAP 6 H 7

Set in the heart of the city along the banks of the Shannon and just a two-minute stroll from the shopping and cultural centre of Limerick. This very welcoming inn provides an excellent base from which to explore many scenic delights in Co. Limerick and Co. Clare.

Room Rate from €69.00 to €80.00
£54.34 to £63.00

DEREK MCDONAGH
GENERAL MANAGER

American Express
Diners
Mastercard
Visa

151 151

HOTELS

Closed 24 - 26 December

B&B rates are per person sharing per night incl. Breakfast

JURYS LIMERICK HOTEL

ENNIS ROAD,
LIMERICK

TEL: 061-327777 FAX: 061-326400
EMAIL: limerick@jurysdoyle.com
WEB: www.jurysdoyle.com

HOTEL ★★★★ MAP 6 H 7

Set in a green leafy garden on the banks of the mighty Shannon and just a 2-minute walk to the principal shopping and business districts, Jurys Limerick Hotel is at once contemporary and timeless in its appeal. It is also within short driving distance of some of Ireland's most dramatic scenic attractions.

B&B from €51.00 to €113.00
£40.17 to £88.99

AILEEN PHELAN
GENERAL MANAGER

American Express
Diners
Mastercard
Visa

95 95

Closed 24 - 27 December

RAILWAY HOTEL

PARNELL STREET,
LIMERICK

TEL: 061-413653 FAX: 061-419762
EMAIL: sales@railwayhotel.ie
WEB: www.railwayhotel.ie

HOTEL ★★ MAP 6 H 7

Family run hotel, owned and managed by the McEnery/Collins Family, this hotel offers Irish hospitality at its best. Personal attention is a way of life, along with an attractive lounge/bar, comfortable en suite accommodation and good home cooked food, one can't ask for more. Ideally situated, opposite rail/bus station, convenient to city centre, it is the perfect stop for the tourist and businessman alike. All major credit cards accepted.

B&B from €31.74 to €44.44
£25.00 to £35.00

PAT & MICHELE MCENERY
OWNERS/MANAGERS

American Express
Diners
Mastercard
Visa

30 30

Closed 25 - 26 December

ROYAL GEORGE HOTEL

O'CONNELL STREET,
LIMERICK

TEL: 061-414566 FAX: 061-317171
EMAIL: royalgeorgehotel@eircom.net
WEB: www.royalgeorge.com

HOTEL R MAP 6 H 7

This 3*** hotel is ideally suited for business or pleasure situated in the heart of Limerick City. Enjoy a night in our traditional Irish pub of distinction, The Sibin, with nightly entertainment. 15 minutes drive from Shannon International Airport. Local attractions include St. Johns Castle, Bunratty Folk Park, the Hunt Museum, Cliffs of Moher and Adare. Secure lock-up carpark. Niteclub - Thursday, Friday, Saturday, complimentary to all residents.

Room Rate from €50.00 to €90.00
£39.38 to £70.88

PAUL O'SHAUGHNESSY
GENERAL MANAGER

American Express
Diners
Mastercard
Visa

54 54

Closed 24 - 26 December

Room rates are per room per night

SHANNON GROVE GUESTHOUSE

ATHLUNKARD,
CORBALLY ROAD,
LIMERICK

TEL: 061-345756 FAX: 061-343838
EMAIL: noreenmarsh@eircom.net
WEB: www.shannongroveguesthouse.com

GUESTHOUSE ★★★ MAP 6 H 7

Shannon Grove Guesthouse is a charming, family-managed, registered 3*** guesthouse, 5 mins from Limerick City, yet away from the bustle of city noise and traffic. 10 beautifully decorated en suite bedrooms, multi channel TV, direct dial phone and secure car parking. Relaxing guest lounge, with tea/coffee facilities provided. Shannon Grove is the ideal location for your stay in Limerick, being in close proximity to a wide range of leisure activities, university, Shannon Airport, Bunratty and King John's Castle, and Lough Derg. Route R463, from Limerick.

B&B from €35.00 to €45.00
£27.56 to £35.44

NOREEN MARSH
OWNER

Mastercard
Visa

10   10

IRISH HOTELS FEDERATION

Closed 15 December - 06 January

WOODFIELD HOUSE HOTEL

ENNIS ROAD,
LIMERICK

TEL: 061-453022 FAX: 061-326755
EMAIL: woodfieldhotel@eircom.net
WEB: www.woodfieldhousehotel.com

HOTEL ★★★ MAP 6 H 7

Reminiscent of days gone by, the stylish Woodfield House Hotel welcomes you with traditional family hospitality. Over the years it has earned a reputation for quality, service and fine cuisine, creating a memorable experience. A combination of convenient ground floor and upper story en suite rooms offers a high standard of comfort to ensure a relaxed stay. All bedrooms include direct dial phone, multi-channel TV, trouser press and hair dryer.

Member of MinOtel Ireland Hotel Group
B&B from €50.15 to €69.20
£39.50 to £54.50

AUSTIN GIBBONS
PROPRIETOR

American Express
Diners
Mastercard
Visa

26   26

aidt Inet FAX

IRISH HOTELS FEDERATION

Open All Year

COURTENAY LODGE HOTEL

NEWCASTLE WEST,
CO. LIMERICK

TEL: 069-62244 FAX: 069-77184
EMAIL: res@courtenaylodge.iol.ie
WEB: www.courtenaylodgehotel.com

HOTEL ★★★ MAP 2 F 6

A warm welcome awaits you at the Courtenay Lodge Hotel situated on the main Limerick to Killarney Road and only 15 mins from the picturesque village of Adare. The newly-built, tastefully decorated, en suite rooms complete with TV, direct dial phone, power showers, trouser press, tea/coffee facilities, etc. ensure a level of comfort second to none. The ideal base for touring the Shannon and South West region and the perfect location for golfers to enjoy some of the most renowned courses.

B&B from €39.00 to €58.00
£30.71 to £45.68

DECLAN O'GRADY
GENERAL MANAGER

American Express
Diners
Mastercard
Visa

39   39

aidc

IRISH HOTELS FEDERATION

Closed 25 December

B&B rates are per person sharing per night incl. Breakfast

DEVON INN HOTEL

TEMPLEGLANTINE,
NEWCASTLE WEST,
CO. LIMERICK
TEL: 069-84122 FAX: 069-84255
EMAIL: devoninnhotel@eircom.net

HOTEL ★★★ MAP 6 F 6

The newly refurbished Devon Inn Hotel offers a superb base to explore the wonderful attractions of the South West. Situated midway between Limerick City and Killarney in the heart of West Limerick. The hotel features 40 excellent bedrooms, a superb restaurant featuring the best of local produce, a choice of two bars and conference and banqueting for up to 400 guests. Private car park. Just over an hour's drive from Shannon Airport and under an hour to Killarney.

Member of Irish Family Hotels

B&B from €44.44 to €57.13
£35.00 to £44.99

WILLIAM SHEEHAN
MANAGER

American Express
Diners
Mastercard
Visa

Weekend specials from €101.57

40 40

Closed 24 - 26 December

RATHKEALE HOUSE HOTEL

RATHKEALE,
CO. LIMERICK
TEL: 069-63333 FAX: 069-63300
EMAIL: rhh@iol.ie

HOTEL ★★★ MAP 6 G 6

Rathkeale House Hotel, located just off the N21 Limerick to Killarney route and 4 miles west of Ireland's prettiest village, Adare. 26 superior en suite rooms, O'Deas Bistro open each evening 6-9.30pm. Chestnut Tree Bar where carvery lunch is available each day. Conference & banqueting facilities for 300 guests. Golf packages a speciality. Local courses, Adare, Adare Manor, Newcastle West (Ardagh), Charleville. Spacious gardens for your relaxation. A warm welcome awaits you.

B&B from €45.00 to €69.00
£35.44 to £54.34

GERRY O'CONNOR
GENERAL MANAGER

American Express
Diners
Mastercard
Visa

Weekend specials from €114.00

26 26

Closed 25 December

ABBEY COURT HOTEL AND TRINITY LEISURE CLUB

DUBLIN ROAD,
NENAGH,
CO. TIPPERARY
TEL: 067-41111 FAX: 067-41022
EMAIL: abycourt@indigo.ie
WEB: www.abbeycourt.ie

HOTEL ★★★ MAP 6 I 8

If you enjoy fine food with flair and attention to detail, coupled with an Irish welcome, then Abbey Court Hotel is your destination. Located off the main Dublin to Limerick Road (N7), the hotel consists of 82 bedrooms, all tastefully decorated with emphasis on luxury and relaxation. Our state of the art leisure club consists of a unique techno gym and 20m pool. Extensive conference and banqueting facilities available. The perfect balance between traditional comfort and a relaxed contemporary atmosphere. Access and facilities for disabled persons.

B&B from €58.00 to €96.00
£45.68 to £75.61

TOM WALSH
MANAGING DIRECTOR

American Express
Diners
Mastercard
Visa

Weekend specials from €126.00

82 82

Open All Year

Room rates are per room per night

ST. DAVID'S COUNTRY HOUSE

PUCKANE,
NENAGH,
CO. TIPPERARY
TEL: 067-24145 FAX: 067-24388

HOTEL N MAP 6 I 8

The Perfect Irish country house: an elegant Victorian home, nestled on the shores of Lough Derg. The house is restored and refurbished to the highest standards and yet retains the cosy relaxed atmosphere of those days gone by. St. David's is set in 17 acres of mature park and woodland. St. David's offers a warm welcome, deliciously good food served with excellent wines and luxurious accommodation at its best.

Room Rates from € 150.00 to € 230.00
£118.12 to £181.11

BERNHARD KLOTZ
PROPRIETOR

American Express
Mastercard
Visa

10 10

HOTELS
FEDERATION

Closed 01 January - 15 April

GRANT'S HOTEL

CASTLE STREET,
ROSCREA,
CO. TIPPERARY
TEL: 0505-23300 FAX: 0505-23209
EMAIL: grantshotel@eircom.net
WEB: www.grantshotel.com

HOTEL ★★★ MAP 7 J 9

Located on the main link road from Dublin to Kerry, Limerick and Clare (N7). Visit Grant's Hotel, 3*** Hotel in the heart of the heritage town of Roscrea. The hotel features 25 en suite bedrooms pleasantly furbished in warm toned colours. Lunch and evening meals served in Kitty's Tavern daily. The award-winning Lemon Tree Restaurant is the ideal place to relax after a day's golfing, fishing or exploring Ely O'Carroll country. Special golf packages available.

B&B from € 45.00 to € 45.00
£35.44 to £35.44

SHARON GRANT
PROPRIETOR

American Express
Diners
Mastercard
Visa

25 25

HOTELS
FEDERATION

Closed 25 December

RACKET HALL COUNTRY HOUSE HOTEL

DUBLIN ROAD,
ROSCREA,
CO. TIPPERARY
TEL: 0505-21748 FAX: 0505-23701
EMAIL: racketh@iol.ie

HOTEL U MAP 7 J 9

Charming family-run olde world country residence set in the heart of the monastic midlands. Situated on the busy N7 just outside the heritage town of Roscrea, this is the ideal location for the avid golfer, hill walker, fishing enthusiast or those who wish to explore the abundant historic sites in the area. The Slieve Bloom Mountains are also only a stone's throw away. This is a very convenient stopping off point from Dublin to Limerick, Shannon, Clare or Kerry. Award winning Lily Bridges Bar and Willow Tree Restaurant.

B&B from € 37.50 to € 49.50
£29.53 to £38.98

EAMONN CUNNINGHAM
MANAGER

American Express
Mastercard
Visa

Weekend specials including 1 round of golf from €95.00

10 10

HOTELS
FEDERATION

Closed 25 December

B&B rates are per person sharing per night incl. Breakfast

TOWER

CHURCH STREET,
ROSCREA,
CO. TIPPERARY
TEL: 0505-21774 FAX: 0505-22425
EMAIL: thetower@eircom.net

GUESTHOUSE ★★★ MAP 7 J 9

The Tower is a unique 3*** guest house offering the facilities of a fully licensed restaurant and bar with à la carte and dinner menus. The 10 bedrooms are furnished to a very high standard. It is situated in the town centre and golfing, pitch & putt, angling and hill-walking are available nearby. Special golf week-ends available on request. Members of Premier Guest Houses and Automobile Association.

Member of Premier Guesthouses
B&B from €29.00 to €35.50
£22.84 to £27.96

GERARD & BRIDIE COUGHLAN
PROPRIETORS

American Express
Diners
Mastercard
Visa

10 10

IRISH HOTELS FEDERATION

Closed 25 - 26 December

TEMPLEMORE ARMS HOTEL

MAIN STREET,
TEMPLEMORE,
CO. TIPPERARY
TEL: 0504-31423 FAX: 0504-31343
EMAIL: info@templemorearmshotel.com
WEB: www.templemorearmshotel.com

HOTEL ★★ MAP 7 J 8

The Templemore Arms Hotel, located in the shadow of one of Ireland's most prominent landmarks, The Devil's Bit, in the centre of the town of Templemore. Recently rebuilt to match the demands of the most discerning guests, it boasts lounge bars, carvery, restaurant, banqueting suite and conference room, providing first class service. Visit the Templemore Arms Hotel and experience an enjoyable getaway.

B&B from €44.44 to €88.88
£35.00 to £70.00

DAN WARD

Mastercard
Visa

10 10

IRISH HOTELS FEDERATION

Closed 25 December

ANNER HOTEL & LEISURE CENTRE

DUBLIN ROAD,
THURLES,
CO. TIPPERARY
TEL: 0504-21799 FAX: 0504-22111
EMAIL: info@annerhotel.com
WEB: www.annerhotel.com

HOTEL ★★★ MAP 7 J 7

The Anner Hotel is situated on its own private grounds with beautiful landscaped gardens. We offer our guests a warm welcome, excellent food and a friendly service in comfortable surroundings. Each room is spaciously furnished and fully fitted with direct dial phone, cable TV, tea/coffee making facilities, trouser press and hairdryer. Our luxurious health & leisure centre boost an 18m pool, kiddies pool, jacuzzi, sauna and gym. Situated on the outskirts of Thurles, 5 mins walk from town.

B&B from €51.00 to €70.00
£40.17 to £55.13

FRANK MULCAHY

American Express
Diners
Mastercard
Visa

Weekend specials from €95.50

64 64

Open All Year

Room rates are per room per night

HAYES HOTEL

LIBERTY SQUARE,
THURLES,
CO. TIPPERARY

TEL: 0504-22122 FAX: 0504-24516
EMAIL: info@hayeshotel.com
WEB: www.hayeshotel.com

HOTEL ★★ MAP 7 J 7

Hayes Hotel, birthplace of the GAA in 1884, is centrally located in Thurles Town. It prides itself on its reputation for good food, friendly atmosphere and the personal attention extended to all our guests. All rooms are en suite with colour TV, DD phone, tea/coffee making facilities. Weekend entertainment provided for our guests. Use of nearby health and leisure club. Local facilities include golf, horse-riding and fishing. Nearby attractions: Holycross Abbey, Rock of Cashel.

B&B from €45.00 to €50.00
£35.44 to £39.38

GERRY MCGOVERN

American Express
Diners
Mastercard
Visa

Open All Year

INCH HOUSE COUNTRY HOUSE AND RESTAURANT

THURLES,
CO. TIPPERARY

TEL: 0504-51348 FAX: 0504-51754
EMAIL: info@inch-house.com
WEB: www.inch-house.com

GUESTHOUSE ★★★★ MAP 3 J 7

Historic 300 year old manor set in a demesne of 250 acres, with fully licenced award winning restaurant. Relax in peace and tranquillity in front of open log fires. Each room has its own individual style with antique furniture combined with modern comforts for the discerning guests. Recommended in Bridgestone 100 Best in Ireland, the Good Hotel Guide, AA 5◆◆◆◆◆ Golf, fishing, shooting and horse-riding can be arranged.

B&B from €50.00 to €50.00
£39.38 to £39.38

NORA EGAN

American Express
Mastercard
Visa

Closed 23 - 29 December

General Tourist Information

❄

Banking

Banks are normally open from Monday to Friday 10.00 to 16.00. Many Banks stay open until 17.00 on Thursdays. Visitors are advised to change their bank notes at banks and Bureaux de Change to get the best exchange rate. Most credit cards, including all cards carrying the Eurocheque symbol, are accepted in hotels, restaurants, petrol stations and most shops. ATMs located at most banks accept major credit cards.

❄

Medical Treatment

Citizens of the European Community are entitled to free hospital treatment in a public ward and should obtain an E111 form prior to departure. When necessary, this should be presented to the doctor or hospital visited, along with identification.
Visitors from other countries should check with their insurance agent or broker before travelling to establish their entitlement to recover additional medical expenses.

❄

Public Holidays

The following are the public holidays
in the Republic of Ireland (those in Northern Ireland differ slightly). Most companies and shops are closed on these days.

January 1st; March 17th; Friday before Easter; Monday after Easter; First Monday in May, June and August; Last Monday in October; Christmas Day; St. Stephen's Day

B&B rates are per person sharing per night incl. Breakfast

Galway, Mayo and Roscommon

There is a special quality about these three counties in the West of Ireland which is unique in Europe. The welcome is heartwarming, the quality of life, people and landscapes are all there for the visitor to enjoy.

The spectaculury beautiful countryside, the coast that has been etched by the Atlantic, the rambling hills and mountains and the lovely lakes and bays that mirror that special light from the clear skies over the countryside. Each county has its own special attractions and rich in all that is best in Irish folklore, music and song. There is something here for everyone. You will not be disappointed

MAJOR ATTRACTIONS

Galway City has a host of attractions on offer, including Galway Irish Crystal Heritage Centre,Royal Tara China, Lynch's Castle, the Spanish Arch, Nora Barnacle House and the Talbhdhearc – Ireland's only Irish-speaking theatre. In Co. Galway you have Thoor Ballylee, the home of the poet W.B. Yeats, and Coole Park Visitor Centre, former home of Lady Gregory, both located just north of Gort. The Battle of Aughrim Interpretative Centre near Ballinasloe gives a fascinating account of one of the most decisive battles in European history. Other major attractions include Aughnanure Castle in Oughterard, Dan O'Hara's Pre-Famine Farm near Clifden, Leenane Cultural Centre, Kylemore Abbey in Letterfrack, Connemara, Glengowla Mines near Oughterard and Ionad Arann, Aran's Heritage Centre on Inishmore.

Amongst the attractions worth a visit in Co. Mayo are the Ceide Fields in Ballycastle, Foxford Woollen Mills,Turlough Park House, Knock Shrine and Folk Museum, Ballintubber Abbey and the Westport Heritage Centre. Westport Heritage Centre Ballintubber Abbey.

While Roscommon can boast the County Heritage and Genealogical centre in Strokestown, Strokestown Park House, Gardens and Famine Museum, Clonalis House in Castlerea, Douglas Hyde Interpretative Centre in Porthard, King House and Boyle Abbey in Boyle and the magnificent Lough Key Forest Park.

For information and accommodation bookings in Counties Galway, Mayo and Roscommon contact:

Ireland West Tourism,
Aras Fáilte, Forster Street, Galway.
Tel: 00353 91 537700
Fax: 00353 91 537733
Email: info@irelandwest.ie

Tourist Information Office,
James Street, Westport, Co. Mayo.
Tel: 00353 98 25711
Fax: 00353 98 26709
Email: westport@irelandwest.ie

Tourist Information Office,
Boyle, Co. Roscommon.
Tel: 00353 79 62145.

ARD EINNE GUESTHOUSE

INISMOR,
ARAN ISLANDS,
CO. GALWAY
TEL: 099-61126 FAX: 099-61388
EMAIL: ardeinne@eircom.net
WEB: www.galway.net/pages/ardeinne

GUESTHOUSE ★★★ MAP 5 D 10

Ard Einne 3*** guesthouse is situated in an area of unrivalled beauty with sweeping panoramic views of Galway/Clare coastlines and Galway Bay from bedroom windows. The warmest of welcomes await you in this family-run, high quality guesthouse. Conveniently situated. Suitable base for cyclists, walkers and tours. Overlooks own beach. Ideal getaway for those looking for a totally unique, relaxing break. Quality home cooked food. Attractive group/individual rates.

B&B from €32.00 to €32.00
£25.20 to £25.20

KEVIN AND ENDA GILL
PROPRIETORS

Mastercard
Visa

2 nights B&B and 1 Dinner
€77.00pps

14 14

HOTELS FEDERATION

Closed 15 December - 01 February

KILMURVEY HOUSE

KILRONAN,
INISMOR, ARAN ISLANDS,
CO. GALWAY
TEL: 099-61218 FAX: 099-61397
EMAIL: kilmurveyhouse@eircom.net
WEB: www.kilmurveyhouse.com

GUESTHOUSE ★★★ MAP 5 D 10

Kilmurvey House is a 150 year-old country house situated at the foot of Dun Aonghus, beside Dun Aongusa visitor centre. 3 minutes walk from a Blue Flag beach in one of the more peaceful locations on the island. We are the ideal setting for cyclists, walkers, botanists and those who just want to relax. Special group rates available.

B&B from €35.00 to €35.00
£27.56 to £27.56

TREASA JOYCE
PROPRIETOR

Mastercard
Visa

12 12

HOTELS FEDERATION

Closed 31 October - 01 April

OSTAN INIS MEAIN

INIS MEAIN,
OILEAN ARAINN,
CO. GALWAY
TEL: 099-73020
EMAIL: bfaherty@iol.ie
WEB: www.aaranislands.com

HOTEL N MAP 5 E 9

The only hotel on Inis Me-in, where a warm welcome awaits you. Enjoy good traditional bar food and a pint in our hotel bar. During the summer the hotel hosts the best traditional music and craic! With a sea view on one side on a sunny day enjoy our beach and go for a swim or you can do some deep sea diving. Come and relax in beautiful comfortable surroundings with all modern facilities.

B&B from €32.00 to €45.00
£25.20 to £35.44

BERNADETTE FAHERTY

Mastercard
Visa

10 10

Open All Year

B&B rates are per person sharing per night incl. Breakfast

PIER HOUSE GUESTHOUSE

LOWER KILRONAN,
ARAN ISLANDS,
CO. GALWAY
TEL: 099-61417 FAX: 099-61122
EMAIL: pierh@iol.ie

GUESTHOUSE ★★★ MAP 5 D 10

Pier House is perfectly located less than 100m from Kilronan Harbour and Village, within walking distance of sandy beaches, pubs, restaurants and historical remains. This modern house is finished to a very high standard, has a private gym for guest use and many other extra facilities. Its bedrooms are well appointed and have perfect sea and landscape views. If it is comfort and old fashioned warmth and hospitality you expect, then Pier House is the perfect location to enjoy it.

B&B from €35.00 to €55.00
£27.56 to £43.32

MAURA & PADRAIG JOYCE
PROPRIETORS

Mastercard

Visa

12 12

Closed 01 November - 01 March

TIGH FITZ

KILLEANY, KILRONAN,
INISHMORE, ARAN ISLANDS,
CO. GALWAY
TEL: 099-61213 FAX: 099-61386
EMAIL: penny@tighfitz.com
WEB: www.tighfitz.com

GUESTHOUSE ★★★ MAP 5 D 10

Tigh Fitz, a family run guest house, bar, lounge, is in Killeany, Inishmore. Offering luxurious accommodation in this unspoilt area of the Aran Isles. Tigh Fitz is unique in its situation, in its spaciousness and proximity to beaches and areas of archaeological and historical remains. In this area are the tall cliffs of Aran and the magnificent pre-historic forts. Tigh Fitz is 1.6km from the Island capital Kilronan and close to the Aer Arann Airstrip.

B&B from €38.00 to €50.80
£30.00 to £40.00

PENNY MAHON
PROPRIETOR

Mastercard

Visa

11 11

Closed 01 November - 28 December

AANDERS GUESTHOUSE

13 SOCIETY STREET,
BALLINASLOE,
CO. GALWAY
TEL: 0905-44937 FAX: 0905-44937
EMAIL: aandersguesthouse@email.com

GUESTHOUSE N MAP 6 I 11

Superior quality guesthouse decorated in old world Georgian charm, situated in the heart of Ballinasloe. Spacious en suite rooms; power shower, TV, direct dial phone, hairdryer plus the added facilities of the renowned Elle Room Hair & Beauty Salon offering a professional hair & beauty service. Special group rates. Ideally based to enjoy a host of other activities locally including golf, fishing, horse riding, kayaking and scenic walks. Gourmet restaurants and bars just a walk away.

B&B from €31.75 to €44.45
£25.01 to £35.01

MARGARET CAMPBELL
PROPRIETOR

Mastercard

Visa

5 5

Closed 24 December - 02 January

B&B rates are per person sharing per night incl. Breakfast

BALLYNAHINCH CASTLE HOTEL

BALLYNAHINCH,
RECESS, CONNEMARA,
CO. GALWAY
TEL: 095-31006 FAX: 095-31085
EMAIL: bhinch@iol.ie
WEB: www.ballynahinch-castle.com

HOTEL ★★★★ MAP 5 D 11

Once home to the O'Flaherty Chieftains, pirate queen Grace O'Malley, Humanity Dick Martin and Maharajah Ranjitsinji, Ballynahinch is now a 4**** hotel. With casual country elegance overlooking the river and ringed by mountains, Ballynahinch offers an unpretentious service and is an ideal centre from which to tour the West. Log fires and a friendly fisherman's pub complement a restaurant offering the best in fresh game, fish and produce. Ballynahinch, the Jewel in Connemara's Crown. AA 2 rosettes.

Member of Manor House Hotels

B&B from €78.10 to €154.00
£61.50 to £121.26

PATRICK O'FLAHERTY
GENERAL MANAGER

American Express
Diners
Mastercard
Visa

40 40

alc Inet FAX

IRISH HOTELS FEDERATION

Closed Christmas Week & February

SILVERSEAS

CAPPAGH ROAD,
BARNA,
CO. GALWAY
TEL: 091-590575 FAX: 091-590575
EMAIL: silverseas@eircom.net

GUESTHOUSE ★★★ MAP 5 F 10

Luxurious quality residence, located on coast road between Salthill and Barna Village, overlooking Galway Bay and landscaped gardens. AA Selected ♦♦♦, family run guesthouse with high standard of accommodation. All rooms en suite with power showers, TV, clock radio, hairdryer and trouser press. Guest sitting room with tea/coffee making facilities, large private car park. Breakfast menu available. Horse riding, golf, surfing, beach nearby, cycling, nature walks, angling, historical tours, Burren, sea cruise, Connemara and Aran Island trips arranged.

B&B from €27.00 to €38.00
£21.26 to £29.93

GEULAH MCGRATH
PROPRIETOR

Mastercard
Visa

8 8

Open All Year

Room rates are per room per night

CARNA BAY HOTEL

CARNA,
CONNEMARA,
CO. GALWAY
TEL: 095-32255 FAX: 095-32530
EMAIL: carnabay@iol.ie
WEB: www.carnabay.com

HOTEL ★★★ MAP 9 D 11

Are you looking for somewhere special? Allow us to plan your carefree days in the most magical scenery in Ireland. Connemara, unique landscape, flora and fauna, unspoilt beaches, mountain ranges. Beautiful Western Way walking routes. Cycling, bicycles provided free. Our kitchen offers the finest fresh Irish produce. 26 well appointed rooms, most with sea or mountain views. Locally: St. McDara's Island, Connemara National Park, Kylemore Abbey, Aran and Inisbofin Ferry 40 mins drive.

Member of Village Inn Hotels
B&B from €50.00 to €80.00
£39.38 to £63.01

PARAIC & MARY CLOHERTY
PROPRIETORS

American Express
Mastercard
Visa

26 26

Closed 23 -27 December

HOTEL CARRAROE

CARRAROE,
CO. GALWAY

TEL: 091-595116 FAX: 091-595187

HOTEL ★★ MAP 5 D 10

The Hotel Carraroe is a 25 bedroomed en suite family run hotel situated in the heart of the Connemara Gaeltacht. The village of Carraroe itself is renowned for its traditional values and music. Daily boat trips to the Aran Islands are from nearby Rossaveal Harbour. Our local friendly staff will provide information on where to fish, play golf, horse ride or tour beautiful Connemara. Enjoy our new Irish Themed Bar.

B&B from €38.09 to €59.68
£30.00 to £47.00

PAT & EILEEN MURRAY
OWNERS

Mastercard
Visa

25 25

Open All Year

CASHEL HOUSE HOTEL

CASHEL,
CO. GALWAY

TEL: 095-31001 FAX: 095-31077
EMAIL: info@cashel-house-hotel.com
WEB: www.cashel-house-hotel.com

HOTEL ★★★★ MAP 5 D 11

Elegance in a wilderness on the shores of the Atlantic. It is set amidst the most beautiful garden in Ireland. Enjoy long walks, bicycle or horseback rides, and fishing. Later, relax in front of a peat fire in this elegant residence appointed with antique furniture and period paintings. Most guestrooms look onto the gardens and some onto the sea. Dine on bounty from the sea and garden - enjoy vintage wine. Also member of Ireland's Blue Book.

Member of Relais & Châteaux
B&B from €85.00 to €123.75
£66.94 to £97.46

MCEVILLY FAMILY
PROPRIETORS

American Express
Mastercard
Visa

☺ Weekend specials from €178.87

32 32

Closed 10 January - 10 February

B&B rates are per person sharing per night incl. Breakfast

ZETLAND COUNTRY HOUSE HOTEL

CASHEL BAY,
CONNEMARA,
CO. GALWAY
TEL: 095-31111 FAX: 095-31117
EMAIL: zetland@iol.ie
WEB: www.zetland.com

HOTEL ★★★★ MAP 5 D 11

Overlooking Cashel Bay this 19th century manor house is renowned for its peace and commanding views. The bedrooms and superb seafood restaurant overlook the gardens and Cashel Bay. Facilities include tennis court and billiard room and there are many activities, hill walking and golf in the surrounding area. Good Hotel Guide recommended, AA Courtesy of Care Award and Gilbeys Gold Medal Winner. 4**** Manor House Hotel, GDS Access Code, US 1-800-44-UTELL

Member of Manor House Hotels

B&B from €85.00 to €102.00
£66.94 to £80.33

JOHN & MONA PRENDERGAST
PROPRIETORS

American Express
Diners
Mastercard
Visa

☺ Weekend specials from €140.00

🛏 🄵 ☎ 🖵 T C ✳ ↺ 🅿 🄰 🄰🄳 ⬤
19   19

IRISH HOTELS FEDERATION

Closed 01 October - 01 April

OYSTER MANOR HOTEL

CLARENBRIDGE,
CO. GALWAY

TEL: 091-796777 FAX: 091-796770
EMAIL: oystermanor@eircom.net
WEB: www.oystermanorhotel.com

HOTEL ★★★ MAP 6 F 10

Located in the famous oyster village of Clarenbridge the Oyster Manor Hotel was opened in May 1996. The building dates back some 150 years and has been tastefully redecorated in mature grounds. The hotel is family run which adds to its relaxing and friendly atmosphere. The hotel boasts a wide reputation for excellent cuisine in the Pearl Restaurant. Music and craic every weekend in the Leanach Bar. Exclusive conference and banqueting facilities available.

B&B from €45.00 to €100.00
£35.44 to £78.76

NED & JULIANNE FORDE
PROPRIETORS

American Express
Diners
Mastercard
Visa

☺ Weekend specials from €105.00

🛏 🄵 ☎ 🖵 T C ⬇ C M ✳ ↺ 🎵 🄿 S
26   26

🄰🄳 ⬤ Inet

IRISH HOTELS FEDERATION

Closed 24 - 26 December

Royal Tara China
VISITOR CENTRE

Only minutes from
Galway city center

**Open 7 days all year
Five Factory Showrooms
Free Guided Factory Tours
Coffee Shop**

www.royal-tara.com
Email:
visitor@royal-tara.com
PH: 353 91 705602

**Royal Tara China
Tara Hall. Mervue
Galway**

Room rates are per room per night

QUALITY HOTEL CLARINBRIDGE

CLARINBRIDGE,
CO. GALWAY

TEL: 091-796988 FAX: 091-796884
EMAIL: clarincourt@eircom.net
WEB: www.qualityclarinbridge.com

HOTEL U   MAP 6 F 10

Superb Country House Hotel, 10 minutes from Galway City, on Galway/Limerick road, set in splendid woodlands in the famous Oyster village of Clarinbridge. Facilities include 51 luxurious bedrooms, an elegant restaurant offering a creative dining experience & Mollie Greaney's bar providing regular entertainment & an excellent bar food menu. Leisure facilities available complimentary at our sister hotel 5 minutes away. Family rooms available. An ideal choice for both business & pleasure. Golfing, fishing & equestrian facilities nearby.

Member of Choice Hotels Ireland
Room Rate from €65.00 to €149.00
£51.19 to £117.35

RHONA KEARNEY
SALES & MARKETING MANAGER

American Express
Diners
Mastercard
Visa

✓ 🛏

☺ Weekend specials from €99.00

51 51

HOTELS
FEDERATION

Closed 24 - 26 December

ABBEYGLEN CASTLE HOTEL

SKY ROAD,
CLIFDEN,
CO. GALWAY

TEL: 095-22832 FAX: 095-21797
EMAIL: info@abbeyglen.ie
WEB: www.abbeyglen.ie

HOTEL ★★★★   MAP 9 C 12

Abbeyglen Castle Hotel was built in 1832 in the heart of Connemara by John D'Arcy of Clifden Castle. It is romantically set in beautiful gardens with waterfalls and streams, has a panoramic view of Clifden and the bay with a backdrop of the Twelve Bens. Abbeyglen provides a long list of indoor/outdoor facilities, cuisine of international fame, unique qualities of peace, serenity and ambience. Complimentary afternoon tea a speciality. AA 2 rosettes for good food and service. Reservations from USA 011 353 95 22832, from Europe 00 353 95 22832.

Member of Manor House Hotels
B&B from €79.00 to €97.00
£62.22 to £76.39

BRIAN/PAUL HUGHES
MANAGER/PROPRIETOR

American Express
Diners
Mastercard
Visa

✓

38 38

HOTELS
FEDERATION

Closed 06 January - 01 February

ALCOCK AND BROWN HOTEL

CLIFDEN,
CONNEMARA,
CO. GALWAY

TEL: 095-21206 FAX: 095-21842
EMAIL: alcockandbrown@eircom.net
WEB: www.alcockandbrown-hotel.com

HOTEL ★★★   MAP 9 C 12

Alcock and Brown Hotel is family owned and operated. Situated in the centre of Clifden Village, featuring Brownes Restaurant with AA Rosette and 2 RAC ribbons for food and service. Ideal base for touring Connemara. Pursuits to be enjoyed are pony trekking, golfing on Connemara championship links course. Sea angling, guided heritage walks and mountain climbing. Numerous sandy beaches nearby. Member of Best Western Hotels - Central Reservations 01-6766776.

Member of Best Western Hotels
B&B from €48.00 to €62.00
£37.80 to £48.83

DEIRDRE KEOGH
MANAGER

American Express
Diners
Mastercard
Visa

✓

19 19

HOTELS
FEDERATION

Closed 22 - 26 December

B&B rates are per person sharing per night incl. Breakfast

ARDAGH HOTEL & RESTAURANT

**BALLYCONNEELY ROAD,
CLIFDEN,
CO. GALWAY**
TEL: 095-21384 FAX: 095-21314
EMAIL: ardaghhotel@eircom.net
WEB: www.commerce.ie/ardaghhotel

HOTEL ★★★ MAP 9 C 12

A quiet family-run 3*** hotel, 2km from Clifden on Ardbear Bay, AA and RAC recommended. Bedrooms individually decorated with television, telephone and tea/coffee facilities. Award-winning restaurant, 3 AA rosettes & 3 dining seals by RAC, specialises in lobsters, salmon, oysters and Connemara lamb with homegrown vegetables and a wide selection of wines. Local amenities: golf, fishing and beaches. Reservations by post, phone, fax, email and website. Superior suites with bay view available.

Member of Irish Country Hotels

B&B from €66.65 to €90.00
£52.49 to £70.88

STEPHANE & MONIQUE BAUVET
PROPRIETOR/MANAGER/CHEF

American Express
Diners
Mastercard
Visa

☺ Weekend specials from €110.00

17 17

Closed 28 October - 28 March

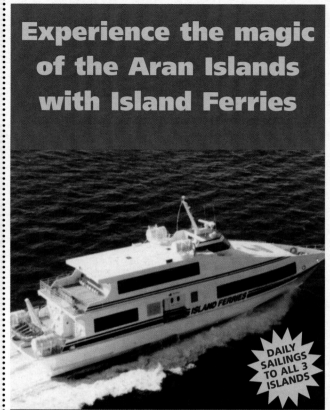

Experience the magic of the Aran Islands with Island Ferries

DAILY SAILINGS TO ALL 3 ISLANDS

All aspects of your trip can be arranged - Accommodation, Meals, Mini-bus Tours, Bicycle Hire, Heritage Centre Visits, etc.

**Excellent individual, family and group rates available.
Special packages available off-season.
Free Travel Pass accepted.
Credit Card Bookings welcome.**

aran
WITH
ISLAND FERRIES

For information / reservations contact us at:
**Tel: 091 568903 / 572273 (after 7pm)
Fax 091 568538 Email: island@iol.ie
Web: www.aranislandferries.com**

Room rates are per room per night

BEN VIEW HOUSE

BRIDGE STREET,
CLIFDEN, CONNEMARA,
CO. GALWAY
TEL: 095-21256 FAX: 095-21226
EMAIL: benviewhouse@ireland.com
WEB: www.connemara.net/benviewhouse

GUESTHOUSE ★★ MAP 9 C 12

Charming mid 19th century town house of immense character. Owned and managed by our family since 1926. We have been extending traditional family hospitality to our guests since then. Recommended by Frommer and Le Petit Fute Guides. Enjoy all the modern comforts and special ambience of this elegant guesthouse, surrounded by antiques and old world atmosphere. Wishing all our guests a pleasant and safe journey.

B&B from €24.13 to €31.74
£19.00 to £25.00

EILEEN MORRIS
PROPRIETOR

American Express
Mastercard
Visa

Midweek specials from €72.37

9   9

HOTELS
FEDERATION

Closed 24 - 26 December

BENBAUN HOUSE

LYDONS,
WESTPORT ROAD, CLIFDEN,
CO. GALWAY
TEL: 095-21462 FAX: 095-21462
EMAIL: benbaunhouse@eircom.net
WEB: www.connemara.net/benbaunhouse

GUESTHOUSE ★★★ MAP 9 C 12

We invite you to enjoy the affordable luxury of Benbaun, set well back from the road in mature, leafy gardens, 2 mins walk from Clifden town centre. Newly refurbished to a very high standard. We offer a variety of en suite rooms with TV, DD phone, hairdryers and a hospitality trolley in the study. Breakfast is special, a feast offering tempting choices. Whether you're sightseeing, fishing, rambling, golfing, Benbaun House is where you'll find a home away from home.

B&B from €25.00 to €35.00
£19.69 to £27.56

DR BRENDAN LYDON
PROPRIETOR

Mastercard
Visa

14   14

S   Inet

HOTELS
FEDERATION

Closed 01 November - 01 April

BUTTERMILK LODGE

WESTPORT ROAD,
CLIFDEN,
CO. GALWAY
TEL: 095-21951 FAX: 095-21953
EMAIL: buttermilk@anu.ie
WEB: www.buttermilklodge.com

GUESTHOUSE ★★★ MAP 9 C 12

A warm friendly home from home, 400m from Clifden Town Centre (5 minutes walk). Our spacious en suite rooms have satellite TV, direct dial phone, radio/alarm clock and hairdryer. Your warm welcome includes tea/coffee and home baking by the turf fire where there is always a cuppa available. Our breakfast options, tasteful décor and many extra touches bring our guests back. Internet access for guests. Irish Tourist Board 3***, AA ◆◆◆◆ and RAC ◆◆◆◆◆.

B&B from €25.00 to €40.00
£19.69 to £31.50

CATHRIONA & PATRICK O'TOOLE
PROPRIETORS/HOSTS

Mastercard
Visa

Midweek specials from €70.00

11   11

HOTELS
FEDERATION

Closed 07 January - 01 February

B&B rates are per person sharing per night incl. Breakfast

BYRNE'S MAL DUA HOUSE

GALWAY ROAD,
CLIFDEN, CONNEMARA,
CO. GALWAY
TEL: 095-21171 FAX: 095-21739
EMAIL: info@maldua.com
WEB: www.maldua.com

GUESTHOUSE ★★★★ MAP 9 C 12

Byrne's Mal Dua House, winner of RAC Little Gem Award for 2001, offers luxury and personalized hospitality in a relaxed, friendly atmosphere. All rooms offer luxury and comfort. Reception rooms and balcony overlooking landscaped gardens, invite you to enjoy our light menu, afternoon tea & select wines. RAC ◆◆◆◆◆. AA ◆◆◆◆◆. Member of Premier Guesthouse & Les Routiers. Karen Brown Guide. Courtesy minibus. Bicycles for rental. Web access. Use of nearby health & leisure centre. Ground floor rooms available. Non smoking.

B&B from €39.00 to €63.00
£30.71 to £49.62

THE BYRNE FAMILY

American Express
Diners
Mastercard
Visa

Any 3 days from €113.00

14 14

Open All Year

CLIFDEN HOUSE

BRIDGE STREET,
CLIFDEN,
CO. GALWAY
TEL: 095-21187 FAX: 095-21701
EMAIL: info@clifdon.com
WEB: www.clifdon.com

HOTEL ★★ MAP 6 F 10

This period town house of almost 200 years offers spacious airy rooms with views over the Twelve Bens. Newly renovated in 2001 it is an ideal base for touring Connemara, fishing and golfing or simply enjoying the delights of Clifden's bars and restaurants which is just a short walk away. We have private car parking. The treasures of Connemara await you. Welcome to Clifden House.

B&B from €32.00 to €50.00
£25.20 to £39.38

MICHAEL PRENDERGAST

American Express
Mastercard
Visa

Midweek specials from €75.00

12 12

Closed 01 November - 31 March

CONNEMARA COUNTRY LODGE

WESTPORT ROAD,
CLIFDEN,
CO. GALWAY
TEL: 095-22122 FAX: 095-21122
EMAIL: connemara@unison.ie
WEB: www.bedandbreakfastgalway.com

GUESTHOUSE ★★ MAP 6 F 10

Delightful Georgian home with spacious bedrooms, 2 mins walk from Clifden, on extensive grounds with large private car park. All bedrooms are en suite with TV, tea/coffee making facilities, telephones and hairdryers. Why not join Mary for an evening of traditional Irish music and song in her large lounge - a truly unique experience - as Mary is a well known performer. Her home and ballad singing have recently been recorded for broadcasting on American TV. French and German spoken.

B&B from €25.39 to €38.09
£20.00 to £30.00

MARY CORBETT
PROPRIETRESS

10 10

Open All Year

DUN RI GUESTHOUSE

HULK STREET,
CLIFDEN,
CO. GALWAY
TEL: 095-21625 FAX: 095-21635
EMAIL: dunri@anu.ie
WEB: www.connemara.net/dun-ri

GUESTHOUSE ★★★ MAP 9 C 12

Centrally located in picturesque Clifden. Dun Ri is newly built and specially designed to offer a high standard of accommodation. The spacious and luxurious bedrooms are all en suite. Facilities include TV, phone, hairdryer and tea/coffee. Private parking is available. Ideal base to enjoy all Connemara has to offer - golf, fishing, walking, sandy beaches, cycling, horse riding, excellent restaurants and pubs.

B&B from €25.00 to €35.00
£19.69 to £27.56

MICHAEL KING
PROPRIETOR

Mastercard

Visa

10 10

Closed 01 November - 01 March

ERRISEASK HOUSE HOTEL & RESTAURANT

BALLYCONNEELY,
CLIFDEN,
CO. GALWAY
TEL: 095-23553 FAX: 095-23639
EMAIL: erriseask@connemara-ireland.com
WEB: www.erriseask.connemara-ireland.com

HOTEL ★★★ MAP 9 C 11

This 3*** hotel is situated on the shores of Mannin Bay with its own private beach. Only 10 minutes drive from Clifden on the R341, ideally situated for exploring the Galway coast, walk along the numerous sandy beaches & bay for hours. An extensive à la carte menu is available in our award winning restaurant or you may enjoy a snack in the bar by the open turf fire. Open to residents and non residents. Local amenities include guided heritage walks, climbing, sea angling, Connemara Link Course, pony trekking, cycling, and deep sea diving.

B&B from €66.04 to €88.90
£52.01 to £70.01

GERALDINE CONNEELY
PROPRIETOR

American Express

Mastercard

Visa

Weekend specials from €127.00

12 12

Closed 01 November - 01 March

FOYLES HOTEL

CLIFDEN,
CONNEMARA,
CO. GALWAY
TEL: 095-21801 FAX: 095-21458
EMAIL: foyles@anu.ie
WEB: www.foyleshotel.com

HOTEL U MAP 9 C 12

Foyles Hotel, formerly Clifden Bay Hotel, is situated on the square in Clifden. Connemara's longest established hotel, it has been owned and managed by the Foyle Family since 1917. Facilities include, direct dial phone, tea/coffee tray, multi-channel colour TV and hair dryers in all bedrooms. There is a pleasant patio garden to the rear of the hotel. Golf, horse riding, deep sea fishing and tennis are all available locally. Logis of Ireland, Central Reservations tel. 01-668 9743.

B&B from €45.00 to €65.00
£35.44 to £51.19

EDDIE FOYLE
PROPRIETOR

American Express

Diners

Mastercard

Visa

Weekend specials from €115.00

28 28

Closed 02 November - 01 April

B&B rates are per person sharing per night incl. Breakfast

JOYCES WATERLOO HOUSE

GALWAY ROAD,
CLIFDEN, CONNEMARA,
CO. GALWAY
TEL: 095-21688 FAX: 095-22044
EMAIL: pkp@joyces-waterloo.com
WEB: www.joyces-waterloo.com

GUESTHOUSE ★★★ MAP 9 C 12

Romantic lodge on edge of Clifden Town (10 mins walk). Relax with a genuine Irish coffee in front of a glowing fire after settling into your spacious 4 poster or king-size en suite room embellished with special touches. South facing superior rooms are furnished with sofas in bay windows to enjoy glorious countryside views. A refreshing relaxed home, tempered with our knowledge of local activities. Superb breakfast menu, and our evening meals are a must. Secure private parking. AA ◆◆◆◆.

Member of Premier Guesthouses of Ireland

B&B from €25.00 to €45.00
£19.69 to £35.44

PATRICIA & P.K. JOYCE
HOSTS

Mastercard

Visa

🛏🐾☎️⬜🇹🇨➤CM✳☂🔅⬜🅿🅂⬇
8 8

Open All Year

O'GRADY'S SUNNYBANK GUESTHOUSE

CHURCH HILL,
CLIFDEN,
CO. GALWAY
TEL: 095-21437 FAX: 095-21976
EMAIL: info@sunnybankhouse.com
WEB: www.sunnybankhouse.com

GUESTHOUSE ★★★★ MAP 9 C 12

Restored 19th Century residence of 4**** rating uniquely situated one hundred metres from town centre. The guesthouse is surrounded by landscaped gardens which contain many interesting features. It is owned and run by the O'Grady Family who have long experience in the restaurant and hospitality industry and are recipients of many awards of excellence. AA ◆◆◆◆◆. Galtee Breakfast Award. Amenities include swimming pool, sauna, tennis court. "Sunnybank, for that something a little special".

Member of Premier Guesthouses

B&B from €40.00 to €57.00
£31.50 to £44.89

SHANE O'GRADY
PROPRIETOR

Mastercard

Visa

🛏🐾☎️⬜🇹✳🔅🪑🔅⬜🅿🅂
8 8

Closed 06 November - 01 April

QUAY HOUSE

BEACH ROAD,
CLIFDEN,
CO. GALWAY
TEL: 095-21369 FAX: 095-21608
EMAIL: thequay@iol.ie
WEB: www.thequayhouse.com

GUESTHOUSE N MAP 9 C 12

The Quay House is Clifden's oldest building, c.1820. It now comprises 14 individually furnished rooms, some with balconies and working fireplaces, and has a wonderful collection of Georgian furniture and family portraits. Its just 7 minutes walk into town. Fishing, golf, pony-trekking, etc. are all nearby. Owned by Julia and Paddy Foyle whose family have been innkeepers in Connemara since 1917. Staying at the Quay House is a completely different experience.

B&B from €57.15 to €82.55
£45.00 to £65.00

JULIA & PADDY FOYLE
OWNERS

Mastercard

Visa

🛏🐾☎️⬜🇹🇨➤CM✳🔅⬜🅿🅂🇾
14 14
☕

Closed 07 November - 12 March

Room rates are per room per night

ROCK GLEN COUNTRY HOUSE HOTEL

CLIFDEN,
CONNEMARA,
CO. GALWAY
TEL: 095-21035 FAX: 095-21737
EMAIL: rockglen@iol.ie
WEB: www.connemara.net/rockglen-hotel

HOTEL ★★★★ MAP 9 C 12

A delightful 4★★★★ Country House Hotel run by the Roche family. It has spectacular views, tasteful décor and open fires. The restaurant with 3 AA Rosettes is well known for its excellent cuisine. The bedrooms are quiet and offer all facilities for your comfort. A short drive to Connemara's 27 hole golf links, horse riding, trekking, fishing & hill walking. Clifden has many art galleries and shops where you can buy local handcrafts, tweeds, linens and gifts. Visit Kylemore Abbey, the Victorian Gardens and National Park. National AA Courtesy and Care award winners 2000.

Member of Manor House Hotels

B&B from € 78.00 to € 96.00
£61.43 to £75.61

JOHN & EVANGELINE ROCHE
PROPRIETORS

American Express
Mastercard
Visa

26   26

Closed 24 November - 15 February

STATION HOUSE HOTEL

CLIFDEN,
CONNEMARA,
CO. GALWAY
TEL: 095-21699 FAX: 095-21667
EMAIL: info@stationhousehotel.com
WEB: www.stationhousehotel.com

HOTEL ★★★ MAP 9 C 12

Modern hotel adjacent to the old station house which has been restored as a pub and restaurant. Rooms are spacious, warm and designed for the modern traveller. Leisure centre with indoor pool and conference facilities for 250. A heritage site complete with museum, old railway buildings, a village of crafts, antique and designer shops and 11 holiday homes complete what is the most exciting resort complex in Ireland. A warm, friendly and relaxed atmosphere awaits you at the Station House.

Member of Sweeney Hotels

B&B from € 50.79 to € 82.53
£40.00 to £65.00

CIAN LANDERS
GENERAL MANAGER

American Express
Diners
Mastercard
Visa

78   78

Closed 24 - 25 December

PASS INN HOTEL

KYLEMORE,
CONNEMARA,
CO. GALWAY
TEL: 095-41141 FAX: 095-41377
EMAIL: passinn@indigo.ie
WEB: www.kylemore-pass-inn-hotel.com

HOTEL ★★ MAP 9 D 12

Family owned and managed where you are assured a warm welcome, comfortable & restful holiday. Beautifully situated on a 4 acre site overlooking mountains and Kylemore Lake. Ideal base for leisure activities including fishing, diving, pony trekking and hiking. In both restaurant & lounge bar each window affords a view of magnificent scenery, serves vegetarian menu & local caught fish a speciality, also when available organic produce. Restaurant (and 1st Floor Bedrooms) Non-Smoking.

B&B from € 44.44 to € 63.49
£35.00 to £50.00

ROSE RIMA
OWNER

American Express
Diners
Mastercard
Visa

11   11

Closed 01 November - 15 March

B&B rates are per person sharing per night incl. Breakfast

ST. CLERANS

CRAUGHWELL,
CO. GALWAY

TEL: 091-846555 FAX: 091-846600
EMAIL: stclerans@iol.ie
WEB: www.merv.com

GUESTHOUSE ★★★★   MAP 6 G 10

The Georgian style house is situated 35km east of Galway City. It was considered by the late owner, film director John Huston, to be 'one of the most beautiful houses in Ireland'. American entertainer and present owner, Merv Griffin, has carefully restored St. Clerans to its original splendour and decorated the house with art treasures from around the world. St. Clerans provides a calm and serene location for true relaxation.

Member of Ireland's Blue Book

B&B from €184.00 to €248.00
£144.89 to £195.28

SEAMUS DOOLEY
GENERAL MANAGER

American Express
Mastercard
Visa

🐎 🐕 ☎ 🖵 T 🖥 CM ✿ U J P 🅿 a/c inet
12   12

IRISH
HOTELS
FEDERATION

Open All Year

CONNEMARA COAST HOTEL

FURBO,
CO. GALWAY

TEL: 091-592108 FAX: 091-592065
EMAIL: sinnott@iol.ie
WEB: www.sinnotthotels.com

HOTEL ★★★★   MAP 6 F 10

Perched on the shores of Galway Bay and just 10 mins from the West's most vibrant city. The Connemara Coast is an ideal base offering many options for your precious leisure time. Experience unspoilt sea and landscapes within sight of the Aran Islands and Connemara magic. Luxurious public areas, ample free secure car parking, an award winning bar and leisure centre provide a unique setting to relax and enjoy Galway at its best.

B&B from €57.50 to €115.00
£45.29 to £90.57

PAUL O'MEARA
GENERAL MANAGER

American Express
Diners
Mastercard
Visa

☺   Weekend specials from €125.00

🐎 🐕 ☎ 🖵 T 🍽 C ✎ CM ✿ � 🏊 ⌂ ♉
112 112
Q U J ♫ P S 🅰 a/c 🔌 🍴 FAX

IRISH
HOTELS
FEDERATION

Open All Year

A STAR OF THE SEA

125 UPPER SALTHILL,
SALTHILL,
GALWAY

TEL: 091-525900 FAX: 091-589563
EMAIL: astarsea@iol.ie
WEB: www.astarofthesea.com

GUESTHOUSE N MAP 6 F 10

Luxury family managed guesthouse overlooking Galway Bay, within walking distance of Galway's medieval city and Salthill's sandy beach. An ideal base for holiday makers and business people, offering a very high standard of accommodation. All rooms have en suite, cable TV, hairdryers, tea/coffee. Some of our rooms have stunning views of the sea with balconies. Convenient to Leisureland, tennis, windsurfing, fishing, horseriding and golf. Safe facilities and carpark available.

B&B from €25.00 to €45.00
£19.69 to £35.44

LORRAINE MCEVADDY
OWNER

American Express
Mastercard
Visa

🐎 🐕 🖵 C P ♿
8   8

Open All Year

Room rates are per room per night

ABBEY HOUSE

113 UPPER NEWCASTLE,
GALWAY

TEL: 091-524394 FAX: 091-528217
EMAIL: johndarby@eircom.net
WEB: www.abbeyhousegalway.com

GUESTHOUSE ★★ MAP 6 F 10

Family run guest house located on
the N59 leading to Connemara.
Convenient to city centre. Rooms are
en suite with cable TV, and direct dial
phones. Private car parking. Close to
golf, fishing, tennis, swimming pool,
horse riding, seaside and city centre.
Excellent location for touring
Connemara, Aran Islands and the
Burren. A warm welcome awaits you
from the Darby family.

B&B from €30.00 to €38.00
£23.63 to £29.93

JOHN DARBY

Mastercard
Visa

🛏️ 👤 ☎️ 🖥️ T A ➘ C M ◡ P
12 12

Closed 23 - 28 December

ADARE GUEST HOUSE

9 FATHER GRIFFIN PLACE,
GALWAY

TEL: 091-582638 FAX: 091-583963
EMAIL: adare@iol.ie
WEB: www.adarebedandbreakfast.com

GUESTHOUSE ★★★ MAP 6 F 10

Adare Guesthouse is a family
managed guesthouse, within 5
minutes of city centre (train/bus).
Refurbished with old time pine
furniture & floors, you can enjoy your
multi choice breakfast in our dining
room overlooking our beautiful patio
area. All bedrooms have en suite,
direct dial phones, cable TV &
hairdryers. Tea/coffee & ironing
facilities are available. 2 new suites
built to a high standard with baths,
direct dial fax phone, trouser
press/iron, tea/coffee/cable TV/radio.
Safe facilities available.

B&B from €31.74 to €48.88
£25.00 to £38.50

GRAINNE & PADRAIC CONROY
PROPRIETORS

American Express
Mastercard
Visa

🛏️ 👤 ☎️ 🖥️ T C ➘ ❄️ P S
11 11

Closed 24 - 27 December

ANNO SANTO HOTEL

THREADNEEDLE ROAD,
SALTHILL,
GALWAY

TEL: 091-523011 FAX: 091-522110
EMAIL: annosant@iol.ie
WEB: www.annosantosalthill.com

HOTEL ★★ MAP 6 F 10

Small family run hotel located in quiet
residential area. Galway's major
tennis/badminton and squash club
lies opposite the hotel. The golf club
is also close by (1km), while Galway
City and beaches are within easy
reach. We are also on a main bus
route. All rooms are en suite, TV,
tea/coffee and direct dial telephone.
Your hosts, the Vaughan Family,
provide high class service in
comfortable bedrooms at budget
prices.

B&B from €33.50 to €56.00
£26.38 to £44.10

GERARD & JOANNA VAUGHAN
PROPRIETORS

American Express
Diners
Mastercard
Visa

🛏️ 👤 ☎️ 🖥️ T C ➘ C M ❄️ J P S 🖥️ a/c
14 14

Closed 20 December - 20 January

B&B rates are per person sharing per night incl. Breakfast

ARDAWN HOUSE

31 COLLEGE ROAD, GALWAY

TEL: 091-568833 FAX: 091-563454
EMAIL: ardawn@iol.ie
WEB: www.galway.net/pages/ardawn-house/

GUESTHOUSE ★★★★ MAP 6 F 10

Ardawn House is a luxurious haven for the discerning visitor to Galway. Located within five minutes walking of city centre, train & bus. Antiques, fresh flowers, silver and china help to make our multi choice home cooked breakfast famous. All bedrooms have en suite, direct dial phones, cable TV & hairdryers. Tea/coffee & ironing facilities are also available. Highly recommended in Guide du Routard, AA and many other guide books.

B&B from €35.00 to €60.00
£27.56 to £47.25

MIKE & BREDA GUILFOYLE
PROPRIETORS

American Express
Mastercard
Visa

6 6

IRISH HOTELS FEDERATION

Closed 22 - 26 December

ARDILAUN HOUSE HOTEL, CONFERENCE CENTRE & LEISURE CLUB

TAYLOR'S HILL, GALWAY

TEL: 091-521433 FAX: 091-521546
EMAIL: ardilaun@iol.ie
WEB: www.ardilaunhousehotel.ie

HOTEL ★★★★ MAP 6 F 10

The Ardilaun is a privately owned 89 bedroomed 4**** hotel, in 5 acres of beautiful grounds. All rooms en suite with *direct dial phone *TV *Trouser press *Tea and coffee making facilities *Hairdryer *Award winning restaurant *New leisure club *Deck level pool *Hydro-spa *Jacuzzi *Sauna *Steamroom *Aerobics *Hi-tech gym *Sun-room therapy suites *Billiard room *Golf *Tennis *Beach & city within 5 minutes drive. Conference centre, 6 Syndiacte rooms - Board room & facilities for 350 persons.

B&B from €65.00 to €110.00
£51.19 to £86.63

T.A. MCCARTHY O'HEA
GENERAL MANAGER

American Express
Diners
Mastercard
Visa

Midweek specials from €180.00

89 89

IRISH HOTELS FEDERATION

Closed 22 - 28 December

ASHFORD MANOR

NO 7 COLLEGE ROAD, GALWAY

TEL: 091-563941 FAX: 091-563941
EMAIL: ashfordmanor@esatclear.ie
WEB: www.galwaynet/pages/ashford

GUESTHOUSE ★★★ MAP 6 F 10

Centrally located in the heart of Galway's City centre, Ashford Manor offers a unique combination of stylish en suite accommodation in a prestigious location at affordable prices. All rooms include multi-channel TV, radio, direct dial phone, professional hairdryer and tea/coffee facilities. Car parking. Credit cards accepted. Featured in holiday programme "Bon Voyage". Beside train and bus station. Ideal base for touring Connemara, The Burren and The Aran Islands.

B&B from €29.00 to €48.00
£22.84 to £37.80

CORINNE MANNION
PROPRIETOR

American Express
Mastercard
Visa

5 5

Open All Year

Room rates are per room per night

BRENNANS YARD HOTEL

LOWER MERCHANTS ROAD,
GALWAY

TEL: 091-568166 FAX: 091-568262
EMAIL: info@brennansyardhotel.com
WEB: www.brennansyardhotel.com

HOTEL ★★★ MAP 6 F 10

A refurbished city centre hotel, Brennans Yard is a charming, intimate hotel with excellent standards of accommodation, food and service. Our en suite bedrooms have been individually designed and are furnished with antique pine furniture. In Terry's Restaurant, you can dine in discreet elegance and choose from a wide range of dishes prepared from the freshest ingredients. The Spanish Bar offers an intimate, warm and lively atmosphere. Bookable worldwide through UTELL International.

B&B from €47.62 to €66.67
£37.50 to £52.50

CONNIE FENNELL
GENERAL MANAGER

American Express
Diners
Mastercard
Visa

🛏️📞💻📠©🅲CM🎵🅿️ⓐⓛⓒ
45 45

HOTELS FEDERATION

Closed 24 - 29 December

CORRIB GREAT SOUTHERN HOTEL

RENMORE,
GALWAY

TEL: 091-755281 FAX: 091-751390
EMAIL: res@corrib-gsh.com
WEB: www.greatsouthernhotels.com

HOTEL ★★★★ MAP 6 F 10

This 4**** hotel overlooks Galway Bay. It has 180 rooms, all en suite with radio, TV, direct dial phone, hairdryer, tea/coffee making facilities and trouser press. Leisure facilities include indoor heated swimming pool, steam room, jacuzzi, gym. Evening entertainment and children's play centre during summer months. Currach Restaurant and O'Malley's Bar. Convention centre accommodates up to 800 delegates. Bookable through central reservations 01-214 4800 or UTELL International.

Room Rate from €210.00 to €240.00
£165.36 to £188.98

MICHEAL CUNNINGHAM
GENERAL MANAGER

American Express
Diners
Mastercard
Visa

😊 Weekend specials from €140.00

🛏️📞💻📠🅣🅐🅢©🅲CM❄️🌐
180 180
🏠🍴🎵🅿️🅢ⓐⓛⓒ📠♿ Inet FAX

HOTELS FEDERATION

Closed 24 - 26 December

CORRIB HAVEN

107 UPPER NEWCASTLE,
GALWAY

TEL: 091-524171 FAX: 091-524171
EMAIL: corribhaven@eircom.net

GUESTHOUSE ★★★ MAP 6 F 10

Corrib Haven's motto is quality hospitality for discerning people. AA Selected ◆◆◆◆. It is new, purpose built, located in Galway City on the N59 leading to Connemara. All rooms en suite, power showers, posture sprung beds, cable TV, video, direct dial phones. Tea/coffee facility, breakfast menu, private parking. Convenient to city centre, good restaurants, nightly entertainment. Ideal for touring Connemara, Aran Islands. Smooth professionalism with personal warmth to our visitors. Non-smoking.

B&B from €25.00 to €40.00
£19.69 to £31.50

FRANK KELLY
OWNER

Mastercard
Visa

🛏️📞💻🅣🅟🅢
9 9

HOTELS FEDERATION

Closed 24 - 27 December

B&B rates are per person sharing per night incl. Breakfast

EYRE SQUARE HOTEL

FORSTER STREET,
OFF EYRE SQUARE,
GALWAY

TEL: 091-569633 FAX: 091-569641

EMAIL: eyresquarehotel@eircom.net
WEB: www.byrne-hotels-ireland.com

HOTEL ★★★ MAP 6 F 10

The Eyre Square Hotel is situated right in the heart of Galway adjacent to both bus and rail stations. The Eyre Square Hotel caters for both the tourist and business person offering a very high standard of accommodation, rooms en suite with direct dial phone, satellite TV and tea/coffee making facilities. Enjoy excellent cuisine in our Red's Bistro or visit the lively Red Square pub. A warm and friendly welcome awaits you at the Eyre Square Hotel.

Member of Byrne Hotel Group

B&B from €44.44 to €101.58
£35.00 to £80.00

JOHN HUGHES
GENERAL MANAGER

American Express
Diners
Mastercard
Visa

😊 Weekend specials from €107.93

52 52

Inet
IRISH HOTELS FEDERATION

Closed 25 - 26 December

FLANNERYS HOTEL

DUBLIN ROAD,
GALWAY

TEL: 091-755111 FAX: 091-753078

EMAIL: flanneryshotel@eircom.net
WEB: www.flanneryshotel.net

HOTEL ★★★ MAP 6 F 10

Flannerys Hotel is long established in Galway as an hotel offering comfort and style within relaxed surroundings. A welcome choice for business traveller or leisure guest. We take pride in ensuring that a special emphasis is placed on guest comfort enhanced by a genuinely caring and efficient service. Recently refurbished, the interior features tasteful decor, excellent restaurant and relaxing cocktail bar. Sample a selection of 136 rooms and suites. Member of Best Western.

Member of Best Western Hotels

B&B from €50.80 to €95.25
£40.01 to £75.02

MARY FLANNERY
PROPRIETOR

American Express
Diners
Mastercard
Visa

136 136

Open All Year

FORSTER COURT HOTEL

FORSTER STREET,
GALWAY

TEL: 091-564111 FAX: 091-539839

EMAIL: sales@forstercourthotel.com
WEB: www.forstercourthotel.com

HOTEL N MAP 6 F 10

This new hotel is excellently located in Galway City centre and is easily accessed by all major approach roads. The hotel is impeccably finished incorporating every comfort for our guests. It comprises 48 stylish en suite guest rooms, all designed to cater for your every need. Enjoy dining in the intimacy of Elwood's Restaurant or why not relax in our extensive bar. The Forster Court Hotel gives you Freedom of the City.

B&B from €50.00 to €120.00
£39.38 to £94.51

JONATHAN MURPHY
GENERAL MANAGER

American Express
Mastercard
Visa

😊 Weekend specials from €125.00

48 48
Inet FAX
IRISH HOTELS FEDERATION

Closed 24 - 26 December

Room rates are per room per night

GALWAY BAY HOTEL, CONFERENCE & LEISURE CENTRE

THE PROMENADE,
SALTHILL,
GALWAY

TEL: 091-520520 FAX: 091-520530
EMAIL: info@galwaybayhotel.net
WEB: www.galwaybayhotel.net

HOTEL ★★★★ MAP 6 F 10

This AA**** Hotel situated on Galway's City Seafront at the Promenade, Salthill, has all the advantages of a city location while being situated on a beautiful beach overlooking the famous Galway Bay. All bedrooms are designed for maximum guest comfort. The hotel has a fully equipped leisure centre and swimming pool. Enjoy dining in The Lobster Pot Restaurant which offers modern style cuisine with strong emphasis on fresh fish and lobster from the lobster tank.

B&B from € 70.00 to € 108.00
£55.13 to £85.06

DAN MURPHY
GENERAL MANAGER

American Express
Diners
Mastercard
Visa

Weekend specials from €100.00

153 153

Open All Year

GALWAY GREAT SOUTHERN HOTEL

EYRE SQUARE,
GALWAY

TEL: 091-564041 FAX: 091-566704
EMAIL: res@galway-gsh.com
WEB: www.greatsouthernhotels.com

HOTEL ★★★★ MAP 6 F 10

A blend of 19th century elegance & modern amenities, Galway Great Southern (built in 1845) overlooks Eyre Square in Galway City. It offers a wide range of facilities including The Oyster Room Restaurant, cocktail bar & O'Flaherty's Pub. Rooftop leisure facilities include indoor heated swimming pool, steamroom, sauna. Accommodation includes well appointed en suite bedrooms plus level 5, a range of luxurious suites. Bookable worldwide through UTELL International or Central Res. 01-214 4800

Room Rate from € 230.00 to € 254.00
£181.11 to £200.00

FERGAL O'CONNELL
GENERAL MANAGER

American Express
Diners
Mastercard
Visa

Weekend specials from €145.00

108 108

Closed 24 - 26 December

GALWAY RYAN HOTEL & LEISURE CENTRE

DUBLIN ROAD,
GALWAY CITY EAST,
GALWAY

TEL: 091-753181 FAX: 091-753187
EMAIL: ryan@indigo.ie
WEB: www.ryan-hotels.com

HOTEL ★★★ MAP 6 F 10

This hotel offers the ultimate in relaxation and leisure facilities. 96 en suite rooms, the air-conditioned Oranmore Room, 2 air-conditioned meeting rooms, Toddy's Bar and a relaxing lobby lounge. A magnificent leisure centre with a 2,500 sq ft. pool incorporating 60ft. swimming lanes, lounger, geyser and toddlers' pools, steam room, jacuzzi, sauna, multi purpose sports hall, aerobics studio, a state of the art gym and floodlit tennis courts. Parking. AA, RAC & Egon Ronay recommended.

B&B from € 66.00 to € 91.00
£51.98 to £71.67

SIOBHAN BURKE
RESIDENT MANAGER

American Express
Diners
Mastercard
Visa

Weekend specials from €140.00

96 96

Open All Year

B&B rates are per person sharing per night incl. Breakfast

GLENLO ABBEY HOTEL

**BUSHYPARK,
GALWAY**

TEL: 091-526666 FAX: 091-527800
EMAIL: info@glenloabbey.ie
WEB: www.glenlo.com

HOTEL ★★★★★ MAP 6 F 10

Glenlo Abbey Hotel - an 18th century country residence, is located on a 138 acre lake side golf estate just 4km from Galway City. Now a Bord Failte rated 5***** hotel, Glenlo Abbey is a haven for all discerning travellers. All 46 rooms have a marbled bathroom, personal safe, direct dial phone, trouser press, cable TV, radio and 24 hour room service. The Pullman Restaurant, two unique Orient Express carriages, offers a totally new dining experience. Other activities include fishing, etc.

Member of Small Luxury Hotels

Room Rate from €145.00 to €310.00
£114.20 to £244.14

PEGGY & JOHN BOURKE
PROPRIETORS

American Express
Diners
Mastercard
Visa

46 46

Open All Year

GLENOAKS HOTEL

**BISHOP O'DONNELL ROAD,
GALWAY**

TEL: 091-589680 FAX: 091-589509
EMAIL: info@glenoakshotel.com
WEB: www.glenoakshotel.com

HOTEL N MAP 6 F 10

A new family run hotel offering the visitor a warm welcome. Located 1.5 miles from Eyre Square and a leisurely walk from the shores of Galway Bay, makes this the ideal location for business or pleasure. All bedrooms are en suite with multi channel TV, direct dial telephone, hairdryer and tea/coffee making facilities

B&B from €45.00 to €90.00
£35.44 to £70.88

HANLEY BROTHERS

American Express
Mastercard
Visa

20 20

Closed 23 - 28 December

HARBOUR HOTEL

**THE HARBOUR,
GALWAY**

TEL: 091-569466 FAX: 091-569455
EMAIL: info@galwayharbourhotel.com
WEB: www.galwayharbourhotel.com

HOTEL N MAP 6 F 10

The Harbour Hotel opened in March 2001. Located in the city centre adjacent to the waterfront area. Offering guests secure, on-site parking. This contemporary style hotel offers 96 superior rooms, bar, restaurant, and meeting rooms for 2-70 people. The Harbour prides itself on outstanding levels of service and quality. AA recommended.

Room Rate from €75.00 to €190.00
£59.07 to £149.64

JOHN LALLY
PROPRIETOR

American Express
Diners
Mastercard
Visa

96 96

Closed 24 - 27 December

Room rates are per room per night

HOTEL SACRE COEUR

LENABOY GARDENS,
SALTHILL,
GALWAY

TEL: 091-523355 FAX: 091-523553

HOTEL ★★ MAP 6 F 10

Hotel Sacre Coeur is a family owned and managed hotel where a Cead Mile Failte awaits you. All of our 40 rooms are en suite, direct dial telephone, with colour TV and tea/coffee making facilities. Within five minutes walk of the hotel we have Salthill's magnificent promenade, tennis club and a wonderful 18 hole golf course. Renowned for its friendly service and excellent food you will enjoy your stay at the Sacre Coeur.

B&B from €41.00 to €48.00
£32.29 to £37.80

SEAN OG DUNLEAVY
MANAGER

Mastercard
Visa

40 40

Closed 22 - 31 December

HOTEL SPANISH ARCH

QUAY STREET,
GALWAY

TEL: 091-569600 FAX: 091-569191
EMAIL: emcdgall@iol.ie
WEB: www.irishholidays.com/sp-index.html

HOTEL ★★★ MAP 6 F 10

Situated in the heart of Galway this is a 20 bedroomed boutique style hotel. Rooms of unsurpassed elegance designed by Easter McDonagh. Victorian bar features original wooden panelled walls from the home of Lilly Langtree, confidante to King Edward VII. The original 16th Century stone wall can be found in the bar where locals and visitors mingle and enjoy late nightly music. Claddagh Loft Organic Restaurant & Cogars Organic Bistro boast world bronze medalist Chef Padraic Kielty. Secure car park nearby. (Reduced fee payable).

Room Rate from €190.50 to €228.60
£150.03 to £180.04

EASTER MCDONAGH GALLAGHER
MANAGING DIRECTOR

American Express
Mastercard
Visa

20 20

Closed 25 - 26 December

IMPERIAL HOTEL

EYRE SQUARE,
GALWAY

TEL: 091-563033 FAX: 091-568410
EMAIL: imperialhtl@hotmail.com

HOTEL ★★★ MAP 6 F 10

A bustling hotel in the centre of Galway City with modern comfortable 3 star bedrooms. Located in the main shopping area surrounded by a large choice of restaurants, pubs and quality shops. Five minutes walk from the new Galway Theatre, main bus and rail terminals. Beside main taxi rank with multi storey parking nearby. Full service hotel; friendly and informative staff. No service charge. R.A.C. 3 ***.

B&B from €50.00 to €82.50
£39.38 to £64.97

KEVIN FLANNERY
GENERAL MANAGER

American Express
Diners
Mastercard
Visa

84 84

Closed 24 - 27 December

B&B rates are per person sharing per night incl. Breakfast

INISHMORE GUESTHOUSE

109 FR. GRIFFIN ROAD,
LOWER SALTHILL,
GALWAY

TEL: 091-582639 FAX: 091-589311
EMAIL: inishmorehouse@eircom.net
WEB: www.galwaybaygolfholidays.com

GUESTHOUSE ★★★ MAP 6 F 10

A charming family residence with secure carpark within 5 minutes walk of city and beach. All rooms contain direct dial phone, multi-channel TV and hairdryers. Tea/coffee and ironing facilities available. German spoken. An ideal base for touring the Aran Islands, Burren and Connemara. All day tours can be organised. Golf holidays, sea angling trips and coarse or game fishing arranged. Recommended by many leading travel guides. Specialise in Golf Package Holidays.

B&B from €26.00 to €50.00
£20.48 to £39.38

MARIE & PETER
PROPRIETORS

Mastercard
Visa

6   6

Closed 23 December - 07 January

JAMESONS HOTEL

SALTHILL,
GALWAY

TEL: 091-528666 FAX: 091-528626
EMAIL: jamesons@iol.ie
WEB: www.galway.net/pages/jamesons

HOTEL ★★★ MAP 6 F 10

Jamesons Hotel is located in the heart of Salthill, overlooking Galway Bay. All rooms are en suite with special jacuzzi suites available. We offer excellent cuisine in the pleasant surroundings of our restaurant. Live entertainment 7 nights a week in summer and at weekends over the winter period. Conference suites facilitating up to 60 people. Private car parking. Special weekend rates available.

B&B from €25.00 to €100.00
£19.69 to £78.76

JONATHAN POWELL
GENERAL MANAGER

American Express
Diners
Mastercard
Visa

20   20

Open All Year

JURYS INN GALWAY

QUAY STREET,
GALWAY

TEL: 091-566444 FAX: 091-568415
EMAIL: jurysinngalway@jurysdoyle.com
WEB: www.jurysdoyle.com

HOTEL ★★★ MAP 6 F 10

Beside the historic Spanish Arch, overlooking Galway Bay, and just a few minutes walk through twisting medieval street to the buzz of Galway's commercial and shopping districts. Convenient also to main access routes to the haunting landscape of Connemara and the Atlantic Coast. There couldn't be a better location!

Room Rate from €64.00 to €94.00
£50.40 to £74.03

KAREN CREMINS
GENERAL MANAGER

American Express
Diners
Mastercard
Visa

128   128

Closed 24 - 26 December

Room rates are per room per night

KNOCKREA GUEST HOUSE

**55 LOWER SALTHILL,
GALWAY**

TEL: 091-520145 FAX: 091-529985
EMAIL: knockrea@eircom.net
WEB: www.galway.net/pages/knockrea/

GUESTHOUSE ★★★ MAP 6 F 10

A 3*** family run guesthouse established 1950. Refurbished to a high standard with pine floors throughout. Car park at rear. 1km from city centre on bus route. 300 metres from Salthill Promenade. Restaurants, theatres, golf, tennis, horseriding close by. Perfect base for touring Connemara, Burren and Aran Islands. Within walking distance of Spanish Arch and Quay Street. Irish pub music entertainment available locally. All rooms en suite, TV and direct dial phone. Frommers Guide recommended.

B&B from € 25.00 to € 45.00
£19.69 to £35.44

EILEEN STORAN
PROPRIETOR

Mastercard
Visa

6 6

IRISH HOTELS FEDERATION

Closed 23 - 26 December

LOCHLURGAIN HOTEL

**22 MONKSFIELD,
UPPER SALTHILL,
GALWAY**

TEL: 091-529595 FAX: 091-522399
EMAIL: lochlurgain@eircom.net
WEB: www.lochlurgain.com

HOTEL U MAP 6 F 10

Welcome to Lochlurgain. Completely refurbished elegant Town House Hotel, AA***. Beside church off Main St, 5 minutes beach and leisure centre. City centre 5 minutes. Fresh home cooked food served. Seafood also featured. Enjoy comfort, peace, tranquillity and relaxation. Lochlurgain is 62 miles/100km north of Shannon Airport. One hour from the Burren and Connemara. On parle francais. Bed, breakfast and dinner breaks, please ask for details. Peadar and Joan Cunningham welcome you.

B&B from € 40.00 to € 85.00
£31.50 to £66.94

PEADAR & JOAN CUNNINGHAM
PROPRIETORS

Mastercard
Visa

2 B&B & 2 Dinner from €130.00

10 10

IRISH HOTELS FEDERATION

Closed 28 October - 11 March

MARIAN LODGE GUESTHOUSE

**KNOCKNACARRA ROAD,
SALTHILL UPPER,
GALWAY**

TEL: 091-521678 FAX: 091-528103
EMAIL: celine@iol.ie
WEB: www.marian-lodge.com

GUESTHOUSE ★★★ MAP 6 F 10

AA ♦♦♦♦ "A home from home". Family run. Period furniture. Adjacent to promenade/beach in Salthill Upr. Private parking. Daily tours arranged Connemara/Burren/Aran Islands. City bus route. Home baking. Bedrooms en suite, cable TV, DD phone, clock radio, orthopaedic beds, hairdryers, tea/coffee facilities. Iron, trouser press available. Large family rooms. Children welcome. Convenient to nightly entertainment, Leisureland, Aquarium, tennis, windsurfing, fishing, horse-riding, bird sanctuary. Beside golf course, driving range, hair salon, restaurant, pubs and shops.

B&B from € 38.00 to € 38.00
£29.93 to £29.93

CELINE MOLLOY

Mastercard
Visa

6 6

IRISH HOTELS FEDERATION

Closed 23 - 28 December

B&B rates are per person sharing per night incl. Breakfast

MENLO PARK HOTEL AND CONFERENCE CENTRE

TERRYLAND,
HEADFORD ROAD,
GALWAY
TEL: 091-761122 FAX: 091-761222
EMAIL: menlopkh@iol.ie
WEB: www.menloparkhotel.com

HOTEL ★★★ MAP 6 F 10

Situated near Galway's City centre the Menlo Park offers the best of modern facilities with old fashioned hospitality. All rooms have TV/satellite, welcome tray, power showers, ironing centres, rich colour schemes. Executive rooms also feature king beds, sofas, work desks. Contemporary chic but casual restaurant; MP's Bar and Lounge. Bar food/carvery all day. Entertainment, traditional and folk at weekends. Easy access, free parking. Computer point in some bedrooms.

B&B from €50.00 to €105.00
£39.38 to £82.69

DAVID KEANE
MANAGER

American Express
Diners
Mastercard
Visa

😊 Weekend specials from €110.00

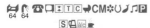
64 64

Closed 24 - 26 December

OCEAN CREST HOUSE

NO 6 OCEAN WAVE,
SEAPOINT PROMENADE, SALTHILL,
GALWAY
TEL: 091-589028 FAX: 091-529399
EMAIL: oceanbb@iol.ie
WEB: www.oceanbb.com

GUESTHOUSE ★★★ MAP 6 F 10

We chose this site and built this guesthouse to provide what our guests love, a taste of subtropical elegance, overlooking Galway Bay and beaches with panoramic views of the Burren Mountains. We are walking distance from the bustling medieval city of Galway and across the road we have the Promenade. Our bedrooms are beautifully appointed with multi channel TV, en suite facilities, phone, trouser press, hair dryers, hospitality tray and armchairs.

B&B from €25.00 to €45.00
£19.69 to £35.44

LORRAINE MCEVADDY
MANAGER

American Express
Mastercard
Visa

6 6

Closed 24 - 28 December

PARK HOUSE HOTEL & PARK ROOM RESTAURANT

FORSTER STREET,
EYRE SQUARE,
GALWAY
TEL: 091-564924 FAX: 091-569219
EMAIL: parkhousehotel@eircom.net
WEB: www.parkhousehotel.ie

HOTEL ★★★★ MAP 6 F 10

An oasis of luxury and hospitality in the heart of Galway City centre. We are Bord Failte 4****, AA 4 star and RAC 4 star. All 57 rooms are en suite with bath and shower, direct dial phone, ISDN line, multi channel TV, tea/coffee making facilities, trouser press, awards of excellence winning restaurant over many years. Les Routiers Restaurant of the Year Ireland 1998-1999. Our high standards are your guarantee. Private residents' car park on hotel grounds.

B&B from €60.00 to €140.00
£47.25 to £110.26

EAMON DOYLE & KITTY CARR
PROPRIETORS

American Express
Diners
Mastercard
Visa

57 57

Closed 24 - 26 December

Room rates are per room per night

RADISSON SAS HOTEL

LOUGH ATALIA ROAD,
GALWAY

TEL: 091-538300 FAX: 091-538380
EMAIL: sales.galway@radissonsas.com
WEB: www.radissonsas.com/gwyzhie

HOTEL N MAP 6 F 10

The Radisson SAS Hotel is ideally located on the waterfront on Lough Atalia Road, near the railway station. The hotel has 200 well appointed rooms featuring The Radisson SAS room style concepts Maritime, Scandinavian and Classic. The hotel has one main all day restaurant and bar, 12 meeting rooms (largest up to 1,000 guests for a standing reception), leisure centre with gym, sauna, jacuzzi, steam bath and a swimming pool.

Member of Radisson SAS Hotels and Resorts

Room Rate from €170.00 to €292.00
£133.86 to £229.92

JÜRGEN WIRTZ
GENERAL MANAGER

American Express
Diners
Mastercard
Visa

☺ Weekend break-away B&B €127.00
per night in double room

200 200

Inet FAX

IRISH HOTELS FEDERATION

Open All Year

ROCKBARTON PARK HOTEL

ROCKBARTON PARK,
SALTHILL,
GALWAY

TEL: 091-522286 FAX: 091-527692
EMAIL: tyson'shotel@eircom.net
WEB: www.rockbartonhotel.com

HOTEL ★★ MAP 6 F 10

Owned and managed by the Tyson Family, fully licensed, in a quiet residential cul de sac. 200 metres from seafront and Leisureland Centre. Golf, tennis, badminton and squash just 5 minutes walk. Tyson's Restaurant offers a homely comfortable atmosphere noted for fresh local fish and prime steaks, prepared and cooked delightfully by chef/proprietor Terry. Bar food also available. Friendly service.

Member of Logis of Ireland

B&B from €38.00 to €58.00
£29.93 to £45.68

PATRICIA AND TERRY TYSON
PROPRIETORS

American Express
Diners
Mastercard
Visa

☺ Weekend specials from €90.00

10 10

IRISH HOTELS FEDERATION

Closed 23 - 31 December

SALT LAKE GUESTHOUSE

40 LOUGH ATALIA ROAD,
GALWAY

TEL: 091-564572 FAX: 091-569544
EMAIL: oceanbb@iol.ie
WEB: www.oceanbb.com

GUESTHOUSE ★★★ MAP 6 F 10

Salt Lake House is a beautifully purpose-built guesthouse with exquisite views of Lough Atalia (inlet of Galway Bay). We offer luxurious accommodation within easy reach of Galway City centre, only minutes from bus/train station. Each room is beautifully appointed with en suite facilities, multi-channel TV (12 channels), armchairs and table, hospitality tray, iron and board and hairdryer.

B&B from €25.00 to €45.00
£19.69 to £35.44

LORRAINE McEVADDY
MANAGER

American Express
Mastercard
Visa

7 7

Closed 24 - 30 December

B&B rates are per person sharing per night incl. Breakfast

SALTHILL COURT HOTEL

**SALTHILL,
GALWAY**

TEL: 091-522711 FAX: 091-521855
EMAIL: salthillhotel@eircom.net
WEB: www.byrne-hotels-ireland.com

HOTEL ★★★ MAP 6 F 10

A Byrne Hotel, 50m from Salthill's sandy beach. Live entertainment most nights, every night from June to Sept (Thu-Sun rest of year). All rooms en suite, direct dial phone, tea making facilities, hair dryer. Excellent cuisine and service. 100m from Leisureland and indoor swimming pool. Overlooking Galway Bay with large car park. Ideal location for family holidays and over 55s in off season. Less than 2 miles from the medieval city of Galway. Many sporting activities nearby.

Member of Byrne Hotel Group
B&B from € 44.45 to € 95.23
£35.01 to £75.00

JOEY HALLINAN
GENERAL MANAGER

American Express
Diners
Mastercard
Visa

75 75

Closed 23 - 26 December

SKEFFINGTON ARMS HOTEL

**EYRE SQUARE,
GALWAY**

TEL: 091-563173 FAX: 091-561679
EMAIL: info@skeffington.ie
WEB: www.skeffington.ie

HOTEL ★★★ MAP 6 F 10

The Skeffington Arms Hotel has been caring for guests for over 100 years. Overlooking Eyre Square, within walking distance of rail and bus terminal, it enjoys an enviable position in the heart of Galway. This privately owned hotel is justifiably proud of its new bars and à la carte menu which is very popular with both locals and guests alike. The bedrooms, which are newly refurbished have multi-channel TV, tea/coffee making facilities, direct dial phone and bath/shower en suite.

B&B from € 50.80 to € 95.25
£40.00 to £75.00

SINEAD LALLY
RESERVATIONS MANAGER

American Express
Mastercard
Visa

23 23

Closed 25 - 26 December

SPINNAKER HOUSE HOTEL

**KNOCKNACARRA,
SALTHILL,
GALWAY**

TEL: 091-525425 FAX: 091-526650
EMAIL: spinnakerhousehotel@eircom.net

HOTEL ★★ MAP 6 F 10

The newly refurbished Spinnaker Hotel is a family run hotel overlooking Galway Golf Course and has spectacular views of Galway Bay and the Burren. All 20 rooms, most with private balconies, are newly built with en suite facilities, telephone, TV and tea/coffee maker. Within 2km of the hotel we have beaches, fishing, horse riding, golf and tennis clubs, Leisureland complex and the ferry port to the Aran Islands.

B&B from € 34.92 to € 62.87
£27.50 to £49.50

TOM O'DWYER
PROPRIETOR

American Express
Mastercard
Visa

20 20

Closed 25 - 26 December

Room rates are per room per night

VICTORIA HOTEL

VICTORIA PLACE,
EYRE SQUARE,
GALWAY
TEL: 091-567433 FAX: 091-565880
EMAIL: victoriahotel@eircom.net
WEB: www.byrnehotel.com

HOTEL ★★★ MAP 6 F 10

The Victoria Hotel is centrally located just 100 yards off Eyre Square, within walking distance of all shops, theatres, pubs and cinemas. Each of the 57 spacious en suite rooms is beautifully appointed with direct dial phone, trouserpress and hairdryer. The hotel restaurant serving à la carte dinner along with a lively bar serving lunches will all add up to make your stay at the Victoria as enjoyable as possible. The Victoria is your enclave in the city, dedicated to pleasing you.

B&B from €57.14 to €107.93
£45.00 to £85.00

ANNE MARIE HALLINAN
MANAGER

American Express
Mastercard
Visa

57 57

Open All Year

WATERFRONT HOTEL

SALTHILL,
GALWAY
TEL: 091-588100 FAX: 091-588107
EMAIL: info@waterfront.ie
WEB: www.waterfront.ie

HOTEL U MAP 6 F 10

Our superbly located Hotel sits on the shores of Galway Bay in the delightful suburb of Salthill, just 5 minutes from Galway's vibrant city centre. Each of our spacious 64 en suite rooms offers a dazzling, panoramic ocean view, and is amply furnished with a large lounge or kitchenette. Adjacent to the Hotel is the famous Kitty O'Shea's Bar and Restaurant. Family rooms and free, secure car parking. Reservations: Call Save 1850 588 488

Room Rate from €57.00 to €171.00
£44.89 to £134.67

KEN BERGIN
GENERAL MANAGER

American Express
Mastercard
Visa

Weekend specials from €95.00

64 64

Closed 23 - 29 December

WEST WINDS

5 OCEAN WAVE,
SALTHILL,
GALWAY
TEL: 091-520223 FAX: 091-520223
EMAIL: westwinds@eircom.net
WEB: www.travelaccommodation.co.uk/westwind.htm

GUESTHOUSE ★★★ MAP 6 F 10

Westwinds is a charming family-managed guesthouse overlooking Galway Bay, 10 minutes walk from Galway City, an ideal base for all travellers wishing to explore the Burren, Connemara and the Aran Islands. We are situated at the city end of Salthill Promenade, restaurants, nightly entertainment and all other amenities 5-10 minutes walk. All rooms have en suite bathrooms with power shower, hairdryer, cable TV, tea/coffee making facility. Our hospitality awaits!

B&B from €25.40 to €44.45
£20.01 to £35.01

RITA & PATRICK JOYCE
PROPRIETORS

American Express
Mastercard
Visa

Midweek specials from €73.66

8 8

Closed 1 December - 01 April

B&B rates are per person sharing per night incl. Breakfast

WESTWOOD HOUSE HOTEL

**DANGAN,
UPPER NEWCASTLE,
GALWAY**
TEL: 091-521442 FAX: 091-521400
EMAIL: westwoodreservations@eircom.net
WEB: www.westwoodhousehotel.com

HOTEL ★★★★ MAP 6 F 10

The 4**** Westwood House Hotel stands amidst a rural landscape of greenery combining a mellow taste of the countryside with the city's cutting edge. Air conditioned throughout, the hotel features 58 superbly appointed bedrooms, the award winning Meridian Restaurant, split level bar, conference and banqueting facilities and complimentary private car parking.

*B&B from €50.00 to €130.00
£39.37 to £102.37*

RACHAEL COYLE
GENERAL MANAGER

American Express
Diners
Mastercard
Visa

Weekend specials from €126.00

58 58

Inet FAX

Closed 24 - 26 December

WHITE HOUSE

**2 OCEAN WAVE,
SEAPOINT PROMENADE, SALTHILL,
GALWAY**
TEL: 091-529399 FAX: 091-529399
EMAIL: oceanbb@iol.ie
WEB: www.oceanbb.com

GUESTHOUSE ★★★ MAP 6 F 10

New and beautiful purpose-built guest house in Galway's finest location, overlooking Galway Bay and the Burren Mountains, minutes walk to Galway's medieval city and Salthill's new hotel, the Galway Bay. Large bedrooms with armchairs and tables, iron and board, multi-channel TV, hospitality tray and hairdryer.

*B&B from €25.00 to €45.00
£19.69 to £35.44*

LORRAINE MCEVADDY
MANAGER

American Express
Mastercard
Visa

6 6

Closed 24 - 28 December

LADY GREGORY HOTEL

**ENNIS ROAD,
GORT,
CO. GALWAY**
TEL: 091-632333 FAX: 091-632332
EMAIL: ladygregoryhotel@eircom.net
WEB: www.ladygregoryhotel.com

HOTEL ★★★ MAP 6 G 9

Situated in the west of Ireland near Coole Park, home of Lady Gregory in the town of Gort, with its many historic and local attractions. A warm friendly welcome awaits you as you enter the architectural splendour of the Lady Gregory Hotel. 48 beautifully appointed rooms, Copper Beech Restaurant, lively Jack B Yeats Bar and magnificent Gregory Suite. Relax in our Kiltatan Reading Room. Discounted green fees available from reception for Gort Golf Course located less than 1 hour from Shannon Airport. www.globalgolf.com.

*B&B from €57.15 to €107.95
£45.00 to £85.00*

LEONARD MURPHY
GENERAL MANAGER

American Express
Diners
Mastercard
Visa

48 48

Inet FAX

Closed 24 - 27 December

Room rates are per room per night

SULLIVAN'S ROYAL HOTEL

THE SQUARE,
GORT,
CO. GALWAY
TEL: 091-631257 FAX: 091-631916
EMAIL: jsullinsauc@eircom.net
WEB: www.irelandmidwest.com

HOTEL ★★ MAP 6 G 9

Sullivan's Hotel is family run and managed, fully licensed and open all year round. Situated on main west of Ireland road, in close proximity to Coole Park, home of Lady Gregory, Thoore Ballylee, Kilmacduagh and the Burren. TV and telephone in all bedrooms, en suite rooms, meals served all day - bar food, à la carte dinner at reasonable rates. Available locally: golf, pony trekking, fishing. Dining Pub of the Year Award 2000 & 2001.

Room Rate from €38.10 to €63.50
£30.01 to £50.01

JOHNNY & ANNIE SULLIVAN
PROPRIETORS

American Express
Diners
Mastercard
Visa

12 12

IRISH HOTELS FEDERATION

Open All Year

DOONMORE HOTEL

INISHBOFIN ISLAND,
CO. GALWAY
TEL: 095-45804 FAX: 095-45804
EMAIL: reservations@doonmorehotel.com
WEB: www.doonmorehotel.com

HOTEL ★★ MAP 9 C 12

Uniquely situated on a beautiful and historic island, commanding magnificent views of the surrounding sea and islands. Inishbofin, a haven for artists, fishermen, bird watchers, nature lovers or those who just wish to escape from the hectic pace of life. Fine sandy beaches. Sea trips and boat angling can be arranged. Facilities for divers. Excellent shore fishing. Doonmore Hotel is owned and managed by the Murray Family, unpretentious but friendly and comfortable.

B&B from €30.00 to €44.00
£23.63 to £34.65

AILEEN MURRAY
MANAGER

American Express
Mastercard
Visa

19 19

alc

Closed 30 September - 28 March

MERRIMAN INN & RESTAURANT

MAIN STREET,
KINVARA,
CO. GALWAY
TEL: 091-638222 FAX: 091-637686
EMAIL: merrimanhotel@eircom.net
WEB: www.merrimanhotel.com

HOTEL ★★★ MAP 6 G 10

Located in the picturesque fishing village of Kinvara, The Merriman opened in April '97. Named after the famous Irish Poet, Brian Merriman, this 32 bedroomed hotel has one of the largest thatched roofs in Ireland. Overlooking Galway Bay, the Burren, the hills of Connemara, Kinvara is an ideal touring base. Dunguaire Castle, a short stroll away, where an enjoyable medieval banquet can be experienced. Excellent restaurant & bar provide for friendly, comfortable & value for money hotel.

B&B from €45.00 to €57.50
£35.44 to £45.28

RITA HUBAN
MANAGER

American Express
Diners
Mastercard
Visa

32 32

alc

IRISH HOTELS FEDERATION

Closed 22 December - 31 January

B&B rates are per person sharing per night incl. Breakfast

LEENANE HOTEL

LEENANE,
CONNEMARA,
CO. GALWAY
TEL: 095-42249 FAX: 095-42376
EMAIL: leenanehotel@eircom.net
WEB: www.connemara.net/leenanehotel

HOTEL U MAP 9 D 12

On the shores of Killary Harbour, Ireland's only Fjord, lies Ireland's oldest Coaching Inn. The Leenane Hotel, recently refurbished to the highest of standards, boasts the most spectacular views in Ireland. Being a family-run hotel, we understand the appreciation for traditional home-cooking. Fresh seafood from the harbour and vegetables and herbs from the hotel garden are brought in every day. The hotel's position makes it without doubt the best base for exploring Connemara, the most romantic and unspoiled region of Ireland.

B&B from €32.00 to €70.00
£25.20 to £55.12

CONOR FOYLE
MANAGER

Mastercard

Visa

☺ Week partial board from €375.00

🛏 👤 ☎ 🖵 T C ⌨ CM ❄ ☎ ⟳ ♫ P
S 🅰 alc ☕
29 29

Closed 03 November - 27 March

PORTFINN LODGE

LEENANE,
CO. GALWAY
TEL: 095-42265 FAX: 095-42315
EMAIL: rorydaly@anu.ie
WEB: www.anu.ie/portfinn

GUESTHOUSE ★★ MAP 9 D 12

Portfinn Lodge is a family run guest house offering 8 comfortable rooms en suite including double and triple bedrooms, a guest lounge and a restaurant which has an international reputation for its fresh seafood. Rory and Brid Daly will be delighted to make you feel welcome. An ideal centre from which beaches, walking, angling, watersports etc. are easily reachable. When in Connemara, stay at Portfinn.

B&B from €25.00 to €34.00
£19.69 to £26.78

BRID & RORY DALY
OWNERS

Mastercard

Visa

🛏 👤 ☎ T C CM ❄ ⟳ P 🅰 alc
8 8

Closed 01 November - 31 March

ROSLEAGUE MANOR HOTEL

LETTERFRACK,
CONNEMARA,
CO. GALWAY
TEL: 095-41101 FAX: 095-41168
EMAIL: rosleaguemanor@eircom.net
WEB: www.rosleague.com

HOTEL ★★★★ MAP 9 C 12

Rosleague is a Regency manor now run as a first class country house hotel by Mark Foyle and Eddie Foyle. It lies 7 miles north west of Clifden on the coast overlooking a sheltered bay and surrounded by the Connemara Mountains and beside the National Park. It is renowned for its superb cuisine personally supervised by the owners with all the amenities expected by todays discerning guest. Also a member of Ireland's Blue Book.

Member of I.C.H.R.A. (Blue Book)
B&B from €76.20 to €114.30
£60.01 to £90.02

MARK FOYLE/EDDIE FOYLE
MANAGER/OWNER

American Express

Mastercard

Visa

✓

☺ Weekend specials from €145.00

🛏 👤 ☎ 🖵 T C CM ❄ 🅢 ⟳ ⟳ P S
🅰 alc
15 15

Closed 01 November - 01 April

Room rates are per room per night

MEADOW COURT HOTEL

CLOSTOKEN,
LOUGHREA,
CO. GALWAY
TEL: 091-841051 FAX: 091-842406
EMAIL: meadowcourthotel@eircom.net
WEB: www.meadowcourthotel.com

HOTEL ★★★ MAP 6 H 10

Newly extended and refurbished the Meadow Court Hotel's en suite rooms have full facilities, multi channel TV, hair dryer and garment press. Superb dining is on offer in our award-winning restaurant renowned for its outstanding cuisine. Enjoy after dinner drinks in our Derby Bar. Situated on the main Galway Dublin Road 2 miles from Loughrea, 18 miles from Galway, convenient to all local 18-hole golf courses, angling, horseriding, water sports. Banqueting & conference facilities. Carpark.

B&B from €38.00 to €63.50
£29.93 to £50.01

TOM & DAVID CORBETT
DIRECTORS

American Express
Mastercard
Visa

😊 Midweek room only rate available

21 21

S ♿ aic 🔌 Inet

IRISH HOTELS FEDERATION

Closed 25 December

O'DEAS HOTEL

BRIDE STREET,
LOUGHREA,
CO. GALWAY
TEL: 091-841611 FAX: 091-842635
EMAIL: odeashotel@eircom.net
WEB: www.commerce.ie/odeashotel

HOTEL ★★★ MAP 6 H 10

O'Deas Hotel is a family hotel, a Georgian town house hotel, of character with open fires and within walking distance of Loughrea's game fishing lake. It is an ideal touring base situated on the N6 (exactly halfway between Clonmacnoise, 35 miles to the east and the Cliffs of Moher, 35 miles to the west). The start of the Burren country is just 12 miles away. Galway City 20 miles.

Member of MinOtel of Ireland
B&B from €50.00 to €63.00
£39.38 to £49.62

MARY O'NEILL
PROPRIETOR/MANAGER

American Express
Mastercard
Visa

32 32

aic 🔌

IRISH HOTELS FEDERATION

Open All Year

PEACOCKES HOTEL & COMPLEX

MAAM CROSS,
CONNEMARA,
CO. GALWAY
TEL: 091-552306 FAX: 091-552216
EMAIL: peacockes@eircom.net
WEB: www.peacockeshotel.com

HOTEL ★★★ MAP 6 F 10

Newly built, nestling between the lakes and mountains at the crossroads to Connemara. Peacockes Hotel is the ideal base for hillwalking, cycling, golfing, fishing, horse riding or watersports. After a day's travel, relax with a drink by the open turf fire in the Bogdale Bar or enjoy a sumptuous meal in our Quiet Man Restaurant. Visit our 20m high viewing tower, extensive craft shop and replica Quiet Man cottage.

B&B from €45.00 to €85.00
£35.44 to £66.94

EIMEAR KILLIAN
GENERAL MANAGER

American Express
Diners
Mastercard
Visa

😊 Weekend specials from €105.00

25 25

S ♿ aic 🔌

IRISH HOTELS FEDERATION

Closed 23 - 26 December

B&B rates are per person sharing per night incl. Breakfast

MORAN'S CLOONABINNA HOUSE HOTEL

MOYCULLEN,
CONNEMARA,
CO. GALWAY
TEL: 091-555555 FAX: 091-555640
EMAIL: cbinnia@iol.ie

HOTEL ★★★ MAP 6 F 11

A hidden jewel, 16km from Galway City just off route N59. Overlooking Ross Lake and the rolling hills of Connemara. Quality food and magnificent views. It is the warmth and genuine hospitality of the Moran Family that make a visit to this delightful hotel a memorable experience. Angling centre on hotel grounds, own boats and gillies. 60,000 acres of internationally renowned lake and river systems. Atlantic Ocean 20 minutes. 5 golf courses and many walking routes nearby.

B&B from €60.00 to €75.00
£47.24 to £59.05

PETER MORAN
PROPRIETOR

Mastercard
Visa

☺ Weekend specials from €92.00

20   20

Open All Year

ORANMORE LODGE HOTEL, CONFERENCE & LEISURE CENTRE

ORANMORE,
CO. GALWAY

TEL: 091-794400 FAX: 091-790227
EMAIL: orlodge@eircom.net
WEB: www.oranmorelodge.com

HOTEL ★★★ MAP 6 G 10

This manor house hotel 8km from Galway City in the picturesque village of Oranmore, overlooking Galway Bay and on the edge of oyster country. 3km from Galway Airport. Equestrian, golfing and walking pursuits all within 3km of the hotel. Full leisure facilities with a 17m swimming pool and computerised TechnoGym. Your host and his efficient staff radiate a welcome and warmth reminiscent of the old country houses of Ireland.

B&B from €45.00 to €115.00
£35.44 to £90.57

BRIAN J. O'HIGGINS
PROPRIETOR

American Express
Diners
Mastercard
Visa

☺ Weekend specials from €115.00

56   56

Closed 23 - 27 December

QUALITY HOTEL AND LEISURE CENTRE GALWAY

ORANMORE,
CO. GALWAY

TEL: 091-792244 FAX: 091-792246
EMAIL: qualityhotelgalway@eircom.net
WEB: www.qualityhotelgalway.com

HOTEL ★★★ MAP 6 G 10

This luxury hotel is ideally located on the N6 approach to Galway, adjacent to the picturesque village of Oranmore & just 5 mins drive from Galway City. Facilities include spacious rooms, Furey's Well traditional pub with regular entertainment & all day menu, Furey's Relish Restaurant, residents' lounge & a superb leisure centre with a 20m pool, jacuzzi, hi-tech gym, steamroom, sauna, therapy suite & solarium. Rooms to accommodate up to 2 adults & 2 children. Golf, karting, horseriding nearby.

Member of Choice Hotels Ireland
Room Rate from €65.00 to €149.00
£51.19 to £117.35

DERMOT COMERFORD
GENERAL MANAGER

American Express
Diners
Mastercard
Visa

☺ Weekend specials from €99.00

93   93

Closed 24 - 26 December

Room rates are per room per night

BOAT INN

THE SQUARE,
OUGHTERARD,
CO. GALWAY
TEL: 091-552196 FAX: 091-552694
EMAIL: info@theboatinn.com
WEB: www.theboatinn.com

GUESTHOUSE ★★★   MAP 5 E 11

3*** guesthouse in the heart of
Oughterard, just 25 minutes from
Galway. 5 minutes to Lough Corrib
and redesigned 18 hole golf course.
Ideal base to explore Connemara. The
Boat Bar and Restaurant offer an
imaginative choice of food, drink and
wine. Enjoy the continental feel of our
terrace and rear gardens. Live music
in the bar. All bedrooms en suite with
TV, radio, phone and tea coffee
making facilities.

B&B from €31.75 to €38.00
£25.01 to £29.93

MICHAEL MURPHY
PROPRIETOR

American Express
Diners
Mastercard
Visa

🛏️ 📞 ☎️ 📺 T C 🔌 C M ✳️ ☋ ⌣ ♫🅿️ alc

Closed 25 - 26 December

CONNEMARA GATEWAY HOTEL

OUGHTERARD,
CO. GALWAY

TEL: 091-552328 FAX: 091-552332
EMAIL: gateway@iol.ie
WEB: www.sinnotthotels.com

HOTEL ★★★   MAP 5 E 11

Set in its own grounds, just 16 miles
from Galway City at the gateway to
Connemara. The emphasis here is on
warmth and hospitality. Full of
character and style, turf fires, a pine
panelled lobby, Cottage bar, indoor
heated swimming pool, meeting
facilities and all bedrooms en suite
with tea/coffee making facilities, make
this an ideal place from which to
explore all that Galway/Connemara
has to offer. Excellent golf and fishing
nearby.

Member of Sinnott Hotels Ireland
B&B from €49.00 to €90.00
£38.59 to £70.88

JOHN BRODERICK
MANAGER

American Express
Diners
Mastercard
Visa

✓ 🍴♨

☺ Weekend specials from €110.00

🛏️ 📞 ☎️ 📺 T /A C 🔌 C M ✳️ ☋ ⌣🅿️ 🛶 ☋
♫🅿️🅿️🅂 alc 🔲 🔵 ⛵

HOTELS
FEDERATION

Closed 24 - 28 December

CORRIB HOUSE HOTEL

BRIDGE STREET,
OUGHTERARD,
CO. GALWAY

TEL: 091-552329 FAX: 091-552522
EMAIL: chhotel@gofree.indigo.ie

HOTEL U   MAP 5 E 11

Character at the gateway to
Connemara the Corrib House Hotel is
17 miles from Galway City and 1
mile from Connemara. 28
comfortable en suite rooms, turf fires
and our renowned Owenriff Restaurant
with superb food and wine list. 4
championship golf courses within 30
miles, the world famous fishing on
Lough Corrib (1 mile) and
magnificent walking and hiking - a
few of the pastimes available while
staying with us.

B&B from €36.00 to €49.00
£28.35 to £38.59

LIZ O'MALLEY
MANAGER

American Express
Diners
Mastercard
Visa

✓ 🍴♨

🛏️ 📞 ☎️ 📺 T C 🔌 C M ✳️ ☋ ⌣ ♫🅿️🅂
🔲 alc

HOTELS
FEDERATION

Closed 23 - 28 December

B&B rates are per person sharing per night incl. Breakfast

CORRIB WAVE GUEST HOUSE

**PORTACARRON,
OUGHTERARD, CONNEMARA,
CO. GALWAY**
TEL: 091-552147 FAX: 091-552736
EMAIL: cwh@gofree.indigo.ie
WEB: www.corribwave.com

GUESTHOUSE ★★★ MAP 5 E 11

Panoramic lakeside guest house - the home of Michael & Maria Healy. As our guests, you are assured of a warm welcome to a family home with every comfort and Irish hospitality, superb home cooking, excellent wines, beautiful en suite bedrooms (all with double and single beds), TVs, hairdryers. Spectacular views, turf fire, peace & tranquillity. Angling specialists, boats, engines. Boatmen for hire. Wild brown trout, salmon, pike, lakeside walks. 18 hole golf 1km. Colour brochure on request.

Room Rate from €32.50 to €35.00
£25.60 to £27.56

MARIA & MICHAEL HEALY
PROPRIETORS

Mastercard

Visa

3 B&B & 3 Dinner from €155-€160

9 9

IRISH HOTELS FEDERATION

Closed 15 November - 15 March

CURRAREVAGH HOUSE

**OUGHTERARD,
CONNEMARA,
CO. GALWAY**
TEL: 091-552312 FAX: 091-552731
EMAIL: currarevagh@ireland.com

GUESTHOUSE ★★★★ MAP 5 E 11

A charming country mansion, built in 1842, situated beside Lough Corrib in 60 hect. of private woodlands. The relaxing atmosphere & classically simple menus receive much international praise. Own fishing, boats, tennis court, with golf & riding locally. Recommendations: Egon Ronay, Guide Michelin, Footprint Guide, Lonely Planet, Karen Brown's Irish Country Inn's, Good Food Guide, Good Hotel Guide & many other international hotel & food guides. You should stay at least 3 nights to absorb the atmosphere and gently explore Connemara.

Member of Ireland's Blue Book
B&B from €72.60 to €95.70
£57.16 to £75.35

HARRY & JUNE HODGSON
PROPRIETORS

Mastercard

Visa

Week partial board from €682.00

15 15

IRISH HOTELS FEDERATION

Closed 20 October - 27 March

LAKE HOTEL

**OUGHTERARD,
CO. GALWAY**

TEL: 091-552275 FAX: 091-552794

HOTEL ★★ MAP 5 E 11

Situated in the picturesque fishing and golfing village of Oughterard, within easy access to Connemara's rugged hills and hidden lakes and only 20 minutes drive to the City of Galway. Choice of 4 Championship Golf Courses and numerous Fishing Lakes. Family Run Hotel under the personal supervision of the McDonnell Family.

B&B from €40.00 to €50.00
£31.50 to £39.38

GERRY MCDONNELL & FAMILY
PROPRIETORS

American Express

Diners

Mastercard

Visa

18 18

IRISH HOTELS FEDERATION

Open All Year

Room rates are per room per night

MOUNTAIN VIEW GUEST HOUSE

AUGHNANURE,
OUGHTERARD,
CO. GALWAY
TEL: 091-550306 FAX: 091-550133
EMAIL: tricia.oconnor@eircom.net

GUESTHOUSE ★★★ MAP 5 E 11

Situated just off the N59, 24km from Galway City and within 2.4km of Oughterard, with the Connemara Mountains in the distance and Lough Corrib nearby. Leisure activities include; golf at the renowned Oughterard Golf Club, established walks along scenic routes, boating or fishing on Lough Corrib. Guests can relax in the lounge with open turf fire and sample some of the cuisine before retiring to en suite bedrooms with TV, direct dial phone, tea/coffee making facilities and hairdryer.

B&B from € 25.00 to € 31.00
£19.69 to £24.41

RICHARD & PATRICIA O'CONNOR
PROPRIETORS

Mastercard
Visa

Weekend specials from €70.00

10 10

Closed 24 - 26 December

RIVER RUN LODGE

GLANN ROAD,
OUGHTERARD,
CO. GALWAY
TEL: 091-552697 FAX: 091-552669
EMAIL: rivrun@indigo.ie
WEB: www.connemara-bedandbreakfast.com

GUESTHOUSE ★★★★ MAP 5 E 11

River Run Lodge sits on the Owenriff which flows into Lough Corrib. Just minutes walk from the heart of Oughterard you'll find landscaped gardens, patios and riverside walks. A lodge warmed by light wood and lit by natural hues. Comfortably traditional spacious bedrooms and cosy lounges. A riverside restaurant with menus to rival any city repertoire. Book your slice of peace and quiet in the ideal base for exploring Connemara. AA ◆◆◆◆◆.

B&B from € 40.00 to € 55.00
£31.50 to £43.32

TOM & ANNE LITTLE
PROPRIETORS

American Express
Mastercard
Visa

6 6

Open All Year

ROSS LAKE HOUSE HOTEL

ROSSCAHILL,
OUGHTERARD,
CO. GALWAY
TEL: 091-550109 FAX: 091-550184
EMAIL: rosslake@iol.ie
WEB: www.rosslakehotel.com

HOTEL ★★★ MAP 5 E 11

Ross Lake House is a wonderful Georgian house set in the magnificent wilderness of Connemara. Six acres of mature gardens surround the house creating an air of peace and tranquillity. Hosts Henry and Elaine Reid have beautifully restored this manor house to its former glory. A high quality Irish menu is prepared daily featuring a tempting variety of fresh produce from nearby Connemara hills, streams and lakes as well as fish straight from the Atlantic.

Member of Green Book of Ireland
B&B from € 64.00 to € 134.00
£50.40 to £105.53

ELAINE & HENRY REID
PROPRIETORS

American Express
Diners
Mastercard
Visa

13 13

Closed 31 October - 15 March

B&B rates are per person sharing per night incl. Breakfast

SHANNON OAKS HOTEL & COUNTRY CLUB

PORTUMNA,
CO. GALWAY

TEL: 0509-41777 FAX: 0509-41357
EMAIL: sales@shannonoaks.ie
WEB: www.shannonoaks.ie

HOTEL ★★★ MAP 6 J 9

Shannon Oaks Hotel & Country Club lies adjacent to the 17th century Portumna Castle and estate, by the shores of Lough Derg. All our rooms have satellite television, D.D. phone and an en suite bathroom. A distinguished menu of classic and fusion Irish dishes are available each evening. Our leisure centre, with its indoor heated swimming pool, sauna, steam room and gymnasium provides the stress free atmosphere in which to relax and unwind.

Member of Signature Hotels

B&B from €73.00 to €79.36
£57.49 to £62.50

BARRY MAHER
GENERAL MANAGER

American Express
Diners
Mastercard
Visa

Weekend specials from €152.37

Open All Year

LOUGH INAGH LODGE

RECESS,
CONNEMARA,
CO. GALWAY

TEL: 095-34706 FAX: 095-34708
EMAIL: inagh@iol.ie
WEB: www.commerce.ie/inagh/

HOTEL ★★★★ MAP 5 D 11

Lough Inagh Lodge was built in 1880. It offers all the comforts of an elegant modern hotel in an old world atmosphere, open log fires in the library and oak panelled bar symbolises the warmth of Inagh hospitality. The lodge is surrounded by famous beauty spots including the Twelve Bens Mountain Range and the Connemara National Park. Kylemore Abbey is also nearby.

Member of Manor House Hotels

B&B from €79.00 to €109.00
£62.22 to £85.84

MAIRE O'CONNOR
PROPRIETOR

American Express
Diners
Mastercard
Visa

Weekend specials from €162.00

Closed 09 December - 15 March

RENVYLE HOUSE HOTEL

RENVYLE,
CONNEMARA,
CO. GALWAY

TEL: 095-43511 FAX: 095-43515
EMAIL: renvyle@iol.ie
WEB: www.renvyle.com

HOTEL ★★★ MAP 9 C 12

Historic coastal hotel set amid the magical beauty of sea, lake and mountains, the keynotes are warmth and comfort with award winning fine fare. Turf fires and cosy lounges make you relax and feel at home. Golf, tennis, horse riding, swimming pool, snooker, boating, fishing are the facilities to name but a few. Wonderful walking and cycling routes throughout an area that hosts a vast National Park.

B&B from €51.00 to €96.00
£40.17 to £75.61

ZOE COYLE
SALES & MARKETING MANAGER

American Express
Diners
Mastercard
Visa

Closed 06 January - 14 February

Room rates are per room per night

ELDONS HOTEL

ROUNDSTONE,
CONNEMARA,
CO. GALWAY
TEL: 095-35933 FAX: 095-35722
EMAIL: eldonshotel@eircom.net
WEB: www.connemara.net

HOTEL ★★ MAP 9 C 11

Situated in the village of Roundstone, has a view of the harbour and Twelve Ben's mountain range. We are a newly built, family run hotel, offering bedrooms all with private bathrooms, colour TV and D.D. phones. Locally; 18 hole golf course, sea angling and windsurfing school. Our Beola Restaurant has been operating successfully for many years and is renowned for its fine food, with lobster being its speciality. Credit cards taken. New Annex consisting of 6 superior rooms with a lift.

B&B from € 36.00 to € 65.00
£28.35 to £51.19

ANN & NOLEEN CONNEELY
OWNER/CHEF

American Express
Diners
Mastercard
Visa

19 19

Closed 03 November - 14 March

ROUNDSTONE HOUSE HOTEL

ROUNDSTONE,
CONNEMARA,
CO. GALWAY
TEL: 095-35864 FAX: 095-35944
EMAIL: diar@eircom.net

HOTEL ★★ MAP 9 C 11

Roundstone House Hotel is a family hotel situated in the picturesque village of Roundstone. Roundstone is a fascinating place for a holiday offering a wide range of interests for the holiday makers. Many outdoor activities are available locally including sea angling, watersports, hillwalking, pony trekking and a championship 18 hole golf course nearby. Come to beautiful Roundstone for a holiday to remember.

Member of Village Inn Hotels
B&B from € 42.00 to € 52.00
£33.07 to £40.94

MAUREEN VAUGHAN
PROPRIETOR

American Express
Mastercard
Visa

13 13

Closed 30 October - 28 March

AN CRUISCIN LAN HOTEL

SPIDDAL,
CO. GALWAY

TEL: 091-553148 FAX: 091-553712
EMAIL: info@cruiscinlanhotel.com
WEB: www.cruiscinlanhotel.com

HOTEL N MAP 5 E 10

Newly reconstructed family run hotel situated in the heart of Spiddal. All rooms en suite, colour TV, direct dial phone line. Ideal for canoeing, sea angling and touring Connemara and the Aran Islands. Enjoy a drink in the bar or a meal in our restaurant with panoramic views of Galway Bay.

B&B from € 49.52 to € 113.01
£39.00 to £89.00

JOHN FOYE

Mastercard
Visa

14 14

Closed 23 - 28 December

B&B rates are per person sharing per night incl. Breakfast

BRIDGE HOUSE HOTEL

SPIDDAL,
CONNEMARA,
CO. GALWAY

TEL: 091-553118 FAX: 091-553435

HOTEL ★★ MAP 5 E 10

Enjoy a friendly relaxed atmosphere at Bridge House, a small hotel set in the heart of Spiddal Village - the home of traditional Irish music. Ideally situated to tour the many beauty spots of Connemara. Minutes walk from the sea. Trips to the Aran Islands arranged. All rooms en suite, colour TV, direct dial telephone. Award winning restaurant - fresh seafood a speciality - privately owned - personal service. Discover the difference for yourself.

B&B from €45.00 to €80.00
£35.44 to £63.00

ESTHER FEENEY
MANAGER

American Express
Mastercard
Visa

☺ Weekend specials from €108.00

🛏️ 🔥 ☎ 🛁 T ❄ U P S 🔒 a/c
10   10

IRISH HOTELS FEDERATION

Closed 20 December - 14 March

PARK LODGE HOTEL

PARK,
SPIDDAL,
CO. GALWAY

TEL: 091-553159 FAX: 091-553494
EMAIL: parklodgehotel@eircom.net
WEB: www.parklodgehotelandcottages.com

HOTEL U MAP 5 E 10

The Park Lodge Hotel is owned and run by the Foyle Family. It is situated on the coast road from Galway to Connemara, 16km west of Galway City and just east of Spiddal Village. Most of the 23 bedrooms have a view of Galway Bay. There are also seven detached cottages on the grounds, each self-catering and fully equipped for 5 persons. Cottages open all year.

B&B from €39.00 to €55.00
£30.71 to £43.32

JANE MARIE FOYLE
MANAGER

American Express
Diners
Mastercard
Visa

🛏️ 🔥 ☎ 🛁 △ 🚭 C 🍴 CM ❄ U J P S
23   23

IRISH HOTELS FEDERATION

Closed 01 October - 31 May

TIGH CHUALAIN

KILROE EAST,
SPIDDAL,
CO. GALWAY

TEL: 091-553609 FAX: 091-553049

GUESTHOUSE ★★★ MAP 5 E 10

Tigh Chualain is a charming, family run 3*** guesthouse, 16km west of Galway City and 2km west of Spiddal Village, en route to the Aran Islands' Ferry. Overlooking Galway Bay, with a nearby Blue Flag beach it is in the heart of the Connemara Gaeltacht. An obvious starting point for exploring the rugged beauty of Connemara with its manifold attractions. All bedrooms are en suite with direct dial telephone and colour TV.

B&B from €25.39 to €27.93
£20.00 to £22.00

NORA & COLM FOLAN
PROPRIETORS

☺ Midweek specials from €69.84

🛏️ 🔥 ☎ 🛁 C ❄ J P
9   9

Closed 31 October - 31 March

Room rates are per room per night

ACHILL CLIFF HOUSE HOTEL

KEEL,
ACHILL ISLAND,
CO. MAYO
TEL: 098-43400 FAX: 098-43007
EMAIL: info@achillcliff.com
WEB: www.achillcliff.com

HOTEL ★★★ MAP 9 C 14

Family run hotel with a warm welcome. AA ◆◆◆◆. Spacious smoke free rooms with everything a guest could ask for. Fully licenced restaurant with good selection of fine wines. Fresh local produce with seafood a speciality. Dining room looks out on to magnificent scenery. Ideal base for walking, climbing, fishing, sightseeing, painting, photography, writing. Beside bus stop. Friendly host recommends a 3 day stay. A perfect place to rest, relax and refresh.

Member of Premier Guesthouses

B&B from €35.00 to €70.00
£27.56 to £55.13

JJ & TERESA MCNAMARA
PROPRIETORS

American Express
Mastercard
Visa

☺ 3 B&B & 2 Dinners €189.00

🛏🛎☎🖥T C CM📷 J P S 🔲alc ☕
10 10

Inet

IRISH HOTELS FEDERATION

Closed 23 -27 December

GRAYS GUEST HOUSE

DUGORT,
ACHILL ISLAND,
CO. MAYO
TEL: 098-43244

GUESTHOUSE ★★★ MAP 9 C 14

Vi McDowell welcomes you to Grays where you are assured of a restful holiday, with good food, comfort and personal attention. Turf fires and electric blankets. Late dinner is served at 7pm. There are three lounges, colour TV, table tennis room and croquet lawn and swings in an enclosed garden. Art Gallery for use of artists staying in guesthouse.

B&B from €32.00 to €40.00
£25.20 to £31.50

VI MCDOWELL
OWNER/MANAGER

🛏🛎🖥T A🛇C CM☀🔍U J P 🍴
15 15

S ♀ ☕

Closed 24 - 26 December

OSTAN OILEAN ACLA

ACHILL SOUND,
CO. MAYO

TEL: 098-45138 FAX: 098-45198
EMAIL: reservations@achillislandhotel.com
WEB: www.achillislandhotel.com

HOTEL U MAP 9 C 14

Enjoy the panoramic views of Achill Island from our new luxury hotel situated at the gateway to Achill Island. In our elegant Seafood Restaurant choose from a wide range of local produce. Relax and enjoy a drink in our friendly traditional bar. Convenient to Blue Flag beaches, the highest cliffs in Europe, golf courses, pitch and putt course, outdoor activities. A warm friendly welcome awaits you at Óstán Oileán Acla.

B&B from €45.00 to €70.00
£35.44 to £55.13

MICHAEL MCLOUGHLIN

American Express
Mastercard
Visa

🛏🛎☎🖥T🛇C♨CM☀U J 🎵P
26 26

S 🔲alc ☕

IRISH HOTELS FEDERATION

Open All Year

B&B rates are per person sharing per night incl. Breakfast

BELLEEK CASTLE

BELEEK,
BALLINA,
CO. MAYO

TEL: 096-22400 FAX: 096-71750
EMAIL: belleekcastlehotel@eircom.net
WEB: www.belleekcastle.com

HOTEL U MAP 10 F 15

Historic, romantic, set in 1000 acres of woodland on banks of River Moy - Wine/dine till midnight - Gourmet organic food enthusiasts welcomed - 'Perchance to Dream' in a four poster. For your added pleasure: tour of 16c castle armoury, giant fossil exhibits, Spanish Armada Bar, dramatic artifacts and timbers salvaged from Galleons wrecked off Irish west coast 1588. Sporting: international surfing, golf, fishing, tennis, riding, ten stables in castle.

B&B from €53.77 to €99.86
£42.35 to £78.65

MARSHALL & JACQUELINE DORAN

American Express
Mastercard
Visa

15 15

Closed 24 - 27 December

DOWNHILL HOUSE HOTEL

BALLINA,
CO. MAYO

TEL: 096-21033 FAX: 096-21338
EMAIL: thedownhillhotel@eircom.net
WEB: www.downhillhotel.ie

HOTEL ★★★ MAP 10 F 15

3*** Downhill House Hotel, privately owned country house hotel beside Europe's best salmon fishing River Moy. The addition of the new garden wing offers the guest a perfect blend of olde world charm and new world comfort. Set in tranquil gardens, offering excellent cuisine with superb facilities on site. Eagles Leisure Club incorporates two swimming pools, steamroom, sauna, jacuzzi and floodlit tennis courts. Conference centre, piano bar with national and international entertainment. Six 18-hole golf courses nearby. Fishing - river, lake and deep sea.

Member of D'Arcy Marketing
B&B from €66.50 to €81.00
£52.37 to £63.79

MICHAEL MCKEIGUE
GENERAL MANAGER

American Express
Diners
Mastercard
Visa

☺ Weekend specials from €145.00

62 62

DOWNHILL INN

SLIGO ROAD,
BALLINA,
CO. MAYO

TEL: 096-73444 FAX: 096-73411
EMAIL: thedownhillinn@eircom.net
WEB: www.downhillinn.com

HOTEL ★★★ MAP 10 F 15

A family-run 3*** hotel, located 1 mile outside Ballina Town on the main Sligo Road (N59). Contemporary in its design with 45 well-appointed triple rooms. All rooms are en suite with multi-channel TV, hairdryer, tea/coffee facilities and DD phone. The region offers superb fishing on the River Moy, Lough Conn and Killala Bay. An excellent selection of golf courses: Enniscrone, Ballina, Carne, to mention but a few. Enjoy a drink at the bar or a meal in our Terrace Restaurant. Rest assured!

Member of Holiday Ireland Hotels
B&B from €39.00 to €48.00
£30.71 to £37.80

JOHN RAFTERY/NICOLA MOYLETT
PROPRIETORS

American Express
Mastercard
Visa

☺ Weekend specials from €100.00

45 45

Closed 22 December - 03 January

Closed 22 - 27 December

REGANS BARTRA HOUSE HOTEL

PEARSE STREET,
BALLINA,
CO. MAYO
TEL: 096-22200 FAX: 096-22111
EMAIL: bartrahotel@eircom.net

HOTEL ★★ MAP 10 F 15

Bartra House Hotel, situated in Ballina, is a family business run by brothers Paul and Noel Regan. Located near the famous River Moy and with two golf courses within easy reach, it is the ideal base for such holidays. The hotel boasts 17 bedrooms all en suite, with colour television and telephone. Our restaurant is famous for its superb food and service and our function room can cater for up to 200 people for dinner.

B&B from € 47.00 to € 51.00
£37.02 to £40.17

PAUL AND NOEL REGAN
DIRECTORS

American Express
Diners
Mastercard
Visa

17 17

Closed 25 December

ROCKS

FOXFORD ROAD,
BALLINA,
CO. MAYO
TEL: 096-22140
EMAIL: therocks@eircom.net

GUESTHOUSE ★★ MAP 10 F 15

Built and designed by the present owners. This beautiful residence offers good hospitality and atmosphere. All rooms en suite with hairdryers, TV and internal phone system. Guest tea & coffee room and guest lounge. Large landscaped gardens - front & rear - children's playground and barbeque. Ideal location for touring the scenic North West. All fishing arranged on River Moy - Lough Conn - estuary and sea with gillie and boats. Pony riding, golf, swimming and mountain climbing nearby.

B&B from € 25.00 to € 30.00
£19.69 to £23.63

MARGARET CUMISKEY

6 6

Open All Year

STELLA MARIS HOTEL

BALLYCASTLE,
CO. MAYO

TEL: 096-43322 FAX: 096-43965
EMAIL: info@stellamarisireland.com
WEB: www.stellamarisireland.com

HOTEL P MAP 9 E 16

Overlooking Bunatrahir Bay and picturesque Downpatrick Head, Stella Maris is a luxurious boutique hotel in tranquil Ballycastle. The former Coast Guard station and subsequent convent is strategically located between the world renowned golf links of Enniscrone and Carne/Belmullet. Tasteful antique furnishings in well appointed oceanfront rooms. Sea and fresh water fishing nearby.

B&B from € 70.00 to € 108.00
£55.13 to £85.06

FRANCES KELLY/TERENCE MCSWEENEY
PROPRIETORS

American Express
Diners
Mastercard
Visa

12 12

Closed 01 October - 01 April

B&B rates are per person sharing per night incl. Breakfast

JENNINGS HOTEL & TRAVELLERS FRIEND

OLD WESTPORT ROAD,
CASTLEBAR,
CO. MAYO
TEL: 094-23111 FAX: 094-23111
EMAIL: patj@anu.ie
WEB: www.travellersfriendhotel@anu.ie

HOTEL ★★★ MAP 9 E 14

Jennings Hotel & The Travellers Friend, Hotel & Theatre is a luxurious family 3*** facility. Contemporary style new rooms & suites with aircon, data-ports, VCR and trouser press. Combine with a new 1920s style restaurant & new conference rooms to provide excellent facilities for meetings/banquets. New bars and carvery in 2001. Personalised service, excellent cuisine, theatre shows, afford total comfort without compromise. Dedicated Business Centre. Adjacent to Institute of Technology, Mayo General Hospital and Aldi Shopping Centre.

Member of MinOtel Ireland Hotel Group
B&B from €50.00 to €80.00
£39.38 to £63.01

PAT AND MARY JENNINGS
PROPRIETORS

American Express
Mastercard
Visa

27 27
alc Inet

IRISH HOTELS FEDERATION

Closed 24 - 25 December

KENNYS GUESTHOUSE

LUCAN STREET,
CASTLEBAR,
CO. MAYO
TEL: 094-23091
EMAIL: kennys@castlebar.ie
WEB: www.castlebar.ie/stay/kennys

GUESTHOUSE ★★★ MAP 9 E 14

Our family-managed guesthouse is tastefully decorated and furnished to a very high standard. All guests rooms are en suite with direct dial phone, TV and hairdryer. Relax in our residents' lounge with complimentary tea/coffee or avail of the numerous facilities nearby e.g. organised walks, fishing trips, bowling, swimming, golf, fine restaurants and entertainment. Ideal base to explore the unspoilt areas in the West. Private car parking. Reasonable prices for business or leisure.

B&B from €28.00 to €38.00
£22.05 to £29.93

SUSANNA & RAYMOND KENNY
OWNERS/PROPRIETORS

Mastercard
Visa

8 8

IRISH HOTELS FEDERATION

Open All Year

WELCOME INN HOTEL

NEW ANTRIM STREET,
CASTLEBAR,
CO. MAYO
TEL: 094-22288 FAX: 094-21766
EMAIL: welcomeinn@eircom.net
WEB: www.welcomeinnhotel.net

HOTEL ★★ MAP 9 E 14

The Welcome Inn Hotel is a professionally managed family hotel in the capital town of County Mayo. We provide first class service at reasonable rates. We have ultra modern facilities combined with a very friendly and welcoming attitude. Ours is an ideal base from which to tour and view some of the world's most breathtaking scenery. We look forward to welcoming you. A member of Irish Family Hotels Marketing Group Int. Tel 353 - 458 67307.

Member of Irish Family Hotels
B&B from €45.00 to €63.00
£35.44 to £49.62

ANN MCHUGH
DIRECTOR

American Express
Mastercard
Visa

40 40
alc

IRISH HOTELS FEDERATION

Closed 24 - 27 December

Room rates are per room per night

RIVERSIDE GUESTHOUSE & RESTAURANT

CHURCH STREET,
CHARLESTOWN,
CO. MAYO
TEL: 094-54200 FAX: 094-54207
EMAIL: riversiderestaurant@eircom.net
WEB: www.riversiderest.com

GUESTHOUSE P   MAP 10 G 14

Situated on the intersection of N17 & N5 primary routes. 10 minutes to Knock International Airport, 20 minutes to Knock Shrine. Ideal base for touring Mayo, Sligo, Roscommon and Galway. A charming family run guesthouse with all rooms en suite and with TV. Modern Irish food served and prepared in our Olde World restaurant by award winning chef/owner Anthony Kelly and his wife Anne. Special restaurant licence to serve all alcohol to diners. A warm Irish welcome awaits you.

Member of Restaurant Association of Ireland
B&B from €35.50 to €58.50
£27.96 to £46.07

ANTHONY & ANNE KELLY
PROPRIETORS

Mastercard

Visa

🛏️ 🛎️ ⬜TCCMP🔲alc
8   8

HOTELS
FEDERATION

Closed 01 - 25 November

ASHFORD CASTLE

CONG,
CO. MAYO
TEL: 092-46003 FAX: 092-46260
EMAIL: ashford@ashford.ie
WEB: www.ashford.ie

HOTEL ★★★★★   MAP 9 E 12

5***** Ashford Castle has long been considered one of Ireland's most outstanding properties - and has adapted the facilities to cater for the demands of today's discerning clientele. Now a total resort, guests can enjoy complimentary golf and the health club facilities which comprise a fully equipped gymnasium, sauna, steamroom and whirlpool. Other sports to be enjoyed are horseback riding outdoor & indoor, falconry, cruising and fishing on Lough Corrib. Nightly entertainment is provided.

Member of Relais & Châteaux
Room Rate from €194.00 to €466.00
£152.79 to £367.00

BILL BUCKLEY
MANAGER

American Express

Diners

Mastercard

Visa

🛏️ 🛎️ 📞⬜TC🛒CM❄️🔲🔍
83 83
U🚲🎵🔲P🔲alc

HOTELS
FEDERATION

Closed 06 January - 24 February

LYDONS LODGE HOTEL

CONG,
CO. MAYO
TEL: 092-46715 FAX: 092-46523
EMAIL: lydonslodge@eircom.net
WEB: www.lydonslodgefreeservers.com

HOTEL ★★   MAP 9 E 12

Lydons Lodge combines the most modern amenities with old world charm. Located in Cong, village of 'Quiet Man' film fame it offers salmon, pike and famous Lough Corrib wild brown trout fishing. Boats, engines and boatmen can be arranged. Choice of 3 local golf clubs, horse riding and tennis. Minutes' walk from Ashford Castle and Gardens. Hill walks and mountain climbing with spectacular lake views, an archaeological and geological paradise. Traditional music and bar food.

B&B from €32.00 to €50.00
£25.20 to £39.38

FRANK & CARMEL LYDON
OWNERS

American Express

Diners

Mastercard

Visa

🛏️ 🛎️ 📞⬜TCMU🎵🔲alc
11 11

HOTELS
FEDERATION

Closed 05 November - 01 February

 B&B rates are per person sharing per night incl. Breakfast

RYAN'S HOTEL

CONG,
CO. MAYO

TEL: 092-46243 FAX: 092-46634
EMAIL: michaelv@indigo.ie

HOTEL ★★ MAP 9 E 12

The idyllic riverside setting of Ryan's Hotel is more than matched by the outstanding service and lovely surroundings inside. Just a few minutes' walk from the famous free brown trout fishing lake Lough Corrib, the hotel is ideally situated for touring the west coast including the breathtaking views of Connemara. Because of its unique beauty, Cong was chosen by John Ford for his film The Quiet Man.

Member of MinOtel Ireland Hotel Group

B&B from €45.00 to €57.00
£35.44 to £44.89

MICHAEL & GERALDINE RYAN
OWNERS

Mastercard

Visa

12 12

TEACH IORRAIS

GEESALA,
BALLINA,
CO. MAYO

TEL: 097-86888 FAX: 097-86855
EMAIL: teachior@iol.ie
WEB: www.teachiorrais.com

HOTEL ★★★ MAP 10 F 15

Situated in an area of unrivalled beauty, Teach Iorrais is an exclusive and luxurious hotel in Co. Mayo. The hotel boasts 31 exquisite en suite bedrooms which are decorated to the highest standard and offer awe-inspiring views of the surrounding Neiphinn Mountains and the Atlantic Ocean. An Neiphinn Restaurant offers the best of fine dining in a relaxing and intimate environment. Our theme bar, Beear Synge, is one of the Irish Pubs of Distinction. Carne Links Golf Course located 15 minutes drive from hotel.

B&B from €46.00 to €62.00
£36.22 to £48.81

PATRICIA GAUGHAN
MANAGER

American Express

Diners

Mastercard

Visa

☺ Weekend specials from €100.31

31 31

S 🅿 alc

IRISH HOTELS FEDERATION

CILL AODAIN HOTEL

MAIN STREET,
KILTIMAGH,
CO. MAYO

TEL: 094-81761 FAX: 094-81838
EMAIL: cillaodain@eircom.net

HOTEL ★★ MAP 10 F 14

This RAC 3*** hotel is set in the centre of historic Kiltimagh. Furnished with flair and imagination, panelled lounges and open fires. The restaurant which has received many accolades is open each evening. The rooms, with all amenities, are individually furnished and decorated. Kiltimagh is one of Ireland's most famous small towns. 5km off Galway to Sligo Road. Ideally situated for visiting Knock Village. Member of Village Inns of Ireland.

Member of Village Inn Hotels

B&B from €37.00 to €57.00
£29.00 to £45.00

TONY MCDERMOTT
INNKEEPER

American Express

Diners

Mastercard

Visa

12 12

alc

Room rates are per room per night

BELMONT HOTEL

KNOCK,
CO. MAYO

TEL: 094-88122 FAX: 094-88532
EMAIL: belmonthotel@eircom.net
WEB: www.belmonthotel.ie

HOTEL ★★★ MAP 10 G 13

A haven of hospitality nestled at the rear entrance to Knock Shrine off N17. The hotel radiates Old Country Warmth from the moment you arrive. Recently RAC 3*** accreditation is added to Irish Tourist Board 3*** and AA 3*** status. Our An Bialann Restaurant is the recipient of 3 AA Rosette Awards. All day carvery is available and our specially developed Natural Health Therapy packages compliment our services. All rooms tastefully furnished with direct dial phone, TV, tea/coffee making facilities.

Member of Logis of Ireland

B&B from €39.00 to €54.00
£30.71 to £42.53

TERENCE EGAN
MANAGER

American Express
Diners
Mastercard
Visa

63 63

IRISH HOTELS FEDERATION

Open All Year

KNOCK HOUSE HOTEL

BALLYHAUNIS ROAD,
KNOCK,
CO. MAYO

TEL: 094-88088 FAX: 094-88044
EMAIL: hotel@knock-shrine.ie
WEB: www.knock-shrine.ie

HOTEL ★★★ MAP 10 G 13

Knock House Hotel opened in May 1999 and is located in 100 acres of parkland, behind the famous Marian Shrine, just minutes from the Basilica. The foyer of local limestone and a glazed area give unparalleled views of the surrounding countryside. 6 guestrooms have been especially designed to cater for wheelchair users. The Four Seasons Restaurant is ideal for snacks and full meals.

B&B from €48.00 to €62.00
£37.80 to £48.83

BRIAN CROWLEY
MANAGER

Diners
Mastercard
Visa

68 68

IRISH HOTELS FEDERATION

Open All Year

KNOCK INTERNATIONAL HOTEL

MAIN STREET,
KNOCK,
CO. MAYO

TEL: 094-88466 FAX: 094-88428

HOTEL ★★ MAP 10 G 13

Knock International Hotel was opened in 1986 by Mary and Edward Curry, who have been catering for pilgrims for years at Fairfield Restaurant. Set in its own gardens only minutes from Knock Shrine. Also only 10 minutes from Knock Airport. The Currys are joined in the operations by their family and the hotel is especially suited for weddings and functions. Credit cards, Access, Visa.

B&B from €35.55 to €40.63
£28.00 to £32.00

MR & MRS EDWARD CURRY
OWNERS

Mastercard
Visa

10 10

IRISH HOTELS FEDERATION

Closed 13 October - 29 March

B&B rates are per person sharing per night incl. Breakfast

HEALY'S RESTAURANT AND HOTEL

PONTOON,
FOXFORD,
CO. MAYO
TEL: 094-56443 FAX: 094-56572
EMAIL: healyspontoon@eircom.net
WEB: www.irelandmayohotel.com

HOTEL ★★ MAP 9 F 14

In the heart of Mayo, Ireland's best location for golf and fishing. Owner managed. Healy's Restaurant "probably the best food in the West". Scenically overlooking Lough Cullen/Conn. 10 minutes from the River Moy, one of Western Europe's best salmon rivers. Healys is 30 minutes from Enniscrone Golf Links which now has 27 holes, 30 minutes from Westport Championship Golf Course and one hour from the magic Carne Golf Links in Belmullet.

B&B from € 32.00 to €39.00
£25.20 to £30.71

JOHN DEVER
PROPRIETOR

American Express
Diners
Mastercard
Visa

Closed 25 December

PONTOON BRIDGE HOTEL

PONTOON,
FOXFORD,
CO. MAYO
TEL: 094-56120 FAX: 094-56688
EMAIL: relax@pontoonbridge.com
WEB: www.pontoonbridge.com

HOTEL ★★★ MAP 10 F 14

Family managed hotel on the shores of Lough Conn and Cullin in the centre of Mayo. Famous for trout and salmon fishing - River Moy, golf, horseriding, scenery, central for touring. Twin Lakes Restaurant. Live musical entertainment nightly during season. Tennis court, sandy beaches, conference facilities. Families welcome. School of flyfishing, landscape painting and cookery. Leisure Centre opening Spring 2002.

B&B from € 57.00 to €82.00
£44.89 to £64.58

BREETA GEARY
GENERAL MANAGER

American Express
Mastercard
Visa

Closed 24 - 26 December

ARDMORE COUNTRY HOUSE HOTEL AND RESTAURANT

THE QUAY,
WESTPORT,
CO. MAYO
TEL: 098-25994 FAX: 098-27795
EMAIL: ardmore@anu.ie
WEB: www.ardmorecountryhouse.com

HOTEL ★★★★ MAP 9 E 13

Ardmore Country House and Restaurant is a small luxurious 4**** hotel, owned and managed by Pat & Noreen Hoban and family, offering warm hospitality. Ardmore House is idyllically situated overlooking Clew Bay with breathtaking sunsets, in the shadow of Croagh Patrick. The Restaurant offers the best of local produce, including fresh fish from Clew Bay, organic vegetables and herbs from local producers and a selection of Irish farmhouse cheeses. All bedrooms are non-smoking.

B&B from € 80.00 to € 115.00
£63.01 to £90.57

NOREEN & PAT HOBAN

American Express
Mastercard
Visa

Closed 01 February - 01 March

Room rates are per room per night

ATLANTIC COAST HOTEL

THE QUAY,
WESTPORT,
CO. MAYO
TEL: 098-29000 FAX: 098-29111
EMAIL: achotel@iol.ie
WEB: www.atlanticcoasthotel.com

HOTEL ★★★★ MAP 9 E 13

Recently established as one of Westport's finest and most popular hotels, situated on the waterfront at Westport Quay overlooking Clew Bay. Superb contemporary cuisine in our unique top floor award winning restaurant -The Blue Wave. The Atlantic Club features pool, gym, sauna, steamroom & massage, including seaweed hydrotherapy bath treatments. Championship golf, angling, scenic walks, islands & Blue Flag beaches nearby. Your perfect base to explore beautiful Westport. Callsave: 1850 229000

B&B from €50.00 to €89.00
£39.38 to £70.09

JOHN VARLEY
GENERAL MANAGER

American Express
Mastercard
Visa

😊 Weekend specials from €127.00

85 85

Closed 23 - 27 December

AUGUSTA LODGE

GOLF LINKS ROAD,
WESTPORT,
CO. MAYO
TEL: 098-28900 FAX: 098-28995
EMAIL: info@augustalodge.ie
WEB: www.augustalodge.ie

GUESTHOUSE ★★★ MAP 9 E 13

Augusta Lodge is a purpose-built 3*** guesthouse situated just 5 minutes walk from the town centre of Westport. A warm and friendly welcome awaits you in this family run guesthouse and Liz and Dave will ensure that your stay is a memorable one. A golfer's haven with tee times and green fees arranged at Westport and adjacent courses. Putting green on site for guests use. Listed in all leading guides.

B&B from €23.00 to €38.00
£18.11 to £29.93

LIZ O'REGAN

Mastercard
Visa

10 10

Closed 23 - 27 December

CASTLECOURT HOTEL CONFERENCE AND LEISURE CENTRE

CASTLEBAR STREET,
WESTPORT,
CO. MAYO
TEL: 098-25444 FAX: 098-28622
EMAIL: info@castlecourthotel.ie
WEB: www.castlecourthotel.ie

HOTEL ★★★ MAP 9 E 13

Perfectly located in the heart of Westport, a genuine welcome awaits you at this spectacular hotel which is run by the Corcoran family since 1971. The hotel has been completely refurbished and extended and guests can enjoy 140 bedrooms (deluxe rooms available), indoor heated swimming pool, children's pool, spa, sauna, steamroom, sunbed, children's creche, health suites for aromatherapy and massage, hairdressing salon, 200 car parking spaces, conservatory concourse and an award winning restaurant.

Member of Holiday Ireland Hotels
B&B from €55.00 to €100.00
£43.32 to £78.76

JOSEPH & ANNE CORCORAN
MANAGERS

American Express
Diners
Mastercard
Visa

😊 Weekend specials from €119.00

140 140

Closed 24 - 26 December

B&B rates are per person sharing per night incl. Breakfast

CENTRAL HOTEL

THE OCTAGON,
WESTPORT,
CO. MAYO
TEL: 098-25027 FAX: 098-26316
EMAIL: centralhotel@anu.ie
WEB: www.thecentralhotel.com

HOTEL ★★★ MAP 9 E 13

A warm friendly newly renovated hotel located in the heart of Westport's beautiful town. 54 superbly appointed rooms all en suite with tea/coffee making facilities, irons, TV, hair dryer and DD phone. Enjoy dining in the Wyatt Bistro or our acclaimed bar menu in J. W's Bar - famous for its clam chowder and fresh seafood. 4**** leisure facilities available 50 yards from the hotel. Padraig and his team are there to offer you a personal service with good old fashioned hospitality.

Member of Logis of Ireland
B&B from €52.00 to €76.00
£40.95 to £59.85

PADRAIG MCCARTHY
GENERAL MANAGER

American Express
Mastercard
Visa

:/Ⅰ

☺ Weekend specials from €140.00

54 54

Closed 24 - 26 December

CLEW BAY HOTEL

JAMES STREET,
WESTPORT,
CO. MAYO
TEL: 098-28088 FAX: 098-25783
EMAIL: info@clewbayhotel.com
WEB: www.clewbayhotel.com

HOTEL ★★★ MAP 9 E 13

Enjoy our warm friendly family run hotel situated in Westport Town centre. Our newly renovated hotel has 28 en suite rooms finished to the highest standard of comfort. Guests can enjoy the Old World charm of the Tubber Bar that features traditional music. The Riverside Restaurant overlooking the Carrowbeg River offers an imaginative menu, modestly priced. Local attractions include Westport Leisure Park, golfing, angling, pony trekking, scenic walks/drives, beaches.

Member of Village Inn Hotels
B&B from €45.00 to €65.00
£35.44 to £51.19

DARREN MADDEN & MARIA RUDDY
PROPRIETORS

Mastercard
Visa

☺ Weekend specials from €115.00

28 28

Closed 22 - 27 December

HOTEL WESTPORT, CONFERENCE & LEISURE CENTRE

THE DEMESNE,
NEWPORT ROAD, WESTPORT,
CO. MAYO
TEL: 098-25122 FAX: 098-26739
EMAIL: reservations@hotelwestport.ie
WEB: www.hotelwestport.ie

HOTEL ★★★ MAP 9 E 13

This uniquely comfortable, friendly hotel is set in its own tranquil parklands, in the heart of Westport Town, offering a unique experience in relaxation and leisure. Our state of the art conference centre and ultra modern swimming pool/leisure centre offer an excellent range of accommodation with delightful food, wine, entertainment for your business or leisure break. Local attractions: golf, scenic walks/drives, cycling, angling, pony trekking, beaches. Callsave: 1850 53 63 73

B&B from €83.00 to €102.00
£65.37 to £80.33

GERRY WALSHE
GENERAL MANAGER

American Express
Diners
Mastercard
Visa

:/ⅡⅠ

☺ Weekend specials from €126.00

129 129

Open All Year

Room rates are per room per night

KNOCKRANNY HOUSE HOTEL

WESTPORT,
CO. MAYO

TEL: 098-28600 FAX: 098-28611
EMAIL: info@khh.ie
WEB: www.khh.ie

HOTEL ★★★★ MAP 9 E 13

Situated on a hillside overlooking picturesque town of Westport, Knockranny House Hotel enjoys unrivalled views of Clew Bay & Croagh Patrick. The hotel is full of character with log fires creating a warm and relaxed atmosphere. The restaurant 'La Fougère' offers excellent cuisine with an emphasis on fresh seafood and the finest local ingredients. Westport is a charming town with a lot to offer. Local activities include golf, angling, horse riding, water sports and much more.

B&B from € 89.00 to € 115.00
£70.08 to £90.57

GERALDINE & ADRIAN NOONAN
PROPRIETORS

American Express
Mastercard
Visa

54 54

S alc Inet FAX

IRISH HOTELS FEDERATION

Closed 23 - 27 December

KNOCKRANNY LODGE

KNOCKRANNY,
WESTPORT,
CO. MAYO

TEL: 098-28595 FAX: 098-28805
EMAIL: knockranny@anu.ie
WEB: www.anu.ie/knockrannylodge

GUESTHOUSE ★★★★ MAP 9 E 13

Knockranny Lodge is a beautifully appointed 4**** guesthouse. It has the peace and tranquillity of the country and yet is only 5 mins walk to town. Relax and enjoy a cup of tea or coffee in our welcoming lounge. All of our en suite bedrooms have direct dial phone, multi-channel TV, trouserpress and hairdryer. Private tennis court and car park. We have full use of swimming pool and leisure complex in nearby sister hotel. AA ◆◆◆◆◆

B&B from € 35.00 to € 60.00
£27.56 to £47.25

MARY MCDERMOTT

American Express
Diners
Mastercard
Visa

12 12

Closed 01 December - 30 January

OLDE RAILWAY HOTEL

THE MALL,
WESTPORT,
CO. MAYO

TEL: 098-25166 FAX: 098-25090
EMAIL: railway@anu.ie
WEB: www.anu.ie/railwayhotel

HOTEL ★★★ MAP 9 E 13

Get away from it all and be pampered in this tastefully appointed 18th Century coaching inn. Standard and superior accommodation. Renowned for traditional country fare and fine wines. Genuine hospitality and warm welcome in relaxing intimate surroundings. Conservatory restaurant, residents' lounge and library, turf fires, original antique furniture adorn. Patio and garden area. Organic vegetable garden for restaurant. Recommended in all leading guides, Egon Ronay, AA Rosette winner.

B&B from € 45.00 to € 90.00
£35.44 to £70.88

KARL ROSENKRANZ
OWNER/MANAGER

American Express
Diners
Mastercard
Visa

15 15

alc

IRISH HOTELS FEDERATION

Open All Year

B&B rates are per person sharing per night incl. Breakfast

QUAY WEST

QUAY ROAD,
WESTPORT,
CO. MAYO
TEL: 098-27863 FAX: 098-27863

GUESTHOUSE N   MAP 9 E 13

Quay West is a purpose built house situated 10 minutes walk from town and 5 minutes from the harbour and directly opposite Westport Woods Hotel where guests can enjoy the superb leisure facilities at discounted rates. Rooms are en suite with power showers, orthopaedic beds and TV. Lounge for guest comfort with tea/coffee facilities. Perfect base for touring beautiful Mayo, Connemara and relaxing in some of Westport's famous pubs and restaurants.

B&B from €23.00 to €38.00
£18.11 to £29.93

DAVID KELLY
PROPRIETOR

Mastercard
Visa

🛏🐾⌨TC⌣PS
6   6

Closed 24 - 27 December

WESTPORT INN HOTEL

TOWN CENTRE,
MILL STREET, WESTPORT,
CO. MAYO
TEL: 098-29200 FAX: 098-29250
EMAIL: info@westportinn.ie
WEB: www.westportinn.ie

HOTEL N   MAP 9 E 13

Westport's newest and liveliest hotel offering a rate per room. Located in the centre of Westport, this charming Inn is 3*** standard with all bedrooms equipped with DD phone, TV, iron/board, tea/coffee making facilities and hairdryer. The original structure has been retained to give a sense of the past, while being right up to date in its approach. Secure parking available. Home of WITS nightclub. Up to 3 adults or 2 adults and 2 children per room.

Room Rate from €50.00 to €125.00
£39.38 to £98.45

BRENDAN KEALY
PROPRIETOR

American Express
Diners
Mastercard
Visa

✓

☺ Weekend specials from €108.00

🛏🐾☎⌨🅱C⌨CM⌣♪PS🅰
34   34
[ald] [Inet]

Open All Year

WESTPORT WOODS HOTEL & LEISURE CENTRE

QUAY ROAD,
WESTPORT,
CO. MAYO
TEL: 098-25811 FAX: 098-26212
EMAIL: info@westportwoodshotel.com
WEB: www.westportwoodshotel.com

HOTEL ★★★   MAP 9 E 13

Friendly, cosy hotel with fabulous 'Beech Club' leisure centre, set in mature woodland, overlooking private lake. Enjoy unforgettable family holidays with our famous Kiddies Club or treat yourself to a terrific theme break, ranging from golf and murder mystery to bridge and short mat bowls. Glorious "young at heart" getaways are a speciality in this welcoming establishment. Situated on the road to the harbour, the hotel is ideally located for lots of fascinating day trips - Kylemore Abbey, Achill, Clare Island, Croagh Patrick plus lots more.

Member of Brian McEniff Hotels
B&B from €50.00 to €99.00
£39.38 to £77.97

MICHAEL LENNON &
JOANNE MCENIFF

American Express
Mastercard
Visa

☺ Murder Mystery weekends from €159.00

🛏🐾☎T🅰C⌨CM❄🄿🄶□
111   111
🌊⌣♪PS🅰ald

Open All Year

WHITEHOUSE HOTEL

**BALLINLOUGH,
CO. ROSCOMMON**

TEL: 0907-40112 FAX: 0907-40993
EMAIL: thewhitehousehotel@eircom.net
WEB: www.white-house-hotel.com

HOTEL N   MAP 10 H 13

Located on the Roscommon Mayo border stands the all-new luxurious Whitehouse Hotel. Enjoy our lunchtime carvery in the bar whilst our Blue Room Restaurant offers the finest in contemporary and traditional cuisine. Frequent live music and traditional sessions throughout the year add to the ambience of this unique hotel. The hotel is just a short drive from Lough O'Flynn and within 6 miles of Ballyhaunis and Castlerea Golf Clubs.

Member of Protelier
B&B from €50.00 to €95.00
£39.37 to £74.81

MARTIN DALY
GENERAL MANAGER

American Express
Diners
Mastercard
Visa

19 19

Inet

Closed 25 December

FOREST PARK HOTEL

**DUBLIN ROAD,
BOYLE,
CO. ROSCOMMON**
TEL: 079-62229 FAX: 079-63113

HOTEL ★★   MAP 10 I 14

Newly refurbished family run hotel on the main Dublin-Sligo Road. Located 1km from town centre. All rooms are en suite with tea and coffee making facilities. Full restaurant & bar facilities available daily. Ideal touring centre close to Lough Key Forest Park, Boyle Abbey, Arigna Drive & King House. Available locally are 9 Hole Golf, Fishing, Walking, Cycling & Animal Farm. Close to Knock & Sligo Airports.

B&B from €44.44 to €63.49
£35.00 to £50.00

ROSALEEN & FINIAN DWYER
PROPRIETORS

American Express
Diners
Mastercard
Visa

12 12

Closed 24 - 26 December

ROYAL HOTEL

**BRIDGE STREET,
BOYLE,
CO. ROSCOMMON**
TEL: 079-62016 FAX: 079-64949

HOTEL ★★   MAP 10 I 14

Royal Hotel is over 250 years old. Under the new ownership since December 1999 of Nelson Chung & Adrian Bouchier, General Manager, it consists of 16 en suite bedrooms. Coffee shop open daily serving hot food from 8 a.m to 6 p.m. Chung's famous Chinese restaurant is also part of the hotel opening at 6 p.m. nightly until late. AA***. Private car park. Member of MinOtel Marketing Group, Ballycanew, Co. Wexford. Tel.353-55-27291. Fax:353-55-27398

Member of MinOtel Ireland Hotel Group
B&B from €50.79 to €60.95
£40.00 to £48.00

ADRIAN BOUCHIER & NELSON CHUNG

Mastercard
Visa

16 16

alc Inet FAX

Open All Year

B&B rates are per person sharing per night incl. Breakfast

SHANNON KEY WEST HOTEL

**THE RIVER EDGE,
ROOSKEY,
CO. ROSCOMMON**

TEL: 078-38800 FAX: 078-38811
EMAIL: shnkywst@iol.ie
WEB: www.keywest.firebird.net

HOTEL ★★★ MAP 11 J 13

Situated on N4 Dublin Sligo route, 2km from Dromod Train Station, this beautiful 40 bedroom hotel with Greek, Georgian and modern architecture offers panoramic views of Shannon River from both bedrooms and roof gardens. All rooms are well appointed with direct dial phone - modem compatible. Rooskey Inn and Kilglass Restaurants offer excellent choice of cuisine. Leisure club and tennis court. Enjoy scenic trips on Shannon Queen. While away your time in elegant and peaceful surroundings.

Member of Best Western Hotels

B&B from €50.00 to €59.00
£39.38 to £46.47

JOHN LIKELY
MANAGING DIRECTOR

American Express
Mastercard
Visa

39 39

PS 🅰ⓐ

IRISH HOTELS FEDERATION

Closed 24 - 26 December

ABBEY HOTEL

**GALWAY ROAD,
ROSCOMMON TOWN**

TEL: 0903-26240 FAX: 0903-26021
EMAIL: cmv@indigo.ie

HOTEL ★★★ MAP 10 I 12

This eighteenth century manor has been carefully transformed into an exceedingly well appointed country house hotel beautifully set in four acres of private lawns. The Abbey offers excellent accommodation. The old wing rooms are a special feature and a fine restaurant is open to non residents. The hotel is three star rated by Bord Fáilte, AA and RAC. Recommended in most guide books. Roscommon Town is on these holiday routes - Dublin/Westport, Shannon/Donegal and Belfast/Galway.

Member of Coast and Country Hotels

B&B from €60.00 to €75.00
£47.25 to £59.07

TOMMY & ANYA GREALY
MANAGER/MANAGERESS

American Express
Diners
Mastercard
Visa

25 25

IRISH HOTELS FEDERATION

Closed 25 - 26 December

GLEESONS TOWNHOUSE & RESTAURANT

**MARKET SQUARE,
ROSCOMMON TOWN**

TEL: 0903-26954 FAX: 0903-27425
EMAIL: gleerest@iol.ie
WEB: www.gleesonstownhouse.com

GUESTHOUSE ★★★ MAP 10 I 12

Magnificent Townhouse/Restaurant in a tastefully restored listed 19th Century Town House with an attractive finish of cut limestone and blue Bangor quarry slates. Located in the town centre next door to the Tourist Office/Museum. We offer superb accommodation with all 19 rooms built to a 4 star standard. Private car parking. Experience "The Manse" Restaurant where all the old values of guest satisfaction comfort and value for money prevail. Fully licensed for beers/spirits/wine. Anglers/Golf facility centre on-site. Conference facilities available.

Member of Premier Guesthouses of Ireland

B&B from €35.00 to €45.00
£27.56 to £35.44

MARY & EAMONN GLEESON
PROPRIETORS

American Express
Diners
Mastercard
Visa

☺ Weekend specials from €89.00

19 19

🅰ⓐ 📶 Inet

IRISH HOTELS FEDERATION

Closed 25 - 26 December

Room rates are per room per night

O'GARA'S ROYAL HOTEL

CASTLE STREET,
ROSCOMMON TOWN

TEL: 0903-26317 FAX: 0903-26225

HOTEL ★★ MAP 10 | 12

O'Gara's Royal Hotel family run, situated on the Dublin to Castlebar/Westport route. 19 bedrooms en suite, radio, direct dial phone, TV, video, hair dryer. Comfortable modern dining room with good food and friendly service. Coffee dock/carvery. Spacious lounge bar with pleasant surroundings. Private car park. A warm welcome awaits you. Available 3 new conference rooms fully equipped with the latest facilities. Golfing holidays a speciality with a number of top golf courses locally.

B&B from €32.00 to €45.00
£25.20 to £35.44

AILEEN & LARRY O'GARA
PROPRIETORS

American Express
Mastercard
Visa

19 19

HOTELS
FEDERATION

Open All Year

REGANS

MARKET SQUARE,
ROSCOMMON TOWN

TEL: 0903-25339 FAX: 0903-27833
EMAIL: info@regans.com
WEB: www.regansbar.com

GUESTHOUSE ★★★ MAP 10 | 12

Regan's is a family run 3*** licenced guesthouse situated in Roscommon Town Centre. It provides a central base to explore the town and environs. Regans boasts a fine bar, restaurant and 14 en suite bedrooms, all with satellite TV and direct dial phone facilities. We have also added a new dimension by way of two bedroom self-catering apartments. Our restaurant offers good quality food at a reasonable price. Also available is a fully equipped conference room. A warm welcome awaits you.

B&B from €31.75 to €38.00
£25.00 to £30.00

EAMON & DOMINIC REGAN
MANAGERS

American Express
Mastercard
Visa

14 14

Closed 24 - 26 December

B&B rates are per person sharing per night incl. Breakfast

NORTH WEST
Atlantic and Lakelands

Ireland's North West spans a huge variety of landscape, from the rolling drumlins and tranquil lakes of counties Cavan and Monaghan in the east, to the lovely valleys of Leitrim and Sligo and the dramatic wild landscape of Co. Donegal in the west. Three of the counties, Donegal, Leitrim and Sligo bathe their feet in the restless Atlantic and the Shannon Erne Waterway connects the other great water courses in the region, the Shannon and the Erne Rivers.

FESTIVALS AND EVENTS
The North West offers many unexplored peaceful beauty spots, but lively action too. Festivals and events abound, from the Letterkenny and Ballyshannon Folk Festivals, Sligo International Choral Festival, the Mary from Dungloe International Festival, to the Yeats International Summer School, the Mullaghamore Lobster Festival, the North Leitrim Walking Festival and the Monaghan Jazz Festival.

MAJOR ATTRACTIONS
Two major attractions are Bundoran's Waterworld and the Visitor Centre at Carrowmore near Sligo, the largest and most important megalithic site in Europe. Not to

Lough Muckno Park, Co. Monaghan

be missed in Co. Donegal are the Lakeside Museum at Dunlewy, Glencolumbkille Folk Museum, Glenveagh National Park, Donegal Castle, the Vintage Car Museum in Buncrana and Parian China and Celtic Weave in Ballyshannon.

In Co. Cavan, visit the Cavan Crystal and Cavan County Museum and explore Swan Island Visitor Farm and Moon River Cruises on the Shannon in Co. Leitrim. In Co. Monaghan, visit the Patrick Kavanagh Centre in Inniskeen, also worth a visit are Ireland's only motor sport activity centre at Rally School Ireland in Scotstown and the award winning Monaghan County Museum. Near Sligo town, follow the sculpture trail through Hazelwood Forest Park, pamper yourself at the Celtic Seawee

Tra Na Rosann Bay, Co. Donegal

Baths at Strandhill and visit Yeats Grave at Drumcliffe Church and Heritage Centre.

Alternatively, discover our culture in the lively traditional music sessions that are held in pubs throughout the region.

For further information and assistance in planning your holiday and making accommodation reservations please contact:–

The North West Tourism Authority,
Temple Street, Sligo.
Tel: 071 61201. Fax: 071 60360
OR
Tourist Information Office,
Derry Road, Letterkenny, Co. Donegal.
Tel: 074 21160. Fax: 074 25180.

GUINNESS.

Sligo Arts Festival, Co. Sligo.
June

Guinness Mary from Dungloe International Festival, Co. Donegal.
July / August

Yeats International Summer School, Co. Sligo.
August

Event details correct at time of going to press

CO. DONEGAL
ARDARA / BALLYBOFEY

General Tourist Information

Banking
Banks are normally open from Monday to Friday 10.00 to 16.00. Many Banks stay open until 17.00 on Thursdays. Visitors are advised to change their bank notes at banks and Bureaux de Change to get the best exchange rate. Most credit cards, including all cards carrying the Eurocheque symbol, are accepted in hotels, restaurants, petrol stations and most shops. ATMs located at most banks accept major credit cards.

Medical Treatment
Citizens of the European Community are entitled to free hospital treatment in a public ward and should obtain an E111 form prior to departure. When necessary, this should be presented to the doctor or hospital visited, along with identification.
Visitors from other countries should check with their insurance agent or broker before travelling to establish their entitlement to recover additional medical expenses.

Public Holidays
The following are the public holidays in the Republic of Ireland (those in Northern Ireland differ slightly). Most companies and shops are closed on these days.

January 1st; March 17th; Friday before Easter; Monday after Easter; First Monday in May, June and August; Last Monday in October; Christmas Day; St. Stephen's Day

---

WOODHILL HOUSE

ARDARA,
CO. DONEGAL

TEL: 075-41112 FAX: 075-41516
EMAIL: yates@iol.ie
WEB: www.woodhillhouse.com

GUESTHOUSE ★★★ MAP 13 H 18

An historic country house, the site dates back to the 17th century. The house is set in its own grounds, overlooking the Donegal Highlands. There is a quality restaurant, with fully licensed bar and occasional music. The area, famous for its Donegal tweeds and woollen goods, also offers salmon and trout fishing, pony trekking, golf, boating, cycling, bathing beaches, many archaeological sites, Sheskinmore Wildlife Reserve, Slieve League and some of the most unspoiled scenery in Europe.

B&B from €45.00 to €60.00
£35.44 to £47.25

NANCY & JOHN YATES
OWNERS

American Express
Diners
Mastercard
Visa

99

Closed 24 - 27 December

JACKSON'S HOTEL

BALLYBOFEY,
CO. DONEGAL

TEL: 074-31021 FAX: 074-31096
EMAIL: bjackson@iol.ie
WEB: www.jacksons-hotel.ie

HOTEL ★★★ MAP 13 J 19

Jackson's award winning family run hotel is situated in its own gardens with all 87 bedrooms en suite with mod cons. Relax at the log fire at reception or enjoy breathtaking views of the River Finn and Drumboe Woods. Close to Glenveagh National Park and ideal for golf, fishing, hill walking and horse riding. Indulge in fine cuisine in the Bally Buffet Bistro or Garden Restaurant. Leisure club with swimming pool, jacuzzi, sauna, sun beds, massage and gym.

B&B from €55.25 to €66.75
£43.51 to £52.57

MARGARET & BARRY JACKSON
PROPRIETORS

American Express
Diners
Mastercard
Visa

87 87

Open All Year

B&B rates are per person sharing per night incl. Breakfast

KEE'S HOTEL

STRANORLAR,
BALLYBOFEY,
CO. DONEGAL
TEL: 074-31018 FAX: 074-31917
EMAIL: info@keehotel.ie
WEB: www.keeshotel.ie

HOTEL ★★★ MAP 13 J 19

This charming historic family run hotel in its pleasant village situation overlooking the Blue Stack Mountains has that special atmosphere, a combination of excellent facilities, caring staff and management, which draws guests back time and again. The elegant Looking Glass Restaurant awarded 2 AA Rosettes of Excellence. The Old Gallery Restaurant for more casual dining. Delightful en suite rooms with TV, tea/coffee facilities, hairdryer, trouser press. Comprehensive leisure club.

B&B from €63.00 to €74.00
£49.62 to £58.28

RICHARD & VICKY KEE

American Express
Diners
Mastercard
Visa

☺ Weekend specials from €129.00

53 53

Open All Year

DOHERTY'S POLLAN BEACH HOTEL

ARDAGH,
BALLYLIFFIN,
CO. DONEGAL
TEL: 077-78991 FAX: 077-78991
EMAIL: pollanbeachhotel@eircom.net
WEB: www.pollanbeachhotel.com

UNDER CONSTRUCTION - OPENING MARCH 2002

HOTEL P MAP 14 K 21

Doherty's Pollan Beach Hotel is situated 100yds from sandy beach with childrens playground. All bedrooms are en suite, equipped with modern facilities. Most bedrooms have sea views. Spacious dining room and bar overlooking the beach and Atlantic ocean. The hotel overlooks the two 18 hole golf courses in Ballyliffin, the Classic Old Links and the New Glasheady Links. Ideal for: golf, fishing, cycling and walking. 40 minutes drive from city of Derry airport, 2 hours drive from Belfast International. Perfect retreat for short break.

B&B from €57.14 to €76.18
£45.00 to £60.00

VINCENT AND KATHLEEN DOHERTY
PROPRIETORS

American Express
Diners
Mastercard
Visa

20 20
alc Inet

Open All Year

Room rates are per room per night

DORRIANS IMPERIAL HOTEL

MAIN STREET,
BALLYSHANNON,
CO. DONEGAL

TEL: 072-51147 FAX: 072-51001

EMAIL: info@dorriansimperialhotel.com
WEB: www.dorriansimperialhotel.com

HOTEL U   MAP 13 1 17

Town centre family run hotel (built 1781). All rooms en suite with TV, phone and tea/coffee making facilities. Gym. Private car park. Hotel recently renovated, embracing old and new decor, elevator. Ideally suited for touring North West and North East Ireland. Ideally located for golfing and fishing. Sligo 45km, Belfast 202 km, Dublin 216km.

Member of Logis of Ireland
B&B from €50.75 to €70.00
£39.97 to £55.13

BEN & MARY DORRIAN
PROPRIETORS

Mastercard

Visa

☺ Weekend specials from €120.00

47 47

Closed 22 - 31 December

FORGE

ROSSNOWLAGH ROAD,
BALLYSHANNON,
CO. DONEGAL

TEL: 072-22070 FAX: 072-22075

EMAIL: theforgeguesthouse@eircom.net

GUESTHOUSE N   MAP 13 1 17

Crafted with care, easy on the eye, this unique Irish country guesthouse and restaurant is definitely worth a visit. Ideally located about 3 miles from Ballyshannon and the same from Rossnowlagh Beach. With 10 superb en suite bedrooms you can relax in comfort. We have combined traditional charm, modern design and gracious hospitality. Dedicated to the highest standard 'The Forge' Restaurant features contemporary creative cuisine that will excite your palate.

B&B from €40.00 to €45.00
£31.50 to £35.44

COLM & FIONA ROPER

American Express

Mastercard

Visa

☺ Weekend specials from €100.00

10 10

Closed 19 November - 9 December

OSTAN GWEEDORE HOTEL & LEISURE COMPLEX

BUNBEG,
CO. DONEGAL

TEL: 075-31177 FAX: 075-31726

EMAIL: ostangweedore@ireland.com
WEB: www.ostangweedore.com

HOTEL ★★★   MAP 13 1 20

Luxury hotel, all major guides approved, with 36 bedrooms & 3 executive suites, leisure centre with 19m swimming pool, children's pool, sauna, steam room & jacuzzi. Our award winning restaurant, overlooking the Atlantic, specialises in salmon & lobster fresh from the ocean. The Library Bar is the ideal place to relax with a quiet drink and a good book. 9-hole golf course & fishing available locally.

B&B from €50.80 to €70.00
£40.01 to £55.13

CHARLES BOYLE
MANAGING DIRECTOR

American Express

Mastercard

Visa

☺ Weekend specials from €153.00

36 36

Closed 01 December - 31 January

B&B rates are per person sharing per night incl. Breakfast

OSTAN RADHARC NA MARA

SEA VIEW HOTEL,
BUNBEG,
CO. DONEGAL
TEL: 075-31159 FAX: 075-32238
EMAIL: ostanradharcnamara@eircom.net

HOTEL ★★ MAP 13 I 20

In an area where nature remains untouched, the air is rich and pure, ensuring a heavy appetite. In the Seaview Hotel, guests are treated to wonderful food. The à la carte menu always includes a seasonal selection of fresh, local seafood dishes, with salmon, trout, lobster and oysters a speciality.

B&B from €38.00 to €44.44
£29.93 to £35.00

JAMES BOYLE
GENERAL MANAGER

Mastercard
Visa

37 37

alc

Closed 23 - 28 December

ALLINGHAM ARMS HOTEL

MAIN STREET,
BUNDORAN,
CO. DONEGAL
TEL: 072-41075 FAX: 072-41171
EMAIL: allinghamarmshotel1@eircom.net
WEB: www.tyrconnell-group.com

HOTEL ★★★ MAP 13 I 17

Hospitality is a Donegal tradition and nowhere is the tradition more honoured than at the Allingham Arms Hotel. The Allingham's comfortable rooms, good food and considerate personal attention contribute to the stress-free atmosphere which many clients feel is a holiday in itself. Entertainment at weekends and nightly during the summer season.

B&B from €45.00 to €60.00
£35.44 to £47.25

PETER MCINTYRE
MANAGER

American Express
Diners
Mastercard
Visa

117 117

alc

Closed 22 - 27 December

GRAND CENTRAL HOTEL

MAIN STREET,
BUNDORAN,
CO. DONEGAL
TEL: 072-42722 FAX: 072-42656
EMAIL: grandcentral@eircom.net

HOTEL ★★★ MAP 13 I 17

Situated in Bundoran, Co. Donegal we provide the perfect base for touring Donegal, Sligo, Leitrim and Northern Ireland. The hotel consists of 62 bedrooms, all tastefully decorated with the emphasis on luxury and relaxation. Large family rooms and rooms with facilities for the disabled are also available. Our restaurant and bar is known locally for its varied and interesting dishes and boasts a reputation for excellence in both cuisine and service. Multi purpose gym available with steam room.

B&B from €44.44 to €69.84
£35.00 to £55.00

GEORGINA WHITTLE
MANAGER

American Express
Diners
Mastercard
Visa

62 62

alc

Open All Year

Room rates are per room per night

GREAT NORTHERN HOTEL

BUNDORAN,
CO. DONEGAL

TEL: 072-41204 FAX: 072-41114
EMAIL: reservations@greatnorthernhotel.com
WEB: www.greatnorthernhotel.com

HOTEL ★★★★ MAP 13 I 17

The Great Northern Hotel and Leisure Centre, Bundoran is situated in the middle of its own 18 hole championship golf course overlooking Donegal Bay. This hotel has all en suite bedrooms, a restaurant, grill room, lounge, ballroom and syndicate rooms. Leisure centre with swimming pool, gymnasium, private jacuzzi, sauna, steam room, plunge pool, beauty salon and hairdressing salon. We now offer a new state of the art conference centre.

Member of Brian McEniff Hotels
B&B from €85.00 to €88.00
£66.94 to £69.31

PHILIP MCGLYNN
GENERAL MANAGER

American Express
Mastercard
Visa

 Weekend specials from €165.00

96 96

Open All Year

HOLYROOD HOTEL

MAIN STREET,
BUNDORAN,
CO. DONEGAL

TEL: 072-41232 FAX: 072-41100
EMAIL: hrood@indigo.ie
WEB: www.holyroodhotel.com

HOTEL ★★★ MAP 13 I 17

The Holyrood Hotel situated on the main street of Bundoran, just a few minutes walk from the beach. All rooms are luxuriously furnished with multi-channel TV, DD phone, bath/shower, hairdryer and tea/coffee making facilities. Entertainment available at our Waterfront Bar. Leisure centre available at sister hotel nearby.

Member of Brian McEniff Hotels
B&B from €57.14 to €60.95
£45.00 to £48.00

SEANNIE & AUDREY MCENIFF

American Express
Diners
Mastercard
Visa

 Weekend specials from €120.63

100 100

Closed 23 - 26 December

MCGRORYS OF CULDAFF

CULDAFF,
INISHOWEN,
CO. DONEGAL

TEL: 077-79104 FAX: 077-79235
EMAIL: mcgr@eircom.net
WEB: www.mcgrorys.ie

GUESTHOUSE ★★★ MAP 14 L 21

Modern family run guesthouse, bar and restaurant, incorporating Mac's Backroom Bar (famous live music venue). Specialising in music, all tastes are catered for from traditional sessions to Rock and Jazz. The restaurant at McGrorys offers great food in a stylish setting and includes locally sourced seafood. Situated on the scenic Inishowen Peninsula, McGrorys is an ideal base for golfing, angling and leisure breaks.

B&B from €45.00 to €60.00
£35.44 to £47.25

JOHN & NEIL MCGRORY/
ANNE DOHERTY

American Express
Mastercard
Visa

10 10

Closed 23 - 27 December

B&B rates are per person sharing per night incl. Breakfast

CENTRAL HOTEL, CONFERENCE & LEISURE CENTRE

THE DIAMOND,
DONEGAL

TEL: 073-21027 FAX: 073-22295
EMAIL: centralhotel@eircom.net
WEB: www.whites-hotelsireland.com

HOTEL ★★★ MAP 13 I 18

The Central Hotel, Conference & Leisure Centre is a 3★★★ hotel based in the centre of Donegal Town, with views of Donegal Bay. It is an ideal base for discovering our beautiful countryside and unspoilt beaches. There is also horse riding, golfing and angling near by. Our leisure centre has a fully equipped gym, indoor swimming pool, steam room, jacuzzi and solarium. An experience you won't forget.

Member of White's and Associated Hotels

B&B from €63.49 to €76.18
£50.00 to £60.00

MICHAEL NAUGHTON
GENERAL MANAGER

| American Express |
| Diners |
| Mastercard |
| Visa |

☺ Weekend specials from €146.02

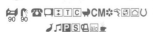
90 90

Open All Year

HARVEY'S POINT COUNTRY HOTEL

LOUGH ESKE,
DONEGAL TOWN,
CO. DONEGAL

TEL: 073-22208 FAX: 073-22352
EMAIL: reservations@harveyspoint.com
WEB: www.harveyspoint.com

HOTEL ★★★ MAP 13 I 18

If you enjoy fine food cooked with flair and attention to detail, coupled with a warm Irish welcome, then Harvey's Point is your destination. Hidden in the hills of Donegal, this exclusive, 20 bedroomed hotel is situated on the shores of Lough Eske, 6km from Donegal Town. Michelin Guide listed, AA 3 Rosette award 1992-2000, RAC Blue Ribbon award 2000. Closed Sunday, Monday & Tuesday nights from 1st November to 31st March.

B&B from €70.00 to €100.00
£55.13 to £78.76

DEIRDRE MCGLONE & MARK GYSLING
PROPRIETORS

| American Express |
| Diners |
| Mastercard |
| Visa |

☺ Weekend specials from €189.00

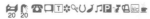
20 20

Open All Year

MILL PARK HOTEL, CONFERENCE CENTRE & LEISURE CLUB

THE MULLINS, KILLYBEGS ROAD,
DONEGAL TOWN,
CO. DONEGAL

TEL: 073-22880 FAX: 073-22640
EMAIL: millparkhotel@eircom.net
WEB: www.millparkhotel.com

HOTEL ★★★ MAP 13 I 18

The warm welcome of an open fire mixed with the tranquil gentle flow of the millstream welcomes you to the Mill Park Hotel. A few minutes from Donegal Town the hotel is a perfect base for touring the North West of Ireland & its many attractions. The hotel has 43 luxurious bedrooms. With a fully equipped Leisure Centre.The heart of the hotel is the unique styled Granary, along with the restaurant, bars & lounges. Cead Mile Failte.

Member of Village Inn Hotels

B&B from €49.50 to €89.50
£38.98 to £70.49

TONY MCDERMOTT

| American Express |
| Diners |
| Mastercard |
| Visa |

☺ Weekend specials from €125.00

43 43

Closed 24 - 26 December

Room rates are per room per night

SAINT ERNAN'S HOUSE HOTEL

DONEGAL TOWN,
CO. DONEGAL

TEL: 073-21065 FAX: 073-22098
EMAIL: info@sainternans.com
WEB: www.sainternans.com

HOTEL ★★★★ MAP 13 I 18

Saint Ernan's House Hotel is situated on its own wooded island and joined to the mainland by a causeway. This graceful house offers a homely atmosphere where good food and tranquillity is a way of life. Golfing, swimming and angling are close by. The surrounding countryside offers beautiful scenic tours of mountains, sea and lakes. Saint Ernan's is the perfect respite from the hectic pace of life. Children under 6 not catered for. Member of Irish Country Houses and Restaurants Association.

Member of Ireland's Blue Book

B&B from €115.00 to €125.00
£90.57 to £98.45

BRIAN O'DOWD
PROPRIETOR

Mastercard

Visa

🛏️🔥☎️🖥️T☀️🏊🎣P🛎️
10 10

Closed 29 October - 10 April

OSTAN NA TRA (BEACH HOTEL)

DOWNINGS,
LETTERKENNY,
CO. DONEGAL

TEL: 074-55303 FAX: 074-55907

HOTEL ★ MAP 13 J 21

The Beach Hotel is family run, situated on the breathtaking Atlantic Drive, having safe Downings Beach at the back door. In the heart of Rosguill golf enthusiasts can avail of both Carrigart and Rosapenna 18 hole championship course. Ideally placed for angling, diving and walking, within easy driving distance of Glenveagh National Park, Glebe Gallery, Horn Head and Letterkenny. Sea trips to Tory Island, and diving for wrecks and shark fishing easily arranged.

B&B from €30.00 to €40.00
£23.63 to £31.50

CHARLIE & MAIREAD MCCLAFFERTY

Mastercard

Visa

😊 Week partial board from €380.00

🛏️🔥T🅰️©CM☀️♨️🎣♫PS🅱️alc
20 14

Closed 01 November - 01 April

ROSAPENNA HOTEL

DOWNINGS,
CO. DONEGAL

TEL: 074-55301 FAX: 074-55128
EMAIL: rosapenna@eircom.net
WEB: www.rosapenna.ie

HOTEL ★★★★ MAP 13 J 21

Rosapenna is a 4**** hotel situated in North West Donegal beside the fishing village of Downings. Set in 700 acres between Sheephaven and Mulroy Bays, the hotel has its own 18 hole course designed by Old Tom Morris of St. Andrews in 1893. New private pool, whirlpool, steam room, spacious lounges and a magnificent dining room overlooking the bay all contribute to a relaxing atmosphere. Fresh seafood, locally caught, served daily. Rosapenna, a place to remember and return to.

B&B from €70.00 to €80.00
£55.13 to £63.01

HILARY & FRANK CASEY
OWNERS

American Express

Diners

Mastercard

Visa

😊 3 B&B & 3 Dinners & Green Fees
from €315.00

🛏️🔥☎️🖥️TCCM☀️♨️🏊U🅱️P🅱️
53 53

Closed 28 October - 15 March

B&B rates are per person sharing per night incl. Breakfast

ARNOLDS HOTEL

**DUNFANAGHY,
CO. DONEGAL**

TEL: 074-36208 FAX: 074-36352
EMAIL: arnoldshotel@eircom.net
WEB: www.arnoldshotel.com

HOTEL ★★★ MAP 13 J 21

Situated at the entrance to the village and overlooking Sheephaven Bay and Horn Head, the hotel has been in the Arnold Family for three generations. Good food, the friendly relaxed atmosphere and our helpful staff are just some of the compliments we receive from our guests who return each year. We are an ideal base for touring North West Donegal, Glenveagh National Park and Gardens. GDS Access Code UI Toll Free 1-800-44-UTELL.

Member of Irish Country Hotels

B&B from €52.00 to €70.00
£40.95 to £55.12

ARNOLD FAMILY
PROPRIETORS

American Express
Diners
Mastercard
Visa

☺ Midweek specials from €149.00

30 30

Closed 03 November - 15 March

ATLANTIC HOUSE

**MAIN STREET,
DUNGLOE,
CO. DONEGAL**

TEL: 075-21061 FAX: 075-21061
EMAIL: jcannon@iol.ie

GUESTHOUSE ★★ MAP 13 I 19

The Atlantic House is family run. It is within easy access of the airport, golf courses, pitch 'n putt course, shopping and lots of beaches to choose from. There is also lake fishing, sea angling and hill walking close by. We have one of the most beautiful coastlines in Ireland as well as some of the most beautiful scenery to offer the tourist who just wants a quiet, peaceful holiday.

B&B from €26.00 to €32.00
£20.48 to £25.20

JAMES & MARY CANNON
OWNERS

Mastercard
Visa

☺ Midweek specials from €70.00

10 10

Closed 20 - 30 December

OSTAN NA ROSANN

**MILL ROAD,
DUNGLOE,
CO. DONEGAL**

TEL: 075-22444 FAX: 075-22400
EMAIL: ostannarosann@iol.ie
WEB: www.ostannarosann.com

HOTEL ★★★ MAP 13 I 19

The hotel is situated in the rugged area of the Rosses amidst some of the finest scenery in Ireland and is an ideal location for golf, fishing, riding, walking and sailing. All 48 bedrooms are en suite and come fully equipped with TV, tea/coffee making facilities, hairdryer and direct dial phone. The hotel features a leisure centre with a splendid heated indoor swimming pool. The function room can cater for up to 330 people. Fresh local produce is used in all our menus.

B&B from €50.00 to €65.00
£39.37 to £51.18

LEWIS CONNON
GENERAL MANAGER

American Express
Mastercard
Visa

48 48

Open All Year

Room rates are per room per night

OSTAN GHLEANN CHOLM CILLE

MALINMORE,
GLENCOLMCILLE,
CO. DONEGAL

TEL: 073-30003 FAX: 073-30222
EMAIL: reception@glenhotel.com
WEB: www.glenhotel.com

HOTEL ★★ MAP 13 G 18

This is a family run hotel situated on the tip of the scenically splendid Sliabh Liag Peninsula in South West Donegal. Overlooking the Atlantic Coast and Rathlin O'Beirne Island. To complement the beautiful surroundings, we offer the finest cuisine and a beautiful location. A warm welcome is assured with 37 guest bedrooms each with full modern amenities. Our restaurant offers the finest Irish cuisine and locally produced foods. The hotel Tavern offers the opportunity to relax and unwind in front of a real turf fire. Access for Disabled Persons.

B&B from €38.10 to €57.15
£30.01 to £45.01

SHARON O'HARE

Mastercard
Visa

37 37

Closed 15 January - 15 March

HIGHLANDS HOTEL

GLENTIES,
CO. DONEGAL

TEL: 075-51111 FAX: 075-51564
EMAIL: highlandhotel@eircom.net
WEB: www.thehighlandshotel.com

HOTEL ★★ MAP 13 I 19

The Highlands Hotel is renowned for its warm and friendly atmosphere and good food. An attractive family run hotel ideally situated depending on what pastime you prefer, whether it be fishing, golfing, horse-riding or relaxing on the beautiful sandy beach of Nairn. Famous for its excellent cuisine the hotel offers a wide ranging choice of à la carte menus. Special rates for families and golfing weekends are our speciality.

B&B from €44.00 to €44.00
£34.65 to £34.65

JOHNNY, CHRISTINE & SINEAD BOYLE

American Express
Mastercard
Visa

😊 Weekend specials from €103.00

25 25

Open All Year

AN CHUIRT

GWEEDORE COURT HOTEL & HERITAGE CENTRE, GWEEDORE,
CO. DONEGAL

TEL: 075-32900 FAX: 075-32929
EMAIL: anchuirt@eircom.net
WEB: www.anchuirt-hotel.ie

HOTEL N MAP 13 I 20

An Chuirt, the Gweedore Court Hotel, is beautifully situated in the heart of the Donegal Gaeltacht, which boasts some of the most breathtaking views to be found. Reconstructed on the site of the old Gweedore Hotel, An Chuirt offers the very best in comfort and service. The building provides a suitable blend of modern convenience and elegant touches of the past.

B&B from €64.00 to €76.00
£50.40 to £59.85

DONAL COX
GENERAL MANAGER

Mastercard
Visa

19 19

Closed 23 - 27 December

B&B rates are per person sharing per night incl. Breakfast

BAY VIEW HOTEL & LEISURE CENTRE

MAIN STREET,
KILLYBEGS,
CO. DONEGAL
TEL: 073-31950 FAX: 073-31856
EMAIL: bvhotel@iol.ie
WEB: www.bayviewhotel.ie

HOTEL ★★★   MAP 13 H 18

One of Donegal's newest hotels, overlooking the splendour of Donegal Bay. We offer 38 en suite bedrooms with satellite TV, hair dryer, trouser press, tea/coffee makers, D.D. Theme bar and carvery, seafood restaurant. Fully equipped leisure centre, indoor swimming pool. Deep sea angling, fresh water fishing, golf, hill walking. Scenic boat trips. An ideal touring base. Wheelchair accessible rooms. Lift.

B&B from €55.00 to €80.00
£43.32 to £63.01

MICHAEL HEFFERNAN &
AIDAN MCHUGH

American Express
Mastercard
Visa

☺ Weekend specials from €100.00

38 38

HOTELS
IRISH HOTELS FEDERATION

Closed 25 - 27 December

MOORLAND GUESTHOUSE

LAGHEY,
DONEGAL TOWN,
CO. DONEGAL
TEL: 073-34319 FAX: 073-34319
EMAIL: wasch@indigo.ie

GUESTHOUSE ★★★   MAP 13 I 18

Have a break from the hustle and bustle. A guesthouse with family character, situated in a wild, high moor/hill landscape. We offer good cuisine. Available on the premises:- cosmetic treatment, reflexology, massage, lymphatic drainage, chiropody and sauna. The ideal starting point for unlimited walks, angling, bicycle tours, riding and touring. Excellent golf links and sandy bathing beaches nearby. Very quiet and remote. German spoken.

B&B from €25.00 to €32.00
£19.69 to £25.20

ROSEMARIE & WALTER SCHAFFNER
PROPRIETORS

Mastercard
Visa

8 8

HOTELS
IRISH HOTELS FEDERATION

Open All Year

CASTLE GROVE COUNTRY HOUSE HOTEL

BALLYMALEEL,
LETTERKENNY,
CO. DONEGAL
TEL: 074-51118 FAX: 074-51384
EMAIL: marytsweeney@hotmail.com
WEB: www.castlegrove.com

HOTEL ★★★★   MAP 13 J 19

Castle Grove is a 17th century country house set on its own rolling estate overlooking Lough Swilly. Its bedrooms are spacious and with all modern facilities. Downstairs in both drawing room and library you find a perfect blend of old and new. The dining room offers excellent cuisine, much of its produce from the Walled Garden. To the discerning guest Castle Grove has to be visited to be appreciated. While here you can fish, golf, or simply enjoy the locality.

B&B from €51.00 to €83.00
£40.17 to £65.37

RAYMOND & MARY T. SWEENEY
OWNERS

American Express
Diners
Mastercard
Visa

☺ Weekend specials from €133.00

15 15

Closed 23 - 28 December

Room rates are per room per night

QUALITY LETTERKENNY COURT HOTEL

MAIN STREET,
LETTERKENNY,
CO. DONEGAL
TEL: 074-22977 FAX: 074-22928
EMAIL: stay@irishcourthotels.com
WEB: www.irishcourthotels.com

HOTEL N MAP 13 J 19

The Quality Letterkenny Court Hotel, opened in Nov '99. 84 luxurious bedrooms, 30 of which are apartment-style luxury suites. All rooms have direct dial phone, hair dryer, tea/coffee making facilities, cable TV. Dillons Bar serves food all day. Private car parking.

Member of Irish Court Hotels

B&B from €45.00 to €110.00
£35.00 to £85.00

SEAN LYNE
PROPRIETOR

American Express
Diners
Mastercard
Visa

84   84

Closed 25 December

SILVER TASSIE HOTEL

RAMELTON ROAD,
LETTERKENNY,
CO. DONEGAL
TEL: 074-25619 FAX: 074-24473
EMAIL: silvertassie@eircom.net
WEB: www.silvertassiehotel.com

HOTEL ★★★ MAP 13 J 19

Nestled in the beautiful hills of Donegal overlooking Lough Swilly. The Silver Tassie Hotel combines old world charm with modern comfort and elegance. Our spacious and plush bedrooms offer unrivalled comfort and luxury with an old country house feel. Our restaurant has a reputation for the best food around. Friendly service in relaxed surroundings with open fires. Ideal touring base with local golf courses, fishing and hill walking.

B&B from €40.00 to €65.00
£31.50 to £51.19

CIARAN & ROSE BLANEY

Mastercard
Visa

☺ Weekend specials from €99.00

11   11

Closed 24 - 25 December

MALIN HOTEL

MALIN,
INISHOWEN,
CO. DONEGAL
TEL: 077-70645 FAX: 077-70770
EMAIL: malinhotel@eircom.net
WEB: www.inishowen.com

HOTEL ★★ MAP 14 L 21

Situated on the scenic Inishowen Peninsula. Ideal area for walking, cycling, painting etc. Golf locally (10 minutes drive), golf driving range nearby. Provides extensive variety of good homecooked food. All rooms en suite, DD phone, colour TV, tea/coffee making facilities and hair dryer.

B&B from €38.10 to €44.45
£30.00 to £35.00

MARTIN & BRIDIE MCLAUGHLIN
PROPRIETORS

Mastercard
Visa

10   10

Open All Year

B&B rates are per person sharing per night incl. Breakfast

FORT ROYAL HOTEL

**RATHMULLAN,
LETTERKENNY,
CO. DONEGAL**

TEL: 074-58100 FAX: 074-58103
EMAIL: fortroyal@eircom.net
WEB: www.fortroyalhotel.com

HOTEL ★★★ MAP 14 K 20

One of the most beautifully situated hotels in Ireland with 7 hectares of lovely grounds and gardens beside Lough Swilly include a sandy beach, hard tennis court, par 3 golf course. Especially friendly welcome accounts for the large number of regular visitors from all parts of the world to this peaceful unspoilt part of Donegal. Awarded two rosettes for food by AA. Member of Manor House Hotels, Irish Tourist Board and AA ***. GDS Access Code: UI Toll Free 1-800-44-UTELL

Member of Manor House Hotels
B&B from €67.00 to €80.00
£52.77 to £63.01

TIM & TINA FLETCHER
PROPRIETOR/MANAGER

American Express
Diners
Mastercard
Visa

☺ Weekend specials from €160.00

15 15

Closed 01 November - 31 March

RATHMULLAN HOUSE

**LOUGH SWILLY,
RATHMULLAN,
CO. DONEGAL**

TEL: 074-58188 FAX: 074-58200
EMAIL: info@rathmullanhouse.com
WEB: www.rathmullanhouse.com

HOTEL ★★★★ MAP 14 K 20

A country house with a glorious seaside setting on Lough Swilly amid award winning gardens which stretch down to a sandy beach. Inside, elegant sitting-rooms are in period style. Bedrooms vary in size and cost, from family rooms to luxurious suites. Renowned for good food. Indoor heated pool, steamroom and tennis. 4 golf courses nearby. Special weekend and half board rates on request. Member of Blue Book. RAC**** (Comfort Award). Dublin - 3.5 hours, Belfast - 2 hours.

Member of Ireland's Blue Book
B&B from €77.00 to €88.00
£60.64 to £69.31

ROBIN & BOB WHEELER
HOSTS

American Express
Diners
Mastercard
Visa

☺ Weekend specials from €200.00

24 24

Closed 02 January - 15 February

SAND HOUSE HOTEL

**ROSSNOWLAGH,
CO. DONEGAL**

TEL: 072-51777 FAX: 072-52100
EMAIL: info@sandhouse-hotel.ie
WEB: www.sandhouse-hotel.ie

HOTEL ★★★★ MAP 13 I 17

A delightful seaside setting overlooking the Atlantic Ocean on Donegal Bay. This small 4* luxury hotel, a transformed mid 19th century fishing lodge, is an oasis of comfort and relaxation on a 2 mile golden sandy beach. It combines elegant accommodation, open log fires and an award winning restaurant. A splendid location to explore the spectacular Donegal landscapes. Nearby 3 Ch'ship golf links courses. Described as one of Ireland's west coast treasures. Dublin 3.5hrs, Shannon 4hrs.

Member of Manor House Hotels
B&B from €70.00 to €115.00
£55.13 to £90.57

PAUL DIVER
MANAGER

American Express
Diners
Mastercard
Visa

60 60

Closed 01 December - 01 February

Room rates are per room per night

COMMERCIAL & TOURIST HOTEL

BALLINAMORE,
CO. LEITRIM

TEL: 078-44675 FAX: 078-44679
EMAIL: commercialhotel@oceanfree.net
WEB: www.hotelcommercial.com

HOTEL ★★ MAP 11 J 15

Ideally situated in the centre of the beautiful town of Ballinamore in the heart of Lovely Leitrim. Completely rebuilt to 3*** standard. Large comfortable bedrooms with queen size beds, all en suite with DD phone. Your ideal base for breathtaking tours or business.

B&B from € 35.00 to € 45.00
£27.56 to £35.44

MARY & FRED WALSH

Mastercard
Visa

☺ Midweek specials from €100.00

28 28

FAX

IRISH HOTELS FEDERATION

Closed 25 December

GLENVIEW GUESTHOUSE

AUGHOO,
BALLINAMORE,
CO. LEITRIM

TEL: 078-44157 FAX: 078-44814
EMAIL: glenvhse@iol.ie

GUESTHOUSE ★★ MAP 11 J 15

Glenview House, 2 miles south of Ballinamore is a holiday haven, 500m from the Shannon-Erne Waterway with its boating, canoeing, fishing and tranquil walks. Exclusive restaurant, private tennis court, games room, museum and play area. Enjoy golf, boat trips, cycling and hill walking locally. Self catering houses within grounds.

B&B from € 35.55 to € 38.09
£28.00 to £30.00

TERESA KENNEDY

Mastercard
Visa

6 6

alc

IRISH HOTELS FEDERATION

Open All Year

RIVERSDALE FARM GUESTHOUSE

BALLINAMORE,
CO. LEITRIM

TEL: 078-44122 FAX: 078-44813

WEB: www.riversdaleguesthouse.com

GUESTHOUSE ★★★ MAP 11 J 15

Riversdale is an impressive residence beautifully situated in parkland overlooking the Shannon-Erne Waterway. Spacious rooms and lounges mean a comfortable and peaceful ambience. We have our own heated indoor pool, squash court, sauna and fitness suite for when the weather is unkind - or hot! Local golf, horse riding, walking, riverbus, boat trips and scenic drives. Wide choice of interesting day trips. Brochure available - special family suites.

B&B from € 38.00 to € 45.00
£29.93 to £35.44

THE THOMAS FAMILY OWNERS

Mastercard
Visa

☺ Midweek Specials from €99.00

13 13

PS

IRISH HOTELS FEDERATION

Closed 16 - 31 December

B&B rates are per person sharing per night incl. Breakfast

AISLEIGH GUEST HOUSE

DUBLIN ROAD,
CARRICK-ON-SHANNON,
CO. LEITRIM

TEL: 078-20313 FAX: 078-20313
EMAIL: aisleigh@eircom.net
WEB: homepage.eircom.net/~aisleigh

GUESTHOUSE ★★★ **MAP 10 I 14**

A warm welcome awaits you at our family run guest house situated 1km from the centre of the picturesque town of Carrick on Shannon, Ireland's best kept secret. Facilities include en suite bedrooms with TV, direct dial telephones (fax also available) games room, and sauna. Local genealogy a speciality. Nearby there is golfing, swimming, tennis, squash, cruising, fishing (tackle & bait supplies) horse riding, walking, cycling, etc.

B&B from € 25.00 to € 25.00
£19.69 to £19.69

SEAN & CHARLOTTE FEARON
OWNERS

American Express
Mastercard
Visa

Open All Year

BUSH HOTEL

CARRICK-ON-SHANNON,
CO. LEITRIM

TEL: 078-20014 FAX: 078-21180
EMAIL: info@bushhotel.com
WEB: www.bushhotel.com

HOTEL ★★★ **MAP 10 I 14**

An hotel of ambience, style and comfort, the Bush Hotel (one of Ireland's oldest) has recently undergone major refurbishment whilst retaining its olde world character and charm. Centrally located in the town centre, the hotel backs onto courtyard, gardens and N4 by-pass with private access and parking. 28 en suite bedrooms, theme bars, coffee shop, restaurant overlooking courtyard. Amenities: National Parks, period houses, River Shannon.

B&B from € 44.00 to € 57.00
£34.65 to £44.89

JOSEPH DOLAN
MANAGING DIRECTOR

American Express
Mastercard
Visa

Closed 24 - 31 December

LANDMARK HOTEL

CARRICK-ON-SHANNON,
CO. LEITRIM

TEL: 078-22222 FAX: 078-22233
EMAIL: landmarkhotel@eircom.net
WEB: www.thelandmarkhotel.com

HOTEL U MAP 10 I 14

Overlooking the majestic River Shannon and its picturesque marinas. This beautifully appointed property is just a stroll from the town. Luxurious accommodation, Boardwalk Café & Bar, Ferrari's themed Restaurant offering innovative cuisine. Extensive leisure centre - 20m deck level pool, sauna, steamroom, jacuzzi & fully equipped gym. This unique unspoilt location invites you to enjoy river cruising, golf, hill walking, equestrian, watersports, scenic drives and places of historic interest.

B&B from € 76.00 to € 122.00
£59.85 to £96.08

SIOBHAN SMYTH
OPERATIONS MANAGER

American Express
Mastercard
Visa

☺ Midweek specials from €171.00

Closed 24 - 25 December

Room rates are per room per night

GLEBE HOUSE	MARKREE CASTLE	CASTLE ARMS HOTEL

BALLINAMORE ROAD,
MOHILL,
CO. LEITRIM
TEL: 078-31086 FAX: 078-31886
EMAIL: glebe@iol.ie
WEB: www.glebehouse.com

COLLOONEY,
CO. SLIGO

TEL: 071-67800 FAX: 071-67840
EMAIL: markree@iol.ie
WEB: www.markreecastle.ie

ENNISCRONE,
CO. SLIGO

TEL: 096-36156 FAX: 096-36156
EMAIL: castlearmshotel@eircom.net
WEB: www.castlearmshotel.com

GUESTHOUSE ★★★ MAP 11 J 14 | **HOTEL ★★★ MAP 10 H 15** | **HOTEL ★★ MAP 10 F 15**

Dating back to 1823 this lovely Georgian former rectory set in fifty acres of woods and farmland has been completely restored by the Maloney Family. Enjoy the tranquillity of this peaceful part of Ireland. Plenty to see and do. Visit the stately homes and gardens, sample golf, horse riding, pony trekking, fishing and cruising. Or take to the country roads by bike or on foot. Assistance given with genealogy. 10% discount on bookings if more than one night. Special discount for seniors.

Charles and Mary Cooper have restored Sligo's oldest inhabited house and made it a spectacular family hotel. Home of the Cooper family since 1640 and set in the middle of a large estate, Markree boasts spectacular plasterwork, a fine Irish oak staircase yet has all the comforts of a 3* hotel. Good food, peace, quiet, lots of space and warm family welcome. Riding is also available on the estate.

The Castle Arms Hotel is a family run hotel and upholds the tradition of offering a warm and friendly welcome with excellent home cooking. It is adjacent to a three mile long sandy beach, an 18 hole championship golf links, aqua leisure centre, seaweed and steam health baths, tennis courts and many other amenities. For more information contact a member of the Grimes family at 096-36156.

| *B&B from €36.00 to €40.00* | *B&B from €92.00 to €157.50* | *B&B from €35.00 to €40.00* |
| *£28.35 to £31.50* | *£72.45 to £124.02* | *£27.56 to £31.50* |

LAURA MALONEY
MANAGER

American Express
Mastercard
Visa

CHARLES COOPER
OWNER

American Express
Diners
Mastercard
Visa

LIAM & SHANE GRIMES

Mastercard
Visa

Weekend specials from €90.00

Weekend specials from €100.00

7 7

 30 30

27 27

| Open All Year | Closed 24 - 27 December | Closed 01 November - 01 March |

B&B rates are per person sharing per night incl. Breakfast

BEACH HOTEL AND LEISURE CLUB

THE HARBOUR,
MULLAGHMORE,
CO. SLIGO
TEL: 071-66103 FAX: 071-66448
EMAIL: beachhot@iol.ie
WEB: www.beachhotelmullaghmore.com

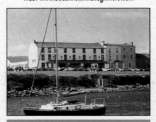

HOTEL ★★   MAP 13 H 17

Set in the centre of the picturesque seaside village of Mullaghmore, overlooking the Atlantic Ocean. All rooms en suite (bath & shower), direct dial phone, TV & tea/coffee facilities. The hotel boasts an excellent leisure club; heated indoor swimming pool, jacuzzi, sauna, steam room & gymnasium. Discount at 5 golf courses, sea, game & coarse angling, horse riding, watersports & boat trips locally. Free Kiddies Club. Murder Mystery & activity weekends. "Fall under the spell of the Beach Hotel".

B&B from €32.00 to €64.00
£25.20 to £50.40

COLM & AUDRI HERRON
PROPRIETORS
American Express
Mastercard
Visa

☺ Weekend specials from €77.00

Open All Year

PIER HEAD HOTEL

MULLAGHMORE,
CO. SLIGO
TEL: 071-66171 FAX: 071-66473
EMAIL: pierhead@eircom.net
WEB: www.pierheadhotel.com

HOTEL ★★   MAP 13 H 17

With its unique setting in the picturesque seaside/fishing resort of Mullaghmore this family run hotel offers superb bay & harbour views. All rooms en suite, café style bar, restaurant, function rooms and conference facilities. Regular entertainment by top Irish and international artistes. Next door is the renowned Olde Quay Bar & upstairs Seafood Restaurant with its attractive stone façade and old world nautical charm, making it a popular haunt for locals and tourists alike.

B&B from €44.44 to €57.14
£35.00 to £45.00

JOHN MCHUGH
American Express
Diners
Mastercard
Visa

Open All Year

YEATS COUNTRY HOTEL AND LEISURE CLUB

ROSSES POINT,
CO. SLIGO
TEL: 071-77211 FAX: 071-77203
EMAIL: yeatscountry@eircom.net
WEB: www.cisl.ie/sligoaccommodation/yeats

HOTEL ★★★   MAP 10 H 16

A family run, 3*** hotel. All rooms en suite, cable TV, direct dial phone, tea/coffee facilities, hairdryer. 3km of sandy beaches and Sligo's 18 hole ch'ship golf courses at concession rates locally. Amenities include deluxe leisure club with 18m swimming pool, sauna, jacuzzi, steam room and hi-tech gymnasium. Also available tennis, basketball, indoor bowling. Supervised creche and indoor play areas on bank holiday weekends/July/August. Local activities: golf, yachting, fishing, scenic drives.

Member of Brian McEniff Hotels
B&B from €40.00 to €105.00
£31.50 to £82.69

FIONA MCENIFF
MANAGING DIRECTOR
American Express
Diners
Mastercard
Visa

Closed 02 January - 02 February

CLARENCE HOTEL

**WINE STREET,
SLIGO**

**TEL: 071-42211 FAX: 071-45823
EMAIL: clarencehotel@eircom.net**

HOTEL U   MAP 10 H 16

Listed for its striking architectural design, the hotel is situated in the centre of Sligo. Its location makes it the perfect base to explore one of Ireland's most beautiful counties. You will find all of Sligo's business, shopping and historic centres just steps away with a modern new entertainment complex adjoining the hotel. Our restaurant, a gourmet delight, atmospheric throughout brings an exciting dimension to wining and dining in Sligo. All rooms en suite with all amenities.

**B&B from €44.44 to €63.49
£35.00 to £50.00**

CARMEL FOLEY
MANAGING DIRECTOR

American Express
Diners
Mastercard
Visa

11 11

Open All Year

HOTEL SILVER SWAN

**HYDE BRIDGE,
SLIGO**

**TEL: 071-43231 FAX: 071-42232
EMAIL: hotelsilverswan@eircom.net**

HOTEL U   MAP 10 H 16

Uniquely situated on the banks of the Garavogue River and close to shops, art gallery and theatre. All rooms recently refurbished and our de-luxe rooms have aero-spa baths. Relax and watch the swans glide by as you dine in the Cygnet Restaurant renowned for excellent French cuisine with a special emphasis on fresh oysters, lobster and game in season.

**B&B from €35.55 to €50.79
£28.00 to £40.00**

MICHAEL HIGGINS
MANAGER

American Express
Diners
Mastercard
Visa

Weekend specials from €95.23

29 29

Closed 25 - 28 December

INNISFREE HOTEL

**HIGH STREET,
SLIGO**

**TEL: 071-42014 FAX: 071-45745
EMAIL: innisfreehotelsligo@eircom.net**

HOTEL ★★   MAP 10 H 16

Located in the heart of Sligo Town, this comfortable hotel has a special, friendly atmosphere. All rooms are en suite with TV, direct dial phone and tea making facilities. Excellent food served all day or visit the lively Ark Bar with its seafaring theme. Convenient to theatre and shops. Explore W.B. Yeats' breathtaking countryside, the Lake Isle of Innisfree, Glencar, Lisadell, renowned for its golf courses and seaside resorts. Specialising in commercial traveller rates and golf holidays.

**B&B from €45.00 to €50.00
£35.44 to £39.38**

GERRY & CATHERINE GURN
OWNERS

American Express
Mastercard
Visa

Midweek specials from €115.00

19 19

Closed 23 - 27 December

B&B rates are per person sharing per night incl. Breakfast

LISADORN

DONEGAL ROAD,
SLIGO

TEL: 071-43417 FAX: 071-46418
EMAIL: cjo'connor@eircom.net

GUESTHOUSE ★★★ MAP 10 H 16

Sligo Town's first and only 3*** guesthouse situated on the N15 within 5 minutes of town centre. Ideal base for North bound traffic. All rooms en suite, remote control colour TVs, direct dial telephones, fax, hairdryers and hospitality tray. Beside pitch & putt and 10 minutes to Rosses Point. Beside Sligo's Tennis & Squash Club. In the heart of Yeats' Country. It's the ultimate in luxury accommodation. A friendly welcome and service is guaranteed.

B&B from €25.00 to €32.00
£19.69 to £25.20

CYRIL O'CONNOR
PROPRIETOR

Mastercard
Visa

7 7

Open All Year

RIVERSIDE QUALITY HOTEL

MILBROOK,
SLIGO

TEL: 071-48080 FAX: 071-48060
EMAIL: stay@irishcourthotels.com
WEB: www.irishcourthotels.com

HOTEL N MAP 10 H 16

Opened in October 1999, this 66 bedroomed hotel is situated in the centre of Sligo Town overlooking the River Garavogue. All rooms are en suite with cable TV, direct dial telephone, hair dryer. Indoor swimming pool, gym, jacuzzi, sauna & steam room. The mill bar serves food all day or you can dine in the Waterfront Restaurant offering excellent cuisine. Ideal base for touring the north west region.

Member of Irish Court Hotels
B&B from €45.00 to €110.00
£35.00 to £85.00

TADHG LYNE
PROPRIETORS

American Express
Diners
Mastercard
Visa

66 66

Closed 25 - 25 December

SLIGO PARK HOTEL & LEISURE CENTRE

PEARSE ROAD,
SLIGO

TEL: 071-60291 FAX: 071-69556
EMAIL: sligopk@leehotels.ie
WEB: www.leehotels.ie

HOTEL ★★★ MAP 10 H 16

Situated one mile south of Sligo on the Dublin Road, the Sligo Park Hotel is set on seven acres of gardens. A 3*** hotel with 110 bedrooms, the hotel has one of the finest leisure centres in the country. In the heart of the Yeats country, the Sligo Park is surrounded by some of the most scenic countryside in Ireland ranging from the majestic Benbulben to the gentle waters of Lough Gill. For that special break, the Sligo Park has all the facilities for your enjoyment.

Member of Lee Hotels
B&B from €55.00 to €88.00
£43.32 to £69.31

MICHELE HAUGH
GENERAL MANAGER

American Express
Diners
Mastercard
Visa

110 110

Open All Year

Room rates are per room per night

SLIGO'S SOUTHERN HOTEL & LEISURE CENTRE

STRANDHILL ROAD,
SLIGO

TEL: 071-62101 FAX: 071-60328
EMAIL: reservations@sligosouthernhotel.com
WEB: www.sligosouthernhotel.com

HOTEL ★★★   MAP 10 H 16

The Sligo Southern Hotel is situated in the heart of Sligo Town, adjacent to the railway and bus stations. The Sligo Southern Hotel blends old world intimacy with every modern convenience. All 99 rooms are en suite, cable TV, phone, hairdryers, tea/coffee making facilities. Indoor swimming pool, gym, jacuzzi, sauna and steam room. Entertainment most nights in high season. Reservations 1 850 520052 or Free phone NI & UK 0800 783 9024.

Member of Brian McEniff Hotels
B&B from €48.00 to €79.00
£37.80 to £62.22

KEVIN MCGLYNN
MANAGER

American Express
Diners
Mastercard
Visa

Weekend specials from €83.00

Closed 24 - 26 December

TOWER HOTEL

QUAY STREET,
SLIGO

TEL: 071-44000 FAX: 071-46888
EMAIL: towersl@iol.ie
WEB: www.towerhotelgroup.ie

HOTEL ★★★   MAP 10 H 16

A Tower Group Hotel - located in the heart of Sligo Town, the hotel has immediate access to Sligo's shopping facilities and has a host of lively bars on its doorstep. It also makes an ideal base from which to play the great links courses of the North West. With 60 bedrooms it is small enough to offer a truly personal service. The Links Bar and Lady Eleanor Restaurant offer the perfect relaxation after a busy day touring or a rewarding day's golf.

Member of Tower Hotel Group
B&B from €50.00 to €67.50
£39.38 to £53.16

GARRET MARRINAN
GENERAL MANAGER

American Express
Diners
Mastercard
Visa

Weekend specials from €99.00

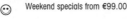

Closed 24 - 27 December

OCEAN VIEW HOTEL

STRANDHILL,
CO. SLIGO

TEL: 071-68115 FAX: 071-68009
EMAIL: oceanviewhotel@eircom.net
WEB: www.ovhotel.com

HOTEL ★★★   MAP 10 H 16

Ocean View Hotel, nestling at the foot of Knocknarea Mountain, overlooking the Atlantic, is a long established family hotel which offers a unique blend of all modern comforts with old-fashioned courtesy and charm. Its Rollers Restaurant is renowned for its home oak-smoked salmon and fresh local produce. Bar food also available. This picturesque area invites you to stroll its sandy beaches, pony trek, golf, explore the hidden glens, visit the oldest megalithic tombs in Europe.

Member of Village Inn Hotels
B&B from €49.00 to €66.00
£38.59 to £51.98

SHAY BURKE/JEAN BURKE
PROPRIETORS

American Express
Diners
Mastercard
Visa

Closed 01 November - 28 February

B&B rates are per person sharing per night incl. Breakfast

CAWLEY'S

EMMET STREET,
TUBBERCURRY,
CO. SLIGO
TEL: 071-85025 FAX: 071-85963

GUESTHOUSE ★★   MAP 10 G 15

Cawley's, a large 3 storey family run guesthouse. We offer high standards in accommodation with tastefully decorated rooms. Our home cooking and personal service makes this premises your home for the duration of your stay. Private parking, landscaped gardens, easily accessed by air, rail and bus. Local amenities include fishing, 9 hole golf, horse riding. Seaside resorts close by. Major credit cards accepted.

B&B from €32.00 to €45.00
£25.20 to £35.44

JEAN CAWLEY
PROPRIETOR

American Express
Mastercard
Visa

10 10

IRISH
HOTELS
FEDERATION

Closed 25 - 26 December

General Tourist Information

❄

POPULATION
The population of the Republic of Ireland (26 counties) is over 3.5 million. Dublin is the largest City with over one million inhabitants, Cork the second largest City and Limerick, Capital of the Shannon Region, is the third.

❄

LANGUAGE
Almost everyone in Ireland speaks English. The country is bilingual, English and Irish (the Gaelic language) are spoken, especially in the West.

❄

WEATHER
Influenced by the Gulf Stream, Ireland has a mild temperate climate with summer temperatures generally ranging from 14 to 16 degree Celsius (60-70 degree Fahrenheit). The temperatures in Spring and Autumn are generally around 10 degree Celsius (50 degree Fahrenheit) and in Winter between 4 and 7 degrees Celsius (30-40 degree Fahrenheit).

Room rates are per room per night

MINOTEL
Ireland

MINOTEL IRELAND HOTEL GROUP

BALLYCANEW, GOREY, CO. WEXFORD

TEL: 353-55-27 291   FAX: 353-55-27 398
EMAIL: info@minotel.iol.ie

MinOtel Ireland is a marketing consortium of carefully chosen Owner/Manager style Hotels located throughout Ireland. The Hotels are chiefly 3* standard with their own individual characteristics. The Member Hotels are exposed by MinOtel Ireland to a range of Tour Operator Programmes including:– Car Tours, Fly-Drive, Coach Tours, Activity Holidays, Short Breaks, etc. MinOtel Ireland has established business links with the Trade in Britain, Europe and North America. Central Reservations/Accounts is an essential service which the Ireland Office provides.

MinOtel International represents over 700 Hotels in 32 countries and the combined initiatives of MinOtel gives Irish Hotels exposure in over a million pieces of MinOtel publications, at the World's major Travel Fairs, in Tour Operator Programmes and on the Internet. The MinOtel Europe Voucher operates on a B+B basis and is accepted at all MinOtel hotels throughout Europe.

Enquiries are invited and will be attended to promptly.

IRELAND FOR

Golf

HOTELS & GUESTHOUSES

Golfing in Ireland is not quite like
golfing any other place else on earth.

Here the game has become part of
the national culture and is for
everyone. That includes you.

Ireland's rugged landscape, perched on the
edge of the Atlantic ocean, has provided
many great golf courses.

And they are relatively uncrowded.
So get in the swing - come golfing in Ireland.

WHERE TO STAY WHEN YOU PLAY!

We invite you to sample the golf, the countryside and the friendship of the Irish people and then to stay in some of Ireland's most charming accommodation. We have listed a range of hotels and guesthouses which are either situated on or close to a golf course. Your host will assist you if necessary in arranging your golfing requirements including tee reservations and green fee charges. A full description of the hotels and guesthouses can be had by looking up the appropriate page number. Premises are listed in alphabetical order in each county.

ACCOMMODATION	COURSES	BE OUR GUEST PAGE NUMBER	GOLF ON SITE	ALL INCLUSIVE PACKAGE	TUITION AVAILABLE	CART AVAILABLE	ARRANGE TEE OFF TIMES	ADVANCE RESERVATIONS	CLUBS FOR HIRE	TRANSPORT	PREFERENTIAL GREEN FEES	CADDY AVAILABLE
North												
ANTRIM												
Adair Arms Hotel	Galgorm Castle, Moyola Park	30		•	•	•	•	•	•	•	•	•
Bayview Hotel	Royal Portrush, Portstewart, Castlerock, Ballycastle, Bushfoot, Gracehill	30		•	•	•	•	•	•	•	•	•
Bushmills Inn	Royal Portrush, Portstewart, Castlerock, Ballycastle, Bushfoot, Gracehill	31		•	•	•	•	•	•	•	•	•
Causeway Coast Hotel & Conference Centre	Royal Portrush, Portstewart, Castlerock, Ballycastle, Bushfoot, Gracehill	33		•	•	•	•	•	•	•	•	•
Comfort Hotel Portrush	Royal Portrush, Portstewart, Castlerock, Ballycastle, Bushfoot, Gracehill	34		•	•	•	•	•	•	•	•	•
Crockatinney Guest House	Ballycastle, Royal Portrush, Bushfoot, Grace Hill, Stranocum, Portstewart	30		•		•	•	•	•		•	•
Hilton Templepatrick		36	🚩18	•	•	•	•	•	•	•	•	•
Magherabuoy House Hotel	Royal Portrush, Valley, Portstewart, Castlerock, Bushfoot, Ballycastle	34		•	•	•	•	•	•	•	•	•
BELFAST												
Fitzwilliam International Hotel	Allen Park, Massereene Golf Club	39		•	•	•	•	•	•		•	
DERRY												
Brown Trout Golf & Country Inn	Royal Portrush, Portstewart, Castlerock	42	🚩9	•		•	•	•	•	•	•	•
Edgewater Hotel	Portstewart, Royal Portrush	45			•		•	•	•	•	•	
Walsh's Hotel	The Royal Portrush, Moyola, Portstewart, Brown Trout Golf Course	45								•		
DOWN												
Burrendale Hotel and Country Club	Royal County Down, Kilkeel, Downpatrick, Ardglass, Spa	48							•		•	

🚩18 = Full 18 Hole   🚩9 = 9 Hole   🚩3 = Par 3

WHERE TO STAY WHEN YOU PLAY!

ACCOMMODATION	COURSES	BE OUR GUEST PAGE NUMBER	GOLF ON SITE	ALL INCLUSIVE PACKAGE	TUITION AVAILABLE	CART AVAILABLE	ARRANGE TEE OFF TIMES	ADVANCE RESERVATIONS	CLUBS FOR HIRE	TRANSPORT	PREFERENTIAL GREEN FEES	CADDY AVAILABLE
DOWN Continued												
Royal Hotel	Bangor, Clandeboye, Blackwood	46		•								
FERMANAGH												
Mahons Hotel	Castle Hume, Enniskillen	51		•	•	•	•	•		•	•	•

East Coast
DUBLIN

ACCOMMODATION	COURSES	BE OUR GUEST PAGE NUMBER	GOLF ON SITE	ALL INCLUSIVE PACKAGE	TUITION AVAILABLE	CART AVAILABLE	ARRANGE TEE OFF TIMES	ADVANCE RESERVATIONS	CLUBS FOR HIRE	TRANSPORT	PREFERENTIAL GREEN FEES	CADDY AVAILABLE
Aberdeen Lodge	St. Margarets, Portmarnock, Woodbrook, Dun Laoghaire, Sea Point, Druids Glen	60		•	•	•	•	•	•	•	•	•
Arlington Hotel	St. Margarets, Portmarnock, Island, Luttrellstown, Citywest, Royal Dublin	63					•	•	•	•	•	•
Ashview House	St. Margarets, Dublin Country Golf, Hollystown, Ashbourne, Corrstown	117		•	•	•	•	•	•	•	•	•
Bracken Court Hotel	Balbriggan, Seapoint, Baltray, The Island, Donabate, Malahide	56		•	•	•	•	•	•	•	•	•
Carnegie Court Hotel	Forrest Little, Balheary, St. Margarets, Swords Open, Corballis, Hollywood Lakes	116		•	•	•	•	•	•	•	•	•
Carriage House	St. Margarets, Portmarnock, Skerries, Balbriggan, Hollywood, Luttrellstown, The Island	113		•	•	•	•	•	•	•	•	•
Cassidys Hotel	Royal Dublin, Lutterellstown, St. Anne's, Clontarf, Portmarnock, St. Margaret's Golf and Country Club	70			•	•	•	•	•	•		•
Charleville Lodge	St. Margarets, Luttrellstown, The Links, Portmarnock, The Island Golf Links	72		•	•	•	•	•	•	•	•	•
Clarion Hotel Dublin IFSC	Clontarf, Portmarnock, St. Anne's, Royal Dublin, St. Margaret's	73				•	•	•	•	•	•	•
Clarion Stephens Hall Hotel and Suites	St. Margaret's, Portmarnock Links, Citywest, Luttrellstown Castle	73		•	•	•	•	•	•	•	•	•
Clontarf Castle Hotel	Royal Dublin, Clontarf, St. Annes, St. Margaret's, Portmarnock	74		•					•		•	
Court Hotel	Druids Glen, European, Roundwood, Woodbrook, Charlesland, Powerscourt	111		•	•		•	•	•	•	•	•
Deer Park Hotel and Golf Courses		111	▶18	•		•	•	•				

DUBLIN Continued

▶18 = Full 18 Hole   ▶9 = 9 Hole   ▶3 = Par 3

WHERE TO STAY WHEN YOU PLAY!

ACCOMMODATION	COURSES	BE OUR GUEST PAGE NUMBER	GOLF ON SITE	ALL INCLUSIVE PACKAGE	TUITION AVAILABLE	CART AVAILABLE	ARRANGE TEE OFF TIMES	ADVANCE RESERVATIONS	CLUBS FOR HIRE	TRANSPORT	PREFERENTIAL GREEN FEES	CADDY AVAILABLE
Georgian Hotel	K Club, Druids Glen, St. Margaret's, Portmarnock	80		•		•	•	•		•	•	•
Gresham Royal Marine	Dun Laoghaire, Woodbrook, Killiney, Greystones, Seapoint, Druids Glen	110				•			•			
Harrington Hall	Portmarnock Old Course & Links, St. Margarets, Royal Dublin, Powerscourt, Sutton	83					•					
Hedigan's	Clontarf, Royal Dublin, St. Annes, Howth, Portmarnock, Sutton	84				•	•	•		•	•	
Hilton Dublin	St. Margarets, Druids Glen	85	•								•	
Holiday Inn Dublin Airport	Hollystown, St. Margaret's, Portmarnock, Malahide, Forest Little, The Island	58				•	•	•	•	•	•	•
King Sitric Fish Restaurant & Accommodation	Deerpark, Howth, Royal Dublin, Portmarnock, St. Margaret's, The Island	111					•	•	•	•	•	
Kingston Hotel	Powerscourt, Charlesland, Old Conna, European, Druids Glen, Portmarnock	110		•		•	•	•	•	•	•	•
Le Meridien Shelbourne	St. Margaret's, Druids Glen	91		•		•	•	•		•	•	•
Merrion Hall	Portmarnock, Royal Dublin, Elm Park, Castle, Milltown, Druids Glen	93		•		•	•	•	•	•	•	•
Plaza Hotel	Ballinascorney, Citywest, Newlands, K-Club, Powerscourt, Tulfarris	100		•	•	•	•	•	•	•	•	•
Portmarnock Hotel & Golf Links	Portmarnock, St. Margaret's, Royal Dublin, Malahide, The Island	114	18 •	•	•	•	•	•	•	•	•	•
Raglan Lodge	Elm Park, Royal Dublin, Portmarnock, Leopardstown	102				•	•	•	•	•		
Redbank House Guesthouse & Restaurant	Skerries, Laytown, Bettystown, Baltray, Portmarnock, St. Margaret's	115		•		•	•	•	•	•	•	•
Regency Airport Hotel	Malahide, Clontarf, Hollystown, St. Annes, Royal Dublin	103				•	•	•				
Spa Hotel	Hermitage, Citywest, Knockanally, Lucan, Luttrellstown, Highfield	113		•		•	•	•		•	•	•
Stillorgan Park Hotel	Druids Glen, Portmarnock, Woodbrook, Woodenbridge, Powerscourt, European	56		•		•	•	•	•	•	•	•
Waterside Hotel	Donabate, Turvey, Beaverstown, Belcarrick, Island/Corballis	58	•			•	•	•		•	•	•
Westin Dublin	Powerscourt, Portmarnock, K Club, St. Margaret's, Druids Glen, The Island	109					•	•	•	•	•	•

18 = Full 18 Hole   9 = 9 Hole   3 = Par 3

WHERE TO STAY WHEN YOU PLAY!

ACCOMMODATION	COURSES	BE OUR GUEST PAGE NUMBER	GOLF ON SITE	ALL INCLUSIVE PACKAGE	TUITION AVAILABLE	CART AVAILABLE	ARRANGE TEE OFF TIMES	ADVANCE RESERVATIONS	CLUBS FOR HIRE	TRANSPORT	PREFERENTIAL GREEN FEES	CADDY AVAILABLE
DUBLIN Continued												
White Sands Hotel	Malahide, St. Margarets, Luttrellstown	114		•	•	•	•	•	•	•	•	•
LOUTH												
Ballymascanlon House Hotel		119	⚑18	•	•	•	•	•	•	•	•	•
Fairways Hotel	Ballymascanlon, Dundalk, Killin Park, Greenore, Warrenpoint, Carnbeg	120		•	•	•	•	•	•	•	•	•
Hotel Imperial	Ballymascanlon, Dundalk, Greenore	121		•	•	•	•	•	•		•	•
McKevitt's Village Hotel	Greenore	118		•	•	•	•	•	•		•	•
MEATH												
Conyngham Arms Hotel	Sea Point, Ardee, Headfort, Royal Tara	125		•	•	•	•	•	•		•	•
Neptune Beach Hotel & Leisure Club	Laytown & Bettystown, Sea Point, County Louth/Baltray, Royal Tara	122			•	•	•	•	•	•	•	•
Newgrange Hotel	Navan, Royal Tara	125		•	•	•	•	•	•		•	
Old Darnley Lodge Hotel	Royal Tara, Delvin Castle, Headfort, Trim, The Glebe	122		•	•	•	•	•	•		•	•
WICKLOW												
Arklow Bay Hotel	European, Arklow, Woodenbridge, Blainroe	126		•	•	•	•	•	•	•		•
Charlesland Golf Hotel & Country Club	Druids Glen, Powerscourt, Glen of the Downs, Delgany, Greystones, Woodbrook	135	⚑18	•	•	•	•	•	•	•	•	
Chester Beatty Inn	Druids Glen, Woodenbridge, Blainroe, European, Powerscourt, Charlesland	128		•	•	•	•	•	•	•		
Cullenmore Hotel	Druids Glen, Charlesland, Wicklow, Blainroe, European Club, Delgany	129							•	•	•	•
Glendalough Hotel	The European Club, Woodenbridge, Charlesland, Druid's Glen, Blainroe	134		•		•	•	•	•	•	•	
Glenview Hotel	Charlesland, Druids Glen, Delgany, Powerscourt, Glen-O-The-Downs	134					•	•	•	•	•	
Gormanstown Manor	Wicklow Golf Club, Blainroe, European, Druids Glen, Arklow, Woodenbridge	137	⚑3	•				•			•	

⚑18 = Full 18 Hole   ⚑9 = 9 Hole   ⚑3 = Par 3

WHERE TO STAY WHEN YOU PLAY!

ACCOMMODATION	COURSES	BE OUR GUEST PAGE NUMBER	GOLF ON SITE	ALL INCLUSIVE PACKAGE	TUITION AVAILABLE	CART AVAILABLE	ARRANGE TEE OFF TIMES	ADVANCE RESERVATIONS	CLUBS FOR HIRE	TRANSPORT	PREFERENTIAL GREEN FEES	CADDY AVAILABLE
WICKLOW Continued												
Hunter's Hotel	Druid's Glen, European, Blainroe, Powerscourt, Woodenbridge, Delgany	136			•	•	•	•	•	•	•	•
Lawless's Hotel	Woodenbridge, Coolattin, European, Blainroe, Arklow, Druids Glen, Tulfarris	129					•	•	•	•	•	•
Rathsallagh House, Golf and Country Club	Mount Juliet, Carlow, K Club, Mount Wolseley, Druids Glen, Powerscourt	133	18		•	•	•	•	•	•	•	
Royal Hotel and Leisure Centre	Woodbrook, Charlesland, Delgany, The European Club, Druids Glen	132				•	•	•	•	•	•	
Summerhill House Hotel	Powerscourt, Druids Glen, Kilternan, Old Conna	133			•	•	•	•	•	•	•	•
Tinakilly Country House and Restaurant	European, Druid's Glen, Blainroe, Woodenbridge, Wicklow, Delgany	136			•	•	•	•	•	•	•	
Tulfarris Hotel & Golf Resort	K Club, Druids Glen, City West, Rathsallagh	131	18				•	•	•	•	•	
Valley Hotel and Restaurant	Woodenbridge, European, Arklow, Courtown, Blainroe	137								•	•	
Woodenbridge Hotel	Woodenbridge, Blainroe, Arklow, European Club, Mill Brook, Glenmalure	138		•		•	•	•	•	•	•	
Woodland Court Hotel	Powerscourt, Woodbrook, Druids Glen, Charlesland, Old Conna, Kilternan	132		•			•	•	•		•	

Midlands & Lakelands

CAVAN

ACCOMMODATION	COURSES	PAGE	GOLF ON SITE	ALL INCL.	TUITION	CART	ARRANGE TEE	ADVANCE RES.	CLUBS HIRE	TRANSPORT	PREF. GREEN FEES	CADDY
Cabra Castle Hotel		142	9	•	•	•	•	•	•	•		
Park Hotel	Cavan Golf Club, Headfort Golf Club, Kells	142	9	•	•		•	•	•	•		
Slieve Russell Hotel, Golf & Country Club		141	18	•	•	•	•	•	•	•	•	

KILDARE

ACCOMMODATION	COURSES	PAGE	GOLF ON SITE	ALL INCL.	TUITION	CART	ARRANGE TEE	ADVANCE RES.	CLUBS HIRE	TRANSPORT	PREF. GREEN FEES	CADDY
Curragh Lodge Hotel	Cill Dara, K Club, Curragh, Rathsallagh, Naas, Killeens	144		•			•	•	•		•	
Glenroyal Hotel, Leisure Club & Conference Centre	Knockanally, K Club, Killeen, Castlewarden, Bodenstown, City West, Carton	145		•			•	•	•		•	
Hazel Hotel	Cill Dara, Portarlington, Curragh, Heath, Athy	146		•	•	•	•	•	•	•		
K Club	Luttrellstown Castle, Druids Glen, Portmarnock Links, Rathsallagh, Hermitage	148	18	•	•	•	•	•	•	•	•	

🚩18 = Full 18 Hole   🚩9 = 9 Hole   🚩3 = Par 3

WHERE TO STAY WHEN YOU PLAY!

ACCOMMODATION	COURSES	BE OUR GUEST PAGE NUMBER	GOLF ON SITE	ALL INCLUSIVE PACKAGE	TUITION AVAILABLE	CART AVAILABLE	ARRANGE TEE OFF TIMES	ADVANCE RESERVATIONS	CLUBS FOR HIRE	TRANSPORT	PREFERENTIAL GREEN FEES	CADDY AVAILABLE
LONGFORD												
Longford Arms Hotel	Longford, Glasson, Ballyconnell, Carrick-on-Shannon	150		•		•	•	•		•	•	
MONAGHAN												
Four Seasons Hotel & Leisure Club	Rossmore, Nuremore, Armagh, Castleblaney	151		•	•		•	•	•			•
Glencarn Hotel and Leisure Centre	Castleblayney, Mannon Castle, Rossmore	151		•				•	•		•	
Nuremore Hotel & Country Club	Nuremore, Baltray, Headfort, Dundalk, Greenore, Royal County Down	151	🚩18	•	•	•	•	•	•	•	•	•
OFFALY												
Bridge House Hotel & Leisure Club	Esker Hills, Tullamore	154		•	•	•	•	•	•	•	•	•
Brosna Lodge Hotel	Birr, Esker Hills, Tullamore, Glasson, Portumna, Ballinasloe	152		•			•	•	•		•	
Doolys Hotel	Birr, Esker Hills, Roscrea	153		•	•		•	•	•		•	•
Kinnitty Castle Demesne	Birr, Glasson, Esker Hill, Roscrea, Tullamore and Castle Barna	153		•	•	•	•	•	•	•	•	
Moorhill House Hotel	Esker Hills, Tullamore, Daingean, Mount Temple, Birr, Glasson	155		•	•	•	•	•	•	•	•	•
Tullamore Court Hotel	Tullamore, Esker Hills, Castle Barna, Mount Temple, Glasson, Birr	156		•	•	•	•	•	•	•	•	•
WESTMEATH												
Austin Friar Hotel	Mullingar	158		•	•	•	•	•	•		•	•
Bloomfield House Hotel & Leisure Club	Mullingar, Glasson, Mount Temple, Esker Hills, Athlone, Tullamore	158		•	•	•	•	•	•	•	•	•
Creggan Court Hotel	Glasson Golf & Country Club, Athlone, Moate, Mount Temple	156		•					•			
Greville Arms Hotel	Mullingar, Glasson, Mount Temple, Tullamore, Longford, Esker Hills	158		•	•	•	•	•	•	•	•	•
Hodson Bay Hotel	Athlone, Glasson, Mountemple, Ballinasloe, Roscommon, Esker Hills	156	🚩18	•	•	•	•	•	•	•	•	
Royal Hoey Hotel	Mount Temple, Glasson, Hodson Bay	157		•	•	•	•	•	•	•	•	

🚩18 = Full 18 Hole   🚩9 = 9 Hole   🚩3 = Par 3

ACCOMMODATION	COURSES	BE OUR GUEST PAGE NUMBER	GOLF ON SITE	ALL INCLUSIVE PACKAGE	TUITION AVAILABLE	CART AVAILABLE	ARRANGE TEE OFF TIMES	ADVANCE TEE RESERVATIONS	CLUBS FOR HIRE	TRANSPORT	PREFERENTIAL GREEN FEES	CADDY AVAILABLE
South East												
CARLOW												
Dolmen Hotel and River Court Lodges	Mount Wolseley, Kilkea Castle, Carlow	162				•	•	•	•		•	
Mount Wolseley Hotel, Golf and Country Club	Carlow, Rathsallagh, Coolatin, Kilkea Castle, Killerig Castle, Mount Juliet	163	⚑18	•	•	•	•	•	•	•	•	•
Seven Oaks Hotel	Mount Wolseley, Kilkea Castle, Killerig Castle, Carlow	162					•	•	•		•	•
KILKENNY												
Avalon Inn	Castlecomer, Carlow, Kilkenny, Kilkee Castle, Athy and Mount Juliet	163				•	•	•	•	•		
Bambricks Troysgate House	Kilkenny, Callan, Mount Juliet, Castlecomer	164		•			•	•	•	•	•	•
Brannigans Glendine Inn	Kilkenny, Mount Juliet, Callan, Castlecomer, Pococke, Gowran (New 18 hole Golf Course)	165				•	•	•	•	•		•
Butler House	Kilkenny, Mount Juliet, Carlow, Killerig Castle, Waterford, Kilkea Castle	165				•	•	•	•	•		•
Carrolls Hotel	Mount Juliet, Callan, Mountain View, Kilkenny	171						•	•			
Club House Hotel	Kilkenny (18), Mount Juliet (18), Callan (18), Castlecomer (9) Gowran Park (18) and Borris (9)	165				•	•	•	•	•		•
Hibernian Hotel	Mount Juliet, Kilkenny City, Callan, Carlow, Faithlegg, Waterford Castle	166		•		•	•	•	•	•		•
Hotel Kilkenny	Kilkenny, Gowran, Callan, Mount Juliet, Castlecomer	166		•			•	•	•		•	
Kilford Arms	Mount Juliet, Kilkenny, Callan, Gowran, Castlecomer, Borris	167		•	•		•	•	•		•	
Kilkenny Ormonde Hotel	Mount Juliet, Kilkenny, Gowran	167					•	•	•		•	
Kilkenny River Court	Mount Juliet, Callan, Castlecomer, Gowran, Kilkenny	168		•			•	•	•	•		•
Metropole Hotel	Kilkenny, Callan, Castlecomer and Carrick-on-Suir	169		•		•	•	•	•	•	•	•
Mount Juliet Estate		171	⚑18	•		•		•	•	•	•	•

⚑18 = Full 18 Hole   ⚑9 = 9 Hole   ⚑3 = Par 3

WHERE TO STAY WHEN YOU PLAY!

ACCOMMODATION	COURSES	BE OUR GUEST PAGE NUMBER	GOLF ON SITE	ALL INCLUSIVE PACKAGE	TUITION AVAILABLE	CART AVAILABLE	ARRANGE TEE OFF TIMES	ADVANCE RESERVATIONS	CLUBS FOR HIRE	TRANSPORT	PREFERENTIAL GREEN FEES	CADDY AVAILABLE
TIPPERARY SOUTH												
Cahir House Hotel	Cahir Park, Carrick-on-Suir, Clonmel, Ballykisteen, Dundrum, Tipperary, Thurles	172	•	•	•	•	•	•	•	•	•	•
Cashel Palace Hotel	Cahir Park, Thurles, Ballykisteen, Dundrum	173				•	•	•	•	•	•	•
Dundrum House Hotel		173 ▸18	•	•	•	•	•	•	•	•	•	•
Glen Hotel	Tipperary Golf Club, Ballykisteen, Dundrum, Cahir Park	177	•	•	•	•	•	•	•	•	•	•
Hearns Hotel	Clonmel, Cahir, Carrick-on-suir	175	•	•	•	•	•	•	•	•	•	
Hotel Minella & Leisure Centre	Clonmel, Dungarvan, Kilkenny, Waterford, Thurles, Faithlegg	175	•				•	•	•		•	•
Mulcahys	Clonmel, Cahir, Carrick-on-Suir, Slieve na mbán at Lisranagh, Dungarvan	176	•	•	•	•	•	•	•	•	•	•
WATERFORD												
Arlington Lodge Country House & Restaurant	Waterford Castle, Faithlegg, Waterford, Tramore	186	•	•	•	•	•	•	•	•	•	•
Barnawee Bridge Guesthouse	Gold Coast, Dungarvan, West Waterford, Lismore, Youghal, Waterford Castle	181	•	•	•	•	•	•	•		•	•
Belfry Hotel	Waterford Castle Golf Club, Waterford Golf Club, Faithlegg, Tramore	186	•	•	•	•	•	•	•	•	•	•
Bridge Hotel	Waterford Castle, Faithlegg, Waterford, Tramore, New Ross	187	•	•	•	•	•	•	•	•	•	•
Clonea Strand Hotel, Golf & Leisure	Gold Coast, West Waterford, Dungarvan, Lismore	181 ▸18	•	•	•	•	•	•	•	•	•	•
Dooley's Hotel	Waterford, Tramore, Faithlegg, Waterford Castle, Dunmore, Carrick-on-Suir	188	•	•	•	•	•	•	•	•	•	•
Faithlegg House Hotel	Waterford Castle, Tramore, Waterford Golf Club	184 ▸18	•	•	•	•	•	•	•	•	•	•
Grand Hotel	Tramore, Dunmore East, Faithlegg	185	•	•	•	•	•	•	•	•	•	•
Granville Hotel	Waterford, Faithlegg, Waterford Castle, Tramore, Dunmore East	188	•	•	•	•	•	•	•	•	•	•
Hanoras Cottage	Clonmel, Carrick-on-Suir, Dungarvan, West Waterford, Gold Coast, Cahir Park	180	•	•	•	•	•	•	•	•	•	•
Ivory's Hotel	Dunmore East, Faithlegg, Waterford, Waterford Castle, Tramore, Williamstown	189	•	•	•	•	•	•	•	•	•	•

▸18 = Full 18 Hole   ▸9 = 9 Hole   ▸3 = Par 3

WHERE TO STAY WHEN YOU PLAY!

ACCOMMODATION	COURSES	BE OUR GUEST PAGE NUMBER	GOLF ON SITE	ALL INCLUSIVE PACKAGE	TUITION AVAILABLE	CART AVAILABLE	ARRANGE TEE OFF TIMES	ADVANCE RESERVATIONS	CLUBS FOR HIRE	TRANSPORT	PREFERENTIAL GREEN FEES	CADDY AVAILABLE
WATERFORD Continued												
Lawlors Hotel	Dungarvan, West Waterford, Gold Coast	182		•	•	•	•	•	•	•	•	•
Majestic Hotel	Tramore, Waterford, Faithlegg, Waterford Castle, Mount Juliet, Dunmore East	185		•	•	•	•	•	•		•	•
Ocean Hotel	Waterford, Waterford Castle, Faithlegg, Dunmore East, Tramore	183		•		•	•	•	•	•	•	•
O'Shea's Hotel	Tramore, Faithlegg, Waterford Castle, Waterford, Dungarvan	185		•	•	•	•	•	•	•	•	•
Rice Guesthouse Batterberry's Bar	Dunmore East, Faithlegg, Waterford Castle, Tramore	190					•	•	•	•	•	
Sands Hotel	Tramore, Waterford, Faithlegg	186						•				
Three Rivers Guest House	Faithlegg, Dunmore East, Tramore, Waterford Castle, Waterford, Mount Juliet	181		•	•	•	•	•	•	•		•
Tower Hotel & Leisure Centre	Waterford Castle, Waterford, Faithlegg, Tramore	191		•	•	•	•	•	•		•	•
Waterford Castle Hotel & Golf Club	Waterford Castle Golf Club, Faithlegg, Tramore, Waterford Golf Club	191	🏴18	•	•	•	•	•	•			•
Woodlands Hotel	Waterford Castle, Waterford, Faithlegg, Tramore, Dunmore East	192		•	•	•	•	•	•			•
WEXFORD												
Bayview Hotel	Courtown Harbour, Ballymoney, Coolattin, Enniscorthy, Woodenbridge, Arklow	192				•	•	•	•		•	•
Clarion Brandon House Hotel & Leisure Centre	New Ross, Mount Juliet, Faithlegg, Rosslare Strand, Waterford, Enniscorthy	197		•		•	•	•	•		•	•
Coral Gables	St. Helens, Rosslare and Wexford	200				•	•	•	•		•	•
Danby Lodge Hotel	St. Helens Bay, Rosslare Strand, Wexford	199		•	•	•	•	•	•		•	•
Ferrycarrig Hotel	St. Helen's, Rosslare, Wexford, Enniscorthy	202		•			•	•	•		•	•
Hotel Rosslare	Rosslare Strand, St. Helens Bay	201		•			•	•	•		•	•
Murphy - Floods Hotel	Enniscorthy	194		•			•	•			•	

🏴18 = Full 18 Hole   🏴9 = 9 Hole   🏴3 = Par 3

WHERE TO STAY WHEN YOU PLAY!

ACCOMMODATION	COURSES	BE OUR GUEST PAGE NUMBER	GOLF ON SITE	ALL INCLUSIVE PACKAGE	TUITION AVAILABLE	CART AVAILABLE	ARRANGE TEE OFF TIMES	ADVANCE RESERVATIONS	CLUBS FOR HIRE	TRANSPORT	PREFERENTIAL GREEN FEES	CADDY AVAILABLE
WEXFORD Continued												
Riverside Park Hotel	Enniscorthy, Rosslare, St. Helens	195	•	•		•		•	•		•	•
St. Martins	St. Helens, Wexford, Rosslare Strand, Enniscorthy	201	•	•	•	•	•	•	•		•	•
Talbot Hotel Conference and Leisure Centre	St. Helens, Wexford, Rosslare, Enniscorthy and Courtown	203	•	•	•	•	•	•	•		•	•
Tuskar House Hotel	St. Helen's, Rosslare Strand, Wexford, Mount Juliet, Waterford, Enniscorthy	202	•	•	•	•	•	•	•		•	•
Whites Hotel	Wexford, Rosslare, St. Helen's Bay, Enniscorthy	204	•	•	•	•	•	•	•		•	•
Whitford House Hotel	St. Helen's Bay, Wexford, Rosslare, Rathaspeck (par 3 golf)	204	•	•	•	•	•	•	•		•	•

South West

CORK

ACCOMMODATION	COURSES	PAGE	GOLF ON SITE	ALL INCLUSIVE PACKAGE	TUITION AVAILABLE	CART AVAILABLE	ARRANGE TEE OFF TIMES	ADVANCE RESERVATIONS	CLUBS FOR HIRE	TRANSPORT	PREFERENTIAL GREEN FEES	CADDY AVAILABLE
Abbey Hotel	Killarney, Kenmare, Macroom, Lee Valley, Dooks	207	•					•			•	
Actons Hotel	Kinsale, Old Head of Kinsale, Fota Island, Bandon, Harbour Point, Little Island	236	•	•		•	•	•	•		•	•
Aherne's Townhouse & Seafood Restaurant	Youghal, Waterford Castle, Old Head Kinsale, Little Island, Dungarvan, Fota Island	248		•	•	•	•	•	•		•	•
Ashlee Lodge	Lee Valley, Harbour Point, Fota Island, Muskerry, Cork, Mallow	210	•	•	•	•	•	•	•	•	•	•
Ballylickey Manor House	Bantry, Glengarriff	207					•	•		•		•
Blarney Castle Hotel	Blarney, Muskerry, Lee Valley, Fota Island, Harbour Point, Cork	211	•	•	•	•	•	•			•	•
Blarney Park Hotel	Lee Valley, Harbour Point, Fota, Muskerry, Mallow	211		•	•	•	•	•			•	•
Carrigaline Court Hotel	Old Head of Kinsale, Monkstown, Kinsale, Douglas, Fota Island, Cork	212	•	•		•	•	•	•		•	•
Casey's of Baltimore	Skibbereen	208	•					•	•		•	•
Castle Hotel & Leisure Centre	Macroom Golf Course, 18 hole Parklands Course	241	•				•	•	•		•	
Celtic Ross Hotel Conference & Leisure Centre	Skibbereen, Bandon, Lisselan, Bantry, Kinsale	245	•	•	•	•	•	•	•		•	•

🏌18 = Full 18 Hole   🏌9 = 9 Hole   🏌3 = Par 3

WHERE TO STAY WHEN YOU PLAY!

ACCOMMODATION	COURSES	BE OUR GUEST PAGE NUMBER	GOLF ON SITE	ALL INCLUSIVE PACKAGE	TUITION AVAILABLE	CART AVAILABLE	ARRANGE TEE OFF TIMES	ADVANCE RESERVATIONS	CLUBS FOR HIRE	TRANSPORT	PREFERENTIAL GREEN FEES	CADDY AVAILABLE
CORK Continued												
Christy's Hotel	Muskerry, Lee Valley, Fota Island, Harbour Point, Mallow	211		•	•	•	•	•	•	•	•	•
Clarion Hotel & Suites Cork	Fota Island, Frankfield (Cork City), Muskerry (Blarney), Lee Valley	222		•	•	•	•	•	•	•	•	•
Colla House Hotel	Coosheen, Bantry, Skibbereen	245		•					•	•	•	•
Commodore Hotel	East Cork, Midleton, Cobh	217		•			•				•	
Deerpark Hotel	Charleville	214					•	•	•	•		
Devonshire Arms Hotel & Restaurant	Youghal, West Waterford, Fota Island, Harbour Point, Lismore	248		•	•	•	•	•	•	•	•	•
Dunmore House Hotel	Macroom, Bandon, Skibbereen, Monkstown, The Island and Foto Island	214	🚩9	•	•	•	•	•	•	•	•	•
Eldon Hotel	Skibbereen, Bantry, Glengarriff, Schull, Clonakilty	247		•	•	•	•	•	•	•	•	•
Fernhill Golf & Country Club	Douglas, Monkstown, Harbour Point, Kinsale - Old Head, Cork, Fota	213	🚩18	•	•	•	•	•	•	•	•	•
Glengarriff Eccles Hotel	Bantry Bay, Glengarriff, Ring of Kerry	235		•				•			•	
Gresham Metropole	Fota Island, Little Island, Harbour Point, Muskerry, Kinsale	225			•	•	•	•	•	•	•	•
Harbour Lodge	Kinsale, Old Head of Kinsale, Bandon, Fota, Cork, Harbour Point	237			•	•	•	•	•	•	•	•
Hayfield Manor Hotel	Fota Island, Cork, Harbour Point, Douglas, Old Head of Kinsale	226		•	•	•	•	•	•	•	•	•
Hibernian Hotel And Leisure Centre	Mallow, Lee Valley, Charleville, Doneraile, Fota Island	242		•				•			•	
Imperial Hotel	Fota Island, Douglas, Cork , Muskerry, Lee Valley, Monkstown	226		•	•	•	•				•	
Innishannon House Hotel	Old Head Of Kinsale, Bandon, Kinsale, Lee Valley, Lisalawn, Farran Galway	236				•	•	•	•	•	•	•
Kierans Folkhouse Inn	Kinsale, Farrangalway, Fota, Lee Valley, Harbour Point, Old Head of Kinsale	238		•	•	•	•	•	•	•	•	•
Long Quay House	Kinsale Golf Club, Old Head Golf Links, Ringenane Kinsale	239		•	•	•	•	•	•	•	•	•
Lotamore House	Cork, Harbour Point, Fota Island, Water Rock, Lee Valley, Kinsale	229		•					•	•	•	•

🚩18 = Full 18 Hole 🚩9 = 9 Hole 🚩3 = Par 3

WHERE TO STAY WHEN YOU PLAY!

ACCOMMODATION / COURSES	BE OUR GUEST PAGE NUMBER	GOLF ON SITE	ALL INCLUSIVE PACKAGE	TUITION AVAILABLE	CART AVAILABLE	ARRANGE TEE OFF TIMES	ADVANCE RESERVATIONS	CLUBS FOR HIRE	TRANSPORT	PREFERENTIAL GREEN FEES	CADDY AVAILABLE
CORK Continued											
Maryborough House Hotel — Douglas, Fota Island, Cork, Kinsale Old Head, Harbour Point, Monkstown	229	•	•	•	•	•	•	•	•	•	•
Midleton Park Hotel — Fota Island, Cork - Little Island, Harbour Point, Water Rock, East Cork	244	•	•	•	•	•	•	•	•	•	•
Munster Arms Hotel — Bandon, Lisselan, Old Head, Kinsale, Douglas	209	•	•	•	•	•	•	•	•	•	•
Old Bank House — Old Head of Kinsale, Kinsale, Farringalway, Little Island, Fota, Lee Valley	239	•	•	•	•	•	•	•	•	•	•
Quality Hotel and Leisure Centre — Dunmore, Kinsale, Bandon, Skibbereen, Lisselan	216	•								•	
Quality Hotel Cork — Fota Island Golf Course, Cork Golf Course, Blarney Golf Course	230	•	•	•	•	•	•	•	•	•	•
Quayside House — Kinsale Golf Club (18 & 9 hole course)	239	•	•	•	•	•	•	•	•	•	•
Seven North Mall — Cork, Douglas, Fota Island, Harbour Point, Monkstown, Muskerry	231		•	•	•	•	•	•	•	•	
Trident Hotel — Kinsale Golf Club, Fota Island, Old Head Golf Links, Lee Valley	240	•	•	•	•	•	•	•	•	•	•
Victoria Hotel — Lee Valley, Macroom	242		•	•	•	•	•	•			•
Victoria Hotel — Fota Island, Cork Golf Club, Monkstown Golf Club, Douglas, Lee Valley	232		•	•	•	•	•	•			•
Vienna Woods Hotel — Cork, Harbour Point, Fota, Old Head of Kinsale, Water Rock	233	•	•	•	•	•	•	•	•	•	•
Walter Raleigh Hotel — Fota Island, Youghal, West Waterford, Water Rock, Harbour Point, Gold Coast	249	•	•	•	•	•	•	•	•		•
WatersEdge Hotel — Fota Island, Harbour Point, Cobh, Water Rock, East Cork, Old Head of Kinsale	217		•	•	•	•	•	•	•	•	•
West Cork Hotel — Skibbereen, West Carbery	248			•	•	•	•	•		•	•
Westlodge Hotel — Bantry, Bantry Bay	210	•				•	•	•	•	•	•
White House — Kinsale (18) and (9), Old Head, Bandon, Carrigaline, Muskerry	240			•	•	•	•	•		•	
White Lady Hotel — Kinsale, Old Head of Kinsale, Farringalway, Ringenane	241		•	•	•	•	•	•	•	•	•

KERRY

18 = Full 18 Hole   9 = 9 Hole   3 = Par 3

WHERE TO STAY WHEN YOU PLAY!

Accommodation	Courses	Be Our Guest Page Number	Golf on Site	All Inclusive Package	Tuition Available	Cart Available	Arrange Tee Off Times	Advance Tee Reservations	Clubs for Hire	Transport	Preferential Green Fees	Caddy Available
Abbey Gate Hotel	Tralee, Ballybunion, Killarney, Dooks, Waterville, Kerries.	291			•	•		•	•	•	•	•
Aghadoe Heights Hotel	Waterville, Ballybunion, Kenmare, Killarney, Beaufort, Ring of Kerry	268						•	•	•	•	•
Arbutus Hotel	Killarney, Ballybunion, Waterville, Dooks, Tralee, Ring of Kerry	268			•			•	•	•	•	•
Ashville Guesthouse	Killarney, Ross, Dunloe, Beaufort, Waterville, Dooks, Ballybunion	269						•	•	•	•	•
Ballyroe Heights Hotel	Barrow, Ballybunion, Dooks, Ardfert, Ballyheigue, The Kerries	291			•	•	•	•	•	•	•	•
Ballyseede Castle Hotel	Tralee, Ballybunion, Killarney, Kerries,	292			•	•	•	•	•	•	•	•
Barrow Country House	Tralee, Ballybunion, Killarney, Waterville, Dooks, Dingle	292			•	•	•	•	•	•	•	•
Benners Hotel	Ceann Sibéal (Dingle), Dooks and Castlegregory	255			•	•	•	•	•	•	•	•
Bianconi	Killarney, Beaufort, Dunloe, Killorglin, Dooks, Waterville	288			•	•	•	•	•	•	•	•
Brandon Court Hotel	Tralee, Dooks, Kerries, Ballybunion, Ring of Kerry, Killarney	292			•	•	•	•	•	•	•	•
Brandon Hotel	Tralee, Ballybunion, Waterville, Dooks, Killarney, Ring of Kerry	293			•	•	•	•	•	•	•	•
Brookhaven Country House	Waterville, Dooks, Parknasilla, Tralee, Kenmare, Ballybunion, Ring of Kerry	295					•		•	•	•	•
Butler Arms Hotel	Waterville, Dooks, Killarney, Tralee, Ballybunion, Ring of Kerry	296			•	•	•		•	•	•	•
Caragh Lodge	Dooks, Beaufort, Tralee, Killarney, Waterville, Ballybunion	253			•			•	•			
Carrig House	Dooks, Killarney, Beaufort, Killorglin	288			•			•	•	•		
Castlelodge Guesthouse	Killarney Golf Course, Ross Golf Course	270						•	•	•		
Castlerosse Hotel & Leisure Centre	Killarney (3 courses), Beaufort	271	⚑9		•	•	•	•	•	•	•	•
Cliff House Hotel	Ballybunion Old Course and Cashen Course, Tralee, Killarney, Lahinch and Waterville	249			•	•	•	•	•	•	•	•
Davitts	Kenmare, Ring of Kerry	263						•	•	•	•	

422

⚑18 = Full 18 Hole   ⚑9 = 9 Hole   ⚑3 = Par 3

WHERE TO STAY WHEN YOU PLAY!

ACCOMMODATION	COURSES	BE OUR GUEST PAGE NUMBER	GOLF ON SITE	ALL INCLUSIVE PACKAGE	TUITION AVAILABLE	CART AVAILABLE	ARRANGE TEE OFF TIMES	ADVANCE RESERVATIONS	CLUBS FOR HIRE	TRANSPORT	PREFERENTIAL GREEN FEES	CADDY AVAILABLE
KERRY Continued												
Derrynane Hotel	Ring of Kerry, Kenmare, Waterville, Parknasilla, Beaufort	251						•	•		•	
Dingle Skellig Hotel	Ceann Sibeál Dingle, Castlegregory, Tralee Golf Club, Killarney, Dooks	258		•		•	•	•	•	•	•	
Earls Court House	Killarney, Waterville, Ballybunion, Tralee, Beaufort, Dooks, Old Head	272				•	•	•	•	•	•	•
Eviston House Hotel	Ballybunion, Beaufort, Killarney, Waterville, Dooks, Tralee	273		•		•	•	•	•	•	•	•
Foley's Townhouse	Killarney, Barrow, Beaufort, Dooks, Ballybunion, Waterville	274						•	•			
Fuchsia House	Killarney, Ballybunion, Waterville, Beaufort, Tralee, Dooks, Old Head	274		•	•	•	•	•	•	•	•	•
Gleann Fia Country House	Killarney, Tralee, Ballybunion, Waterville, Beaufort, Dooks	275				•	•	•	•	•	•	•
Glencar House Hotel	Killarney, Beaufort, Dooks, Waterville, Killorglin	262		•		•	•	•	•	•	•	•
Gormans Clifftop House and Restaurant	Ceann Sibeál	259						•	•			
Grand Hotel	Tralee, Ballybunion, Waterville, Dingle, Dooks, Killarney	294		•		•	•	•	•	•	•	•
Grove Lodge Guesthouse	Killarney, Killorglin, Dooks, Beaufort, Gap of Dunloe, Dingle	288				•	•	•	•	•	•	•
Harty Costello Town House	Ballybunion, Tralee, Listowel, Ballyheigue, Killarney	250				•	•	•	•	•	•	•
Holiday Inn Killarney	Killarney Golf & Fishing Club, Ross, Dunloe, Beaufort	276		•		•	•	•	•	•	•	•
International Best Western Hotel	Killarney, Beaufort, Killorglin, Dooks, Ballybunion, Tralee	277		•		•	•	•	•	•	•	•
Kathleens Country House	Killarney, Waterville, Tralee, Dooks, Ballybunion, Beaufort	278		•		•	•	•	•	•	•	•
Kenmare Bay Hotel	Ring of Kerry, Kenmare, Killarney, Tralee, Ballybunion, Waterville	264		•		•	•	•	•	•	•	•
Killarney Avenue Hotel	Killarney, Ballybunion, Tralee, Waterville, Beaufort	278		•		•	•	•	•	•	•	•
Killarney Heights Hotel	Killarney, Beaufort, Waterville, Dooks, Ballybunion, Tralee	279		•		•	•	•	•	•	•	•
Killarney Lodge	Killarney, Waterville, Ballybunion, Tralee, Dooks, Beaufort	279				•	•	•	•	•	•	

18 = Full 18 Hole   9 = 9 Hole   3 = Par 3

WHERE TO STAY WHEN YOU PLAY!

Accommodation	Courses	Be Our Guest Page Number	Golf On Site	All Inclusive Package	Tuition Available	Cart Available	Arrange Tee Off Times	Advance Reservations	Clubs For Hire	Transport	Preferential Green Fees	Caddy Available
KERRY Continued												
Killarney Park Hotel	Killarney, Ballybunion, Tralee, Waterville, Dooks, Beaufort	280				•	•	•	•	•	•	•
Killarney Royal	Killarney, Tralee, Dooks, Waterville, Beaufort, Ross.	280				•	•	•	•	•	•	•
Killeen House Hotel	Killarney, Waterville, Tralee, Dooks, Ballybunion, Beaufort	281	•	•	•	•	•	•	•	•	•	•
Kingfisher Lodge Guesthouse	Beaufort, Dunloe, Castlerosse, Killarney, Ross	281	•		•	•	•	•	•	•	•	
Lake Hotel	Killarney (3 courses), Beaufort, Dooks, Ballybunion, Waterville, Tralee	282	•	•	•	•	•	•	•	•	•	•
Lakelands Farm Guesthouse	Waterville Golf Course	296			•	•	•	•	•	•	•	•
Lime Court	Killarney, Ballybunion, Waterville, Dooks, Beaufort, Tralee	282			•	•	•	•	•	•	•	•
Listowel Arms Hotel	Ballybunion, Listowel, Tralee, Killarney, Lahinch, Waterville	289	•	•	•	•	•	•	•	•	•	
Marine Links Hotel	Ballybunion, Old Course & Cashen, Tralee, Killarney, Lahinch, Dooks	250	•	•	•	•	•	•	•	•		
Moorings	Waterville Golf Links	289	•		•	•	•	•	•	•	•	•
Muckross Park Hotel	Beaufort, O'Mahony's Point, Killeen, Fossa, Ross, Ring of Kerry, Tralee, Ballybunion, Waterville, Dooks	283				•		•	•		•	
Old Weir Lodge	Killarney, Waterville, Ballybunion, Tralee, Dooks, Beaufort	284		•		•	•	•	•	•		
Parknasilla Great Southern Hotel	Ring of Kerry, Waterville, Killarney, Dooks	290 ⛳9		•			•	•	•	•	•	•
Randles Court Clarion Hotel	Killarney, Tralee, Beaufort, Dooks, Ring of Kerry	284		•		•	•	•	•	•	•	
Rivermere	Killarney (O'Mahony's Point and Killeen), Dooks, Ballybunion, Waterville, Tralee, Ring of Kerry	285		•		•	•	•	•	•	•	
Riversdale House Hotel	Kenmare, Killarney, Waterville, Parknasilla, Dooks, Ring of Kerry	266		•		•	•	•	•	•	•	
Ross Hotel	Killarney, Ballybunion, Tralee, Waterville, Dooks, Beaufort	285		•		•	•	•	•	•	•	
Scarriff Inn	Waterville, Kenmare, Sneem, Killorglin, Tralee, Ballybunion	252	•		•	•	•	•	•	•	•	•
Sheen Falls Lodge	Kenmare, Ring of Kerry	267	•	•		•	•	•	•	•	•	•

⛳18 = Full 18 Hole   ⛳9 = 9 Hole   ⛳3 = Par 3

WHERE TO STAY WHEN YOU PLAY!

ACCOMMODATION	COURSES	BE OUR GUEST PAGE NUMBER	GOLF ON SITE	ALL INCLUSIVE PACKAGE	TUITION AVAILABLE	CART AVAILABLE	ARRANGE TEE OFF TIMES	ADVANCE RESERVATIONS	CLUBS FOR HIRE	TRANSPORT	PREFERENTIAL GREEN FEES	CADDY AVAILABLE
KERRY Continued												
Smerwick Harbour Hotel	Ceann Sibeál (Dingle) 18 hole links, par 72, 6500yrds	261	•	•	•	•	•	•	•	•	•	•
Smugglers Inn	Waterville, Killarney, Dooks, Tralee, Ballybunion, Kenmare, Parknasilla	296		•	•	•	•	•	•	•		•
Tralee Townhouse	Ardfert, Ballybeggin, Ballyheigue, The Kerries	295		•		•	•	•	•		•	•
Tuscar Lodge	Killarney Golf Club, Beaufort, Dooks, Killorglin	287		•		•	•	•	•		•	•

Shannon
CLARE

ACCOMMODATION	COURSES	BE OUR GUEST PAGE NUMBER	GOLF ON SITE	ALL INCLUSIVE PACKAGE	TUITION AVAILABLE	CART AVAILABLE	ARRANGE TEE OFF TIMES	ADVANCE RESERVATIONS	CLUBS FOR HIRE	TRANSPORT	PREFERENTIAL GREEN FEES	CADDY AVAILABLE
Atlantic Hotel	Lahinch Championship Course and Castle, Woodstock, Ennis, Spanish Point	313		•	•	•	•	•	•	•	•	•
Ballinalacken Castle Country House & Restaurant	Lahinch, Lahinch Castle, Woodstock, Galway Bay, Dromoland Castle, Ennis.	303		•	•	•	•	•	•			•
Bellbridge House Hotel	Spanish Point, Lahinch, Doonbeg	318		•		•	•	•	•	•	•	•
Bunratty Castle Hotel and Conference Centre	Shannon, Dromoland, Lahinch, Limerick	300	•		•	•	•	•	•			•
Burkes Armada Hotel	Spanish Point, Lahinch, Kilkee	318	•		•	•	•	•	•			•
Dough Mor Lodge	Lahinch Golf Club (36 holes), Doonbeg G.C.	314					•	•	•			
Falls Hotel	Lahinch, Dromoland, Ennis, Kilkee, Shannon	308		•		•	•	•	•			•
Fitzpatrick Bunratty	Shannon, Dromoland, Woodstock, Ballykisteen, Limerick County	302	•				•	•	•	•		•
Greenbrier Inn Guesthouse	Lahinch Championship Golf Links, Lahinch Castle Golf Links, Doonbeg Championship Golf Links	314			•	•		•	•			•
Grovemount House	Lahinch	309			•	•	•	•	•			
Halpin's Townhouse Hotel	Ballybunion, Lahinch, Kilkee, Doonbeg, Woodstock, Shannon	309		•		•	•	•	•	•		•
Kilkee Bay Hotel	Kilkee, Kilrush, Doonbeg	309	•		•	•	•	•	•		•	•
Kincora Hall Hotel	East Clare, Lahinch, Limerick County Golf & Country Club	310	•			•	•	•	•		•	•

 ⚑18 = Full 18 Hole   ⚑9 = 9 Hole   ⚑3 = Par 3

WHERE TO STAY WHEN YOU PLAY!

ACCOMMODATION	COURSES	BE OUR GUEST PAGE NUMBER	GOLF ON SITE	ALL INCLUSIVE PACKAGE	TUITION AVAILABLE	CART AVAILABLE	ARRANGE TEE OFF TIMES	ADVANCE RESERVATIONS	CLUBS FOR HIRE	TRANSPORT	PREFERENTIAL GREEN FEES	CADDY AVAILABLE
CLARE Continued												
Kincora House and Gallery Restaurant	Lahinch, Lahinch Castle, Woodstock, Galway Bay, Dromoland Castle, Ennis	316			•		•	•	•	•	•	•
Liscannor Bay Hotel	Lahinch (Links), Lahinch (Castle), Spanish Point, Doonbeg	316		•	•		•	•	•			•
Magowna House Hotel	Woodstock, Ennis, Lahinch, Dromoland Castle, Shannon, Doonbeg	306		•	•		•	•	•	•		
Oak Wood Arms Hotel	Shannon, Dromoland	320		•	•		•	•	•	•	•	
Old Ground Hotel	Lahinch, Woodstock, Ennis, Dromoland, Shannon, East Clare	307		•		•	•	•	•	•		•
Sancta Maria Hotel	Lahinch Links, Lahinch Castle, Doonbeg, Woodstock, Dromoland, Spanish Point	315		•		•	•	•	•	•		•
Shamrock Inn Hotel	Lahinch Championship Course, Spanish Point, Woodstock, Ennis	315		•		•	•	•	•	•	•	•
Temple Gate Hotel	Woodstock, Ennis, Lahinch, East Clare, Shannon, Dromoland	307		•	•	•	•	•	•	•	•	•
Tinarana House Hotel and Health Resort	East Clare, Portumna, Nenagh	312		•			•	•	•			
Westbrook House	Woodstock, Ennis, Dromoland, Shannon, Lahinch and East Clare Golf Clubs	308		•	•		•	•	•		•	•
Woodstock Hotel		308	18	•	•		•	•	•		•	•
LIMERICK												
Adare Manor Hotel & Golf Resort		321	18	•	•	•	•	•	•	•	•	•
Castletroy Park Hotel	Castletroy, Limerick County (Ballyneety), Dromoland, Adare	323		•			•	•	•	•		•
Courtenay Lodge Hotel	Newcastle West, Adare Manor, Adare Golf Club, Ballybunion, Charleville, Dingle (Ceann Sibeál)	328		•		•	•	•	•	•	•	•
Devon Inn Hotel	Newcastle West, Killeline, Ballybunion, Killarney, Tralee	329		•			•	•	•	•		•
Dunraven Arms Hotel	Adare, Adare Manor, Limerick, Ballybunion, Lahinch	322			•			•	•	•		•
Fitzgeralds Woodlands House Hotel and Leisure Club	Adare Manor, New Adare, Newcastle West, Ardagh, Charleville, Ballyneety	322		•	•			•	•	•		
Greenhills Hotel Conference/Leisure	Ballyneety, Shannon, Castletroy, Ballykisten, Dromoland, Limerick	325		•		•	•	•	•	•	•	•

18 = Full 18 Hole   9 = 9 Hole   3 = Par 3

WHERE TO STAY WHEN YOU PLAY!

ACCOMMODATION	COURSES	BE OUR GUEST PAGE NUMBER	GOLF ON SITE	ALL INCLUSIVE PACKAGE	TUITION AVAILABLE	CART AVAILABLE	ARRANGE TEE OFF TIMES	ADVANCE RESERVATIONS	CLUBS FOR HIRE	TRANSPORT	PREFERENTIAL GREEN FEES	CADDY AVAILABLE
LIMERICK Continued												
Gresham Ardhu	Limerick, Castletroy, Adare, Shannon, Ballykisteen, Limerick County	326			•	•	•	•	•	•	•	•
Jurys Limerick Hotel	Castletroy, Limerick (Ballyclough), Co. Limerick (Ballyneety), Shannon	327	•		•	•	•	•	•	•	•	•
Rathkeale House Hotel	Adare, Adare Manor, Killeline, Newcastle West, Charleville, Ballybunion	329				•	•	•	•	•	•	•
TIPPERARY NORTH												
Abbey Court Hotel and Trinity Leisure Club	Birr, Nenagh, Roscrea, Portumna	329	•		•	•	•	•	•	•	•	•
Anner Hotel & Leisure Centre	Thurles, Dundrum, Templemore	331					•	•	•	•	•	•
Racket Hall Country House Hotel	Roscrea Golf Club	330	•		•	•	•	•	•	•	•	•
St. David's Country House	Nenagh, Portumna	330			•			•			•	•
West												
GALWAY												
Abbey House	Barna, Galway, Galway Bay, Athenry, Oughterard	348	•					•				
Abbeyglen Castle Hotel	Connemara	340	•	•	•	•	•		•	•		
Adare Guest House	Galway Bay, Oughterard	348	•		•	•	•	•	•	•	•	•
Alcock and Brown Hotel	Connemara	340	•		•	•	•	•	•	•	•	
Anno Santo Hotel	Glenlo, Athenry, Galway, Oughterard, Galway Bay	348	•				•	•	•	•	•	•
Ardagh Hotel & Restaurant	Connemara	341				•	•	•		•		
Ardilaun House Hotel, Conference Centre & Leisure Club	Galway, Oughterard, Galway Bay Golf & Country, Athenry, Lahinch, Connemara, Barna Golf Club	349	•		•	•	•	•	•	•	•	•
Ballynahinch Castle Hotel	Connemara Championship Golf Course	337	•				•	•	•	•	•	
Ben View House	Connemara	342					•	•	•	•	•	

= Full 18 Hole   = 9 Hole   = Par 3

WHERE TO STAY WHEN YOU PLAY!

ACCOMMODATION	COURSES	BE OUR GUEST PAGE NUMBER	GOLF ON SITE	ALL INCLUSIVE PACKAGE	TUITION AVAILABLE	CART AVAILABLE	ARRANGE TEE OFF TIMES	ADVANCE RESERVATIONS	CLUBS FOR HIRE	TRANSPORT	PREFERENTIAL GREEN FEES	CADDY AVAILABLE
GALWAY Continued												
Byrne's Mal Dua House	Connemara Golf Club, Oughterard Golf Club	343		•	•	•	•	•	•	•		•
Connemara Coast Hotel	Barna, Oughterard, Galway Bay	347		•	•	•	•	•		•	•	•
Connemara Gateway Hotel	Oughterard, Barna Golf and Country	366		•	•	•	•	•				•
Corrib House Hotel	Oughterard, Connemara Isles, Galway Bay, Bearna, Ballyconneely	366		•	•	•	•	•		•		•
Corrib Wave Guest House	Oughterard	367		•	•	•	•	•	•	•	•	•
Dun Ri Guesthouse	Connemara	344		•	•	•	•	•	•	•	•	•
Eldons Hotel	Connemara	370					•	•	•			
Forster Court Hotel	Galway, Barna, Galway Golf & Country, Athenry	351					•	•				
Foyles Hotel	Connemara	344		•	•	•	•	•	•	•	•	•
Galway Bay Hotel, Conference & Leisure Centre	Galway, Galway Bay, Athenry, Bearna, Gort	352		•	•	•	•	•	•	•	•	•
Galway Ryan Hotel & Leisure Centre	Galway Bay, Galway, Athenry, Oughterard, Roscam, Rosshill	352				•	•	•	•			•
Glenlo Abbey Hotel	Glenlo Abbey, Galway, Bearna, Oughterard, Galway Bay, Connemara	353 ▶9		•	•	•	•	•	•			•
Hotel Sacre Coeur	Bearna, Galway, Athenry, Tuam, Oughterard, Galway Bay	354		•	•	•	•	•		•	•	•
Inishmore Guesthouse	Barna, Galway Bay, Oughterard, Athenry, Salthill	355		•	•	•	•	•	•	•	•	•
Lady Gregory Hotel	Gort	361		•	•	•	•	•	•	•	•	•
Lake Hotel	Oughterard Golf Club and other local championship courses	367		•	•	•	•	•	•	•	•	•
Lochlurgain Hotel	Bearna, Galway, Athenry, Gort, Oughterard and Galway Bay	356		•	•	•	•	•	•	•	•	•
Menlo Park Hotel and Conference Centre	Barna, Galway Bay, Galway, Athenry, Oughterard, Connemara	357		•	•	•	•	•	•	•	•	•
Mountain View Guest House	Oughterard, Galway, Connemara, Westport	368		•	•	•	•	•	•	•	•	•

▶18 = Full 18 Hole ▶9 = 9 Hole ▶3 = Par 3

WHERE TO STAY WHEN YOU PLAY!

ACCOMMODATION	COURSES	BE OUR GUEST PAGE NUMBER	GOLF ON SITE	ALL INCLUSIVE PACKAGE	TUITION AVAILABLE	CART AVAILABLE	ARRANGE TEE OFF TIMES	ADVANCE RESERVATIONS	CLUBS FOR HIRE	TRANSPORT	PREFERENTIAL GREEN FEES	CADDY AVAILABLE
GALWAY Continued												
O'Deas Hotel	Loughrea, Curragh, Gort, Galway Bay	364		•		•	•	•	•			
Peacockes Hotel & Complex	Oughterard, Ballyconneely, Glenlo Abbey, Barna, Westport	364		•		•	•	•	•	•	•	•
Quality Hotel and Leisure Centre Galway	Athenry, Galway, Galway Bay, Loughrea, Glenlo Abbey, Gort, Barna	365		•		•	•	•	•	•	•	•
Quality Hotel Clarinbridge	Athenry, Galway, Galway Bay, Loughrea, Glenlo Abbey, Gort	340		•		•	•	•	•	•		
Renvyle House Hotel	Connemara, Westport, Oughterard, Pebble Beach	369 9		•		•	•	•	•		•	•
River Run Lodge	Oughterard	368		•		•	•	•	•		•	•
Rosleague Manor Hotel	Connemara, Ballyconneely	363		•		•	•	•			•	•
Shannon Oaks Hotel & Country Club	Portumna, Galway Bay, Birr, Glasson, Gort, Lahinch	369		•		•	•	•	•			
Westwood House Hotel	Barna, Oughterard, Ballyconneely, Galway Bay Golf and Country Club	361		•		•	•	•	•	•	•	•
MAYO												
Ardmore Country House Hotel and Restaurant	Westport, Castlebar, Ballinrobe, Enniscrone, Belmullet, Clew Bay	379		•		•	•	•	•	•		•
Atlantic Coast Hotel	Westport, Enniscrone, Carne, Ballyconneely, Castlebar, Ballinrobe	380		•	•	•	•	•	•	•	•	•
Belmont Hotel	Claremorris, Ballinrobe, Castlebar and Ballyhaunis	378		•			•	•	•	•		
Castlecourt Hotel Conference and Leisure Centre	Westport, Ballinrobe, Castlebar, Belmullet, Clew Bay, Enniscrone	380		•	•	•	•	•	•	•		•
Central Hotel	Westport Golf Club	381		•	•	•	•	•	•	•		•
Daly's Hotel	Belmullet, Castlebar, Westport, Balla, Enniscrone, Three Oaks			•	•	•	•	•	•	•		•
Downhill House Hotel	Ballina, Enniscrone, Carne (Belmullet), Rosses Point, Strandhill, Westport	373			•	•	•	•	•	•	•	•
Healy's Restaurant and Hotel	Castlebar, Ballina, Westport, Enniscrone, Carne, Swinford, Ballinrobe, Mulrany	379		•		•	•	•	•	•		•
Hotel Westport, Conference & Leisure Centre	Westport, Castlebar, Ballinrobe, Carne	381		•	•	•	•	•	•	•	•	•

18 = Full 18 Hole   9 = 9 Hole   3 = Par 3

WHERE TO STAY WHEN YOU PLAY!

ACCOMMODATION	COURSES	BE OUR GUEST PAGE NUMBER	GOLF ON SITE	ALL INCLUSIVE PACKAGE	TUITION AVAILABLE	CART AVAILABLE	ARRANGE TEE OFF TIMES	ADVANCE RESERVATIONS	CLUBS FOR HIRE	TRANSPORT	PREFERENTIAL GREEN FEES	CADDY AVAILABLE
MAYO Continued												
Jennings Hotel & Travellers Friend	Castlebar, Westport, Three Oaks, Ballinrobe, Belmullet, Enniscrone	375		•	•	•	•	•	•	•	•	•
Knock House Hotel	Ballyhaunis, Claremorris	378		•			•	•		•	•	
Knockranny House Hotel	Westport, Castlebar, Ballinrobe, Clew Bay, Achill, Mulranny	382		•	•	•	•	•	•	•	•	•
Knockranny Lodge	Westport	382			•	•	•	•	•	•	•	•
Regans Bartra House Hotel	Enniscrone, Ballina, Cairn, Rosses Point, Strandhill	374		•		•	•	•	•	•	•	•
Ryan's Hotel	Westport, Clifden (Ballyconneely), Galway, Ballinrobe	377		•	•	•	•	•	•	•	•	•
Teach Iorrais	Carne Links Golf Course	377		•			•	•		•	•	
Westport Inn Hotel	Westport, Enniscrone, Clifden, Ballinrobe	383		•	•	•	•	•	•	•	•	•
Westport Woods Hotel & Leisure Centre	Westport, Castlebar, Ballinrobe, Clew Bay, Carne (Belmullet)	383		•	•	•	•	•	•	•	•	•
ROSCOMMON												
Abbey Hotel	Roscommon, Glasson, Athlone	385		•	•	•	•	•	•	•	•	•
Gleesons Townhouse & Restaurant	Roscommon Golf Club	385			•	•	•	•	•	•	•	•
O'Gara's Royal Hotel	Roscommon, Glasson, Longford, Athlone	386		•			•	•		•	•	
Royal Hotel	Roscommon, County Sligo, Strandhill, Carrick-on-Shannon, Woodbrook	384						•			•	
North West												
DONEGAL												
Arnolds Hotel	Dunfanaghy 18 Hole Links, Cloughaneely 9 Hole Park Land.	395				•	•	•	•	•	•	•
Bay View Hotel & Leisure Centre	Narin (Portnoo), Donegal Murvagh	397		•		•	•	•			•	•
Castle Grove Country House Hotel	Portsalon, Letterkenny, Rosapenna, Ballyliffin	397		•			•	•	•		•	•

🏌18 = Full 18 Hole 🏌9 = 9 Hole 🏌3 = Par 3

430

WHERE TO STAY WHEN YOU PLAY!

ACCOMMODATION	COURSES	BE OUR GUEST PAGE NUMBER	GOLF ON SITE	ALL INCLUSIVE PACKAGE	TUITION AVAILABLE	CART AVAILABLE	ARRANGE TEE OFF TIMES	ADVANCE RESERVATIONS	CLUBS FOR HIRE	TRANSPORT	PREFERENTIAL GREEN FEES	CADDY AVAILABLE
DONEGAL Continued												
Fort Royal Hotel	Portsalon, Rosapenna	399	◣₃	•			•	•				
Great Northern Hotel	Donegal, Strandhill, Rosses Point	392	◣₁₈	•	•	•	•	•	•	•	•	•
Highlands Hotel	Nairn, Portnoo	396		•		•	•	•	•	•	•	•
Holyrood Hotel	Bundoran, Murvagh, Strandhill, Rosses Point, Castle Hume, Enniscrone	392		•	•	•	•	•	•	•	•	•
Jackson's Hotel	Ballybofey, Stranorlar	388		•	•	•	•	•				
McGrorys of Culdaff	Ballyliffen Golf Club	392		•	•	•	•	•	•	•	•	•
Ostan Na Rosann	Cruit Island	395		•			•	•	•		•	
Ostan Na Tra (Beach Hotel)	Rosapenna Golf Club, St Patricks, Carrigart	394					•	•				
Rosapenna Hotel	Rosapenna, Portsalon, Dunfanaghy	394	◣₁₈	•	•	•	•	•			•	•
Sand House Hotel	Donegal Murvagh, Bundoran, Rosses Point	399		•	•	•	•	•	•	•	•	•
SLIGO												
Castle Arms Hotel	Enniscrone, Ballina, Strandhill, Rosses Point, Tubbercurry	402		•	•	•	•	•	•	•		•
Innisfree Hotel	Strandhill, Rosses Point	404						•		•		•
Ocean View Hotel	Strandhill, Sligo	406				•			•			•
Sligo Park Hotel & Leisure Centre	Rosses Point Links Course, Strandhill Links Course	405		•			•	•	•	•	•	
Sligo's Southern Hotel & Leisure Centre	Rosses Point, Strandhill, Bundoran, Enniscrone	406		•	•	•	•					•
Tower Hotel	Co.Sligo(Rosses Pt), Strandhill, Enniscrone, Donegal	406		•	•	•	•	•	•			
Yeats Country Hotel and Leisure Club	Co. Sligo, Strandhill, Enniscrone, Bundoran	403		•	•	•	•	•			•	•

 ₁₈ = Full 18 Hole   ◣₉ = 9 Hole   ◣₃ = Par 3

IRELAND FOR

Fishing

HOTELS & GUESTHOUSES

Ireland is accepted as being the outstanding angling holiday resort in Europe. Whether you are a competition angler, a serious specimen hunter, or just fishing while on holiday, you are sure to enjoy yourself here. With over 14,000km of rivers feeding over 4,000 lakes and with no part of Ireland over 112km from sea. Ireland can, in truth, be called an angler's dream.

So come on and get hooked!

ANGLING FOR A PLACE TO STAY!

We invite you to sample the fishing, the countryside and the friendship of the Irish people and then to stay in some of Ireland's most charming accommodation. We have listed a range of hotels and guesthouses which are either situated with or near angling facilities. Your host will assist you in arranging your angling itinerary. A full description of the hotels and guesthouses can be had by looking up the appropriate page number. Premises are listed in alphabetical order in each county.

ACCOMMODATION	TYPES OF FISH	Be Our Guest Page Number	Coarse Fishing	Game Fishing	Sea Fishing	Bait and Tackle	Boats for Hire	Drying Room	Packed Lunches	Gillie	Tackle Room	Freezer	Permits Required
North													
ANTRIM													
Bushmills Inn	Roach, Bream, Haddock, Salmon, Cod, Plaice, Whiting, Sea Trout	31	•	•	•	•	•	•	•	•		•	•
DERRY													
Brown Trout Golf & Country Inn	Salmon, Trout, Pike, Bream	42	•	•			•		•	•		•	•
Walsh's Hotel	Salmon, Pike, Trout, Roach	45	•	•									
DOWN													
Royal Hotel	Cod, Skate, Mackerel, Haddock, Whiting	46			•	•	•		•			•	
FERMANAGH													
Killyhevlin Hotel	Roach, Bream, Pike, Salmon, Trout, Mackerel, Pollock, Ling, Cod	50	•	•	•	•	•	•	•	•			•
Mahons Hotel	Roach, Bream, Pike, Perch, Trout, Salmon, Pollock, Cod, Conger, Mackerel	51	•	•	•	•	•	•	•	•		•	•
East Coast													
DUBLIN													
Bracken Court Hotel	Pike, Perch, Roach, Tench, Bream, Salmon, Brown Trout, Rainbow Trout, Sea Trout, Mackerel	56	•	•	•	•	•		•	•			•
Gresham Royal Marine	Cod, Plaice, Pollock, Ling, Dab	110			•	•	•		•	•			
Stillorgan Park Hotel	Bass, Sea Trout	56		•	•				•	•		•	•

ANGLING FOR A PLACE TO STAY!

ACCOMMODATION	TYPES OF FISH	BE OUR GUEST PAGE NUMBER	COARSE FISHING	GAME FISHING	SEA FISHING	BAIT AND TACKLE	BOATS FOR HIRE	DRYING ROOM	PACKED LUNCHES	GILLIE	TACKLE ROOM	FREEZER	PERMITS REQUIRED
WICKLOW													
Royal Hotel and Leisure Centre	Trout, Salmon, Cod, Plaice, Pollock	132		•	•	•	•					•	•
Valley Hotel and Restaurant	Brown Trout, Pike, Perch, Roach, Rainbow Trout	137		•	•	•						•	• •
Midlands & Lakelands													
CAVAN													
Sharkeys Hotel	Pike, Perch, Bream, Rudd	142	•		•	•	•	•	•		•		
KILDARE													
Hazel Hotel	Pike, Rudd, Roach, Eel, Tench, Perch, Salmon, Trout	146	•	•	•			•			•		• •
K Club	Salmon, Trout, Carp, Tench, Bream, Rudd	148	•	•	•		•	•	•		•	•	•
LONGFORD													
Longford Arms Hotel	Perch, Pike, Eel, Bream, Salmon, Trout	150	•	•		•	•		•		•		
MONAGHAN													
Glencarn Hotel and Leisure Centre	Perch, Bream, Pike, Trout	151	•	•				•			•		
OFFALY													
Brosna Lodge Hotel	Bream, Tench, Rudd, Roach, Perch, Brown Trout, Pike, Salmon	152	•	•		•	•	•	•	•	•	•	
Doolys Hotel	Trout, Salmon	153		•		•			•			•	
WESTMEATH													
Austin Friar Hotel	Pike, Trout	158	•	•		•	•	•			•	•	
Creggan Court Hotel	Bream, Eel, Pike, Salmon, Trout, Tench, Rudd, Roach	156	•	•		•	•	•	•		•		
Greville Arms Hotel	Pike, Trout	158	•	•		•	•			•	•		

ANGLING FOR A PLACE TO STAY!

ACCOMMODATION	TYPES OF FISH	BE OUR GUEST PAGE NUMBER	COARSE FISHING	GAME FISHING	SEA FISHING	BAIT AND TACKLE	BOATS FOR HIRE	DRYING ROOM	PACKED LUNCHES	GILLIE	TACKLE ROOM	FREEZER	PERMITS REQUIRED
WESTMEATH Continued													
Hodson Bay Hotel	Bream, Perch, Pike, Brown Trout	156	•	•		•	•			•	•		•	•
Royal Hoey Hotel	Pike, Bream, Perch, Salmon, Trout, Cod, Mackerel	157	•	•	•	•	•	•	•	•	•	•	•	•

South East

ACCOMMODATION	TYPES OF FISH	BE OUR GUEST PAGE NUMBER	COARSE FISHING	GAME FISHING	SEA FISHING	BAIT AND TACKLE	BOATS FOR HIRE	DRYING ROOM	PACKED LUNCHES	GILLIE	TACKLE ROOM	FREEZER	PERMITS REQUIRED
CARLOW													
Dolmen Hotel and River Court Lodges	Pike, Salmon, Trout	162	•	•		•	•			•	•		•	•
Seven Oaks Hotel	Bream, Perch, Roach, Pike, Eel, Salmon, Trout	162	•	•		•			•	•			•	•
KILKENNY													
Bambricks Troysgate House	Pike, Bream, Tench, Salmon, Brown Trout	164	•	•		•			•	•			•	•
Butler House	Brown Trout, Salmon	165		•		•			•	•			•	•
Kilford Arms	Salmon, Brown Trout, Trout	167		•		•			•	•		•	•	
Kilkenny River Court	Trout, Salmon	168		•		•			•	•			•	
Mount Juliet Estate	Salmon, Trout	171		•		•		•	•	•	•	•		
TIPPERARY SOUTH													
Cashel Palace Hotel	Perch, Salmon, Brown Trout, Grilse	173	•	•		•	•	•	•	•	•	•	•	•
WATERFORD													
Belfry Hotel	Pike, Bream, Perch, Dace, Flounder, Plaice, Sea Bass, Ray	186	•	•	•	•	•	•	•	•	•	•	•	•
Bridge Hotel	Salmon, Trout, Sea Bass, Plaice, Cod	187	•	•	•	•	•	•	•	•	•	•	•	•
Lawlors Hotel	Roach, Dace, Salmon, Trout, Shark, Mackerel, Codling, Plaice, Brill, Bass, Turbot, Ray	182	•	•	•	•	•	•	•	•			•	•

ANGLING FOR A PLACE TO STAY!

ACCOMMODATION	TYPES OF FISH	BE OUR GUEST PAGE NUMBER	COARSE FISHING	GAME FISHING	SEA FISHING	BAIT AND TACKLE	BOATS FOR HIRE	DRYING ROOM	PACKED LUNCHES	GILLIE	TACKLE ROOM	FREEZER	PERMITS REQUIRED
WEXFORD													
Danby Lodge Hotel	Sea Trout, Bass, Cod	199		•		•			•			•	
Quay House	Bass, Pollock, Coalfish, Codling, Tope, Spurdog, Ballan, Wrasse	197			•	•			•		•	•	
Riverside Park Hotel	Salmon, Trout, Pike, Sea Trout, Shark, Cod, Haddock, Plaice, Bass	195	•	•	•	•			•			•	•
Talbot Hotel Conference and Leisure Centre	Salmon, Trout, Roach, Bass, Cod, Pollock, Ling	203	•	•	•	•			•				•
Whites Hotel	Sea Bass, Salmon, Trout, Bream, Roach	204	•	•	•	•			•				
South West													
CORK													
Aherne's Townhouse & Seafood Restaurant	Salmon, Trout, Shark, Cod, Ling, Conger	248		•	•				•	•		•	•
Ashley Hotel	Pike, Perch, Carp, Bream, Salmon, Sea Trout, Rainbow Trout, Cod, Ling, Plaice, Turbot, Pollock	220	•	•	•	•			•		•	•	•
Casey's of Baltimore	Pike, Ling, Cod, Pollock, Mackerel, Turbot, Skate, Shark	208	•		•	•			•			•	•
Castlehyde Hotel	Bream, Eel, Salmon, Brown Trout, Rainbow Trout	234	•	•		•			•	•		•	•
Celtic Ross Hotel Conference & Leisure Centre	Bream, Roach, Tench, Trout, Salmon, Cod, Shark, Wrasse, Flat Fish	245	•	•	•	•	•	•	•	•		•	•
Colla House Hotel	Shark, Conger Eel, Cod, Mackerel, Ling, Flat Fish	245		•					•			•	
Commodore Hotel	Ling, Cod, Pollock, Conger, Blue Shark	217		•	•	•	•	•	•			•	
Coolcower House	Bream, Rudd, Pike, Perch, Trout	241	•	•		•	•	•	•		•	•	•
Creedon's Hotel	Bream, Pike, Perch	235	•					•	•	•			
Dunmore House Hotel	Bass, Cod, Mackerel, Skate, Whiting, Ling	214			•			•	•			•	
Eldon Hotel	Pike, Bream, Tench, Trout, Salmon, Shark, Ray, Mackerel	247	•	•	•	•			•	•		•	•
Fernhill Golf & Country Club	Salmon, Brown Trout	213		•	•				•	•		•	•

ANGLING FOR A PLACE TO STAY!

ACCOMMODATION	TYPES OF FISH	BE OUR GUEST PAGE NUMBER	COARSE FISHING	GAME FISHING	SEA FISHING	BAIT AND TACKLE	BOATS FOR HIRE	DRYING ROOM	PACKED LUNCHES	GILLIE	TACKLE ROOM	FREEZER	PERMITS REQUIRED
CORK Continued													
Hibernian Hotel And Leisure Centre	Bream, Pike, Perch, Tench, Trout, Salmon	242	•						•	•		•	•
Innishannon House Hotel	Salmon, Sea Trout, Brown Trout, Shark, Cod, Ling, Skate, etc.	236		•	•	•	•	•	•	•		•	•
Kierans Folkhouse Inn	Ling, Cod, Conger, Blue Shark, Sea Bass, Pollock	238			•	•	•		•				•
Longueville House & Presidents' Restaurant	Brown Trout, Salmon	243		•						•		•	•
Maryborough House Hotel	Bream, Perch, Pike, Trout, Rudd, Eel, Salmon, Shark, Ling, Conger, Pollock, Cod, Ray, Wrasse	229	•	•	•	•	•		•	•			•
Midleton Park Hotel	Rainbow Trout, Brown Trout, Salmon, Roach, Shark, Cod	244		•	•	•	•		•			•	
Trident Hotel	Ling, Cod, Conger, Wrasse, Pollock, Mackerel, Blue Shark	240			•	•	•		•	•	•	•	•
Victoria Hotel	Bream, Pike, Perch	242	•		•			•	•		•	•	•
Walter Raleigh Hotel	Shark, Dogfish, Conger Eel, Salmon	249			•	•	•		•	•		•	•
Whispering Pines Hotel	Blue Shark, Conger, Ling, Pollock	233			•	•	•	•	•			•	
White Lady Hotel	Shark fishing our speciality, Cod, Pollock, etc.	241			•	•	•		•				
KERRY													
Abbey Gate Hotel	Salmon, Sea Trout, Brown Trout, Mackerel, Pollock, Dog Fish, etc.	291	•	•	•	•	•	•	•	•		•	•
Aghadoe Heights Hotel	Salmon, Sea Trout, Brown Trout, Mackerel, Pollock, Cod	268		•	•	•			•			•	•
Benners Hotel	Pollock, Mackerel, Cod, Sea Trout, Salmon, Ray, Shark	255			•	•	•			•			•
Brandon Hotel	Cod, Sea Trout	293			•				•				•
Brookhaven Country House	Bream, Pike, Chub, Rudd, Roach, Tench, Salmon, Trout, Pollock, Mackerel, Whiting, Plaice, Ling	295	•	•	•	•	•	•	•	•	•	•	•
Butler Arms Hotel	Salmon, Trout, Bass, Pollock, Cod, Shark, Mackerel, Whiting	296		•	•	•	•		•	•		•	•
Caragh Lodge	Brown Trout, Salmon	253		•					•			•	•

ANGLING FOR A PLACE TO STAY!

ACCOMMODATION	TYPES OF FISH	BE OUR GUEST PAGE NUMBER	COARSE FISHING	GAME FISHING	SEA FISHING	BAIT AND TACKLE	BOATS FOR HIRE	DRYING ROOM	PACKED LUNCHES	GILLIE	TACKLE ROOM	FREEZER	PERMITS REQUIRED
KERRY Continued													
Castlelodge Guesthouse	Trout, Salmon	270		•		•	•						•
Castlerosse Hotel & Leisure Centre	Trout, Salmon	271		•		•	•			•	•	•	•
Derrynane Hotel	Mackerel, Pollock, Shark	251			•	•	•	•	•	•		•	
Dingle Skellig Hotel	Pollock, Garfish, Blue Shark, Tope, Dogfish, Ling, Whiting, Ray	258			•	•	•	•	•		•	•	
Earls Court House	Salmon, Trout	272		•		•	•	•	•	•	•	•	•
Glencar House Hotel	Salmon, Trout, Sea Trout, Tope, Pollock, Cod, Mackerel, Ray, Shark	262		•	•	•	•	•	•	•	•	•	•
Grand Hotel	Perch, Trout, Pike, Salmon, Dog Fish, Pollock, Ray, Monkfish	294	•	•	•	•	•	•	•	•		•	
Inveraray Farm Guesthouse	Salmon, Brown Trout, Perch, Peel	277		•		•	•		•			•	•
Killarney Heights Hotel	Pike, Eel, Trout, Salmon	279	•	•		•			•	•		•	•
Killarney Park Hotel	Brown Trout, Salmon, Sea Trout	280		•		•	•	•	•	•	•	•	
Killarney Royal	Brown Trout, Salmon	280		•		•	•	•	•	•	•	•	
Kingfisher Lodge Guesthouse	Salmon, Trout, Sea Trout, Pollock, Ling, Coalfish, Mackerel, Wrasse, Shark	281		•	•	•	•	•	•	•	•	•	•
Lake Hotel	Salmon, Trout	282		•		•	•		•	•		•	•
Lakelands Farm Guesthouse	Salmon, Sea Trout, Pollock, Bass, Shark, Ling, Mackerel	296		•	•	•	•	•	•	•	•	•	•
Listowel Arms Hotel	Pike, Perch, Eel, Salmon, Trout, Ling, Ray, Bass, Pollock, Cod, Monkfish, Tope	289	•	•	•	•	•		•	•		•	•
Moorings	Salmon, Trout, Cod, Pollock, Mackerel, Shark, Turbot, Sea Trout, Salmon, Plaice	289		•	•	•	•	•	•	•	•	•	•
Muckross Park Hotel	Salmon, Brown Trout, Tench, Rainbow Trout	283	•	•		•	•		•	•		•	
O'Connor's Guesthouse	Salmon, Trout, Bass, Ray, Plaice, Cod, Mackerel	254		•	•	•	•			•		•	
Riversdale House Hotel	Bream, Chub, Dab, Eel, Roach, Rudd, Tench, Brown Trout, Rainbow Trout, Salmon, Bass, Cod	266	•	•		•	•		•	•		•	•

ANGLING FOR A PLACE TO STAY!

ACCOMMODATION	TYPES OF FISH	BE OUR GUEST PAGE NUMBER	COARSE FISHING	GAME FISHING	SEA FISHING	BAIT AND TACKLE	BOATS FOR HIRE	DRYING ROOM	PACKED LUNCHES	GILLIE	TACKLE ROOM	FREEZER	PERMITS REQUIRED
KERRY Continued													
Scarriff Inn	Mackerel, Pollock, Salmon, Pike, Bass	252	•	•	•		•		•	•	•		•
Sheen Falls Lodge	Salmon, Trout, Shark, Mackerel, Pollock, Skate, Conger Eel, Dogfish	267		•	•	•	•	•	•	•	•	•	•
Smerwick Harbour Hotel	Plaice, Turbot, Sole, Mackerel, Cod, Pollock, Conger, Shark	261		•	•	•	•	•	•	•	•	•	
Tuscar Lodge	Salmon, Trout, Pike, Perch, Tench, etc.	287	•	•	•	•		•	•	•	•		•
Shannon													
CLARE													
Atlantic Hotel	Bream, Perch, Pike, Tench, Bass, Blue Shark, Conger Eel, Ling, Salmon, Trout	313	•	•	•	•	•	•	•	•	•	•	•
Bunratty Castle Hotel and Conference Centre	Salmon, Trout, Cod, Mackerel, Bass, Pike, Bream	300	•	•	•				•				
Grovemount House	Roach, Trout	309	•	•			•	•					
Kincora Hall Hotel	Tench, Bream, Roach, Perch, Pike, Wild Brown Trout	310	•	•	•	•	•	•	•	•	•	•	
Woodstock Hotel	Pike, Bream, Tench, Perch, Rudd, Salmon, Rainbow Trout, Brown Trout, Sea Trout, Cod	308	•	•	•	•	•	•	•	•	•		•
LIMERICK													
Adare Manor Hotel & Golf Resort	Salmon, Trout	321		•		•			•	•		•	
Castle Oaks House Hotel & Country Club	Pike, Bream, Tench, Eel, Trout, Salmon	322	•	•	•	•	•	•	•	•	•	•	•
Fitzgeralds Woodlands House Hotel and Leisure Club	Pike, Trout, Salmon	322	•	•		•	•		•			•	•
Gresham Ardhu	Pike, Perch, Roach, Trout, Salmon	326	•	•		•	•		•	•	•	•	•
Leens Hotel	Salmon, Trout, Ray, Bass, Pollock, Cod, Monkfish	321	•	•	•	•		•	•	•	•	•	•
Rathkeale House Hotel	Pike, Perch, Roach, Trout, Salmon	329	•	•		•	•	•	•			•	•

ANGLING FOR A PLACE TO STAY!

ACCOMMODATION	TYPES OF FISH	BE OUR GUEST PAGE NUMBER	COARSE FISHING	GAME FISHING	SEA FISHING	BAIT AND TACKLE	BOATS FOR HIRE	DRYING ROOM	PACKED LUNCHES	GILLIE	TACKLE ROOM	FREEZER	PERMITS REQUIRED
TIPPERARY NORTH													
Abbey Court Hotel and Trinity Leisure Club	Pike, Perch, Bream, Roach, Brown Trout, Salmon	329	•	•		•		•		•			

West

ACCOMMODATION	TYPES OF FISH	BE OUR GUEST PAGE NUMBER	COARSE FISHING	GAME FISHING	SEA FISHING	BAIT AND TACKLE	BOATS FOR HIRE	DRYING ROOM	PACKED LUNCHES	GILLIE	TACKLE ROOM	FREEZER	PERMITS REQUIRED
GALWAY													
Ardilaun House Hotel, Conference Centre & Leisure Club	Salmon, Brown Trout, Sea Trout, Rainbow Trout	349		•	•		•		•			•	•
Ballynahinch Castle Hotel	Salmon, Sea Trout, Brown Trout	337		•			•	•	•	•	•	•	•
Ben View House	Salmon, Trout, Cod, Herring, Whiting, Pollock, Plaice	342		•	•		•		•			•	•
Connemara Gateway Hotel	Brown Trout, Salmon	366		•		•	•	•	•	•			•
Corrib House Hotel	Salmon, Trout, Perch, Pike, Shark, Cod	366	•	•	•		•		•	•		•	•
Corrib Wave Guest House	Pike, Perch, Brown Trout, Salmon	367	•	•	•	•	•	•	•	•	•	•	•
Eldons Hotel	Shark, Pollock, Cod, Mackerel	370			•							•	
Galway Bay Hotel, Conference & Leisure Centre	Bream, Roach, Perch, Rudd, Salmon, Brown Trout, Blue Shark, Cod, Ling, Pollock, Ray	352	•	•	•			•	•			•	
Galway Ryan Hotel & Leisure Centre	Pike, Perch, Bream, Roach, Salmon, Brown Trout	352	•	•		•	•		•	•			•
Glenlo Abbey Hotel	Pike, Bream, Roach, Trout, Salmon, Shark, Cod, Mackerel	353	•	•	•	•	•		•	•		•	•
Lake Hotel	Pike, Perch, Trout, Salmon, All species	367	•	•	•		•	•	•	•	•	•	•
Lough Inagh Lodge	Salmon, Sea Trout, Brown Trout	369		•	•	•	•	•	•	•	•	•	•
Menlo Park Hotel and Conference Centre	Perch, Pike, Trout, Salmon, Mackerel, Pollock, Ray, Tope, Bullhuss, Wrasse	357	•	•	•	•	•	•	•	•	•	•	•
Moran's Cloonabinna House Hotel	Bream, Roach, Rudd, Pike, Wild Brown Trout, Salmon, Sea Trout, Shark, Bass, Pollock, Cod	365	•	•	•	•	•	•	•	•	•	•	•
Mountain View Guest House	Salmon, Trout, Pike, Perch, Bream	368	•	•			•		•	•			•
O'Deas Hotel	Trout, Pike, Perch	364	•	•			•	•	•	•			•

ANGLING FOR A PLACE TO STAY!

ACCOMMODATION	TYPES OF FISH	BE OUR GUEST PAGE NUMBER	COARSE FISHING	GAME FISHING	SEA FISHING	BAIT AND TACKLE	BOATS FOR HIRE	DRYING ROOM	PACKED LUNCHES	GILLIE	TACKLE ROOM	FREEZER	PERMITS REQUIRED
GALWAY Continued													
Peacockes Hotel & Complex	Salmon, Sea Trout, Shark, Cod, Pollock, Mackerel, Ray	364		•	•	•	•	•	•	•	•	•	•
Renvyle House Hotel	Brown Trout, Salmon, Sea Trout, Cod, Shark, Eel, Mackerel, Pollock	369		•	•	•	•	•	•	•			•
River Run Lodge	Pike, Perch, Roach, Salmon, Trout	368	•	•		•	•	•	•	•	•		•
Westwood House Hotel	Pike, Perch, Salmon, Brown Trout, Cod	361	•	•	•	•	•	•	•	•			•
MAYO													
Ardmore Country House Hotel and Restaurant	Brown Trout, Salmon, Sea Trout	379		•		•	•	•	•	•		•	•
Atlantic Coast Hotel	Eel, Pike, Perch, Salmon, Trout, Sea Trout, Brill, Mackerel, Ling, Pollock, Ray, Shark, Herring	380	•	•	•	•	•	•	•	•		•	•
Downhill House Hotel	Pike, Salmon, Trout, Sea Trout, Sole, Bream, Brill, Mackerel, Ling, Cod, Monkfish	373	•	•	•	•	•	•	•	•	•	•	•
Healy's Restaurant and Hotel	Pike, Perch, Salmon, Brown Trout, Sea Trout, Rainbow Trout	379	•	•	•	•	•	•	•	•	•	•	•
Hotel Westport, Conference & Leisure Centre	Pike, Perch, Bream, Salmon, Trout, Pollock, Dog Fish, Cod, Whiting, Blue Shark, Ling, Tope, Skate	381	•	•	•	•	•	•	•	•	•	•	•
Knockranny House Hotel	Pike, Salmon, Trout, Sea Trout	382	•	•	•	•	•	•	•	•		•	•
Ostan Oilean Acla	Cod, Ling, Conger, Shark, Mackerel, Trout, Brill, Whiting, Ray	372		•	•	•	•		•		•		•
Regans Bartra House Hotel	Perch, Pike, Eel, Bream, Salmon, Trout, Wrasse, Cod, Mackerel, Conger, Eel	374	•	•	•	•	•	•	•	•		•	•
Ryan's Hotel	Brown Trout, Salmon - also Pike, Perch and Roach, Hake, Mackerel, Plaice, Pollock, Ray	377	•	•	•	•	•	•	•	•	•	•	•
Teach Iorrais	Salmon, Trout, Cod, Mackerel	377		•	•	•	•	•	•		•		•
ROSCOMMON													
Gleesons Townhouse & Restaurant	Pike, Perch, Roach, Tench, Hybrids	385	•			•	•	•	•	•	•	•	•
Royal Hotel	Salmon, Trout, Pike, Perch	384	•	•		•	•	•			•	•	
Whitehouse Hotel	Pike, Perch, Rudd, Bream, Tench, Brown Trout	384	•	•			•	•		•	•		•

441

ANGLING FOR A PLACE TO STAY!

ACCOMMODATION	TYPES OF FISH	BE OUR GUEST PAGE NUMBER	COARSE FISHING	GAME FISHING	SEA FISHING	BAIT AND TACKLE	BOATS FOR HIRE	DRYING ROOM	PACKED LUNCHES	GILLIE	TACKLE ROOM	FREEZER	PERMITS REQUIRED
North West													
DONEGAL													
Arnolds Hotel	Brown Trout, Salmon, Sea Trout	395		•	•		•	•	•	•		•	•
Bay View Hotel & Leisure Centre	Pike, Perch, Eel, Shark, Pollock, Cod, Ling, Conger, Marlin, Salmon, Trout	397	•	•	•	•	•	•	•	•			•	
Great Northern Hotel	Pike, Perch, Salmon, Trout, Pollock, Cod, Ling, Plaice, Shark, Sole	392	•	•	•	•	•	•	•	•	•	•	•	
Ostan Na Rosann	Brown Trout, Sea Trout, Salmon, Cod, Mackerel, Shark, Turbot	395		•	•	•	•	•	•	•		•	•	
Ostan Na Tra (Beach Hotel)	Shark, Cod, Haddock, Ling, Conger, Gurnard, Pollock	394			•	•	•	•	•	•			•	

IRELAND FOR
Conferences
HOTELS & GUESTHOUSES

Small meetings or large conferences are part
and parcel of life in Irish hotels and guesthouses.

What makes Ireland special as a venue
is the warmth of the welcome you will receive,
coupled with excellent facilities
which can be tailored to your needs.

If you have an agenda, we can supply
the venue.

SELECT A VENUE FOR YOUR AGENDA

We will be glad to see you and work with you to make your meeting or conference a successful one. Choose from the wide selection of special facilities throughout the country as shown here. A full description of the hotels and guesthouses can be had by looking up the appropriate page number. Premises are listed in alphabetical order in each county.

Accommodation	Contact Person	Be Our Guest Page Number	*500+	*400+	*300+	*200+	*100+	*50+	*3-	Black Out Facilities	Air Conditioning	Interpreting Equipment	Audio Visual Equipment
North													
ANTRIM													
Ballymac	Cathy Muldoon	36						1	1		•		O
Bayview Hotel	Mary O'Neill	30						1	1	•	•	H	H
Bushmills Inn	Stella Minogue	31						1	2	•	•	H	O
Causeway Coast Hotel & Conference Centre	Mary O'Neill	33			1	1	2	2	2	•	•	H	H
Comfort Hotel Portrush	Mary O'Neill	34						1	1	•	•	H	H
Hilton Templepatrick	Wilma Lindsay	36	1			2	5	7	3	•	•	H	O
Magherabuoy House Hotel	Anna Conn	34			1	1	2	2	3		•	H	O
BELFAST													
Dukes Hotel	Yvonne McNally	38					1	2	3	•	•	H	H
Dunadry Hotel and Country Club	Sheree Davis	39			1	1	2	4	5	•	•		O
Fitzwilliam International Hotel	Kellie Service	39				1	2	3	7	•	•	H	O
Lansdowne Hotel	Michael Cafolla	41					1	1	2	•	•	H	O
McCausland Hotel	Adrianne Carr	41						1	2	•	•	H	O
Park Avenue Hotel	Angela Reid	42		1	1	2	3	6	7	•	•	H	O
Wellington Park Hotel	Malachy Toner	42		1	1	2	3	4	9	•	•	H	O
DERRY													
Brown Trout Golf & Country Inn	Bill O'Hara	42							2	•	•		

NUMBER OF ROOMS OF VARIOUS SEATING CAPACITIES

H = Can Arrange Hire   O = Available On Premises

SELECT A VENUE FOR YOUR AGENDA

ACCOMMODATION	CONTACT PERSON	Be Our Guest Page Number	Number of Rooms of Various Seating Capacities							Black Out Facilities	Air Conditioning	Interpreting Equipment	Audio Visual Equipment
			500+	400+	300+	200+	100+	50+	50-				
DERRY Continued													
City Hotel	Averil Clarke	44		1	1	1					•	H	H
Tower Hotel Derry	Ian Hyland	45				1			3	•	•	H	H
Walsh's Hotel	Briege Scullion	45						1			•		O
DOWN													
Burrendale Hotel and Country Club	Fiona O'Hare	48					1	1	6	•	•	H	O
Royal Hotel	Martin Newell	46							1	•			O
FERMANAGH													
Killyhevlin Hotel	David Morrison	50	1			2		2	3	•	•	H	H
East Coast													
DUBLIN													
Aberdeen Lodge	Pat Halpin	60							2	•	•	H	H
Academy Hotel	John Coonan	61							5	•	•	H	O
Airport View	Anne Marie Beggs	57							1	•			H
Alexander Hotel	Siobhan O'Hare	62		1	1	2	4	5	1	•	•	H	O
Arlington Hotel	Michelle Kelly	63							2	•	•	H	O
Ashling Hotel	John Gannon	64				1	1	1	5	•	•	H	H
Becketts Country House Hotel	Emma Mandler	112							1		•	H	O
Belvedere Hotel	Marion Heneghan	66				1					•		
Berkeley Court	Michelle McDermot	66	1			2	1		3	•	•	H	H

H = Can Arrange Hire   O = Available On Premises

SELECT A VENUE FOR YOUR AGENDA

DUBLIN Continued

Columns under "Number of Rooms of Various Seating Capacities": 500+, 400+, 300+, 200+, 100+, 50+, 3-

Accommodation	Contact Person	Be Our Guest Page Number	500+	400+	300+	200+	100+	50+	3-	Black Out Facilities	Air Conditioning	Interpreting Equipment	Audio Visual Equipment
Bracken Court Hotel	Stephen O'Donoghue	56				1		1	2	•		H	O
Brooks Hotel	Anne McKiernan / Tom Reilly	68						1	3	•		H	O
Burlington	John Conmee	68	1	3			3	2	14	•	•	H	H
Buswells Hotel	Aileen Mangan	69						1	3	•		H	O
Camden Court Hotel	Georgia Blake	69							4	•		H	H
Carnegie Court Hotel	Sharon Caffrey	116				1		1	2	•	•	H	O
Cassidys Hotel	Carol/Karen	70						1	3	•	•		H
Clarence Hotel	Patsy Mooney	73							2	•	•	H	O
Clarion Hotel Dublin IFSC	Jane Hurley	73					2	2	7	•	•		O
Clontarf Castle Hotel	Deirdre Kavanagh	74		1			3	2	1	•	•	H	H
Court Hotel	Joe Conlon/Michael Collins	111				1	2	2	5	•	•	O	O
Davenport Hotel	Siobhan O'Hare	75			1	2	2	2	4	•	•	H	O
Eglinton Manor	Rosaleen Cahill O'Brien	77							1	•			
Finnstown Country House Hotel	Jenny Holmes	112				1	1	2	4	•		H	O
Fitzwilliam Hotel	Alice Wildgust	79						2	1	•	•	H	H
Georgian Hotel	Lorraine Loughnane	80							3			H	H
Great Southern Hotel Dublin Airport	Louise Maguire	58			1	1	3	8		•		H	H
Gresham Hotel	Ian Craig	82			1	2	3	8	22	•	•	H	H
Gresham Royal Marine	Banqueting Manager	110		1		1	1	2	4	•		H	H

H = Can Arrange Hire   O = Available On Premises

SELECT A VENUE FOR YOUR AGENDA

DUBLIN Continued

Accommodation	Contact Person	Be Our Guest Page Number	500+	400+	300+	200+	100+	50+	30+	Air Conditioning	Black Out Facilities	Interpreting Equipment	Audio Visual Equipment
Herbert Park Hotel	Siona Arnold	84					2	1	2	•	•	H	H
Hilton Dublin	Karen O'Sullivan	85			1			4	7	•		H	O
Holiday Inn Dublin Airport	Valerie Markey	58						1	6	•	•	H	H
Holiday Inn Dublin City Centre	Sabrina Guida	85				1	2	5	5	•	•	H	O
Jurys Ballsbridge Hotel	Lorraine Morgan	87	1				2	2	8	•	•	H	H
Jurys Inn Custom House	Emily Murray	88					1		3	•	•	H	H
Jurys Montrose Hotel	Nicky Warren	88						2	2	•			
Kingston Hotel	Marge Daly	110					1		1	•	•		H
Lansdowne Hotel	Margaret English	90					1	1	1	•	•	H	O
Le Meridien Shelbourne	Richard Margo	91		1			2	2	6	•		H	H
Mercer Hotel	Caroline Fahy	93					1	1	3	•	•	H	O
Merrion Hall	Pat Halpin	93							2	•	•	H	H
Merrion Hotel	Orla Duff	93							2	•	•	H	O
Mont Clare Hotel	Siobhan O'Hare	94					1	3	6	•	•	H	O
North Star Hotel	David Kiely	96					1	1	1	•	•	H	H
Ormond Quay Hotel	Conor Byrne	97					1		3	•		H	H
Orwell Lodge Hotel	Reception	97						1	2				
Paramount Hotel	Angela Henry	99							1	•	•	H	O
Parliament Hotel	David Kiely	99							1	•	•	H	O

H = Can Arrange Hire   O = Available On Premises

SELECT A VENUE FOR YOUR AGENDA

ACCOMMODATION	CONTACT PERSON	BE OUR GUEST PAGE NUMBER	500+	400+	300+	200+	100+	50+	50-	BLACK OUT FACILITIES	AIR CONDITIONING	INTERPRETING EQUIPMENT	AUDIO VISUAL EQUIPMENT
DUBLIN Continued													
Plaza Hotel	Aine McGuinness	100			1		2	2	8	•	•	H	H
Portmarnock Hotel & Golf Links	Caitriona Loughrey	114				1	2	2	2	•	•	H	H
Radisson SAS St Helen's Hotel	John Coleman	56			1	1	3	6	5	•	•	H	O
Red Cow Moran Hotel	Karen Moran	102	1	1	1	2	5	10	16	•	•	H	O
Regency Airport Hotel	Catherine McGettigan	103		2				1	3	•	•	H	O
Sheldon Park Hotel & Leisure Centre	Aine Gaynor	104	1	1	1	2	3	2	9	•	•	H	O
Spa Hotel	Betty Dolan	113	1	1	1	1	1	1	1	•	•		H
Stephen's Green Hotel	Tina Ward	105							6	•	•	H	O
Stillorgan Park Hotel	Sharon Power	56	1	1	1	2	5	6	10	•	•	H	H
Temple Bar Hotel	Danny Harrington	106						1	4	•		H	H
West County Hotel	Eamon Fennelly	108					1	1	2	•	•		H
Westbury	Gillian Murphy	108				1	2	1	1	•	•	H	H
Westin Dublin	Fiona Burns	109				1	2	2	8	•			H O
LOUTH													
Boyne Valley Hotel & Country Club	Noel Comer	118	1	2	1	2	1	2	3	•		H	O
Carrickdale Hotel & Leisure Complex	Breige Savage/Declan O'Neill/Fiona Clerkin	119	1			1	1	1	4	•	•	H	O
Derryhale Hotel	Liam Sexton	120				1			2	•		H	H
Fairways Hotel	Killian O'Grady/Dara McCarthy	120	1	1	2	2	2	5	10	•	•	H	O
Hotel Imperial	Peter Quinn	121					1	2	2	•			O

H = Can Arrange Hire   O = Available On Premises

SELECT A VENUE FOR YOUR AGENDA

ACCOMMODATION	CONTACT PERSON	BE OUR GUEST PAGE NUMBER	NUMBER OF ROOMS OF VARIOUS SEATING CAPACITIES							BLACK OUT FACILITIES	AIR CONDITIONING	INTERPRETING EQUIPMENT	AUDIO VISUAL EQUIPMENT
			500+	400+	300+	200+	100+	50+	8+				
LOUTH Continued													
McKevitt's Village Hotel	Terry and Kay McKevitt	118					1		1		•		H
Westcourt Hotel	Valerie Sherlock	119			1	1	2	3	5	•	•		O
MEATH													
Ardboyne Hotel	Sharon Crowe	124			1		2	3	4	•	•	H	O
Broadmeadow Country House & Equestrian Centre	Sandra Duff	122							2			H	H
Neptune Beach Hotel & Leisure Club	Martina O'Dwyer	122				1			2	•		H	O
Newgrange Hotel	Lorraine Cunningham	125	1			1	1	1	1	•	•	H	O
Old Darnley Lodge Hotel	Mary Murphy	122				1			1	•	•		O
Station House Hotel	Chris Slattery	124				1				•	•	H	O
WICKLOW													
Arklow Bay Hotel	Monique Freeman	126	1	1	1	1	1	2	2	•	•	H	O
Brooklodge	Suzanne Tallon	129			1		1		2	•	•	H	O
Cullenmore Hotel	Dirk Van der Flier	129						1	2		•		H
Esplanade Hotel	Annie Friel	131					1	1	2	•		H	H
Glendalough Hotel	Patrick Casey	134				1			2	•	•	H	O
Glenview Hotel	Marie O'Halloran	134				1	1	2	2	•	•	H	O
Hunter's Hotel	Nicola Coffey	136							3	•			
La Touche Hotel	Lisa Bradshaw	135	1	1	1	1	1	3	3				H
Lawless's Hotel	Seoirse or Maeve O'Toole	129				1			1	•		H	O

H = Can Arrange Hire O = Available On Premises

SELECT A VENUE FOR YOUR AGENDA

ACCOMMODATION	CONTACT PERSON	Be Our Guest Page Number	500+	400+	300+	200+	100+	50+	5-	Black Out Facilities	Air Conditioning	Interpreting Equipment	Audio Visual Equipment
WICKLOW Continued													
Rathsallagh House, Golf and Country Club	Catherine Lawlor	133					1	4			•	H	O
Royal Hotel and Leisure Centre	Siobhan Ashall	132		1				1		•	•	H	O
Summerhill House Hotel	Fregus O'Grady	133			1		1	5			•	H	H
Tinakilly Country House and Restaurant	Brenda Gilmore	136					1	3		•	•	H	O
Woodenbridge Hotel	Esther and Bill O'Brien	138			1			1		•	•		O
Woodland Court Hotel	Eileen Murphy	132					1	4		•	•	H	O

Midlands & Lakelands

ACCOMMODATION	CONTACT PERSON	Be Our Guest Page Number	500+	400+	300+	200+	100+	50+	5-	Black Out Facilities	Air Conditioning	Interpreting Equipment	Audio Visual Equipment
CAVAN													
Cabra Castle Hotel	Karen Owens	142	1				1	1	2	•	•	H	O
Hotel Kilmore	Sharon Crowe	141	1			2	3	3	4	•	•	H	O
Park Hotel	Mary McMillan	142						2	2	•	•	H	O
Sharkeys Hotel	Goretti Sharkey	142	1					1	1	•	•		O
Slieve Russell Hotel, Golf & Country Club	Bridie Gallagher	141	1	1	3	3	3	4	7	•	•	H	O
KILDARE													
Ambassador Hotel	Sarah McCreesh	144				1	2	2	3	•	•	H	O
Glenroyal Hotel, Leisure Club & Conference Centre	Clare Lyons	145		1	2	2	2	4	7	•	•	H	O
Hazel Hotel	John Kelly	146			1	1	1	1	1	•	•		O
K Club	Kerri Wells	148					1	1	3	•	•	H	O
Keadeen Hotel	Pauline Barry	148	1	1	1	1	3	4	7	•	•	H	O

H = Can Arrange Hire   O = Available On Premises

SELECT A VENUE FOR YOUR AGENDA

Accommodation	Contact Person	Be Our Guest Page Number	500+	400+	300+	200+	100+	50+	30	Black Out Facilities	Air Conditioning	Interpreting Equipment	Audio Visual Equipment
KILDARE Continued													
Standhouse Hotel Leisure & Conference Centre	Shane D'Arcy	144	1	1	2	3	4	4	7	•	•	H	O
Straffan Court Hotel	Emma Gallagher	146					1	1		•			
LONGFORD													
Longford Arms Hotel	Denise Batt	150	1				2	3		•	•	H	H
MONAGHAN													
Four Seasons Hotel & Leisure Club	Orla McKenna	151	1	1	2	2	4	4	5	•	•	H	O
Glencarn Hotel and Leisure Centre	Patrick McFadden/Fiona Dooley/Kathleen Lavelle	151	1	1	1	3	3	3	5	•	•	H	O
Nuremore Hotel & Country Club	Helen Woods	151	1				2	3	4	•	•	H	O
OFFALY													
Bridge House Hotel & Leisure Club	Colm McCabe	154	1	1	2	2	3	4	9	•	•	H	O
Doolys Hotel	Jo Duignan	153				1		1			•		O
Kinnitty Castle Demesne	Enda McDonagh	153					1	1	2	2	•	H	H
Moorhill House Hotel	David or Alan Duffy	155						1	3	•		H	H
Tullamore Court Hotel	Ann Lynch	156	1	1	2	2	3	4	8	•	•	H	O
WESTMEATH													
Austin Friar Hotel	Patrina Mullen	158							1	•	•	H	O
Bloomfield House Hotel & Leisure Club	Ita Kerrigan	158			1	2	4	5	8	•	•	H	O
Creggan Court Hotel	Patricia Flynn	156							1	•	•	H	O
Greville Arms Hotel	John Cochrane	158				1	2	1	2	•		H	H

H = Can Arrange Hire   O = Available On Premises

SELECT A VENUE FOR YOUR AGENDA

Accommodation	Contact Person	Be Our Guest Page Number	\>500+	400+	300+	200+	100+	50+	50-	Black Out Facilities	Air Conditioning	Interpreting Equipment	Audio Visual Equipment
WESTMEATH Continued													
Hodson Bay Hotel	Christina Melican	156	1	1	1	2	3	4	4	•	•	H	O
Royal Hoey Hotel	M. Hoey	157				1	2	3		•	•		O
Shamrock Lodge Hotel and Conference Centre	Pamela Wilson/Karen Smyth	157			1		1		2		•		H	O

South East													
CARLOW													
Dolmen Hotel and River Court Lodges	Nora Duggan	162	1	2	2	2	2	3	8	•	•	H	O
Mount Wolseley Hotel, Golf and Country Club	Kathy Walsh	163					1		3	•	•	H	H
Seven Oaks Hotel	Kathleen Dooley	162	1		1		1	2		•	•		H
KILKENNY													
Butler House	Gabrielle Hickey	165					1	2	2			H	O
Hibernian Hotel	Trish Murphy	166					1	2	2	•	•	H	O
Hotel Kilkenny	Fiona Fields	166		1	1	2	3	4	7	•	•	H	H
Kilford Arms	Pius Phelan	167			1	1	2	3	5			H	H
Kilkenny Ormonde Hotel	Sheena McCanny	167	1		1			2	6	•	•	H	O
Kilkenny River Court	Breda Kehoe	168				1			4	•	•	H	H
Lacken House	Jackie Kennedy	168							1				H
Mount Juliet Estate	Aine O'Hare	171					1	3	2	•	•	H	O
Newpark Hotel	Orla Gray	169		1	1	1	2	2	7	•	•	H	O
Springhill Court Hotel	Suzanne Palmer	170	1	1	1	1	2	2	3	•	•	H	O

H = Can Arrange Hire   O = Available On Premises

SELECT A VENUE FOR YOUR AGENDA

ACCOMMODATION	CONTACT PERSON	BE OUR GUEST PAGE NUMBER	NUMBER OF ROOMS OF VARIOUS SEATING CAPACITIES							BLACK OUT FACILITIES	AIR CONDITIONING	INTERPRETING EQUIPMENT	AUDIO VISUAL EQUIPMENT
			500+	400+	300+	200+	100+	50+	<				
TIPPERARY SOUTH													
Cahir House Hotel	Liam Duffy	172			1	1	1		3	•	•	H	H
Cashel Palace Hotel	Susan Murphy	173						1			•	H	H
Dundrum House Hotel	Dolores Thornton	173		1						•	•	H	O
Glen Hotel	James Coughlan	177				1	1	1	1	•	•	H	
Hotel Minella & Leisure Centre	Elizabeth Nallen	175	1			2	2	4	5	•	•	H	O
Kilcoran Lodge Hotel	Lisa Lindy	172				1	1	1	1	•	•	H	O
WATERFORD													
Arlington Lodge Country House & Restaurant	Liam Heafey	186							1	•	•	H	O
Belfry Hotel	Mairead Casey	186						1	1	•	•	H	H
Bridge Hotel	Catherina Byrne/Rosemary Ahern	187			1	1	2	3	4	•	•	H	O
Clonea Strand Hotel, Golf & Leisure	Mark Knowles or Ann McGrath	181			2	2	3	4	5	•	•	H	H
Dooley's Hotel	Margaret Darrer	188			1	1	2	1	3	•	•	H	O
Faithlegg House Hotel	Tracy McDaid	184				1		1	3	•	•	H	O
Grand Hotel	Majella Scanlon	185				1				•	•	H	H
Granville Hotel	Richard Hurley	188					1	2	1	•		H	H
Jurys Waterford Hotel	Susie Molloy	189	1				2	2	2	•	•	H	H
Lawlors Hotel	William Buckley & Anne Marie Daffy	182		1		2	3	4	5	•	•	H	O
Rhu Glen Country Club Hotel	Rita Fitzgerald	190			1	1	1	1	1	•	•	H	H
Tower Hotel & Leisure Centre	Alicia Maguire	191	1				3	1	2	•	•		H

H = Can Arrange Hire   O = Available On Premises

SELECT A VENUE FOR YOUR AGENDA

Accommodation	Contact Person	Be Our Guest Page Number	Number of Rooms of Various Seating Capacities							Black Out Facilities	Air Conditioning	Interpreting Equipment	Audio Visual Equipment
			500+	400+	300+	200+	100+	50+	50-				
WATERFORD Continued													
Woodlands Hotel	Marguerite Fitzgerald	192	1			1		1	3	•	•	H	H
WEXFORD													
Ashdown Park Hotel Conference & Leisure Centre	Catherine Byrne	196	1							•	•	H	O
Clarion Brandon House Hotel & Leisure Centre	Mary Keating	197			1				2	•	•	H	O
Danby Lodge Hotel	Margaret Parle	199						1			•	H	H
Ferrycarrig Hotel	Caroline Roche	202	1	1	1	1	1		2	•	•	H	H
Hotel Rosslare	Aileen Boyd	201					1				•	H	H
Marlfield House Hotel	Margaret Bowe	196						1			•	H	O
Riverside Park Hotel	Jim Maher	195	1			2		4	1	•	•	H	O
Rosslare Great Southern Hotel	Roisin Buckley	201			1				1	•	•	H	H
Talbot Hotel Conference and Leisure Centre	Niamh Lambert	203			1	1	2	3	4	•	•	H	O
Whites Hotel	Michael Connolly	204			1	1	2	3	7	•		H	H
South West													
CORK													
Actons Hotel	Angela Hess/Anne Marie Cross	236		1					2	•	•	H	H
Aherne's Townhouse & Seafood Restaurant	John Fitzgibbon	248							2	•	•	H	H
Blarney Park Hotel	Aidan Grimes	211				1	2	2	3	•	•	H	H
Carrigaline Court Hotel	Bernadette C. Kirby	212		1					2	•	•	H	O
Celtic Ross Hotel Conference & Leisure Centre	Kate Howey	245				1		1	1	•	•	H	H

H = Can Arrange Hire   O = Available On Premises

SELECT A VENUE FOR YOUR AGENDA

Accommodation	Contact Person	Be Our Guest Page Number	Number of Rooms of Various Seating Capacities							Black Out Facilities	Air Conditioning	Interpreting Equipment	Audio Visual Equipment
			500+	400+	300+	200+	100+	50+	30-				
CORK Continued													
Commodore Hotel	Robert Fitzpatrick	217			1			1				H	O
Doughcloyne Hotel	David Harney	224					1	1	2		•		O
Glengarriff Eccles Hotel	Geraldine Owens	235			1			1	1		•	H	H
Great Southern Hotel	Pat Cussen	218			1				5	•	•	H	O
Gresham Metropole	Fiona Keohane	225	1	1	1	2	2	6	11	•	•	H	H
Hayfield Manor Hotel	Karen Wycherley	226						1	1	•	•	H	O
Hibernian Hotel And Leisure Centre	Catherine Gyves	242			1			2	4		•		O
Imperial Hotel	Elaine O'Driscoll	226		1			1	1	4	•	•	H	H
Innishannon House Hotel	Peter Curran	236					1	1	2		•	H	O
Jurys Cork Hotel	Ann Shanahan	227	1				1	1	5	•	•	H	H
Longueville House & Presidents' Restaurant	Aisling O'Callaghan	243							2		•	H	H
Maryborough House Hotel	Mary Motherway	229		1	1		2	2	5	•	•	H	O
Midleton Park Hotel	Daphne Spillane	244			1			1	3		•	H	H
Quality Hotel and Leisure Centre	Raymond Kelleher	216				1	3	4	1	•	•	H	H
Quality Hotel Cork	Tracy Hoary	230					1	3	4	•	•	H	H
Rochestown Park Hotel	Liam Lally/Claire Cullinane	230	1	1	2	2	3	5	9	•	•	H	O
Silversprings Moran Hotel	Tracey Moran	232	2		4	4	7	11	6	•	•	H	O
Springfort Hall Hotel	Paul Walsh	243				1	1	2	3		•		O
Trident Hotel	Hal McElroy/Una Wren	240			1				4	•	•	H	O

H = Can Arrange Hire   O = Available On Premises

SELECT A VENUE FOR YOUR AGENDA

Accommodation	Contact Person	Be Our Guest Page Number	500+	400+	300+	200+	100+	50+	5+	Black Out Facilities	Air Conditioning	Interpreting Equipment	Audio Visual Equipment
CORK Continued													
Walter Raleigh Hotel	Therese Kelly	249				1		2	3				H
Westlodge Hotel	Eileen M O'Shea	210				1				•	•	H	H
KERRY													
Abbey Gate Hotel	Patrick Dillon	291		1	1	1	2	3	3	•	•	H	O
Aghadoe Heights Hotel	Emma Phillips	268				1		2		•	•		H
Brandon Hotel	Louise Langan	293	1	1	2	2	3	4	4	•	•	H	O
Castlerosse Hotel & Leisure Centre	Michael O'Sullivan	271				1		1			•	H	H
Dingle Skellig Hotel	Colin Aherne	258				1		2		•	•	H	O
Dromhall Hotel	Denise Moynihan	272			1	1	1	1	1	•	•	H	H
Gleneagle Hotel	Cara Fuller	275	2	2	3	3	4	4	4	•	•	H	O
Grand Hotel	Dick Boyle	294		1				3	6	•	•	O	O
Kenmare Bay Hotel	Terry O'Doherty	264		1			1				•	H	O
Killarney Great Southern Hotel	Michele King	279	1			1		2	2	•	•	H	H
Killarney Heights Hotel	Bernadette Cassells	279			1			2		•	•		H
Killarney Park Hotel	Niamh O'Shea	280					1	1	3	•		H	O
Lake Hotel	Tony Huggard/Marie O'Shea/Majella Steinbeck	282						1	2	•		H	O
Listowel Arms Hotel	Kevin O'Callaghan	289			1	1	1	1	2	•	•	H	H
Muckross Park Hotel	Lisa Cronin	283				1		1	1		•	H	H
Parknasilla Great Southern Hotel	Jim Feeney	290						1	1	•		H	H

H = Can Arrange Hire   O = Available On Premises

SELECT A VENUE FOR YOUR AGENDA

ACCOMMODATION	CONTACT PERSON	BE OUR GUEST PAGE NUMBER	500+	400+	300+	200+	100+	50+	30-	BLACK OUT FACILITIES	AIR CONDITIONING	INTERPRETING EQUIPMENT	AUDIO VISUAL EQUIPMENT
KERRY Continued													
Randles Court Clarion Hotel	Tom Randles	284						1		•	•	H	O
Riversdale House Hotel	Joanne O'Sullivan	266	1					1		•	•	H	H
Sheen Falls Lodge	Carmel Flynn	267					1	1	2	•	•	H	O
Shannon													
CLARE													
Bunratty Castle Hotel and Conference Centre	Kathleen McLoughlin	300					1	1	2	•	•	H	H
Burkes Armada Hotel	John J. Burke	318	1		1	1		1			•	H	H
Falls Hotel	Lourda Roche	308			1			2			•	H	H
Fitzpatrick Bunratty	Maria O'Gorman Skelly	302	1		2	1	6	1		•	•	H	O
Halpin's Townhouse Hotel	Pat Halpin	309						2		•	•	H	H
Kilkee Bay Hotel	Eileen O'Dea	309					1	1		•	•	H	H
Kincora Hall Hotel	Matt Sherlock	310					1				•	H	O
Liscannor Bay Hotel	Brian J O'Higgins	316				1		1		•	•	H	H
Magowna House Hotel	Gay Murphy	306				1		1		•	•	H	O
Oak Wood Arms Hotel	Isobel Browne	320			1			3	3	•	•		O
Old Ground Hotel	Clara Clarke	307			1			1	1	•	•	H	O
Shannon Great Southern Hotel	Clodagh Cussen	320				1			3	•	•	H	O
Temple Gate Hotel	John Madden	307				1	1	2	1	•	•	H	O
Tinarana House Hotel and Health Resort	Mary Fahy Stewart	312						1					H

H = Can Arrange Hire   O = Available On Premises

SELECT A VENUE FOR YOUR AGENDA

Accommodation	Contact Person	Be Our Guest Page Number	500+	400+	300+	200+	100+	50+	3+	Black Out Facilities	Air Conditioning	Interpreting Equipment	Audio Visual Equipment
CLARE Continued													
Woodstock Hotel	Therese O'Connor	308				1		1	2	•	•	H	O
LIMERICK													
Adare Manor Hotel & Golf Resort	Yvette Kennedy	321				1	1	1	1	•		H	O
Castletroy Park Hotel	Ursula Cullen, Sales Manager	323		1	2	2	2	2	9	•	•	H	O
Cruises House	Carole Kelly	324						1			•	H	H
Devon Inn Hotel	William Sheehan	329		1	1	1	1	2	1		•	H	O
Dunraven Arms Hotel	Louis Murphy	322		1	1	1	2	4	5	•	•	H	H
Fitzgeralds Woodlands House Hotel and Leisure Club	David or Karen	322		1	1	1	2	3	3	•	•	H	H
Greenhills Hotel Conference/Leisure	Mark Carroll	325	1	1	1	1	2	3	4	•	•	H	O
Gresham Ardhu	Claire Kennedy	326					1	5	5		•	H	H
Jurys Limerick Hotel	Celia McKeogh	327					1		5	•	•	H	H
Rathkeale House Hotel	Gerry O'Connor	329			1		1		1	•	•	H	O
TIPPERARY NORTH													
Abbey Court Hotel and Trinity Leisure Club	Tom Walsh	329		1	1	1	2	3	6	•	•	H	O
Anner Hotel & Leisure Centre	Joan Brett-Moloney	331		1	1	1	2	3			•	H	O
St. David's Country House	Bernhard Klotz	330						1		•	•	O	O
West													
GALWAY													
Ardilaun House Hotel, Conference Centre & Leisure Club	Thomas MacCarthy O'Hea	349			1	1	1	2	3	•	•	H	H

H = Can Arrange Hire O = Available On Premises

SELECT A VENUE FOR YOUR AGENDA

ACCOMMODATION	CONTACT PERSON	BE OUR GUEST PAGE NUMBER	NUMBER OF ROOMS OF VARIOUS SEATING CAPACITIES							BLACK OUT FACILITIES	AIR CONDITIONING	INTERPRETING EQUIPMENT	AUDIO VISUAL EQUIPMENT
			500+	400+	300+	200+	100+	50+	50-				
WEST Continued													
Connemara Coast Hotel	Paul O'Meara	347		1	1	2	2	5	8	•		H	O
Connemara Gateway Hotel	Geraldine Deely	366					1		1	•		H	H
Corrib Great Southern Hotel	Micheal Cunningham	350	1			2		1	3	•	•	H	O
Corrib House Hotel	Liz O'Malley	366					1						H
Galway Bay Hotel, Conference & Leisure Centre	Virginia Connolly	352	1	2	2	2	2	5	5	•	•	H	O
Galway Great Southern Hotel	Fergal O'Connell	352				1	1		3	•	•	H	O
Galway Ryan Hotel & Leisure Centre	Duty Manager	352							2		•	H	H
Lady Gregory Hotel	Brian Morrissey	361			1				2	•	•	H	O
Meadow Court Hotel	Tom Corbett Jnr	364			1					•	•		H
Menlo Park Hotel and Conference Centre	David Keane	357			1	1	2	3	2	•	•	H	O
Oranmore Lodge Hotel, Conference & Leisure Centre	Mary O'Higgins	365			1		1	1	1	•	•	H	H
Park Lodge Hotel	Jane Marie Foyle	371					1	1	1		•	H	H
Peacockes Hotel & Complex	Eimear Killian	364	1				1	1		•	•	H	H
Quality Hotel and Leisure Centre Galway	Rhona Kearney/Dermot Comerford	365						1	6	•		H	H
Quality Hotel Clarinbridge	Rhona Kearney/Martin Brett	340		1			1	1	1	•	•	H	H
Radisson SAS Hotel	Carmel O'Sullivan	358	1						11	•	•	H	O
Renvyle House Hotel	Mairead McManamon	369					2	1	1	•	•	H	O
Shannon Oaks Hotel & Country Club	Barry Maher	369	1					1	2	•	•	H	O
Westwood House Hotel	David Kelly	361			1	1	1	3	3	•	•	H	O

H = Can Arrange Hire   O = Available On Premises

SELECT A VENUE FOR YOUR AGENDA

ACCOMMODATION	CONTACT PERSON	BE OUR GUEST PAGE NUMBER	NUMBER OF ROOMS OF VARIOUS SEATING CAPACITIES 500+	400+	300+	200+	100+	50+	30+	BLACK OUT FACILITIES	AIR CONDITIONING	INTERPRETING EQUIPMENT	AUDIO VISUAL EQUIPMENT
MAYO													
Atlantic Coast Hotel	Catherine O'Grady-Powers	380					1		3	•	•	H	O
Castlecourt Hotel Conference and Leisure Centre	Cynthia Doyle	380	1	1	1	2	2	3	3	•	•	H	O
Central Hotel	Padraig McCarthy	381		1			2	3		•			O
Downhill House Hotel	Kay Devine & Rachel Moylett	373	1		1	1	1	2	4	•	•	H	O
Hotel Westport, Conference & Leisure Centre	Gerry Walshe & Ruth Farrell & Rhona Chambers	381		1			1	3	1	•	•	H	O
Jennings Hotel & Travellers Friend	David McManus	375	1	1	2	2	3	3	4	•	•	H	O
Knock House Hotel	Brian Crowley	378					1	1	1				O
Knockranny House Hotel	Carol Noonan	382	1	1	1	1	2	3	3	•	•	H	O
Ostan Oilean Acla	Michael McLoughlin	372		1				1	1	•	•	O	O
Teach Iorrais	Carmel Gallagher	377				2				•	•	H	H
Westport Woods Hotel & Leisure Centre	Michael Lennon	383				1	1	1	2	•	•	H	H
ROSCOMMON													
O'Gara's Royal Hotel	Larry O'Gara	386					1	2	1	•	•		O
North West													
DONEGAL													
Bay View Hotel & Leisure Centre	Michael Heffernan/Aidan McHugh	397			1				1	•	•		O
Central Hotel, Conference & Leisure Centre	Michael Naughton	393			1	1	1	1	1	•	•	H	O
Dorrians Imperial Hotel	Mary Dorrian	390				1			1	•	•		H
Great Northern Hotel	Philip McGlynn	392	1	1	1	1	1	1	1	•	•	H	O

H = Can Arrange Hire   O = Available On Premises

SELECT A VENUE FOR YOUR AGENDA

ACCOMMODATION	CONTACT PERSON	BE OUR GUEST PAGE NUMBER	NUMBER OF ROOMS OF VARIOUS SEATING CAPACITIES							BLACK OUT FACILITIES	AIR CONDITIONING	INTERPRETING EQUIPMENT	AUDIO VISUAL EQUIPMENT
			500+	400+	300+	200+	100+	50+	<50				
DONEGAL Continued													
Ostan Na Rosann	Lewis Connon	395			1	1	1	1	1	•		H	H
Sand House Hotel	Paul Diver - Manager	399						1	3	•		H	H
LEITRIM													
Bush Hotel	Joseph Dolan	401	1				2	3	5	•			0
Landmark Hotel	Mary Stillman	401		1	1	2			2	•	•	H	0
SLIGO													
Beach Hotel and Leisure Club	Audri Herron	403				1	2			•		H	H
Sligo Park Hotel & Leisure Centre	Bernadette Coffey	405	1					3		•	•	H	0
Sligo's Southern Hotel & Leisure Centre	Kevin McGlynn/Jackie McLoughlin	406			1	1	1	2	4			H	H
Tower Hotel	Garret Marrinan	406					1	1	2	•		H	H

H = Can Arrange Hire   0 = Available On Premises

Heritage Island

is a group of the most prestigious heritage attractions in all of Ireland...

The centres range from historic houses, castles, monuments, museums, galleries, national parks, interpretative centres, gardens and theme parks.

Visitors can avail of big savings by displaying the *Heritage Island Explorer* coupon at the following attractions, which will entitle them to reduced admission, many two for one's and special offers...

Antrim
- The Ulster Museum
- W5 whowhatwherewhenwhy

Armagh
- Armagh Planetarium
- The Argory

Cavan
- Belturbet Station
- Cavan County Museum

Cavan (cont)
- Cavan Crystal

Clare
- Bunratty Castle and Folk Park
- Clare County Museum
- Craggaunowen
- Glor Irish Music Centre

Cork
- Cork City Gaol
- Mizen Vision
- Old Midleton Distillery
- Skibbereen Heritage Centre

Derry
- Springhill House

Donegal
- Donegal County Museum

Down
- Castle Ward
- Exploris Aquarium
- Mount Stewart House and Gardens

Down (cont)
- Rowallane
- Somme Heritage Centre
- St. Patrick Centre
- Ulster Folk & Transport Museum

Dublin
- Dublinia
- Dublin's City Hall, The Story of the Capital
- GAA Museum
- Guinness Storehouse
- Hugh Lane Gallery
- James Joyce Centre

Dublin (cont)
- Old Jameson Distillery
- St. Patrick's Cathedral
- Trinity College Library and Dublin Experience

Fermanagh
- Belleek Pottery Visitor Centre
- Castle Coole
- Enniskillen Castle
- Florence Court
- Marble Arch Caves

Galway
- Dartfield - Galway's Horse Museum & Park
- Galway Irish Crystal Heritage Centre
- Kylemore Abbey and Gardens

Kerry
- Crag Cave
- Kerry the Kingdom

Kildare
- Irish National Stud, Japanese Gardens & St. Fiachra's Garden

Kildare (cont)
- Steam Museum
- Kildare Town Heritage Centre

Limerick
- Adare Heritage Centre
- Croom Mills Visitor Centre

Limerick (cont)
- Hunt Museum, Limerick
- King John's Castle
- Limerick County Museum

Louth
- County Museum, Dundalk

Meath
- Kells Heritage Centre
- Trim Visitor Centre

Monaghan
- Monaghan County Museum

Offaly
- Birr Castle Demesne & Ireland's Historic Science Centre
- Tullamore Dew Heritage Centre

Roscommon
- Cruachán Aí Visitor Centre
- King House
- Lough Key Forest Park
- Strokestown Park

Sligo
- Drumcliffe Church and Visitor Centre
- Michael Coleman Heritage Centre

Tipperary
- Brú Ború

Waterford
- Waterford Crystal Visitor Centre
- Waterford Treasures at the Granary and Reginald's Tower

Westmeath
- Athlone Castle Visitor Centre
- Belvedere House, Gardens and Park

Wexford
- Dunbrody
- Hook Lighthouse
- Irish National Heritage Park

Wicklow
- Avondale House
- National Sealife Centre
- Powerscourt House and Gardens
- Russborough

Heritage Island members confirmed as at August 2001. Heritage Island cannot accept responsibility for any errors or omissions.

HERITAGE ISLAND
EXPLORER

Display this coupon at any Heritage Island Centre to qualify for reduced admission. Touring Guide available at Tourist Information Offices throughout Ireland, or contact www.heritageisland.com

✂ CUT ALONG DOTTED LINE

For full details on centres, opening times, discounts and special offers see Heritage Island Touring Guide 2002 available at Tourist Information Centres, nationwide.

Heritage Island,
37 Main Street,
Donnybrook, Dublin 4.
Tel: + 353 1 260 0055
Fax: + 353 1 260 0058
E mail: heritage.island@indigo.ie
Web: www.heritageisland.com

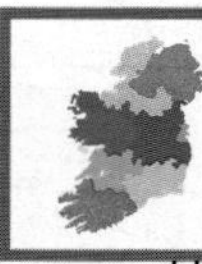

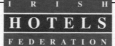

IRISH
HOTELS
FEDERATION

KEY TO MAPS

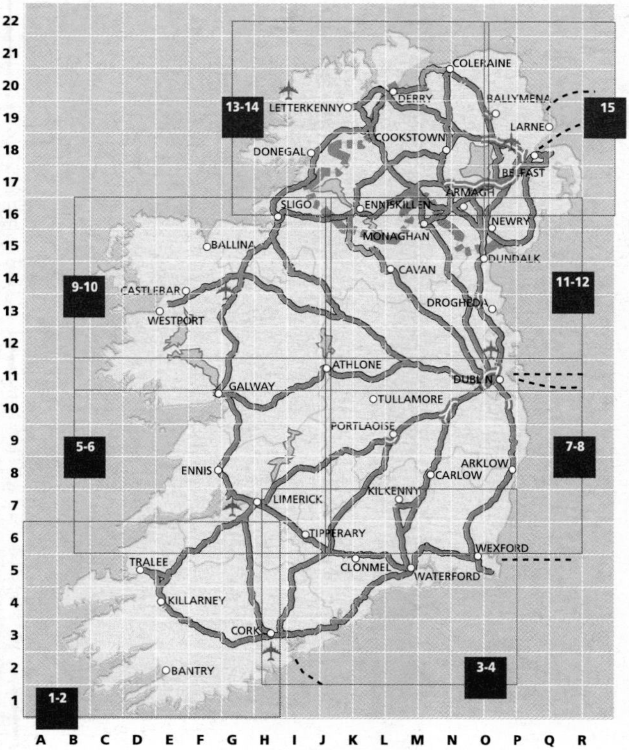

22
21
20
19
18
17
16
15
14
13
12
11
10
9
8
7
6
5
4
3
2
1
A B C D E F G H I J K L M N O P Q R
13-14
15
9-10
11-12
5-6
7-8
1-2
3-4
COLERAINE
DERRY
BALLYMENA
LETTERKENNY
LARNE
COOKSTOWN
DONEGAL
BELFAST
ARMAGH
SLIGO
ENNISKILLEN
NEWRY
MONAGHAN
BALLINA
DUNDALK
CAVAN
CASTLEBAR
WESTPORT
DROGHEDA
ATHLONE
DUBLIN
GALWAY
TULLAMORE
PORTLAOISE
ENNIS
ARKLOW
CARLOW
KILKENNY
LIMERICK
TIPPERARY
WEXFORD
TRALEE
CLONMEL
WATERFORD
KILLARNEY
CORK
BANTRY

LEGEND

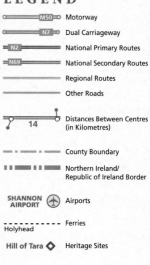

- M50 Motorway
- N7 Dual Carriageway
- N2 National Primary Routes
- N69 National Secondary Routes
- Regional Routes
- Other Roads
- 14 Distances Between Centres (in Kilometres)
- County Boundary
- Northern Ireland/ Republic of Ireland Border
- SHANNON AIRPORT — Airports
- Holyhead — Ferries
- Hill of Tara — Heritage Sites

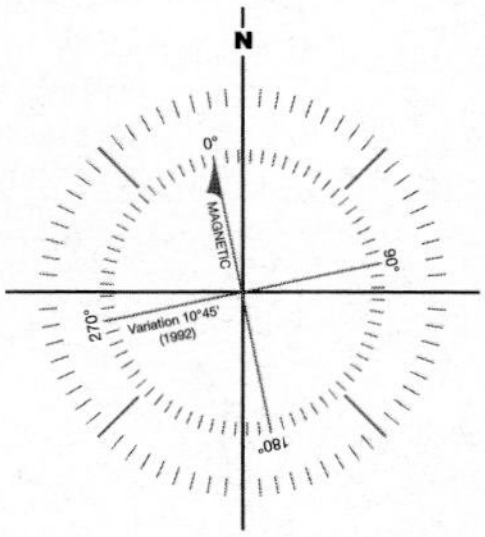

N
0°
MAGNETIC
90°
270°
Variation 10°45' (1992)
180°

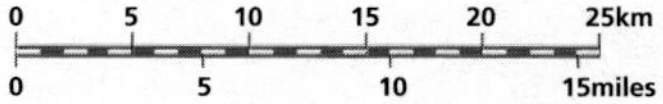

0 5 10 15 20 25km
0 5 10 15miles

SCALE 1 : 625 000

DISTANCE CHART
in Kilometres

	ARMAGH	ATHLONE	BELFAST	CARLOW	CLIFDEN	CORK	DERRY	DUBLIN	DUNDALK	ENNISKILLEN	GALWAY	KILKENNY	KILLARNEY	LARNE	LIMERICK	PORTLAOISE	ROSSLARE HARBOUR	SHANNON AIRPORT	SLIGO	TRALEE	WATERFORD	WEXFORD
ATHLONE	159																					
BELFAST	66	224																				
CARLOW	211	108	248																			
CLIFDEN	316	171	370	256																		
CORK	380	219	423	187	287																	
DERRY	114	225	118	309	303	460																
DUBLIN	129	124	167	82	296	256	233															
DUNDALK	45	142	82	166	314	340	158	84														
ENNISKILLEN	81	127	135	240	237	346	98	175	101													
GALWAY	238	92	303	177	79	206	277	216	233	192												
KILKENNY	245	121	282	39	248	148	335	114	200	242	169											
KILLARNEY	388	229	430	235	295	89	480	303	348	356	214	196										
LARNE	105	264	40	287	411	462	122	206	121	174	343	320	470									
LIMERICK	279	119	320	138	184	101	369	192	238	245	105	114	109	356								
PORTLAOISE	208	71	250	37	229	174	287	82	167	192	150	50	221	285	109							
ROSSLARE HARBOUR	282	201	320	93	348	206	385	151	237	324	269	100	272	356	204	130						
SHANNON AIRPORT	293	134	345	163	172	126	357	216	261	261	93	138	134	380	24	134	229					
SLIGO	148	116	203	224	167	336	134	213	171	68	142	237	345	240	235	187	319	224				
TRALEE	382	222	423	242	288	121	472	296	341	349	208	216	32	460	103	213	291	127	338			
WATERFORD	285	167	324	74	296	126	383	156	240	290	217	48	192	359	124	97	81	148	283	211		
WEXFORD	264	184	301	76	330	187	365	132	219	306	250	81	254	338	187	113	19	209	299	272	61	
WICKLOW	185	138	222	61	311	256	293	56	140	221	232	100	303	259	193	82	118	216	238	296	135	100

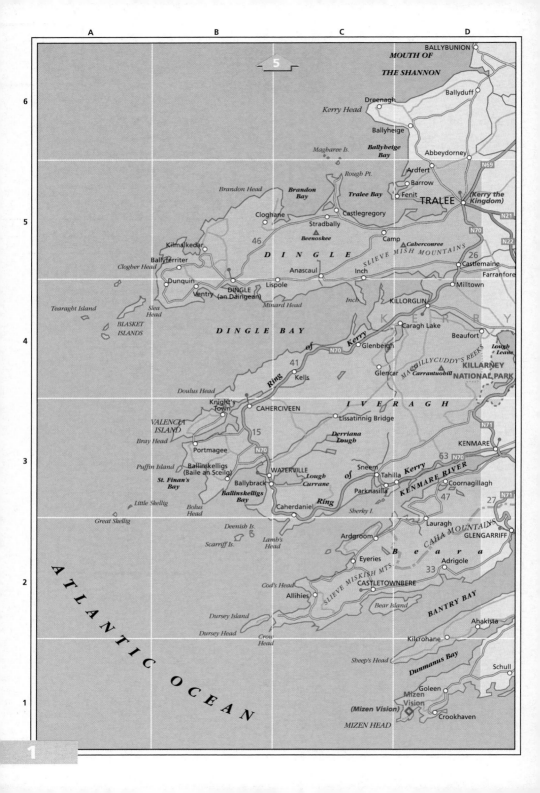

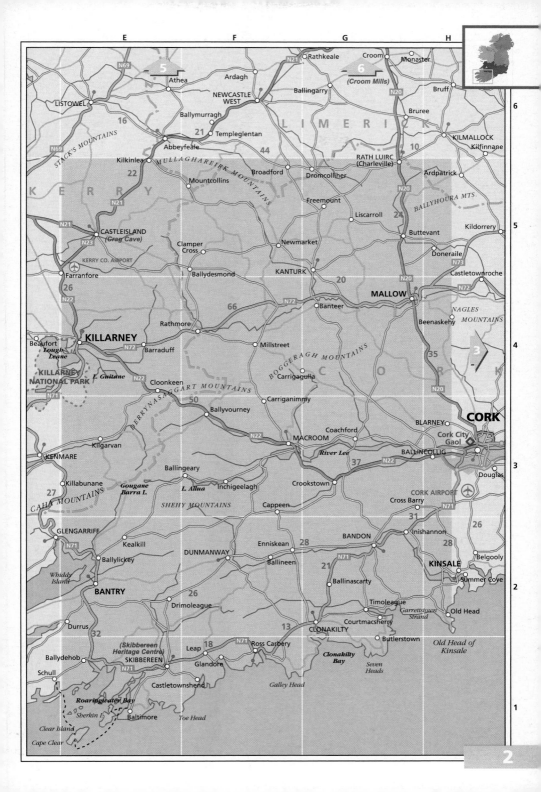

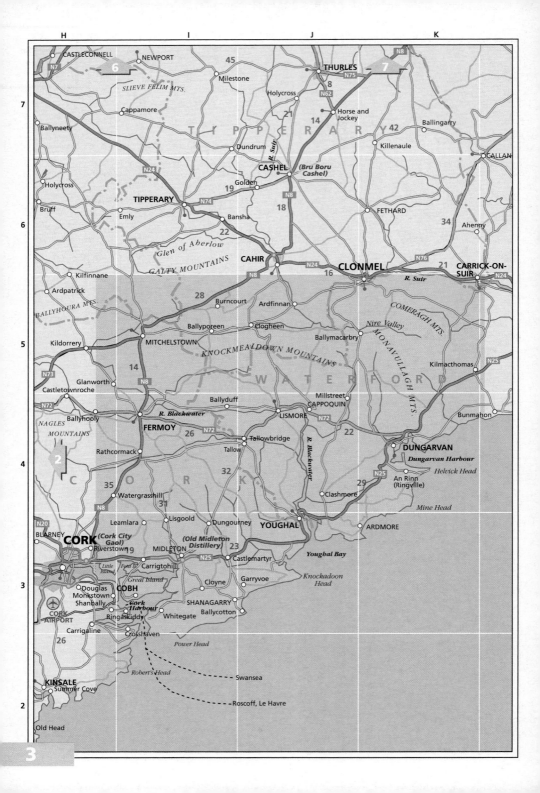

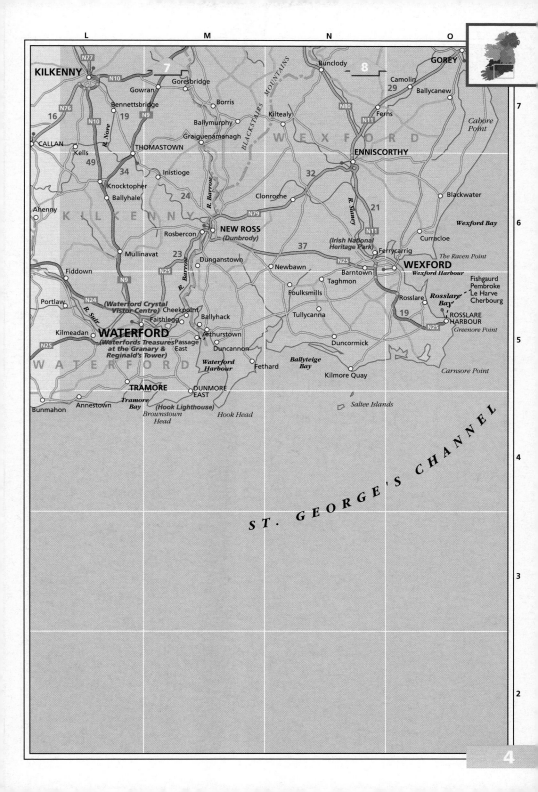

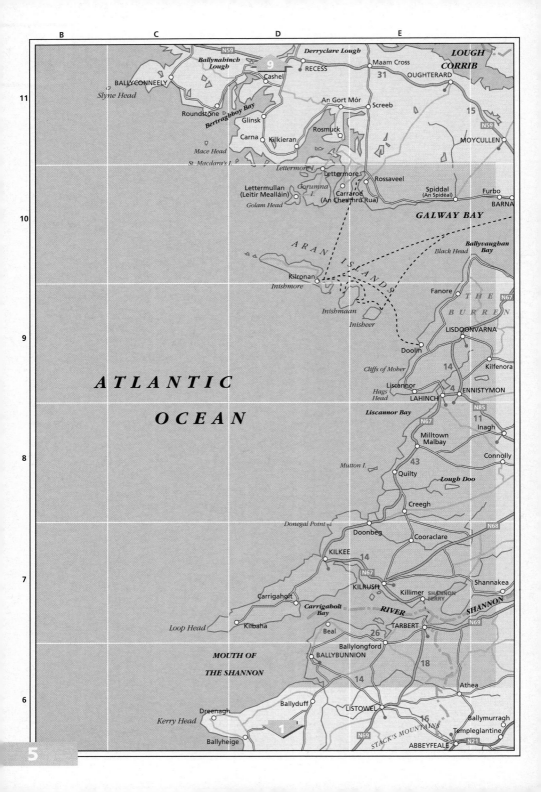

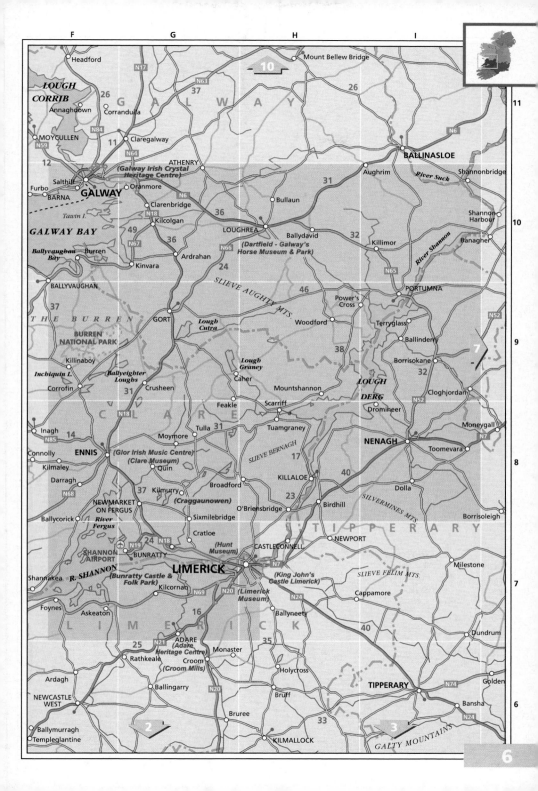

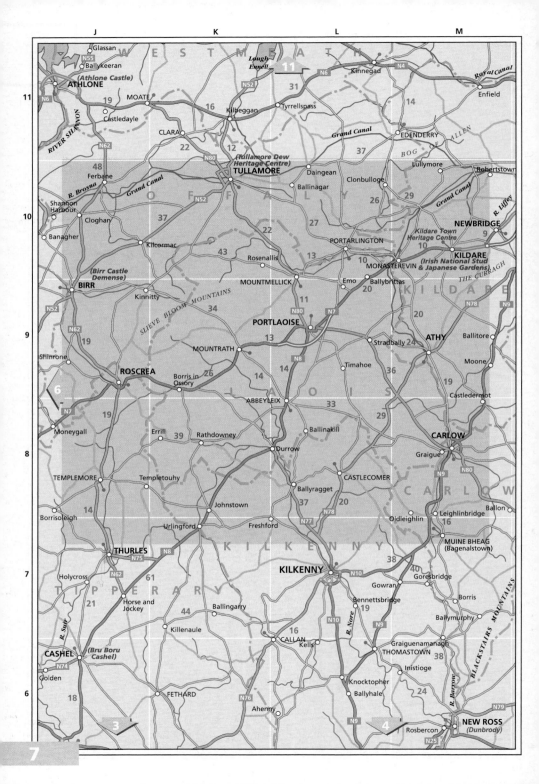

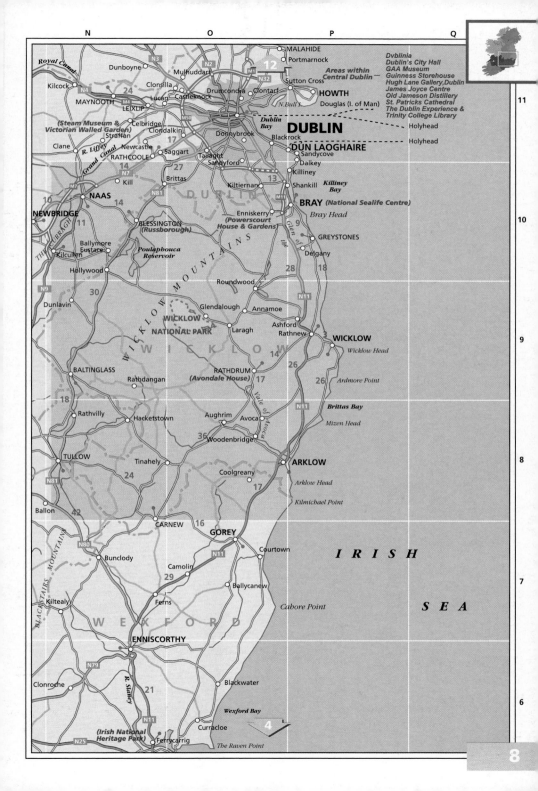

MALAHIDE
Portmarnock
Dunboyne
Royal Canal
N3
Mulhuddart
M1
12
Kilcock
N4
Clonsilla
Castleknock
Drumcondra
Clontarf
N32
Sutton Cross
Areas within
Central Dublin
MAYNOOTH
Lucan
HOWTH
LEIXLIP
M4
M50
N.Bull I.
Douglas (I. of Man)
(Steam Museum &
Victorian Walled Garden)
Celbridge
Clondalkin
*Dublin
Bay*
DUBLIN
Straffan
Donnybrook
Clane
R. Liffey
Newcastle
17
Blackrock
DÚN LAOGHAIRE
RATHCOOLE
Saggart
Tallaght
Sandyford
Sandycove
Grand Canal
14
27
Dalkey
Killiney
NAAS
Kill
Brittas
13
Shankill
*Killiney
Bay*
N7
N81
Kiltiernan
M7
14
D U B L I N
NEWBRIDGE
11
BRAY (National Sealife Centre)
Enniskerry
(Powerscourt
House & Gardens)
Bray Head
BLESSINGTON
(Russborough)
9
Ballymore
Eustace
GREYSTONES
Kilcullen
*Poulaphouca
Reservoir*
Delgany
Hollywood
28
18
N9
30
Roundwood
Dunlavin
Glendalough
Annamoe
N11
WICKLOW
Ashford
Rathnew
NATIONAL PARK
Laragh
3
WICKLOW
Wicklow Head
W I C K L O W
BALTINGLASS
14
26
Rathdangan
RATHDRUM
(Avondale House)
17
26
Ardmore Point
18
Rathvilly
Hacketstown
Aughrim
Avoca
N11
Brittas Bay
36
Mizen Head
Woodenbridge
TULLOW
Tinahely
ARKLOW
8
24
Coolgreany
Arklow Head
N81
17
Kilmichael Point
Ballon
42
CARNEW
16
I R I S H
GOREY
N80
N11
Courtown
Bunclody
Camolin
S E A
29
7
Kiltealy
Ballycanew
Ferns
Cahore Point
W E X F O R D
ENNISCORTHY
N79
6
Clonroche
R. Slaney
21
Blackwater
N11
Wexford Bay
4
(Irish National
Heritage Park)
Curracloe
N25
Ferrycarrig
The Raven Point

*Dvblinia
Dublin's City Hall
GAA Museum
Guinness Storehouse
Hugh Lane Gallery,Dublin
James Joyce Centre
Old Jameson Distillery
St. Patricks Cathedral
The Dublin Experience &
Trinity College Library*

Holyhead
Holyhead

Blackstairs Mountains
The Curragh
Vale of Avoca
Glen of the Dargle
WICKLOW MOUNTAINS

10
11

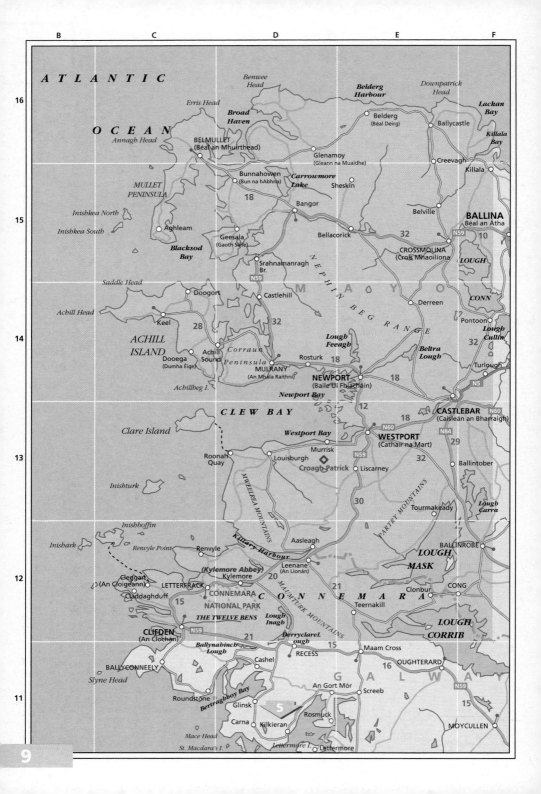

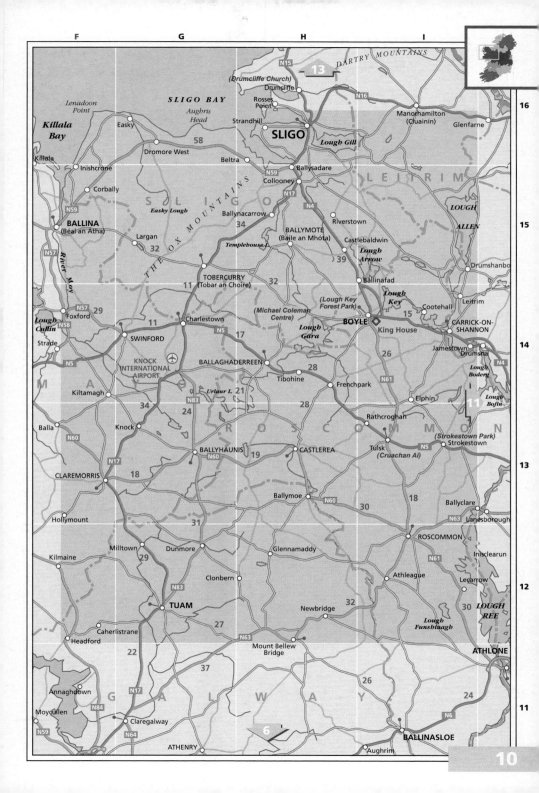

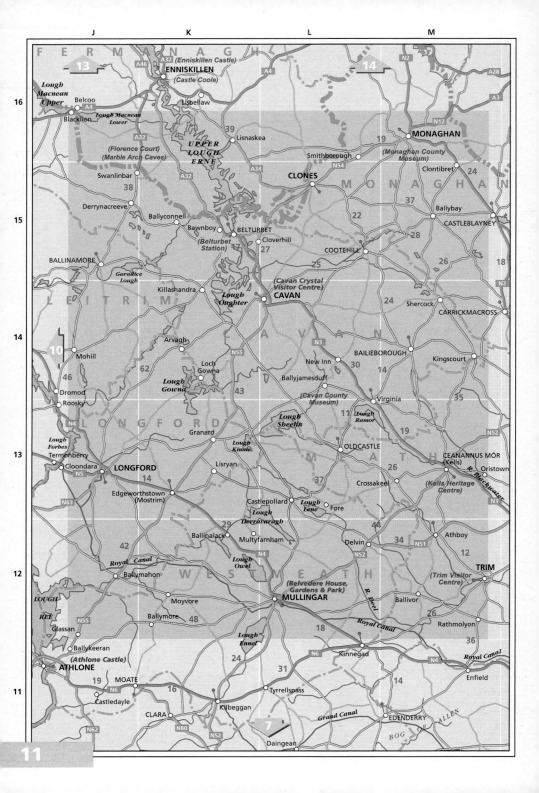

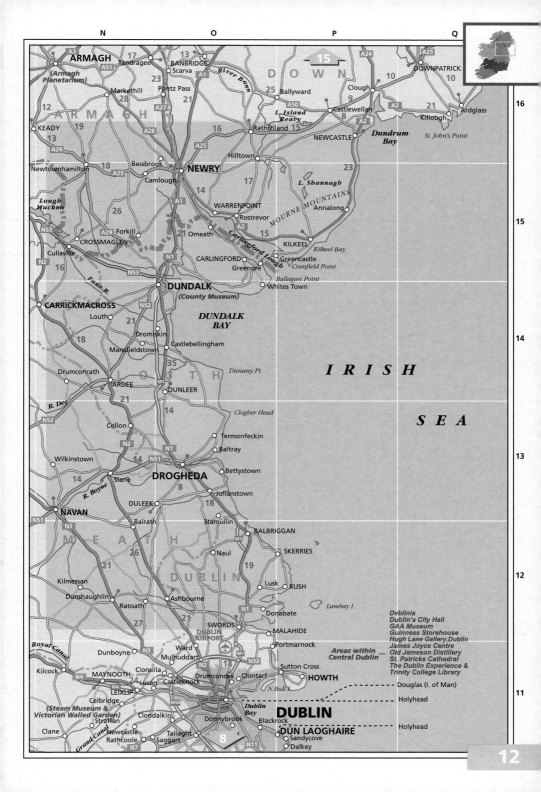

N   O   P   Q

ARMAGH   17   Tandragee   13   BANBRIDGE   A24   A25   **DOWNPATRICK**   16

A3   A51   Scarva   A1   *River Bann*   D O W N   **15**

(Armagh Planetarium)   23   Pontz Pass   25   Ballyward   Clough   10   10

Markethill   28   A27   21   Castlewellan   A50   A2   21   Ardglass   16

A R M A G H   12   A28   16   Rathfriland   L. Island Reavy   9   A2   8   Killough

KEADY   19   A29   Hilltown   15   **NEWCASTLE**   *St. John's Point*

13   A29   A25   *Dundrum Bay*

Newtownhamilton   18   Bessbrook   **NEWRY**   17   23   **15**

A25   Camlough   14   *L. Shannagh*   M O U R N E

Lough Muckno   26   A1   **WARRENPOINT**   Annalong   M O U N T A I N S

N53   A29   Forkill   Rostrevor   A2

CROSSMAGLEN   21   Omeath   15   **KILKEEL**

Cullaville   N1   *Carlingford Lough*   *Kilkeel Bay*   **14**

N2   16   *Fane R.*   **CARLINGFORD**   Greencastle   *Cranfield Point*

N53   Greenore   *Ballagan Point*

DUNDALK   Whites Town

(County Museum)

CARRICKMACROSS   *DUNDALK BAY*   I R I S H   **13**

Louth   21   N52

Dromiskin   *Dunany Pt.*

18   Mansfieldstown   Castlebellingham

L   O   U   T   H   S E A

Drumconrath   35   M1   *Clogher Head*

ARDEE   **DUNLEER**

R. Dee   21

N52   14   Termonfeckin

Collon   N2   Baltray   **13**

Wilkinstown   N1   Bettystown

14   N51   **DROGHEDA**   N1

R. Boyne   Slane   8   Julianstown

NAVAN   **DULEEK**   18   **12**

N51   N3   Balrath   Stamullin

M E A T H   **BALBRIGGAN**   M1

26   Naul   **SKERRIES**

21   19

Kilmessan   D U B L I N   Lusk   **RUSH**   **12**

Dunshaughlin   Ashbourne   *Lambay I.*

Ratoath   N1   Donabate

27   **SWORDS**   *Dvblinia*
   Dublin's City Hall
   GAA Museum

Dunboyne   N3   **DUBLIN AIRPORT**   **MALAHIDE**   *Guinness Storehouse*
   Hugh Lane Gallery,Dublin

Kilcock   Ward   Mulhuddart   M1   Portmarnock   *Areas within*   *James Joyce Centre*
   Old Jameson Distillery

N4   **MAYNOOTH**   Clonsilla   N2   N32   Sutton Cross   *Central Dublin*   *St. Patricks Cathedral*
   The Dublin Experience &
   Trinity College Library

Royal Canal   Lucan   Castleknock   Drumcondra   Clontarf   **HOWTH**

LEIXLIP   M50   M4   *N.Bull I.*   Douglas (I. of Man)

Celbridge   *Dublin Bay*   Holyhead

(Steam Museum & Victorian Walled Garden)   Straffan   Clondalkin   Donnybrook   Blackrock   **DUBLIN**   **11**

Clane   Newcastle   Tallaght   **DÚN LAOGHAIRE**   Holyhead

Rathcoole   Saggart   N11   Sandycove

Grand Canal   N7   **8**   Dalkey

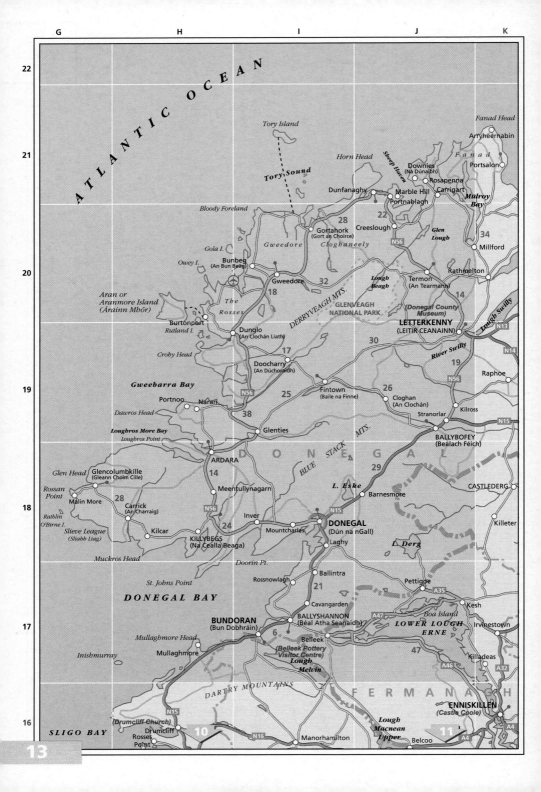

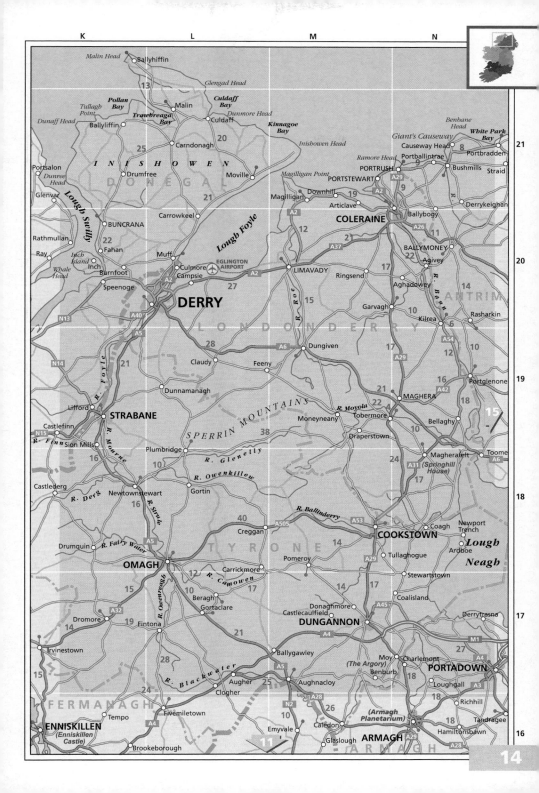

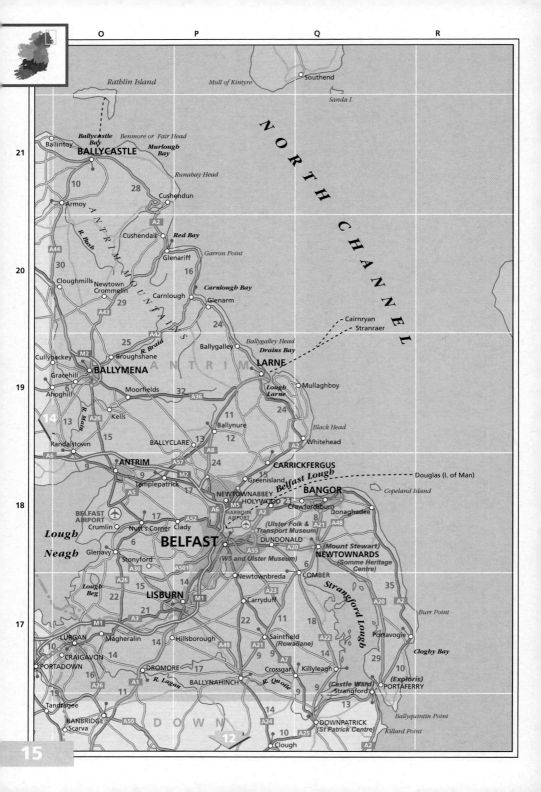

GUINNESS

Holiday Competition

Guinness invite you to Be Our Guest in any of the hotels or guesthouses featured in Ireland's favourite and most successful accommodation guide. (Value of prize €1,250).

[Excluding peak periods and subject to availability]

Simply complete the sentence below in 10 words or less:

I would like to win this wonderful prize because

_____

_____

Replies clearly marked Holiday Competition to:

Irish Hotels Federation, 13 Northbrook Road, Dublin 6, Ireland.

Closing Date for Entries 31st August 2002

(Photocopies not accepted)

Name: _____

Address: _____

_____

irelandhotels.com
log on and book in

IRISH
HOTELS
FEDERATION

Throughout the year, Ireland has a great range of social, cultural and sporting events. The big cities and even the smallest villages have festivals, whether in honour of a goat, as at Puck Fair, or to celebrate the oysters in Galway.

Listed below is a small selection of well known events/festivals which take place. There are, of course, many others, whether music or sport. **Please contact your nearest Irish Tourist Board office for confirmation of dates and a full calendar of events. (TBC = Dates to be Confirmed)**

FEBRUARY

02 February	Ireland v Wales (6 Nations) Rugby International, Lansdowne Road, Dublin
27 February - 03 March	Dublin Boat Show

MARCH

27 February - 03 March	Dublin Boat Show
02 March	Ireland v Scotland (6 Nations) Rugby International, Lansdowne Road, Dublin
15 - 18 March	St. Patrick's Festival 2002, Dublin
19 - 24 March	The Irish Masters Snooker Tournament, Goffs, Kill, Co. Kildare
23 March	Ireland v Italy (6 Nations) Rugby International, Lansdowne Road, Dublin
T.B.C.	Dublin Film Festival, Dublin
29 March - 01 April	Kerry Arts Easter Weekend Festival, Tralee, Co. Kerry
30 March - 01 April	Circuit of Ireland Rally, Enniskillen, Co. Fermanagh & Bundoran, Co. Donegal

APRIL

T.B.C.	Dublin Film Festival, Dublin
29 March - 01 April	Kerry Arts Easter Weekend Festival, Tralee, Co. Kerry
30 March - 01 April	Circuit of Ireland Rally, Enniskillen, Co. Fermanagh & Bundoran, Co. Donegal
23 - 26 April	Irish National Hunt Festival, Punchestown, Co. Kildare

MAY

02 - 05 May	Cork International Choral Festival, Cork
09 - 12 May	International Mussel Fair, Bantry, Co. Cork

MAY (CONTINUED)

18 - 19 May	A.I.M.S. Choral Festival, New Ross, Co. Wexford
23 - 27 May	Fleadh Nua, Ennis, Co. Clare
29 May - 02 June	Writers' Week, Listowel, Co. Kerry
30 May - 03 June T.B.C.	Murphy's Cat Laughs Comedy Festival, Kilkenny City

JUNE

29 May - 02 June	Writers' Week, Listowel, Co. Kerry
30 May - 03 June T.B.C.	Murphy's Cat Laughs Comedy Festival, Kilkenny City
09 June T.B.C	Tesco/Evening Herald Women's Mini Marathon, Dublin City
12 - 17 June	Guinness Bloomsday Festival, Dublin
13 - 23 June	Eigse Carlow 2002 Arts Festival, St. Patrick's College, Carlow
27 - 30 June	Murphy's Irish Open, Fota Island, Cork
28 - 30 June	Budweiser Irish Derby Weekend, The Curragh Racecourse, Co. Kildare
30 June - 06 July	Synge Summer School, Rathdrum, Co. Wicklow

JULY

30 June - 06 July	Synge Summer School, Rathdrum, Co. Wicklow
04 - 07 July	The Smurfit European Open, K Club, Co. Kildare
07 - 14 July T.B.C	Willie Clancy Summer School, Miltown Malbay, Co. Clare
08 - 13 July T.B.C	Bard Summer School, Clare Island, Co. Mayo
09 - 14 July	Galway Film Fleadh, Galway City
13 - 19 July	Cork Ford Week, Crosshaven, Cork
16 - 28 July	Galway Arts Festival, Galway City
27 July - 10 August	Yeats International Summer School, Sligo
28 July - 06 August T.B.C	Mary from Dungloe International Festival, Dungloe, Co. Donegal
29 July - 04 August	Guinness Galway Race Meeting, Galway

AUGUST

27 July - 10 August	Yeats International Summer School, Sligo
28 July - 06 August T.B.C.	Mary from Dungloe International Festival, Dungloe, Co. Donegal
29 July - 04 August	Guinness Galway Race Meeting, Galway
07 - 11 August	Kerrygold Horse Show 2002, Royal Dublin Society, Dublin
09 - 18 August	Kilkenny Arts Festival, Kilkenny City
10 - 12 August	Guinness Puck Fair, Killorglin, Co. Kerry
15 August	Connemara Pony Show, Clifden, Co. Galway
23 -25 August	Fleadh Ceoil Na hEireann, Listowel, Co. Kerry
23 -28 August T.B.C.	Rose of Tralee International Festival, Tralee, Co. Kerry
30 August- 06 October	Matchmaking Festival, Lisdoonvarna, Co. Clare
31 August - 01 September	Cape Clear Island International Storytelling Festival, Cape Clear Island, West Cork

SEPTEMBER

30 August - 06 October T.B.C.	Matchmaking Festival, Lisdoonvarna, Co. Clare
31 August - 01 September	Cape Clear Island International Storytelling Festival, Cape Clear Island, West Cork
07 - 09 September T.B.C.	Guinness Clarenbridge Oyster Festival, Clarenbridge, Co. Galway
08 September	Guinness All Ireland Hurling Championship Final, Croke Park, Dublin
18 - 29 September	Waterford International Festival of Light Opera, Waterford

SEPTEMBER (CONTINUED)

22 September	Bank of Ireland All Ireland Football Championship Final, Croke Park, Dublin
23 - 29 September	Listowel Racing Festival, Listowel, Co. Kerry
24 - 26 September T.B.C.	National Ploughing Championships, Ballacolla, Co. Laois
26 - 29 September	Guinness Galway International Oyster Festival, Galway City
28 September - 06 October	Ballinasloe International Horse Fair and Festival, Ballinasloe, Co. Galway

OCTOBER

30 August - 06 October T.B.C.	Matchmaking Festival, Lisdoonvarna, Co. Clare
28 September - 06 October	Ballinasloe International Horse Fair and Festival, Ballinasloe, Co. Galway
T.B.C.	Dublin Theatre Festival, Dublin
10 - 13 October	26th International Gourmet Festival, Kinsale, Co. Cork
14 - 21 October	Cork Film Festival, Cork City
17 October - 03 November	Wexford Festival Opera, Wexford
25 - 28 October	Guinness Cork Jazz Festival, Cork City
28 October	Dublin City Marathon, Dublin City

INDEX OF HOTELS & GUESTHOUSES **GUINNESS.**

A

19TH GREEN
Killarney, Co.Kerry 267

A STAR OF THE SEA
Galway City, Co.Galway 347

AANDERS GUESTHOUSE
Ballinasloe, Co.Galway 336

AARONMOR GUESTHOUSE
Dublin City, Co.Dublin 59

ABBERLEY COURT HOTEL
Dublin City, Co.Dublin 59

ABBEY COURT HOTEL AND TRINITY
LEISURE CLUB
Nenagh, Co.Tipperary North.............329

ABBEY GATE HOTEL
Tralee, Co.Kerry 291

ABBEY HOTEL
Ballyvourney, Co.Cork 207

ABBEY HOTEL
Roscommon Town, Co.Roscommon 385

ABBEY HOTEL
Dublin City, Co.Dublin 60

ABBEY HOUSE
Galway City, Co.Galway 348

ABBEY LODGE
Killarney, Co.Kerry 267

ABBEYGLEN CASTLE HOTEL
Clifden, Co.Galway 340

ABBEYLEIX MANOR HOTEL
Abbeyleix, Co.Laois 148

ABERDEEN LODGE
Dublin City, Co.Dublin 60

ABRAE COURT
Dublin City, Co.Dublin 60

ACADEMY HOTEL
Dublin City, Co.Dublin 61

ACH NA SHEEN GUESTHOUSE
Tipperary Town, Co.Tipperary South 178

ACHILL CLIFF HOUSE HOTEL
Achill Island, Co.Mayo 372

ACHILL HOUSE
Cork City, Co.Cork 218

ACORN HOUSE
Cork City, Co.Cork 219

ACTONS HOTEL
Kinsale, Co.Cork 236

ADAIR ARMS HOTEL
Ballymena, Co.Antrim.............30

ADAMS TRINITY HOTEL
Dublin City, Co.Dublin 61

ADARE GUEST HOUSE
Galway City, Co.Galway 348

ADARE MANOR HOTEL
& GOLF RESORT
Adare, Co.Limerick.............321

AGHADOE HEIGHTS HOTEL
Killarney, Co.Kerry 268

AHERLOW HOUSE HOTEL
Glen Of Aherlow, Co.Tipperary South..177

AHERNE'S TOWNHOUSE & SEAFOOD
RESTAURANT
Youghal, Co.Cork 248

AILSA LODGE
Rosslare Harbour, Co.Wexford 199

AIRPORT LODGE
Cork Airport, Co.Cork 218

AIRPORT VIEW
Blakes Cross, Co.Dublin 57

AISHLING HOUSE
Dublin City, Co.Dublin 61

AISLEIGH GUEST HOUSE
Carrick-on-Shannon, Co.Leitrim 401

AISLING HOUSE
Killarney, Co.Kerry 268

AISLING HOUSE
Ashbourne, Co.Meath 121

ALCOCK AND BROWN HOTEL
Clifden, Co.Galway 340

ALEXANDER HOTEL
Dublin City, Co.Dublin 62

ALEXANDRA GUEST HOUSE
Limerick City, Co.Limerick 323

ALLINGHAM ARMS HOTEL
Bundoran, Co.Donegal 391

ALPINE HOUSE
Dingle, Co.Kerry 254

AMBASSADOR HOTEL
Kill, Co.Kildare 144

AMBASSADOR HOTEL
Cork City, Co.Cork 219

AN CHUIRT
Gweedore, Co.Donegal 396

AN CRUISCIN LAN HOTEL
Spiddal, Co.Galway 370

AN TINTAIN GUESTHOUSE
Multyfarnham, Co.Westmeath 159

ANCHOR GUEST HOUSE
Dublin City, Co.Dublin 62

ANGLESEA TOWN HOUSE
Dublin City, Co.Dublin 62

ANNAGH LODGE GUESTHOUSE
Newbridge, Co.Kildare 147

ANNER HOTEL & LEISURE CENTRE
Thurles, Co.Tipperary North 331

ANNO SANTO HOTEL
Galway City, Co.Galway 348

ANTOINE HOUSE
Cork City, Co.Cork 220

ARAN VIEW HOUSE HOTEL
& RESTAURANT
Doolin, Co.Clare 303

ARBUTUS HOTEL
Killarney, Co.Kerry 268

ARBUTUS LODGE HOTEL
Cork City, Co.Cork 220

ARD EINNE GUESTHOUSE
Aran Islands, Co.Galway 334

ARDAGH HOTEL & RESTAURANT
Clifden, Co.Galway 341

ARDAGH HOUSE
Killenaule, Co.Tipperary South 178

ARDAGH HOUSE
Dublin City, Co.Dublin 63

ARDAWN HOUSE
Galway City, Co.Galway 349

ARDBOYNE HOTEL
Navan, Co.Meath 124

ARDENODE HOTEL
Ballymore Eustace, Co.Kildare 143

ARDILAUN GUESTHOUSE
Ennis, Co.Clare 304

ARDILAUN HOUSE HOTEL, CONFERENCE
CENTRE & LEISURE CLUB
Galway City, Co.Galway 349

ARDMORE COUNTRY HOUSE HOTEL AND
RESTAURANT
Westport, Co.Mayo 379

ARD-NA-SIDHE
Caragh Lake, Co.Kerry 252

ARKLOW BAY HOTEL
Arklow, Co.Wicklow.............126

ARLINGTON HOTEL
Dublin City, Co.Dublin 63

ARLINGTON LODGE COUNTRY
HOUSE & RESTAURANT
Waterford City, Co.Waterford 186

ARNOLDS HOTEL
Dunfanaghy, Co.Donegal 395

ASHBERRY LODGE
Kenmare, Co.Kerry 262

ASHBOURNE HOUSE HOTEL
Ashbourne, Co.Meath 121

ASHBURN HOTEL
Lurgan, Co.Armagh 37

ASHDOWN PARK HOTEL CONFERENCE &
LEISURE CENTRE
Gorey, Co.Wexford.............196

ASHFIELD HOUSE
Dublin City, Co.Dublin 63

ASHFORD CASTLE
Cong, Co.Mayo 376

ASHFORD MANOR
Galway City, Co.Galway 349

ASHLEE LODGE
Blarney, Co.Cork.............210

ASHLEY HOTEL
Cork City, Co.Cork 220

ASHLING HOTEL
Dublin City, Co.Dublin 64

ASHVIEW HOUSE
The Ward, Co.Dublin 117

ASHVILLE GUESTHOUSE
Killarney, Co.Kerry 269